Moral Psychology

Moral Psychology

Volume 2: The Cognitive Science of Morality: Intuition and Diversity

edited by Walter Sinnott-Armstrong

A Bradford Book
The MIT Press
Cambridge, Massachusetts
London, England

MIT Press books may be purchased at special quantity discounts for business or sales promotional use. For information, please e-mail special_sales@mitpress.mit.edu or write to Special Sales Department, The MIT Press, 55 Hayward Street, Cambridge, MA 02142.

This book was set in Stone Sans and Stone Serif by SNP Best-set Typesetter Ltd., Hong Kong and was printed and bound in the United States of America.

Library of Congress Cataloging-in-Publication Data

Moral psychology / edited by Walter Sinnott-Armstrong.
   v.   cm.
"A Bradford Book."
Includes bibliographical references and index.
Contents: v. 1. The evolution of morality : adaptations and innateness—v. 2. The cognitive science of morality : intuition and diversity—v. 3. The neuroscience of morality : emotion, disease, and development.
ISBN 978-0-262-19561-4 (vol. 1 : hardcover : alk. paper)—ISBN 978-0-262-69354-7 (vol. 1 : pbk. : alk. paper)—ISBN 978-0-262-19569-0 (vol. 2 : hardcover : alk. paper)—ISBN 978-0-262-69357-8 (vol. 2 : pbk. : alk. paper)—ISBN 978-0-262-19564-5 (vol. 3 : hardcover : alk. paper)—ISBN 978-0-262-69355-4 (vol. 3 : pbk. : alk. paper)
1. Ethics. 2. Psychology and philosophy. 3. Neurosciences. I. Sinnott-Armstrong, Walter, 1955–
BJ45.M66   2007
170—dc22   2006035509

10 9 8 7 6 5 4 3 2 1

This volume is dedicated to all of my students who challenged and inspired me, especially Jana Schaich Borg, Jon Ellis, and Laura Donohue.

Contents

Acknowledgments   xi
Introduction   xiii
Walter Sinnott-Armstrong

1 | Moral Intuition = Fast and Frugal Heuristics?   1
Gerd Gigerenzer

1.1 | Fast, Frugal, and (Sometimes) Wrong   27
Cass R. Sunstein

1.2 | Moral Heuristics and Consequentialism   31
Julia Driver and Don Loeb

1.3 | Reply to Comments   41
Gerd Gigerenzer

2 | Framing Moral Intuitions   47
Walter Sinnott-Armstrong

2.1 | Moral Intuitions Framed   77
William Tolhurst

2.2 | Defending Ethical Intuitionism   83
Russ Shafer-Landau

2.3 | How to Apply Generalities: Reply to Tolhurst and
Shafer-Landau   97
Walter Sinnott-Armstrong

3 | Reviving Rawls's Linguistic Analogy: Operative Principles and the
Causal Structure of Moral Actions   107
Marc D. Hauser, Liane Young, and Fiery Cushman

3.1 | Reviving Rawls's Linguistic Analogy Inside and Out   145
Ron Mallon

3.2 | Resisting the Linguistic Analogy: A Commentary on Hauser, Young, and Cushman   157
Jesse J. Prinz

3.3 | On Misreading the Linguistic Analogy: Response to Jesse Prinz and Ron Mallon   171
Marc D. Hauser, Liane Young, and Fiery Cushman

4 | Social Intuitionists Answer Six Questions about Moral Psychology   181
Jonathan Haidt and Fredrik Bjorklund

4.1 | Does Social Intuitionism Flatter Morality or Challenge It?   219
Daniel Jacobson

4.2 | The Social Intuitionist Model: Some Counter-Intuitions   233
Darcia Narvaez

4.3 | Social Intuitionists Reason, in Conversation   241
Jonathan Haidt and Frederick Bjorklund

5 | Sentimentalism Naturalized   255
Shaun Nichols

5.1 | Normative Theory or Theory of Mind? A Response to Nichols   275
James Blair

5.2 | Sentimental Rules and Moral Disagreement: Comment on Nichols   279
Justin D'Arms

5.3 | Sentiment, Intention, and Disagreement: Replies to Blair and D'Arms   291
Shaun Nichols

6 | How to Argue about Disagreement: Evaluative Diversity and Moral Realism   303
John M. Doris and Alexandra Plakias

6.1 | Against Convergent Moral Realism: The Respective Roles of Philosophical Argument and Empirical Evidence   333
Brian Leiter

6.2 | Disagreement about Disagreement   339
Paul Bloomfield

6.3 | How to Find a Disagreement: Philosophical Diversity and
Moral Realism   345
Alexandra Plakias and John M. Doris

7 | Moral Incoherentism: How to Pull a Metaphysical Rabbit out of a
Semantic Hat   355
Don Loeb

7.1 | Metaethical Variability, Incoherence, and Error   387
Michael B. Gill

7.2 | Moral Semantics and Empirical Inquiry   403
Geoffrey Sayre-McCord

7.3 | Reply to Gill and Sayre-McCord   413
Don Loeb

8 | Attributions of Causation and Moral Responsibility   423
Julia Driver

8.1 | Causal Judgment and Moral Judgment: Two Experiments   441
Joshua Knobe and Ben Fraser

8.2 | Can You Be Morally Responsible for Someone's Death If Nothing
You Did Caused It?   449
John Deigh

8.3 | Kinds of Norms and Legal Causation: Reply to Knobe and
Fraser and Deigh   459
Julia Driver

References   463
Contributors   499
Index to Volume 1   501
Index to Volume 2   529
Index to Volume 3   559

Acknowledgments

Many people deserve my thanks for assistance as these volumes grew. For financial support of the conference that sowed the seeds for this project, I am grateful to several institutions at Dartmouth College, including the Leslie Center for the Humanities, the Dickey Center for International Understanding, the Master of Arts in Liberal Studies program, the Dean of the Faculty, the Department of Psychological and Brain Sciences, the Social Brain Science Project, the Cognitive Neuroscience Center, the Department of Philosophy, and the Institute for Applied and Professional Ethics. For help in making these essays more accessible to students, I thank Cate Birtley, Cole Entress, and Ben Shear, Dartmouth students who served as my Presidential Scholars. I also greatly appreciate the devotion and editorial skills of Kier Olsen DeVries, who worked long and hard to put the essays from these diverse authors into a single form for the publisher. Tom Stone, my editor at MIT Press, also has my gratitude for his spirited encouragement. Last but not least, I thank my family—Liz, Miranda, and Nick—for their love and patience while I spent many nights and weekends on this project.

Introduction

Walter Sinnott-Armstrong

Moral judgments, emotions, and actions can be studied in many ways. One method cites patterns in observations as evidence of evolutionary origins. That method was exemplified in the chapters of the first volume in this collection. A second method uses similar patterns in observations as evidence of cognitive processes employed in forming the moral judgments, emotions, or actions. That method will be exemplified in the papers in this volume. It can be described as cognitive science.

Cognitive scientists need not say anything about how their proposed cognitive processes evolved in order to reach fascinating and important results. Nonetheless, no cognitive model can be acceptable if it is incompatible with what we know about evolution. Moreover, a cognitive model can derive additional support from a plausible story about how a cognitive process evolved to where it is today. In these ways and more, the papers on cognitive science in this volume are connected to the views on the evolution of morality that were canvassed in the preceding volume.

Similarly, although cognitive scientists do not have to mention brain mechanisms, connections to known brain mechanisms can validate a postulated cognitive model, and any cognitive model must be rejected if it conflicts with what we know about the brain and how it works. The cognitive science of moral judgment, emotion, and action cannot be done thoroughly in isolation from brain science. Hence, the papers on cognitive science in this volume are also connected to those on neuroscience in the following volume.

Nonetheless, this particular volume focuses on cognitive science rather than on evolution or on brain science. The various chapters here illustrate the diversity of approaches within cognitive science.

One very common view in cognitive science claims that the mind often works by means of heuristics—fast and frugal procedures for forming beliefs, reaching decisions, and performing actions. A major debate about heuristics concerns their reliability. Daniel Kahneman, Amos Tversky, and their collaborators emphasize that heuristics often lead to biases and at least apparent irrationality. In contrast, Gerd Gigerenzer is well-known for emphasizing the usefulness and reliability of heuristics in proper circumstances. In his chapter in this volume, Gigerenzer applies his general approach to moral decisions and intuitions and argues that moral intuitions are nothing more than fast and frugal heuristics of a special sort. He claims that this view is much more realistic than competing views, including some forms of consequentialism, whose standards of rationality cannot be met by real cognitive agents.

Cass Sunstein comments that even good heuristics can produce a kind of irrationality, and he argues that prescriptive treatments of moral heuristics should avoid controversial assumptions about morality. Julia Driver and Don Loeb then claim that Gigerenzer has misinterpreted traditional consequentialism. In his reply, Gigerenzer admits that heuristics produce some errors, but so do all available policies, so heuristics can still reduce errors more than any realistic alternative in some environments. According to Gigerenzer, what we need to study is when—that is, in which environments—specific heuristics lead to better results than any realistic alternative.

Since heuristics predict and explain framing effects, Gigerenzer's chapter leads right into the next chapter, which is by Walter Sinnott-Armstrong and is on framing effects in moral judgment. Framing effects are, basically, variations in beliefs as a result of variations in wording and order. Sinnott-Armstrong emphasizes that, when such variations in wording and order cannot affect the truth of beliefs, framing effects signal unreliability. Hence, if framing effects are widespread enough in moral intuitions, moral believers have reason to suspect that those intuitions are unreliable. Sinnott-Armstrong cites empirical evidence that framing effects are surprisingly common in moral judgments, so he concludes that moral believers have reason to suspect that their moral intuitions are unreliable. This result creates a need for confirmation and thereby undermines traditional moral intuitionism as a response to the skeptical regress problem in moral epistemology.

William Tolhurst and Russ Shafer-Landau both defend moral intuitionism against Sinnott-Armstrong's argument. Tolhurst argues that Sinnott-Armstrong's grounds support only a suspension of belief about whether moral intuitions are reliable or unreliable. Shafer-Landau canvasses different ways of understanding Sinnott-Armstrong's argument and concludes that none of them undermine traditional moral intuitionism. In reply,

Sinnott-Armstrong reformulates his argument in ways that are intended to avoid the criticisms of Tolhurst and Shafer-Landau.

Moral intuitions are also often understood by means of analogy to Noam Chomsky's universal grammar, an analogy suggested by John Rawls.[1] This analogy is developed in chapter 3, by Marc Hauser, Liane Young, and Fiery Cushman. This research group uses a very large Web-based survey as well as data on brain-damaged patients[2] to adjudicate among four models of moral judgment.[3] They conclude that at least some forms of moral judgment are universal and mediated by unconscious and inaccessible principles. This conclusion supports the analogy to linguistics and suggests that these principles could not have been learned from explicit teaching.

In his comment on Hauser et al., Ron Mallon argues that no evidence points to a specialized moral faculty or supports a strong version of the linguistic analogy. Jesse Prinz then emphasizes several disanalogies between morality and language and shows how to account for the data of Hauser et al. without admitting that morality is innate. In their reply, Hauser, Young, and Cushman specify how Mallon and Prinz have misread their linguistic analogy; then they discuss some new evidence for their model.

One of the psychological models criticized by Hauser, Young, and Cushman was presented by Jonathan Haidt and claims that initial moral intuitions are emotional, whereas moral reasoning normally comes later and serves social purposes. Since its original formulation, Haidt's social intuitionist model of moral judgment has been subjected to numerous criticisms.[4] In their wide-ranging chapter here, Haidt and Fredrik Bjorklund develop their view in new ways, summarize the evidence for their view, and respond to criticisms. They discuss where moral beliefs and motivations come from, how moral judgment works, how morality develops, and why moral beliefs vary. In their philosophical conclusion, they argue against monistic theories and for an anthropocentric view of moral truth that is supposed to be neither relativistic nor skeptical insofar as it shows how some moral codes can be superior to others.[5]

Both commentators suggest that Haidt and Bjorklund's theory is more relativistic than Haidt and Bjorklund admit. Daniel Jacobson also argues that social intuitionism in moral psychology coheres best with a kind of sentimentalism in metaethics, rather than with Haidt and Bjorklund's anthropocentric view. Darcia Narvaez then claims that social intuitionism addresses only a small sample of moral judgment, reasoning, and decision. Haidt and Bjorklund reply that their topic is moral judgment rather than moral decision making and which judgments get classified as moral judgments is under dispute. They also point out how their model can account for more moral reasoning than their critics realize and can avoid extreme versions of moral relativism.

Emotions are also central to morality according to Shaun Nichols, who summarizes his recent book, *Sentimental Rules*, in the next chapter.[6] Nichols holds that emotions play a key role in everyday moral judgment, but emotions cannot be the whole story, since normal people have similar emotional reactions to harms that are not caused by immoral actions. Nichols also argues that philosophical attempts to analyze moral judgments in terms of emotions, such as Allan Gibbard's prominent version of sentimentalism, conflict with recent studies of moral judgments by young children. Nichols concludes that core moral judgment depends on a body of rules—a normative theory. This postulated theory is used to explain recent observations of young children, as well as the relation of moral judgments to conventional judgments and rules regarding disgusting actions.

In his comment, Justin D'Arms defends his own version of sentimentalism against Nichols's arguments and counters that sentimentalists can explain moral disagreement better than Nichols can. James Blair then grants the force of Nichols's arguments against Blair's previous views but questions whether Nichols's postulated normative theory is needed for all moral judgments and decisions, and he suggests that the normative theory's work might be done by the theory of mind, since an agent's intention marks the difference between what is harmful and what is morally wrong. In response, Nichols argues that intention is not enough to explain the difference between being harmful and being wrong and that the only kind of disagreement that D'Arms can explain that he can't is fundamental moral disagreement among nonobjectivists, which is dubious for independent reasons.

Several preceding essays already mentioned moral disagreement, but this crucial topic is explored directly in the next chapter, by John Doris and Alexandra Plakias.[7] Doris and Plakias argue that intractable moral disagreements create serious problems for moral realism. Then they canvass a variety of evidence for such fundamental moral disagreements, including studies of attitudes toward honor and violence in the American South and a new study of Chinese responses to punishing innocent people. Doris and Plakias list possible defusing explanations (ignorance, partiality, irrationality, and prior theoretical commitments) and argue that none of these explanations defuses the disagreement in the cases under discussion, so the moral disagreement is truly fundamental and, hence, creates trouble for moral realism.

Brian Leiter questions whether moral disagreements can be explained away by partiality or irrationality, and he suggests that the history of philosophy (especially Friedrich Nietzsche) is enough by itself to reveal fundamental moral disagreements. Paul Bloomfield then argues that fundamental moral disagreements do not undermine moral realism, because moral realists can accommodate and explain moral divergence, and because widespread moral agreement can exist alongside the documented moral disagreements. In their reply, Plakias and Doris compare disagreements among philosophers with disagreements among everyday people, and disagreements over principles with disagreements over particular cases, as problems for moral realism.

The following chapter, by Don Loeb, also concerns moral realism, but he approaches moral realism from the perspective of the semantics of moral language. Loeb argues that moral language should be studied empirically and that, when we see how moral language actually works, it looks like moral vocabulary contains too much semantic incoherence for moral terms to refer to real properties, as moral realists claim. The crucial incoherence arises from the observation that ordinary people use moral language both to make factual assertions and also to do something incompatible with making such assertions.

Michael Gill suggests that these different uses of moral language are confined to isolated areas of moral thought, so variability need not yield incoherence or undermine moral realism about some areas of morality. Geoffrey Sayre-McCord then asks whether semantic theories in metaethics might be trying to capture not what ordinary people think and say but only what "we" think and say, where the pronoun "we" identifies a group that can properly be seen as making genuine moral judgments. Loeb replies by questioning whether Gill can divide moral language and thought into semantically insulated pockets and whether Sayre-McCord can nonarbitrarily identify a group that makes genuine moral judgments and avoids incoherence.

Morality includes not only rules about which acts are morally wrong but also standards of when agents are responsible for doing such acts. One common claim is that an agent is morally responsible for a harm only if that agent's action or omission caused that harm. Julia Driver defends this standard in the final chapter of this volume. Driver responds to both philosophical and empirical challenges to this standard and suggests that our causal judgments are based on prior judgments of whether the purported cause is unusual either statistically or normatively. Driver also argues that, while psychological research into the folk concepts can be interesting and helpful, it cannot replace more traditional methods of philosophy.

In response, Joshua Knobe, who was criticized by Driver, and Ben Fraser report the results of two new experiments that are supposed to undermine Driver's suggestion that causal judgments follow judgments of what is unusual or atypical, along with the alternative suggestion that Knobe's previous empirical results can be explained by conversational pragmatics. John Deigh then argues that Driver's claim that moral responsibility entails causation is refuted by legal cases, including one where medical personnel at a jail release a psychotic killer and another where every member of a group is complicit in and, hence, responsible for a harm that only some members of that group caused. Driver replies that her theory is compatible with Knobe and Fraser's new findings and also with Deigh's examples, if criminal responsibility is distinguished from moral responsibility.

These brief summaries cannot, of course, do justice to the rich empirical detail, careful philosophical arguments, and variety of profound issues that arise in these chapters. All together, these chapters show how much contemporary cognitive science has to contribute to moral theory.

Notes

1. This linguistic analogy is discussed further in the chapters by Sripada and Prinz in the first volume of this collection.

2. Hauser's studies of moral judgments by people with brain damage are relevant to the debate between Kennett and Roskies in the third volume of this collection.

3. Two of these models are defended by Haidt and Bjorklund in this volume and by Greene in the third volume of this collection.

4. Compare the chapter by Greene in the third volume of this collection.

5. A similar view is developed and defended by Flanagan, Sarkissian, and Wong in the first volume of this collection.

6. Moral emotions are also discussed by Moll et al. and by Greene in the third volume of this collection.

7. The extent and importance of moral disagreement are also discussed in the chapters by Sripada and Prinz in the first volume of this collection.

Moral Psychology

1 Moral Intuition = Fast and Frugal Heuristics?

Gerd Gigerenzer

Ordinary Men

On July 13, 1942, the men of Reserve Police Battalion 101, stationed in Poland, were wakened at the crack of dawn and driven to the outskirts of a small Polish village. Armed with additional ammunition, but with no idea what to expect, the 500 men gathered around their well-liked commander, Major Wilhelm Trapp (Browning, 1993). Nervously, Trapp explained that he and his men had been assigned a frightfully unpleasant task, not to his liking, but the orders came from the highest authorities. There were some 1,800 Jews in the village, who were said to be involved with the partisans. The order was to take the male Jews of working age to a work camp. The women, children, and elderly were to be shot on the spot. As he spoke, Trapp had tears in his eyes and visibly fought to control himself. He and his men had never before been confronted with such a task. Concluding his speech, Trapp made an extraordinary offer: If any of the older men did not feel up to the task that lay before them, *they could step out.*

Trapp paused for a moment. The men had a few seconds to decide. A dozen men stepped forward. The others went on to participate in the massacre. Many of them, however, after they had done their duty once, vomited or had other visceral reactions that made it impossible to continue killing and were then assigned to other tasks. Almost all were horrified and disgusted by what they were doing. Yet why did only a mere dozen men out of 500 declare themselves unwilling to participate in the mass murder?

One might first think of anti-Semitism. That, however, is unlikely, as the historian Christopher Browning (1993) documents in his seminal book *Ordinary Men.* Most of the battalion members were middle-aged family men, considered too old to be drafted into the German army, and drafted instead into the police battalion. By virtue of their age, their formative years had taken place in the pre-Nazi era, and they knew different political standards and moral norms. They came from the city of Hamburg, by reputation one of the least nazified cities in Germany, and from a social class that had been anti-Nazi in its political culture. These men would not have seemed to be a promising group of mass murderers on behalf of the Nazi vision.

The extensive interviews with the men indicate that the primary reason was not conformity with authority either. Unlike in the Milgram experiment, where an authoritative researcher told students to apply electric shocks to other people, Major Trapp explicitly allowed for "disobedience." The men who stepped out experienced no sanctions from him. If neither anti-Semitism nor fear of authority was the explanation, what else had turned ordinary men into mass killers? The documents collected on this case reveal a different reason. Most policemen's behavior seemed to follow a social heuristic:

Don't break ranks.

The men felt "the strong urge not to separate themselves from the group by stepping out" (Browning, 1993, p. 71), even if this conformity meant violating the moral imperative "Don't kill innocent people." For most, it was easier to shoot rather than to break ranks. Browning ends his book with a disturbing question: "Within virtually every social collective, the peer group exerts tremendous pressures on behavior and sets moral norms. If the men of Reserve Police Battalion 101 could become killers under such circumstances, what group of men cannot?" From a moral point of view, nothing can justify this behavior. In trying to understand why certain situations can promote or inhibit morally significant actions, however, we can find an explanation in social heuristics.[1]

Organ Donors

Since 1995, some 50,000 people in the United States have died waiting for a suitable organ donor (Johnson & Goldstein, 2003). Although most Americans say they approve of organ donation, relatively few sign a donor card. Here neither peer pressure, nor obedience, nor fear of being punished seems to be at issue. Why are only 28% of Americans but a striking 99.9% of French citizens donors? Do Americans fear that if emergency room doctors know that the patients are potential organ donors, they won't work as hard to save them? Or are Americans more anxious about a postmortem opening of their bodies than the French? Yet why are only 17% of British citizens but 99.9% of Hungarians donors?

If moral behavior is the result of deliberate moral reasoning, then the problem might be that Americans and the British are not aware of the need for organs. This view calls for an information campaign to raise people's awareness so that they change their behavior. Dozens of such campaigns have been launched in the United States and the United Kingdom with limited success. If moral behavior is the result of stable preferences, as postulated by rational choice theory, then Americans and the British might simply find too little utility in donation. Yet that does not seem to be the case either. Something stronger than preferences and deliberate reasoning appears to guide behavior. The differences between nations seem to be produced by a simple rule, the *default rule*:

If there is a default, do nothing about it.

In explicit-consent countries such as the United States and the United Kingdom, the law is that nobody is a donor without registering to be one. You need to opt in. In presumed-consent countries such as France and Hungary, everyone is a donor unless they opt out. The majority of citizens in these and other countries seem to follow the same default rule, and the striking differences between nations result as a consequence. However, not everyone follows the default rule. Among those who do not, most opt in but few opt out. The 28% of Americans who opted in and the 0.1% of French citizens who opted out illustrate this asymmetry. The perceived rationale behind the rule could be that the existing law is interpreted as a reasonable recommendation; otherwise it would not have been chosen by the policymakers. From a rational choice perspective, however, the default should have little effect because people will override the default if it is not consistent with their preference. After all, one only needs to sign a form to opt in or to opt out. However, the empirical evidence demonstrates that it is the default rule rather than alleged preferences that explains most people's behavior.

Fast and Frugal Heuristics

The two examples illustrate the general thesis of this essay: Morally significant actions (moral actions, for short) can be influenced by simple heuristics. The resulting actions can be morally repulsive, as in the case of mass killing, or positive, as when people donate organs or risk their lives to save that of another person. The underlying heuristic, however, is not good or bad per se.

The study of heuristics will never replace the need for moral deliberation and individual responsibility, but it can help us to understand which environments influence moral behavior and how to possibly modify them to the better. One and the same heuristic can produce actions we might applaud *and* actions we condemn, depending on where and when a person relies on it. For instance, the don't-break-ranks heuristic can turn a soldier simultaneously into a loyal comrade and into a killer. As an American rifleman recalls about comradeship during World War II: "The reason you storm the beaches is not patriotism or bravery. It's that sense of not wanting to fail your buddies. There's sort of a special sense of kinship" (Terkel, 1997, p. 164). Similarly, the default rule can turn a person into an organ donor or none. What appears as inconsistent behavior—how can such a nice guy act so badly, and how can that nasty person be so nice?—can result from the same underlying heuristic.

In this essay, I will look at moral actions through the lens of the theory of fast and frugal heuristics (Gigerenzer, Todd, & the ABC Research Group, 1999; Gigerenzer & Selten, 2001; Payne, Bettman, & Johnson, 1993). This theory is based on the work on bounded rationality by Nobel laureates Herbert Simon and Reinhard Selten. A heuristic is called "fast" if it can make a decision within little time, and "frugal" if it searches for only little information. The science of heuristics centers on three questions:

1. *Adaptive toolbox*   What heuristics do people have at their disposal? What are their building blocks, and which evolved (or learned) abilities do these exploit?
2. *Ecological rationality*   What environmental structures can a given heuristic exploit, that is, where is it successful and where will it fail? A heuristic is not good or bad, rational or irrational, per se, but only relative to environmental structures.
3. *Design of heuristics and environments*   How can heuristics be designed to solve a given problem? How can environments be designed to support the mind in solving a problem?

The first question is descriptive, concerning the content of *Homo sapiens'* adaptive toolbox. The tools in the toolbox are the heuristics, and the term "adaptive" refers to the well-documented fact that people tend to adjust the heuristics they use to the environment or problem they encounter. The second question is normative. The rationality of a heuristic is not logical, but ecological—it is conditional on environmental structure. The study of ecological rationality has produced results that appear logically impossible or counterintuitive, such as when a judgment based on only one reason is as good as or better than one based on more reasons or when partial ignorance leads to more accurate inferences about the world than more knowledge does (Gigerenzer, 2004). For instance, environmental structures such as high predictive uncertainty, small samples, and skewed cue validities allow the simple "take the best" heuristic, which ignores most information, to make more accurate predictions than do multiple regression or neural networks that integrate all information and use sophisticated calculation (Brighton, 2006; Chater, Oaksford, Nakisa, & Redington, 2003; Martignon & Hoffrage, 2002). Less can be more. The third question concerns cognitive (environmental) engineering. It draws on the results of the study of ecological rationality to design heuristics for given problems, such as whether or not a child should be given antibiotics (Fischer et al., 2002), or to design environments so that they fit the human mind, such as determining how to represent DNA evidence in court so that judges and jurors understand it (Hoffrage, Hertwig, & Gigerenzer, 2000).

Heuristics are embedded in (social) environments. For the reserve policemen, the environment included Major Trapp and the other men; the organ donors' environment is shaped by the legal default. Their actions are explained by both heuristics *and* their respective environments. This type of explanation goes beyond accounts of moral action in terms of personality traits such as an authoritarian personality, attitudes such as anti-Semitism, or prejudices against minorities or majorities. Unlike traits, attitudes, and preferences, which are assumed to be fairly stable across situations, heuristics tend to be highly context sensitive (Payne et al., 1993). A single policeman isolated from his comrades might not have hesitated to step forward.

If moral action is based on fast and frugal heuristics, it may conflict with traditional standards of morality and justice. Heuristics seem to have little in common with consequentialist views that assume that people (should) make an exhaustive analysis of the consequences of each action, nor with the striving for purity of heart that Kant considered to be an absolute obligation of humans. And they do not easily fit a neo-Aristotelian theory of virtue or Kohlberg's sophisticated postconventional moral reasoning. The closest cousin within moral philosophy seems to be rule utilitarianism (rather than act utilitarianism), which views a particular action as being right if it is consistent with some moral rule, such as "keep promises" (Downie, 1991). As mentioned before, heuristics provide explanations of actual behavior; they are not normative ideals. Their existence, however, poses normative questions.

What can be gained from analyzing moral actions in terms of fast and frugal heuristics? I believe that there are two goals:

1. *Explanation of moral actions*   The first result would be a theory that explains the heuristic processes underlying moral actions, just as for judgment and decision making in general. Such a theory is descriptive, not normative.

2. *Modification of moral actions*   The adaptive nature of heuristics implies that moral actions can be changed from outside, not just from inside the mind. Changes in environments, such as institutions and representations, can be sufficient to foster desired behavior and reduce moral disaster.

To illustrate the second goal, consider again the case of organ donation. A legal system aware of the fact that heuristics rather than reasoned preferences tend to guide behavior can make the desired option the default. In the United States, simply switching the default would save the lives of many patients who otherwise wait in vain for a donor. At the same time, this measure would save the expenses of current and future donor campaigns, which are grounded on an inadequate theory of mind. Setting proper defaults provides a simple solution for what looks like a complex moral problem. Similarly, consider once again the men of Reserve Police Battalion 101. With his offer, Major Trapp brought the Judaeo-Christian commandment "Don't murder," with which the Hamburg men grew up, into conflict with the "Don't break ranks" heuristic. With knowledge of the heuristic guiding his men's behavior, Major Trapp could have made a difference. He could have framed his offer the other way around, so that not breaking ranks no longer conflicted with not killing. Had he asked those who *felt up to the task* to step out, the number of men who participated in the killing might have been considerably smaller. This cannot be proven; yet, like Browning, I suspect that situational factors *can* shape moral behavior, as the prison experiments by Philip Zimbardo and the obedience experiments by Stanley Milgram indicate. These cases exemplify how a theory of heuristics could lead to instructions on how to influence moral action "from outside."

What are the limits of the heuristics approach? I do not believe that my analysis promises a normative theory of moral behavior. Yet the present descriptive analysis can put constraints on normative theories. A normative theory that is uninformed as to the workings of the mind, or is impossible to implement in a mind (or machine), will most likely not be useful for making our world better (see below).

Embodiment and Situatedness

Heuristics allow us to act fast—a requirement in situations where deferring decisions until more information is available can do harm to a person, such as in emergency unit decisions. Heuristics are frugal, that is, they ignore part of the information, even when it is available. Finally, heuristics can perform well because they are embodied and situated. Let me illustrate these features by an example that has nothing to do with moral action.

How does a player catch a fly ball? If you follow a classical information-processing approach in cognitive science, you assume that the player needs a more or less *complete representation* of the environment and a sophisticated computer to calculate the trajectory from this representation. To obtain a complete representation, the player would have to estimate the ball's initial velocity, angle, and distance, taking account of air resistance, wind speed, direction of wind, and spin. The player would then calculate the trajectory and run to the point where the ball will hit the ground. All this creates a nice optimization model, but there is no empirical evidence for it. No mind or machine can solve the problem this way. In the real world, players do not compute trajectories; instead, they rely on a number of simple heuristics. One is the *gaze heuristic*, which works if the ball is already high up in the air:

Fixate your gaze on the ball, start running, and adjust your speed so that the angle of gaze remains constant.

The gaze heuristic *ignores* all causal information necessary to compute the trajectory. It does not need a complete representation, even if it could be obtained. The heuristic uses only one piece of information, the angle of gaze. Yet it leads the player to the point where the ball will land. If you ask players how they catch a ball, most do not know the heuristic or can describe only one building block, such as "I keep my eye on the ball." The heuristic is composed of building blocks that draw on specific abilities. "Fixate your gaze on the ball" is one building block of the heuristic, which exploits the evolved ability to track a moving object against a noisy background. In general, a fast and frugal heuristic is a rule that is anchored in both mind and environment:

1. *Embodiment* Heuristics exploit evolved abilities, such as the human ability for group identification, imitation, or cheating detection (e.g., Cosmides & Tooby, 2004). The gaze heuristic exploits the ability of object tracking, that is, the ability to track a moving target against a noisy background, which emerges in three-month-old infants (Rosander & Hofsten, 2002). The default heuristic exploits a set of evolved abilities that deal with cooperation in small groups of people, such as imitation and trust.

2. *Situatedness* Heuristics exploit environmental structures, such as social institutions or the redundancy of information. The gaze heuristic even manipulates the environment, that is, it transforms the complex relation between player and ball into a simple, linear one.

Evolved abilities allow heuristics to be simple. Today's robots cannot trace moving objects against noisy backgrounds as well as humans; thus, the gaze heuristic is only simple for the evolved brains of humans, fish, flies, and other animals using it for predation and pursuit. The embodiment of heuristics poses a problem for the view that mental software is largely independent of the hardware and that mental processes can be realized in quite different physical systems. For instance, Hilary Putnam (1960) used Alan Turing's work as a starting point to argue for a distinction between the mind and the brain in terms of the separation of software from hardware. For many psychologists, this seemed a good basis for the autonomy of psychology in relation to neurophysiology. The rhetoric was that of cognitive systems that describe the thought processes "of everything from man to mouse to microchip" (Holland, Holyoak, Nisbett, & Thagard, 1986, p. 2). In contrast, heuristics do not function independently of the brain; they exploit it. Therefore, the heuristics used by "man and microchip" should not be the same. In summary, heuristics are simple because they exploit human brains—including their evolved abilities. This position is inconsistent with the materialistic ideal of reducing the mind to the brain, and also with the dualistic ideal of analyzing the mind independent of the brain, and vice versa.

Environmental structures allow heuristics to function well. When a clear criterion of success exists, one can mathematically analyze in which environments a given heuristic will succeed or fail. For instance, the gaze heuristic only works well when the ball is already high up in the air, not beforehand. In the latter case, the third building block of the heuristic needs to be changed into "adjust your speed so that the image of the ball is rising at a constant speed" (Shaffer, Krauchunas, Eddy, & McBeath, 2004). This illustrates that one does not need to develop a new heuristic from scratch for every new situation but can perhaps just modify one building block. The analysis of the situations in which a given heuristic works and fails is called the study of its "ecological rationality." The study of ecological rationality is difficult to generalize to moral action, unless criteria for success are supplied. Such criteria need to be precise; vague notions such as happiness and pleasure are insufficient for a mathematical analysis of ecological rationality.

Moral Action and Heuristics

I propose three hypotheses. First, moral intuitions as described in the social intuitionist theory (e.g., Haidt, 2001) can be explicated in terms of fast and frugal heuristics (Gigerenzer, 2007). Let me elaborate with a frequently posed distinction: Is moral judgment based on reasons or feelings? According to the philosophical theory of intuitionism, "a person who can grasp the truth of true ethical generalizations does not accept them as the result of a process of ratiocination; he just sees without argument that they are and must be true, and true of all possible worlds" (Harrison, 1967, p. 72). This view makes strong assumptions (that ethical generalizations are synthetic and a priori) and is hard to refute, as Harrison describes in detail. However, the idea that moral judgments are caused by perception-like, self-evident moral intuitions (not necessarily moral truths) has become the fundament of the social intuitionist approach to moral judgment. In this view, "moral reasoning does not cause moral judgment; rather moral reasoning is usually a post hoc construction, generated after a judgment has been reached" (Haidt, 2001, p. 814). Just like its philosophical sibling, social intuitionist theory makes a descriptive claim, and the evidence presented includes the sudden appearance in consciousness of moral judgments, after which people are "morally dumbfounded," that is, they mostly cannot tell how they reached a judgment (Haidt, Algoe, Meijer, Tam, & Chandler, 2000; Nisbett & Wilson, 1977). The unresolved issue in this theory is that "moral intuition" remains an unexplained primitive term.[2]

I agree with the proposition that in many cases moral judgments and actions are due to intuitive rather than deliberative reasoning. I also grant that there are important exceptions to this hypothesis, such as Benjamin Franklin's (1772/1987) "moral algebra" and the professional reasoning of judges. However, reasons given in public can be post hoc justification. What intuitionist theories could gain from the science of heuristics is to explicate intuition in terms of fast and frugal heuristics. This would provide an understanding of how intuitions are formed.

Here is my second hypothesis: Heuristics that underlie moral actions are largely the same as those for underlying behavior that is not morally tinged. They are constructed from the same building blocks in the adaptive toolbox. That is, one and the same heuristic can solve both problems that we call moral and those we do not. For instance, the "do what the majority do" heuristic (Laland, 2001) guides behavior in a wide range of situations, only some of which concern moral issues:

If you see the majority of your peers behave in a certain way, engage in the same action.

This heuristic produces social facilitation and guides behavior through all states of development from childhood to teenage and adult life. It virtually guarantees social acceptance in one's peer group. It can steer consumer behavior (what clothes to wear, what CDs to buy) and moral action as well (to donate to a charity, to discriminate against minorities). Teenagers tend to buy Nike shoes because their peers do, and skinheads hate foreigners for no other reason than that their peers hate them as well. The second hypothesis implies that moral intuitions are based on reasons, just as in cognitive heuristics, thus questioning the original distinction made between feelings and reasons. By explicating the processes underlying "feeling" or "intuition," the feeling/reason distinction is replaced by one between the conscious versus unconscious reasons that cause moral judgments.

The third hypothesis is that the heuristics underlying moral action are generally unconscious. If one interviews people, the far majority are unaware of their underlying motives. Rather, they often stutter, laugh, and express surprise at their inability to find supporting reasons for their likes and dislikes, or they invent post hoc justifications (Haidt, 2001; Haidt & Hersh, 2001; Nisbett & Wilson, 1977; Tetlock, 2003). This lack of awareness is similar to decision making outside the moral domain. As mentioned before, baseball players are often unaware of the heuristics they use, and consumers are not always able to explain why they bought a particular car, dress, or CD. Because of their simplicity and transparency, however, heuristics can be easily made conscious, and people can learn to use or to avoid them.

The view that moral action is based on fast and frugal heuristics also has three methodological implications:

1. *Study social groups in addition to isolated individuals* Heuristics exploit evolved abilities and social motives, such as the human potential for imitation, social learning, and feelings of guilt (Gigerenzer & Hug, 1992). The methodological implication is to study behavior in situations where these heuristics can unfold, such as in the presence of peers (e.g., Asch's [1956] conformity experiments). Compare the situation that the men of Reserve Police Battalion 101 faced with the hypothetical moral dilemmas in which an individual has to choose either to kill one person or otherwise let twenty people be killed by someone else (e.g., Williams, 1988). Here, the

experimental participant is studied in isolation. Heuristics such as *"don't break ranks"* and *"do what the majority do"* can hardly be detected.

2. *Study natural environments in addition to hypothetical problems* The science of heuristics aims for theoretical statements that involve the pairing of heuristics with environments, where the environment may select a heuristic or the heuristic may shape the environment (Gigerenzer et al., 1999). The methodological implication is to study moral intuitions in natural environments, or in experimental models thereof (e.g., Zimbardo's prison experiments and Milgram's obedience studies) rather than using hypothetical problems only. Toy problems such as the "trolley problems" eliminate characteristic features of natural environments, such as uncertainty about the full set of possible actions and their consequences, and do not allow the search for more information and alternative courses of action. I am not suggesting that hypothetical moral problems are of no use but that the present focus on hypothetical problems in experimental moral psychology as well as in moral philosophy creates a limited opportunity for understanding moral action. Because heuristics used tend to be very sensitive to social context, the careful analysis of natural environments is essential. This focus on the environment contrasts with those cognitive theories that assume, implicitly or explicitly, that morality is located within the individual mind, like a trait or a set of knowledge structures. For instance, in Kohlberg's (1971) rational cognitive theory, inspired by Piaget's (1932/1965) step model, moral development is a process that can be fully described internally, from egoistic to conventional to postconventional forms of reasoning. In these internalistic views, the structure of the environment appears of little relevance.

3. *Analyze moral behavior in addition to self-reports* People are typically unaware of the heuristics underlying their moral judgments or understand only part of them. The methodological implication is that asking people for reasons will rarely reveal the heuristics on which they actually base their decisions. Observation and analysis of behavior are indispensable if one wants to understand what drives people.

I will illustrate these points with judgments of trustworthiness in the legal context. The results of the following case study indicate that (1) legal decision makers use fast and frugal heuristics, (2) their heuristics have the same structure (not content) as heuristics used to solve nonmoral problems, (3) magistrates are largely unaware of this fact and believe their decisions are based on elaborate reasoning, and (4) the heuristics appear to be shaped by the social institution in which the decision makers operate.

Bail Decisions and Due Process

One of the initial decisions of the legal system is whether to bail the defendant unconditionally or to make a punitive decision such as custody or imprisonment. The bail decision is not concerned with the defendant's guilt but with his or her moral trustworthiness: whether or not the defendant will turn up at the court hearing, try to silence witnesses, or commit another crime. In the English system, magistrates are responsible for making this decision. About 99.9% of English magistrates are members of the local community without legal training. The system is based on the ideal that local justice be served by local people.

In England and Wales, magistrates make decisions on some two million defendants per year. They sit in court for a morning or afternoon every one or two weeks and make bail decisions as a bench of two or three. The Bail Act of 1976 and its subsequent revisions (Dhami & Ayton, 2001) require that magistrates pay regard to the nature and seriousness of the offense; to the character, community ties, and bail record of the defendant; and to the strength of the prosecution case, the likely sentence if convicted, and any other factor that appears to be relevant. Yet the law is silent on how magistrates should weigh and integrate these pieces of information, and the legal institutions do not provide feedback on whether their decisions were in fact appropriate or not. The magistrates are left to their own intuitions.

How do magistrates actually make these millions of decisions? To answer this question, several hundred trials were observed in two London courts over a four-month period (Dhami, 2003). The average time a bench spent with each case was less than 10 minutes. The analysis of the actual bail decisions indicated a fast and frugal heuristic that accounts for 95% of all bail decisions in Court A (see figure 1.1, left; cross-validation performance: 92%). When the prosecution requested conditional bail, the magistrates also made a punitive decision. If not, or if no information was available, a second reason came into play. If a previous court had imposed conditions or remanded in custody, then the magistrates also made a punitive decision. If not, or if no information was available, they followed the action of the police.

The bail decisions in Court B could be modeled by the same heuristic, except that one of the reasons was different (see figure 1.1, right). The benches in both courts relied on the same defensive rationale, which is known as "passing the buck." The magistrates' heuristics raise an ethical issue. In both London courts, they violate due process. Each bench based

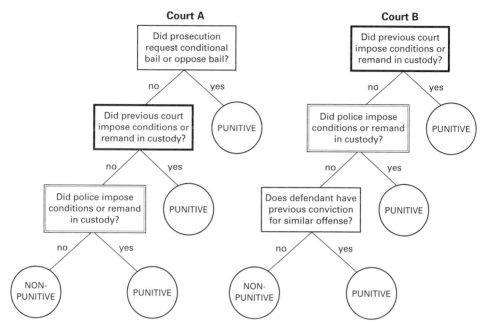

Figure 1.1
Models of fast and frugal heuristics for bail decisions in two London courts (adapted from Dhami, 2003).

a punitive decision on one reason only, such as whether the police had imposed conditions or imprisonment. One could argue that the police or prosecution had already looked at all the evidence concerning the defendant, and therefore magistrates simply used their recommendation as a shortcut (although this argument would make magistrates dispensable). However, the reasons guiding the heuristics were *not* correlated with the nature and seriousness of the offense or with other pieces of information relevant for due process.

The bail study investigated magistrates in their original social context (a bench of two or three laypeople) and in their natural environment (magistrates work in an institution that provides no systematic feedback about the quality of their decisions, and they can only be proven wrong if they bailed a defendant who then committed an offense; see below). Are its results consistent with the three hypotheses? With respect to the first hypothesis, the bail study can, at best, provide proof of the existence of fast and frugal heuristics but does not allow the conclusion that a substantial part of moral action is based on them. The answer to the second hypothesis, that the structure of moral heuristics mirrors that of other heuristics, however, is positive. The two bail heuristics have the same structure as a class of cognitive heuristics called "fast and frugal trees" (Katsikopoulos & Martignon, 2004). Unlike in a full tree, a decision is possible at each node of the tree. For three binary reasons with values [0, 1], where "1" allows for an immediate decision, the general structure of a fast and frugal tree is as follows:

Consider the first reason: If the value is "1," stop search and choose the corresponding action. Otherwise,
Consider the second reason. If the value is "1," stop search and choose the corresponding action. Otherwise,
Consider the third reason: If the value is "1," choose action A; otherwise choose B.

Fast and frugal trees are a subclass of heuristics that employ sequential search through reasons (Gigerenzer, 2004). The bail heuristics embody a form of one-reason decision making: Although more than one reason may be considered, the punitive decision itself is based on only one reason. The decision is noncompensatory, which means that reasons located further down the tree cannot compensate for or overturn a decision made higher up in the tree. In other words, the heuristic makes no trade-offs. Note that sequential heuristics can embody interactions, such as that bail is given only if neither prosecution, nor previous court, nor police opposed bail. Fast and frugal trees play a role in situations beyond the trustworthiness of a defendant, such as in medical decision making (Fischer et al., 2002; Green & Mehr, 1997).

Third, are magistrates aware of what underlies their judgments? When asked to explain their decisions, their stories were strikingly different. A typical answer was that they thoroughly examined all the evidence on a defendant in order to treat the individual fairly and without bias, and that they based their decision on the full evidence. For instance, one explained that the decision "depends on an enormous weight of balancing information, together with our experience and training" (Dhami & Ayton, 2001, p. 163). Another said that "the decisions of magistrates are indeed complex, each case is an 'individual case'" (Dhami, 2001, p. 255). Furthermore, magistrates actually asked for information concerning the defendant, which they subsequently ignored in their decisions. Unless the magistrates deliberately deceived the public about how they make bail decisions (and I have no grounds to assume so), one must conclude on the basis of the models in figure 1.1 that they are largely unaware of the heuristics they use. This dissociation between the reported reasons and the actual reasons (as modeled in the bail heuristics) is consistent with what Konecni and Ebbesen (1984) refer to as the "mythology of legal decision making" (p. 5).

Models of Moral Heuristics

There is a classical distinction between rationalist and nonrationalist theories of moral judgment. Is moral judgment the result of reasoning and reflection, as in Kohlberg's (1969) and Piaget's (1932/1965) theories? Or is it an intuitive process, as in Haidt's (2001) social intuitionism perspective, based on Hume's ideas? Rationalist theories assume that reasoning comes first and that moral intuition is its product, whereas social intuitionist theories assume that moral intuition typically comes first and reasoning is a post hoc attempt to justify an intuition to an audience. I suggest that the intuitions can be explicated by heuristics relying on reasons. The opposition is not between intuition and reasoning, in my view, but between the (unconscious) reasons underlying intuition and the conscious, after-the-fact reasons. The magistrates' judgments, for instance, can be explained by a simple heuristic based on three reasons, yet they believed they were engaging in highly complex reasoning. This point fits well with the social intuitionist view of moral judgment, where rationalization is ex post facto rather than the cause of the decision (Haidt, 2001). Moreover, the heuristics perspective can extend the intuitionist view in two directions: It provides an analysis of the heuristic process and of the environment.

Why Processes Models Are Essential

Unlike views that treat intuition as an unexplained primitive notion or attribute it to feelings as opposed to reasons, the heuristics perspective asks to specify models of what underlies moral intuition. The descriptive goal of the heuristics program is to spell out what the heuristics underlying intuition are and how they differ from the post hoc rationalization of one's judgment. This is a call for *models* and for going beyond mere *labels* for heuristics, such as "availability" and "representativeness" (Kahneman & Tversky, 1996). Mere labels and ying–yang lists of dichotomies such as "System 1 versus System 2" can account post hoc for everything and nothing (Gigerenzer, 1996, 1998; Gigerenzer & Regier, 1996). For decades, these surrogates for theories have hindered progress in the psychology of judgment. We instead need testable theories of cognitive processes, such as shown in figure 1.1. It is a striking paradox that many cognitive and social psychologists practice "black-box behaviorism." They don't seem to dare or care to open the box more than an inch, and they throw in a "one-word explanation" (e.g., salience, availability) before quickly shutting it again. B. F. Skinner would have been happy to see cognitive psychologists voluntarily abstain from theories of cognitive processes.

Models of heuristics demonstrate that the dichotomy between intuitions and reasons has its limits. Like conscious reasoning, sequential search heuristics—as shown in figure 1.1—rely on reasons. After all, one could make the bail heuristics public, implement them into a computer program, and replace the entire British bail system. Moral intuitions can be based on reasons, even if the latter are unconscious. These reasons, however, need not be the same as those given post hoc in public. In addition, moral intuition can ignore most or even all reasons, as in the case of simply copying the moral action of one's peers.

Yet why do we need models of heuristic processes underlying moral intuitions? Could one not simply say that people behave *as if* they were maximizing justice, well-being, or happiness? Consider the task of catching a ball again. Could one not simply say, as the biologist Richard Dawkins (1989) put it, "When a man throws a ball high in the air and catches it again, he behaves as if he had solved a set of differential equations in predicting the trajectory of the ball" (p. 96)? As-if theories do not describe how people actually solve a problem, in courts or sports. However, not knowing the heuristics can have unwanted consequences. I once gave a talk on the gaze heuristic, and a professor of business administration came up to me and told me the following story. Phil (not his real name) played baseball for the local team. His coach scolded him for being lazy, because Phil sometimes trotted over, as others did, toward the point where the ball came down. The angry coach insisted that he instead run as fast as he could. However, when Phil and his teammates tried to run at top speed, they often missed the ball. Phil had played as an outfielder for years and had never understood how he caught the ball. Unaware of the gaze heuristic and the other heuristics players use, the coach assumed something like the as-if model and did not realize that the heuristic dictates the speed at which a player runs, and that running too fast will impede performance. Phil's case illustrates that knowing the heuristic can be essential to correcting wrong conclusions drawn from an as-if model.

I argue that in the moral domain it is equally important to analyze the processes underlying people's helpful or harmful behavior in order to improve a situation. For instance, by starting with the assumption that the magistrates behaved as if they were maximizing the welfare of defendants and society, one would miss how the system works and not be able to improve it. Now that we have—for the first time—a good model of the magistrates' underlying heuristics, it is possible to assess the system and ask the critical questions. Are magistrates necessary at all? And, if the answer is positive, how can one improve their heuristics as well as a legal system that supports defensive justice rather than due process?

Institutions Shape Intuitions

The science of heuristics emphasizes the analysis of the "external" environment, in addition to the "internal" heuristics. Heuristics that shape moral intuitions are in part a consequence of the external environment, and vice versa. How does an institution shape heuristics?

The legal institution in which magistrates operate seems to support their mental dissociation. The law requests that magistrates follow due process. The magistrates' official task is to do justice to a defendant and the public, that is, to minimize the two possible errors one can make. This first error occurs when a suspect is released on bail and subsequently commits another crime, threatens a witness, or does not appear in court. The second error occurs when a suspect who would not have committed any of these offenses is imprisoned. However, as mentioned before, English legal institutions collect no systematic information about the quality of magistrates' decisions. Even if statistics were kept about when and how often the first error occurs, it would be impossible to do the same for the second error, simply because one cannot find out whether an imprisoned person would have committed a crime if he or she had been bailed. That is, the magistrates operate in an institution that does not or cannot provide feedback about how well they protect the defendant and the public. They effectively cannot learn how to solve the intended task, and the bail heuristics suggest that they instead try to solve a different one: to protect themselves rather than the defendant. Magistrates can only be proven to have made a bad decision if a suspect who was released committed an offense or crime while on bail. If this happens, the bail heuristic protects them against accusations by the media or the victims. The magistrates in Court A, for instance, can always argue that neither the prosecution, nor a previous court, nor the police had imposed or requested a punitive decision. Thus, the event was not foreseeable. An analysis of the institution can help to understand the nature of the heuristics people use and why they believe they are doing something else.

More generally, consider an institution that requires their employees to perform a duty. The employees can commit two kinds of errors: false alarms and misses. If an institution (1) does not provide systematic feedback concerning false alarms and misses but (2) blames the employees if a miss occurs, the institution fosters employees' self-protection over the protection of their clients, and it supports self-deception. I call this environmental structure a "split-brain institution." The term is borrowed from the fascinating studies of people whose corpus callosum—the connection between the right and left cerebral hemispheres—has been severed (Gazzaniga, 1985). Split-brain patients confabulate post hoc stories with the left (verbal) side of their brain to rationalize information or phenomena perceived by the right (nonverbal) side of their brain, which they are apparently unaware of. The analogy only holds to a point. Unlike a split-brain patient, a split-brain institution can impose moral sanctions for confabulating and punishment for awareness of what one does. If magistrates were fully aware of their heuristics, a conflict with the ideal of due process would ensue. Medical institutions often have a similar split-brain structure. Consider a health system that allows patients to visit a sequence of specialized doctors but does not provide systematic feedback to these doctors concerning the efficacy of their treatments, and in which doctors are likely to be sued by the patient for having overlooked a disease but not for overtreatment and overmedication. Such a system fosters doctors' self-protection over the protection of their patients and supports similar self-deception as in the case of the magistrates.

Should We Rely on Moral Heuristics?

The answer seems to be "no." Heuristics ignore information, do not explore all possible actions and their consequences, and do not try to optimize and find the best solution. Thus, for those theories that assume that all consequences of all possible actions should be taken into account to determine the best action, fast and frugal heuristics appear to be questionable guidelines. Even social intuitionists who argue against rationalist theories as a valid descriptive theory are anxious not to extend their theory to the normative level. For instance, Haidt (2001) is quick to point out that intuition is not about how judgments should be made, and he cites demonstrations that "moral intuitions often bring about nonoptimal or even disastrous consequences in matters of public policy, public health, and the tort system" (p. 815). Understanding nonrational intuitions may be "useful in helping decision makers avoid mistakes and in helping educators design programs (and environments) to improve the quality of moral judgment and behavior" (p. 815). The same negative conclusion can be derived from the heuristics-and-biases program (Kahneman, Slovic, & Tversky, 1982; Kahneman & Tversky, 2000), where heuristics are opposed to the laws of logic, probability, or utility maximization, and only the latter are defended as normative. Sunstein (2005), for instance, applies this approach to moral intuitions and emphasizes that heuristics lead to mistaken and even absurd moral judgments. Just as Kahneman and Tversky claimed to know the only correct answer to a reasoning problem (a controversial claim; see Gigerenzer 1996, 2000), Sunstein has a clear idea of what is right and wrong for many moral issue he discusses, and he holds people's moral heuristics responsible for their negligence, wrong-doing, and evil. Despite laudable attempts to propose models of heuristics, he relies on vague terms such as "availability" and "dual-process models." Yet, without some degree of precision, one cannot spell out in what environment a given heuristic would work or not work. All these views seem to converge to a unanimous consensus: Heuristics are always second-best solutions, which describe what people do but do not qualify as guidelines for moral action.

The view that heuristics can be prescriptive, not only descriptive, distinguishes the study of the adaptive toolbox from the heuristics-and-biases program. Both programs reject rational choice or, more generally, optimization as a general descriptive theory, arguing instead that people often use heuristics to make decisions. However, the heuristics-and-biases program stops short when it comes to the question of "ought." The study of ecological rationality, in contrast, offers a more radical revision of rational choice, including its prescriptive part. The gaze heuristic illustrates that ignoring all causal variables and relying on one-reason decision making can be ecologically rational for a class of problems that involve the interception of moving objects. More generally, today we know of conditions under which less information is better than more, for instance, when relying on only one reason leads to predictions that are as good as or better than by weighting and adding a dozen reasons (Czerlinski, Gigerenzer, & Goldstein, 1999; Hogarth & Karelaia, 2005; Martignon & Hoffrage, 1999). We also understand situations where limited cognitive capacities can enable language learning (Ellman, 1993) and covariation detection (Kareev, 2000) better than larger capacities do (Hertwig & Todd, 2003). Simple heuristics, which ignore part of the available information, are not only faster and cheaper but also more accurate for environments that can be specified precisely. I cannot go into detail here, but the general reason for these counterintuitive results are that, unlike logic and rational choice models, heuristics exploit evolved abilities and structures of environments, including their uncertainty (Gigerenzer, 2004). This opens up the possibility that when it comes to issues of justice and morals, there are situations in which the use of heuristics, as opposed to an exhaustive analysis of possible actions and consequences, is preferable.

Can heuristics be prescriptive? As I said earlier, unlike in inferences and predictions where a clear-cut criterion exists, in the moral domain one can only analyze the situations in which a heuristic is ecologically rational if a normative criterion is introduced. For inference tasks, such as classification and paired comparison, heuristics are evaluated by predictive accuracy, frugality, speed, and transparency. Some of these criteria may be relevant for moral issues. For instance, transparent rules and laws may be seen as a necessary (albeit not sufficient) condition for creating trust and reassurance in a society, whereas nontransparent rules and arbitrary punishments are the hallmark of totalitarian systems. Transparency also implies that the number of laws is few, as in the Ten Commandments of Christianity. In many situations, however, there is no single agreed norm. But I believe that one should face rather than deny normative uncertainty.

Last but not least, the science of heuristics can provide a better understanding of the limits of normative theories of morality. I illustrate this point with versions of consequentialism and similar theories that are based on the moral ideal of maximization.

The Problem with Maximization Theories

The idea that rational choice means the maximization of the expected value has been attributed to the seventeenth-century French mathematicians Blaise Pascal and Pierre Fermat and dated to their exchange of letters in 1654. Pascal used the calculus for a moral problem: whether or not to believe in God (Daston, 1988). He argued that this decision should not be based on blind faith or blind atheism but on considering the consequences of each action. There are two possible errors. If one believes in God but he does not exist, one will forgo a few worldly pleasures. However, if one does not believe in God but he exists, eternal damnation and suffering will result. Therefore, Pascal argued, however small the probability that God exists, the known consequences dictate that believing in God is rational. What counts are the consequences of actions, not the actions themselves. "Seek the greatest happiness of the greatest number"—the slogan associated with Jeremy Bentham—is a version of this maximization principle, a form of hedonistic utilitarianism where the standard is not the agent's own happiness but that of the greatest number of people. Today, many forms of utilitarianism and consequentialism exist, both normative and descriptive (see Smart, 1967).

My question is, can utilitarianism and consequentialism provide (1) a norm and (2) a description of moral action in the real world? I emphasize the "real world" as opposed to a textbook problem such as the trolley problem, where I assume, for the sake of argument, that the answer is "yes." When I use the term *consequentialism* in the following, I refer to theories that postulate maximizing, implicitly or explicitly: "in any form of direct consequentialism, and certainly in act-utilitarianism, the notion of the right action in given circumstances is a maximizing notion" (Williams, 1988, p. 23; see also Smart, 1973). Just as in Pascal's moral calculus, and Daniel Bernoulli's maximization of subjective expected utility, this form of consequentialism is about the *optimal* (best) action, not just one that is good enough. It demands optimizing, not satisficing.

To find the action with the best consequences is not a simple feat in the real world. It requires determining the set of all possible actions, all possible consequences, their probabilities, and their utilities. There are at least four interpretations of this process of maximizing:

- a conscious mental process (e.g., to think through all possible actions and consequences),
- an unconscious mental process (the brain does it for you, but you don't notice the process, only the result),
- an *as-if* theory of behavior (people behave *as if* they computed the action with the highest utility; no claim for a conscious or unconscious mental process), and
- a normative goal (maximizing determines which action one ought to choose; no claim as a model of either process or behavior).

Proponents of consequentialism have emphasized that their theory is not just a fiction created by some philosophers and economists and handed down to moral scholars. It is written into law (Posner, 1972). According to U.S. tort law, an action is called "negligent" and the actor is likely to pay damages if the probability of resulting harm multiplied by the cost of harm to others exceeds the benefit of the action to the actor. This is known as the "Learned Hand formula," named after Judge Learned Hand, who proposed the formula for determining negligence in 1947. If the expected damage is less than the expected benefit, the actor is not liable for damages, even if the risked harm came to pass.

Yet there is a second part to this story. Although Judge Learned Hand has been acclaimed as an early proponent of maximization and consequentialism, he also held the view that "all such attempts [to quantify the determinants of liability] are illusory; and, if serviceable at all, are so only to center attention upon which one of the factors may be determinate in any given situation" (Moisan v. Loftus, 178 F.2d 148, 149 [2d Cir 1949]; see Kysar et al., 2006). Here, Judge Hand seems to favor one-reason decision making, such as fast and frugal decision trees and Take The Best (Gigerenzer & Goldstein, 1996). This second part illustrates some of the problems with maximization in the real world, which I will now turn to.

Computational Limits

By definition, consequentialism (in the sense of maximization) can only give guidelines for moral action *if the best action can actually be determined by a mind or machine.* I argue that this is typically not the case in the real world. To the degree that this is true, consequentialism is confined to well-defined moral problems with a limited time horizon and a small set of possible actions and consequences that do not allow uncertainty and surprises. Moral textbook problems in the philosophical literature have this impoverished structure (Williams, 1988).

Consider, in contrast, a moral game that has the structure of chess—a choice set of about 30 possible actions per move, a temporal horizon of a sequence of some 20 moves, and two players. One player acts, the other reacts, and so on, with 10 moves for each person. For each move, both players can choose to act in 1 out of the 30 possible ways—to tell the truth, to lie, to cheat, to form an alliance, to withhold information, to insult, to threaten, to blackmail, and so on. The opponent then responds with 1 of the 30 possible actions, and so on. The game is well defined; no negotiation of rules or self-serving changes are allowed. Every action in this game of social chess depends on those of the other person, so one has to look ahead to understand the consequences of one's own action. Can one determine the best sequence of actions in this game? Although the game looks like a somewhat impoverished human interaction, no mind or machine can enumerate and evaluate all consequences. A simple calculation will illustrate this.

For each action, there are 30 possibilities, which makes in 20 moves 30^{20} sequences, which amounts to some

350,000,000,000,000,000,000,000,000,000

possible sequences of moves. Can a human mind evaluate all of these consequences? No. Can our fastest computers do it? Deep Blue, the IBM chess computer, can examine some 200 million possible moves per second. How long would it take Deep Blue to think through all consequences in social chess and choose the move that maximizes utility? Even at its breathtaking speed, Deep Blue would need some 55,000 billion years to think 20 moves ahead and pick the best one. (Recall that the Big Bang is estimated to have occurred only some 14 billion years ago.) But 20 moves are not yet a complete game of chess or of human interaction. In technical terms, social chess is "computationally intractable" for minds and machines.

If we increased the number of people interacting from two to three or more, we would encounter a new obstacle for maximization. Just as the predictive power of physics ends with a three-body problem—such as earth, moon, and sun, moving under no influence other than their mutual gravitation—there is no best way to predict the dynamics of the mutual attractions of three or more people. This computational problem arises both in competitive and cooperative games if they are played in an uncertain world rather than in a small closed one. My conclusion is that consequentialism, understood as the maximization of some measure of utility or happiness, can only work with a limited time perspective and limited interactions. Beyond these limits, consequentialism can neither be prescriptive nor descriptive.

When Maximization Is Out of Reach

More generally, situations for which maximization—in consequentialism or other moral theories—is impossible, include the following:

1. *Computationally intractable problems* These are well-defined problems, such as chess and the computer games Tetris and Minesweeper. No mind or machine can compute the optimal solution in real time. For instance, when former chess world champion Kasparov played against the IBM chess program Deep Blue, both had to rely on heuristics. The reason is not simply because people or computers have limited cognitive capacities but because the problem is computationally intractable. This is not necessarily bad news. Games where we know the optimal solution (such as tic-tac-toe) are boring for exactly this reason. The same holds for moral issues. If social chess were computable, part of our emotional life would become obsolete. We would always know how to behave optimally, as would our partners. There would be fewer things to hope for, and less surprise, joy, disappointment, and regret.

2. *The criterion cannot be measured with sufficient precision* For instance, there is no way to optimize the acoustics of a concert hall because experts consistently disagree about what constitutes good acoustics. The same applies to many moral criteria. The criterion of consequentialist theory—"happiness," "pleasure," or "utility"—is at least as difficult to measure as the acoustics of a concert hall, and for similar reasons. People, including

experts, will not agree what consequences make them and others most happy, and there are societies where happiness means little in comparison to religious faith and loyalty to one's national and cultural identity. Thus, the criterion of the greatest happiness for everyone may become increasingly fuzzy the farther one travels from one's social group. The same problem arises for norms of egalitarianism. Moral philosophers have long discussed what should be equal: opportunity, rights, income, welfare, capabilities, or something else? A heuristic may focus on those few that can be observed most easily in a given situation (Messick, 1993). However, the general problem of optimizing equality has no solution because of lack of sufficient precision.

3. *Multiple goals or criteria* Optimization is, in general, impossible for problems with multiple criteria. One cannot maximize several criteria simultaneously (unless one combines them by, say, a linear function). For instance, even if the traveling salesman problem could be solved (it cannot for large numbers of cities), its real-world equivalent has multiple criteria, not only the shortest route. These can involve the fastest route, the cheapest route, and the most scenic route. Multiple criteria or goals, however, are characteristic of moral dilemmas. Examples are paternity cases where one wants to find the truth but also protect the child from being uprooted, while doing justice to the rights of the genetic parents and the foster family. Similarly, when happiness is not of one kind, but of several, one cannot maximize all of these simultaneously.

4. *Calculative rationality can be seen as morally unacceptable* In certain domains, the idea of choosing the option with the best anticipated consequences can violate people's moral sense. These include kinship, friendship, and mate choice. When a man (or woman) proceeds rationally by empirically investigating all potential partners, the possible consequences of living with them, and the probabilities and utilities of each consequence, moral outrage from those being investigated can result. In 1611, for instance, the astronomer Johannes Kepler began a methodical search for his second wife after an arranged and unhappy first marriage. He investigated 11 possible replacements within 2 years. Friends urged him to marry Candidate No. 4, a woman of high status and tempting dowry, but she eventually rejected him for toying with her too long. The attempt to rationally determine the best alternative can be perceived as morally repulsive. Former First Lady Barbara Bush, in contrast, seemed to have undertaken little comparative study: "I married the first man I ever kissed. When I tell this to my children, they just about throw up" (Todd & Miller, 1999).

5. *Optimization can destroy trust*   If an employer tried to optimize and dismissed his employees and subcontracters every year in order to hire the best ones, he might destroy loyalty, identification, and trust (Baumol, 2004). In contrast, heuristics such as satisficing entail an implicit promise to current employees that as long as their performance and development continue to be satisfactory, that is, meet an aspiration level, no changes will be made. This makes it attractive for employees to adapt their services to the needs of the firm. The value in commitments holds outside of business environments. When a university admits a graduate student, it is typically understood that there is no annual contest among students inside and outside the university for reallocating stipends competitively to the students who look best at any point in time. Rather, the support will be continued for the next several years, as long as the student's performance continues to meet standards of acceptability.

6. *Ill-defined problems*   Most problems in the real world are ill-defined, that is, the set of possible actions is not known, their consequences cannot be foreseen, the probabilities and utilities are unknown, and the rules of the game are not fixed but are negotiated during the game. In these situations, maximization—of collective happiness or anything else—is, by definition, impossible.

The fact that maximization (optimization) is typically out of reach in the real world is widely ignored in philosophy, economics, and the cognitive sciences. This state of affairs has been called the "fiction of optimization" (Klein, 2001; see also Selten, 2001). Several tools for rescuing maximization are in use. One is to assume that people are unboundedly rational, that is, that they know all actions, consequences, and other information needed to calculate the best option. A second tool is to edit a computationally intractable real-world problem into one that is small enough so that the optimization calculus can be applied. However, as Herbert Simon (1955, p. 102) argued long ago, there is a complete lack of evidence that in real-world situations of any complexity, these computations can be or actually are performed. In contrast, in applied sciences such as robotics and machine learning, it is common wisdom that in order to solve real-world problems, one needs to develop heuristic methods.

Toward an Investigation of Moral Heuristics

In this essay, I argued that many—not all—moral actions can be understood as based on fast and frugal heuristics. Specifically, moral intuitions can be explicated by models of heuristics. These heuristics are strong enough to act upon, yet people are typically not aware of their underlying rationale. Understanding heuristics requires an analysis of the social environment in which people act, because heuristics take advantage of environments and environments select heuristics. Analyzing the environment also helps to understand systematic discrepancies between the reasons people give for their moral intuitions and the underlying heuristics. To the degree that moral action is guided by heuristics, it can be influenced by changing the conditions that trigger a given heuristic. This includes the framing of an offer, as illustrated in the case of Major Trapp, and the choice of the default, as in the case of organ donation. Unlike theories that focus on traits, preferences, attitudes, and other internal constructs, the science of heuristics emphasizes the interaction between mind and social environment. Knowing the heuristics that guide people's moral actions can be of help in designing change that might otherwise be out of reach.

Notes

I thank Lael Schooler, Walter Sinnott-Armstrong, Masanori Takezawa, Rona Unrau, and the members of the LIFE Max Planck International Research School for their helpful comments.

1. Browning (1993, p. xvii). I chose this sensitive example because it is one of the best-documented mass murders in history, with the unique feature that the policemen were given the opportunity not to participate in the killing. My short account cannot do justice to the complexity of the situation, and I recommend consulting Browning's book, including the afterword, in which he deals with his critics such as Daniel Goldhagen. Browning (e.g., pp. 209–216) offers a multilayered portrayal of the battalion during their first and subsequent mass killings. The largest group of policemen ended up doing whatever they were asked to, avoiding the risk of confronting authority or appearing to be cowards, yet not volunteering to kill. Increasingly numbed by the violence, they did not think that what they were doing was immoral, because it was sanctioned by authority. In fact, most tried not to think at all. A second group of "eager" killers who celebrated their murderous deeds increased in numbers over time. The smallest group were the nonshooters, who, with the exception of one lieutenant, neither protested against the regime nor reproached their comrades.

2. Some psychologists do invoke a "dual-process model" that postulates an "intuitive system" and a "reasoning system" to account for the difference between moral intuition and reasoning. In my opinion, however, this amounts to a redescription of the phenomenon rather than an explanation; contrary to what its name suggests, this model does not specify any process underlying intuition or reasoning but consists of a list of dichotomies (Gigerenzer & Regier, 1996).

1.1 | Fast, Frugal, and (Sometimes) Wrong

Cass R. Sunstein

For many problems, Gerd Gigerenzer celebrates heuristics. He believes that they are simple, fast, frugal, and remarkably accurate. He emphasizes that heuristics can be prescriptive, in the sense that they may well lead to good outcomes in the real world. In the moral domain, Gigerenzer is properly cautious about whether heuristics produce moral or immoral behavior. What I would like to do here is to emphasize the imperfect reliability of heuristics in general and to suggest that their imperfect reliability raises serious cautionary notes about some of Gigerenzer's broader claims.

Let us begin with Gigerenzer's illuminating remarks about the "gaze heuristic," which enables baseball players (and others) to make otherwise difficult catches. Gigerenzer, who has often explored this particular heuristic, is quite right to emphasize that people who use heuristics are often not aware that they are doing so. But even a casual understanding of sports requires some qualification of Gigerenzer's claims. Stupid tennis players tend to use fast and frugal heuristics, which contribute to their stupid tennis. Often they think, for example, that they should hit the ball hard and deep whenever the opportunity arises—an intuition, or thought, that can get them into serious trouble. Stupid athletes adopt simple heuristics that make them dumb. By contrast, smart tennis players are immensely flexible, and they are able to rethink their rules of thumb as the occasion demands. The best athletes have an exceedingly complex set of heuristics, fast but not at all simple, which they deploy as the situation requires. The moral domain is not so very different (see Nussbaum, 2003). It is pervaded by fast heuristics, as Gigerenzer suggests, but they often misfire, and good moral agents are aware of that fact.

My own treatment of moral heuristics, criticized by Gigerenzer, emphasizes the immense importance of moral framing and the possibility that people use "simple heuristics that make us good" (Sunstein, 2005). For morality, as for issues of fact and logic, it is important to see that many heuristics do point us in the right direction—and hence to stress, as did Tversky and Kahneman (1974) and later Gigerenzer, that heuristics can lead to excellent judgments in the actual world. If people believe that they ought not to lie, or harm innocent people, they will often do the right thing—especially in light of the fact that case-by-case inquiries into the morality of lying, or harming innocent people, could produce self-serving conclusions that produce grievous moral wrong. (The case of Nazi massacres, explored by Gigerenzer, can be understood as an example.) Moral heuristics, understood as simple rules of thumb, might well have a rule-utilitarian defense, in the sense that they might, on balance, produce morally preferable behavior even if they lead to unfortunate results in particular cases.

But no one should deny that in many contexts, moral and other heuristics, in the form of simple rules of thumb, lead to moral error on any plausible view of morality. Consider, for example, the idea, emphasized by Gigerenzer, that one ought to do as the majority does, a source of massive moral blunders (see Sunstein, 2003). Or consider the fast and frugal idea that one ought not to distort the truth—a heuristic that generally works well but that also leads (in my view) to moral error when, for example, the distortion is necessary to avoid significant numbers of deaths. Or consider the act–omission distinction, which makes moral sense in many domains but which can lead to unsupportable moral judgments as well.

Gigerenzer notes, usefully, that it may be possible to modify people's judgments, including their moral judgments, by altering the background. The idea is hardly original, but it is true that a default rule in favor of organ donations might well increase what, on one view, is morally desirable behavior. Indeed there are many applications of this point. If default rules matter, an employer, including the state qua employer, could dramatically increase charitable contributions by presuming that (for example) each employee would like to devote 2% of wages to charitable causes. Of course, the use of default rules to steer behavior raises normative questions of its own. The only point is that default rules greatly matter to choices, including those with a moral component.

Thus far, then, Gigerenzer's general argument seems both plausible and illuminating, and I am merely underlining the possibility that even good heuristics will go wrong, for morality as for other questions. But on an important issue, Gigerenzer seems to me to miss some of the complexity of moral argument. His objections to maximization theories treat moral judgments as involving a kind of moral arithmetic, and this is a most contentious understanding.

To be sure, Gigenenzer is correct to stress the cognitive difficulties of undertaking a full ex ante calculation of the consequences of social actions. Human beings do not have unlimited cognitive abilities, and hence they are often unable to specify the effects of one or another course of action. Gigerenzer believes that satisficers, using moral heuristics, have important advantages over optimizers. For some questions, this is undoubtedly correct. But to understand the relationship between heuristics and the moral domain, much more must be said. Three points are especially important here.

First: Gigerenzer does not mention that many people are rule consequentialists; they know exactly what Gigerenzer emphasizes, and they favor clear and simple moral rules for that very reason (Hooker, 2000). A complex consequentialist calculus might lead to error, even if it would be preferable if properly applied. Because people are self-serving, and because their on-the-spot judgments are unreliable, they might do best to follow simple moral rules or one-reason decision making. There are interesting relationships between Gigerenzer's understanding of heuristics and a rule-utilitarian approach to morality.

Second: Consequentialism can be specified in many different ways. Utilitarianism is one form of consequentialism, but because it requires all goods and bads to be described along the metric of utility, it is controversial, even among consequentialists. When Gigerenzer speaks of the limits of maximization theories, and even of consequentialism, he appears to be operating under a utilitarian framework, without exploring the problem of plural and incommensurable goods. We might, for example, endorse a form of consequentialism that sees rights violations (so understood on nonutilitarian grounds) as a set of (very) bad consequences (see Sen, 1982). Gigerenzer's exploration of moral problems does not recognize the complexities in consequentialist accounts of morality.

Third: Many people are not consequentialists at all (see Scheffler, 1994). Consider the injunction to treat people as ends, not means, an injunction that runs afoul of many versions of consequentialism (but see Sen, 1982). Hence—and this is the most important point—it is not enough for Gigerenzer to show that moral heuristics do a good (enough) real-world job of achieving what we would achieve if we were optimizers with unlimited abilities of calculation. Perhaps some heuristics, in some contexts, violate deontological commands.

Return to Gigerenzer's first example: Should a Nazi massacre be evaluated in utilitarian or consequentialist terms? To make the calculation, does it matter if, for example, there were many more Nazis than Jews, and that many Germans had a great deal to gain, economically and otherwise, from mass murders? Many people would respond that this moral atrocity counts as such whatever the outcome of a utilitarian or consequentialist calculus—and hence that Gigerenzer's emphasis on the impossibility of ex ante calculations is often beside the point (or worse). Perhaps many moral heuristics, followed by most people and even most soldiers (putting Nazi soldiers to one side), should be seen as fast and frugal ways not of satisficing rather than optimizing but of ensuring that people do what is required by nonconsequentialist accounts of morality.

The existence of plural and conflicting accounts of the foundations of morality makes it all the more difficult to argue that moral heuristics function well. If certain fast and frugal heuristics are defensible on utilitarian or consequentialist grounds, they might still be objectionable from the moral point of view. In my view, it is for this reason productive to explore heuristics that might be defensible, or indefensible, on the basis of *any* view of what morality requires or on the basis of the least contentious views of what morality requires (Sunstein, 2005).

Gigerenzer seems to think that moral heuristics might be shown to be prescriptive if a full consequentialist calculus is not possible, but this thought too quickly treats morality as a problem of arithmetic. If morality ought not to be so understood, as many people believe, then it is not clear what is shown by Gigerenzer's emphasis on the cognitive problems associated with optimizing. I emphasize that prescriptive treatments of moral heuristics are likely to be productive, but they should steer clear of the most contentious arguments about the foundations of morality.

1.2   Moral Heuristics and Consequentialism

Julia Driver and Don Loeb

Professor Gerd Gigerenzer's work on fast and frugal heuristics is fascinating and has been extremely influential, in a very positive way, on research in the psychology of human action. There is much in Gigerenzer's work that we agree with. For example, he has effectively demonstrated that people often perform intentional actions using heuristics rather than complicated decision procedures. Further, he has plausibly argued for various ways in which these heuristics work, focusing on actual cases—such as the way persons normally go about catching balls, which relies in part on the gaze heuristic. We agree that much moral action is not guided by any process of conscious decision making or calculation, and we find interesting and promising the suggestion that fast and frugal heuristics are sometimes responsible for people's actions and moral judgments.

Furthermore, knowing how the mind works in solving problems or accomplishing tasks is useful for anyone concerned about ethics. Gigerenzer's suggestions about institutional design, the recognition of programmed responses that lead to good or bad results, and the ways these can be modified are all very constructive indeed. While we have reservations about certain elements of his descriptive argument, we will, for the most part, leave such issues to the psychologists and focus on normative matters. When it comes to such matters, however, there is much that we disagree with. In particular, we think, his treatment of prescriptive issues blurs significant distinctions and unfairly characterizes traditional philosophical methods of reasoning about ethics. Most importantly, we think, his attack on consequentialism is seriously misguided. Before turning to these prescriptive matters, however, we offer a few concerns about the descriptive claims.

Some Worries about Gigerenzer's Descriptive Claims

In a couple of cases, Gigerenzer's descriptive claims seem less than fully warranted. For example, in a fascinating and illuminating discussion of the behavior of bail magistrates in London, he shows that the vast number of these magistrates' decisions fit a much simpler, tree-like decision procedure, rather than the multifactor analysis they believe themselves to be employing. While we can think of unanswered questions about the magistrates' decisions, we do not wish to (and indeed are not in a position to) claim that Gigerenzer's analysis is incorrect. Still, we think it unfair to suggest that instead of trying to do justice, the magistrates' "heuristics suggest that they instead try to solve a different [problem]: to protect themselves rather than the defendant" (p. 32). There is often a difference between what people do and what they are *trying* to do. And without better evidence, we should be reluctant to suggest that well-meaning people are following the CYA (try to avoid anticipated criticisms) heuristic.[1]

Another place in which we are suspicious of Gigerenzer's descriptive claims involves his defense of the claim that "knowing the heuristic can be essential to correcting wrong conclusions drawn from an as-if model" (p. 16). He discusses the case of a baseball-playing professor who, on the advice of his coach, began to run as fast as he could toward fly balls, with disastrous results. "The coach," we are told, "assumed something like the as-if model" (p. 16) and did not realize that knowing the heuristic was essential to correcting this error. The former claim seems implausible; the as-if model seems to recommend advising the player not to change a thing. We suggest that a player who behaves as if he intends to catch the ball is much more likely to succeed than one who attempts to employ the gaze heuristic instead. While *following* the heuristics can lead to success, *attending* to them may well lead to failure.[2]

Finally, Gigerenzer hypothesizes that even intuitions are based on reasons (in the form of heuristics) and thus that we can substitute a *conscious* versus *unconscious* reasoning distinction for the more traditional *feeling* versus reason distinction found in philosophical and psychological debates about how moral decisions are made. However, we must be careful here. That heuristics underlie some of our intuitive responses does not show that reasoning, in any ordinary sense of the term, underlies them. That there is a reason (in the sense of an explanation or cause) for our behaving a certain way—even an explanation having to do with the behavior's effectiveness at achieving some end—does not mean that we have unconsciously reasoned to that end. By analogy, and as Gigerenzer would be the first to acknowledge, evolution produces results that often resemble products of reasoning, but this is an illusion.

Worries about Gigerenzer's Prescriptive Claims

We now turn to Gigerenzer's discussion of the possibility that heuristics can be prescriptive, as well as descriptive. Here we think Gigerenzer treads on much more hazardous ground. He begins with a horrifying example involving Nazi policemen who had to decide whether or not to take part in a massacre. A surprisingly small number decided not to participate. Professor Gigerenzer attributes the majority's shocking failure to remove themselves from the massacre to a heuristic, "Don't break ranks." Their behavior can be explained, though not justified, by this heuristic, he thinks. Indeed, the example makes quite clear that Gigerenzer does not think the mere fact that we tend to *employ* a given heuristic makes it morally acceptable to do so.

However, that leaves unclear what Gigerenzer means when he claims that in some cases, heuristics can be prescriptive. We think that there are at least two dimensions along which heuristics might be thought to have normative significance. An understanding of the way heuristics work and the concrete environments in which they do so might be claimed to be useful in helping to *identify* normative goals. Alternatively, such an understanding might be thought useful in helping us to design institutions and in other ways help people to realize certain normative goals, once such goals have been identified independently.

Gigerenzer is clearly making the second of these claims, and we see no reason to dispute it. Heuristics are extremely useful because they allow people to reach decisions or to act in short periods of time, which is often necessary to ensure good outcomes. Moreover, they do so in a way that is economical in the sense that they make use of only a fraction of the available information relevant to a given decision. This not only fosters quicker action but sometimes, at least, results in better decisions relative to those outcomes. As one of us argued in another context, more information is not always better; indeed, sometimes it is much worse (Loeb, 1995). Without the gaze and similar heuristics we would be terrible at catching balls.

Moreover, the concept of ecological rationality is an interesting and useful one. For example, Gigerenzer writes, "The gaze heuristic illustrates that ignoring all causal variables and relying on one-reason decision making can be ecologically rational for a class of problems that involve the interception of moving objects" (p. 19). In the case of moral heuristics, ecological rationality means that they "exploit environmental structures, such as social institutions" (p. 8). Gigerenzer seems to mean by this that our determination of the rationality of a heuristic—and perhaps also whether or not it is morally good or bad—will depend upon the agent's environment. It is context sensitive and depends upon features external to the agent. Professor Driver, in *Uneasy Virtue* (2001), argued that moral virtue is like this. What makes a trait a moral virtue has nothing to do with the internal psychological states of the agent; rather it has to do with externalities such as what consequences are typically produced by the trait. Indeed, virtuous agents can be unaware of their true reasons for action, the considerations that are actually moving them to perform their good deeds. It may be that morally virtuous persons are those who are sensitive to the reasons that would justify one heuristic over another in a certain situation and so are responsive to the *right* heuristics. Heuristics underlie good actions as well as bad ones, and what makes a heuristic a good one will depend on how it plays out in the real world, what it accomplishes when employed by an individual in a given situation. On her view, good effects make for a good heuristic.

But what about the first of the two claims? Can heuristics help us to *choose* normative goals—in particular, moral ones? Can they help us to identify the fundamental principles of morality (or for irrealists like Loeb, in deciding what to value)? Gigerenzer's answer seems to be that they cannot do so directly, but they can do so indirectly by placing limitations on what counts as an acceptable moral theory. An acceptable theory must be one that could in fact be used by real people in the real world. Real people aren't supercomputers, and even if we were, we'd rely on heuristics to solve complex problems. "Simple heuristics," Gigerenzer tells us, ". . . are not only faster and cheaper but also more accurate for environments that can be specified precisely" (p. 19).

Accuracy, as Gigerenzer uses the term, is success in accomplishing a particular task, whether it be catching a ball, playing chess, or behaving morally. But this raises an important question for Gigerenzer. Is he suggesting that if morality's requirements can be reduced to precisely specifiable goals, then sometimes heuristics may help us to achieve them? Or is he making the stronger claim that the requirements of morality *must* themselves involve specifiable goals—the sort for which "ecologically rational" heuristics are most likely to be useful? The stronger claim seems to beg the question against approaches to ethics that do not function this way. To take a central example, deontological approaches focus more on the permissibility and impermissibility of certain behaviors, behaviors whose normative status is not centrally focused on outcomes. Such approaches are, for the most part at least, incompatible with evaluations along the lines of ecological rationality.[3] Ironically, there is a sense in which Gigerenzer's approach fits better with a morality of consequences than it does with a morality of rules.

However, consequentialist moral theories are especially problematic, according to Gigerenzer. It does not appear that his rejection of such theories reflects a belief that they are not well suited to heuristics. We are confident that most consequentialists would applaud the use of heuristics well adapted to achieving good consequences. Instead, Gigerenzer's criticism seems to rely on independent grounds. One is that "consequentialism . . . can only give guidelines for moral action *if the best action can actually be determined by a mind or machine,*" something he thinks "is typically not the case in the real world" (p. 22). He illustrates this with a simple two-player game, which despite its simplicity winds up with so many possible moves that even our most powerful computers would take about 4 times the 14 billion years since the Big Bang to compute it.

But here Gigerenzer overlooks an important distinction philosophers have drawn between the *indeterminable* and the *indeterminate.* Gigerenzer has argued that we are not *able to determine* the answers to the questions posed by consequentialism. What he has not argued is that *there are no determinate answers* to such questions. As long as there are facts about what states of affairs are best (and thus about what actions it is right to perform) consequentialism can still serve as a *criterion of rightness.* Consequentialists distinguish between such a criterion and a *decision procedure.* And most would reject the idea that consequentialism sets out a decision procedure of the sort Gigerenzer has in mind.[4]

However, perhaps this misses the point of Gigerenzer's objection. Of what use is a moral theory that does not provide us with concrete guidance about how to behave? In the real world, he seems to think, consequentialist theories are impractical in just the way that good heuristics are practical. But this suggests a fundamental misunderstanding of the theory. No consequentialist recommends that we always use a complicated consequentialist decision procedure to decide what to do. Consider the father of utilitarianism, Jeremy Bentham. After outlining an admittedly complicated consequentialist decision procedure, he then goes on to remark, "It is not to be expected that this process should be strictly pursued previously to every moral judgement. . . ."[5]

The reason has to do with efficiency. Bentham and other consequentialists fully recognize that there are computational limits. And overall utility depends in part on the costs of calculating![6] In most cases, we are better off *not* calculating but instead relying on what consequentialists have dubbed "rules of thumb"—rules that would function much like Gigerenzer's heuristics. "Don't kill another person" is a pretty good one. Of course, there will be situations in which one is permitted to kill—in self-defense, for example. However, by and large, "Don't kill another person" is a pretty good heuristic.

What is the standard according to which a heuristic is or is not a good one to follow? As suggested earlier, the consequentialist has an answer: Heuristics are good insofar as their employment will lead to good outcomes. The best are those that get us as close as we can to *optimal* outcomes. It is, of course, an empirical issue what these are. And just as one can use optimality to evaluate someone's actions, one can use it to evaluate policy, including policy regarding which heuristics to use (or, as in the organ donation case, to exploit). The policies or heuristics that are optimific—*as far as we can reasonably tell*—are the ones we should choose, given the limits of our computational abilities. However, these may not tell us to maximize the good. Indeed, it would be very surprising if they did, given the costs of calculation, our proneness to unrecognized special pleading and other biases, our lack of information, and the difficulty of the calculations. In some contexts, even random selection will turn out to be the best policy to choose. Although optimality provides us with a criterion of rightness, it need not (and typically should not) serve as a procedure for making decisions.

Of course, even if there are determinate answers to questions about best consequences, a moral theory based on them would hardly be plausible if we stood little chance of even getting close to the right answers. But the situation is not nearly so bleak. Although social chess involves many possible moves, most of them are irrelevant to any given decision, whether about a specific action or about what sorts of policies to adopt. I can be reasonably sure that killing my neighbor's infant child will not lead to good results, without considering whether the child would have grown up to be as evil, and as well positioned to *do* evil, as someone like Hitler. Like the so-called "butterfly effect" of urban legend, such possibilities are too remote to worry about in the real world. Of course we will sometimes make mistakes; we are only human. But what *makes them* mistakes, the consequentialist will argue, is their failure to produce good outcomes. There is little doubt that things would have gone better if Hitler's mother had strangled him at birth. However, we cannot blame her for failing to know this. And the consequentialist can still argue that the *reason* it would have been better is that Hitler's behavior wound up causing such awful consequences in terms of human suffering.

At times, Gigerenzer seems to be endorsing a satisficing strategy. At one point, he claims that a strategy of optimization will destroy trust and loyalty, since, for example, employees would fear being fired whenever an employer thought she could hire someone more productive.[7] Satisficing would not have this destructive effect, he writes, since ". . . heuristics such as satisficing entail an implicit promise to current employees that as long as their performance and development continue to be satisfactory . . . no changes will be made" (p. 25).

The satisficing strategy is deeply problematic. Whatever intuitive plausibility it has rests on its being disguised maximization. Consider the following scenario (which, sadly, no one has actually confronted us with). Suppose that we are presented with the option of taking the money in one of two hands. Which hand is up to us. In one hand there is $10; in the other hand there is $1,000. Which is the rational choice? Most would argue that if—all other things being equal—we took the $10 as opposed to the $1,000, we would be crazy. This is because the $1,000 is the better option. One maximizes one's own prudential good by taking the $1,000, so, prudentially, that's what one ought to do. However, if the hand holding the $10 is right next to us, whereas we need to swim over shark-infested waters to reach the hand holding the $1,000—well, that's a different story, because the cost to us of getting the $1,000 as opposed to the $10 has to be factored in. Of course, we would say under these circumstances that the $10 is "good enough," but this does not mean that we are rejecting maximization at all. It just means we recognize that money isn't the only good thing we should be concerned with. Keeping away from sharks is another good. But the point is that *both* of these are goods because of their contributions to happiness, pleasure, or some other form of utility. Or so the consequentialist would argue.

Gigerenzer also criticizes consequentialism as unworkable because there is so much disagreement over what makes people happiest. Again, this doesn't count against the theory or against maximization. Consider an analogy with buying stocks. Presumably, the goal of investment is to acquire the most money. There is disagreement about which stocks will produce the most return. Thus, many financial advisors will advise that one "diversify one's portfolio" so as to minimize risk and increase the chance of favorable return. As a practical matter, this is what one does. This does not mean that one rejects the *goal* of maximization, merely because one recognizes that one cannot know ahead of time which stock is the most profitable. If one *could* know that a given stock will be most profitable, then it would be rational to invest in that stock as opposed to the others. But, in the real world, we just don't know. Under these conditions of epistemic uncertainty, one wouldn't pick just one good and run with it. In the moral case, as in the stock case, it is often better to "diversify one's portfolio."[8]

Professor Gigerenzer himself says that heuristics can never replace normative theory. And he is always careful to say, for example, that we must study natural environments *as well as* contrived examples. However, he shows little patience for such examples, at one point referring to "toy problems such as the 'trolley problems,'" which "eliminate characteristic features of natural environments" (p. 11). But (although trolley problems represent only a tiny fraction of the sorts of cases moral philosophers attend to) there is a reason why philosophers use examples that eliminate some of the complexities of everyday life. The aim is to consider which of a number of possibly morally relevant factors present in everyday situations really *are* morally relevant, to make judgments about what their relevance is by looking at them in isolation, and to abstract from those features of everyday moral choices that may distract us or tempt us to special pleading.

For example, some people have thought that a fetus becomes a person (a being with a right to life) at the moment when it is born. Any number of changes occur at birth, but is any of them morally relevant? To answer, we must look at these features one at a time. At birth, the child begins to breathe on its own. But don't people who depend on respirators have a right to life? If so, then being able to breathe on one's own is not necessary for having such a right. Is it sufficient? Lab rats can breathe on their own, but most of us feel that they do not have a right to life.

In fact, reflection of this sort seems the *only* way to answer the questions that Gigerenzer admits cannot be answered by heuristics alone. Of course, much more sophisticated examples of moral reasoning can be found in the vast philosophical literature on normative ethics, as a brief perusal of any edition of *Philosophy and Public Affairs* (or any of a plethora of other excellent sources) will demonstrate. The best such work makes use of the most accurate available scientific understanding of human nature and the environments in which we are likely to find ourselves, and Professor Gigerenzer's fine work on heuristics has a place in that understanding. Although science cannot take the place of moral thinking, it is certainly of great relevance to such thinking, as long as it is not applied in a hasty and shortsighted way.

Conclusion

We see a great deal of value in Gigerenzer's discoveries. As philosophers, we have much to learn from psychologists, and we do not, and should not, pretend that we can do without their help. However, the converse is also true. When psychologists try to draw philosophical conclusions from their fascinating discoveries about the mind, they ought to make sure they know their philosophy before doing so, and moral philosophy is more complex and nuanced than Gigerenzer's treatment suggests.

Notes

1. Interestingly, Gigerenzer allows that "the professional reasoning of judges" is an exception to his claim that, "in many cases, moral judgments and actions are due to intuitive rather than deliberative reasoning" (p. 9). For over a year Professor Loeb clerked for a Justice on the Michigan Supreme Court, who quite openly claimed to follow his "gut" first, developing a rationale for his view only *after* coming to an intuitive conclusion.

2. Perhaps Gigerenzer's point is only that, had the *coach* understood the heuristic, he would not have given the player such bad advice. However, this illustrates that if we are to use the science of heuristics to improve our success, we must attend carefully to questions about the circumstances in which it is wise to attend to them.

3. This may be too quick. In a good society, "Follow the law" or "Follow widely accepted moral standards" might produce good results by deontological standards. However, few, if any, societies have had standards good enough to satisfy most deontologists.

4. Gigerenzer claims that there are at least four interpretations of consequentialism: "a conscious mental process," "an unconscious mental process," "an *as-if* theory of behavior," and "a normative goal" (p. 21). But although he cites J. J. C. Smart's claim in *The Encyclopedia of Philosophy* (1967) that it is important to distinguish between utilitarianism as a normative and a descriptive theory, when philosophers talk about utilitarianism, they almost always have in mind the normative ideal (as did Smart himself in his famous monograph, "An outline of a system of utilitarian ethics," cited by Gigerenzer).

5. Bentham (1789/1907, chapter IV). Bentham was not alone in this. Mill, Sidgwick, and Moore also held that the decision procedure is not to be followed all of the time.

6. Thus, no serious consequentialist would recommend Kepler's "methodical search for his second wife" (p. 24), in part *because* of the bad feelings to which it would give rise. Even if Kepler had been an egoist, he should have realized (as any sensible person

would) that his method was likely to lead to a prudentially bad outcome. Consequentialist views of morality and prudence *require* taking these bad consequences into account!

7. As in the case of Kepler, an employer who behaved in such a way would be a very poor optimizer, since the consequences of destroyed trust and loyalty are as relevant as any others.

8. The fact that "there are societies where happiness means little in comparison to religious faith and loyalty to one's national and cultural identity" does not make "the criterion . . . increasingly fuzzy" (p. 24) unless a crude moral relativism is presupposed. According to eudemonistic utilitarianism, faith and loyalty are only valuable insofar as they contribute to utility.

Gerd Gigerenzer

I would like to thank Professors Julia Driver, Don Loeb, and Cass Sunstein for their thoughtful comments. They correctly point out that I have not done justice to the complexity of moral philosophy, and, if I may add, the same can be said with respect to moral psychology. Rather, the question I tried to answer in my essay was this: What picture of morality emerges from the science of heuristics? Sunstein (2005) has written a pioneer article arguing that people often rely on "moral heuristics." Here we are in agreement with each other, and Driver and Loeb also find it a promising proposition. Note that I prefer to speak of "fast and frugal heuristics" instead of "moral heuristics," since one interesting feature is that the same heuristic can guide behavior in both moral and other domains.

Do Heuristics Lead to Moral Errors?

Sunstein also points to the imperfect reliability of heuristics. He emphasizes that his comment bears on the debate between those who emphasize cognitive errors (such as Kahneman and Tversky) and those who emphasize the frequent success of heuristics (such as myself). Here I would like to insert a clarification. Some philosophers have contended that the difference between the two programs was that one describes the dark side and the other the bright side of the mind (e.g., Samuels, Stich, & Bishop, 2002), although the distinctions are deeper and more interesting (e.g., Bishop, 2000). Cognitive errors have been measured against logical rationality as opposed to ecological rationality and explained by vague labels such as "availability" as opposed to precise models of heuristics. Let me illustrate these differences with reference to the term "sometimes" in Sunstein's title. He is right; heuristics sometimes lead us astray, and sometimes they make us smart or good. However, we can do better and work on defining exactly what "sometimes" means. That is the goal of the program of ecological rationality: to identify the structures of environments in which a given heuristic succeeds and fails. This goal can be achieved only with precise models of heuristics.

For instance, we know that "Imitate the majority" is successful in relatively stable environments but not in quickly changing ones (Boyd & Richerson, 2005), that "tit for tat" succeeds if others also use this heuristic but can fail otherwise, and that heuristics based on one good reason are as accurate as or better than consideration of many reasons when predictability is low and the variability of cue validities high (e.g., Hogarth & Karelaia, 2006; Martignon & Hoffrage, 2002). To the best of my knowledge, no such work has been undertaken in moral psychology and philosophy.

Thus, I agree with Sunstein that heuristics make errors, but I emphasize that there are already some quantitative models that predict the amount of error (e.g., Goldstein & Gigerenzer, 2002). Moreover, making errors is not specific to heuristics. All policies, even so-called optimal ones, make them. And there is a more challenging insight. We know today of situations where, in contrast to an "optimizing" strategy, a heuristic makes *fewer* errors (see below). In the real world, the equation "optimizing = best" and "heuristic = second best" does not always hold.

Institutions Shape Heuristics

Driver and Loeb find my suggestion unfair that English magistrates are more involved in trying to protect themselves than to ensure due process. My intention was not to issue a moral verdict against magistrates, who seemed to be unaware of the differences between what they think they do and in fact do, but to illustrate how institutions elicit heuristics. The study of the adaptive toolbox is not about the mind per se but about the mind–environment system. Features of the English legal institution, such as lack of feedback for magistrates' errors, are part of the system, as is the "passing the buck" heuristic. The distinction between a moral theory that focuses on the individual mind versus one that focuses on the mind–environment system is an important one, which goes beyond magistrates' bail decisions.

Consider medicine. Is it morally right that physicians make patients undergo tests that they themselves wouldn't take? I once lectured to a group of 60 physicians, including presidents of physicians' organizations and health insurance companies. Our discussion turned to breast cancer screening, in which some 75% percent of American women over 50 participate. A gynecologist remarked that after a mammogram, it is she, the physician, who is reassured: "I fear not recommending a mammogram to a woman who may later come back with breast cancer and ask me 'Why didn't you do a mammogram?' So I recommend that each of my patients be screened. Yet I believe that mammography screening should not be recommended. But I have no choice. I think this medical system is perfidious, and it makes me nervous" (Gigerenzer, 2002, p. 93). Did she herself participate in mammography screening? "No," she said, "I don't." The organizer then asked all 60 physicians the same question (for men: "If you were a woman, would you participate?"). The result was an eye-opener: Not a single female doctor in this group participated in screening, and no male physician said he would do so if he were a woman. Nevertheless, almost all physicians in this group recommended screening to women.

Once again, my intention is not to pronounce a moral judgment on doctors or magistrates. A gynecologist who knows that there is still a debate in medical science as to whether mammography screening has a very small or zero effect on mortality reduction from breast cancer but has proven harms (e.g., biopsies and anxieties after frequent false positives, surgical removal and treatment of cancers that a woman would have never noticed during her lifetime) may or may not decide upon screening. Yet in an environment where doctors feel the need to protect themselves against being sued, they may—consciously or unconsciously—place self-protection first and recommend screening. At present, the United States in particular has created such environments for medical doctors and their patients. For many doctors, it is a no-win situation.

A physician who does not employ this double standard can be severely punished. A young Vermont family doctor and his residency were recently put to trial because the doctor, following national guidelines, explained the pros and cons of prostate-specific antigen (PSA) screening to a patient, after which the patient declined to have the test (and later died of an incurable form of prostate cancer). Note that the benefits of PSA testing are highly controversial, whereas the potential harms (such as impotence and incontinence after radical prostatectomy) in the aftermath of a positive PSA test result are well documented. The prosecution argued that the physician should have simply administered the test without informing the patient, as is established practice in Vermont and most other parts of the United States. A jury found the doctor's residency liable for $1 million (Merenstein, 2004). After this experience, the family doctor said that he now has no choice but to overtreat patients, even at the risk of doing unnecessary harm, in order to protect himself.

These cases illustrate how institutions can create moral split brains, in which a person is supposed to do one thing, or even believes that he is doing it, but feels forced to do something else.

Maximization

It is interesting how economic theories resemble some moral theories: The common denominator is the ideal of maximization of a form of utility. One motivation for studying heuristics is the fact that maximization or, more generally, optimization is limited. The limits of optimization are no news to the departments of computer science where I have held talks, whereas during talks to economists and other social scientists, my pointing out these limits typically generates defensive rhetoric. In my chapter, I outlined some of these limits in consequentialist theories that rely on maximization. As my commentators correctly noted, these limits do not apply to all forms of consequentialism. For instance, if certain versions of consequentialism maintain that actions should be judged by their outcomes, and that one should choose a good-enough action (rather than the best one), the arguments I made do not apply.

Driver and Loeb defend maximization by introducing the distinction between the indeterminable and the indeterminate. Even if there is no procedure known to mind or machine to determine the best action, as long as a best action exists, consequentialism can still serve as a criterion of rightness. In economics, optimization is similarly defended. I must admit that I fail to understand the logic. Take the example of chess, where maximization is out of reach for mind and machine, but where a best strategy exists. Even if someone were to stumble over the best action by accident, we would not recognize it as such and be able to prove that it is indeed the best. How can maximization serve as a norm for rightness if we can neither determine nor, after the fact, recognize the best action?

Rethinking the Relation between Heuristics and Maximization

The ecological perspective also provides a new look on norms. It is a common belief that heuristics are always second best, except when there are time constraints. Yet that is not always so. Heuristics can also be "better than optimal." It is important to understand what that phrase means. Driver and Loeb introduce the analogy of buying stocks. Nobody can know which stocks will produce the most returns, they argue; therefore, simple heuristics such as "Diversify one's portfolio" would be practical. This does not mean that one should reject maximization, they explain, because if one *could* know the future, one would pick the best portfolio. Let me outline my view on the matter, which I believe is systematically different.

First, I always use the term "maximization" for a process or, as Driver and Loeb call it, a "decision procedure," whereas in this passage, it seems to refer to the outcome (knowing the stock results), not to the process of estimating their future performance. In economics, "maximization" refers to the (as-if) process.[1] For instance, the economist Harry Markowitz received a Noble Prize for his theoretical work on portfolios that maximize return and minimize risks. Nevertheless, for his own retirement investments, he relied on a simple heuristic, the $1/N$ rule, which simply allocates equal amounts of money to each option. He explicitly defended his decision to prefer a simple heuristic to his optimal theory (Zweig, 1998). How could he do that? The answer is that maximization (as a process) is not always better than a fast and frugal heuristic. For instance, a recent study compared a dozen "optimal" asset allocation policies (including Markowitz's) with the $1/N$ rule in 7 allocation problems (DeMiguel, Garlappi, & Uppal, 2006). One problem consisted of allocating one's money to the 10 portfolios tracking the sectors comprising the Standard & Poor's 500 index, and another one to 10 American industry portfolios. What was the result? Despite its simplicity, the $1/N$ rule typically made higher gains than the complex policies did.

To understand this result, it is important to know that the complex policies base their estimates on existing data, such as the past performance of industry portfolios. The data fall into two categories, information that is useful for predicting the future and arbitrary information or error that is not. Since the future is unknown, it is impossible to distinguish between these, and the optimization strategies end up including arbitrary information. These strategies do best if they have data over a long time period and for a small number of assets. For instance, with 50 assets to allocate one's wealth, the complex policies would need a window of 500 years to eventually outperform the $1/N$ rule. The simple rule, in contrast, ignores all previous information, which makes it immune to estimation errors. It bets on the wisdom of diversification by equal allocation. This is not a singular case; there are many cases known where some form of maximization leads to no better or even worse outcomes than heuristics—even when information is free (e.g., Hogarth, in press; Dawes, 1979; Gigerenzer, Todd, & the ABC Research Group, 1999).

Thus, it is important to distinguish clearly between maximization as a process and maximization as an outcome. Only in some situations does the first imply the second; in others, maximization does not lead to the best outcome, or even to a good one. One can think of a two-by-two table with the process (optimization vs. heuristic) listed in the rows and the outcome (good or bad) in the columns. None of the table cells are empty; both optimization and heuristics entail good or bad outcomes. The challenging question is one of ecological rationality: When does a procedure succeed and when does it not?

Description and Prescription

My analysis of moral behavior concerns how the world *is*, rather than how it *should* be. As mentioned in my essay, although the study of moral intuitions will never replace the need for individual responsibility, it can help us to understand which environments influence moral behavior and find ways of making changes for the better. In this sense, the fields of moral psychology and moral philosophy are interdependent. A necessary condition of prescribing efficient ways to improve on a present state—on lives saved, due process, or transparency—is an understanding of how the system in question works. Sunstein suggests going further and trying to find heuristics that might be defensible or indefensible on the basis of any view or morality, or the least contentious one. This is a beautiful goal, and if he can find such universal heuristics, I would be truly impressed. Yet Sunstein's goal is not in the spirit of ecological rationality, where every strategy has its limits and potential, and there is no single best one for all situations. My proposal is to study the combinations of heuristics and institutions that shape our moral behavior. The idea of an adaptive toolbox may prove fruitful for moral psychology, and moral philosophy as well.

Note

1. The distinction between process and outcome is also important for understanding the term "as-if model," which refers to the process, not the outcome. Driver and Loeb suggest that the as-if model refers to a player "who behaves as if he intends to catch the ball" (the decision outcome). The as-if model I describe, however, refers to a player who behaves as if he were calculating the ball's trajectory (the decision process).

2 | Framing Moral Intuitions

Walter Sinnott-Armstrong

If you think that affirmative action is immoral, and I disagree, then it is hard to imagine how either of us could try to convince the other without appealing at some point either implicitly or explicitly to some kind of moral intuition. The same need for intuition arises in disputes about other moral issues, including sodomy, abortion, preventive war, capital punishment, and so on. We could never get started on everyday moral reasoning about any moral problem without relying on moral intuitions. Even philosophers and others who officially disdain moral intuitions often appeal to moral intuitions when refuting opponents or supporting their own views. The most sophisticated and complex arguments regularly come down to: "But surely *that* is immoral. Hence, . . ." Without some move like this, there would be no way to construct and justify any substantive moral theory.[1] The importance of moral theory and of everyday moral reasoning thus provides lots of reasons to consider our moral intuitions carefully.

Moral Intuitions

I define a "moral intuition" as a strong immediate moral belief.[2] "Moral" beliefs are beliefs that something is morally right or wrong, good or bad, virtuous or vicious, and so on for other moral predicates. Moral beliefs are "strong" when believers feel confident and do not give them up easily. Moral beliefs are "immediate" when the believer forms and holds them independent of any process of inferring them from any other belief either at the time when the belief originated or during the later times when the belief is maintained. Moral intuitions in this sense might arise after reflection on the facts of the situation. They might result from moral appearances that are not full beliefs. Nonetheless, they are not inferred from those facts or appearances. The facts only specify which case the intuition is about. The appearances merely make acts seem morally right or wrong, and so on. People do not always believe that things really are as they appear, so moral belief requires an extra step of endorsing the appearance of this case. When this extra step is taken independently of inference, and the resulting belief is strong, the resulting mental state is a moral intuition.

In this minimal sense, most of us have some moral intuitions. We can react immediately even to new cases. Sometimes I ask students, for example, whether it is morally wrong to duck to avoid an arrow when the arrow will then hit another person (Boorse & Sorensen, 1988). Most students and others who consider such cases for the first time quickly form strong opinions about the moral wrongness of such acts, even though they cannot cite any principle or analogy from which to infer their moral beliefs.

In addition to *having* moral intuitions, most of us think that our own moral intuitions are *justified*. To call a belief "justified" is to say that the believer ought to hold that belief as opposed to suspending belief, because the believer has adequate epistemic grounds for believing that it is true (at least in some minimal sense). Our moral intuitions do not seem arbitrary to us. It seems to us as if we ought to believe them. Hence, they strike us as justified.

Moral Intuitionism

The fact that our moral intuitions *seem* justified does not show that they really *are* justified. Many beliefs that appear at first sight to be justified turn out after careful inspection to be unjustified. To determine whether moral beliefs really are justified, we need to move beyond psychological description to the normative epistemic issue of how we ought to form moral beliefs.

There are only two ways for moral intuitions or any other beliefs to be justified:

A belief is justified *inferentially* if and only if it is justified only because the believer is able to infer it from some other belief.
A belief is justified *noninferentially* if and only if it is justified independently of whether the believer is able to infer it from any other belief.

Whether a belief is justified inferentially or noninferentially depends not on whether the believer *actually* bases the belief in an actual inference but instead on whether the believer is *able* to infer that belief from other beliefs.

A moral intuition might be justified inferentially. What makes it a moral intuition is that it is not actually based on an *actual* inference. What makes it justified inferentially is that its epistemic status as justified depends on the believer's *ability* to infer it from some other belief. People often form beliefs immediately without actual inference, even though they are able to justify those beliefs with inferences from other beliefs if the need arises. If they are justified only because of this ability to infer, then these moral intuitions are justified inferentially.

However, if every moral belief were justified inferentially, a regress would arise: If a believer needs to be able to infer a moral belief from some other belief, the needed inference must have premises. Either none or some of those premises are moral. If none of the premises is moral, then the inference could not be adequate to justify its moral conclusion.[3] On the other hand, if even one of the premises is moral, then it would have to be justified itself in order for the inference to justify its conclusion. If this moral premise is also justified inferentially, then we would run into the same problem all over again. This regress might go on infinitely or circle back on itself, but neither alternative seems attractive. That's the problem.

To stop this regress, some moral premise would have to be justified non-inferentially. *Moral skeptics* argue that no moral belief is justified noninferentially, so no moral belief is justified. To avoid skepticism, *moral intuitionists* claim that some moral intuitions are justified noninferentially. Moral intuitionists do not only claim that some moral beliefs are justified apart from any actual inference. That would not be enough to stop the skeptical regress. To avoid skepticism, moral intuitionists need to claim that some moral beliefs are justified independently of the believer's ability to infer those moral beliefs from any other beliefs.

A variety of moral intuitionists do make or imply this claim. First, some *reliabilists* claim that a moral belief (or any other belief) is justified whenever it results from a process that is in fact reliable, even if the believer has no reason at all to believe that the process is reliable (Shafer-Landau, 2003). If so, and if some reliable processes are independent of inferential ability, then some moral beliefs are justified noninferentially. Another kind of moral intuitionism claims that some moral beliefs are justified only because they appear or seem true and there is no reason to believe they are false (Tolhurst, 1990, 1998). If moral appearances or seemings are not endorsed, then they are not beliefs, so they cannot serve as premises or make the believer able to infer the moral belief. Such *experientialists*, thus, also claim that some moral beliefs are justified noninferentially. Third, *reflectionists* admit that moral intuitions are justified only if they follow reflection that involves beliefs about the subject of the intuition, but they deny that the believer needs to infer or even be able to infer the moral beliefs from those other beliefs in order for the moral belief to be justified (Audi, 2004). If so, the moral believer is justified noninferentially. Since moral intuitionism as I define it is endorsed by these and other prominent moral philosophers, I cannot be accused of attacking a straw man.

This kind of moral intuitionism is openly normative and epistemic. It specifies when moral beliefs are justified—when believers ought to hold them. It does not merely describe how moral beliefs are actually formed. Hence, this normative epistemic kind of moral intuitionism is very different from the descriptive psychological theory that Jonathan Haidt calls "social intuitionism" (Haidt, 2001, this volume). One could adopt Haidt's social intuitionism and still deny moral intuitionism as I define it. Or one could deny Haidt's social intuitionism and yet accept moral intuitionism under my definition. They are independent positions.

The kind of moral intuitionism that will concern me here is the normative epistemic kind because that is what is needed to stop the skeptical regress. Even if Haidt is right about how moral beliefs are *formed*, that by itself will not address the normative issue of whether or how moral beliefs can be *justified*. To address that issue, we need to ask whether the normative epistemic kind of moral intuitionism is defensible.

The Need for Confirmation

It is doubtful that psychological research by itself could establish any positive claim that a belief *is* justified. Nonetheless, such a claim presupposes certain circumstances whose denial can undermine it. By denying such circumstances, psychological research might thus establish negative conclusions about when or how moral beliefs are *not* justified (where this merely denies that they ought to be believed and does not make the positive claim that they ought not to be believed). For example, suppose I believe that I am next to a pink elephant, and I know that I believe this only because I took a hallucinogenic drug. This fact about the actual origin of my belief is enough to show that my belief is not justified. My belief in the elephant might be true, and I might have independent ways to confirm that it is true. I might ask other people, take an antidote to the hallucinogen, or feel the beast (if I know that the drug causes only visual but not tactile illusions). Still, I am not justified without some such confirmation. Generally, when I know that my belief results from a process that is likely to lead to error, then I need some confirmation in order to be justified in holding that belief.

Hallucinogenic drugs are an extreme case, but the point applies to everyday experiences as well. If I am standing nearby and have no reason to believe that the circumstances are abnormal in any way, then I seem justified in believing that someone is under six feet tall simply by looking without inferring my belief from any other belief. In contrast, if a stranger is too far away and/or surrounded by objects of unknown or unusual size, and if my vision is all that makes me believe that he is under six feet tall, then my belief will often be false, so this process is unreliable. Imagine that I see him five hundred yards away next to a Giant Sequoia tree, and he looks as if he is under six feet tall. This visual experience would not be enough by itself to make me justified in believing that he is under six feet tall. Of course, I can still be justified in believing that this stranger is under six feet tall if I confirm my belief in some way, such as by walking closer or asking a trustworthy source. However, if I do not and cannot confirm my belief in any way, then I am not justified in holding this belief instead of suspending belief while I wait for confirmation.

The kinds of confirmation that work make me able to justify my belief by means of some kind of inference. If I ask a trustworthy source, then I can use a form of inference called "appeal to authority." If I walk closer to the stranger, then I can infer from my second-order belief that I am good at assessing heights from nearby. Similarly, if I touch the pink elephant, then I can infer from my background belief that my senses are usually accurate when touch agrees with sight. And so on for other kinds of confirmation. Since confirmation makes me able to infer, when I need confirmation, I need something that gives me an ability to infer. In short, I need inferential confirmation.

We arrive, therefore, at a general principle:

If the process that produced a belief is not reliable in the circumstances, and if the believer ought to know this, then the believer is not justified in forming or holding the belief without inferential confirmation.

This principle probably needs to be qualified somehow, but the basic idea should be clear enough: A need for confirmation and, hence, inference is created by evidence of unreliability.

This general principle is not about moral beliefs in particular, but it does apply to moral beliefs among others. When it is restricted to moral beliefs, its instance can serve as the first premise in *the master argument*:

(1) If our moral intuitions are formed in circumstances where they are unreliable, and if we ought to know this, then our moral intuitions are not justified without inferential confirmation.

(2) If moral intuitions are subject to framing effects, then they are not reliable in those circumstances.

(3) Moral intuitions are subject to framing effects in many circumstances.

(4) We ought to know (3).

(5) Therefore, our moral intuitions in those circumstances are not justified without inferential confirmation.

I just argued for the general principle that implies Premise 1. What remains is to argue for the rest of the premises.

What Are Framing Effects?

Premise 2 says that framing effects bring unreliability. This premise follows from the very idea of framing effects. Many different kinds of phenomena have been labeled framing effects (for a typology, see Levin, Schneider, & Gaeth, 1998). What I have in mind are effects of wording and context on moral belief.

A person's belief is subject to a *word* framing effect when whether the person holds the belief depends on which words are used to describe what the belief is about. Imagine that Joseph would believe that Marion is fast if he is told that she ran one hundred meters in ten seconds, but he would not believe that she is fast (and would believe that she is not fast and is slow) if he is told that it took her ten seconds to run one hundred meters (or that it took her ten thousand milliseconds to run one hundred meters). His belief depends on the words: "ran" versus "took her to run" (or "seconds" vs. "milliseconds"). This belief is subject to a word framing effect.

Whether Marion is fast can't depend on which description is used. Moreover, she cannot be both fast and slow (relative to the same contrast class). At least one of Joseph's beliefs must be false. He gets it wrong either when his belief is affected by one of the descriptions or when it is affected by the other. In this situation on this topic, then, he cannot be reliable in the sense of having a high probability of true beliefs. If your car started only half of the time, it would not be reliable. Similarly, Joseph is not reliable if at most half of his beliefs are true. That is one way in which framing effects introduce unreliability.

The other kind of framing effect involves *context*. Recall the man standing next to a Giant Sequoia tree. In this context, the man looks short.

forms a moral belief about that act should judge that the act is morally wrong regardless of the context from which the believer views the act. If the moral wrongness of an act did vary with the believer's context, we could never say whether any act is morally wrong, because there are so many different believers in so many different contexts.

Since wording and context of belief do *not* affect what is morally wrong, if wording or context of belief *does* affect moral beliefs about what is morally wrong, then those moral beliefs will often be incorrect. Moral beliefs that vary in response to factors that do not affect truth—such as wording and belief context—cannot reliably track the truth. Unreliability comes in degrees, but the point still holds: Moral beliefs are unreliable to the extent that they are subject to framing effects.

Framing Effects on Moral Intuitions

The crucial question now asks: To what extent *are* moral intuitions subject to framing effects? The third premise in the master argument claims that moral intuitions are subject to framing effects in many circumstances. To determine whether this premise is true, we need to determine the extent to which moral judgments vary with framing. Here is where we need empirical research.

Kahneman and Tversky

Framing effects were first explored by Tversky and Kahneman (1981). In a famous experiment, they asked some subjects this question:

Imagine that the U.S. is preparing for an outbreak of an unusual Asian disease which is expected to kill 600 people. Two alternative programs to fight the disease, A and B, have been proposed. Assume that the exact scientific estimates of the consequences of the programs are as follows: If program A is adopted, 200 people will be saved. If program B is adopted, there is a 1/3 probability that 600 people will be saved, and a 2/3 probability that no people will be saved. Which of the two programs would you favor? (p. 453)

The same story was told to a second group of subjects, but these subjects had to choose between these programs:

If program C is adopted, 400 people will die. If program D is adopted, there is a 1/3 probability that nobody will die and a 2/3 probability that 600 people will die. (p. 453)

It should be obvious that programs A and C are equivalent, as are programs B and D. However, 72% of the subjects who chose between A and B favored

However, if the man were standing next to a Bonsai tree, he mig
tall. If Josephine believes that the man is short when she sees the
the first context, but she would believe that the man is tall if she
man in the second context, then Josephine's belief is subject to a
framing effect.

A special kind of context framing effect involves *order*. Imagi
Josephine sees the man both next to a Sequoia and also next to a
but her belief varies depending on the order in which she sees these
If she sees the man next to the Sequoia first, then she continues to
that the man is short even after she sees the man next to the Bc
she sees the man next to the Bonsai first, then she continues to
that the man is tall even after she sees the man next to the Sequo
impressions rule. The order affects the context of her belief, so
Josephine's belief is subject to a context framing effect.

In both cases, at least one of Josephine's beliefs must be false. T
cannot be both short and tall (for a man). Hence, Josephine's beliefs
topic cannot be reliable, since she uses a process that is inaccurate
half the time. Thus, context framing effects also introduce unrelial

The point applies as well to moral beliefs. Suppose your friend p
to drive you to the airport at an agreed time. When the time arr
decides to go fishing instead, and you miss your flight. His act c
described as breaking his promise or as intentionally failing to k
promise, but how his act is described cannot affect whether hi
morally wrong. It morally wrong for him to break his promise in th
cumstances if and only if it is also morally wrong for him to intent
fail to keep his promise in these circumstances. What is morally w
not affected by such wording.

It is also not affected by the context of belief. Imagine that te
later you tell me about your friend's failure. Then I form a mora
about your friend's failure. Whether my belief is correct depends o
happened at the earlier time, not at the later time when I form my
My later context cannot affect any of the factors (such as the a
cumstances or consequences and the agent's beliefs or intention
determine whether your friend's act was morally wrong. Of cou
context of the action does affect its moral wrongness. If your frie
to drive you to the airport because he needs to take his child to th
pital to save her life, then his failure to keep his promise is not
wrong. However, that is the *agent's* context. The *believer's* context,
trast, does not affect moral wrongness. If it is morally wrong for you
to go fishing in the context in which he went fishing, then anyor

A, but only 22% of the subjects who chose between C and D favored C. More generally, subjects were risk averse when results were described in positive terms (such as "lives saved") but risk seeking when results were described in negative terms (such as "lives lost" or "deaths").

The question in this experiment was about choices rather than moral wrongness. Still, the subjects were not told how the policies affect them personally, so their choices seem to result from beliefs about which program is morally right or wrong. If so, the subjects had different moral beliefs about programs A and C than about programs B and D. The only difference between the pairs is how the programs are described or framed. Thus, descriptions seem to affect these moral beliefs. Descriptions cannot affect what is really morally right or wrong in this situation. Hence, these results suggest that such moral beliefs are unreliable.

Moral intuitionists could respond that moral intuitions are still reliable when subjects have consistent beliefs after considering all relevant descriptions. It is not clear that adding descriptions or adding more thought removes framing effects. (I will discuss this below.) In any case, moral believers would still need to know that their beliefs are consistent and that they are aware of all relevant descriptions before they could be justified in holding moral beliefs. That would make them able to confirm their moral beliefs, so this response would not undermine the main argument, which concludes only that moral believers need confirmation for any particular moral belief.

To see how deeply this point cuts, consider Quinn's argument for the traditional doctrine of doing and allowing, which claims that stronger moral justification is needed for doing or causing harm than for merely allowing harm to happen. When the relevant harm is death, this doctrine says, in effect, that killing is worse than letting die. In support of this general doctrine, Quinn appeals to moral intuitions of specific cases:

In Rescue I, we can save either five people in danger of drowning at one place or a single person in danger of drowning somewhere else. We cannot save all six. In Rescue II, we can save the five only by driving over and thereby killing someone who (for an unspecified reason) is trapped on the road. If we do not undertake the rescue, the trapped person can later be freed. (Quinn 1993, p. 152; these cases derive from Foot, 1984)

Most people judge that saving the five is morally wrong in Rescue II but not in Rescue I. Why do they react this way? Quinn assumes that these different intuitions result from the difference between killing and letting die or, more generally, between doing and allowing harm. However, Horowitz uses a different distinction (between gains and losses) and a different theory (prospect theory from Kahneman & Tversky, 1979) to develop an alternative explanation of Quinn's moral intuitions:

> In deciding whether to kill the person or leave the person alone, one thinks of the person's being alive as the *status quo* and chooses this as the neutral outcome. Killing the person is regarded as a negative deviation. . . . But in deciding to save a person who would otherwise die, the person being dead is the *status quo* and is selected as the neutral outcome. So saving the person is a positive deviation. . . . (Horowitz, 1998, pp. 377–378)

The point is that we tend to reject options that cause definite negative deviations from the status quo. That explains why most subjects rejected program C but did not reject program A in the Asian disease case, despite the equivalence between those programs. It also explains why we think that it is morally wrong to "kill" in Rescue II but is not morally wrong to "not save" in Rescue I, since killing causes a definite negative deviation from the status quo. This explanation clearly hinges on what is taken to be the status quo, which in turn depends on how the options are described. Quinn's story about Rescue I describes the people as already "in danger of drowning," whereas the trapped person in Rescue II can "later be freed" if not for our "killing" him. These descriptions affect our choice of the neutral starting point. As in the Asian disease cases, our choice of the neutral starting point then affects our moral intuitions.

Horowitz's argument leaves many ways for opponents to respond. Some moral intuitionists argue that, even if the difference between gains (or positive deviations) and losses (or negative deviations) does explain our reactions to Quinn's cases, this explanation does not show that our moral intuitions are incoherent or false or even arbitrary, as in the Asian disease case. Horowitz claims, "I do not see why anyone would think the distinction [between gains and losses] is morally significant, but perhaps there is some argument I have not thought of" (Horowitz, 1998, p. 381). As Mark van Roojen says, "Nothing in the example shows anything wrong with treating losses from a neutral baseline differently from gains. Such reasoning might well be appropriate where framing proceeds in a reasonable manner" (Van Roojen, 1999, p. 854).[4] Indeed, Frisch (1993) found that subjects who were affected by frames often could give justifications for differentiating the situations so described. Nonetheless, the framing also "might well" *not* be reasonable, so there still might be a *need* for some reason to believe that the framing is reasonable. This need produces the epistemological dilemma: If there is *no* reason to choose one baseline over the other, then our moral intuitions seem arbitrary and unjustified. If there *is* a reason to choose one baseline over the other, then either we have access to that reason or we do not. If we have access to the reason, then we are able to draw an inference from that reason to justify our moral belief. If we do not have access to that reason, then we do not seem justified in our moral belief. Because framing effects so often lead to incoherence and error, we cannot be justified in trusting a moral intuition that relies on framing effects unless we at least can be aware that this intuition is one where the baseline is reasonable. Thus, Horowitz's explanation creates serious trouble for moral intuitionism whenever framing effects could explain our moral intuitions.

A stronger response would be to show that prospect theory is not the best explanation of our reactions to Quinn's cases.[5] Kamm (1998a) argues that the traditional distinction between doing and allowing harm, rather than prospect theory's distinction between gains and losses, is what really drives our intuitions in these cases. These distinctions overlap in most cases, but we can pull them apart in test cases where causing a harm prevents a greater loss, such as this one:

Suppose we frame Rescue II so that five people are in excellent shape but need a shot of a drug, the last supply of which is available only now at the hospital, to prevent their dying of a disease that is coming into town in a few hours. Then not saving them would involve losses rather than no-gains. We still should not prevent these five losses of life by causing one loss in this case. So even when there is no contrast between a loss and no-gain in a case, we are not permitted to do what harms (causes a foreseen loss) in order to aid (by preventing a loss). (Kamm, 1998a, p. 477)

Here a failure to save the five is supposed to involve losses to the five, because they are alive and well at present, so the baseline is healthy life. There are, however, other ways to draw the baseline. The disease is headed for town, so the five people are doomed to die if they do not get the drug (just as a person is doomed when an arrow is headed for his heart, even if the arrow has not struck yet). That feature of the situation might lead many people to draw the baseline at the five people being dead. Then not saving them would involve no-gains rather than losses, contrary to Kamm's claim. Thus, prospect theory can explain why people who draw such a baseline believe that we should not cause harm to save the five in this case. Kamm might respond that the baseline was not drawn in terms of who is doomed in the Asian flu case. (Compare her response to Baron at Kamm 1998a, p. 475.) However, prospect theory need not claim that the baseline is always drawn in the same way. People's varying intuitions can be explained by variations in where they draw the baseline, even if they have no consistent reason for drawing it where they do. Thus, Horowitz's explanation does seem to work fine in such cases.[6]

Psychologists might raise a different kind of problem for Horowitz's argument. Framing effects in choices between risks do not always carry over into choices between definite effects, and they get weaker in examples with smaller groups, such as six hundred people versus six people (Petrinovich & O'Neill, 1996, pp. 162–164). These results together suggest that special features of Asian disease cases create the framing effects found by Kahneman and Tversky. Those features are lacking from Quinn's cases, which do not involve probabilities or large numbers. This asymmetry casts doubt on Horowitz's attempt to explain our reactions to Quinn's cases in the same way as our reactions to Asian disease cases.

Finally, some opponents might respond that Horowitz's claim applies only to the doctrine of doing and allowing, and not to other moral intuitions. However, the doctrine of doing and allowing is neither minor nor isolated. It affects many prominent issues and is strongly believed by many philosophers and common people, who do not seem to be able to infer it from any other beliefs. Similar framing effects are explained by prospect theory in other cases involving fairness in prices and tax rates (Kahneman, Knetsch, & Thaler, 1986) and future generations (Sunstein, 2004, 2005) and other public policies (Baron, 1998). There are still many other areas of morality, but, if moral intuitions are unjustified in these cases, doubts should arise about a wide range of other moral intuitions as well.

To see how far framing effects extend into other moral intuitions, we need to explore whether framing effects arise in different kinds of moral conflicts, especially moral conflicts without probabilities or large numbers. Then we need to determine the best explanation of the overall pattern of reactions. This project will require much research. There are many studies of framing effects outside of morality, especially regarding medical and economic decisions. (Kühberger, 1998, gives a meta-analysis of 248 papers.) However, what we need in order to assess the third premise of the master argument are studies of framing effects in moral judgments in particular. Luckily, a few recent studies do find framing in a wider array of moral intuitions.

Petrinovich and O'Neill

Petrinovich and O'Neill (1996) found framing effects in various trolley problems. Here is their description of the classic side-track trolley case:

A trolley is hurtling down the tracks. There are five innocent people on the track ahead of the trolley, and they will be killed if the trolley continues going straight ahead. There is a spur of track leading off to the side. There is one innocent person on that spur of track. The brakes of the trolley have failed and there is a switch that can be activated to cause the trolley to go to the side track. You are an innocent bystander (that is, not an employee of the railroad, etc.). You can throw the switch, saving five innocent people, which will result in the death of the one innocent person on the side track. What would you do? (p. 149)

This case differs from Rescues I–II in important respects. An agent who saves the five and lets the one drown in Rescue I does not cause the death of the one. That one person would die in Rescue I even if nobody were around to rescue anyone. In contrast, if nobody were around to throw the switch in the side-track trolley case, then the one person on the side track would not be harmed at all. Thus, the death of the one is caused by the act of the bystander in the side-track trolley case but not in Rescue I. In this respect, the side-track trolley case is closer to Rescue II. It is then surprising that, whereas most people agree that it *is* morally wrong to kill one to save five in Rescue II, most subjects say that it is *not* morally wrong to throw the switch in the side-track trolley case.

The question raised by Petrinovich and O'Neill is whether this moral intuition is affected by wording. They asked 387 students in one class and 60 students in another class how strongly they agreed or disagreed with given alternatives in twenty-one variations on the trolley case. Each alternative was rated on a 6-point scale: "strongly agree" (+5), "moderately agree" (+3), "slightly agree" (+1), "slightly disagree" (–1), "moderately disagree" (–3), "strongly disagree" (–5).[7]

The trick lay in the wording. Half of the questionnaires used "kill" wordings so that subjects faced a choice between (1) "... throw the switch which will result in the death of the one innocent person on the side track ..." and (2) "... do nothing which will result in the death of the five innocent people ...". The other half of the questionnaires used "save" wordings, so that subjects faced a choice between (1*) "... throw the switch which will result in the five innocent people on the main track being saved ..." and (2*) "... do nothing which will result in the one innocent person being saved ...". These wordings did not change the facts of the case, which were described identically before the question was posed.

The results are summarized in table 2.1 (from Petrinovich & O'Neill, 1996, p. 152). The top row shows that the average response was to agree slightly with action (such as pulling the switch) when the question was asked in the save wording but then to disagree slightly with action when the question was asked in the kill wording.

These effects were not due to only a few cases: "Participants were likely to agree more strongly with almost any statement worded to Save than one worded to Kill." Out of 40 relevant questions, 39 differences were

Table 2.1
Means and standard deviations (in parentheses) of participants' levels of agreement with action and inaction as a function of whether the questions incorporating action and inaction were framed in a kill or save wording[a]

	Saving Wording	Killing Wording
Action	0.65	−0.78
	(0.93)	(1.04)
Inaction	0.10	−1.35
	(1.04)	(1.15)

[a]Positive mean values in the table indicate agreement, and negative values indicate disagreement.
Source: Petrinovich & O'Neill, 1996, p. 152.

significant. The effects were also not shallow: "The wording effect . . . accounted for as much as one-quarter of the total variance, and on average accounted for almost one-tenth when each individual question was considered." Moreover, wording affected not only strength of agreement (whether a subject agreed slightly or moderately) but also whether subjects agreed or disagreed: "the Save wording resulted in a greater likelihood that people would absolutely agree" (Petrinovich & O'Neill, 1996, p. 152).

What matters to us, of course, is that these subjects gave different answers to the different questions even though those questions were asked about the same case. The facts of the case—consequences, intentions, and so on—did not change. Nor did the options: throwing the switch and doing nothing. All that varied was the wording of the dependent clause in the question. That was enough to change some subjects' answers. However, that wording cannot change what morally ought to be done. Thus, their answers cannot track the moral truth.

Similar results were found in a second experiment, but this time the order rather than the wording of scenarios was varied. One hundred eighty-eight students were asked how strongly they agreed or disagreed (on the same scale of +5 to −5) with each of the alternatives in the moral problems on one form. There were three pairs of forms.

Form 1 posed three moral problems. The first is the side-track trolley problem. In the second, the only way to save five dying persons is to scan the brain of a healthy individual, which would kill that innocent person. In the third, the only way to save five people is to transplant organs from a healthy person, which would kill that innocent person. All of the options were described in terms of who would be saved. Form 1R posed the same three problems in the reverse order: transplant, then scan, then side-track. Thirty students received Form 1, and 29 students received Form 1R.

The answers to Form 1 were not significantly different from the answers to Form 1R, so there was no evidence of any framing effect. Of course, that does not mean that there was no framing effect, just that none was found in this part of the experiment.

A framing effect was found in the second part of the experiment using two new forms: 2 and 2R. Form 2 began with the trolley problem where the only way to save the five is to pull a switch. In the second moral problem on Form 2, "You can push a button which would cause a ramp to go underneath the train; the train would jump onto tracks on the bridge and continue, saving the five, but running over the one" (Petrinovich & O'Neill, 1996, p. 156). In the third problem on Form 2, the only way to stop the trolley from killing the five is to push a very large person in front of the trolley. All of the options were described in terms of who would be saved. Form 2R posed the same three problems in the reverse order: Person, then Button, then Trolley. Thirty students received Form 2, and 29 received Form 2R.

The results of this part of the experiment are summarized in their table 3 and figure 2 (Petrinovich & O'Neill 1996, pp. 157–158; see table 2.2 and figure 2.1.)

Participants' agreement with action in the Trolley and Person dilemmas were significantly affected by the order. Specifically, "People more strongly approved of action when it appeared first in the sequence than when it appeared last" (Petrinovich & O'Neill, 1996, p. 157). The order also significantly affected participants' agreement with action in the Button dilemma (whose position in the middle did not change when the order changed). Specifically, participants approved more strongly of action in the Button dilemma when it followed the Trolley dilemma than when it followed the Person dilemma.

Why were such framing effects found with Forms 2 and 2R but not with Forms 1 and 1R? Petrinovich and O'Neill speculate that the dilemmas in Forms 1 and 1R are so different from each other that participants' judgments on one dilemma does not affect their judgments on the others. When dilemmas are more homogeneous, as in Forms 2 and 2R, participants who already judged action wrong in one dilemma will find it harder to distinguish that action from action in the other dilemmas, so they will be more likely to go along with their initial judgment, possibly just in order to maintain coherence in their judgments.

Table 2.2
Means and standard deviations of ratings for forms 2 and 2R of participants' level of agreement with action and inaction in each of the dilemmas as a function of the order in which the dilemma appeared

Dilemma	Order	Action/Inaction	Mean	SD
Trolley	First	Action	3.1	2.6
	Third	Action	1.0	2.9
	First	Inaction	−1.9	2.7
	Third	Inaction	−1.1	3.1
Person	First	Action	−.86	3.4
	Third	Action	−1.7	4.1
	First	Inaction	−.10	3.5
	Third	Inaction	0.0	3.6
Button[a]	Trolley	Action	2.7	2.8
	Person	Action	.65	3.3
	Trolley	Inaction	−.65	3.3
	Person	Inaction	−2.0	2.8

Positive values indicate agreement, and negative values indicate disagreement.
[a]For the Button dilemma, Order refers to the preceding Dilemma.
Source: Petrinovich & O'Neill, 1996, p. 157.

However, Petrinovich and O'Neill's third pair of forms suggests more subtle analysis. Forms 3 and 3R presented five heterogeneous moral problems (boat, trolley, shield, shoot, shark) in reverse order. Participants' responses to action and inaction in the outside dilemmas did not vary with order. Nonetheless, in the middle shield dilemma, "participants approved of action more strongly (2.6) when it was preceded by the Boat and Trolley dilemmas than when it was preceded by the Shoot and Shark dilemmas (1.0)" (Petrinovich & O'Neill, 1996, p. 160). Some significant framing effects, thus, occur even in heterogeneous sets of moral dilemmas.

In any case, the order of presentation of moral dilemmas does affect many people's moral judgments at least within homogeneous sets of moral problems. Of course, the truth or falsity of moral judgments about actions and inactions in those dilemmas does not depend on which dilemmas preceded or followed the dilemmas in question. Thus, framing effects show ways in which our moral intuitions do not reliably track the truth.

Haidt and Baron

Two more experiments by the Jonathans (Haidt and Baron) also found framing effects in yet another kind of situation. Their first case did not

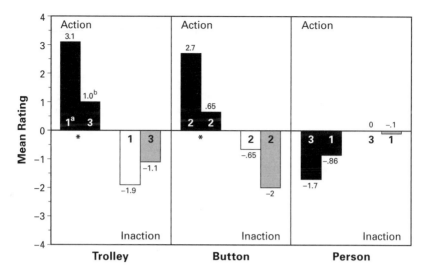

Figure 2.1
Mean ratings for each question for Form 2 and 2R for the Action and Inaction choices in each dilemma. [a]indicates the Order in which the Dilemma appeared in the sequence of questions (1 = first dilemma posed, 2 = second dilemma posed, and 3 = third dilemma posed). [b]indicates the mean rating (positive values indicate agreement with the option, and negative values indicate disagreement). *indicates that the two means differed significantly ($p < .05$). (Reprinted from Petrinovich & O'Neill, 1996, p. 158)

involve killing but only lying. It is also more realistic than most of the other cases in such experiments:

Nick is moving to Australia in two weeks, so he needs to sell his 1984 Mazda MPV. The car has only 40,000 miles on it, but Nick knows that 1984 was a bad year for the MPV. Due to a manufacturing defect particular to that year, many of the MPV engines fall apart at about 50,000 miles. Nevertheless, Nick has decided to ask for $5000, on the grounds that only one-third of the 1984 MPV's are defective. The odds are two out of three that his car will be reliable, in which case it would certainly be worth $5000.

Kathy, one of Nick's best friends, has come over to see the car. Kathy says to Nick: "I thought I read something about one year of the MPV being defective. Which year was that?" Nick gets a little nervous, for he had been hoping that she wouldn't ask. Nick is usually an honest person, but he knows that if he tells the truth, he will blow the deal, and he really needs the money to pay for his trip to Australia. He thinks for a moment about whether or not to tell the truth. Finally, Nick says, "That was 1983. By 1984 they got it all straightened out." Kathy believes him. She likes the car, and they close the deal for $4700. Nick leaves the country and never finds out whether or not his car was defective. (Haidt & Baron, 1996, pp. 205–206)

Some of the subjects received a different ending:

Nick is trying to decide whether or not to respond truthfully to Kathy's question, but before he can decide, Kathy says, "Oh, never mind, that was 1983. I remember now. By 1984, they got it all straightened out." Nick does not correct her, and they close the deal as before. (Haidt & Baron, 1996, p. 206)

The difference is that Nick actively lies in the first ending whereas he merely withholds information in the second ending. The first version is, therefore, called the act version, and the second is called the omission version.

The relation between Kathy and Nick was also manipulated. In the personal version (as above), Kathy and Nick are best friends. In the intermediate version, Kathy is only "a woman Nick knows from the neighborhood." In the anonymous version, Kathy just "saw Nick's ad in the newspaper." Each of these role versions were divided into act and omission versions.

The six resulting stories were distributed to 91 students who were asked to rate Nick's "goodness" from +100 (maximally good) to 0 (morally neutral) to –100 (maximally immoral). Each subject answered this question about both an act version and an omission version of one of the role variations. Half of the subjects received the act version first. The other half got the omission version first.

The subject's responses are summarized in table 2.3 (from Haidt & Baron, 1996, p. 207). Thus, subjects judged Nick more harshly when he lied than when he withheld information, but the distinction became less important when Nick was good friends with Kathy. They also tended to judge Nick more harshly (for lying or withholding) when he was good friends with Kathy than when they were mere neighbors or strangers. None of this is surprising.

What is surprising is an order effect: "Eighty per cent of subjects in the omission-first condition rated the act worse than the omission, while only 50 per cent of subjects in the act-first condition made such a distinction" (Haidt & Baron, 1996, p. 210). This order effect had not been predicted by Haidt and Baron, so they designed another experiment to check it more carefully.

In their second experiment, Haidt and Baron varied roles within subjects rather than between subjects. Half of the subjects were asked about the act and omission versions with Kathy and Nick as strangers, then about the

Table 2.3
Mean ratings, and percentage of subjects who rated act or omission worse, experiment 1

	Anonymous	Solidarity Intermediate	Personal	Whole Sample
N	31	27	33	91
Act	−53.8	−56.9	−66.3	−59.3
Omission	−27.4	−37.2	−50.8	−38.8
Delta	26.4	19.7	15.5	20.5
Act-worse	74%	67%	52%	64%
Omit-wose	0%	0%	3%	1%

Source: Haidt & Baron, 1996, p. 207.

act and omission versions with Kathy and Nick as casual acquaintances, and finally about the act and omission versions with Kathy and Nick as close friends. The other half of the subjects were asked these three pairs in the reverse order: friends, then acquaintances, and finally strangers.[8] Within each group, half were asked to rate the act first, and the others were asked to rate the omission first.

Haidt and Baron also added a second story that involved injury (but not death or lying). The protagonists are two construction workers, Jack and Ted. The action begins as Ted is operating a crane to move a load of bricks. Here is how the omission version ends:

Jack is sitting 30 yards away from the crane eating his lunch. He is watching Ted move the bricks, and he thinks to himself: "This looks dangerous. I am not sure if the crane can make it all the way. Should I tell him to stop?" But then he thinks "No, why bother? He probably knows what he is doing." Jack continues to eat his lunch. A few yards short of its destination, the main arm of the crane collapses, and the crane falls over. One of Ted's legs is broken.

Here is the act version:

Jack is standing 30 yards away from the crane, helping Ted by calling out signals to guide the bricks to their destination. Jack thinks to himself: "[same thoughts]." Jack motions to Ted to continue on the same course [same ending]. (Haidt & Baron, 1996, pp. 208–209)

Haidt and Baron also manipulated the relation between Jack and Ted. Half of the subjects were asked about the act and omission versions with Jack as Ted's boss (the authority version), then about the act and omission versions with Jack as Ted's coworker (the equal version), and finally about the act and omission versions with Jack as Ted's employee (the subordinate version). The other half of the subjects were asked these three pairs in the reverse order: subordinate, then equal, and finally authority. Within each group, half were asked to rate the act first, and the others were asked to rate the omission first.

The subjects were 48 + 21 students. Because positive ratings were not needed, the scale was truncated to 0 (morally neutral, neither good nor bad) to –100 (the most immoral thing a person could ever do).

The results are summarized in tables 2.4 and 2.5 (from Haidt & Baron, 1996, p. 210). This experiment replicates the unsurprising results from Experiment 1.

More importantly for our purposes, a systematic order effect was found again: "a general tendency for subjects to make later ratings more severe than earlier ratings." This effect was found, first, in the role variations: "In the Mazda story, 88 per cent of subjects lowered their ratings as Nick changed from stranger to friend, yet only 66 percent of subjects raised their

Table 2.4

Mean ratings, and percentage of subjects who rated act or omission worse, experiment 2, Mazda story ($N = 67$)

	Anonymous	Solidarity Intermediate	Personal
Act	–49.2	–54.9	–63.1
Omission	–40.3	–46.9	–57.3
Delta	9.0	7.9	5.9
Act-worse	58%	57%	43%
Omit-worse	2%	0%	0%

Source: Haidt & Baron, 1996, p. 210.

Table 2.5

Mean ratings, and percentage of subjects who rated act or omission worse, experiment 2, Crane story ($N = 68$)

	Subordinate	Hierarchy Equal	Authority
Act	–41.2	–42.4	–51.9
Omission	–30.4	–31.8	–44.4
Delta	10.8	10.6	7.5
Act-worse	52%	53%	43%
Omit-worse	3%	3%	4%

Source: Haidt & Baron, 1996, p. 210.

ratings as Nick changed from friend to stranger." Similarly, "In the Crane story, 78 per cent of those who first rated Jack as a subordinate lowered their ratings when Jack became the foreman, while only 56 percent of those who first rated Jack as the foreman raised their ratings when he became a subordinate." The same pattern recurs in comparisons between act and omission versions: "In the Crane story, 66 per cent of subjects in the omission-first condition gave the act a lower rating in at least one version of the story, while only 39 per cent of subjects in the act-first condition made such a distinction." In both kinds of comparisons, then, "subjects show a general bias towards increasing blame" (Haidt & Baron, 1996, p. 211).

These changes in moral belief cannot be due to changes in the facts of the case, because consequences, knowledge, intention, and other facts held constant. The descriptions of the cases were admittedly incomplete, so subjects might have filled in gaps in different ways (Kuhn, 1997). However, even if that explains how order affected their moral judgments, order still *did* affect their moral judgments. The truth about what is morally right or wrong in the cases did not vary with order. Hence, moral beliefs fail to track the truth and are unreliable insofar as they are subject to such order effects.

Together these studies show that moral intuitions are subject to framing effects in many circumstances. That is the third premise of the master argument.[9]

The Final Premise

Only one premise remains to be supported. It claims that we ought to know that moral intuitions are subject to framing effects in many circumstances. Of course, those who have not been exposed to the research might not know this fact about moral intuitions. However, this psychological research—like much psychological research—gives more detailed arguments for a claim that educated people ought to have known anyway. Anyone who has been exposed to moral disagreements and to the ways in which people argue for their moral positions has had experiences that, if considered carefully, would support the premise that moral intuitions are subject to framing effects in many circumstances. Those people ought to know this.

Maybe children and isolated or uneducated adults have not had enough experiences to support the third premise of the master argument, which claims that moral framing effects are common. If so, then this argument cannot be used to show that *they* are not justified noninferentially in trusting their moral intuitions. However, if these were the only exceptions, moral intuitionists would be in an untenable position. They would be claiming that the only people who are noninferentially justified in trusting their moral intuitions are people who do not know much, and they are justified in this way only because they are ignorant of relevant facts. If they knew more, then they would cease to be justified noninferentially. To present such people as epistemic ideals—by calling them "justified" when others are not—is at least problematic. If it takes ignorance to be justified noninferentially, then it is not clear why (or how) the rest of us should aspire to being justified noninferentially.

In any case, if you have read this far, you personally know some of the psychological studies that support the third premise in the master argument. So do moral intuitionists who have read this far. Thus, both they and you ought to know that moral intuitions are subject to framing effects in many circumstances. The last premise and the master argument, therefore, apply to them and to you. They and you cannot be justified noninferentially in trusting moral intuitions. That is what the master argument was most concerned to show.

Responses

Like all philosophical arguments, the master argument is subject to various responses. Some responses raises empirical issues regarding the evidence for moral framing effects. Others question the philosophical implications of those studies.

Psychologists are likely to object that I cited only a small number of studies that have to be replicated with many more subjects and different moral problems. Additional studies are needed not only to increase confidence but also to understand what causes moral framing effects and what does not. Of course, all of the reported results are statistically significant. Moreover, the studies on moral judgments and choices fit well with a larger body of research on framing effects on decisions and judgments in other areas, especially medical and economic decisions (surveyed in Kühberger, 1998, and Kühberger, Schulte-Mecklenbeck, & Perner, 1999). Therefore, I doubt that future research will undermine my premise that many moral beliefs are subject to framing effects. Nonetheless, I am happy to concede that more research on moral framing effects is needed to support the claim that moral beliefs are subject to framing effects in the ways that these initial studies suggest. I encourage everyone (psychologists *and* philosophers) to start doing the research. In the meantime, the trend of the research so far is clear and not implausible. Hence, at present we have an adequate reason to accept, at least provisionally, the premise that many moral beliefs are subject to framing effects.

More specifically, critics might object that moral believers might not be subject to framing effects when scenarios are fully described. Even if subjects' moral intuitions are not reliable when subjects receive only one description—such as killing or saving—their moral intuitions still might be reliable when they receive both descriptions, so they assess the scenarios within both frames. Most intuitionists, after all, say that we should look at a moral problem from various perspectives before forming a moral judgment. This objection is, however, undermined by Haidt and Baron's second study. Because of its within-subjects design, subjects in that study *did* receive both descriptions, yet they were still subject to statistically significant framing effects. Admittedly, the descriptions were not given within a single question, but the questions were right next to each other on the page and were repeated in each scenario, so subjects presumably framed the scenarios in both ways. Moreover, in a meta-analysis, Kühberger (1998, p. 36) found "stronger framing effects in the less-frequently used within-subjects comparisons." It seems overly optimistic, then, to assume that adding frames will get rid of framing effects.[10]

The scenarios are still underdescribed in various ways. Every scenario description has to be short enough to fit in an experiment, so many possibly relevant facts always have to be left out. These omissions might seem to account for framing effects, so critics might speculate that framing effects would be reduced or disappear if more complete descriptions were provided. Indeed, Kühberger (1995) did not find any framing effects of wording in the questions when certain problems were fully described. A possible explanation is that different words in the questions lead subjects to fill in gaps in the scenario descriptions in different ways. Kuhn (1997) found, for example, that words in questions led subjects to change their estimates of unspecified probabilities in medical and economic scenarios. If probability estimates are also affected by words and order in moral scenarios, this might explain how such framing affects moral judgments, and these effects would be reasonable if the changes in probability estimates are great enough to justify different moral judgments. Nonetheless, even if this is the process by which framing effects arise, moral intuitions would still be unreliable. Wording and context would still lead to conflicting moral judgments about a single description of a scenario. Thus, it is not clear that this response undermines the master argument, even if the necessary empirical claims do hold up to scrutiny.

Another response emphasizes that the studies do not show that everyone is affected by framing. Framing effects are not like visual illusions that are shared by everyone with normal vision. In within-subjects studies, there are always some subjects who maintain steady moral beliefs without being affected by frames.

But who are they? They might be the subjects who thought more about the problems. Many subjects do not think carefully about scenarios in experimental conditions. They just want to get it over with, and they do not have much at stake. Some moral intuitionists, however, require careful reflection before forming the moral intuitions that are supposed to be justified noninferentially. If moral intuitions that are formed after such careful reflection are not subject to framing effects, then moral intuitionists might claim that the master argument does not apply to the moral intuitions that they claim to be justified noninferentially. In support of this contention, some studies have found that framing effects are reduced, though not eliminated, when subjects are asked to provide a rationale (Fagley & Miller, 1990) or take more time to think about the cases (Takemura, 1994) or have a greater need for cognition (Smith & Levin, 1996) or prefer a rational thinking style (McElroy & Seta, 2003). In contrast, a large recent study (LeBoeuf & Shafir, 2003) concludes, "More thought, as indexed here [by need for cognition], does not reduce the proclivity to be framed" (p. 77). Another recent study (Shiloh, Salton, & Sharabi, 2002) found that subjects who combined rational and intuitive thinking styles were among those *most* prone to framing effects. Thus, it is far from clear that framing effects will be eliminated by the kind of reflection that some moral intuitionists require.

Moreover, if analytic, systematic, or rational thinking styles do reduce framing effects, this cannot help to defend moral intuitionism, because subjects with such thinking styles are precisely the ones who are able to form inferences to justify their moral beliefs. The believers who form their beliefs without inference and those who claim to be justified noninferentially are still subject to framing effects before they engage in such reasoning. That hardly supports the claim that any moral belief is justified noninferentially. To the contrary, it suggests that inference is needed to correct for framing effects. Thus, these results do not undermine the master argument. They support it.

Finally, suppose we do figure out which people are not subject to moral framing effects. Moral intuitionism still faces a dilemma: If we can tell that we are in the group whose moral intuitions are reliable, then we can get inferential confirmation; if we cannot tell whether we are in the group whose moral intuitions are reliable, then we are not justified. Either way, we cannot be justified independently of inferential confirmation.

To see the point, imagine that you have a hundred old thermometers.[11] You know that many of them are inaccurate, though you don't know exactly how many. It might be eighty or fifty or ten. You pick one at random, put it in a tub of water, which you have not felt. The thermometer reads 90°. Nothing about this thermometer in particular gives you any reason to doubt its accuracy. You feel lucky, so you become confident that the water is 90°. Are you justified? No. Since you believe that a significant number of the thermometers are unreliable, you are not justified in trusting the one that you happen to randomly pick. You need to check it. One way to check it would be to feel the water or to calibrate this thermometer against another thermometer that you have more reason to trust. Such methods might provide confirmation, and then your belief might be justified, but you cannot be justified without some kind of confirmation.

In addition to having confirmation, you need to know that it is confirmation. To see why, imagine that the thermometers are color coded. Their tops are red, yellow, green, and blue. All of the blue and green thermometers are accurate, some but not all of the yellow ones are accurate, but none of the red ones are accurate. However, you are completely unaware of any relation between colors and accuracy. Then you randomly pick a blue one, see its top, and trust it. Even though you know it is blue, and its being blue would give you good evidence that it is accurate if you knew that all the blue thermometers are accurate, still, if you do not know that its being blue is good evidence of its accuracy, then you are unjustified in trusting this thermometer. Thus, it is not enough to have a belief that supports accuracy. You need to know that it supports accuracy.

These thermometers are analogous to the processes by which believers form immediate moral beliefs. According to moral intuitionism, some moral believers are justified in forming immediate moral beliefs on the basis of something like (though not exactly like) a personal moral thermometer that reliably detects moral wrongness and rightness. However, the analogy to the hundred thermometers shows that, if we know that a large number of our moral thermometers are broken or unreliable in many situations, then we are not justified in trusting a particular moral thermometer without confirmation. Maybe we got lucky and our personal moral thermometer is one of the ones that works fine, but we are still not justified in trusting it, if we know that lots of moral thermometers do not work, and we have no way of confirming which ones do work. This standard applies to moral beliefs, because we do know that lots of moral thermometers do not work. That's what framing effects show: Our moral beliefs must be unreliable when they vary with wording and context. The range of framing effects among immediate moral beliefs thus shows that many of our moral thermometers are unreliable. It doesn't matter that we do not know exactly how many are unreliable or whether any particular believer is unreliable. The fact that moral framing effects are so widespread still reveals enough unreliability to create a need for confirmation of moral beliefs, contrary to moral intuitionism.

Critics might complain that, if my own moral intuition is reliable and not distorted, then I am justified in trusting it, because it is mine. But recall the colored thermometers. Merely knowing a feature that is correlated with accuracy is not enough to make me justified. I also need to know that this feature is correlated with accuracy. The same standard applies if the feature that is correlated with accuracy is being my own intuition. In the moral case, then, I need to know that my moral intuition is reliable. If I know that, then I have all the information I need in order to make me able to justify my belief with an inference. Thus, I am not justified noninferentially in trusting my own moral intuition.

This point also applies to those who respond that some moral intuitions are not subject to framing effects. All that moral intuitionists claim is that some moral intuitions are reliable. The studies of framing effects show that some moral intuitions are not reliable. Maybe some are and others are not. Thus, the studies cannot refute the philosophical claim. More specifically, the studies suggest *which* moral intuitions are not subject to framing effects. Recall the transplant case in Petrinovich and O'Neill's nonhomogeneous Forms 1 and 1R. They found no framing effects there—so maybe moral intuitions like these are justified noninferentially, even if many others are not.

This response runs into the same dilemma as above: If a particular moral intuition is in a group that is reliable or based on a reliable process, then the person who has that moral intuition either is or is not justified in believing that it is in the reliable group. If that person is not justified in believing that it is in the reliable group, then he is not justified in trusting it. However, if he is justified in believing that this moral intuition is in the reliable group, then he is able to justify it by an inference from this other belief. Either way, the moral believer is not justified independently of inferential confirmation. That is all that the master argument claims.

This argument might not seem to apply to moral intuitionists who claim only that general prima facie (or pro tanto) moral principles can be justified noninferentially. Standard examples include "It is prima facie morally wrong to kill" and "It is prima facie morally wrong to lie." If such moral principles are justified by intuitive induction from specific cases, as Ross (1939, p. 170) claimed, then they will be just as unreliable as the specific cases from which they are induced. However, if moral intuitions of general principles are supposed to be justified directly without any reference at all to specific cases, then the above experiments might seem irrelevant, because those experiments employ particular cases rather than general principles. This response, however, runs into two problems. First, such general principles cannot be applied to concrete situations without framing the information about those situations. What counts as killing depends on the baseline, as we saw. However, if such general principles cannot be applied without framing effects, then it seems less important whether their abstract formulations are subject to framing effects. In any case, even though current studies focus on concrete examples rather than general principles, general principles could be subject to framing effects as well. They are also moral intuitions after all. Hence, since many other moral intuitions are subject to framing effects, it seems reasonable to suppose that these are, too, unless we have some special reason to believe that they are exempt. But if we do have a special reason to exempt them, then that reason makes us able to infer them in some way—so we arrive back at the same old dilemma in the end.

Finally, some moral intuitionists might accuse me of forgetting that believers can be *defeasibly* justified without being *adequately* justified. A believer is defeasibly justified whenever the following conditional is true: The believer would be adequately justified if there were no defeater. If moral believers would be adequately justified in the absence of any framing effect, then, even if framing effects actually keep moral believers from being adequately justified apart from inferential confirmation, those moral believers still might be defeasibly justified apart from inferential confirmation.

However, it is crucial to distinguish two kinds of defeaters. An *overriding* defeater of a belief provides a reason to believe the opposite. In contrast, an *undermining* defeater takes the force out of a reason without providing any reason to believe the opposite. For example, my reason to trust a newspaper's prediction of rain is undermined but not overridden by my discovery that the newspaper bases its prediction on a crystal ball. This discovery leaves me with no reason at all to believe that it will rain or that it will not rain. Similarly, the fact that moral intuitions are subject to framing effects cannot be an overriding defeater, because it does not provide any reason to believe that those moral intuitions are false. Thus, framing effects must be undermining defeaters. But then, like the discovery about the crystal ball, moral framing effects seem to leave us with no reason to trust our immediate moral beliefs before confirmation.

Moral intuitionists can still say that some immediate moral beliefs are defeasibly justified if that means only that they *would* be adequately justified *if* they were not undermined by the evidence of framing effects. This conditional claim is compatible with their actually not being justified at all, but only appearing to be justified. Such moral believers might have no real reason at all for belief but only the misleading appearance of a reason, as with the newspaper's weather prediction based on a crystal ball. That claim is too weak to worry about.

Besides, even if we did have some reason to trust our moral intuitions apart from any inferential ability, this would not make them adequately justified. Skeptics win if no moral belief is adequately justified. Hence, moral intuitionists cannot rest easy with the claim that moral intuitions are merely defeasibly justified apart from inferential ability.

Conclusions

I am not claiming that no moral beliefs or intuitions are justified. That academic kind of moral skepticism does not follow from what I have said here. Moreover, I do not want to defend it. My point here is not about *whether* moral beliefs are justified but rather about *how* they can be justified. I have not denied that moral beliefs can be justified inferentially. Hence, I have not denied that they can be justified.

What I am claiming is that no moral intuitions are justified noninferentially. That is enough to show why moral intuitionism (as I defined it) is false. Moral intuitionists claim that moral intuitions are justified in a special way: without depending on any ability to infer the moral belief from any other belief. I deny that any belief is justified in that way.

Behind my argument lies another claim about methodology. I am also claiming that empirical psychology has important implications for moral epistemology, which includes the study of whether, when, and how moral beliefs can be justified. When beliefs are justified depends on when they are reliable or when believers have reasons to believe that they are reliable. In circumstances where beliefs are based on processes that are neither reliable nor justifiably believed to be reliable, they are not justified. Psychological research, including research into framing effects, can give us reason to doubt the reliability of certain kinds of beliefs in certain circumstances. Such empirical research can, then, show that certain moral beliefs are not justified. Moral intuitionists cannot simply dismiss empirical psychology as irrelevant to their enterprise. They need to find out whether the empirical presuppositions of their normative views are accurate. They cannot do that without learning more about psychology and especially about how our moral beliefs are actually formed.

Notes

1. For a systematic critique of attempts to justify moral theories without appealing to moral intuitions, see Sinnott-Armstrong (2006).

2. Some defenders of moral intuitions do not count anything as a moral intuition unless it is true or probable or justified. Such accounts create confusion when we want to ask whether moral intuitions are reliable or justified, because an affirmative answer is guaranteed by definition, but skeptics can still ask whether any people ever have any "real" moral intuitions. To avoid such double-talk, it is better to define moral intuitions neutrally so that calling something a moral intuition does not entail by definition that it has any particular epistemic status, such as being true or probable or justified.

3. Contrary to common philosophical dogma, there is a logically valid way to derive a moral "ought" from "is," but such derivations still cannot make anyone justified in believing their conclusions. See Sinnott-Armstrong (2000).

4. Van Roojen might admit that Horowitz's argument undermines moral intuitionism, since he defends a method of reflective equilibrium that is coherentist rather than foundationalist.

5. Another possible explanation is change in beliefs about probabilities. See Kuhn (1997). However, this would not cover all of the moral cases and would not save the reliability of moral intuitions anyway.

6. Kamm gives many other examples and arguments, but I cannot do justice to her article here. For further criticisms, see Levy (forthcoming).

7. To disagree with an alternative is, presumably, to see it as morally wrong. However, this is not clear, since subjects were asked what they would do—not what was wrong.

8. To make it clearer that Nick would not have told the truth if Kathy had not interrupted, the omission version was changed to read, ". . . Nick decides to lie to Kathy, but [before Nick can speak] Kathy says, 'Oh, never mind, that was 1983.'"

9. Unger (1996) argues that many other moral intuitions change when intervening cases are presented between extremes. If so, these cases present more evidence of framing effects. A final bit of evidence for framing effects comes from philosophical paradoxes, such as the mere addition paradox (Parfit, 1984). In Parfit's example,

when people compare A and B alone, most of them evaluate A as better. In contrast, when people consider B+ and A– in between A and B, most of them do not evaluate A as better than B. The fact that Parfit's paradox still seems paradoxical to many philosophers after long reflection shows how strong such framing effects are.

10. For more on framing effects when both frames are presented, see Armstrong, Schwartz, Fitzgerald, Putt, and Ubel (2002), Druckman (2001), and Kühberger (1995).

11. My analogy to thermometers derives from Goldman (1986, p. 45). The same point could be made in terms of fake barns, as in Goldman (1976).

2.1 Moral Intuitions Framed

William Tolhurst

In "Framing Moral Intuitions," Walter Sinnott-Armstrong argues that moral intuitions are unreliable and hence not justified in the absence of inferential confirmation. Since moral intuitionism is committed to the view that moral intuitions are sometimes justified independently of inferential confirmation, he concludes that moral intuitionism is false. I shall argue that Sinnott-Armstrong fails to justify either conclusion.

Justification

The issue concerns the justification of moral intuitions, so we need to begin with Sinnott-Armstrong's understanding of justification:

> To call a belief "justified" is to say that the believer ought to hold that belief as opposed to suspending belief, because the believer has adequate epistemic grounds for believing that it is true (at least in some minimal sense). (p. 48)

On this view, in judging a person to be justified in holding a belief, we are saying that she ought to hold the belief and it would be a mistake for her not to believe it, a mistake that renders her a less than optimal epistemic agent because, given that she has adequate epistemic grounds, believing is the best option. I have no quarrel with this definition even though it implies that those who fail to believe everything they have adequate grounds for believing (i.e., most of us) have made a mistake that renders us less than optimal epistemic agents. This is something we all knew anyway, and we need to be reminded. After all, epistemic humility is a virtue, and some of us are inclined to forget.

In this essay, I argue that a proper regard for epistemic humility requires us to disagree with Sinnott-Armstrong because the grounds for believing that moral intuitions are unreliable are too weak to show that we ought to believe this. In the absence of adequate reasons to believe they are reliable, suspending belief is the best response.

The Master Argument

The framework for Sinnott-Armstrong's case against moral intuitions is provided by the following argument:

(1) If our moral intuitions are formed in circumstances where they are unreliable, and if we ought to know this, then our moral intuitions are not justified without inferential confirmation.

(2) If moral intuitions are subject to framing effects, then they are not reliable in those circumstances.

(3) Moral intuitions are subject to framing effects in many circumstances.

(4) We ought to know (3).

(5) Therefore, our moral intuitions in those circumstances are not justified without inferential confirmation. (p. 52)

It is not entirely clear from the above statement how the conclusion is supposed to follow from the premises. Presumably, the occurrence of "those circumstances" in step 5 refers to the many circumstances in which moral intuitions are subject to framing effects. A person might know that moral intuitions are subject to framing effects in many cases without knowing which cases they are. If so, she would not know of each of the many circumstances that it is one in which moral intuition is unreliable, nor is there any reason to believe that she should know this. Hence, it does not follow that her intuitions *in those circumstances* are not justified without inferential confirmation. Of course, if she should know that moral intuitions are subject to framing effects in many circumstances, then, given step 1, she should know that her moral intuitions are unreliable in many circumstances. But from this it doesn't follow that she ought to know that her intuitions in those cases are unjustified without inferential justification. That would follow only if she ought to have known of each of the cases that it was one in which her moral intuitions were subject to framing effects. Nonetheless, the gist of the argument is clear—we ought to know that moral intuitions are unreliable in many circumstances, and, this being so, we ought to know that moral intuitions are unreliable and in need of independent inferential justification, which Sinnott-Armstrong defines as follows:

A belief is justified *inferentially* if and only if it is justified only because the believer is able to infer it from some other belief.

A belief is justified *noninferentially* if and only if it is justified independently of whether the believer is able to infer it from any other belief. (p. 48)

The Problematic Inference

The main problem with the argument is the inference from "Many of our moral intuitions are unreliable" to "Our moral intuitions are unreliable." What counts as "many" varies from one situation to another. Suppose I found out that one hundred 2005 Honda Accords had serious defects that rendered them unreliable. I think a hundred cars is a lot of cars; I don't know anyone who owns a hundred cars, so as far as I'm concerned, if someone owns a hundred cars, then they own many cars. This being so, if a hundred 2005 Honda Accords are defective, then many Honda Accords are defective. However, if many Honda 2005 Accords are defective, then surely 2005 Honda Accords are unreliable. Obviously, this is bad reasoning. What counts as many cars depends on context as does what counts as reliable. In the context of car ownership, owning a hundred cars counts as owning many cars. When it comes to judging the reliability of a particular kind of car, one hundred is not enough.

In like manner, ascriptions of reliability are also context dependent. In a discussion of the unreliability caused by word framing effects, Sinnott-Armstrong observes that a person influenced by word framing "cannot be reliable in the sense of having a high probability of true beliefs" and goes on to note, "If your car started only half of the time, it would not be reliable" (Sinnott-Armstrong, p. 52). What Sinnott-Armstrong says is surely true given the reliability of today's cars. Relative to today's cars, such a car would be very unreliable. Suppose, however, that we are talking about a time in automotive history (perhaps imaginary) when cars were much less reliable than they are now. Suppose at this time most cars start only a third of the time. In this context one might well describe a car that starts half the time as very reliable. Thus, the truth of judgments of reliability may be context dependent because what counts as a high probability of success (either true belief or a car's starting) can depend on a comparison class. In making these observations, I do not suggest that Sinnott-Armstrong's argument is fallacious; my point concerns how we are to understand what he means by "many circumstances" in the context of the master argument. In order for the argument to work, he must show that the probability that one's moral intuitions are influenced by framing effects is high enough to render them unreliable and hence unjustified without supposing that he means "a suitably high percentage of the circumstances in which moral intuitions are formed." Our disagreement concerns whether he has adequately shown this.

The Prevalence of Framing Effects

After an extended discussion of a number of psychological studies of framing effects, Sinnott-Armstrong concludes:

Together these studies show that moral intuitions are subject to framing effects in many different circumstances. . . . Only one premise remains to be supported. It claims that we ought to know that moral intuitions are subject to framing effects in many circumstances. Of course, those who have not been exposed to the research might not know this fact about moral intuitions. However, this psychological research—like much psychological research—gives more detailed arguments for a claim that educated people ought to have known anyway. Anyone who has been exposed to moral disagreements and to the ways in which people argue for their moral positions has had experiences that, if considered carefully, would support the premise that moral intuitions are subject to framing effects in many circumstances. (Sinnott-Armstrong, p. 67)

Let's grant that moral intuitions evoked as the result of framing effects are unreliable and that moral intuitions are subject to framing effects in many circumstances. How does this provide us with adequate reason to believe that moral intuitions are so unreliable that they are not justified in the absence of inferential justification? How does the fact that they are disturbingly prevalent in these studies show that moral intuitions formed in the world outside the psych lab are unreliable? The subjects in these studies were probably college students, many of whom were probably freshmen. Why should we take the responses of this population to be a reliable indicator of the reliability of all of us?

Furthermore, the studies were designed to elicit framing effects in the subjects. The situations in which we generally form our spontaneous moral beliefs are not. Indeed, the framing effects reported in these studies were word framing effects and order effects elicited in response to narratives designed to evoke them. Many of our spontaneous moral beliefs are evoked by perceptions of the situations in which we find ourselves. Hence, these moral intuitions cannot be affected by word framing because they are not a response to a verbal description. They may, of course be affected by context framing, but these experiments do not provide grounds for believing that intuitions that are responses to nonverbal input are likely to result from context framing effects. It is, of course, also possible for moral intuitions formed in response to nonverbal input to be influenced by order effects, but it is not clear how the experimental data on order effects provide grounds for judging the likelihood of order effects in response to nonverbal cues. This being so, we don't have clear evidence that moral intuitions formed in response to nonverbal cues are likely to be affected by framing effects. However, what about moral intuitions that are formed in response to verbal input; do the studies show these moral intuitions to be unreliable and in need of inferential justification? Whether our moral intuitions are reliable depends on how frequent framing effects are outside the experimental setting. Putting aside questions of just who "we" are and just how many of "us" there are, we would need to know the baseline reliability of our moral intuitions and the frequency of framing effects in moral intuitions outside the psychology lab to have adequate reason to believe that they are unreliable absent inferential confirmation. Thus, the data on framing effects reported in psychological studies seem to be too weak to justify the belief that our moral intuitions are unreliable in the absence of inferential justification. We can be confident that the baseline is greater than zero and less than 100%. I must confess that I have no idea what the baseline reliability is, nor do I have any idea what the overall frequency of framing effects outside of psychology labs is. Nothing Sinnott-Armstrong has provided by way of argument gives us sufficient reason to believe that the percentage of moral intuitions formed in ordinary circumstances that result from framing effects is a significant fraction of all such moral intuitions. Of course, neither do we have any reason to think that the proportion of false and unreliable intuitions is not significant— we just don't know whether moral intuitions are unreliable. We don't have adequate grounds to believe they are and we don't have adequate grounds to believe they are not. Because of this, we also don't have adequate grounds to believe that ethical intuitionism is false. Instead, we should withhold belief until we do have adequate grounds.

A Response to a Response

In addressing possible responses to the argument, Sinnott-Armstrong considers the possibility that one might be able to tell that some moral intuitions are not influenced by framing effects:

> . . . suppose we do figure out which people are not subject to moral framing effects. Moral intuitionism still faces a dilemma: If we can tell that we are in the group whose moral intuitions are reliable, then we can get inferential confirmation; if we cannot tell whether we are in the group whose moral intuitions are reliable, then we are not justified. Either way, we cannot be justified independently of inferential justification. (Sinnott-Armstrong, pp. 70–71)

The argument rests on a mistake. Showing that someone's moral intuitions are not subject to framing effects does not, in and of itself, provide inferential confirmation. The knowledge that one is immune to framing effects is a defeater that defeats an undermining defeater that provides reason for believing one is unreliable. It neutralizes the undermining defeater without providing a belief from which one can infer the truth of the moral intuition. Hence, it does not provide inferential justification for the moral intuition.

If the Argument Worked, Would It Undermine Itself?

Some of the reasons given for thinking that moral intuitions are subject to framing seem to apply with strength to epistemic intuitions. If this is so, and if the argument works, it would call into question any epistemic intuitions that functioned as premises of the argument. One might then appeal to other epistemic intuitions to provide inferential justification, but these would, in turn, require inferential support, so we would be faced with worries about vicious infinite regresses and circularity. I am confident that Sinnott-Armstrong can address these worries; my point is that, in order for the argument to provide adequate grounds for the conclusions, he must address them.

A Final Note

In this essay I have focused on a number of concerns; I would like to conclude by noting two important areas of agreement. The first is that framing effects raise important questions about the reliability of intuitions generally, and moral intuitions in particular, and, second, this being so, moral epistemologists can no longer pursue their goals with blithe disregard for the work of empirical psychology.

2.2 | Defending Ethical Intuitionism

Russ Shafer-Landau

Ethical intuitionism is the view that there are noninferentially justified moral beliefs. A belief is noninferentially justified provided that its justification does not depend on a believer's ability to infer it from another belief. I believe that some moral beliefs are noninferentially justified. Therefore, I believe that ethical intuitionism is true.

Here is a plausible intuition: The deliberate humiliation, rape, and torture of a child, for no purpose other than the pleasure of the one inflicting such treatment, is immoral. It might be that a person arrives at such a belief by having inferred it from others. And so that belief, if justified, can be justified inferentially. However, while the justification of this belief can proceed inferentially, it need not. Were the believer to have come to the belief spontaneously, or after reflection, rather than by inference, she might still be justified in her belief, even without reliance on other, supporting beliefs. Such a belief would be epistemically overdetermined—justified both inferentially and noninferentially.

That is not an argument; it is just an assertion of an intuitionist position. Walter Sinnott-Armstrong, in his very provocative and stimulating paper,[1] seeks to cast doubt on this position. If he is right, then any justified moral belief must be justified inferentially. Why does he believe that?

The beginnings of an answer are provided in his *Master Argument*:

(1) If our moral intuitions are formed in circumstances where they are unreliable, and if we ought to know this, then our moral intuitions are not justified without inferential confirmation.

(2) If moral intuitions are subject to framing effects, then they are not reliable in those circumstances.

(3) Moral intuitions are subject to framing effects in many circumstances.

(4) We ought to know (3).

(5) Therefore, our moral intuitions in those circumstances are not justified without inferential confirmation. (p. 52)

I think that this argument is sound. Yet the argument, as it stands, does not undermine ethical intuitionism. Its conclusion is a qualified one, but the rejection of ethical intuitionism is meant to be unqualified. The argument tells us only that moral intuitions (understood, in Sinnott-Armstrong's sense, as strong immediate moral beliefs) are, in many circumstances, unjustified. I don't know of any philosopher who would disagree with that. However, the argument, to do its desired work, must tell us that moral intuitions are *never* justified without inferential confirmation. Clearly, Sinnott-Armstrong takes himself to have provided a perfectly general argument against ethical intuitionism. Shortly after the presentation of the Master Argument, Sinnott-Armstrong claims that "the main argument . . . concludes only that moral believers need [inferential] confirmation for any particular moral belief" (p. 55). But neither the Master Argument, nor any argument offered in the intervening pages, substantiates that sweeping conclusion.

There is a natural way to modify the argument, however, such that it yields the desired anti-intuitionist conclusion. The following argument would span the gap between Sinnott-Armstrong's actual conclusion and the one he'd most like to vindicate. Call this "*The Amended Argument*":

(1)   If a moral belief is subject to a framing effect, then that belief is justified only if the believer is able to confirm that there is no framing effect.
(2)   All moral beliefs are subject to framing effects.
(3)   Therefore, all moral beliefs are justified only if the believer is able to confirm that there is no framing effect.
(4)   Such confirmation is a form of inferential justification.
(5)   Therefore, all moral beliefs are justified, if they are, only inferentially.
(6)   Therefore, ethical intuitionism is false.

Suppose we at least provisionally grant premise (1) and accept premise (4) of the Amended Argument. Premise (2), however, is problematic.

To see why, we need first to be clear about how to understand a belief's being subject to a framing effect. A belief is subject to a framing effect if the truth value of a person's belief would not alter, but the possession or content of the belief *would* alter, were different descriptions used to elicit the belief, or a different context relied on to form the belief. Being subject to such effects is a dispositional notion that denotes a susceptibility to alteration.

There are two basic ways to understand this susceptibility. We might understand "being subject to framing effects" to mean that there is some logically or metaphysically possible situation in which one's belief alters because of wording or context. This reading would vindicate premise (2).

However, this isn't Sinnott-Armstrong's meaning,[2] for if it were, there would be no need to have presented the summaries of the empirical studies surrounding framing effects and moral beliefs. We can know a priori that there are conceivable or metaphysically possible circumstances in which moral beliefs alter because of frames. We don't need empirical research to substantiate that point.[3]

Alternatively, we might understand "being subject to framing effects" probabilistically. A natural suggestion here would be something like this: A belief is subject to framing effects provided that its content (but not its truth value) is likely to change if formed under alternative contexts that are likely to be confronted in the actual world. On this particular reading, however, premise (2) would be false; many moral beliefs would remain invulnerable to change for most people. Consider the example I provided at the top of this essay: The deliberate humiliation, rape, and torture of a child, for no purpose other than securing the rapist's pleasure, is immoral. For most people, there aren't *any* changes in wording or context that will lead them to abandon their belief in this claim. There are plenty of other beliefs held with a like degree of conviction. On the probabilistic understanding of what it is to be subject to framing effects, this kind of invulnerability marks such beliefs as being relevantly immune to framing effects.

What this shows is that the natural way to amend the master argument is not the best way. The Amended Argument's second premise is either obviously true (thus placing pressure on its first premise and making the introduction of all empirical research superfluous) or false. Indeed, Sinnott-Armstrong never endorses the Amended Argument and never claims that all moral intuitions are subject to framing effects. He even cites some evidence of moral beliefs that are immune to framing effects (Petronovich & O'Neill, 1996, discussion of Form 1 and 1R). However, if some moral beliefs are impervious to such undermining effects, then why think that *all* justified moral beliefs must be justified inferentially? Why can't these relevantly invulnerable beliefs, at least, be justified noninferentially?

I don't think that Sinnott-Armstrong answers this question until the end of his article, when he is offering replies to anticipated criticisms. I think that we can reconstruct the real argument against intuitionism as follows:

The Real Argument

(1) If moral beliefs are subject to framing effects in many circumstances, then, for any one of my moral beliefs, it is justified only if I am able to inferentially confirm it.

(2) Moral beliefs are subject to framing effects in many circumstances.

(3) Therefore, for any one of my moral beliefs, it is justified only if I am able to inferentially confirm it.

Since, for purposes of this argument, it doesn't matter who I happen to be—the conclusion generalizes across all agents—the falsity of ethical intuitionism follows directly.

Let us see what can be said for the Real Argument's second premise before considering the support for its first.

I believe that the second premise is true. Still, the premise could do with a bit of elucidation. For instance, the size of the class of moral beliefs that are thus vulnerable presumably matters a good deal to the plausibility of the argument. If only a small number of moral beliefs are unreliable in many circumstances, then this would presumably weaken any allegiance we'd otherwise feel towards the Real Argument's first premise. Imagine, for instance, that only one moral belief was subject to framing effects in many circumstances. It's hard to see how the argument's first premise, amended to refer to just this one belief in its antecedent, could be plausibly defended.

Thus, the extent of the class of vulnerable moral beliefs matters a good deal to the plausibility of the Real Argument. And it isn't clear to me that the few studies that Sinnott-Armstrong summarizes provide a good basis for thinking that this class is large. It's not that they indicate that the class is small. I think it fair to say that, as yet, we simply do not have a sufficient number of relevant experiments to give us much indication of how many of our moral beliefs are subject to framing effects.

That isn't just because the number of experiments that Sinnott-Armstrong cites is quite small, for each experiment might have canvassed a very large number of moral beliefs, on the part of a very large number of subjects. However, the total number of subjects in the experiments cited is not more than a few hundred, and the number of moral beliefs is far smaller. Further, the experimental subjects are (almost) all college or university students, and so are not necessarily reflective of the entire population of those who hold moral beliefs. Further, the beliefs in question are not clearly moral intuitions—no mention is made of how strongly they are held, and no mention is made of whether the beliefs whose variability was measured were immediately formed or, rather, formed through a (possibly quick) inferential process.

Still, leaving all this aside, we might make a plug for the relevance of the experimental evidence here by claiming that many of the moral beliefs subject to framing effects are highly general. It is true that we each hold thousands of moral beliefs, and true that the experiments that Sinnott-Armstrong cites assess the vulnerability of only a tiny fraction of them. Yet if most of our moral beliefs rely on only a few very general moral beliefs, then if many of these latter are subject to framing effects, we might well impute a like vulnerability to many of the remainder. For instance, if (as a study cited by Sinnott-Armstrong indicates) endorsement of the doctrine of double effect were subject to framing effects, then presumably all of the more particular beliefs that rest on this doctrine would be similarly variable.

Yet it isn't clear to me that most of our moral beliefs do rely on a small number of very general moral beliefs. This may be the proper order of justification, if most foundationalist versions of moral epistemology are correct. However, the reliance at issue here has to do with the origin of belief, rather than its justificatory status. It concerns whether people hold their more particular moral beliefs because they hold the moral general ones. And the answer is far from clear. It's possible, of course, that agents have well-developed and coherent, ordered sets of moral beliefs, and come to their more particular beliefs because they see that they are implied by the more general ones that they hold. But this sounds more like an idealization than a description of most doxastic practices. If that is so, then even if we take the experiments at face value, it's not clear that we can assume that many more particular moral beliefs are subject to framing effects, even if some number of highly general beliefs are thus susceptible.

The last caveat I'd mention in interpreting the data that Sinnott-Armstrong presents has to do with the circumstances in which beliefs are subject to framing effects. The second premise of the Real Argument alleges that moral beliefs are subject to such effects in many circumstances. This may be true. However, the experimental evidence does not support this. The experiments are all conducted in one basic kind of circumstance—that of a controlled experiment situated in someone's lab. There may be difficulties with extrapolating from questionnaires administered in such situations. In any event, since the experiments were not conducted in a variety of circumstances, but rather only in a single kind of circumstance, it isn't clear that they can substantiate the Real Argument's second premise.

I think that it's high time to stop nipping at Sinnott-Armstrong's heels and to proceed to a discussion of the Real Argument's first premise. Let us grant its second premise, and suppose, perhaps quite reasonably, that the reservations I've just expressed amount to minor quibbles that can be easily addressed.

The first premise, recall, says that

(1)   If moral beliefs are subject to framing effects in many circumstances, then, for any one of my moral beliefs, it is justified only if I am able to inferentially confirm it.

Why think that this is true?

Here is one argument that makes an appearance in various forms throughout the paper. If there is no reason that supports my current moral belief, then I am unjustified in holding it. If there is a reason, then either I have access to it or I don't. If I don't, then I am again unjustified in holding it. If I do have such access, then I am able to draw an inference from that reason in support of my particular belief. And if I am thus able to draw an inference, then the justification for my belief is inferential. So if my moral belief is justified, then its justification must be inferential (pp. 56, 70, 72).

This argument does not work. It moves too quickly from an ability to draw an inference to the requirement that such inferences be drawn as a precondition of epistemic justification. A belief is inferentially justifiable provided that its justification *depends on* an agent's ability to infer it from another belief. However, one cannot establish the relevant dependence relation just by pointing out the availability of an inferential link. That I *can* infer my belief from others does not mean that I *must* do so in order for it to be justified. Beliefs might be noninferentially justified, even if they are also inferentially justifiable.

Here is another argument:

(1)   "Generally, when I know [or ought to know] that my belief results from a process that is likely to lead to error, then I need some confirmation in order to be justified in holding that belief" (Sinnott-Armstrong, this volume, pp. 50–51).

(2)   Because of the empirical evidence cited in Sinnott-Armstrong's article, I know (or ought to know) that my moral intuitions result from a process that is likely to lead to error.

(3)   Therefore, I need some confirmation in order to be justified in holding my moral intuitions.

Sinnott-Armstrong does not explicitly affirm the argument's second premise, so he may reject it. I think he'd be right to do that. The problem with this argument is that I don't, in fact, know that my intuition-forming processes are likely to lead to error. What Sinnott-Armstrong's cited experiments reveal, if we take them at face value, is that some such processes are unreliable. It's not clear that my very own processes, whatever they happen to be, are likely to be unreliable. I don't know whose processes, or which processes, are likelier than not to lead to error. In fact, the studies that Sinnott-Armstrong cites do not discuss the different processes that lead to noninferential moral belief. They note that some subjects alter their beliefs due to framing effects, but they make no mention of the processes that generate these changes. And so we are in no position to justifiably believe that the processes that generate my (or your) moral intuitions are likely to be unreliable. The argument's first premise may well be true. However, its second is as yet inadequately supported.

Sinnott-Armstrong never clearly announces the argument that is to take us from the limited conclusion of the Master Argument, to the quite general anti-intuitionism that he advocates, so my reconstruction of the Real Argument must be to some extent tentative. Yet, assuming that it is faithfully done, we are still in need of a defense of its first premise. As I read him, the central argument for the conditional is this. My own belief might be highly reliably formed, and even invulnerable to framing effects, but so long as the beliefs of others are not, and I know this (or ought to know this), I need to know that my beliefs are of the reliable kind, rather than the unreliable kind, before being justified in holding them. And gaining such knowledge is a matter of inferentially confirming the original belief.

The same argument can be made intrapersonally as well as interpersonally. If any of my own moral beliefs are subject to framing effects—and surely some of them are, and surely I know, or ought to know, that they are—then even if a given one is immune to such effects, I need to confirm its status as such before I can be justified in holding it. (Both of these arguments can be found at pp. 69–70).

This is a variation on a familiar and powerful argument against foundationalism: If there is a chance that my belief is mistaken, and I know, or ought to know, of this chance, then the original belief is justified only if I enlist other beliefs to confirm it. However, for every one of my beliefs, there is a chance of its being mistaken. And I know, or I ought to know, this. Therefore, the justification of every belief requires inferential confirmation. Therefore, there are no self-evident or basic beliefs. Therefore, foundationalism is false.

Here is a reply. Some beliefs are formed after quite careful, but noninferential, reflection.[4] These beliefs may be immune to framing effects. These, at least, may be candidates for noninferential justification, even if less well-considered beliefs are not. Sinnott-Armstrong disagrees: Those best able to carefully reflect on their beliefs are also those most able to inferentially support them (p. 70). But this reply is suspect. That I can enlist other beliefs to support an initial belief does not mean that its justification depends on my doing so. For all that has been said, certain beliefs may be justified solely on the basis of an agent's having arrived at them via careful (noninferential) reflection. Sinnott-Armstrong again disagrees. Why couldn't a believer be noninferentially justified in his moral belief? Because "[t]he believers who form their beliefs without inference and those who claim to be justified noninferentially are still subject to framing effects before they engage in such reasoning" (p. 70). Perhaps. However, the experiments that Sinnott-Armstrong cites do not support such a broad claim. They support instead the claim that some moral beliefs of some people are subject to framing effects. We don't, as yet, have a general argument that shows the impossibility of noninferential justification for moral beliefs.

That's not the end of the story, however, since Sinnott-Armstrong offers a follow-up argument. It takes the form of a dilemma (p. 70). Some people are subject to framing effects; others are not. If we can tell that we are in the former group, then an inferential confirmation of our intuitions is available. If we cannot tell which group we are in, then our intuitions are not justified. Thus, any justified intuition must be justified inferentially.

It is true that if we can tell that we are among the epistemically fortunate, then we have available to us an inferential justification of our intuitions. However, all that shows is that such an awareness is sufficient for an intuition's (defeasible) justification. It doesn't show that it is necessary. Sinnott-Armstrong presumably means to show that it is necessary by relying on the other horn of the dilemma. If we cannot tell which group we are in, then our intuitions are unjustified. Thus, our intuitions are justified only if we can tell which group we are in. Since discerning our grouping is an inferential matter, our intuitions are justified only inferentially, if at all.

The argument for this crucial claim relies on the example of the thermometers. So long as we know, or even suspect, that some of these instruments are unreliable, then we are not justified in trusting any one of them until we can confirm its accuracy. These thermometers are meant to be analogous to our capacity to form intuitions. None of our intuitions is justified until we can determine that we are free of framing effects and other impediments to doxastic reliability. And such determination is a matter of inferential confirmation. So our intuitions are justified only if they are inferentially confirmed.

The reliance on the thermometer analogy is a bit puzzling. In the example, we don't know whether ten or fifty or eighty percent of the thermometers are unreliable. We just know that some are. If the argument from analogy is going to work, then we don't need to know just what percentage of our beliefs is subject to framing effects. All we need to know is that some nonnegligible percentage is.

But we already knew that. We knew that because we knew the rough extent of moral disagreement in the world. On the assumption (that Sinnott-Armstrong accepts) that there is moral truth, contradictory moral claims indicate unreliability on someone's part. And there are plenty of contradictory moral claims out there, advanced by legions of adherents each. The evidence about framing effects was presumably introduced in order to establish the unreliability of some moral beliefs in some circumstances. However, the extent of moral disagreement has long been clear, as has the pressure it has placed on ethical intuitionism.

That's not to say that the evidence about framing effects is useless. It can help to explain why some moral beliefs are unreliable. The fact of moral disagreement doesn't offer such an explanation—it only indicates the existence of unreliability (supposing some kind of ethical objectivism to be true). Still, the more particular explanation of unreliability does not create a novel difficulty for intuitionism. The basic question is this: Knowing that my moral beliefs might be unreliable, must I be able to inferentially confirm them before being justified in holding them? Intuitionists have faced this question many times before, and it isn't clear why any successful answer they have earlier provided will not do for the present case.

In his presentation of the thermometer analogy, Sinnott-Armstrong is insisting on a classic internalist constraint on epistemic justification: A belief (as to the thermometer's reliability, or as to an action's moral status) is justified only if we have accessible evidence that supports it. That is why it is puzzling that he should rely on an example first introduced by Alvin Goldman, who is perhaps most responsible for the growing challenge to internalism over the past thirty years. Goldman himself rejects the epistemic principle that justification must be inferential. In the book from which the thermometer example is taken,[5] Goldman defends an externalist, reliabilist account of knowledge.

Let us consider some replies to Sinnott-Armstrong's analogy. The first is concessive. We might accept that epistemic justification is basically an internalist notion, and so concede the lesson that Sinnott-Armstrong wants us to take from the thermometer example. However, it is now a common view in epistemology to have bifurcated accounts according to which justification is construed as internalists would do, while arguing that knowledge is best understood as externalists prefer. On externalist views, knowledge does not require epistemic justification, but rather some other feature, such as warrant, which indicates a well-functioning, reliable belief-forming mechanism or process. If any such view were true, Sinnott-Armstrong's arguments, even if successful, would undermine only an intuitionist account of epistemic justification, but would not touch the intuitionist's central claim about knowledge: namely, that it can be had without inferential support.

Rather than pursue the niceties of the bifurcated account, which is founded on a concession, let us see whether we can resist Sinnott-Armstrong's claim about justification itself. One way to do this starts with a focus on the class of moral beliefs that are agreed by (nearly) everyone to be true.

There are such beliefs. Those endorsing Rossian prima facie duties are among them. That such beliefs do not by themselves allow us to determine what is right or wrong in a situation is neither here nor there. They are genuine moral beliefs, and the evidence about framing effects casts no doubt on their reliability. Neither does this evidence impugn the reliability of more specific, entirely uncontroversial moral beliefs, of the sort I introduced at the beginning of the essay. These are beliefs that are (for almost everyone) not subject to framing effects: They are invulnerable to change under realistic circumstances.

However, if there are classes of moral beliefs that are in fact highly reliable, then it isn't clear why their justification must proceed inferentially. Insisting that it do so sounds like simply insisting that internalism, not externalism, is the correct account of epistemic justification. I assume that Sinnott-Armstrong would reply by slightly amending an argument that we'd earlier seen. In that argument, either we can class ourselves as among those who are invulnerable to framing effects, or we are unable to do so. Our ability to sort ourselves into the relevant class entails an inferential justification of our beliefs. Our inability to do so entails a lack of justification for our beliefs. A variation on this theme would focus on the reliability of our beliefs, rather than our reliability as epistemic agents. Either we can identify a belief as free of framing effects or we can't. If we can't, then we are unjustified in holding it without inferential confirmation. If we can, then an inferential justification is available to us. Thus, if we are justified in holding any such belief, we are justified only inferentially.

The reply to this variation should recall the reply to the original argument. It is true that if we can tell whether we, or certain of our beliefs, are free from framing effects, then we have all the materials of an inferential confirmation. However, that does not show that such confirmation is *required* for the justification of those beliefs. What is supposed to show that? The other horn of the dilemma, whose contrapositive states that we are justified in a belief only if we can tell which group we (or our beliefs) belong to. But why think that this second-order belief is required in order for the initial belief to be justified? Why not think, instead, that the need for inferential confirmation arises only when the credibility of a belief is relevantly in question? If (nearly) everyone agrees in a given belief, then, rare contexts aside (as when one is arguing with a very intelligent inter-locutor who refuses to accept the existence of an external world or the immorality of genocide), its credibility is *not* relevantly in question. That *other* moral beliefs are subject to framing effects does not provide enough evidence for thinking that a particular belief, which everyone accepts, is thus vulnerable. Thus, the need for inferential confirmation doesn't (as yet) arise for such beliefs. We may well be noninferentially justified in some of our moral beliefs.

What is thought to trigger the need for inferential confirmation is the second-order belief—one that everyone ought to have—that one's intu-itions might be mistaken. However, it isn't clear that possession of such a belief is enough to establish the need for confirmation. Belief in the falli-bility of one's intuitions is not enough to serve as an epistemic underminer. Or, if it is, Sinnott-Armstrong has not provided an adequate argument for securing this claim. The only argument we get for this view is one by analogy, the one that invokes the thermometers. But there are (at least) four principles that we might extract from the thermometer example:

(A) If there is any chance that one's belief is mistaken, and one knows (or ought to know) this, then one's belief is justified only if one is able to inferentially confirm it.

(B) If there is a substantial chance that one's belief is mistaken, and one knows (or ought to know) this, then one's belief is justified only if one is able to inferentially confirm it.

(C) If, given one's other beliefs, one's belief stands a substantial chance of being mistaken, then one's belief is justified only if one is able to confirm it.

(D) If one thinks that one's belief stands a substantial chance of being mistaken, then one's belief is justified only if one is able to confirm it.

Sinnott-Armstrong has given no argument for preferring (A) to (B), (C), or (D). (A) is what is needed to make trouble for intuitionism. For it is true that, with regard to any of my (nontautologous) moral beliefs, there is at least some chance of its being mistaken. And so, given (A), all of my justified moral beliefs must be justified inferentially. However, the truth of (B), (C), or (D) does not threaten intuitionism. Consider (B). Sinnott-Armstrong has presented no evidence that there is a substantial chance that certain of our moral beliefs are mistaken—namely, those, such as the claim about child torture cited at the top of this essay, that strike many as conceptual constraints on what could qualify as moral or immoral behavior. (B) may well be true. But when applied to the class of moral beliefs about which there is near universal agreement, we as yet have no reason to suppose that it generates an implication incompatible with ethical intuitionism.

Now consider (C) and (D). For almost every believer, there is a class of moral beliefs that, given her other beliefs, do *not* stand a substantial chance of being mistaken. These are (among others) the ones agreed to by nearly everyone. These beliefs are also such that they will rarely, if ever, be directly regarded by the believer as subject to a substantial chance of being mistaken. Thus, the antecedents of (C) and (D) are false with regard to such beliefs, and so nothing can be inferred about whether their justification must proceed inferentially.

In short, the thermometer example creates difficulty for ethical intuitionism only if we are to apply principle (A), rather than (B), (C), or (D), to the case. However, we haven't yet seen good reason to do so. Therefore, we don't, as yet, have a determinative argument against ethical intuitionism.

I think we can lend further support to this conclusion if we imagine a modification of the thermometer example. Suppose we had 10,000 thermometers, and only one of them malfunctioned. Further, we know this, or we ought to know this. Under these conditions, it isn't at all clear that one needs to confirm one's readings before they are justified.

Why not say the very same thing with regard to certain moral intuitions? Only one in 10,000 (if that) would deny that the sort of torture I described at the outset is immoral. There is a chance that this iconoclast is correct and that we are all deluded. However, that is not enough to establish the need to inferentially confirm all of our moral beliefs. That there are intuitions subject to framing effects is not enough to undermine any initial credibility possessed by moral intuitions that (nearly) everyone shares. Nor is it the case that one's justification for believing such intuitions must stem from their widespread support. Rather, *the call for doxastic confirmation arises only in certain circumstances.* Sinnott-Armstrong has sought to defend the view that, when it comes to moral beliefs, every circumstance is such a circumstance. He has done this by means of the thermometer example.

But if I am right, that example falls short of establishing his desired conclusion.

I have tried to reconstruct, and then to undermine, Sinnott-Armstrong's central arguments against ethical intuitionism. Success on this front, if I have achieved that much, is no guarantee of intuitionism's truth. If Sinnott-Armstrong's arguments are sound, then ethical intuitionism is false. But of course it doesn't follow that if Sinnott-Armstrong's arguments are unsound, then ethical intuitionism is true. Intuitionists need both to defend against criticisms of their view and also to provide positive arguments on its behalf. There is still plenty of work to be done.

Notes

My thanks to Walter Sinnott-Armstrong and Pekka Väyrynen for extremely helpful comments on an earlier draft of this essay.

1. "Framing Moral Intuitions" (this volume).

2. As he has indicated in correspondence.

3. Further, understanding the relevant vulnerability this way places a substantial argumentative burden on premise (1), since it's quite contentious to claim that the mere conceptual or metaphysical possibility of doxastic change entails the need for a belief's confirmation.

4. See Audi (2004, pp. 45ff.) for a defense of the idea that careful reflection need not proceed inferentially.

5. Goldman (1986, p. 45).

How to Apply Generalities: Reply to Tolhurst and Shafer-Landau

Walter Sinnott-Armstrong

Good news: My commentators raise important issues.
Bad news: Most of their points are critical.
Good news: Many of their criticisms depend on misunderstandings.
Bad news: Many of their misunderstandings are my fault.
Good news: I can fix my argument.

Reformulation

My basic point was and is that studies of framing effects give us reason to believe that moral intuitions in general are not reliable. This claim is not about any particular belief content or state. What is reliable or unreliable is, instead, a general class of beliefs (or their source). A class of beliefs is reliable only when a high enough percentage of beliefs in that class are true.

One class of beliefs is moral intuitions, defined as strong and immediate moral beliefs. When we ask whether moral intuitions in general are reliable, the question is whether enough beliefs in that class are true.

Any particular belief falls into many such classes. For example, my belief that it is morally wrong to torture a child just for pleasure falls into the class of moral intuitions. It also falls into the narrower class of moral intuitions with which almost everyone agrees. The percentage of true beliefs in the former class might be low, even if the percentage of true beliefs in the latter class is high.

How can we apply information about the reliability of general classes to particular beliefs within those classes? Just as we do outside of morality. Suppose we know that 70% of voters in Texas in 2004 voted for Bush, and all we know about Pat is that Pat voted in Texas in 2004. Then it is reasonable for us to assign a .7 probability to the claim that Pat voted for Bush. If we later learn that Pat is a woman, and if we know that less than

50% of women voters in Texas in 2004 voted for Bush, then it will no longer be reasonable for us to assign a .7 probability to the claim that Pat voted for Bush. Still, even if Pat is a woman, if we do not know that fact about Pat but know only that Pat voted in Texas in 2004, then it is reasonable for us to assign a probability of .7 to the claim that Pat voted for Bush. And even if we know that Pat is a woman, if we do not know whether being a woman decreases or increases the probability that a person voted for Bush, then it is also reasonable for us to assign a probability of .7 to the claim that Pat voted for Bush. The probability assignment based on what we know about the larger class remains reasonable until we gain additional information that we have reason to believe changes the probability.

The same pattern holds for moral beliefs. If we know that 30% of moral beliefs are false, and if all we know about a particular belief is that it is a moral belief, then it is reasonable to assign a .3 probability that the particular belief is false. If we later add the information that almost everyone agrees with this moral belief, and if we know that less than 10% of moral beliefs that almost everyone agrees with are false, then it is no longer reasonable to assign a .3 probability that this belief is false. However, even if almost everyone agrees with this moral belief, if we do not know of this agreement, or if we do not have any reason to believe that such agreement affects the probability that a moral belief is false, then it remains reasonable to assign a .3 probability that this moral belief is false.

Now we need a principle to take us from reasonable probability assignments to justified belief. I suggest this one: If it is reasonable for a person to assign a large probability that a certain belief is false, then that person is not epistemically justified in holding that belief. This standard is admittedly vague, but its point is clear in examples. If it is reasonable for us to assign a large probability that Pat did not vote for Bush, then we are not epistemically justified in believing that Pat did vote for Bush.

The same standard applies to immediate beliefs. Imagine that, when subjects watch movies of cars on highways, their beliefs about a car's speed vary a lot depending on whether the car is described as a car or as a sports car and also on whether the car they saw before this one was going faster or slower than this one. We test only a few hundred students in a lab. We do not test ourselves or anyone in real life. Nonetheless, these studies still provide some reason to believe that our own immediate visual estimates of car speeds on highways are not reliable in general. Our estimates might be reliable, but if we have no reason to believe that our speed estimates are better than average or that such estimates are more reliable in real life than in the lab, then it is reasonable for us to believe that our estimates are often inaccurate. If the rate of error is high enough, then we are not justified in forming a particular belief on this immediate visual basis alone without any confirmation.

The situation with moral beliefs is analogous. Evidence of framing effects makes it reasonable for informed moral believers to assign a large probability of error to moral intuitions in general and then to apply that probability to a particular moral intuition until they have some special reason to believe that the particular moral intuition is in a different class with a smaller probability of error. But then their special reasons make them able to justify the moral belief inferentially. Thus, they are never justified epistemically without some such inferential ability.

More formally:

(1)   For any subject S, particular belief B, and class of beliefs C, if S is justified in believing that B is in C and is also justified in believing that a large percentage of beliefs in C are false, but S is not justified in believing that B falls into any class of beliefs C* of which a smaller percentage is false, then S is justified in believing that B has a large probability of being false. (generalized from cases like Pat's vote)

(2)   Informed adults are justified in believing that their own moral intuitions are in the class of moral intuitions.

(3)   Informed adults are justified in believing that a large percentage of moral intuitions are false. (from studies of framing effects)

(4)   Therefore, if an informed adult is not justified in believing that a certain moral intuition falls into any class of beliefs of which a smaller percentage is false, then the adult is justified in believing that this particular moral intuition has a large probability of being false. (from 1–3)

(5)   A moral believer cannot be epistemically justified in holding a particular moral belief when that believer is justified in believing that the moral belief has a large probability of being false. (from the standard above)

(6)   Therefore, if an informed adult is not justified in believing that a certain moral intuition falls into any class of beliefs of which a smaller percentage is false, then the adult is not epistemically justified in holding that moral intuition. (from 4–5)

(7)   If someone is justified in believing that a belief falls into a class of beliefs of which a smaller percentage is false, then that person is able to infer that belief from the premise that it falls into such a class. (by definition of "able to infer")

(8)   Therefore, an informed adult is not epistemically justified in holding a moral intuition unless that adult is able to infer that belief from some premises. (from 6–7)

(9)   If a believer is not epistemically justified in holding a belief unless the believer is able to infer it from some premises, then the believer is not justified noninferentially in holding the belief. (by definition of "noninferentially")

(10)   Therefore, no informed adult is noninferentially justified in holding any moral intuition. (from 8–9)

(11)   Moral intuitionism claims that some informed adults are noninferentially justified in holding some moral intuitions. (by definition)

(12)   Therefore, moral intuitionism is false. (from 10–11)

This reformulation is intended to answer fair questions by both commentators about how my argument was supposed to work. In addition, this reformulation avoids the criticisms by my commentators.

Replies to Tolhurst

Tolhurst: "A person might know that moral intuitions are subject to framing effects in many cases without knowing which cases they are" (p. 78).

Reply: Granted, but I do not need to know which cases are subject to framing effects. My argument as reformulated claims only that it is reasonable to ascribe probabilities to particular members of a class on the basis of percentages within the whole class when the ascriber has no relevant information other than that this case is a member of the class. That claim holds for the probability that Pat voted for Bush, so it should also hold for the probability that a given moral intuition is mistaken.

Tolhurst: "What counts as 'many' varies from one situation to another. . . . ascriptions of reliability are also context dependent" (p. 79).

Reply: Granted, and also for "large" probability in my new version. The context affects how large is large enough. Suppose we know that 45% of women voters in Texas in 2004 voted for Bush, and all we know about Pat is that she is a woman who voted in Texas in 2004. It would then be reasonable for us to believe that it is more likely than not that Pat did not vote for Bush, but I think we would still not be epistemically justified in forming the belief that Pat did not vote for Bush. (Maybe we should bet even money that Pat did not vote for Bush, but that's because failing to bet has opportunity costs which failing to believe does not have and which could not make belief justified epistemically.) We should instead suspend belief on Pat's vote and wait until more information comes in. At least in this context, a belief is not epistemically justified if it is reasonable for the believer to assign a probability of error as high as .45.

The standards are much higher in some other areas. Scientists do not call a result statistically significant unless the probability that it is due to chance is less than .05. In this way, they seem to prescribe suspending belief until the evidence warrants a probability assignment over .95. Thus, if moral beliefs are to be justified in anything like the way scientific beliefs are justified, then it has to be reasonable to assign them a probability of at least .95.

Critics might respond that this standard is too high for moral beliefs. Then these critics have to give up the claim that moral beliefs are justified in the same way or to the same degree as scientific beliefs. In any case, it would still be implausible to call a moral believer epistemically justified whenever it is reasonable for that believer to assign a probability over .5 if moral beliefs need to meet even the weak standards for beliefs about Pat's vote.

I do not need or want to commit myself to any exact cutoff, since precise numbers are unavailable for moral beliefs anyway. Instead, I use only the admittedly vague standard that a moral believer cannot be epistemically justified in holding a particular moral belief when it is reasonable for that believer to assign a large probability that the moral belief is false. What shows that the probability of error in moral intuitions is too large to meet an appropriate standard is the size and range of framing effects in the studies (along with other evidence of unreliability). If someone denies that those results are large enough, then my only recourse is to recite the details of the studies, to evoke the high costs of mistaken moral intuitions, and to remind critics that only a minimal kind of confirmation is needed. Critics who still insist that the rate of error is not large enough even to create a need for minimal confirmation must be willing to take big chances with their moral beliefs.

Tolhurst: "Why should we take the responses of . . . [subjects who are college students] to be a reliable indicator of the reliability of all of us?" (p. 80; cf. Shafer-Landau, this volume, p. 86).
Reply: There is no reason to think that college students are more subject to framing effects than other humans. Indeed, they might be less subject to framing effects if they are more reflective.

Tolhurst: "Furthermore, the studies were designed to elicit framing effects in the subjects. The situations in which we generally form our spontaneous moral beliefs are not" (p. 80).
Reply: Actually, some of the experimenters were surprised by the framing effects. The other experiments were designed to find out whether there are framing effects. Those effects would not have been elicited if we were not

subject to framing. It is also not clear that everyday situations are not designed to elicit framing effects, since we are all subject to a lot of moral rhetoric throughout our lives. Even when we encounter a new situation without having heard anything about it, our reactions to that situation still can be affected by the moral problem that we faced right before it. The order effects in the studies I cited suggest that our moral beliefs are probably often affected in this way even in real life.

Tolhurst: "Some of the reasons given for thinking that moral intuitions are subject to framing seem to apply with strength to epistemic intuitions. If this is so, and if the argument works, it would call into question any epistemic intuitions that functioned as premises of the argument" (p. 82).
Reply: I do not claim that moral intuitions are not justified. All I claim is that moral intuitions are not justified noninferentially. Analogously, if epistemic intuitions are not justified noninferentially, they can still be justified. Then there is nothing wrong with using them in my argument.

Replies to Shafer-Landau

Shafer-Landau: "If . . . [knowledge does not require epistemic justification], Sinnott-Armstrong's arguments, even if successful, would undermine only an intuitionist account of epistemic justification but would not touch the intuitionist's central claim about knowledge: namely, that it can be had without inferential support" (p. 92).
Reply: Let's stick to one topic at a time. I am inclined to think that knowledge does require at least the possibility of justified belief (for reasons given in Sinnott-Armstrong, 2006, pp. 60–63). If so, my argument extends to intuitionist claims about moral knowledge. Still, I do not depend on that extension here. I will be satisfied for now if my argument succeeds for justified belief.

Shafer-Landau: "We already knew that [some nonnegligible percentage of our beliefs are subject to framing effects]. . . . because we knew the rough extent of moral disagreement in the world" (p. 91).
Reply: I happily admit that framing effects are not our only evidence of unreliability in moral intuitions. I discuss evidence from disagreement elsewhere (Sinnott-Armstrong, 2002, 2006, chapter 9). These other kinds of evidence do not undermine but support my conclusion here that moral intuitions are unreliable.

Shafer-Landau: "As yet, we simply do not have a sufficient number of relevant experiments to give us much indication of how many of our moral beliefs are subject to framing effects. . . . Further, the beliefs in question are not clearly moral intuitions. . . . The experiments are all conducted in one basic kind of circumstance—that of a controlled experiment situated in someone's lab" (p. 87).

Reply: I agree that we need more and better experiments, but I bet that future experiments will confirm the results I cite. After all, similar patterns have already been found in hundreds of experiments on framing effects outside of morality. And there is no reason to think that we should not extrapolate from lab to real world here just as we successfully do in other areas of psychology. Finally, when participants are asked for confidence levels or justifications, their responses suggest that the moral beliefs in question were strong and immediate, so they were intuitions. Anyway, Shafer-Landau admits these objections are merely "nipping at [my] heels" (p. 87), and he himself "believe[s] that the second premise is true" (p. 86), that is, that many moral intuitions are subject to framing effects in many circumstances.

Shafer-Landau: "The studies that Sinnott-Armstrong cites do not discuss the different processes that lead to noninferential moral belief" (p. 89).

Reply: A process is unreliable if its outputs are often false, regardless of exactly what the process is. The studies of framing effects do show that the processes employed by subjects in those studies had many false outputs. Hence, I do not need to discuss exactly what the processes are in order to show that they are unreliable.

Shafer-Landau: "It's not clear that my very own processes, whatever they happen to be, are likely to be unreliable" (p. 88).

Reply: I do not need to claim that my or your intuition-forming processes are in fact unreliable. I do not even need to claim that they are likely to be unreliable in a statistical sense of "likely." All I need to claim (and so all I do claim here) is that the evidence of framing effects make it reasonable for me or you to believe that my or your intuition-forming processes are unreliable unless I or you have special evidence to the contrary. Thus, if I ever say that my or your intuitive processes are likely to be unreliable, the relevant kind of likelihood is epistemic rather than statistical, and the claim is conditional on the absence of special counterevidence.

Shafer-Landau: "Some beliefs are formed after quite careful, but noninferential, reflection [note citing Audi]. These beliefs may be immune to framing effects" (p. 89).

Reply: The evidence actually suggests that reflection removes some but not all framing effects, as I said (p. 70). Of course, one could guarantee reliability by describing the process in terms like "adequate reflection" if reflection is not adequate when it is unreliable. But then the question just shifts to whether I have reason to believe that I reflected adequately in a particular case. Besides, as Audi characterizes moral reflection, it involves a transition from beliefs about a case to a moral judgment about that case. I see no reason not to count that transition as an inference. (See Sinnott-Armstrong, forthcoming.) If the transition to what Audi calls a "conclusion of reflection" is an inference, then beliefs based on reflection are not justified noninferentially.

Shafer-Landau: "[Beliefs] endorsing Rossian prima facie duties are ['agreed by (nearly) everyone to be true']. . . . [T]he evidence about framing effects casts no doubt on their reliability. . . . Neither does this evidence impugn the reliability of more specific, entirely uncontroversial moral beliefs, of the sort I introduced at the beginning of the essay [about 'the deliberate humiliation, rape, and torture, of a child' just for pleasure]" (p. 92; cf. p. 94).

Reply: The evidence from framing effects does cast initial doubt on the reliability of such uncontroversial moral beliefs insofar as the evidence creates a presumption that needs to be rebutted. Because such beliefs fall into a class with a large percentage of falsehoods, it is reasonable to ascribe that same probability of falsehood unless and until the believer has reason to believe that such uncontroversial moral beliefs are more reliable than average.

Of course, that presumption can be successfully rebutted in many cases. I believe that it is morally wrong to torture a child just for pleasure. I also agree that such beliefs are epistemically justified. My point is not about whether they are justified but only about how they are justified. In my view, they are justified inferentially because we know that they are special in some way that gives us reason to believe that they are less likely to be wrong than other moral intuitions. If so, these inferentially justified beliefs pose no problem for my argument against intuitionism, which claims that such beliefs are justified noninferentially.

Shafer-Landau: "[Sinnott-Armstrong's argument] moves too quickly from an ability to draw an inference to the requirement that such inferences be drawn as a precondition of epistemic justification" (p. 88).

Reply: I cite the availability of inferential confirmation only in order to respond to the common objection that if this requirement were imposed, nobody could be justified in believing anything. I never say that the possibility or availability of inferential confirmation shows that an ability to infer is required or needed. What shows that it is required is, instead, that a moral believer is not justified in those cases where it is lacking, as in the thermometer analogy.

Shafer-Landau: "The reliance on the thermometer analogy is a bit puzzling. In the example, we don't know whether ten or fifty or eighty percent of the thermometers are unreliable. We just know that some are" (pp. 90–91).

Reply: Actually, in my example, "You know that *many* of them are inaccurate" (p. 71; emphasis added). The numbers matter to my argument, since I do not assume that a very small chance of error is enough to trigger a need for inferential confirmation. Hence, I can agree with Shafer-Landau's claims about his modified example where we know that only one in 10,000 thermometers fail (p. 94).

Shafer-Landau: "What is thought to trigger the need for inferential confirmation is the second-order belief—one that everyone ought to have—that one's intuitions might be mistaken" (p. 93).

Reply: This misrepresents my argument again. In my view, what triggers the need for confirmation is not a mere possibility of mistake. Instead, the trigger is that moral intuitions of people like you actually are *often* mistaken. That's why I cite empirical evidence. No experiments would be needed if my argument rested only on what is possible.

Shafer-Landau: "Why not think, instead, that the need for inferential confirmation arises only when the credibility of a belief is relevantly in question? If (nearly) everyone agrees in a given belief, then, rare contexts aside (as when one is arguing with a very intelligent interlocutor who refuses to accept the existence of an external world or the immorality of genocide), its credibility is *not* relevantly in question" (p. 93; cf. p. 94).

Reply: I can agree that the need for inferential confirmation arises only when the credibility of a belief is relevantly in question. My point is that, when we know that moral beliefs in general are too likely to be false, then all particular moral beliefs are relevantly in question until we have some reason to think they are special. Such a special reason might be provided by a justified belief that "(nearly) everyone agrees in a given belief." However, if everyone in fact agrees with a given belief, but I do not believe or have any reason to believe in this fact of agreement, then the fact by itself cannot make anyone epistemically justified when the credibility of a belief is already in question. That was shown by analogy with Pat's vote.

Conclusion

These replies are way too quick to be conclusive. Still, I hope they suggest why none of what Tolhurst and Shafer-Landau say touches my argument as reformulated. Other problems for my argument might arise. However, until then, I conclude again that moral intuitionism fails.

3 Reviving Rawls's Linguistic Analogy: Operative Principles and the Causal Structure of Moral Actions

Marc D. Hauser, Liane Young, and Fiery Cushman

The thesis we develop in this essay is that all humans are endowed with a *moral faculty*. The moral faculty enables us to produce moral judgments on the basis of the causes and consequences of actions. As an empirical research program, we follow the framework of modern linguistics.[1] The spirit of the argument dates back at least to the economist Adam Smith (1759/1976), who argued for something akin to a moral grammar, and more recently to the political philosopher John Rawls (1971). The logic of the argument, however, comes from Noam Chomsky's thinking on language specifically and the nature of knowledge more generally (Chomsky, 1986, 1988, 2000; Saporta, 1978).

If the nature of moral knowledge is comparable in some way to the nature of linguistic knowledge, as defended recently by Harman (1977), Dwyer (1999, 2004), and Mikhail (2000, in press), then what should we expect to find when we look at the anatomy of our moral faculty? Is there a grammar, and, if so, how can the moral grammarian uncover its structure? Are we aware of our moral grammar, its method of operation, and its moment-to-moment functioning in our judgments? Is there a universal moral grammar that allows each child to build a particular moral grammar? Once acquired, are different moral grammars mutually incomprehensible in the same way that a native Chinese speaker finds a native Italian speaker incomprehensible? How does the child acquire a particular moral grammar, especially if her experiences are impoverished relative to the moral judgments she makes? Are there certain forms of brain damage that disrupt moral competence but leave other forms of reasoning intact? And how did this machinery evolve, and for what particular adaptive function? We will have more to say about many of these questions later on, and Hauser (2006) develops others. However, in order to flesh out the key ideas and particular empirical research paths, let us turn to some of the central questions in the study of our language faculty.

Chomsky, the Language Faculty, and the Nature of Knowing

Human beings are endowed with a language faculty—a mental "organ" that learns, perceives, and produces language. In the broadest sense, the language faculty can be thought of as an instinct to acquire a natural language (Pinker, 1994). More narrowly, it can be thought of as the set of principles for growing a language.

Prior to the revolution in linguistics ignited by Chomsky, it was widely held that language could be understood as a cultural construction learned through simple stimulus–response mechanisms. It was presumed that the human brain was more or less a blank slate upon which anything could be imprinted, including language. Chomsky, among others, challenged this idea with persuasive arguments that human knowledge of language must be guided in part by an innate faculty of the mind—the faculty of language. It is precisely because of the structure of this faculty that children can acquire language in the absence of tutelage, and even in the presence of negative or impoverished input.

When linguists refer to these principles as the speaker's "grammar," they mean the rules or operations that allow any normally developing human to unconsciously generate and comprehend a limitless range of well-formed sentences in their native language. When linguists refer to "universal grammar" they are referring to a theory about the set of all principles available to each child for acquiring a natural language. Before the child is born, she doesn't know which language she will meet, and she may even meet two if she is born in a bilingual family. However, she doesn't need to know. What she has is a set of principles and parameters that prepares her to construct different grammars that characterize the world's languages—dead ones, living ones, and those not yet conceived. The environment feeds her the particular sound patterns (or signs for those who are deaf) of the native language, thereby turning on the specific parameters that characterize the native language.

From these general problems, Chomsky and other generative grammarians suggested that we need an explicit characterization of the language faculty, what it is, how it develops within each individual, and how it evolved in our species, perhaps uniquely (Anderson & Lightfoot, 2000; Fitch, Hauser, & Chomsky, 2005; Hauser, Chomsky, & Fitch, 2002; Jackendoff, 2002; Pinker, 1994). We discuss each of these issues in turn.

What Is It?
The faculty of language is designed to handle knowledge of language. For English speakers, for instance, the faculty of language provides the princi-

ples upon which our knowledge of the English language is constructed. To properly understand what it means to know a language, we must distinguish between *expressed* and *operative* knowledge. Expressed knowledge includes what we can articulate, including such things as our knowledge that a fly ball travels a parabolic arc describable by a quadratic mathematical expression. Operative knowledge includes such things as our knowledge of how to run to just the right spot on a baseball field in order to catch a fly ball. Notice that in the case of baseball, even though our expressed knowledge about the ball's parabolic trajectory might be used to inform us about where to run if we had a great deal of time and sophisticated measuring instruments, it is of little use in the practical circumstances of a baseball game. In order to perform in the real world, our operative knowledge of how to run to the right spot is much more useful. Our brain must be carrying out these computations in order for us to get to the right spot even though, by definition, we can't articulate the principles underlying this knowledge. In the real-world case of catching a baseball, we rely on operative as opposed to expressed knowledge.

One of the principal insights of modern linguistics is that knowledge of language is operative but not expressed. When Chomsky generated the sentence "Colorless green ideas sleep furiously," he intentionally produced a string of words that no one had ever produced before. He also produced a perfectly grammatical and yet meaningless sentence. Most of us don't know what makes Chomsky's sentence, or any other sentence, grammatical. We may express some principle or rule that we learned in grammar school, but such expressed rules are rarely sufficient to explain the principles that actually underlie our judgments. It is these unconscious or operative principles that linguists discover—and that never appear in the schoolmarm's textbook—that account for the patterns of linguistic variation and similarities. For example, every speaker of English knows that "Romeo loves Juliet" is a well-formed sentence, while "Him loves her" is not. Few speakers of English know why. Few native speakers of English would ever produce this last sentence, and this includes young toddlers just learning to speak English. When it comes to language, therefore, what we think we know pales in relation to what our minds actually know. Similarly, unconscious principles underlie certain aspects of mathematics, music, object perception (Dehaene, 1997; Jackendoff, 2005; Lerdahl & Jackendoff, 1996; Spelke, 1994), and, we suggest, morality (Hauser, 2006; Mikhail, 2000, in press).

Characterizing our knowledge of language in the abstract begins to answer the question "What is the faculty of language?", but in order to achieve a more complete answer we want to explain the kinds of processes of the mind/brain that are specific to language as opposed to shared with other problem-oriented tasks including navigation, social relationships, object recognition, and sound localization. The faculty of language's relationship to other mind-internal systems can be described along two orthogonal dimensions: whether the mechanism is necessary for language and whether the mechanism is unique to language. For example, we use our ears when we listen to a person speaking and when we localize an ambulance's siren, and deaf perceivers of sign language accomplish linguistic understanding without using their ears at all. Ears, therefore, are neither necessary for nor unique to language. However, once sound passes from our ears to the part of the brain involved in decoding what the sound is and what to do with it, separate cognitive mechanisms come in to play, one for handling speech, the other nonspeech. Speech-specific perceptual mechanisms are unique to language but still not necessary (again, consider the deaf).

Once the system detects that we are in a language mode, either producing utterances or listening to them, a system of rules is engaged, organizing meaningless sound and/or gesture sequences (phonemes) into meaningful words, phrases, and sentences, and enabling conversation as either internal monologue or external dialogue. This stage of cognitive processing is common to both spoken and sign language. The hierarchical structure of language, together with its recursive and combinatorial operations, as well as interfaces to phonology and semantics, appear to be unique properties of language *and* necessary for language. We can see, then, that the faculty of language is comprised of several different types of cognitive mechanisms: those that are unique versus those that are shared and those that are necessary versus those that are optionally recruited.

To summarize, we have now sketched the abstract system of knowledge that characterizes the faculty of language, and we have also said something about the different ways in which cognitive mechanisms can be integrated into the faculty of language. There remains one more important distinction that will help us unpack the question "What is the faculty of language": the distinction between linguistic competence, or what the language faculty enables, and linguistic performance, or what the rest of the brain and the environment constrain. Language competence refers to the unconscious and inaccessible principles that make sentence production and comprehension possible. What we say, to whom, and how is the province of linguistic performance and includes many other players of the brain, and many factors external to the brain, including other people, institutions, weather, and distance to one's target audience. When we speak about the language faculty, therefore, we are speaking about the normal, mature individual's *competence* with the principles that underlie her native language. What this individual chooses to say is a matter of her *performance* that will be influenced by whether she is tired, happy, in a fight with her lover, or addressing a stadium-filled audience.

How Does It Develop?

To answer this question, we want to explain the child's path to a mature state of language competence, a state that includes the capacity to create a limitless range of meaningful sentences and understand an equally limitless range of sentences generated by other speakers of the same language. Like all biological phenomena, the development of language is a complex interaction between innate structure, maturational factors, and environmental input. While it is obvious that much of language is learned—for instance, the arbitrary mapping between sound and concept—what is less obvious is that the learning of language is only possible if the learner is permitted to make certain initial assumptions. This boils down to a question of the child's initial state—of her unconscious knowledge of linguistic principles prior to exposure to a spoken or signed language. It has to be the case that some innate structure is in place to guide the growth of a particular language, as no other species does the same (even though cats and dogs are exposed to the same stuff), and the input into the child is both impoverished and replete with ungrammatical structure that the child never repeats.

Consider the observation that in spoken English, people can use two different forms of the verb "is" as in "Frank is foolish" and "Frank's foolish." We can't, however, use the contracted form of "is" wherever we please. For example, although we can say "Frank is more foolish than Joe is," we can't say "Frank is more foolish than Joe's." How do we know this? No one taught us this rule. No one listed the exceptions. Nonetheless, young children never use the contracted form in an inappropriate place. The explanation, based on considerable work in linguistics (Anderson & Lightfoot, 2000), is that the child's initial state includes a principle for verb contraction—a rule that says something like " 's is too small a unit of sound to be alone; whenever you use the contracted form, follow it up with another word." The environment—the sound pattern of English—triggers the principle, pulling it out of a hat of principles as if by magic. The child is born knowing the principle, even though she is not consciously aware of the knowledge she holds. The principle is operative but not expressed.

There are two critical points to make about the interplay between language and the innate principles and parameters of language learners. First, the principles and parameters are what make language learning possible. By guiding children's expectations about language in a particular fashion, the principles and parameters allow children to infer a regular system with infinite generative capacity from sparse, inconsistent, and imperfect evidence. However, the principles and parameters do not come for free, and this brings us to the second point: The reason that principles and parameters make the child's job of learning easier is because they restrict the range of possible languages. In the example described above, the price of constraining a child's innate expectations about verb contraction is that it is impossible for any language to violate that expectation.

To summarize, the development of the language faculty is a complex interaction of innate and learned elements. Some elements of our knowledge of language are precisely specified principles, invariant between languages. Other elements of our knowledge of language are parametrically constrained to a limited set of options, varying within this set from language to language. Finally, some elements of our knowledge of language are unconstrained and vary completely from language to language. We note here that, although we have leaned on the principles and parameters view of language, this aspect of our argument is not critical to the development of the analogy between language and morality. Other versions of the generative grammar perspective would be equally appropriate, as they generally appeal to language-specific, universal computations that constrain the range of cultural variation and facilitate acquisition.

How Did It Evolve?

To answer this question, we look to our history. Which components of our language faculty are shared with other species, and which are unique? What problems did our ancestors face that might have selected for the design features of our language faculty? Consider the human child's capacity to learn words. Much of word learning involves vocal imitation. The child hears her mother say, "Do you want candy?" and the child says "Candy." "Candy" isn't encoded in the mind as a string of DNA. But the capacity to imitate sounds is one of the human child's innate gifts. Imitation is not specific to the language faculty, but without it, no child could acquire the words of his or her native language, reaching a stunning level of about 50,000 for the average high school graduate. To explore whether vocal imitation is unique to humans, we look to other species. Although we share 98% of our genes in common with chimpanzees, chimpanzees show no evidence of vocal imitation. The same goes for all of the other apes and all of the monkeys. What this pattern tells us is that humans evolved the capacity for vocal imitation some time after we broke off from our common ancestor with chimpanzees—something like 6 to 7 million years ago. However, this is not the end of our exploration. It turns out that other species, more distantly related to us than any of the nonhuman primates, are capable of vocal imitation: all Passerine songbirds, parrots, hummingbirds, some bats, cetaceans, and elephants. What this distribution tells us is that vocal imitation is not unique to humans. It also tells us, again, that vocal imitation in humans didn't evolve from the nonhuman primates. Rather, vocal imitation evolved independently in humans, some birds, and some marine mammals.

To provide a complete description of the language faculty, addressing each of the three questions discussed, requires different kinds of evidence. For example, linguists reveal the deep structure underlying sentence construction by using grammaticality judgments and by comparing different languages to reveal commonalities that cut across the obvious differences. Developmental psychologists chart the child's patterns of language acquisition, exploring whether the relevant linguistic input is sufficient to account for their output. Neuropsychologists look to patients with selective damage, using cases where particular aspects of language are damaged while others are spared, or where language remains intact and many other cognitive faculties are impaired. Cognitive neuroscientists use imaging techniques to understand which regions of the brain are recruited during language processing, attempting to characterize the circuitry of the language organ. Evolutionary biologists explore which aspects of the language faculty are shared with other species, attempting to pinpoint which components might account for the vast difference in expressive power between our system of communication and theirs. Mathematical biologists use models to explore how different learning mechanisms might account for patterns of language acquisition, or to understand the limiting conditions for the evolution of a universal grammar. This intellectual collaboration is beginning to unveil what it means to know a particular language and to use it in the service of interacting with the world. Our goal is to sketch how similar moves can be made with respect to our moral knowledge.

Rawls and the Linguistic Analogy

In 1950, Rawls completed his PhD, focusing on methodological issues associated with ethical knowledge and with the characterization of a person's moral worth. His interest in our moral psychology continued up until the mid-1970s, focusing on the problem of justice as fairness, and ending quite soon after the publication of *A Theory of Justice*.

Rawls was interested in the idea that the principles underlying our intuitions about morality may well be unconscious and inaccessible.[2] This perspective was intended to parallel Chomsky's thinking in linguistics. Unfortunately, those writing about morality in neighboring disciplines, especially within the sciences, held a different perspective. The then dominant position in developmental psychology, championed by Piaget and Kohlberg, was that the child's moral behavior is best understood in terms of the child's articulations of moral principles. Analogizing to language, this would be equivalent to claiming that the best way to understand a child's use of verb contraction is to ask the child why you can say "Frank is there" but can't ask "Where Frank's?", presuming that the pattern of behavior must be the consequence of an articulatable rule.

The essence of the approach to morality conceived by Piaget, and developed further by Kohlberg, is summarized by a simple model: The perception of an event is followed by reasoning, resulting finally in a judgment (see figure 3.1); emotion may emerge from the judgment but is not causally related to it. Here, actions are evaluated by reflecting upon specific principles and using this reflective process to rationally deduce a specific judgment. When we deliver a moral verdict, it is because we have considered different possible reasons for and against a particular action and, based on this deliberation, alight upon a particular decision. This model might be termed "Kantian," for, although Kant never denied the role of intuition in our moral psychology, he is the moral philosopher who carried the most weight with respect to the role of rational deliberation about what one ought to do.

The Piaget/Kohlberg tradition has provided rich and reliable data on the moral stages through which children pass, using their justifications as

Model 1:

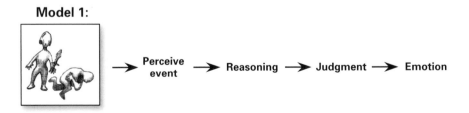

Figure 3.1
The Kantian creature and the deliberate reasoning model

primary evidence for developmental change. In recent years, however, a number of cognitive and social psychologists have criticized this perspective (Macnamara, 1990), especially its insistence that the essence of moral psychology is *justification* rather than *judgment*. It has been observed that even fully mature adults are sometimes unable to provide any sufficient justification for strongly felt moral intuitions, a phenomenon termed "moral dumbfounding" (Haidt, 2001). This has led to the introduction of a second model, characterized most recently by Haidt (2001) as well as several other social psychologists and anthropologists (see figure 3.2). Here, following the perception of an action or event, there is an unconscious emotional response which immediately causes a moral judgment; reasoning is an afterthought, offering a post hoc rationalization of an intuitively generated response. We see someone standing over a dead person, and we classify this as murder, a claim that derives from a pairing between any given action and a classification of morally right or wrong. Emotion triggers the judgment. We might term this model "Humean," after the philosopher who famously declared that reason is "slave to the passions"; Haidt calls it the social intuitionist model.

A second recent challenge to the Piaget/Kohlberg tradition is a hybrid between the Humean and Kantian creatures, a blend of unconscious emotions and some form of principled and deliberate reasoning (see figure 3.3); this view has most recently been championed by Damasio based on neurologically impaired patients (S. W. Anderson, Bechara, Damasio, Tranel, & Damasio, 1999; Damasio, 1994; Tranel, Bechara, & Damasio, 2000) and by Greene (this volume) based on neuroimaging work (Greene, Nystrom, Engell, Darley, & Cohen, 2004; Greene, Sommerville, Nystrom, Darley, & Cohen, 2001).[3] These two systems may converge or diverge in their assessment of the situation, run in parallel or in sequence, but both are precursors to the judgment; if they diverge, then some other mechanism must intrude, resolve the conflict, and generate a judgment. On Damasio's view,

Model 2:

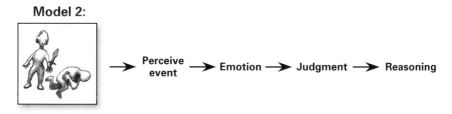

Figure 3.2
The Humean creature and the emotional model.

Model 3:

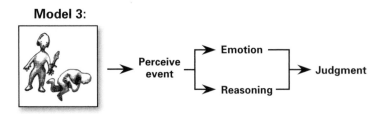

Figure 3.3
A mixture of the Kantian and Humean creatures, blending the reasoning and emotional models.

every moral judgment includes both emotion and reasoning. On Greene's view, emotions come into play in situations of a more personal nature and favor more deontological judgments, while reason comes into play in situations of a more impersonal nature and favors more utilitarian judgments.

Independent of which account turns out to be correct, this breakdown reveals a missing ingredient in almost all current theories and studies of our moral psychology. It will not do merely to assign the role of moral judgment to reason, emotion, or both. We must describe computations underlying the judgments that we produce. In contrast to the detailed work in linguistics focusing on the principles that organize phonology, semantics, and syntax, we lack a comparably detailed analysis of how humans and other organisms perceive actions and events in terms of their causal-intentional structure and the consequences that ensue for self and other. As Mikhail (2000, in press), Jackendoff (2005), and Hauser (2006) have noted, however, actions represent the right kind of unit for moral appraisal: discrete and combinable to create a limitless range of meaningful variation.

To fill in this missing gap, we must characterize knowledge of moral codes in a manner directly comparable to the linguist's characterization of knowledge of language. This insight is at the heart of Rawls's linguistic analogy. Rawls (1971) writes, "A conception of justice characterizes our moral sensibility when the everyday judgments we make are in accordance with its principles" (p. 46). He went on to sketch the connection to language:

A useful comparison here is with the problem of describing the sense of grammaticalness that we have for the sentences of our native language. In this case, the aim is to characterize the ability to recognize well-formed sentences by formulating clearly expressed principles which make the same discriminations as the native speaker. This is a difficult undertaking which, although still unfinished, is known to require theoretical constructions that far outrun the ad hoc precepts of our explicit grammatical knowledge. A similar situation presumably holds in moral philosophy. There is no reason to assume that our sense of justice can be adequately characterized by familiar common sense precepts, or derived from the more obvious learning principles. A correct account of moral capacities will certainly involve principles and theoretical constructions which go beyond the norms and standards cited in every day life. (pp. 46–47)

We are now ready, at last, to appreciate and develop Rawls's insights, especially his linguistic analogy. We are ready to introduce a "Rawlsian creature," equipped with the machinery to deliver moral verdicts based on principles that may be inaccessible (see figure 3.4; Hauser, 2006); in fact, if the analogy to language holds, the principles will be operative but not expressed, and only discoverable with the tools of science. There are two ways to view the Rawlsian creature in relationship to the other models. Minimally, each of the other models must recognize an appraisal system that computes the causal-intentional structure of an agent's actions and the consequences that follow. More strongly, the Rawlsian creature provides the sole basis for our judgments of morally forbidden, permissible, or obligatory actions, with emotions and reasoning following. To be clear: The Rawlsian model does not deny the role of emotion or reasoning. Rather, it stipulates that any process giving rise to moral judgments must minimally do so on the basis of some system of analysis and that this analysis constitutes the heart of the moral faculty. On the stronger view, the operative principles of the moral faculty do all the heavy lifting, generating a moral verdict that may or may not generate an emotion or a process of rational and principled deliberation.

One way to develop the linguistic analogy is to raise the same questions about the moral faculty that Chomsky and other generative grammarians raised for the language faculty. With the Rawlsian creature in mind, let us unpack the ideas.

Model 4:

Figure 3.4
The Rawlsian creature and action analysis model.

What Is It?

Rawls argued that because our moral faculty is analogous to our linguistic faculty, we can study it in some of the same ways. In parallel with the linguist's use of grammaticality judgments to uncover some of the principles of language competence, students of moral behavior might use *morality* judgments to uncover some of the principles underlying our judgments of what is morally right and wrong.[4] These principles might constitute the Rawlsian creature's universal moral grammar, with each culture expressing a specific moral grammar. As is the case for language, this view does not deny cultural variation. Rather, it predicts variation based on how each culture switches on or off particular parameters. An individual's moral grammar enables him to unconsciously generate a limitless range of moral judgments within the native culture.

To flesh out these general comments, consider once again language. The language faculty takes as input discrete elements that can be combined and recombined to create an infinite variety of meaningful expressions: phonemes ("distinctive features" in the lingo of linguistics) for individuals who can hear, signs for those who are deaf. When a phoneme is combined with another, it creates a syllable. When syllables are combined, they can create words. When words are combined, they can create phrases. And when phrases are combined, they can create sentences that form the power of *The Iliad*, *The Origin of Species*, or *Mad Magazine*. Actions appear to live in a parallel hierarchical universe. Like phonemes, many actions may lack meaning depending upon context: lifting your elbow off the table, raising your ring finger, flexing your knee. Actions, when combined, are often meaningful: lifting your elbow and swinging it intentionally into someone's face, raising your ring finger to receive a wedding band, flexing your knee in a dance. Like phonemes, when actions are combined, they do not blend; individual actions maintain their integrity. When actions are combined, they can represent an agent's goals, his means, and the consequences of his action and inaction. When a series of subgoals are combined, they can create events, including the *Nutcracker* Ballet, the World Series, or the American Civil War. Because actions and events can be combined into an infinite variety of strings, it would be a burdensome and incomplete moral theory that attempted to link a particular judgment with each particular string individually. Instead of recalling that it was impermissible for John to attack Fred and cause him pain, we recall a principle with abstract placeholders or variables such as AGENT, INTENTION, BELIEF, ACTION, RECEIVER, CONSEQUENCE, MORAL EVALUATION. For example, the principle might generate the evaluation "impermissible" when intention is extended over an action that is extended over a harm (see figure 3.5). In reality, the principle will be far more complicated and abstract and include other parameters. See Mikhail (2000, in press) for one version of how such representational structures might be constructed and evaluated in more detail.

By breaking down the principle into components, we achieve a second parallel with language: To attain its limitless range of expressive power, the moral faculty must take a finite set of elements and recombine them into new, meaningful expressions or principles. These elements must not blend like paint. Combining red and white paint yields pink. Although this kind of combination gives paint, and color more generally, a vast play space for variation, once combined we can no longer recover the elements. Each contributing element or primary color has lost its individually distinctive contribution. Not so for language or morality. The words in "John kisses Mary" can be recombined to create the new sentence "Mary kisses John." These sentences have the same elements (words), and their ordering is uniquely responsible for meaning. Combining these elements does not, however, dilute or change what each means. John is still the same person in these two sentences, but in one he is the SUBJECT and in the other he is the OBJECT. The same is true of morality and our perception of the causes and consequences of actions. Consider the following two events: "Mother gratuitously hits 3-year-old son" versus "Three-year-old son gratuitously hits mother." The first almost certainly invokes a moral evaluation that harming is forbidden, while the second presumably doesn't. In the first case we imagine a malignant cause, whereas in the second we

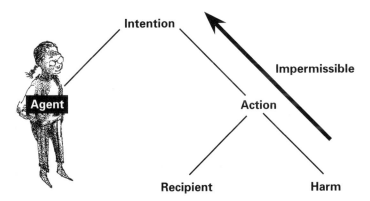

Figure 3.5
Some components of the causes and consequences of morally relevant actions.

imagine a benign cause, focused on the boy's frustration or inability to control anger.

Added on to this layer of description is another, building further on the linguistic analogy: If there is a specialized system for making moral judgments, then damage to this system should cause a selective deficit, specifically, deterioration of the moral sensibilities. To expose our moral knowledge, we must look at the nature of our action and event perception, the attribution of cause and consequence, the relationship between judgment and justification, and the extent to which the mechanisms that underlie this process are specialized for the moral faculty or shared with other systems of the mind. We must also explore the possibility that although the principles of our moral faculty may be functionally imprisoned, cloistered from the system that leads to our judgments, they may come to play a role in our judgments once uncovered. In particular, and highlighting a potentially significant difference between language and morality, once detailed analyses uncover some of the relevant principles and parameters and make these known, we may use them in our day-to-day behavior, consciously, and based on reasoning. In contrast, knowing the abstract principles underlying certain aspects of language plays no role in what we say, and this is equally true of distinguished linguists.

Before moving further, let us make two points regarding the thesis we are defending. First, as Bloom (2004; Pizarro & Bloom, 2003) has argued and as Haidt (2001) and others have acknowledged, it would be foolish to deny that we address certain moral dilemmas by means of our conscious, deliberate, and highly principled faculty of reasoning, alighting upon a judgment in the most rational of ways. This is often what happens when we face new dilemmas that we are ill equipped to handle using intuitions. For example, most people don't have unconsciously generated intuitions, emotionally mediated or not, about stem cell research or the latest technologies for in vitro fertilization, because they lack the relevant details; some may have strong intuitions that such technologies are evil because they involve killing some bit of life or modifying it in some way, independent of whether they have knowledge of the actual techniques, including their costs and benefits. To form an opinion of these biomedical advances that goes beyond their family resemblance to other cases of biological intervention, most people want to hear about the details, understand who or what will be affected and in what ways, and then, based on such information, reason through the possibilities. Of course, once one has this information, it is then easy to bypass all the mess and simply judge such cases as permissible or forbidden. One might, for example, decide, without reasoning, that anything smelling of biomedical engineering is just evil. The main point here is that by setting up these models, we establish a framework for exploring our moral psychology.

The second point builds on the first. On the view that we hold, simplified by model 4 and the Rawlsian creature, there are strong and weak versions. The strong version provides a direct challenge to all three alternative models by arguing that prior to any emotion or process of deliberate reasoning, there must be some kind of unconscious appraisal mechanism that provides an analysis of the causes and consequences of action. This system then either does or doesn't trigger emotions and deliberate reasoning. If it does trigger these systems, they arise downstream, as a result of the judgment. Emotion and deliberate reasoning are not causally related to our initial moral judgments but, rather, are caused by the judgment. On this view, the appraisal system represents our moral competence and is responsible for the judgment. Emotion, on the other hand, is part of our moral performance. Emotions are not specific to the moral domain, but they interface with the computations that are. On this view, if we could go into the brain and turn off the emotional circuits (as arises at some level in psychopathy as well as with patients who have incurred damage to the orbitofrontal cortex; see below), we would leave our moral competence largely intact (i.e., most moral judgments would be normal), but this would cause serious deficits with respect to moral behavior. In contrast, for either models 1 or 3, turning off the emotional circuitry would cause serious deficits for both judgment and behavior. On the weaker version of model 4, there is minimally an appraisal system that analyzes the causes and consequences of actions, leading to an emotion or process of deliberate reasoning. As everyone would presumably acknowledge, by setting our sights on the appraisal system, we will uncover its operative principles as well as its role in the causal generation of moral judgments.

How Does the Moral Faculty Develop?

To answer this question, we need an understanding of the principles (specific grammar in light of the linguistic analogy) guiding an adult's judgments. With these principles described, we can explore how they are acquired.

Rawls, like Chomsky, suggests that we may have to invent an entirely new set of concepts and terms to describe moral principles. Our more classic formulations of universal rules may fail to capture the mind's computations in the same way that grammar school grammar fails to capture the principles that are part of our language faculty. For example, a commonsense approach to morality might dictate that all of the following actions are forbidden: killing, causing pain, stealing, cheating, lying, breaking promises, and committing adultery. However, these kinds of moral absolutes stand little chance of capturing the cross-cultural variation in our moral judgments. Some philosophers, such as Bernard Gert (1998, 2004) point out that like other rules, moral rules have exceptions. Thus, although killing is generally forbidden in all cultures, many if not all cultures recognize conditions in which killing is permitted or at least justifiable. Some cultures even support conditions in which killing is obligatory: In several Arabic countries, if a husband finds his wife in flagrante delicto, the wife's relatives are expected to kill her, thereby erasing the family's shame. Historically, in the American South, being caught in flagrante delicto was also a mark of dishonor, but it was up to the husband to regain honor by killing his spouse. In these cultures, killing is permissible and, one might even say, obligatory. What varies cross-culturally is how the local system establishes how to right a wrong. For each case, then, we want to ask: What makes these rules universal? What aspects of each rule or principle allow for cultural variation? Are there parameters that, once set, establish the differences between cultures, constraining the problem of moral development? Do the rules actually capture the relationship between the nature of the relevant actions (e.g., HARMING, HELPING), their causes (e.g., INTENDED, ACCIDENTAL), and consequences (e.g., DIRECT, INDIRECT)? Are there hidden principles, operating unconsciously, but discoverable with the tools of science? If, as Rawls intuited, the analogy between morality and language holds, then by answering these questions we will have gained considerable ground in addressing the problems of both descriptive and explanatory adequacy.

The hypothesis here is simple: Our moral faculty is equipped with a universal set of principles, with each culture setting up particular exceptions by means of tweaking the relevant parameters. We want to understand the universal aspects as well as the degree of variation, what allows for it, and how it is constrained. Many questions remain open. Does the child's environment provide her with enough information to construct a moral grammar, or does the child show competences that go beyond her exposure? For example, does the child generate judgments about fairness and harm in the absence of direct pedagogy or indirect learning by watching others? If so, then this argues in favor of an even stronger analogy to language, in which the child produces grammatically structured and correct sentences in the absence of positive evidence and despite negative evidence. Thus, from an impoverished environment, the child generates a rich output of grammatical utterances in the case of language and judgments about permissible actions in the case of morality. Further, in the same way that we rapidly and effortlessly acquire our native language, and then slowly and agonizingly acquire second languages later in life, does the acquisition of moral knowledge follow a similar developmental path? Do we acquire our native moral norms with ease and without instruction, while painstakingly trying to memorize all the details of a new culture's mores, recalling the faux pas and punishable violations by writing them down on index cards?

How Did the Moral Faculty Evolve?

Like language, we can address this question by breaking down the moral faculty into its component parts and then exploring which components are shared with other animals and which are unique to our own species. Although it is unlikely that we will ever be able to ask animals to make ethicality judgments, we can ask about their expectations concerning rule followers and violators, whether they are sensitive to the distinction between an intentional and an accidental action, whether they experience some of the morally relevant emotions, and, if so, how they play a role in their decisions. If an animal is incapable of making the intentional–accidental distinction, then it will treat all consequences as the same, never taking into account its origins: Seeing a chimpanzee fall from a tree and injure a group member is functionally equivalent to seeing a chimpanzee leap out of a tree and injure a group member; seeing an animal reach out and hand another a piece of food is functionally the same as seeing an animal reach out for its own food and accidentally drop a piece into another's lap. Finding parallels are as important as finding differences, as both illuminate our evolutionary path, especially what we inherited and what we invented. Critically, in attempting to unravel the architecture of the moral faculty, we must understand what is uniquely human and what is unique to morality as opposed to other domains of knowledge. A rich evolutionary approach is essential.

A different position concerning the evolution of moral behavior was ignited under the name "sociobiology" in the 1970s and still smolders in disciplines ranging from biology to psychology to economics. This position attempts to account for the adaptive value of moral behavior. Sociobiology's primary tenet was that our actions are largely selfish, a behavioral strategy handed down to us over evolution and sculpted by natural selection; the unconscious demons driving our motives were masterfully designed replicators—selfish genes. Wilson (1975, 1998) and other sociobiologists writing about ethics argued that moral systems evolved to regulate individual temptation, with emotional responses designed to facilitate cooperation and incite aggression toward those who cheat. This is an important proposal, but it is not a substitute for the Rawlsian position. Rather, it focuses on a different level or kind of causal problem. Whereas Rawls was specifically interested in the mechanisms underlying our moral psychology (both how we act and how we think we ought to act), Wilson was interested in the adaptive significance of such psychological mechanisms. Questions about mechanism should naturally lead to questions about adaptive significance. The reverse is true as well. The important point is to keep these perspectives in their proper place, never seeing them as alternative approaches to answering a question about moral behavior, or any other kind of behavior. They are complementary approaches.

We want to stress that, at some level, there is nothing at all radical about this approach to understanding our moral nature. In characterizing the moral faculty, our task is to define its anatomy, specifying what properties of the mind/brain are specific to our moral judgments and what properties fall outside its scope but nonetheless play an essential supporting role. This task is no different from that involved in anatomizing other parts of our body. When anatomists describe a part of the body, they define its location, size, components, and function. The heart is located between your lungs in the middle of your chest, behind and slightly to the left of your breastbone; it is about the size of an adult's fist, weighs between 7 and 15 ounces, and consists of four chambers with valves that operate through muscle contractions; the function of the heart is to pump blood through the circulatory system of the body. Although this neatly describes the heart, it makes little sense to discuss this organ without mentioning that it is connected to other parts of the body and depends upon our nutrition and health for its proper functioning. Furthermore, although the muscles of the heart are critical for its pumping action, there are no heart-specific muscles. Anatomizing our moral faculty provides a similar challenge. For example, we would not be able to evaluate the moral significance of an action if every event perceived or imagined flitted in and out of memory without pausing for evaluation. But based on this observation, it would be incorrect to conclude that memory is a specific component of our moral anatomy. Our memories are used for many aspects of our lives, including learning how to play tennis, recalling our first rock concert, and generating expectations about a planned vacation to the Caribbean. Some of these memories reference particular aspects of our personal lives (autobiographical information about our first dentist appointment), some allow us to remember earlier experiences (episodic recall for the smell of our mother's apple pie), some are kept in long-term storage (e.g., travel routes home), and others are short-lived (telephone number from an operator), used only for online work. Of course, memories are also used to recall our own actions that were wrong, to feel bad about them, and to assess how we might change in order to better our moral standing. Our memory systems are therefore part of the support team for moral judgments, but they are not specific to the moral faculty. The same kind of thinking has to be applied to other aspects of the mind.

This is a rough sketch of the linguistic analogy, and the core issues that we believe are at stake in taking it forward, both theoretically and empirically; for a more complete treatment, see Hauser (2006). We turn next to some of the empirical evidence, much of which is preliminary.

Uncommon Bedfellows: Intuition Meets Empirical Evidence

Consider an empirical research program based on the linguistic analogy, aimed at uncovering the descriptive principles of our moral faculty. There are at least two ways to proceed. On the one hand, it is theoretically possible that language and morality will turn out to be similar in a deep sense, and thus many of the theoretical and methodological moves deployed for the one domain will map onto the other. For example, if our moral faculty can be characterized by a universal moral grammar, consisting of a set of innately specified and inaccessible principles for building a possible moral system, then this leads to specific experiments concerning the moral acquisition device, its relative encapsulation from other faculties, and the ways in which exposure to the relevant moral data sets particular parameters. Under this construal, we distinguish between operative and expressed principles and expect a dissociation between our competence and performance—between the knowledge that guides our judgments of right and wrong and the factors that guide what we actually say or do; when confronted with a moral dilemma, what we say about this case or what we actually would do if confronted by it in real life may or may not map on to our competence. On the other hand, the analogy to language may be weak but may nonetheless serve as an important guide to empirical research, opening doors to theoretically distinctive questions that, to date, have few answers. The linguistic analogy has the potential to open new doors because prior work in moral psychology, which has generally failed to make the competence–performance distinction (Hauser, 2006; Macnamara, 1990; Mikhail, 2000), has focused on either principled reasoning or emotion as opposed to the causal structure of action and has yet to explore the possibility of a universal set of principles and parameters that may constrain the range of culturally possible moral systems. In this section, we begin with a review of empirical findings that, minimally, provide support for the linguistic analogy in a weak sense. We then summarize the results and lay out several important directions for future research, guided by the kinds of questions that an analogy to language offers.

Judgment, Justification, and Universality

Philosophers have often used so-called "fantasy dilemmas" to explore how different parameters push our judgments around, attempting to derive not only descriptive principles but prescriptive ones. We aim to uncover whether the intuitions guiding the professional philosopher are shared with others lacking such background and assess which features of the causal structure of action are relevant to subjects' judgments, the extent to which cultural variables impinge upon such judgments, and the degree to which people have access to the principles underlying their assessments of moral actions.

To gather observations and take advantage of philosophical analysis, we begin with the famous trolley problem (Foot, 1967; Thomson, 1970) and its family of mutants. Our justification for using artificial dilemmas, and trolley problems in particular, is threefold. First, philosophers (Fischer & Ravizza, 1992; Kamm, 1998b) have scrutinized cases like these, thereby leading to a suite of representative parameters and principles concerning the causes and consequences of action. Second, philosophers designed these cases to mirror the general architecture of real-world ethical problems, including euthanasia and abortion. In contrast to real-world cases, where there are already well-entrenched beliefs and emotional biases, artificial cases, if well designed, preserve the essence of real-world phenomena while removing any prior beliefs or emotions. Ultimately, the goal is to use insights derived from artificial cases to inform real-world problems (Kamm, 1998b), with the admittedly difficult challenge of using descriptive generalizations to inform prescriptive recommendations.[5] Third, and paralleling work in the cognitive sciences more generally, artificial cases have the advantage that they can be systematically manipulated, presented to subjects for evaluation, and then analyzed statistically with models that can tease apart the relative significance of different parametric variations. In the case of moral dilemmas, and the framework we advocate more specifically, artificial cases afford the opportunity to manipulate details of the dilemma. Although a small number of cognitive scientists have looked at subjects' judgments when presented with trolleyesque problems, the focus has been on questions of evolutionary significance (how does genetic relatedness influence harming one to save many?) or the relationship between emotion and cognition (Greene et al., 2001, 2004; O'Neill & Petrinovich, 1998; Petrinovich, O'Neill, & Jorgensen, 1993). In contrast, Mikhail and Hauser have advocated using these cases to look at the computational operations that drive our judgments (Hauser, 2006; Mikhail, 2000, in press; Mikhail, Sorrentino, & Spelke, 1998).

We have used new Web-based technologies with a carefully controlled library of moral dilemmas to probe the nature of our appraisal system; this approach has been designed to collect a large and cross-culturally diverse sample of responses. Subjects voluntarily log on to the Moral Sense Test (MST) at moral.wjh.edu, enter demographic and cultural background information, and finally turn to a series of moral dilemmas. In our first round of testing, subjects responded to four trolley problems and one control (Hauser, Cushman, Young, Jin, & Mikhail, 2006). Controls entailed cases with no moral conflict, designed to elicit predictable responses if subjects were both carefully reading the cases and attempting to give veridical responses. For example, we asked subjects about the distribution of a drug to sick patients at no cost to the hospital or doctor and with unambiguous benefits to the patients. The four trolley problems are presented below and illustrated in figure 3.6;[6] during the test, we did not give subjects these schematics, though for the third and fourth scenarios, we accompanied the text of the dilemma with much simpler drawings to facilitate comprehension. After these questions were answered, we then asked subjects to justify two cases in which they provided different moral judgments; for some subjects, this was done within a session, whereas for others, it was done across sessions separated by a few weeks. In the data presented below, we focus on subjects' responses to the first dilemma presented to them during the test; this restricted analysis is intentional, designed to eliminate the potential confounds of not only order effects but the real possibility that as subjects read and think about their answers to prior dilemmas they may well change their strategies to guarantee consistency. Though this is of interest, we put it to the side for now.

Scenario 1 Denise is a passenger on a trolley whose driver has just shouted that the trolley's brakes have failed, and who then fainted of the shock. On the track ahead are five people; the banks are so steep that they will not be able to get off the track in time. The track has a side track leading off to the right, and Denise can turn the trolley onto it. Unfortunately there is one person on the right hand track. Denise

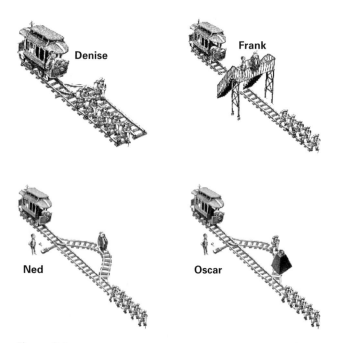

Figure 3.6
The core family of trolley dilemmas used in Internet studies of moral judgments
and justifications.

can turn the trolley, killing the one; or she can refrain from turning the trolley,
letting the five die.

Is it morally permissible for Denise to switch the trolley to the side track?

Scenario 2 Frank is on a footbridge over the trolley tracks. He knows trolleys and
can see that the one approaching the bridge is out of control. On the track under
the bridge there are five people; the banks are so steep that they will not be able to
get off the track in time. Frank knows that the only way to stop an out-of-control
trolley is to drop a very heavy weight into its path. But the only available, sufficiently heavy weight is a large man wearing a backpack, also watching the trolley
from the footbridge. Frank can shove the man with the backpack onto the track in
the path of the trolley, killing him; or he can refrain from doing this, letting the
five die.

Is it morally permissible for Frank to shove the man?

Scenario 3 Ned is taking his daily walk near the trolley tracks when he notices that
the trolley that is approaching is out of control. Ned sees what has happened: The
driver of the trolley saw five men walking across the tracks and slammed on the
brakes, but the brakes failed and they will not be able to get off the tracks in time.
Fortunately, Ned is standing next to a switch, which he can throw, that will tem-

porarily turn the trolley onto a side track. There is a heavy object on the side track. If the trolley hits the object, the object will slow the trolley down, thereby giving the men time to escape. Unfortunately, the heavy object is a man, standing on the side track with his back turned. Ned can throw the switch, preventing the trolley from killing the men, but killing the man. Or he can refrain from doing this, letting the five die.

Is it morally permissible for Ned to throw the switch?

Scenario 4 Oscar is taking his daily walk near the trolley tracks when he notices that the trolley that is approaching is out of control. Oscar sees what has happened: The driver of the trolley saw five men walking across the tracks and slammed on the brakes, but the brakes failed and the driver fainted. The trolley is now rushing toward the five men. It is moving so fast that they will not be able to get off the track in time. Fortunately, Oscar is standing next to a switch, which he can throw, that will temporarily turn the trolley onto a side track. There is a heavy object on the side track. If the trolley hits the object, the object will slow the trolley down, thereby giving the men time to escape. Unfortunately, there is a man standing on the side track in front of the heavy object, with his back turned. Oscar can throw the switch, preventing the trolley from killing the men, but killing the man. Or he can refrain from doing this, letting the five die.

Is it morally permissible for Oscar to throw the switch?

As discussed in the philosophical literature, these cases generate different intuitions concerning permissibility. For example, most agree that Denise and Oscar are permissible, Frank is certainly not, and Ned is most likely not. What is problematic about this variation is that pure deontological rules such as "Killing is impermissible" or utilitarian considerations such as "Maximize the overall good" can't explain philosophical intuition. What might account for the differences between these cases? From 2003–2004—the first year of our project—over 30,000 subjects from 120 countries logged on to our Web site. For the family of four trolley dilemmas, our initial data set included some 5,000 subjects, most of whom were from English-speaking countries (Hauser, Cushman, Young, Jin, & Mikhail, 2006). Results showed that 89% of these subjects judged Denise's action as permissible, whereas only 11% of subjects judged Frank's action as permissible. This is a highly significant difference, and perhaps surprising given our relatively heterogeneous sample, which included young and old (13–70 years), male and female, religious and atheist/agnostic, as well as various degrees of education.

Given the size of the effect observed at the level of the whole subject population (Cohen's $d = 2.068$), we had statistical power of .95 to detect a difference between the permissibility judgments of the two samples at the .05 level given 12 subjects. We then proceeded to break down our sample along several demographic dimensions. When the resultant groups contained more than 12 subjects, we tested for a difference in permissibility score between the two scenarios. This procedure asks: Can we find any demographic subset for which the scenarios Frank and Denise do not produce contrasting judgments? For our data set, the answer was "no." Across the demographic subsets for which our pooled effect predicted a sufficiently large sample size, the effect was detected at $p < .05$ in every case but one: subjects who indicated Ireland as their national affiliation (see table 3.1). In the case of Ireland the effect was marginally significant at $p = .07$ with a sample size of 16 subjects. Given our findings on subjects' judgments, the principled reasoning view would predict that these would be accompanied by coherent and sufficient justifications. We asked subjects perceiving a difference between Frank and Denise to justify their responses. We classified justifications into three categories: (1) sufficient, (2) insufficient, and (3) discounted.

A sufficient justification was one that correctly identified any factual difference between the two scenarios and claimed the difference to be the basis of moral judgment. We adopted this extremely liberal criterion so as

Table 3.1

Demographic subsets revealing a difference for Frank vs. Denise

National Affiliation	Religion	Education
Australia	Buddhist	Elementary school
Brazil	Catholic	Middle school
Canada	Christian Orthodox	High school
Finland	Protestant	Some college
France	Jewish	BA
Germany	Muslim	Masters
India	Hindu	PhD
Ireland (p = .07)	None	**Ethnicity**
Israel	**Age**	American Indian
The Netherlands	10–19 yrs	Asian
New Zealand	20–29	Black non-Hispanic
Philippines	30–39	Hispanic
Singapore	40–49	White non-Hispanic
South Africa	50–59	**Gender**
Spain	60–69	Male
Sweden	70–79	Female
United States	80–89	
United Kingdom		

not to prejudge what, for any given individual, counts as a morally relevant distinction; in evaluating the merits of some justifications, we find it clear that some distinctions (e.g., the agent's gender) do not carry any explanatory weight. Typical justifications were as follows: (1) in Denise, the death of one person on the side track is not a necessary means to saving the five, while in Frank, the death of one person is a necessary means to saving the five; (2) in Denise, an existing threat (of the trolley) is redirected, while in Frank, a new threat (of being pushed off the bridge) is introduced; (3) in Denise, the action (flipping the switch) is impersonal, while in Frank, the action (pushing the man) is personal or emotionally salient.

An insufficient justification—category 2—was one that failed to identify a factual difference between the two scenarios. Insufficient justifications typically fell into one of three subcategories. First, subjects explicitly expressed an inability to account for their contrasting judgments by offering statements such as "I don't know how to explain it," "It just seemed reasonable," "It struck me that way," and "It was a gut feeling." Second, subjects explained that death or killing is "inevitable" in one case but not in the other without offering any further explanation of how they reasoned this to be the case. Third, subjects explained their judgment of one case using utilitarian reasoning (maximizing the greater good) and their judgment of the other using deontological reasoning (acts can be objectively identified as good or bad) without resolving their conflicting responses to the two cases. Subjects using utilitarian reasoning referred to numbers (e.g., save five vs. one or choose "the lesser of two evils"). Subjects using deontological reasoning referred to principles, or moral absolutes, such as (1) killing is wrong, (2) playing God, or deciding who lives and who dies, is wrong, and (3) the moral significance of not harming trumps the moral significance of providing aid.[7]

Discounted responses—category 3—were either blank or included added assumptions. Examples of assumptions included the following: (1) people walking along the tracks are reckless, while people working on the track are responsible, (2) a man's body cannot stop a trolley, (3) the five people will be able to hear the trolley approaching and escape in time, and (4) a third option for action such as self-sacrifice exists and should be considered.

When contrasting Denise and Frank, only 30% of subjects provided sufficient justifications. The sufficiency of subjects' justifications was not predicted by their age, gender, or religious background; however, subjects with a background in moral philosophy were more likely to provide sufficient justifications than those without.

In characterizing the possible differences between Denise and Frank, one could enumerate several possible factors including redirected versus introduced threat, a personal versus impersonal act, and harming one as a means versus a by-product. It is possible, therefore, that due to the variety of possible factors, subjects were confused by these contrasting cases, making it difficult to derive a coherent and principled justification. To address this possibility, we turn to scenarios 3 and 4—Ned and Oscar.

These cases emerged within the philosophical literature (Fischer & Ravizza, 1992; Kamm, 1998a; Mikhail, 2000) in order to reduce the number of relevant parameters or distinctions to potentially only one: means versus by-products. Ned is like Frank, in that a bystander has the option of using a person as the means to save five. The person on the loop is a necessary means to save the five since removing him from the loop leaves the bystander with no meaningful options: Flipping the switch does not remove the threat to the five. The man on the loop is heavy enough to slow the trolley down before hitting the five. In Oscar, the man on the loop isn't heavy enough to slow the trolley, but the weight in front of him is. The weight, but not the man, is therefore a sufficient means to stopping the trolley. In both Ned and Oscar, the act—flipping a switch—is impersonal; consequently, on the view that Greene holds (Model 3), these should be perceived as the same. In both scenarios, the act results in redirecting threat. In both, the act results in killing one. In both, action is intended to bring about the greater good. But in Ned, the negative consequence—killing one—is the means to the positive—saving five—whereas in Oscar, the negative consequence is a by-product of a prior goal—to run the trolley into the weight so that it will slow down and stop before the five people up ahead.

Do subjects perceive these distinctions? In terms of judgments, 55% of subjects responded that it is permissible for Ned to flip the switch, whereas 72% responded that it is permissible for Oscar to flip the switch. This is a highly significant difference.

Paralleling our analysis of Frank and Denise, we calculated the necessary sample size to detect a difference between the cases assuming an effect size equal to the effect size of the total subject population (Cohen's $d = 0.3219$). Because of the substantially smaller effect size, a sample of 420 subjects was necessary to achieve statistical power of .95. Employing this stringent criterion, we were able to test a small range of demographic subsets for the predicted dissociation in judgments: males, females, subjects ages 30–39, 40–49, or 50–59, subjects who had completed college and subjects currently enrolled in college, Protestants and subjects indicating no religious affiliation. For every one of these groups, the predicted dissociation in judgments was observed. In order to broaden the cross-cultural sample, we then tested additional demographic subsets for which we predicted statistical power of .8 to pick up a true effect. Again, every group showed the predicted dissociation in judgments. The additional groups were subjects ages 20–29 and 60–69, subjects who had completed high school but not enrolled in college, and Catholics.

Given that the Ned and Oscar cases greatly curtail the number of possible parametric differences, one might expect subjects to uncover the key difference and provide a sufficient justification. In parallel with Denise and Frank, only 13% of subjects provided a sufficient justification, using something like the means/by-product distinction as a core property.

Results from our family of trolley problems leave us with two conclusions: There is a small and inconsistent effect of cultural and experiential factors on people's moral judgments, and there is a dissociation between judgment and justification, suggesting that intuition as opposed to principled reasoning guides judgment. These results, though focused on a limited class of dilemmas, generate several interim conclusions and set up the next phase of research questions.

Consider first our four toy models concerning the causes of our moral judgments. If model 1—and its instantiation in the Kantian creature—provides a correct characterization, then we would have expected subjects to generate sufficient justifications for their judgments. Since they did not, there are at least two possible explanations. The first is that something about our task failed to elicit principled and sufficient explanations. Perhaps subjects didn't understand the task, didn't take it seriously, or felt rushed. We think these accounts are unlikely for several reasons. With few exceptions, our analyses revealed that subjects were serious about these problems, answering them as best as they could. It is also unlikely that subjects felt rushed given that they were replying on the Internet and were given as much time as they needed to answer. It is of course possible that if we had handed each subject a range of possible justifications that they would have arrived at the correct one. However, given their choice, we would not be able to distinguish between a principle that was truly responsible for their judgment as opposed to a post hoc rationalization. As Haidt has argued in the context of an emotionally mediated intuitive model, people often use a rational and reasoned approach as a way to justify an answer delivered intuitively. The second possibility, consistent with the Rawlsian creature, is that subjects decide what is permissible, obligatory, or forbidden based on unconscious and inaccessible principles. The reason why we observed a dissociation between judgment and justification is that subjects lack access to the reasons—the principles that make up the universal moral grammar.

Our results, especially the fact that some subjects tended to see a difference between Ned and Oscar, also generates difficulties for both models 2 and 3. For subjects who see a difference between these cases, the difference is unlikely to be emotional, at least in the kind of straightforward way that Greene suggests in terms of his personal–impersonal distinction.[8] Both Ned and Oscar are faced with an action that is impersonal: flipping a switch. If Ned and Oscar act, they flip a switch, causing the trolley to switch tracks onto the loop, killing one person in each case but saving five. For Ned, the action of flipping a switch isn't bad. Flipping a switch so that the trolley can hit the man constitutes an action that can be more neutrally translated as "using a means to an end." If the heavy man had not been on the track, Ned would have no functionally meaningful options: Flipping the switch, certainly an option in the strict sense, would serve no purpose as the trolley would loop around and hit the five people. In contrast, if the heavy man had not been on the looped track when Oscar confronted the dilemma, he could have still achieved his goal by flipping the switch and allowing the trolley to hit the heavy weight and then stop. The difference between Ned and Oscar thus boils down to a distinction between whether battery to one person was an intended means to saving five as opposed to a foreseen consequence. This distinction, often described as the "principle of double effect," highlights the centrality of looking at the causes and consequences of an action and how these components feed into our moral judgments.

The results discussed thus far lead, we think, to the intriguing possibility that *some* forms of moral judgment are universal and mediated by unconscious and inaccessible principles. They leave open many other questions that might never have been raised had it not been for an explicit formulation of the linguistic analogy and a contrast between the four toy models and their psychological ingredients. For example, why are some moral judgments relatively immune to cross-cultural variation? Are certain principles and parameters universally expressed because they represent statistical regularities of the environment, social problems that have recurred over the millennia and thus been selected for due to their consistent and positive effects on survival and reproduction? Is something like the principle of double effect at the right level of psychological abstraction, or does the moral faculty operate over more abstract and currently unimaginable computations? Even though people may not be able to retrieve sufficient justifications for some of their judgments, do these principles enter into future judgments once we become aware of them? Do results like these lead to any specific predictions with respect to the moral organ—the circuitry involved in computing whether an action is permissible, obligatory, or forbidden? In the next section, we describe a suite of ongoing research projects designed to begin answering these questions.

Universality, Dilemmas, and the Moral Organ

The Web-based studies we have conducted thus far are limited in a number of ways. Most importantly, they are restricted to people who not only have access to the Web and know how to use it but are also largely from English-speaking countries. Early Web-based studies were criticized for being uncontrolled and unreliable. These criticisms have been addressed in several ways. First, a number of experimental psychologists such as Baron and Banaji (Baron & Siepmann, 2000; Greenwald, Nosek, & Banaji, 2003; Kraut, Olson, Banaji, Bruckman, Cohen, & Cooper, 2004; Schmidt, 1997) have systematically contrasted data collected on the Web with data collected using more standard paper-and-pencil tests in a room with an experimenter. In every case, the pattern of results is identical. Similarly, our results on the Web are virtually identical to those that Mikhail and colleagues (1998) collected with the same dilemmas, but using paper-and-pencil questionnaires. Second, in looking over our data sets, we are rarely forced to throw out data from subjects who produce obviously faulty data, such as entering graduate degrees in the early teen years or linking nationality to the Antarctic. Third, for every test we administer on the Web, we include several control questions or dilemmas designed to test whether subjects understand the task and are taking it seriously.

In terms of cross-cultural diversity, we are currently stretching our reach in two different directions. First, we have already constructed translations of our Web site into Arabic, Indonesian, French, Portuguese, Chinese, Hebrew, and Spanish and have launched the Chinese and Spanish Web sites. Second, we have initiated a collaboration with several anthropologists, economists, and psychologists who are studying small-scale societies in different parts of the world. Under way is a study with Frank Marlowe designed to test whether the Hadza, a small and remote group of hunter-gatherers living in Tanzania, show similar patterns of responses as do our English-speaking, Internet-sophisticated, largely Westernized and industrialized subjects. This last project has forced us to extend the range of our dilemmas, especially since the Hadza, and most of the other small-scale societies we hope to test, would be completely unfamiliar with trolleys. Instead of trolleys, therefore, we have mirrored the architecture of these problems but substituted herds of stampeding elephants as illustrated below (see figure 3.7). Like Denise, the man in the jeep has the option of watching the herd run over and kill five people or of driving toward the herd, turning them away from the five and around the grove where they will run over and kill one person. Similarly, in a case designed to mirror Frank, a person can throw a heavy person out of a tree to stop the herd and thereby save the five people up ahead. Marlowe's preliminary data suggest that the Hadza judge these cases as do Web-savvy Westerners and, also, fail to give sufficient justifications. Though preliminary, these results provide further support for the universality of some of our moral intuitions.

Changing the content of these dilemmas not only is relevant for testing small-scale societies that are unfamiliar with trolleys but also makes precisely the right move for extending the reach of our empirical tests. In

Figure 3.7
A content manipulation of the familiar bystander trolley problem, designed for field testing among hunter-gatherer populations. Here, a man in a jeep has an opportunity to drive toward the herd of stampeding elephants, causing them to move around the grove, saving the five but killing the one person.

particular, we have now constructed several hundred dilemmas, each carefully articulated in terms of the text, while systematically manipulating the content of the dilemma, the nature of the action, the consequences of action as opposed to inaction, the degree to which the consequences are a direct or indirect result of the action, and so forth. More specifically, we have mined the rich philosophical literature on moral dilemmas, including cases of harm, rescue, and distribution of limited resources, to derive a series of relevant parameters and potential principles for building a library of dilemmas that can be presented to subjects on the Web, in the field, and in hospital settings with patient populations.

The strongest opposition to the strict Kantian creature has been the Humean creature. And yet, as we have tried to argue throughout, it is not at all clear how our emotions play a role. As suggested in the first section, *that* emotions play a role is undebatable. To more precisely identify where, when, and how emotions play a role in our moral judgments, we have initiated a suite of collaborative projects with cognitive neuroscientists using patient populations with selective brain damage, functional neuroimaging, and transcranial magnetic stimulation. Here, we give only a brief sketch of some preliminary results and their potential significance for fleshing out the details of our moral psychology.

Over the past 15 or more years, Antonio Damasio (1994, 2000) has amassed an impressive body of data on the neurobiology of emotion and how it bears on our decision making. Some of the most intriguing results come from his studies of patients with damage to the orbitofrontal and ventromedial prefrontal cortex. Based on a wide variety of tests, it appears that these patients often make inappropriate decisions *because* of insufficient input from the emotional circuitry of the brain. This also leads to what appear to be inappropriate moral decisions. On the face of it, this might be taken as evidence for the Humean creature. In the absence of emotional input, moral judgments are often at odds with what nonpatients say. However, because there have been insufficient, in-depth tests of their moral psychology, it is not clear how extensive the deficit is, nor whether it is due to performance or competence. Given the lack of clarity, we teamed up with Damasio, Ralph Adolphs, Daniel Tranel, and Michael Koenigs (2007) and began testing these patients[9] on a large battery of moral dilemmas, including the original family of trolley problems, several additional permutations, and many other dilemmas aimed at different aspects of our moral psychology. For several dilemmas, these patients showed a completely normal pattern of judgments. This shows that emotions are not necessary for a variety of moral situations. However, in cases where a highly aversive action is in conflict with the generation of a significant utilitarian outcome, and the action involves personal contact with another, these patients deviate significantly from normals, favoring the utilitarian outcome. That is, in this selective set of moral problems, emotions appear causally necessary. When the circuitry subserving social emotions is damaged, a hyper-utilitarian emerges.

These results only skim the surface of possibilities and only present a rough picture of the different computations involved in both recognizing a moral dilemma and arriving at a judgment. Crucially, by laying out the possible theoretical issues in the form of our four toy models, and by taking advantage of empirical developments in cognitive neuroscience, we will soon be in a exquisite position to describe the nature of our moral judgments, how they are represented, and how they break down due to acquired or inherited deficits.

Sweet Justice! Rawls and Twenty-first-century Cognitive Science

In 1998, Rawls wrote *Justice as Fairness*, one of his last books. In some sense, it represents the finale to his work in political philosophy, providing the interested reader with an update on his thinking since 1971 when he published *A Theory of Justice*. For the observant reader, there is something missing in this final installment: The linguistic analogy has been completely purged! This is odd on at least two counts. First, linguistics as a discipline was stronger than it had ever been, and certainly in a far more mature state than it was in the 1970s. Not only had there been considerable theoretical developments but work in linguistics proper had joined forces with other neighboring disciplines to provide beautiful descriptions of the neural architecture and its breakdown, the patterns of development, the specificity of the machinery, and the historical and evolutionary patterns of change. Building the analogy would have been, if anything, easier in 1998 than it was at the time Rawls first began writing about language and morality; fortunately, other philosophers including Gert, Dwyer, and Mikhail have picked up where Rawls left off. Second, our understanding of cognitive processes more generally, and moral psychology more specifically, had grown considerably since Piaget and Kohlberg's writings between 1960 and 1980. In particular, many of the issues that Rawls was most deeply interested in concerning principles of justice qua fairness were being explored by political scientists and economists, in both developed and developing countries—an empirical march that continues today (Camerer, 2003; Frohlich & Oppenheimer, 1993; Henrich, Boyd, Bowles,

Camerer, Fehr, & Gintis, 2004). It is in part because of these developments that the time is ripe to bring them back and flesh out their empirical implications.

As stated earlier, there is a strong and weak version of the linguistic analogy. On the strong version, language and morality work in much the same way: dedicated and encapsulated machinery, innate principles that guide acquisition, distinctions between competence and performance, inaccessible and unconscious operative principles, selective breakdown due to damage to particular areas of the brain, and constraints on the evolvable and learnable languages and moralities.[10] On the weak version, the linguistic analogy is merely a heuristic for posing the right sorts of questions about the nature of our moral competence. On this version, it matters little whether morality works like language. What matters is that we ask about the principles that guide mature competence, work out how such knowledge is acquired, understand whether and how competence interacts with both mind internal and external factors to create variation in performance, and assess how such knowledge evolved and whether it has been specially designed for the moral sphere. These are large and important questions, and, to date, we have few answers for them.[11]

Providing answers will not be trivial, and for those interested in moral knowledge and the linguistic analogy in particular, one must recognize that the state of play is far worse than it was when Chomsky and other generative grammarians began writing about language in the 1950s. In particular, whereas linguists have been cataloguing the details of the world's languages, dissecting patterns of word order, agreement, and so on, we have nothing comparable in the moral domain. In the absence of a rich description of adult moral competence, we can't even begin to work out the complexity of the computations underlying our capacity to create and comprehend a limitless variety of morally meaningful actions and events. And without this level of descriptive adequacy, we can't move on to questions of explanatory adequacy, focused in particular on questions of the initial state of competence, interfaces with other mind internal and external factors, and issues of evolutionary uniqueness. On a positive note, however, by raising such questions and showing why they matter, we gain considerable traction on the kinds of data sets that we will need to collect. It is this traction that we find particularly exciting and encouraging in terms of working out the signature of our moral faculty.

Let us end on a note concerning descriptive as opposed to prescriptive ethics. Rawls's linguistic analogy is clearly targeted at the descriptive level, even though many of his critics considered him to be saying more

(Mikhail, 2000, in press). Showing how the descriptive level connects to the prescriptive is a well-worn and challenging path. Our own sense, simple as it may be, is that by understanding the descriptive level we will be in a stronger position to work out the prescriptive details. This is no more (or less) profound than saying that an understanding of human nature, how it evolved, and how it has changed over recent times provides a foundation for understanding our strengths and weaknesses and the kinds of prescriptive policies that may or may not rub up against our innate biases. As an illustration, consider the case of euthanasia and the distinction made by the American Medical Association (AMA) between mercy killing and removing life support. This example, well-known to moral philosophers (Kagan, 1988; Rachels, 1975), is precisely the kind of case that motivated the development of the trolley problems. It is an example that plays directly into the action versus inaction bias (Baron, 1998). The AMA blocks a doctor's ability to deliver an overdose to a patient with a terminal and insufferable illness but allows the doctor to remove life support (including the withdrawal of food and fluids), allowing the patient to die. The AMA allows passive euthanasia but blocks active euthanasia. Although this policy feeds into an inherent bias that we appear to have evolved in which actions are perceived as more harmful than inactions, even when they lead to the same consequences, it is clear that many in the medical community find the distinction meaningless. The intuition that the distinction is meaningless appears even stronger in a different context: James Rachels's example of a greedy uncle who intends to end his nephew's life in order to inherit the family's money, and in one case drowns him in the bathtub and in another lets him drown. His intent is the same in both cases, and the consequences are the same as well. Intuitively, we don't want to let the uncle off in the second case, but convict him of a crime in the first. And the intuition seems to be the same among medical practitioners. Indications that this is the case come from several lines of evidence, including the relatively high rate of unreported (and illegal!) mercy killings going on every day in hospitals in the United States, the fact that many patients diagnosed with some terminal illness often "die" within 24 hours of the diagnosis, and the fact that some countries, such as The Netherlands and Belgium, have abandoned the distinction between active and passive euthanasia altogether. All in all, intuition among medical practitioners appears to go against medical policy.

The fact that intuition rides against policy doesn't mean, in general, that we should allow intuition to have its way in all cases. As Jonathan Baron and others have pointed out, intuition often flies in the face of what ultimately and rationally works out to be the better policy from the stand-point of human welfare. However, ignoring intuition altogether, and going for rational deliberate reasoning instead, is also a mistake. Providing a deeper understanding of the nature of our intuitive judgments, including the principles that underlie them, how they evolved, how they develop, and the extent to which they are immune to reason and unchangeable, will only serve to enhance our prescriptive policies.

The issue of immunity or penetrability of our intuitive system brings us back to Rawls, and perhaps the most significant difference between lan-guage and morality. Looking at the current landscape of research in lin-guistics makes it clear that the principles underlying adult competence are phenomenally complex, abstract, and inaccessible to conscious awareness. The fact that those studying these principles understand them and have access to them doesn't have any significant impact on their performance, or what they use such principles for in their day-to-day life, from writing and reading to giving lectures and schmoozing at a café or pub. On the other hand, our strong hunch is that once we begin to uncover some of the principles underlying our moral judgments, they most certainly will impact our behavior. Although the principle of double effect may not be at the right level of abstraction, it is the kind of principle that, once we are aware of it, may indeed change how we behave or how we perceive and judge the behavior of others. In this sense, our moral faculty may lack the kind of encapsulation that is a signature feature of the language faculty. This wouldn't diminish the usefulness of Rawls's linguistic analogy. Rather, it would reveal important differences between these domains of knowledge and serve to fuel additional research into the nature of the underlying mechanisms, especially the relationship between competence and perfor-mance, operative and expressed principles, and so on. In either case, it would entail a gift to Rawls's deep insight about the nature of our moral psychology, an instance of sweet justice.

Notes

We would like to extend our deepest thanks to John Mikhail for helping us to clarify many of the links between language and morality, and rebuilding Rawls's analogy. Also, thanks to Walter Sinnott-Armstrong for organizing a terrific conference among philosophers, biologists, and psychologists, and for giving us extensive comments on this paper; thanks too to three undergraduates in his class for helping us clarify the issues for a more general readership. Hopefully, none of our commentators will be too disappointed. Marc Hauser was funded by a Guggenheim fellowship during the writing of this chapter.

1. The description of judgments is not meant to exclude others including what is virtuous, ideal, and indecent. Throughout, however, we refer to judgments of permissible, obligatory, and forbidden actions, largely because these are the ones that we have focused on empirically. However, the Rawlsian theory that we favor will ultimately have to encompass judgments of actions that are morally right or wrong, good or bad, and above and beyond the call of duty. In parallel, most of the examples we will target concern harming. However, if the theory is to have sufficiently broad appeal, it will have to encompass harmless acts that are treated as moral infractions. For example, many of the dilemmas that we are currently exploring concern cases of rescue and resource contributions to those in need, as well as actions that are treated as morally impermissible because they are disgusting. It is too early to say whether the Rawlsian view we favor can do the work necessary to account for these other cases, but our hunch is that it will.

2. Rawls' views on the linguistic analogy are presented in section 9 of *A Theory of Justice*, but the precursor to this discussion originates in his thesis and the several papers that followed. For example, in his thesis he states, "The meaning of explication may be stated another way: ordinarily the use of elaborate concepts is intuitive and spontaneous, and therefore like 'cause,' 'event,' 'good,' are applied intuitively or by habit, and not by consciously applied rules. . . . Sometimes, instead of using the term 'explication' one can use the phrase 'rational reconstruction' and one can say that a concept is rationally reconstructed whenever the correct rules are stated which enable one to understand and explain all the actual occasions of its use" (pp. 72–73). Further on, he states that moral principles are "analogous to functions. Functions, as rules applied to a number, yield another number. The principles, when applied to a situation yield a moral rule. The rules of common sense morality are examples of such secondary moral rules" (p. 107). See Mikhail (2000) for a more comprehensive discussion of Rawls's linguistic analogy, together with several important extensions.

3. Our characterization of the Kantian creature is completely at odds with Greene's characterization. For Greene, whose ideas are generally encapsulated by Model 3, Kant is aligned with deontological views and these are seen as emotional. Although we think this is at odds with Kant, and others who have further articulated and studied his ideas, we note here our conflict with Greene's views.

4. Throughout the rest of this paper, when we use the terms "right," "wrong," "permissible," and so forth, we are using these as shorthand for "morally right," "morally wrong," "morally permissible," and so forth.

5. We should note that, as it is for Kamm, this is a methodological move. The moral faculty presumably handles real-world cases in the same way; the problem is that it may be more difficult to separate out competence–performance issues when it comes to real-world problems where people have already decided.

6. There are many permutations of these trolley problems, and in our research we have played around with framing effects (e.g., using "saving" as opposed to "killing"), the location of a bystander (e.g., Denise is on the trolley as opposed to on the side, next to the switch), and so on; in general, these seem to have small effects on overall judgments as long as the wording is held constant across a set of different dilemmas (e.g., if a permissibility question is framed with "saving," then all contrasting dilemmas use "saving" as well).

7. Our analyses of justifications are only at the crudest stage and may blur distinctions that certain subjects hold but do not make explicit. For example, subjects who justify their answers by saying that killing is wrong may have a more nuanced view concerning cause and effect, seeing Denise as carrying out an act that doesn't kill someone, whereas Frank's act clearly does. At present, we take the methodologically simpler view, using what people said as opposed to probing further on the particular meanings they assigned to different pieces of the justification.

8. It is possible that a different take on emotional processing could be used to account for the difference between Ned and Oscar; for example, as Sinnott-Armstrong suggested to us, a difference between imagining the victim jumping off the track in Ned frustrates our attempt to stop the trolley, which may be negatively coded, whereas the same event in Oscar would make things easier, and may be positively coded.

9. At present, we have tested six patients with frontal damage. The extent and location of damage is quite similar across patients.

10. Though not addressed explicitly in this paper, it is important to distinguish—as Chomsky has—between the internal computations underlying language and morality [I-language and I-morality] and the external representations of these computations in the form of specific E-languages (Korean, English, French) and E-moralities (permissible infanticide, polygyny).

11. Since the writing of this chapter in 2005, most of the references to our own work have changed from in preparation to in print, and dozens of other papers by our colleagues have emerged, transforming this rich landscape.

Ron Mallon

Marc Hauser, Liane Young, and Fiery Cushman's paper is an excellent contribution to a now resurgent attempt (Dwyer, 1999; Harman, 1999; Mikhail, 2000) to explore and understand moral psychology by way of an analogy with Noam Chomsky's pathbreaking work in linguistics, famously suggested by John Rawls (1971). And anyone who reads their paper ought to be convinced that research into our innate moral endowment is a plausible and worthwhile research program. I thus begin by agreeing that even if the linguistic analogy turns out to be weak, it can do titanic work in serving "as an important guide to empirical research, opening doors to theoretically distinctive questions that, to date, have few answers" (p. 125). Granting the importance of the empirical investigation of moral judgment generally, and of research designed to probe the linguistic analogy specifically, I will nonetheless argue that there is simply no evidence that there is a specialized moral faculty, no evidence that the stronger version of the linguistic analogy is correct.

What Is the Moral Faculty?

On the strong version of the linguistic analogy, Hauser et al. suggest that the moral faculty may be

1. A specialized system
2. Innate
3. Universal (i.e., species-typical)
4. Upstream of moral judgment (weak processing view)
5. Causally responsible for moral judgment, independent of emotion and reasoning (strong processing view).[1]

I am inclined to agree with them that there must be action appraisals that are upstream of moral judgment and that the capacity for such appraisals may well be substantially innate. However, I am skeptical that there is any evidence that such appraisals involve a specialized moral faculty (1).

What do Hauser et al. mean by suggesting that there is a specific moral faculty? While they do not say a lot about what would make the moral faculty specialized, what I think they have in mind here is that there is a distinct mental subsystem that

- Properly functions in the domain of morality.
- Is functionally (computationally) discrete in that it makes use of only limited sorts of information (i.e., it exhibits information encapsulation) and in that its operational principles and processes are opaque to conscious reasoning.
- Is physiologically discrete—it is some sort of "organ" with a particular brain location.

These commitments lead them to talk of "specialized" moral systems (p. 120), "dedicated and encapsulated machinery" that exhibits "selective breakdown due to damage to particular areas of the brain" (p. 139). Before going on to argue against such a faculty, let's pause to ask what exactly they take the moral faculty to do.

Hauser et al. suggest the moral faculty is an "appraisal system" (p. 117) for "action analysis" (p. 117). Somewhat puzzlingly, they then go on to explain that actions can be combined to create events (p. 118 ff). This is puzzling because the appraisal system is not the system that produces actions, but the one that appraises them. The idea that I think they have in mind is that actions have a complex structure that is isomorphic to the complex computational description of the action that we assign to the action prior to moral judgment. If I understand them correctly, then, there are at least two functions involved in what they call "action analysis." The first is the (perhaps automatic and unconscious) assignment of a description to an action. The second is the application of moral principles to such a description to result (directly or indirectly) in moral judgment.[2]

It seems to me that it must be the second of these functions that Hauser et al. want to identify with the moral faculty, for, at first look anyway, the assignment of a description to an action does not look to be specific to the moral domain nor to be informationally encapsulated. It seems we can, for example, assign action descriptions to actions toward which we have no moral reaction. Nor does it seem that moral principles need be involved in such an assignment. Moreover, it seems that such action descriptions are assigned using information from a wide variety of sources (e.g., general knowledge, theory of mind, etc.). This is not a problem for Hauser et al., because the second function, the application of principles or rules to actions resulting in moral judgment, may be functionally discrete. Thus, if there is a specialized moral faculty, it is the computational mechanism that takes action descriptions as inputs, applies moral principles and parameters, and gives moral judgments (or, on the weak processing view, precursors to moral judgment like moral reasoning or emotion) as outputs.

Three Projects in Understanding Moral Judgment

Let's distinguish three different projects in the area of moral judgment: the first one prescriptive, the other two descriptive. First, many people in general, and moral philosophers in particular, are typically interested in what the correct moral assessment of a particular sort of person or act is. The correct *prescriptive* account of moral judgment (if there is one) could, in principle, allow us to understand for any object (e.g., a person or an action) what the appropriate moral evaluation of that object is. It would perhaps tell us that murder is wrong or keeping one's promises is right, but knowing such a theory would also enable us to know the right answer (if there is one) in hard cases like the moral dilemmas many philosophers focus on.

Of course, moral psychologists like Hauser at al. are not primarily interested in the prescriptive project. Rather, they are interesting in a descriptive project of accurately characterizing the capacities that give rise to moral judgment. However, as Shaun Nichols (2005) has recently pointed out (in a similar context), this descriptive project admits of *external* and *internal* readings similar to those that arose in discussions of linguistics. On the *external* view of the linguistic project, a primary aim of the linguist is to produce a descriptively adequate grammar that predicts linguistic intuitions of speakers and is consistent with the developmental and cross-cultural data. Choice of such a grammar might be further constrained by other theoretical considerations such as simplicity, but, crucially, such an adequate grammar could well have principles quite at odds with anything that is subserved by a specific mechanism or actually represented in language users. On the externalist view, a gap between the principles our theory invokes and the psychological mechanisms that subserve the processes our theory describes is perfectly okay, for the external project is psychologically modest (e.g., Stich, 1972). In contrast, the *internal* reading holds that the project of linguistics is to describe the psychological mechanisms (perhaps including the principles and parameters) that actually give rise to—in virtue, perhaps, of their being mentally represented—judgments of grammaticality in a mature, competent native speaker. The internal project is thus psychologically ambitious: It aims, inter alia, to provide a description of the computational mechanisms that instantiate the adult native speaker's competence with language (e.g., Fodor, 1981).

The same distinction can be applied to the project of understanding adult moral capacity. Here, the external project would be to characterize a descriptively adequate set of moral principles that capture our moral judgments, including those regarding trolley cases. Such a project need not be committed to moral principles that can be explicitly articulated but rather can include whatever principles seem to capture and order the relevant intuitive judgments. In contrast, the more psychologically ambitious internal project aims to characterize those computational mechanisms that actually give rise to our moral judgments.

Rereading Rawls, Outside In

Hauser et al. are pursuing the *internal* project of characterizing the underlying mechanisms that explain moral judgment, and they postulate a moral faculty as part of this project. A critic can thus allow them that there are (externally adequate) moral rules that are innate, are universal (i.e., species typical), and figure in the production of moral judgment while nonetheless denying that there is a functionally discrete faculty that computes from action descriptions to moral judgments.[3]

Before I go on to make that argument, however, it is worth noting that Rawls himself seems most plausibly read as interested in the external project. When Rawls (1971) writes, "A correct account of moral capacities will certainly involve principles and theoretical constructions which go beyond the norms and standards cited in every day life" (p. 47), he is not merely indicating that our moral capacities may involve moral principles that go beyond those we can express, as Hauser et al. suggest. Rather, Rawls seems to be noting that the correct description of our moral capacity may outrun what can plausibly be literally attributed to the individual's psychological endowments. Rawls's aim in the passage Hauser et al. cite is, in part, to defend the relevance of his device of the "original position"—a theoretical construction that we ought not regard him as holding to be an actual component (conscious or unconscious) of our processing of moral judgments. While Hauser et al.'s passage from Rawls ends with, "A correct account of moral capacities will certainly involve principles and theoretical constructions which go beyond the norms and standards cited in every-day life" (p. 117), the original sentence and paragraph continue as follows:

it may eventually require fairly sophisticated mathematics as well. This is to be expected, since on the contract view the theory of justice is part of the theory of rational choice. Thus the idea of the original position and of an agreement on principles there does not seem too complicated or unnecessary. Indeed, these notions are rather simple and can serve only as a beginning. (Rawls, 1971, p. 47)

The full passage offers just an inkling of how much theoretical apparatus Rawls thinks may appropriately be invoked in the course of characterizing our moral capacity, apparatus that seems unconstrained by the psychological facts of processing.

It would, of course, be a mistake to assume that Hauser et al.'s use of the linguistic analogy stands or falls with successful Rawls exegesis. However, once we distinguish the external and internal projects, it does raise questions about how the two projects, if both carried out, might relate to one another. In particular, it might well be that an external theory could be developed, setting out principles governing moral judgment within a moral culture and parameters that vary among moral cultures, but that the principles of such a theory are not smoothly reducible to specific principles or a specific faculty operative in psychological processing.

Prying Apart the External and the Internal Projects

It is something of a truism in cognitive science that functionally identified domains like "moral judgment" may be numerously instantiated computationally, so that there is no reason to infer from the seeming coherence of the folk category "moral judgment" that the psychological mechanisms producing such judgments will themselves cohere. Here, I will develop that idea.

Multiple Realizability

A central organizing doctrine of much cognitive science is that cognitive behavioral phenomena can be described at multiple levels (see, e.g., Marr, 1982; Newell, 1982; Pylyshyn, 1984). A typical division of levels of description might involve three levels:

1. A descriptive level: Describes the function performed by the target mechanism.
2. A computational level: Describes the algorithm actually used to compute the function described in (1).

3. Implementation level: Describes the physical materials that implement the computation described in (2).

Within this tradition, one can think of the external descriptive project as offering a high-level description of principles for judgment that adequately characterize the functional domain (1), while the internal project (2) attempts to specify the computational mechanisms that implement or realize those higher level principles.[4]

Most simply, we can imagine that a correct and complete description of our moral capacity (Level 1) invokes simple moral principles that are literally represented in the brain and used in computations to generate moral judgment (Level 2), and this is all carried out in a particular way by a particular, functionally distinct brain region (Level 3). However, an equally familiar point from these discussions in cognitive science is that properties functionally specified at a higher level of description may be realized by a variety of different lower level mechanisms. Thus, the mere fact that we can describe specific jobs for a moral faculty (e.g., action appraisal) ought to give us no confidence at all that there really is some specialized computational faculty (Level 2) or brain region (Level 3) that realizes such a function. Rather, it might well be that multiple or diffuse internal mechanisms operate in such a way that we can accurately describe them (at Level 1) as performing (or computing) the function. The mere possibility of such multiple realizability ought to undermine any easy faith that a principle or set of principles operating in an adequate description of our moral capacities will find smooth reduction to particular psychological mechanisms. Given an adequate description of our moral capacity, there are just too many underlying computational architectures that could play such a role.

Nichols on Double Effect

Nichols (2005) has recently made just this point in just this context, so let me rehearse his idea and then discuss its implications for Hauser's account. Nichols's discussion begins with Gilbert Harman's (1999) suggestion that the doctrine of double effect (DDE) might be "built into" people, forming part of our "universal moral grammar" (p. 114). Nichols goes on to point out that even if the DDE "is externally adequate to a core set of Trolley intuitions, we still need to determine the best internal account" and "it is by no means clear that the appeal to an innate DDE principle is the best explanation" (p. 361). Nichols points out that the DDE includes multiple criteria for assessing the permissibility of an action, for example, it includes both of the following:

1. The requirement that the good outcome of the action be greater than the bad outcome.
2. The requirement that the bad outcome not be intended.

Given such a complex principle, Nichols goes on to sketch how it might be that different faculties may underlie distinct criteria, suggesting that a system for utilitarian calculations may underlie (1) while a distinct system (what he calls "deontological system") may underlie (2).

Now Hauser et al. do not have much faith that the DDE is a principle of universal moral grammar, perhaps because it is not complex and abstract enough (p. 119). But Nichols's point here is entirely generalizable: The mere fact that we can describe principles that seem to capture intuitions about a set of moral cases gives us exactly no reason at all to think that those principles are themselves implemented directly in a computationally discrete way or by a computationally discrete faculty.

A Yawning Gap: How External and Internal Projects May Have Divergent Aims

Hauser and his colleagues invoke the venerable "performance–competence" distinction, but now that we have distinguished internal and external linguistic projects, we can draw this distinction for either project. A natural reading of this distinction on an internal approach is to say that in seeking to characterize a competency, we aim to literally specify the distinct organizations of the various computational mechanisms that constitute a mind. The distinction between competence and performance is just a way of indicating that while our behavioral evidence typically results from a combination of factors, we are trying to draw inferences about *computational competence*—about the computational structure of a particular module or mechanism.

However, even an external approach to morality must make use of such a distinction, for here too the theorists will be faced with distinguishing data that genuinely reveal moral considerations from those that do not. Rawls (1971), for example, privileges "considered judgments" as

those judgments in which our moral capacities are most likely to be displayed without distortion. . . . [Judgments] given when we are upset or frightened, or when we stand to gain one way or the other can be left aside. All these judgments are likely to be erroneous or be influenced by an excessive attention to our own interests. . . . relevant judgments are those given under conditions favorable for deliberation and judgment in general. (pp. 47–48)

In thinking about the principles underlying our moral capacity, Rawls seeks something we can call "domain competence," and he would have us put our "considered judgment" at the core of our enterprise. We can leave it an open question as to whether he is right and also to what extent the kind of data Rawls considers relevant is like the data that Hauser and his colleagues rely upon. Instead, we simply note that a project focused on domain competence might hold very different judgments to be relevant than one focused on computational competence.

To see this, recall that Hauser and his colleagues emphasize the importance of evolution in thinking about the structure of our moral faculty (pp. 123 ff.), but they curiously assign evolution little role in determining our computational competence. For example, Petrinovich, O'Neill, and Jorgensen (1993) report finding that subjects prefer the lives of relatives and friends over strangers in standard trolley scenarios, a finding they take to support sociobiologists' and evolutionary psychologists' suggestions that humans are designed, in part, to be concerned with their own inclusive fitness. Hauser et al. indicate that in contrast with such research that focuses on questions of "evolutionary significance," their research will probe "the computational operations that drive our judgments" (p. 127). However, this begs a crucial question, namely, whether the computational process driving our typical moral judgments are themselves biased by evolution in ways that are at odds with domain competence. Suppose that the data Petrinovich et al. report are correct, and moreover, suppose that much of our moral judgment is underwritten by an evolutionarily designed mechanism M that computes using the following internalized principle:

(K)   The wrongness of a death is directly proportional to the subject's relatedness to me.

The question is, would such a principle be part of the moral faculty Hauser et al. posit? On an external investigation into our domain competence, the answer might well be "no," for the biasing of judgments toward relatives might be thought of as a distortion of, rather than a part of, moral judgment. This seems to be Rawls's view. In contrast, the internal, psychologically ambitious project ought to want to understand mechanism M however it works, and whether or not we would want to say that its computation is part of morality.[5] Notice that from the internal point of view, to consider the computational function of M in cases (e.g., trolley cases without relatives) where it does not employ K is precisely to fail to characterize its computational competence.

This all goes to show simply that the external conception of moral competence and the internal conception can, and likely do, diverge. For example, if the evolutionary hypothesis we have been considering is true, judgments about relatives might be irrelevant to domain competence but central to computational competence. Insofar as our best account of our moral domain competence and our best account of the computational competences of our various cognitive mechanisms fail to neatly align, to that extent it will be wrong to say a specialized faculty underlies our moral domain competence.

Looking to the Data

Of course, all these arguments about the way things might go will be worth nothing if the experimental data support the strong linguistic analogy. And here they look to be in a very strong position, for they do have a very impressive research program gathering data on moral dilemmas within and across cultures. They consider three kinds of data that I will review here: data regarding selective deficits, the aforementioned data regarding judgments about moral dilemmas within and across cultures, and data regarding justifications for those moral judgments. None of these, I argue, provide evidence for a specialized moral faculty.

With regard to the data on selective deficits that they mention in passing, such deficits would, if borne out, support the strong linguistic analogy, for they would show that whatever underlies our capacity for moral appraisal has at least some necessary components that are physically localized in the brain. Here I will only say (in agreement with Jesse Prinz's commentary on Hauser et al. in this volume), that there is, to my knowledge, simply no evidence at this time for selective deficits of a faculty that takes action descriptions as inputs and gives moral judgments (or their precursors) as outputs.

With regard to evidence of converging judgments on moral dilemmas, both within and across cultures, we should note that this sort of evidence is simply the wrong kind of evidence to bear on the question of whether there is a specialized moral faculty or whether the capacities to make these judgments are distributed throughout multiple different psychological mechanisms. These data *do* bear on the claim that *whatever mental faculties* underlie these judgments are innate and universal (i.e., species typical), but they do not give any evidence at all that there is one mental faculty rather than several, hundreds, or thousands. This is worth emphasizing: on an external approach to the data, one can describe shared judgments about moral features as revealing underlying shared principles and differences as resulting from diverse parameters, as a means of organizing the data. But there's no reason at all to think such an organization reveals internal computational or physiological "joints" of the mind.

Finally, the data on justifications look to be either silent on whether, or undermine the case that, a single moral faculty is involved. The data on justifications are silent on whether there is a single moral faculty if one takes the justifications to be wholly unconnected with individual reasons for judgments. On this view, justifications are just post hoc rationalizations of one's prior judgments (Haidt, 2001). But if the justifications are wholly unconnected with the processing mechanisms, the content of the justifications provides no evidence for the features salient in the processing of the moral judgment. On the other hand, suppose that the justifications are based in part on introspective access to the reasons for actions. Then the fact that subjects who provided insufficient justifications sometimes appealed to diverse and unreconciled factors (Hauser et al., p. 131) seems to cohere precisely with Nichols's suggestion that there may be diverse and competing mechanisms in play in producing judgments about trolley cases.

In short, there is simply no evidence that supports positing a specialized moral faculty, and there is some that suggests just the opposite: Our capacities in the moral domain result from the complex interactions of a variety of mental mechanisms not specific to the moral domain.

Conclusion

I have argued that there is no evidence to support the idea that there is a specialized moral faculty. In closing, I simply note how much this grants the linguistic analogy: Implementing mechanisms for our moral capacities might well be innate, and they might even realize universal moral principles, modified by certain parameters, if this is understood as part of an external project. And yet, if the mechanisms themselves are not computationally discrete, if their computational competencies do not smoothly underlie domain competence in moral judgment, then the central idea of the strong linguistic analogy—the idea that there is a unified moral faculty—will simply be wrong. In its place might well be a messy mishmash of mental mechanisms that are not computationally of a piece.[6]

Notes

1. Hauser et al. distinguish between weak and strong processing roles for the moral faculty (pp. 117, 121) and also weak and strong versions of the linguistic analogy

(pp. 125, 139). My argument is against the strong version of the linguistic analogy, and against both processing views insofar as they endorse (1).

2. The computational economy they envisage (p. 119) arises because the principles employed by the moral faculty they envisage encompass an indefinitely large range of action descriptions.

3. Some might find it confusing to think that a moral rule could be innate but not "internal" in the sense described here. However, innateness typically involves a commitment to robust development across a wide variety of circumstances (Stich, 1975; Ariew, 1996; Sober, 1998) along with, in more recent accounts, an attempt to specify the sort of process that gives rise to them (Ariew, 1999; Samuels, 2002; Mallon & Weinberg, 2006). The short of it is: A principle might be innate whether or not it literally figures in a computational process.

4. This is not the only way to map the external and internal projects on to levels of description. For example, one could view the two projects as distinct descriptions of what the computational specification (Level 2) requires. Nothing in the present discussion hangs on the uniqueness of my mapping.

5. When Hauser et al. write that "we find it clear that some distinctions (e.g., the agent's gender) do not carry any explanatory weight" (p. 131), they are making judgments, like Rawls's, that seem to reflect on what sort of considerations are properly considered moral ones. However, there seems little reason to think evolution respected such niceties in making us up, so it is not clear why they think such an exclusion reveals competence (computationally understood).

6. Stich (2006) has recently argued for a similar thesis albeit on distinct grounds.

3.2 Resisting the Linguistic Analogy: A Commentary on Hauser, Young, and Cushman

Jesse J. Prinz

In the eighteenth century, it was popular to suppose that each human capacity was underwritten by a specialized mental faculty. This view was championed by phrenologists well into the nineteenth century and then rejected by behaviorists in the early twentieth century. In contemporary cognitive science, faculties are back in vogue, due largely to the influence of Noam Chomsky's work on universal grammar. In addition to the language faculty, contemporary researchers also postulate dedicated faculties for reasoning about psychology, math, physical objects, biology, and other domains that look like a list of university departments. Conspicuously absent from this list is a faculty dedicated to morality. This was the most popular faculty of all, back in the days when men wore white wigs, and it is long overdue for a comeback. In their stimulating chapter, Marc Hauser, Liane Young, and Fiery Cushman postulate an innate system dedicated to morality, and they speculate that it is interestingly similar to Chomsky's universal grammar. Related views have also been defended by Mikhail (2000), Dwyer (1999), and Rawls (1971). Hauser et al. do much to sharpen the language analogy, and they also bring recent empirical findings to testify in its defense. I applaud these contributions. Their hypothesis deserves serious attention, and their experimental findings provide data that any naturalistic theory of moral psychology must accommodate.

That said, I think it is premature to celebrate a victory for the moral faculty. There are alternative explanations of the current data. Instead of deriving from an innate moral sense, moral judgments may issue from general-purpose emotion systems and socially transmitted rules. Like art, religion, and architecture, morality might be an inevitable by-product of other capacities rather than an ennobling module. In what follows, I raise some questions about the linguistic analogy, I express some doubts about the innateness of a moral faculty, and I sketch a nonnativist interpretation of the experimental findings that Hauser et al. present. I do not take my objections to be decisive. Hauser et al. may be right. Rather, I offer a nonnativist alternative with the hope that the dialogue between faculty theorists and their detractors will help guide research.

The Linguistic Analogy

Hauser et al. believe that there are a number of similarities between morality and language. They say that both capacities

- have an innate universal basis,
- are vulnerable to selective deficits,
- exploit combinatorial representations,
- and operate using unconscious rules.

If all four points of comparison are true, then there is indeed an analogy to be drawn between language and morality. I am skeptical about each point, but before making that case, I must enter a further point of concern. Notice capacities other than language, such as vision and motor control, are underwritten by mechanism that have each of the items on this list. Thus, the "language analogy" might equally be called the "vision analogy" or the "motor analogy." By drawing an analogy with *language* in particular, Hauser et al. are implying further points of comparison that may not hold up when all the evidence is in. Consider five potential disanalogies.

First, language has a critical period. This may be true of some perceptual systems too, but studies of, for example, vision restoration late in life suggest that language may be somewhat unusual in this respect. We don't know if there is a critical period for morality, but there are anecdotal reasons for doubt. Case studies of children who were raised in isolation, such as Genie or the wild boy of Aveyron, do not report profound moral deficits. Moreover, people can also acquire new moral values late in life, as happens with religious conversion, feminist consciousness raising, and a general trend from liberal to more conservative values that can be traced across the life span. Unlike language, learning a second morality does not seem fundamentally different than learning a first.

Second, language is usually learned in the absence of negative or corrective feedback. Is this true in the case of morality? Arguably not. Children are punished for making moral mistakes: They are reprimanded, socially ostracized, or even physically disciplined. Children also hear adults expressing negative moral attitudes toward numerous events. Of course, kids are never explicitly taught that it's worse to push people off of footbridges than to kill them by switching the course of a speeding steam engine, but these specific rules may be extrapolated from cases acquired through explicit instruction, as I will suggest below.

Third, according to leading theories of grammar (e.g., Chomsky's government and binding theory), linguistic rules are parameterized: They have a small set of possible settings that are triggered by experience. Hauser et al. explicitly endorse this view for morality, but it's not clear what the parameters are supposed to be. Consider opposing moral systems, such as liberalism and conservatism. It doesn't look like the conflicting values are simply different settings on the same basic formation rules. Where linguistic parameter settings correspond to structural variations in how to combine primitives, variation in moral values does not seem to be structural in this sense. Consider the moralized political debate on social welfare: Should governments give aid to those in need, or should the distribution of wealth be determined entirely by what individuals manage to attain in the free market? This question concerns a conflict between principles of equality and equity, rather than a conflict between alternative settings for the same basic principle. Or consider the debate about capital punishment; the two positions are dichotomous (pro or con), and they stem from different conceptions of punishment (retribution and deterrence). Similar considerations apply to debates about gender equality, gun control, and the moral permissibility of imperialism. These differences cannot be treated as parametric variations, except by trivializing that idea—that is, treating each contested policy as a parameter in its own right, which can be switched on or off. Haidt and Joseph (2004) argue that political conservatives have moral systems that contain categories of rules (e.g., rules about hierarchy, honor, and purity) that are not part of liberal morality, rather than mere variations on rules of the kind liberals share. Of course, there are some classes of rules that crop up in most moral systems, such as prohibitions against harm, but the variations in these rules are open-ended rather than parametric. Who may you harm? Depending on the culture, it can be an animal, a child, a criminal, a woman, a member of the out-group, a teenager going through a right of passage, a person who is aggressing against you, an elderly person, and so on. The range of exceptions is as varied as the range of possible social groups, and there is equal variation in the degree to which harm is tolerated (brief pain, enduring pain, mutilation, disfigurement, death). If moral rules were parameterized, there should be less variation.

Fourth, when two languages differ in grammar, there is no tendency to think one grammar is right and the other one wrong. We never start wars to snuff out people who place nouns before adjectives. In contrast, participants in moral conflicts assume that their values are the only acceptable values.

Fifth, language uses various levels of representation: phonology, syntax, and semantics, each of which may subdivide into further levels. There doesn't seem to be an analogous range of moral levels of representation.

Of course, Hauser et al. can concede these points of contrast and restrict their analogy to the four similarities laid out above. That would weaken the language analogy, but it wouldn't undermine it. However, each of the four alleged similarities is itself subject to doubt. Let's have a look.

Do moral rules operate unconsciously? To support this claim, Hauser et al. show that people are bad at justifying their moral judgments. However, this is evidence for unconscious rules only if we think those rules should take the form of justifying principles. Suppose that moral rules take the form of simple injunctions: It's horrible to intentionally kill someone; it's pretty bad to let someone die; we have special obligations to people close to us; incest is seriously wrong; stealing is wrong too, but not as bad as physically harming; and so on. These rules are certainly accessible to consciousness. They are usually much more accessible than the rules of language.

Are moral rules combinatorial? This is a bit more complicated. As Hauser et al. point out, we certainly need a combinatorial system for categorizing actions. But notice that action categorization is something we do quite independently of morality. Our capacity to tell whether something was done intentionally, for example, operates in nonmoral contexts, and individuals who lack moral sensitivity (such as psychopaths) are not impaired in recognizing actions or attributing intentions. Psychopaths can recognize that someone is intentionally causing pain to another person. Moral rules take these combinatorial, nonmoral representations of actions as inputs and then assign moral significance to them. The distinctively moral contribution to a rule such as that killing is wrong is not the representation of the action (killing), but the attitude of wrongness. It's an interesting question whether moral concepts such as "wrong" have a combinatorial structure; they may. However, by focusing on the combinatorial structure of action representations, Hauser et al. fail to show that representations specific to the moral domain are combinatorial.

Is morality vulnerable to selective deficits? I just mentioned psychopaths, who seem to have difficulty understanding moral rules. This can be inferred from the fact that psychopaths don't exhibit moral emotions, they engage in antisocial behavior, and they fail to distinguish between moral and conventional rules (Blair, 1995). However, psychopathy is not a selective deficit in morality. Psychopaths have other problems as well. They seem to suffer from a general flattening of affect, which also affects their ability to recognize emotional facial expressions and to recognize emotion intonation in speech (Blair, Mitchell, Richell, Kelly, Leonard, Newman, & Scott, 2002). Psychopaths may also suffer from a range of executive disorders. They tend to be disinhibited, and they make cognitive errors as a result (e.g., errors on maze tasks; Sutker, Moan, & Swanson, 1972). The moral deficit in psychopaths may result from their general emotion deficit. With diminished negative emotions, they don't experience empathy or remorse, and that leads them to be dangerously indifferent to the well-being others. If this analysis is right, then psychopathy is a domain-general problem with moral repercussions. I know of no case in the clinical literature in which morality is impaired without comorbid impairments of other kinds, most notably emotional impairments.

Is morality innate and universal? This question requires a bit more discussion.

Moral Judgments and Innateness

Elsewhere I have defended the claim that morality is not innate (Prinz, volume 1 of this collection, forthcoming-a, forthcoming-b). I will not rehearse all my arguments against nativism here, but I want to highlight some issues of contention that can help focus the debate.

To decide whether moral judgments are innate, we need a theory of what moral judgments are. Hauser et al. review several different accounts of moral judgment, or, at least, how moral judgments relate to reasoning and emotion in information processing. On one model, which I'll call "Reasons First," things proceed as follows: We perceive an event, then reason about it, then form a moral judgment, and that causes an emotion. On an Emotions First model, the sequence goes the other way around: We perceive an event, then we form an emotion that causes a moral judgment, and then we reason about it. On their view, neither of these is right. Instead, they favor an Analysis First model: We first perceive an event, and then analyze it in terms of component features such as INTENTION, AGENT, RECIPIENT, HARM; this leads to a moral judgment, which can then give rise to emotions and reasoning. I think Hauser et al. are absolutely right that moral judgment typically requires action analysis, but they are wrong to deny that other theories leave this part out. One cannot make a moral judgment about an event without first categorizing that event. Only a straw version of the Reasons First and Emotions First models would leave out some kind of action analysis. Still, there are two important differences between the Hauser et al. model and these others. First, for Hauser et al., action analysis is not done by domain-general mechanisms that are used for categorizing actions; rather, it is done by the moral faculty, which analyzes actions using features that may be proprietary to making moral assessments. Second, for Hauser et al., both emotion and reasoning occur after moral judgments are made. So their model is a genuine alternative to these others.

Of these three models, I am most sympathetic to Emotions First, but my view pushes that approach even farther. On the Emotion First model that Hauser et al. consider, emotions *cause* moral judgments. Jonathan Haidt (2001) favors such a view, but he never tells us exactly what moral judgments are. For example, he doesn't tell us what concept is expressed by the word "wrong." Hauser et al. don't tell us the answer to that question either. I think the concept expressed by "wrong" is constituted by a sentiment. A sentiment is the categorical basis of a disposition to experience different emotions. The sentiment that constitutes the concept wrong disposes its possessor to feel emotions of disapprobation. If I judge that stealing is wrong, that judgment is constituted by the fact that I have a negative sentiment toward stealing—a sentiment that disposes me to feel angry at those who steal and guilty if I myself steal. On any given occasion in which I judge that something is wrong, I will likely experience one of these emotions, depending on whether I am the author of the misdeed or someone else is. (And likewise for other moral concepts.) Thus, in place of the Emotions First model, on which emotions cause moral judgments, I favor an Emotion Constitution model, according to which emotions constitute moral judgments. More fully elaborated, I think moral judgment involves the following sequence: First, we perceive an event and categorize it; if that event type matches one toward which we have a stored sentimental attitude, the event triggers the relevant emotion in me (e.g., guilt if it's my action and anger if it's yours). The resulting mental state is a representation of perception of an action together with a sentiment toward that action, and this complex (action representation plus emotion) constitutes the judgment that the action is wrong. The moral judgment is not a further stage in processing following on the heels of the emotion but is constituted by the emotion together with the action representation. After that, I might reason, or put my judgment into words, or reassess the case and adjust my sentiments, and so on.

I can't defend this theory of moral judgment here. The evidence is both philosophical and empirical. The empirical evidence is the same as the evidence used to support the Emotions First model: Emotions seem to occur when people make moral judgments, emotion induction alters moral judgments, and emotion deprivation (as in the case of psychopathy) leads to deficits in moral judgment. However, the Emotion Constitution model has an advantage over the Emotion First model: it is more parsimonious. Rather than saying moral concepts are mental entities that are caused by moral emotions, I say they are constituted by moral emotions. This fits with the pretheoretical intuitions. A person who feels guilty or outraged about some event can be said, *in virtue of those emotions*, to have a moral attitude about that event. This suggests that emotions constitute moral attitudes. Hauser et al. will presumably disagree. For present purposes, I simply want to explore what implications this approach to moral judgment has for nativism.

If moral judgments are constituted by emotions, then the question of whether morality is innate boils down to the question: How do we come to have the emotions we have about things such as stealing, killing, cheating, and so on? A nativist will propose that we are innately disposed to have these emotions in virtue of domain-specific principles (which may be parameterized). Here's a nonnativist alternative: Suppose that a child who has no moral attitudes or moral faculty engages in a form of behavior that her caregivers dislike. The caregivers may get angry at her, and they may punish her in some way. For example, they might scold her or withdraw love and affection. Children rely on the affection of caregivers, and when punished, those all-important attachments are threatened. The emotion elicited by threats to attachment is sadness. Thus, a child who misbehaves will be led to feel bad. Over time, she will associate that feeling of sadness with the action itself; she will anticipate sadness when she considers acting that way again. Once the child associates sadness with that action, we can say she feels regret, remorse, or even guilt about it. These moral emotions can be defined as species of sadness directed at courses of action. The main difference between ordinary sadness and guilt is that guilt promotes reparative behavior. Such behaviors need not be innate. They are a natural coping strategy for dealing with cases where you have angered another person. The child who is punished will also come to have the same anger dispositions as those who punish her. Children are imitative learners. If a child sees her parents get angry about something that she does, she will feel sad about it, but she will also come to feel angry at other people when they engage in that behavior. She will copy her caregiver's reactions. This will also allow children to acquire moral rules concerning behaviors that they have never attempted, such as prohibitions against murder and rape.

When such behaviors are mentioned by caregivers, there is almost always an expression of emotion. When we mention things that we morally oppose, we do not conceal our emotions. Children imitatively pick up these attitudes. Notice that this story explains the transmission of moral rules by appeal to domain-general resources: Children must be able to categorize actions, they must experience sadness when punished, and they must be disposed to imitate anger and other negative emotions expressed by caregivers. If a child has these capacities, she will learn to moralize. She does not need an innate moral sense.

This developmental just-so story is intended as a possible explanation of how one could learn moral rules without having an innate moral faculty. If moral judgments are sentimental, then moral rules are learnable. However, it is one thing to say that moral rules are learnable and another thing to say they are learned. After all, we could be born with innate moral sentiments or sentimental dispositions. Just as we are biologically prepared to fear spiders, we might be biologically prepared to feel angry and guilty about various courses of action. We need a way of deciding whether moral rules are innate or acquired. One way to approach this question is development. Do children acquire certain moral rules more easily? Are others impossible to acquire? Are certain moral rules learned without punishment or other kinds of social interaction that condition emotional responses? I think these are all important open questions for research. I do think that there is extensive evidence for the claim that punishment plays a central role in moral education (Hoffman, 1983), and that leads me to think that moral nativism will be difficult to defend by appeal to a poverty-of-the-stimulus argument, as I mentioned above. I also think that the wide range of moral rules found cross-culturally suggests that children can acquire moral attitudes toward just about anything. However, both of these observations are anecdotal, and it is crucial at this stage to systematically search for innately prepared moral rules.

Trolley Cases

In suggesting that morality may not be innate, I don't want to deny that we are innately disposed to engage in some forms of behavior that are morally praiseworthy. Perhaps helping behavior, reciprocal altruism, and various forms of peacemaking are species typical in the hominid line. But there is a difference between behaving morally and making moral judgments. My hypothesis is that people are not innately equipped with a faculty of moral judgment. Moral concepts, such as right and wrong, are acquired from domain-general mechanisms. The fact that we are innately disposed to do some praiseworthy things is no more evidence for innateness of a moral sense than is the fact that we are disposed to take care of our young. Laudable behavior can exist without the capacity to praise it as such. One of the exciting features of Hauser et al.'s research program is that they are directly investigating moral judgments, rather than morally praiseworthy behavior. Their research on trolley cases can be interpreted as an argument for innate moral judgments.

Here's how I interpret that argument. There are moral judgments about moral dilemmas that are very widespread, homogeneous across different demographics, and demonstrable across cultures. These judgments do not seem to be learned through explicit instruction, and they do not seem to be based on consciously accessible reasoning processes. Together, this pattern is consistent with the conclusion that the judgments issue from an innate moral faculty. It's not a demonstrative argument, of course, but it's a reasonable argument to the best explanation—or at least it would be, if there weren't other equally good nonnativist explanations available.

Here's how a nonnativist might account for the data. On my view, there is a moral rule of the form "Intentionally taking another person's life is wrong." This rule consists of a domain-general action representation (intentionally taking a person's life) and a sentiment (which disposes one to feel angry or guilty if a person is killed by someone else or by oneself). The nonnativist needs to explain how such a rule could come about without being hardwired. That does not look like an insuperable challenge. Societies that allow killing, at least within the in-group, are not very stable. In very small-scale societies, built around extended kin groups, there may not be a need for any explicit rule against killing. We rarely have motives to kill our near and dear, especially if we feel a sense of attachment to them. However, as societies expand to include many nonrelatives, pressure arises to introduce killing norms, and that probably doesn't take much work. If you try and kill your neighbor, he and his loved ones will get pretty miffed. Other members of the community, afraid for their own security, may get upset too, and they will try punish you or banish you. Thus, aggression against others naturally elicits strong reactions, and those reactions condition the emotions of the aggressor. Knowing that aggression can lead to alienation and reprisal, you resist. When you think about aggressing, you feel anticipatory guilt, and, when you imagine others aggressing, you get angry about the harm they will do. Thus, we don't need innate strictures against killing, because the natural nonmoral emotions that are elicited by acts of aggression will instill the sentiments that constitute moral disapprobation. The rules against killing may, at first, be limited to the in-group, because aggression against more distant strangers may go unpunished by the local community. However, when communities become more transient, more diverse, or more dependent on others for trade, strictures against killing generalize, because harming distant strangers can be perceived as a potential threat to members of the local group.

So much for the genealogy of norms against killing. The nonnativist also needs to explain helping norms. Most of us think we should help people in need if we can do so at little personal cost. Is this an innate rule? Not necessarily. It could easily emerge through cultural evolution, because helping confers obvious advantages. If I join a group whose members will help me when I am in need, I will fare better than if I join a group of selfish people. However, helping always introduces free-rider problems. How can I be sure that people in my community will help me? Game theoretic models suggests that the best solution for coping with free riders is punishment. If I penalize people for being unhelpful, then they will be more likely to help in the future. Punishment leads people to feel guilty about free riding and angry at other free riders. Thus, when unhelpful individuals are punished, emotions are conditioned, and a moral attitude is born. In sum, I think the social and emotional consequences essentially guarantee that most societies will end up with moral rules about killing and helping. Nonviolent cooperation may be a precondition to stability in large populations. However, these rules about killing and rules about helping may differ from each other in one respect. Several factors are likely to make killing norms stronger than helping norms. First, in cultural evolution, prohibitions against killing are more vital than prohibitions against unhelpful behavior, because a group whose members kill each other will fare worse than a group of members who go out of their way to help each other. Second, helping also carries more personal cost than refraining from killing. Third, acts of aggression naturally elicit fear and anger, so it is easier to inculcate strong sentiments toward killing. Collectively, these factors essentially guarantee that sentiments toward killing will be stronger than sentiments pertaining to helpful and unhelpful behavior. If the Emotion Constitution model of moral judgment is right, this difference in sentimental intensity is tantamount to a difference in the strength of the respective moral rules.

I have been arguing that we can account for norms about helping and killing without supposing that they are innate. Once they are in place, they can guide behavior, and, on occasion, they will come into conflict. When this happens, there are two factors that will determine which rule will win. One factor is the extent to which actions in the event under consideration can be construed as instances of killing, on the one hand, or helping, on the other. Failure to conform to paradigm cases of either will diminish the likelihood that we will apply our rules about killing and helping. If some course of action is only a borderline case of killing, we may apply our killing rule with less force or confidence. For example, suppose someone causes a death as a side effect of some other action. This is not a paradigm case of killing. In terms of cultural evolution, groups have greater interest in condemning people who form direct intentions to kill than people who kill as a side effect, because the person who will kill intentionally poses a greater threat. Killing without the explicit intention to kill is a borderline case of the rule. The other factor is emotional intensity. For example, if we can help a huge number of people, our helping rule may become emotionally intense. In some cases, emotions may be affected by salience: If attention is drawn to an act of helping or killing, the corresponding rule will be primed more actively, and the emotions will be felt more strongly.

Now at last, we can turn to the trolley cases presented by Hauser et al. These cases are interesting because they pit helping norms against killing norms. We can now see whether the nonnativist, emotion-based theory can explain the results. In the first case, Frank is on top of a footbridge and can push a man into the path of a trolley, thereby saving five people further down on the track. Only 11% of subjects think it's okay to push the man. One explanation is that this is a paradigm case of killing, and the killing rule is, all else being equal, more emotionally intense than the helping rule. It's also a very salient case of killing, because subjects have to imagine Frank pushing someone, and the thought of physical violence attracts attention and increases emotion. In a second case, Denise can pull a lever that will guide a trolley down an alternate track, killing one person, rather than allowing it to kill the five people on the track it is currently on. Here 89% say it's permissible to pull the lever. The numbers change because this is not a paradigm or emotionally intense case of killing. The person who is killed is not physically assaulted, and Denise does not need to form the intention "I want to cause that guy's death."

The next case is a bit puzzling at first. Like Denise, Ned can pull a lever that will send a train on a different track, killing one rather than five. However, unlike the Denise case, in Ned's case the track is a loop that would reconnect with the original track and kill the five people were it not for the fact that the guy on the alternate track is heavy enough to stop the trolley in its tracks. In this situation, only 55% of subjects think Ned is permitted to pull the lever, killing one and saving five. Why would the minor addition of a looping track change permissibility judgments from the Denise case? The answer may be salience. When we imagine a person being used to stop a trolley in its path, the imagery is more violent and more emotionally intense. It is also a more paradigmatic case of killing, because Ned has to explicitly form the intention that the person be crushed; otherwise, the train wouldn't stop.

Hauser et al.'s final case is a slight variant on the Ned case. Here, Oscar can pull a lever that will send a train on a loop track that is obstructed by a large weight; the weight will prevent the train from rejoining the original track where it would kill five, but, unfortunately, there is a man standing in front of the weight who will be killed if the lever is pulled. Seventy-two percent of subjects think this is permissible. These permissibility ratings are higher than in the Ned case, because it is a less paradigmatic case of killing: The death in the Oscar case is an accidental by-product of sending the train into the weight. There is just one remaining question: Why are the permissibility ratings in the Oscar case slightly lower than in the Denise case? The answer may involve salience. In the vignettes, the solitary man in the Oscar case is introduced with a 20-word sentence, and the solitary man in the Denise case is introduced with 10 words. In the Oscar case, that man is crushed between the train and the weight, and in the Denise case, he is killed the same way that the five people on the other track would have been killed. Thus, the Oscar case draws extra attention to the victim. These explanations are sketchy and tentative. I offer them to illustrate a simple point. If one can tell a nonnativist and sentimentalist story about moral rules pertaining to killing and helping, there are resources to explain intuitions about trolley cases. Without ruling out this alternative account, Hauser et al.'s argument for nativism loses its force. At this stage, it's fair to say that both the nativist and the nonnativist accounts are in embryonic stages of development, and both should be considered live options as we investigate the origin of our capacity to make moral judgments.

The account that I have been proposing leads to some predictions. The first is consistent with Hauser et al.'s account, the second is slightly harder for them to accommodate, and the third is more naturally predicted by my account. First, I think that moral rules contain representations of actions, and these representations may take the form of prototypes or exemplars (e.g., a typical murder). I predict that the moral judgments will weaken as we move away from these prototypes. Hauser et al. may agree.

Second, I think that helping and harm norms are socially constructed to achieve stability within large groups, and, consequently, there may be subtle cultural differences as a function of cultural variables. For example, consequentialist thinking may increase for groups that are highly collectivist (hence more focused on what's best for the collective), for groups that are engaged in frequent warfare (hence more desensitized to killing), and for groups that are extremely peaceful (where norms against killing have never needed to be heavily enforced). In highly individualist societies, there is less overt focus on helping behavior, and consequentialist thinking may diminish. Likewise, in highly pluralistic societies, pluralism promotes the construction of strong rules against killing, because such rules are often needed to ensure peace in diverse groups. Hauser et al. report on some cross-cultural work, but there are two limitations of the data they report. First, as they note, their non-American subjects understand English and have access to computers, so they are probably similar to us. Second, Hauser et al. do not report the actual percentages for their cross-cultural samples; so, even if every tested culture tended to say Frank's behavior is less permissible than Denise's, the actual percentages who hold that dominant view may differ. It is important to note that Hauser et al. *can* allow variation in moral judgments. The language analogy predicts that principles will have parameters that get set differently in different contexts. My worry is that this is the wrong kind of variation. In language, switching parameters results in differences that are qualitative and arbitrary. The differences that I am imagining are quantitative and tailored to fit cultural variables. That is suggestive of learning rather than innateness.

Third, the Emotion Constitution model predicts that manipulation of emotions should influence judgments on trolley dilemmas. By making one of the two courses of action more salient, more violent, more personal, or more emotionally evocative in some other way, one should be able to alter the permissibility ratings. Psychopaths should not be influenced to the same degree by emotional manipulations. Such findings would count against Hauser et al.'s nonaffective theory of moral judgment, and they would also count against the view that moral judgments are driven by domain-specific (or at least encapsulated) mechanisms.

If these predictions pan out, they add support for the Emotion Constitution model. That model is compatible with nativism, but it also lends itself to a plausible nonnativist account of how we come to acquire moral rules. In this commentary, I haven't provided strong evidence for the nonnativist view or against the view favored by Hauser et al. Rather, my goal has been to suggest that, at this early stage of inquiry, several models remain compatible with the evidence. Hauser et al. would undoubtedly agree, and, in the coming years, we will need to find ways to test between these options. Let me sum up with a few questions for Hauser et al. that highlight places where their model and my alternative come apart. Why think that the analyses of action that precede moral judgment are carried out by a domain-specific moral faculty? Why think that emotions arise as consequences of moral judgments rather than causes or constituent parts? Why think that moral principles are innate rather than learned solutions to problems facing all cultures? And what is it about language, as opposed to any other faculty, that sheds light on our moral capacities? Hauser et al. have embarked on an important research program, and the linguistic analogy has been a valuable source of inspiration. My hunch is that it will eventually prove more productive to drop that analogy and adopt a model that places greater emphasis on learning. For now, we can make most progress by keeping both approaches on the table.

3.3 On Misreading the Linguistic Analogy: Response to Jesse Prinz and Ron Mallon

Marc D. Hauser, Liane Young, and Fiery Cushman

Oscar Wilde noted "Always forgive your enemies—nothing annoys them so much." Before we forgive our critics, however, we thank Prinz and Mallon for their thoughtful comments, and for taking the linguistic analogy as a serious proposal amid the current excitement at the interface between moral philosophy and moral psychology. What we forgive is their targeted comments on several issues that are either irrelevant to the linguistic analogy or premature given that we know so little about the nature of our moral psychology. Some of the confusion is undoubtedly due to our own exposition, and some to the rapid pace of theoretical and empirical developments that have emerged since we submitted the final draft and received the commentary.

We begin by clarifying the main goals of the linguistic analogy, including, most importantly, its unique set of empirically tractable questions and challenges. Our hope is that this response, guided by Prinz and Mallon's comments, serves as the next installment on a much larger project that, we can all agree, will yield interesting results irrespective of the strength of the analogy. The reason for this is simple: Until the questions that emerge from the analogy are taken seriously, and pitted against the alternatives, we will have only a weak understanding of the mature state of moral knowledge, how it is acquired within the individual and species, and the extent to which it relies upon domain-specific machinery. In this sense, we see the arguments generated in our target essay, and developed more fully elsewhere (Dwyer, 2004; Hauser, 2006; Mikhail, 2000, in press), as analogous to the minimalist program in linguistics (Chomsky, 1995, 2000): a set of fascinating questions with ample room for movement on theoretical, empirical, and methodological fronts.

For a novel research program to breathe, it is important that its claims be properly understood and that challenges be targeted at the proper level. Let us start then by highlighting two important points of agreement: Both

Prinz and Mallon (1) endorse our research program focused on the cognitive systems responsible for generating the basic representations that serve as input to the process of moral judgment and (2) support our position that these systems operate over the representations of actions, intentions, causes, and consequences. By supporting these two points, they at least implicitly support a third which, we submit, follows: Some moral principles are formulated over the core representations that enter into our moral judgments. The primary thrust of the linguistic analogy is to study these systems and bring them to the attention of philosophers and psychologists. It is in this spirit that we turn next to a more detailed look at the linguistic analogy, pinpointing what we perceive as its central assumptions and predictions, together with a body of relevant data. Along the way, we point out some of the challenges raised by Prinz and Mallon, including the nonnativist alternative based on emotions and real-world experiences, and emphasize the need to posit an innate, dedicated moral organ.

Both Prinz and Mallon attribute to us the view that the cognitive systems responsible for generating basic representations used in moral judgment are in fact specific to the domain of morality. This is not our view—indeed, it should have been clear that we hold the opposite position. Moral judgment depends on a wide range of representational inputs generated by cognitive systems adapted for and typically engaged in entirely different functions. Analogous cognitive mechanisms support linguistic competence without being specific to the domain of language. To clarify, take the rather simple phenomenon of speech perception. Although the last fifty years of research has largely assumed that we are endowed with a dedicated neural system for processing speech, neuroimaging studies with normal subjects, together with comparative and developmental studies of other animals and infants, suggest that much of speech perception may derive from very general and ancient auditory mechanisms. For example, a recent study by Vouloumanos, Hauser, and Werker (unpublished manuscript) showed that neonates less than 48 hours old evidenced no preference for human speech over rhesus monkey vocalizations. Similarly, comparative studies of human adults, infants, and cotton-top tamarin monkeys revealed no difference in the capacity to use transitional probabilities to segment a continuous stream of speech (Hauser, Newport, & Aslin, 2001). These results suggest that early stages of speech perception and segmentation are not mediated by processes that are specific to the domain of language.

Though we explicitly recognize the role of domain-general mechanisms, we are nonetheless committed to the existence of some cognitive mechanisms that are specific to the domain of morality. These we term the "moral faculty." These systems are not responsible for generating representations of actions, intentions, causes, and outcomes; rather, they are responsible for combining these representations in a productive fashion, ultimately generating a moral judgment. Our thesis is that the moral faculty applies general principles to specific examples, implementing an appropriate set of representations. We refer to these principles as an individual's "knowledge of morality" and, by analogy to language, posit that these principles are both unconsciously operative and inaccessible.

Mallon notes that we must distinguish between a theory that can adequately account for the pattern of people's moral judgments and a theory that is actually instantiated in people's heads. We fully agree, especially since this captures the parallel distinction in linguistics. To be precise, we must distinguish between a set of principles that are descriptively consistent with people's moral judgments and the principles that people in fact carry around in their heads, doing the work of adjudicating between moral rights and wrongs. As Mallon correctly intuits, we are aiming at principles in the head. But the first step, of course, is to determine the set of principles at the descriptive level.

Consider the following example as an illustration of how first to identify the set of descriptive principles that are operative in guiding moral judgment and then to investigate the extent to which these principles are expressed in the course of justification. In a recent paper (Cushman, Young, & Hauser, 2006) focused on the relationship between operative and expressed principles, we develop the argument that a three-pronged approach is necessary to assess whether particular principles mediate our moral judgments and whether these principles serve as the basis for our justifications. *Prong 1*: Develop a battery of paired dilemmas that isolate psychologically meaningful and morally relevant, principled distinctions. *Prong 2*: Determine whether these targeted principles guide subjects' moral judgments. *Prong 3*: Determine whether subjects invoke these principles when justifying their moral judgments. With this approach, we explored three principles:

Action principle Harm caused by action is morally worse than equivalent harm caused by omission.

Intention principle Harm intended as the means to a goal is morally worse than equivalent harm foreseen as the side effect of a goal.

Contact principle Harm involving physical contact with the victim is morally worse than equivalent harm involving no physical contact.

Based on a sample of approximately 300 subjects, largely from English-speaking, Western countries, analyses revealed support for the three targeted principles in 17 out of 18 paired dilemmas. That is, subjects judged harm caused by action as worse than omission, intended harm as worse than foreseen harm, and harm involving contact as worse than with no contact. When we turned to justifications, 80% of subjects recovered the key distinction for the action–omission cases, 60% for the contact–no contact cases, and only 30% for the intended–foreseen cases. This pattern suggests that the intended–foreseen distinction is operative but results in an intuitive judgment. The other principles are also operative but appear to be at least accessible to conscious awareness, to some extent.

Are the descriptive principles targeted in this study isomorphic to the domain-specific principles that constitute an individual's moral knowledge? At present we cannot say. We know that these principles are descriptively adequate to capture the observed pattern of subjects' moral judgments, but it remains a viable possibility that they exert their influence during the generation of the relevant representations that are external to and feed into moral judgment. Of course, a direct implication of the view that these principles are not specific to morality is that they influence judgments and behaviors outside the moral domain. Identifying nonmoral analogues of these descriptive principles—if indeed they exist—is an important area for future research.

Thinking about the moral faculty from this perspective leads us directly into Mallon's point that evolution may have created particular biases that set initial conditions on the valenced responses. Consider sex and the extent to which degrees of genetic relatedness matter. An agent INTENDS/DESIRES to ±SEXUAL INTERCOURSE with X_r, where X is some sexual partner and r is his or her degree of genetic relatedness to the agent. If we ask whether sexual intercourse is morally permissible with X, the answer depends on r. Evolution appears to have set up a bias, in the sense that r values between .125 and .5 are generally coded as –SEXUAL INTERCOURSE—that is, forbidden. This may be the default setting or bias, open to modification (to some extent) by the local culture. Again, the initial valence settings may have been established on the basis of their statistical effects (e.g., the probability that mating with parents and siblings will reduce fitness) and only later hooked into the emotions as reinforcing agents. In sum, we completely agree with Mallon that evolution has set us up with strong biases. These biases may enter into moral judgments, and at this point, we are agnostic on whether they figure into moral competence or performance.

To summarize thus far, we propose, and Prinz and Mallon agree, that a deeper understanding of the sources of our moral judgments requires further research into the nature of our representations of actions, intentions, causes, and consequences. The system involved in generating such representations is not specific to the moral domain. In parallel to language, however, individuals possess knowledge of morality that is comprised of domain-specific moral principles operating over these representations. Though we are only at the earliest stages of this research program, our empirical studies suggest a methodology to determine candidate principles for domain-specific moral knowledge. Whether the descriptive principles that capture patterns of moral judgment in fact characterize features of the moral faculty or features of the cognitive systems that feed into the moral faculty is presently unknown but, we submit, not unknowable.

What we wish to stress is that the linguistic analogy provides a substantive foundation for constructing testable hypotheses and collecting the relevant data. For example, as a theory, it demands a proper descriptive account of the mature state of moral knowledge. Until we understand our moral psychology at this descriptive level, including some subset of its principles, it is virtually impossible to make progress on other fronts, including, especially, issues of moral acquisition (explanatory adequacy in Chomsky's terms), domain-specificity, characteristic neural breakdown, and evolutionary origins. That is, we need to understand the nature of our mature subject's moral knowledge before we can ask how it evolved, develops, and is instantiated in neural tissue.

A thorough characterization of moral knowledge is particularly critical to adjudicate between nativist and empiricist claims. For example, Prinz states that he doubts there is a critical period for morality in the same way that there is for language or that learning a second moral system is like learning a second language. However, we are only able to determine that there is a critical period for language because we have a relatively deep understanding of the principles underlying the mature state of linguistic knowledge and, thus, can see what happens to the externalization of such knowledge in expressed language as a function of severe developmental isolation. Furthermore, we are only able to contrast native and second language acquisition because we understand *what* is being acquired. On the basis of a clearly characterized linguistic target, sometimes articulated in terms of principles and parameters, we can state that native language acquisition is fast, effortless, untutored, and relatively immune to negative evidence or correction. Second-language acquisition is slow, effortful, tutored, and vulnerable to negative evidence and correction. Surprisingly, no one has ever systematically compared the acquisition of native and second moral systems.

We end here with a discussion of the role of emotions in guiding our moral psychology and behavior. Though many of the questions that emerge from adopting the linguistic analogy have little or nothing to do with the emotions, our perspective puts into play a different way of looking at the role of emotions. To clarify, consider three ways in which emotions might enter into our moral judgments. First, an individual's emotional response to a particular circumstance might influence the representations he forms of the actions, intentions, causes, and consequences associated with that circumstance. Second, an individual's emotional response to a particular circumstance might, itself, be among the representational inputs to the moral faculty. This characterization implies the existence of a domain-specific moral principle such as "If it produces negative affect, it is morally wrong." Finally, it is possible that emotion has no influence upon moral judgment but is only a product of it.

Prinz proposes "the Emotion Constitution model, according to which emotions constitute moral judgments" (p. 162). This corresponds most closely to our second possibility, but with some potential differences. On the one hand is the rather trivial and uncontroversial claim that moral judgments are not synonymous with negative emotion. There are many instances in which we experience a negative emotion in the absence of moral disapproval (e.g., anger from stubbing a toe, disgust from seeing blood). On the other hand, Prinz appears to define moral judgment as a variety of negative emotion, such that the meaning of wrong is the feeling of wrongness. Stranding the problem here simply raises another: How does one determine wrongness in the first place? Prinz's solution is that "the concept expressed by 'wrong' is constituted by a sentiment . . . [which is] the categorical basis of a disposition to experience different emotions" (p. 162). In essence, Prinz is describing a mechanism that has at its disposal some categorical basis (principles) that presumably operates over some set of representations and that outputs emotions that we label as "right" or "wrong" (moral judgments). Ironically, then, what Prinz calls a "sentiment" is apparently identical to what we call the "moral faculty."

What the discussion above boils down to is that for both our perspective and the one Prinz favors, we are left with a binary choice: either emotion plays a role in moral judgments by shaping the representational input into the judgment mechanism (Prinz's sentiment, our moral faculty) or it is merely a consequence of that mechanism. This is an open and empirically tractable question that we have begun to explore. Let us illustrate with some recent patient data, acquired since our original submission, and only briefly discussed.

In collaboration with Michael Koenigs, Daniel Tranel, Ralph Adolphs, and Antonio Damasio (2007), we have explored the nature of moral judgments in six individuals with adult-onset bilateral damage to ventromedial prefrontal cortex (VMPC), an area noted for its critical role in linking emotion to decision making (Bechara, Damasio, Tranel, & Damasio, 1997). VMPC damage is associated with diminished autonomic and subjective response to passive viewing of emotionally charged pictures (Blair & Cipolotti, 2000; Damasio, Tranel, & Damasio, 1990), recall of emotional memories (Tranel, Bechara, Damasio, & Damasio, 1998), contemplation of risky choices (Bechara et al., 1997), and consideration of counterfactual outcomes (e.g., regret; Camille, Coricelli, Sallet, Pradat-Diehl, Duhamel, & Sirigu, 2004). We found that VMPC subjects were more likely to endorse personal or emotionally salient moral violations presented in hypothetical scenarios developed by Greene and colleagues (Greene, Nystrom, Engell, Darley, & Cohen, 2004; Greene, Sommerville, Nystrom, Darley, & Cohen, 2001) than were comparison groups, including normal subjects and brain damaged controls. More specifically, VMPC subjects were more likely to endorse violations that maximized aggregate welfare (e.g., throw a man off a bridge to save five others), resulting in heavily consequentialist judgments. There was no difference between VMPC subjects and comparison groups on either nonmoral or impersonal moral scenarios, showing that many aspects of their decision-making systems are intact and, significantly, that a variety of moral dilemmas can be evaluated in the absence of emotional input. A supplementary analysis of the personal moral scenarios showed that the difference between VMPC participants and comparison groups was restricted to the "difficult" as opposed to "easy" scenarios, as measured by uniformity of judgment within the comparison groups, showing further that even some judgments of emotional moral actions are intact. These analyses suggest that the effect of VMPC damage on moral judgment is both specific to its role in emotion processing and specific to scenarios for which there are no explicit adjudicating norms, that is, scenarios posing "difficult" moral dilemmas. In short, it appears that there may be an important role for emotion in shaping the representational inputs into the moral faculty under highly selective situations.

These data bear on Prinz and Mallon's concern about the notion of a moral organ. Their own view is that current work in neuropsychology does not support the idea of a dedicated, domain-specific moral organ and, if anything, supports the alternative, domain-general view. Although the existing data may be revealing with respect to moral cognition, they don't yet illuminate the linguistic analogy. Consider the existing work on psychopaths and patients with VMPC damage. Neither group shows selective damage in the moral sphere, which Mallon and Prinz take to be strong evidence against a dedicated moral faculty. However, for both theoretical and methodological reasons, we disagree. Many of the current tests of patients thought to have deficits in the moral sphere have not addressed the issues raised by the linguistic analogy. For example, the published work on prefrontal lobe patients is based on moral reasoning tasks, in particular, Kohlberg's battery of tests, which measure moral maturity based on the content of justifications rather than the nature of the judgments. Because of their emphasis on conscious reasoning, these measures aren't particularly revealing with respect to intuitive judgments, such as those tapped by the dilemmas featured in our Web-based experiments, recent functional neuroimaging studies (Greene et al., 2004), and the new collaborative work reviewed above on moral judgment in individuals with VMPC damage (Koenigs et al., 2007). Further, all of the tests administered to psychopaths that are morally relevant focus on the conventional–moral distinction, in which subjects distinguish between unambiguous conventional transgressions and unambiguous moral transgressions, but never between right and wrong. Furthermore, such tests have not included moral dilemmas where there are no obvious norms to adjudicate between different choices, where both choices lead to harm, for example.

At a theoretical level, we are open to the possibility that even the domain-specific components of the moral faculty may be divisible into discrete units. Indeed, some of the evidence we have presented in this discussion point to just such a multisystem model. Some moral principles appear to be available to conscious reflection, while others do not. Patients with emotional deficits show abnormal moral judgments on some dilemmas, but not others. We argue that such evidence, far from delivering a blow to the linguistic analogy, is in fact an encouraging sign of the type of refinements to models of moral judgment that have been occurring for decades in the research on language. The language faculty includes subsystems for phonology, morphology, semantics, and syntax, and even these subsystems can be further divided. For example, recent work on dysgraphic patients (Miceli, Capasso, Banvegnu, & Caramazza, 2004) has revealed individuals with deficits in the representation of vowels, others for consonants, highlighting the distinctive neural foundations for these linguistically specific distinctions.

Let us end as we started with a comment by Oscar Wilde: "I choose my friends for their good looks, my acquaintances for their good characters, and my enemies for their good intellects." We couldn't be more pleased to have such excellent "enemies" as Prinz and Mallon in an area of research that is fueled with excitement, passion, and hope for fundamental discoveries about the nature of moral thought and action. As we have tried to clarify, by drawing on analogy to language, we raise new questions about the nature of our moral psychology. In particular, we force empirically minded researchers interested in the nature of our moral judgments to tackle five distinctive questions: (1) What are the principles that characterize the mature state of moral competence? (2) How is this moral knowledge acquired? (3) How does our moral competence interface with those systems entailed in performance? (4) How did our moral competence evolve? (5) To what extent are the mechanisms underlying our moral competence domain-specific? We are nowhere near any resolution on any of these questions, and thus nowhere near a thumbs up or down for the linguistic analogy. With these questions in mind, however, and with answers forthcoming, we can be confident that our understanding of moral knowledge will rapidly deepen.

4 Social Intuitionists Answer Six Questions about Moral Psychology

Jonathan Haidt and Fredrik Bjorklund

Here are two of the biggest questions in moral psychology: (1) Where do moral beliefs and motivations come from? (2) How does moral judgment work? All other questions are easy, or at least easier, once you have clear answers to these two questions.

Here are our answers: (1) Moral beliefs and motivations come from a small set of intuitions that evolution has prepared the human mind to develop; these intuitions then enable and constrain the social construction of virtues and values, and (2) moral judgment is a product of quick and automatic intuitions that then give rise to slow, conscious moral reasoning. Our approach is therefore some kind of intuitionism. However, there is more: Moral reasoning done by an individual is usually devoted to finding reasons to support the individual's intuitions, but moral reasons passed between people have a causal force. Moral discussion is a kind of distributed reasoning, and moral claims and justifications have important effects on individuals and societies. We believe that moral judgment is best understood as a social process, not as a private act of cognition. We therefore call our model the social intuitionist model (SIM). Please don't forget the social part of the model, or you will think that we think that morality is just blind instinct, no smarter than lust. You will accuse us of denying any causal role for moral reasoning or for culture, and you will feel that our theory is a threat to human dignity, to the possibility of moral change, or to the notion that philosophers have any useful role to play in our moral lives (see the debate between Saltzstein & Kasachkoff, 2004, vs. Haidt, 2004). Unfortunately, if our theory is correct, once you get angry at us, we will no longer be able to persuade you with the many good reasons we are planning on giving you below. So please don't forget the social part.

In the pages that follow, we will try to answer six questions. We begin with the big two, for which our answer is the SIM. We follow up with Question 3: What is the evidence for the SIM? We then address three questions that we believe become answerable in a coherent and consistent way via the SIM. Question 4: What exactly are the moral intuitions? Question 5: How does morality develop? And Question 6: Why do people vary in their morality? Next we get cautious and consider some limitations of the model and some unanswered questions. And finally we throw caution to the wind and state what we think are some philosophical implications of this descriptive model, one of which is that neither normative ethics nor metaethics can be done behind a firewall. There can be little valid ethical inquiry that is not anchored in the facts of a particular species, so moral philosophers had best get a good grasp of the empirical facts of moral psychology.

Question 1: Where Do Moral Beliefs and Motivations Come From?

When a magician shows us an empty hat and then pulls a rabbit out of it, we all know there is a trick. Somehow or other, the rabbit had to be put into the hat. Infants and toddlers certainly seem like empty hats as far as morality is concerned, and then, somehow, by the time they are teenagers, they have morality. How is this trick accomplished? There are three main families of answers: empiricist, rationalist, and moral sense theories.

Most theories, lay and academic, have taken an empiricist approach. As with the magician's rabbit, it just seems obvious that morality must have come from outside in. People in many cultures have assumed that God is the magician, revealing moral laws to people by way of prophets and divinely appointed kings. People are supposed to learn the laws and then follow them. The idea that morality is internalized is made most concrete in the Old Testament, in which Adam and Eve literally ingest morality when they bite into the forbidden fruit. When God finds out they have eaten of the "tree of the knowledge of good and evil," he says "behold, the man has become like one of us, knowing good and evil" (Genesis, 3:22).

In the twentieth century, most people who didn't buy the God theory bought a related empiricist, blank-slate, or "empty-hat" model: Morality comes from society (which Durkheim said was God anyway), via the media and parents. For the behaviorists, morality was any set of responses that society happened to reward (Skinner, 1971). For Freud (1976/1900), morality comes from the father when a boy resolves his oedipal complex by internalizing the father's superego. Some modern parents fear that morality comes from the barrage of images and stories their children see on TV. However, true blank-slate theories began to die when Garcia and Koelling (1966) demonstrated that equipotentiality—the equal ability of any response to get hooked up to any stimulus—was simply not true. It is now universally accepted in psychology that some things are easy to learn (e.g., fearing snakes), while others (fearing flowers or hating fairness) are difficult or impossible. Nobody in psychology today admits to believing in the blank slate, although as Pinker (2002) has shown, in practice many psychologists stay as close to the blank slate as they can, often closer than the evidence allows.

The main alternative to empiricism has long been rationalism—the idea that reason plays a dominant role in our attempt to gain knowledge. Rationalists such as Descartes usually allow for the existence of innate ideas (such as the idea of God or perfection) and for the importance of sense perceptions, but they concentrate their attention on the processes of reasoning and inference by which people can extend their knowledge with certainty outwards from perceptions and innate ideas. Rationalist approaches to morality usually posit relatively little specific content—perhaps a few a priori concepts such as noncontradiction, or harm, or ought. The emphasis instead is on the act of construction, on the way that a child builds up her own moral understanding, and her ability to *justify* her judgments, as her developing mind with its all-purpose information processor becomes more and more powerful. Piaget, for example, allowed that children feel sympathy when they see others suffer. He then worked out the way the child gradually comes to understand and respect rules that help children get along, share, and thereby reduce suffering. "All morality consists in a system of rules, and the essence of all morality is to be sought for in the respect which the individual acquires for these rules" (Piaget, 1965/1932, p. 13).

Lawrence Kohlberg (1969, 1971) built on the foundation Piaget had laid to create the best known theory of moral development. In Kohlberg's theory, young children are egocentric and concrete; they think that right and wrong are determined by what gets rewarded and punished. However, as their cognitive abilities mature around the ages of 6 to 8 and they become able to "decenter," to look at situations through the eyes of others, they come to appreciate the value of rules and laws. As their abstract reasoning abilities mature around puberty, they become able to think about the reasons for having laws and about how to respond to laws that are unjust. Cognitive development, however, is just a prerequisite for moral development; it does not create moral progress automatically. For moral progress to occur, children need plenty of "role-taking opportunities," such as working out disputes during playground games or taking part in student government. Kohlberg's approach to moral development was inspiring to many people in the 1960s and 1970s, for it presented a picture of an active child, creating morality for herself, not just serving as a passive receptacle for social conditioning. Elliot Turiel (1983) continued this work, showing how children figure out that different kinds of rules and practices have different statuses. Moral rules, which are about harm, rights, and justice, have a different foundation and are much less revisable than social-conventional rules, which in turn are different from personal rules. As adults throw rule after rule at children, the children sort the rules into different cognitive bins (domains of social knowledge) and then figure out for themselves how and when to use—or reject—the different kinds of rules.

To give you a sense of a rationalist approach, we report the transcript of a remarkable interview that one of us (J. H.) overheard about the origin of moral rules. The interview was conducted in the bathroom of a McDonald's restaurant in northern Indiana. The person interviewed—the subject—was a Caucasian male roughly 30 years old. The interviewer was a Caucasian male approximately 4 years old. The interview began at adjacent urinals:

Interviewer: Dad, what would happen if I pooped in here [the urinal]?
Subject: It would be yucky. Go ahead and flush. Come on, let's go wash our hands.
[The pair then moved over to the sinks]
Interviewer: Dad, what would happen if I pooped in the sink?
Subject: The people who work here would get mad at you.
Interviewer: What would happen if I pooped in the sink at home?
Subject: I'd get mad at you.
Interviewer: What would happen if YOU pooped in the sink at home?
Subject: Mom would get mad at me.
Interviewer: Well, what would happen if we ALL pooped in the sink at home?
Subject: [pause . . .] I guess we'd all get in trouble.
Interviewer: [laughing] Yeah, we'd all get in trouble!
Subject: Come on, let's dry our hands. We have to go.

If we analyze this transcript from a Kohlbergian perspective, the subject appears to score at the lowest stage: Things seem to be wrong *because* they are punished. However, note the skill and persistence of the interviewer, who probes for a deeper answer by changing the transgression to remove a punishing agent. Yet even when everyone cooperates in the rule violation so that nobody can play the role of punisher, the subject still clings to a notion of cosmic or immanent justice in which, somehow, the whole family would "get in trouble."

Of course, we didn't really present this transcript to illustrate the depth and subtlety of Kohlberg's approach. (For such an overview, see Lapsley, 1996; Kurtines & Gewirtz, 1995.) We presented it to show a possible limitation, in that Kohlberg and Turiel paid relatively little attention to the emotions. In each of his statements, the father is trying to socialize his curious son by pointing to moral emotions. He tries to get his son to *feel* that pooping in urinals and sinks is wrong. Disgust and anger (and the other moral emotions) are watchdogs of the moral world (Haidt, 2003b; Rozin, Lowery, Imada, & Haidt, 1999), and we believe they play a very important role in moral development. This brings us to the third family of approaches: moral sense theories.

When God began to recede from scientific explanations in the sixteenth century, some philosophers began to wonder if God was really needed to explain morality either. In the seventeenth and eighteenth centuries, English and Scottish philosophers such as the third Earl of Shaftesbury, Frances Hutcheson, and Adam Smith surveyed human nature and declared that people are innately sociable and that they are both benevolent and selfish. However, it was David Hume (1975/1777) who worked out the details and implications of this approach most fully:

There has been a controversy started of late . . . concerning the general foundation of Morals; whether they be derived from Reason, or *from Sentiment*; whether we attain the knowledge of them by a chain of argument and induction, or *by an immediate feeling and finer internal sense*; whether, like all sound judgments of truth and falsehood, they should be the same to every rational intelligent being; or whether, *like the perception of beauty and deformity, they be founded entirely on the particular fabric and constitution of the human species.* (p. 2)

We added the italics above to show which side Hume was on. This passage is extraordinary for two reasons. First, it is a succinct answer to Question 1: Where do moral beliefs and motivations come from? They come from *sentiments* which give us an immediate feeling of right or wrong, and which are built into the fabric of human nature. Hume's answer to Question 1 is our answer too, and much of the rest of our essay is an elaboration of this statement using evidence and theories that Hume did not have available to him. However, this statement is also extraordinary as a statement about the controversy "started of late." Hume's statement is just as true in 2007 as it was in 1776. There really is a controversy started of late (in the 1980s), a controversy between rationalist approaches (based on Piaget and Kohlberg) and moral sense or intuitionist theories (e.g., Kagan, 1984; Frank, 1988; Haidt, 2001; Shweder & Haidt, 1993; J. Q. Wilson, 1993). We will not try to be fair and unbiased guides to this debate (indeed, our theory says you should not believe us if we tried to be). Instead, we will make the case for a moral sense approach to morality based on a small set of innately prepared, affectively valenced moral intuitions. We will contrast this approach to a rationalist approach, and we will refer the reader to other views when we discuss limitations of our approach. The contrast is not as stark as it seems: The SIM includes reasoning at several points, and rationalist approaches often assume some innate moral knowledge, but there is a big difference in emphasis. Rationalists say the real action is in reasoning; intuitionists say it's in quick intuitions, gut feelings, and moral emotions.

Question 2: How Does Moral Judgment Work?

Brains evaluate and react. They are clumps of neural tissue that integrate information from the external and internal environments to answer one fundamental question: approach or avoid? Even one-celled organisms must answer this question, but one of the big selective advantages of growing a brain was that it could answer the question better and then initiate a more finely tailored response.

The fundamental importance of the good–bad or approach–avoid dimension is one of the few strings that runs the entire length of modern psychology. It was present at the birth, when Wilhelm Wundt (1907, as quoted by Zajonc, 1980) formulated the doctrine of "affective primacy," which stated that the affective elements of experience (like–dislike, good–bad) reach consciousness so quickly and automatically that we can be aware of liking something before we know what it is. The behaviorists made approach and avoidance the operational definitions of reward and punishment, respectively. Osgood (1962) found that evaluation (good–bad) was the most basic dimension of all judgments. Zajonc (1980) argued that the human mind is composed of an ancient, automatic, and very fast affective system and a phylogenetically newer, slower, and motivationally weaker cognitive system. Modern social cognition research is largely about the disconnect between automatic processes, which are fast and effortless, and controlled processes, which are slow, conscious, and heavily dependent on verbal thinking (Bargh & Ferguson, 2000; Chaiken & Trope, 1999; Wegner & Bargh, 1998).

The conclusion at the end of this string is that the human mind is always evaluating, always judging everything it sees and hears along a "good–bad" dimension (see Kahneman, 1999). It doesn't matter whether we are looking at men's faces, lists of appetizers, or Turkish words; the brain has a kind of gauge (sometimes called a "like-ometer") that is constantly moving back and forth, and these movements, these quick judgments, influence whatever comes next. The most dramatic demonstration of the like-ometer in action is the recent finding that people are slightly more likely than chance to marry others whose first name shares its initial letter with their own, they are more likely to move to cities and states that resemble their names (Phil moves to Philadelphia; Louise to Louisiana), and they are more likely to choose careers that resemble their names (Dennis finds dentistry more appealing; Lawrence is drawn to law; Pelham, Mirenberg, & Jones, 2002). Quick flashes of pleasure, caused by similarity to the self, make some options "just feel right."

This perspective on the inescapably affective mind is the foundation of the SIM, presented in figure 4.1 (from Haidt, 2001). The model is composed of six links, or psychological processes, which describe the relationships among an initial intuition of good versus bad, a conscious moral judgment, and conscious moral reasoning. The first four links are the core of the model, intended to capture the great majority of judgments for most

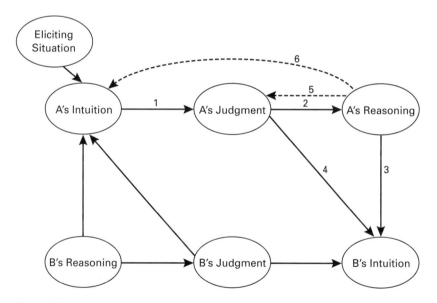

Figure 4.1

The social intuitionist model of moral judgment. The numbered links, drawn for Person A only, are (1) the intuitive judgment link, (2) the post hoc reasoning link, (3) the reasoned persuasion link, and (4) the social persuasion link. Two additional links are hypothesized to occur less frequently, (5) the reasoned judgment link and (6) the private reflection link. (Reprinted from Haidt, 2001)

people. Links 5 and 6 are hypothesized to occur rarely but should be of great interest to philosophers because they are used to solve dilemmas and because philosophers probably use these links far more than most people (Kuhn, 1991). The existence of each link as a psychological process is well supported by research, presented below. However, whether everyday moral judgment is best captured by this particular arrangement of processes is still controversial (Greene, volume 3 of this collection; Pizarro & Bloom, 2003), so the SIM should be considered a hypothesis for now, rather than an established fact. The model and a brief description of the six links are presented next.

Link 1: The Intuitive Judgment Link

The SIM is founded on the idea that moral judgment is a ubiquitous product of the ever-evaluating mind. Like aesthetic judgments, moral judgments are made quickly, effortlessly, and intuitively. We see an act of violence, or hear about an act of gratitude, and we experience an instant flash of evaluation, which may be as hard to explain as the affective response to a face or a painting. That's the intuition. "Moral intuition" is defined as the sudden appearance in consciousness, or at the fringe of consciousness, of an evaluative feeling (like–dislike, good–bad) about the character or actions of a person, without any conscious awareness of having gone through steps of search, weighing evidence, or inferring a conclusion (modified[1] from Haidt, 2001, p. 818). This is the "finer internal sense" that Hume talked about. In most cases this flash of feeling will lead directly to the conscious condemnation (or praise) of the person in question, often including verbal thoughts such as "What a bastard" or "Wow, I can't believe she's doing this for me!" This conscious experience of blame or praise, including a *belief* in the rightness or wrongness of the act, is the moral judgment. Link 1 is the tight connection between flashes of intuition and conscious moral judgments. However, this progression is not inevitable: Often a person has a flash of negative feeling, for example, toward stigmatized groups (easily demonstrated through implicit measurement techniques such as the Implicit Association Test; Greenwald, McGhee, & Schwartz, 1998), yet because of one's other values, one resists or blocks the normal tendency to progress from intuition to consciously endorsed judgment.

These flashes of intuition are not dumb; as with the superb mental software that runs visual perception, they often hide a great deal of sophisticated processing occurring behind the scenes. Daniel Kahneman, one of the leading researchers of decision making, puts it this way:

We become aware only of a single solution—this is a fundamental rule in perceptual processing. All other solutions that might have been considered by the system—and sometimes we know that alternative solutions have been considered and rejected—we do not become aware of. So consciousness is at the level of a choice that has already been made. (quoted in Jaffe, 2004, p. 26)

Even if moral judgments are made intuitively, however, we often feel a need to justify them with reasons, much more so than we do for our aesthetic judgments. What is the relationship between the reasons we give and the judgments we reach?

Link 2: The Post Hoc Reasoning Link

Studies of reasoning describe multiple steps, such as searching for relevant evidence, weighing evidence, coordinating evidence with theories, and reaching a decision (Kuhn, 1989; Nisbett & Ross, 1980). Some of these steps may be performed unconsciously, and any of the steps may be subject to biases and errors, but a key part of the definition of reasoning is that it has steps, at least two of which are performed consciously. Galotti (1989, p. 333), in her definition of everyday reasoning, specifically excludes "any one-step mental processes" such as sudden flashes of insight, gut reactions, and other forms of "momentary intuitive response." Building on Galotti (1989), moral reasoning can be defined as conscious mental activity that consists of transforming given information about people in order to reach a moral judgment (Haidt, 2001, p. 818). To say that moral reasoning is a conscious process means that the process is intentional, effortful, and controllable and that the reasoner is aware that it is going on (Bargh, 1994).

The SIM says that moral reasoning is an effortful process (as opposed to an automatic process), usually engaged in after a moral judgment is made, in which a person searches for arguments that will support an already-made judgment. This claim is consistent with Hume's famous claim that reason is "the slave of the passions, and can pretend to no other office than to serve and obey them" (Hume, 1969/1739, p. 462). Nisbett and Wilson (1977) demonstrated such post hoc reasoning for causal explanations. When people are tricked into doing a variety of things, they readily make up stories to explain their actions, stories that can often be shown to be false. People often know more than they can tell, but when asked to introspect on their own mental processes, people are quite happy to tell more than they can know, expertly crafting plausible-sounding explanations from a pool of cultural theories about why people generally do things (see Wilson, 2002, on the limits of introspection).

The most dramatic cases of post hoc confabulation come from Gazzaniga's studies of split-brain patients (described in Gazzaniga, 1985). When a patient performs an action caused by a stimulus presented to the right cerebral hemisphere (e.g., getting up and walking away), the left hemisphere, which controls language, does not say "Hey, I wonder why I'm doing this!" Rather, it makes up a reason, such as "I'm going to get a soda." Gazzaniga refers to the brain areas that provide a running post hoc commentary on our behavior as the "interpreter module." He says that our conscious verbal reasoning is in no way the command center of our actions; it is rather more like a press secretary, whose job is to offer convincing explanations for whatever the person happens to do. Subsequent research by Kuhn (1991), Kunda (1990), and Perkins, Farady, and Bushey (1991) has found that everyday reasoning is heavily marred by the biased search only for reasons that support one's already-favored hypothesis. People are extremely good at finding reasons for whatever they have done, are doing, or want to do in the future. In fact, this human tendency to search only for reasons and evidence on one side of a question is so strong and consistent in the research literature that it might be considered the chief obstacle to good thinking.

Link 3: The Reasoned Persuasion Link

The glaring one-sidedness of everyday human reasoning is hard to understand if you think that the goal of reasoning is to reach correct conclusions or to create accurate representations of the social world. However, many thinkers, particularly in evolutionary psychology, have argued that the driving force in the evolution of language was not the value of having an internal truth-discovering tool; it was the value of having a tool to help a person track the reputations of others, and to manipulate those others by enhancing one's own reputation (Dunbar, 1996). People are able to reuse this tool for new purposes, including scientific or philosophical inquiry, but the fundamentally social origins of speech and internal verbal thought affect our other uses of language.

Links 3 and 4 are the social part of the SIM. People love to talk about moral questions and violations, and one of the main topics of gossip is the moral and personal failings of other people (Dunbar, 1996; Hom & Haidt, in preparation). In gossip people work out shared understandings of right and wrong, they strengthen relationships, and they engage in subtle or not-so-subtle acts of social influence to bolster the reputations of themselves and their friends (Hom & Haidt, in preparation; Wright, 1994). Allan Gibbard (1990) is perhaps the philosopher who is most sensitive to the social nature of moral discourse. Gibbard took an evolutionary approach to this universal human activity and asked about the functions of moral talk. He concluded that people are designed to respond to what he called "normative governance," or a general tendency to orient their actions with respect to shared norms of behavior worked out within a community. However, Gibbard did not assume that people blindly follow whatever norms they find; rather, he worked out the ways in which people show a combination of firmness in sticking to the norms that they favor, plus persuadability in being responsive to good arguments produced by other people. People strive to reach consensus on normative issues within their "parish," that is, within the community they participate in. People who can do so can reap the benefits of coordination and cooperation. Moral discourse therefore serves an adaptive biological function, increasing the fitness of those who do it well.

Some evolutionary thinkers have taken this adaptive view to darker extremes. In an eerie survey of moral psychology, Robert Wright (1994) wrote:

The proposition here is that the human brain is a machine for winning arguments, a machine for convincing others that its owner is in the right—and thus a machine for convincing its owner of the same thing. The brain is like a good lawyer: given any set of interests to defend, it sets about convincing the world of their moral and logical worth, regardless of whether they in fact have any of either. Like a lawyer, the human brain wants victory, not truth. (p. 280)

This may offend you. You may feel the need to defend your brain's honor. But the claim here is not that human beings can *never* think rationally or that we are *never* open to new ideas. Lawyers can be very reasonable when they are off duty, and human minds can be too. The problem comes when we find ourselves firmly on one side of a question, either because we had an intuitive or emotional reaction to it or because we have interests at stake. It is in those situations, which include most acts of moral judgment, that conscious verbal moral reasoning does what it may have been designed to do: argue for one side.

It is important to note that "reasoned persuasion" does not necessarily mean persuasion via logical reasons. The reasons that people give to each other are best seen as attempts to trigger the right intuitions in others. For example, here is a quotation from an activist arguing against the practice, common in some cultures, of altering the genitalia of both boys and girls either at birth or during initiation rites at puberty: "This is a clear case of *child abuse*. It's a form of *reverse racism* not to *protect* these girls from *barbarous* practices that *rob* them for a lifetime of their *God-given right* to an *intact body"* (Burstyn, 1995). These two sentences contain seven arguments against altering female genitalia, each indicated in italics. But note that each argument is really an attempt to frame the issue so as to push an emotional button, triggering seven different flashes of intuition in the listener. Rhetoric is the art of pushing the ever-evaluating mind over to the side the speaker wants it to be on, and affective flashes do most of the pushing.

Link 4: The Social Persuasion Link

There are, however, means of persuasion that don't involve giving reasons of any kind. The most dramatic studies in social psychology are the classic studies showing just how easily the power of the situation can make people do and say extraordinary things. Some of these studies show obedience without persuasion (e.g., Milgram's, 1963, "shock" experiments); some show conformity without persuasion (e.g., Asch's, 1956, line-length experiments). But many show persuasion. Particularly when there is ambiguity about what is happening, people look to others to help them interpret what is going on and what they should think about what is going on. Sherif (1935) asked people to guess at how far a point of light was moving, back and forth. On this purely perceptual task, people were strongly influenced by their partner's ratings. Latane and Darley (1970) put people into ambiguous situations where action was probably—but not definitely—called for, and the presence of another person who was unresponsive influenced people's interpretations of and responses to potential emergencies. In study after classic study, people adjust their beliefs to fit with the beliefs of others, not just because they assume others have useful information but largely for the simple reason that they interact with these others, or even merely expect to interact (Darley & Berscheid, 1967). Recent findings on the "chameleon effect" show that people will automatically and unconsciously mimic the postures, mannerisms, and facial expressions of their interaction partners and that such mimicry leads the other person to like the mimicker more (Chartrand & Bargh, 1999).

Human beings are almost unique among mammals in being "ultrasocial"—that is, living in very large and highly cooperative groups of thousands of individuals, as bees and ants do (Richerson & Boyd, 1998). The only other ultrasocial mammals are the naked mole rats of East Africa, but they, like the bees and the ants, accomplish their ultrasociality by all being siblings and reaping the benefits of kin altruism. Only human beings cooperate widely and intensely with nonkin, and we do it in part through a set of social psychological adaptations that make us extremely sensitive to and influenceable by what other people think and feel. We have an intense need to belong and to fit in (Baumeister & Leary, 1995), and our moral judgments are strongly shaped by what others in our "parish" believe, even when they don't give us any reasons for their beliefs. Link 4, the social persuasion link, captures this automatic unconscious influence process.

These four links form the core of the SIM. The core of the model gives moral reasoning a causal role in moral judgment, but only when reasoning runs through other people. If moral reasoning is transforming information to reach a moral judgment, and if this process proceeds in steps such as searching for evidence and then weighing the evidence, then a pair of people discussing a moral issue meets the definition of reasoning. Reasoning, even good reasoning, can emerge from a dyad even when each member of the dyad is thinking intuitively and reasoning post hoc. As long as people are at least a little bit responsive to the reasons provided by their partners, there is the possibility that the pair will reach new and better conclusions than either could have on her own. People are very bad at questioning their own initial assumptions and judgments, but in moral discourse other people do this for us. To repeat: Moral judgment should be studied as a *social* process, and in a social context moral reasoning matters.

Can a person *ever* engage in open-minded, non–post hoc moral reasoning in private? Yes. The loop described by the first four links in the SIM is intended to capture the great majority of moral judgments made by the great majority of people. However, many people can point to times in their lives when they changed their minds on a moral issue just from mulling the matter over by themselves, or to dilemmas that were so well balanced that they had to reason things out. Two additional links are included to account for these cases, hypothesized to occur somewhat rarely outside of highly specialized subcultures such as that of philosophy, which provides years of training in unnatural modes of human thought.

Link 5: The Reasoned Judgment Link
People may at times reason their way to a judgment by sheer force of logic, overriding their initial intuition. In such cases reasoning truly is causal and cannot be said to be the "slave of the passions." However, such reasoning is hypothesized to be rare, occurring primarily in cases in which the initial intuition is weak and processing capacity is high. In cases where the reasoned judgment conflicts with a strong intuitive judgment, a person will have a "dual attitude" (Wilson, Lindsey, & Schooler, 2000) in which the reasoned judgment may be expressed verbally, yet the intuitive judgment

continues to exist under the surface, discoverable by implicit measures such as the Implicit Association Test (Greenwald, McGhee, & Schwartz, 1998).

Philosophers have long tried to derive coherent and consistent moral systems by reasoning out from first principles. However, when these reasoned moral systems violate people's other moral intuitions, the systems are usually rejected or resisted. For example, Peter Singer's (1979) approach to bioethical questions is consistent and humane in striving to minimize the suffering of sentient beings, but it leads to the logical conclusion that the life of a healthy chimpanzee deserves greater protection than that of an acephalic human infant who will never have consciousness. Singer's work is a paragon of reasoned judgment, but because his conclusions conflict with many people's inaccessible and unrevisable moral intuitions about the sanctity of human life, Singer is sometimes attacked by political activists and compared, absurdly, to the Nazis. (See also Derek Parfit's, 1984, "repugnant conclusion" that we should populate the world much more fully, and Kant's, 1969/1785, conclusion that one should not tell a lie to save the life of an innocent person.)

Link 6: The Private Reflection Link
In the course of thinking about a situation, a person may spontaneously activate a new intuition that contradicts the initial intuitive judgment. The most widely discussed method of triggering new intuitions is role taking (Selman, 1971). Simply by putting yourself into the shoes of another person you may instantly feel pain, sympathy, or other vicarious emotional responses. This is one of the principle pathways of moral reflection according to Piaget, Kohlberg, and other cognitive developmentalists. A person comes to see an issue or dilemma from more than one side and thereby experiences multiple competing intuitions. The final judgment may be determined either by going with the strongest intuition, or by using reasoning to weigh pros and cons or to apply a rule or principle (e.g., one might think "Honesty is the best policy"). This pathway amounts to having an inner dialogue with oneself (Tappan, 1997), obviating the need for a discourse partner. Is this really reasoning? As long as part of the process occurs in steps, in consciousness, it meets the definition given above for moral reasoning. However, all cases of moral reasoning probably involve a great deal of intuitive processing. William James described the interplay of reason and intuition in private deliberations as follows:

Reason, per se, can inhibit no impulses; the only thing that can neutralize an impulse is an impulse the other way. Reason may, however, make an inference which will excite the imagination so as to set loose the impulse the other way; and thus, though the animal richest in reason might also be the animal richest in instinctive impulses, too, he would never seem the fatal automaton which a merely instinctive animal would be. (quoted in Ridley, 2004, p. 39)

James suggests that what feels to us like reasoning is really a way of helping intuition (impulse, instinct) to do its job well: We consider various issues and entailments of a decision and, in the process, allow ourselves to feel our way to the best answer using a combination of conscious and unconscious, affective and "rational" processes. This view fits the findings of Damasio (1994) that reasoning, when stripped of affective input, becomes inept. Reasoning requires affective channeling mechanisms. The private reflection link describes this process, in which conflicts get worked out in a person's mind without the benefit of social interaction. It is a kind of reasoning (it involves at least two steps), yet it is not the kind of reasoning described by Kohlberg and the rationalists.

Private reflection is necessary whenever intuitions conflict, or in those rare cases where a person has no intuition at all (such as on some public policy issues where one simply does not know enough to have an opinion). Conflicting intuitions may be fairly common, particularly in moral judgment problems that are designed specifically to be dilemmas. Greene (volume 3 of this collection), for example, discusses the "crying baby" problem, in which if you do not smother your child, the child's cries will alert the enemy soldiers searching the house, which will lead in turn to the deaths of you, your child, and the other townspeople hiding in the basement. Gut feelings say "no, don't kill the child," yet as soon as one leans toward making the "no" response, one must deal with the consequence that the choice leads to death for many people, including the baby. Greene's fMRI data show that, in these difficult cases in particular, the dorsolateral prefrontal cortex is active, indicating "cooler" reasoning processes at work. But does a slow "yes" response indicate the victory of the sort of reasoning a philosopher would respect over dumb emotional processes? We think such cases are rather the paradigm of the sort of affective reasoning that James and Damasio described: There is indeed a conflict between potential responses, and additional areas of the brain become active to help resolve this conflict, but ultimately the person decides based on a feeling of rightness, rather than a deduction of some kind.

If you would like to feel these affective channeling mechanisms in action, just look at slavery in the American South from a slaveholder's point of view, look at Auschwitz from Hitler's point of view, or look at the 9/11 attacks from Bin Laden's point of view. There are at least a few supportive reasons on the "other" side in each case, but it will probably cause you pain to examine those reasons and weigh the pros and cons. It is as though our moral deliberations are structured by the sorts of invisible fences that keep suburban dogs from straying over property lines, giving them an electric shock each time they get too near a border. If you are able to rise to this challenge, if you are able to honestly examine the moral arguments in favor of slavery and genocide (along with the much stronger arguments against them), then you are likely to be either a psychopath or a philosopher. Philosophers are one of the only groups that have been found spontaneously to look for reasons on both sides of a question (Kuhn, 1991); they excel at examining ideas "dispassionately."

Question 3: Why Should You Believe Us?

Our most general claim is that the action in morality is in the intuitions, not in reasoning. Our more specific claim is that the SIM captures the interaction between intuition, judgment, and reasoning. What is the evidence for these claims? In this section we briefly summarize the findings from relevant empirical studies.

Moral Judgment Interviews

In the 1980s a debate arose between Elliot Turiel (1983), who said that the moral domain is universally limited to issues of harm, rights, and justice, and Richard Shweder (Shweder, Mahapatra, & Miller, 1987), who said that the moral domain is variable across cultures. Shweder et al. showed that in Orissa, India, the moral domain includes many issues related to food, clothing, sex roles, and other practices Turiel would label as "social conventions." However Turiel, Killen, and Helwig (1987) argued that most of Shweder's research vignettes contained harm, once you understand how Indians construed the violations.

Haidt, Koller, and Dias (1993) set out to resolve this debate by using a class of stories that had not previously been used: harmless taboo violations. They created a set of stories that would cause an immediate affective reaction in people but that upon reflection would be seen to be harmless and unrelated to issues of rights or justice. For example, a family eats its pet dog after the dog was killed by a car; a woman cuts up an old flag to create rags with which to clean her toilet; a man uses a chicken carcass for masturbation, and afterwards he cooks and eats the carcass. These stories were presented to 12 groups of subjects (360 people in all) during interviews modeled after Turiel (1983). Half of the subjects were adults, and half were children (ages 10–12; they did not receive the chicken story); half were of high social class, and half of low; and they were residents of three cities: Recife, Brazil; Porto Alegre, Brazil; and Philadelphia, U.S.A. The basic finding was that the high social class adult groups, which were composed of college students, conformed well to Turiel's predictions. They treated harmless taboo violations as strange and perhaps disgusting, but not morally wrong. They said, for example, that such behaviors would not be wrong in another culture where they were widely practiced. The other groups, however, showed the broader moral domain that Shweder had described. They overwhelmingly said that these actions were wrong and universally wrong, even as they explicitly stated that nobody was harmed. They treated these acts as moral violations, and they justified their condemnation not by pointing to victims but by pointing to disgust or disrespect, or else by pointing simply to norms and rules ("You just don't have sex with a chicken!"). College students largely limited themselves to a mode of ethical discourse that Shweder, Much, Mahapatra, and Park (1997) later called the "ethics of automony" (judgments relating to issues of harm, rights, and justice), while the other groups showed a much broader moral domain including the "ethics of community" (issues of respect, duty, hierarchy, and group obligation) and to a lesser extent the "ethics of divinity" (issues of purity, sanctity, and recognition of divinity in each person).

While conducting these interviews, however, Haidt noticed an interesting phenomenon: Most subjects gave their initial evaluations almost instantly, but then some struggled to find a supporting reason. For example, a subject might say, hesitantly, "It's wrong to eat your dog because . . . you might get sick." When the interviewer pointed out that the dog meat was fully cooked and so posed no more risk of illness than any other meat, subjects rarely changed their minds. Rather, they searched harder for additional reasons, sometimes laughing and confessing that they could not explain themselves. Haidt and Hersh (2001) noticed the same thing in a replication study that asked political liberals and conservatives to judge a series of harmless sexual behaviors, including various forms of masturbation, homosexuality, and consensual incest. Haidt and Hersh called this state of puzzled inability to justify a moral conviction "moral dumbfounding."

We (Haidt, Bjorklund, & Murphy, 2000) brought moral dumbfounding into the lab to examine it more closely. In Study 1 we gave subjects five tasks: Kohlberg's Heinz dilemma (should Heinz steal a drug to save his wife's life?), which is known to elicit moral reasoning; two harmless taboo violations (consensual adult sibling incest and harmless cannibalism of an unclaimed corpse in a pathology lab); and two behavioral tasks that were designed to elicit strong gut feelings: a request to sip a glass of apple juice into which a sterilized dead cockroach had just been dipped and a request to sign a piece of paper that purported to sell the subject's soul to the experimenter for $2 (the form explicitly said that it was not a binding contract, and the subject was told she could rip up the form immediately after signing it). The experimenter presented each task and then played devil's advocate, arguing against anything the subject said. The key question was whether subjects would behave like (idealized) scientists, looking for the truth and using reasoning to reach their judgments, or whether they would behave like lawyers, committed from the start to one side and then searching only for evidence to support that side, as the SIM suggests.

Results showed that on the Heinz dilemma people did seem to use some reasoning, and they were somewhat responsive to the counterarguments given by the experimenter. (Remember the social side of the SIM: People are responsive to reasoning from another person when they do not have a strong countervailing intuition.) However, responses to the two harmless taboo violations were more similar to responses on the two behavioral tasks: Very quick judgment was followed by a search for supporting reasons only; when these reasons were stripped away by the experimenter, few subjects changed their minds, even though many confessed that they could not explain the reasons for their decisions. In Study 2 we repeated the basic design while exposing half of the subjects to a cognitive load—an attention task that took up some of their conscious mental work space—and found that this load increased the level of moral dumbfounding without changing subjects' judgments or their level of persuadability.

Manipulating Intuitions

In other studies we have directly manipulated the strength of moral intuitions without changing the facts being judged, to test the prediction that Link 1 (intuitive judgment) directly causes, or at least influences, moral judgments. Wheatley and Haidt (2005) hypnotized one group of subjects to feel a flash of disgust whenever they read the word "take"; another group was hypnotized to feel disgust at the word "often." Subjects then read six moral judgment stories, each of which included either the word "take" or the word "often." Only highly hypnotizable subjects who were amnesic for the posthypnotic suggestion were used. In two studies, the flash of disgust that subjects felt while reading three of their six stories made their moral judgments more severe. In Study 2, a seventh story was included in which there was no violation whatsoever, to test the limits of the phenomenon: "Dan is a student council representative at his school. This semester he is in charge of scheduling discussions about academic issues. He [tries to take] <often picks> topics that appeal to both professors and students in order to stimulate discussion." We predicted that with no violation of any kind, subjects would be forced to override their feelings of disgust, and most did. However, one third of all subjects who encountered their disgust word in the story still rated Dan's actions as somewhat morally wrong, and several made up post hoc confabulations reminiscent of Gazzaniga's findings. One subject justified his condemnation of Dan by writing "it just seems like he's up to something." Another wrote that Dan seemed like a "popularity seeking snob." These cases provide vivid examples of reason playing its role as slave to the passions.

In another experiment, Bjorklund and Haidt (in preparation) asked subjects to make moral judgments of norm violation scenarios that involved disgusting features. In order to manipulate the strength of the intuitive judgment made in Link 1, one group of subjects got a version of the scenarios where the disgusting features were vividly described, and another group got a version where they were not vividly described. Subjects who got scenarios with vividly described disgust made stronger moral judgments, even though the disgusting features were morally irrelevant.

Another way of inducing irrelevant disgust is to alter the environment in which people make moral judgments. Schnall, Haidt, Clore, and Jordan (2007) asked subjects to make moral judgments while seated either at a clean and neat desk or at a dirty desk with fast food wrappers and dirty tissues strewn about. The dirty desk was assumed to induce low-level feelings of disgust and avoidance motivations. Results showed that the dirty desk did make moral judgments more severe, but only for those subjects who had scored in the upper half of a scale measuring "private body consciousness," which means the general tendency to be aware of bodily states and feelings such as hunger and discomfort. For people who habitually listen to their bodies, extraneous feelings of disgust did affect moral judgment.

Neuroscientific Evidence

A great deal of neuroscience research supports the idea that flashes of affect are essential for moral judgment (see Greene & Haidt, 2002, for a review). Damasio's (1994) work on "acquired sociopathy" shows that damage to the ventromedial prefrontal cortex, an area that integrates affective responses with higher cognition, renders a person morally incompetent, particularly if the damage occurs in childhood (Anderson et al., 1999), suggesting that emotions are necessary for moral learning. When emotion is removed from decision making, people do not become hyperlogical and hyperethical; they become unable to feel the rightness and wrongness of simple decisions and judgments. Joshua Greene and his colleagues at Princeton have studied the brains of healthy people making moral judgments while in an fMRI scanner (Greene, Sommerville, Nystrom, Darley, & Cohen, 2001). They found that the distinctions people make between various classes of moral dilemmas are predicted by whether or not certain brain areas involved in emotional responding are more active. When considering dilemmas with direct physical harm (e.g., pushing one man off of a footbridge to stop a trolley from killing five men), most people have a quick flash of activity in the medial prefrontal cortex and then say that it is not permissible to do this. They make deontological judgments, which they justify with references to rights or to moral absolutes. When they think about cases where the harm is less direct but the outcome is the same (e.g., throwing a switch to shift the train from killing five to killing one), they have no such flash, and most people choose the utilitarian response.

Greene (volume 3 of this collection) makes the provocative argument that deontological judgments are really just gut feelings dressed up with fancy sounding justifications. He suggests that such judgments conform closely to the mechanisms described by the SIM. However, in cases where people override their gut feelings and choose the utilitarian response, Greene believes that the SIM may fail to capture the causal role of moral reasoning. Greene bases this suggestion on evidence of "cognitive conflict" in moral judgment (Greene, Nystrom, Engell, Darley, & Cohen, 2004). For example, people take longer to respond to difficult personal moral dilemmas, such as the crying baby story (described above), than to other types of stories, and when people do choose the utilitarian response to difficult dilemmas, they show a late surge of activity in the dorsolateral prefrontal cortex (suggesting "cognitive" activity), as well as increased activity in the anterior cingulate cortex (indicating a response conflict).

We see no contradiction between Greene's results and the SIM. While some critics erroneously reduce the SIM to the claim that moral reasoning doesn't happen or doesn't matter (see Saltzstein & Kasachkoff, 2004), we point out that the SIM says that reasoning happens between people quite often (link 3), and within individuals occasionally (links 5 and 6). Furthermore, the SIM is not about "cognition" and "emotion"; it is about two kinds of cognition: fast intuition (which is sometimes but not always a part of an emotional response) and slow reasoning. Intuitions often conflict or lead to obviously undesirable outcomes (such as the death of everyone if the crying baby is not smothered), and when they do, the conflict must get resolved somehow. This resolution requires time and the involvement of brain areas that handle response conflict (such as the anterior cingulate cortex). The private reflection link of the SIM is intended to handle exactly these sorts of cases in which a person considers responses beyond the initial intuitive response. According to the definition of reasoning given in the SIM, private reflection is a kind of reasoning—it involves at least two steps carried out in consciousness. However, this reasoning is not, we believe, the sort of logical and dispassionate reasoning that philosophers would respect; it is more like the kind of weighing of alternatives in which feelings play a crucial role (as described by James and Damasio, above). Hauser, Young, and Cushman's finding (this volume) that people usually cannot give a good justification for their responses to certain kinds of trolley problems is consistent with our claim that the process of resolving moral dilemmas and the process of formulating justifications to give to other people are separate processes, even when both can be considered kinds of reasoning.

Question 4: What Exactly Are the Intuitions?

If we want to rebuild moral psychology on an intuitionist foundation, we had better have a lot more to say about what intuitions are and about why people have the particular intuitions they have. We look to evolution to answer these questions. One could perfectly well be an empiricist intuitionist—one might believe that children simply develop intuitions or reactions for which they are reinforced; or one might believe that children have a general tendency to take on whatever values they see in their parents, their peers, or the media. Of course, social influence is important, and the social links of the SIM are intended to capture such processes. However, we see two strong arguments against a fully empiricist approach in which intuitions are entirely learned. The first, pointed out by Tooby, Cosmides, and Barrett (2005), is that children routinely resist parental efforts to get them to care about, value, or desire things. It is just not very easy to shape children, unless one is going with the flow of what they already like. It takes little or no work to get 8-year-old children to prefer candy to broccoli, to prefer being liked by their peers to being approved of by adults, or to prefer hitting back to loving their enemies. Socializing the reverse preferences would be difficult or impossible. The resistance of children to arbitrary or unusual socialization has been the downfall of many utopian efforts. Even if a charismatic leader can recruit a group of unusual adults able to believe in universal love while opposing all forms of hatred and jealousy, nobody has ever been able to raise the next generation of children to take on such unnatural beliefs.

The second argument is that despite the obvious cultural variability of norms and practices, there is a small set of moral intuitions that is easily found in all societies, and even across species. An analogy to cuisine might be useful: Human cuisines are cultural products, and each is unique—a set of main ingredients and plant-based flavorings that mark food as familiar and safe (Rozin, 1982). However, cuisines are built on top of an evolved sensory system including just five kinds of taste receptors on the tongue, plus a more complex olfactory system. The five kinds of taste buds have obvious adaptive benefits: Sweetness indicates fruit and safety; bitterness indicates toxins and danger; glutamate indicates meat. The structure of the human tongue, nose, and brain place constraints on cuisines while leaving plenty of room for creativity. One could even say that the constraints make creativity possible, including the ability to evaluate one meal as better than another.

Might there be a small set of moral intuitions underlying the enormous diversity of moral "cuisines?" Just such an analogy was made by the Chinese philosopher Mencius 2,400 years ago:

There is a common taste for flavor in our mouths, a common sense for sound in our ears, and a common sense of beauty in our eyes. Can it be that in our minds alone we are not alike? What is it that we have in common in our minds? It is the sense of principle and righteousness. The sage is the first to possess what is common in our minds. Therefore moral principles please our minds as beef and mutton and pork please our mouths. (Mencius, quoted in Chan, 1963, p. 56)

Elsewhere Mencius specifies that the roots or common principles of human morality are to be found in moral feelings such as commiseration, shame, respect, and reverence (Chan, 1963, p. 54).

Haidt and Joseph (2004) set out to list these common principles a bit more systematically, reviewing five works that were rich in detail about moral systems. Two of the works were written to capture what is universal about human cultures: Donald Brown's (1991) catalogue *Human Universals* and Alan Fiske's (1992) grand integrative theory of the four models of social relations. Two of the works were designed primarily to explain differences across cultures in morality: Schwartz and Bilsky's (1990) widely used theory of 15 values, and Richard Shweder's theory of the "big 3" moral ethics—autonomy, community, and divinity (Shweder et al., 1997). The fifth work was Frans de Waal's (1996) survey of the roots or precursors of morality in other animals, primarily chimpanzees, *Good Natured*. We (Haidt

& Joseph) simply listed all the cases where some aspect of the social world was said to trigger approval or disapproval; that is, we tried to list all the things that human beings and chimpanzees seem to value or react to in the behavior of others. We then tried to group the elements that were similar into a smaller number of categories, and finally we counted up the number of works (out of five) that each element appeared in. The winners, showing up clearly in all five works, were harm/care (a sensitivity to or dislike of signs of pain and suffering in others, particularly in the young and vulnerable), fairness/reciprocity (a set of emotional responses related to playing tit-for-tat, such as negative responses to those who fail to repay favors), and authority/respect (a set of concerns about navigating status hierarchies, e.g., anger toward those who fail to display proper signs of deference and respect). We believe these three issues are excellent candidates for being the "taste buds" of the moral domain. In fact, Mencius specifically included emotions related to harm (commiseration) and authority (respect, and reverence) as human universals.

We tried to see how much moral work these three sets of intuitions could do and found that we could explain most but not nearly all of the moral virtues and concerns that are common in the world's cultures. There were two additional sets of concerns that were widespread but that had only been mentioned in three or four of the five works: concerns about purity/sanctity (related to the emotion of disgust, necessary for explaining why so many moral rules relate to food, sex, menstruation, and the handling of corpses) and concerns about boundaries between in-group and out-group.[2] Liberal moral theorists may dismiss these concerns as matters of social convention (for purity practices) or as matters of prejudice and exclusion (for in-group concerns), but we believe that many or most cultures see matters of purity, chastity, in-group loyalty, and patriotism as legitimate parts of their moral domain (see Haidt & Graham, 2007; Haidt, 2007).

We (Haidt, Joseph, & Bjorklund) believe these five sets of intuitions should be seen as the foundations of intuitive ethics. For each one, a clear evolutionary story can be told and has been told many times. We hope nobody will find it controversial to suppose that evolution has prepared the human mind to easily develop a sensitivity to issues related to harm/care, fairness/reciprocity, in-group/loyalty, and authority/respect. The only set of intuitions with no clear precursor in other animals is purity/sanctity. However, concerns about purity and pollution require the emotion of disgust and its cognitive component of contamination sensitivity, which only human beings older than the age of 7 have fully mastered (Rozin, Fallon, & Augustoni-Ziskind, 1985). We think it is quite sensible to suppose that most of the foundations of human morality are many millions of years old, but that some aspects of human morality have no precursors in other animals.

Now that we have identified five promising areas or clusters of intuition, how exactly are they encoded in the human mind? There are a great many ways to think about innateness. At the mildest extreme is a general notion of "preparedness," the claim that animals are prepared (by evolution) to learn some associations more easily than others (Seligman, 1971). For example, rats can more easily learn to associate nausea with a new taste than with a new visual stimulus (Garcia & Koelling, 1966), and monkeys (and humans) can very quickly acquire a fear of snakes from watching another monkey (or human) reacting with fear to a snake, but it is very hard to acquire a fear of flowers by such social learning (Mineka & Cook, 1988). The existence of preparedness as a product of evolution is uncontroversial in psychology. Everyone accepts at least that much writing on the slate at birth. Thus, the mildest version of our theory is that the human mind has been shaped by evolution so that children can very easily be taught or made to care about harm, fairness, in-groups, authority, and purity; however, children have no innate moral knowledge—just a preparedness to acquire certain kinds of moral knowledge and a resistance to acquiring other kinds (e.g., that all people should be loved and valued equally).

At the other extreme is the idea of the massively modular mind, championed by evolutionary psychologists such as Pinker (1997) and Cosmides and Tooby (1994). On this view, the mind is like a Swiss army knife with many tools, each one an adaptation to the long-enduring structure of the world. If every generation of human beings faced the threat of disease from bacteria and parasites that spread by physical touch, minds that had a contamination-sensitivity module built in (i.e., feel disgust toward feces and rotting meat and also toward anything that *touches* feces or rotting meat) were more likely to run bodies that went on to leave surviving offspring than minds that had to learn everything from scratch using only domain-general learning processes. As Pinker (2002) writes, with characteristic flair: "The sweetness of fruit, the scariness of heights, and the vileness of carrion are fancies of a nervous system that evolved to react to those objects in adaptive ways" (p. 192).

Modularity is controversial in cognitive science. Most psychologists accept Fodor's (1983) claim that many aspects of perceptual and linguistic processing are the output of modules, which are informationally encapsulated special purpose processing mechanisms. Informational encapsulation means that the module works on its own proprietary inputs. Knowledge contained elsewhere in the mind will not affect the output of the module. For example, knowing that two lines are the same length in the Müller–Lyer illusion does not alter the percept that one line is longer. However, Fodor himself rejects the idea that much of higher cognition can be understood as the output of modules. On the other hand, Dan Sperber (1994) has pointed out that modules for higher cognition do not need to be as tightly modularized as Fodor's perceptual modules. All we need to say is that higher cognitive processes are modularized "to some interesting degree," that is, higher cognition is not one big domain-general cognitive work space. There can be many bits of mental processing that are to some degree module-like. For example, quick, strong, and automatic rejection of anything that seems like incest suggests the output of an anti-incest module, or modular intuition. (See the work of Debra Lieberman, volume 1 of this collection.) Even when the experimenter explains that the brother and sister used two forms of birth control and that the sister was adopted into the family at age 14, many people still say they have a gut feeling that it is wrong for the siblings to have consensual sex. The output of the module is not fully revisable by other knowledge, even though some people overrule their intuition and say, uneasily, that consensual adult sibling incest is OK.

We do not know what point on the continuum from simple preparedness to hard and discrete modularity is right, so we tentatively adopt Sperber's intermediate position that there are a great many bits of mental processing that are modular "to some interesting degree." (We see no reason to privilege the blank-slate side of the continuum as the default or "conservative" side.) Each of our five foundations can be thought of either as a module itself or, more likely, as a "learning module"—a module that generates a multiplicity of specific modules during development within a cultural context (e.g., a child learns to recognize in an automatic and module-like way specific kinds of unfairness, or of disrespect; see Haidt & Joseph, in press, and Sperber, 2005, for details). We particularly like Sperber's point that "because cognitive modules are each the result of a different phylogenetic history, there is no reason to expect them all to be built on the same general pattern and elegantly interconnected" (Sperber, 1994, p. 46). We are card-carrying antiparsimonists. We believe that psychological theories should have the *optimum* amount of complexity, not the *minimum* that a theorist can get away with. The history of moral psychology is full of failed attempts to derive all of morality from a single source (e.g., noncontradiction, harm, empathy, or internalization). We think it makes more sense to look at morality as a set of multiple concerns about social life, each one with its own evolutionary history and psychological mechanism. There is not likely to be one unified moral module, or moral organ. (However, see Hauser et al., this volume, for the claim that there is.)

Question 5: How Does Morality Develop?

Once you see morality as grounded in a set of innate moral modules (Sperber modules, not Fodor modules), the next step is to explain how children develop the morality that is particular to their culture and the morality that is particular to themselves. The first of two main tools we need for an intuitionist theory of development is "assisted externalization" (see Fiske, 1991). The basic idea is that morality, like sexuality or language, is better described as emerging from the child (externalized) on a particular developmental schedule rather than being placed into the child from outside (internalized) on society's schedule. However, as with linguistic and sexual development, morality requires guidance and examples from the local culture to externalize and configure itself properly, and children actively seek out role models to guide their development. Each of the five foundations matures and gets built upon at a different point in development—for example, 2-year-olds are sensitive to suffering in people and animals (Zahn-Waxler & Radke-Yarrow, 1982), but they show few concerns for fairness and equal division of resources until some time after the third birthday (Haidt, Lobue, Chiong, Nishida, & DeLoache, 2007), and they do not have a full understanding of purity and contagion until around the age of 7 or 8 (Rozin, Fallon, & Augustoni-Ziskind, 1986). When their minds are ready, children will begin showing concerns about and emotional reactions to various patterns in their social world (e.g., suffering, injustice, moral contamination). These reactions will likely be crude and inappropriate at first, until they learn the application rules for their culture (e.g., share evenly with siblings, but not parents) and until they develop the wisdom and expertise to know how to resolve conflicts among intuitions.

Take, for example, the game of cooties. All over the United States children play a game from roughly ages 8 to 10 in which some children are said to have "cooties," which are a kind of invisible social germ. Cooties reflects three principal concerns: sex segregation (boys think girls have cooties, and vice versa), social popularity (children who are unattractive and of low social status are much more likely to have cooties), and hygiene (children who are physically dirty are more likely to have cooties). Cooties are spread by physical contact, and they are eliminated by receiving a symbolic "cooties shot," making it clear that cooties relies heavily on children's intuitions about purity, germs, and disease. Cooties is not supported by society at large or by the media—in fact, adults actively oppose cooties, because the game is often cruel and exclusionary. One might still say that cooties is simply learned from other children and passed on as part of peer culture, the way that Piaget (1965/1932) showed that the game of marbles is passed on. And this is certainly correct. But one must still ask: Why do some games persist for decades or centuries while other games (e.g., educational games made up by adults) do not get transmitted at all? Cooties, for example, is found in some form in many widely separated cultures (Hirschfeld, 2002; Opie & Opie, 1969).

The game of cooties is so persistent, stable, and ubiquitous, we believe, because it is a product of the maturation and elaboration of the purity foundation. When children acquire the cognitive ability of contamination sensitivity around the age of 7, they begin applying it to their social world. Suddenly, children who are disliked, and the opposite sex in general, come to be felt to be contaminating—their very touch will infect a person with their dislikable essence. Children's culture is creative, and children mix in other elements of their experience, such as getting vaccines to prevent disease. However, the critical point here is that the cooties game would not exist or get transmitted if not for the purity foundation; the game is both enabled and constrained by the structure of children's minds and emotions. The game is a product of assisted externalization as each cohort of children teaches the game to the next, but only when their minds are ready to hold it (see Sperber & Hirschfeld, 2004, on the cognitive foundations of cultural transmission).

The second crucial tool for an intuitionist theory of moral development is a notion of virtues as constrained social constructions. Virtues are attributes of a person that are to some degree learned or acquired. Philosophers since Aristotle have stressed the importance of habit and practice for the development of virtues, and parents, schools, and religious organizations devote a great deal of effort to the cultivation of virtues in young people. The philosopher Paul Churchland offers an approach to virtue tailored for modern cognitive science. He sees virtues as skills a child develops that help her navigate the complex social world. Virtues are "skills of social *perception*, social *reflection*, *imagination*, and *reasoning*, and social *navigation* and *manipulation* that normal social learning produces" (Churchland,

1998, p. 88). Moral character is then "the individual profile of [a person's] perceptual, reflective, and behavioral skills in the social domain" (Churchland, 1998, p. 89).

Virtues, as sets of culturally ideal skills, clearly vary around the world and across cultures. Even within a single culture, the virtues most highly valued can change over the course of a single generation, as happened in the some parts of the Western world with the so-called "generation gap" of the 1960s. Yet virtues, like gods and ghosts, do not vary wildly or randomly (Boyer, 2001). Lists of focal virtues from around the world usually show a great deal of overlap (Peterson & Seligman, 2004). Virtue theorists such as Churchland are often silent on the issue of constraint, suggesting implicitly that whatever virtues a society preaches and reinforces will be the ones that children develop. Yet such a suggestion is an endorsement of equipotentiality, which has been thoroughly discredited in psychology. There is no reason to suppose that every virtue is equally learnable. Virtue theories can be greatly improved—not vitiated—by adding in a theory of constraint. The constraints we suggest are the five foundations of intuitive ethics.

Some virtues seem to get constructed on a single foundation. For example, as long as people have intuitions about harm and suffering, anyone who acts to relieve harm and suffering will trigger feelings of approval. The virtue of kindness is a social construction that a great many cultures have created to recognize, talk about, and reward people who act to relieve suffering. What it means to be kind will vary to some degree across cultures, but there will be a family resemblance among the exemplars. A similar story can be told for virtues such as honesty (for the fairness foundation), self-sacrifice (in-group), respect (authority), and cleanliness (purity). However, other virtues are much more complex. Honor, for example, is built upon the authority foundation in most traditional cultures (honor is about the proper handling of the responsibilities of high rank), as well as upon fairness/reciprocity (an honorable man pays his debts and avenges insults) and purity (honor is pure and cannot tolerate any stain). But honor is often quite different for women (drawing more heavily on the virtue of chastity, based on the purity foundation; see Abu-Lughod, 1986), and particular notions of honor vary in dramatic yet predictable ways along with the social and economic structure of any given society (e.g., herding vs. agricultural cultures; Nisbett & Cohen, 1996). (For more on foundations, modules, and virtues, see Haidt & Joseph, in press.)

Moral development can now be understood as a process in which the externalization of five (or more) innate moral modules meets up with a particular set of socially constructed virtues. There is almost always a close match, because no culture can construct virtues that do not mesh with one or more of the foundations. (To do so is to guarantee that the next generation will alter things, as they do when converting a pidgin language to a Creole.) Adults assist the externalization of morality by socializing for virtue, but they often overestimate their causal influence because they do not recognize the degree to which they are going with the flow of the child's natural moral proclivities. Adults may also overestimate their influence because children from middle childhood through adolescence are looking more to their peers for moral attunement than to their parents (Harris, 1995). The social parts of the SIM call attention to the ways that moral judgments made by children, especially high-status children, will spread through peer networks and assist in the externalization of intuitions and the construction of virtues.

The five foundations greatly underspecify the particular form of the virtues and the constellation of virtues that will be most valued. As with cuisine, human moralities are highly variable, but only within the constraints of the evolved mind. One of the most interesting cultural differences is the current "culture war" between liberals and conservatives in the United States and in some other Western cultures. The culture war can be easily analyzed as a split over the legitimacy of the last three foundations (Haidt & Graham, 2007; Haidt, 2007). All cultures have virtues and concerns related to harm/care and fairness/reciprocity. However, cultures are quite variable in the degree to which they construct virtues on top of the in-group/loyalty, authority/respect, and purity/sanctity foundations. American liberals in particular seem quite uncomfortable with the virtues and institutions built on these foundations, because they often lead to jingoistic patriotism (in-group), legitimization of inequality (authority), and rules or practices that treat certain ethnic groups as contagious (purity, as in the segregation laws of the American South). Liberals value tolerance and diversity and generally want moral regulation limited to rules that protect individuals, particularly the poor and vulnerable, and that safeguard justice, fairness, and equal rights. Cultural conservatives, on the other hand, want a thicker moral world in which many aspects of behavior, including interpersonal relations, sexual relations, and life-or-death decisions are subject to rules that go beyond direct harm and legal rights. Liberals are horrified by what they see as a repressive, hierarchical theocracy that conservatives want to impose on them. Conservatives are horrified by what they see as the "anything goes" moral chaos that liberals have created, which many see as a violation of the will of God and as a threat to their efforts to instill virtues in their children (Haidt, 2006, chapter 9; Haidt & Graham, 2007).

Question 6: Why do People Vary in Morality?

If virtues are learned skills of social perception, reflection, and behavior, then the main question for an intuitionist approach to moral personality is to explain why people vary in their virtues. The beginning of the story must surely be innate temperament. The "first law of behavioral genetics" states that "all human behavioral traits are heritable" (Turkheimer, 2000, p. 160). On just about everything ever measured, from liking for jazz and spicy food to religiosity and political attitudes, monozygotic twins are more similar than are dizygotic twins, and monozygotic twins reared apart are usually almost as similar as those reared together (Bouchard, 2004). Personality traits related to the five foundations, such as disgust sensitivity (Haidt, McCauley, & Rozin, 1994) or social dominance orientation (which measures liking for hierarchy versus equality; Pratto, Sidanius, Stallworth, & Malle, 1994), are unlikely to be magically free of heritability. The "Big Five" trait that is most closely related to politics—openness to experience, on which liberals are high—is also the most highly heritable of the five traits (McCrae, 1996). Almost all personality traits show a frequency distribution that approximates a bell curve, and some people are simply born with brains that are prone to experience stronger intuitions from individual moral modules (Link 1 in figure 4.1).

Learning, practice, and the assistance of adults, peers, and the media then produce a "tuning up" as each child develops the skill set that is her unique pattern of virtues. This tuning up process may lead to further building upon (or weakening of) particular foundations. Alternatively, individual development might be better described as a broadening or narrowing of the domain of application of a particular module. A moralist is a person who applies moral intuitions and rules much more widely than do other members of his culture, such that moral judgments are produced by seemingly irrelevant cues.

A major source of individual differences may be that all children are not equally "tunable." Some children are more responsive to reward and punishment than others (Kochanska, 1997). Some people tend to use preexisting internal mechanisms for quick interpretation of new information; others have more conservative thresholds and gather more information before coming to a judgment (Lewicki, Czyzewska, & Hill, 1997). Children who are less responsive to reward and who do more thinking for themselves can be modeled as being relatively less influenced by the social persuasion link (link 4 in figure 4.1). They may be slower to develop morally, or they may be more independent and less conventional in their final set of virtues. Individual differences in traits related to reasoning ability, such as IQ or need for cognition (Cacioppo & Petty, 1982), would likely make some people better at finding post hoc arguments for their intuitions (link 2) and at persuading other people via reasoned argument (link 4). Such high-cognition people might also be more responsive themselves to reasoned argument and also better able to engage in reasoning that contradicts their own initial intuitions (links 5 and 6).

A big question in moral personality is the question of behavior: Why do some people act ethically and others less so? Much of modern social psychology is a warning that the causes of behavior should not be sought primarily in the dispositions (or virtues) of individuals (Ross & Nisbett, 1991). John Doris (2002) has even argued that the underappreciated power of situations is a fatal blow for virtue theories. However, we believe such concerns are greatly overstated. The only conception of virtue ruled out by modern social psychology is one in which virtues are global tendencies to act in certain ways (e.g., courageous, kind, chaste) regardless of context. That is the position that Walter Mischel (1968) effectively demolished, showing instead that people are consistent across time within specific settings. Our conception of virtue as a set of skills needed to navigate the social world explicitly includes a sensitivity to context as part of the skill. One reason it takes so long to develop virtues is that they are not simple rules for global behavior. They are finely tuned automatic (intuitive) reactions to complex social situations. They are a kind of expertise.

However, even with that said, it is still striking that people so often fail to act in accordance with virtues that they believe they have. The SIM can easily explain such failures. Recall the Robert Wright quote that the brain is "a machine for winning arguments." People are extraordinarily good at finding reasons to do the things they want to do, for nonmoral reasons, and then mounting a public relations campaign to justify their actions in moral terms. Kurzban and Aktipis (2006) recently surveyed the literature on self-presentation to argue that the modularity of the human mind allows people to tolerate massive inconsistencies between their private beliefs, public statements, and overt behaviors. Hypocrisy is an inevitable outcome of human mental architecture, as is the blindness to one's own hypocrisy.

Unresolved Questions

The SIM is a new theory, though it has very old roots. It seems to handle many aspects of morality quite easily; however, it has not yet been proven to be the correct or most powerful theory of morality. Many questions remain; much new evidence is needed before a final verdict can be rendered in the debate between empiricist, rationalist, and moral sense theories. Here we list some of those questions.

1. *What is the ecological distribution of types of moral judgment?*   The SIM claims that people make the great majority of their moral judgments using quick intuitive responses but that sometimes, not often, people reject their initial intuition after a process of "private reflection" (or, even more rarely, directly reasoned judgment). Rationalist theorists claim that true private moral reasoning is common (Pizarro & Bloom, 2003). An experience sampling or diary study of moral judgment in daily life would be helpful in settling the issue. If moral reasoning in search of truth (with conscious examination of at least one reason on both sides, even when the person has an interest in the outcome) were found to happen in most people on a daily basis, the SIM would need to be altered. If, on the other hand, moral judgments occur several or dozens of times a day for most people, with "cognitive conflicts" or overridden intuitions occurring in less than, say, 5% of all judgments, then the SIM would be correct in saying that private moral reasoning is possible but rare.

2. *What are the causes of moral persuasion and change?*   The SIM posits two links—the reasoned persuasion link and the social persuasion link. These links are similar to the central and peripheral processes of Petty and Caccioppo's (1986) elaboration-likelihood model of persuasion, so a great deal of extant research can be applied directly to the moral domain. However there are reasons to think that persuasion may work differently for moral issues. Skitka (2002) has shown that when people have a "moral mandate"—when they think they are defending an important moral issue—they behave differently, and are more willing to justify improper behavior, than when they have no moral mandate. Further research is needed on moral persuasion.

3. *Are all intuitions externalized?*   We believe the most important ones are, but it is possible that some intuitions are just moral principles that were once learned consciously and now have become automatic. There is no innate knowledge of shoe-tying, but after a few thousand times the act becomes automatic and even somewhat hidden from conscious introspection. Might some moral principles be the same? We do not believe that

the intuitions we have talked about can be explained in this way—after all, were you ever explicitly told not to have sex with your siblings? But perhaps some can. Is it possible to create a moral intuition from scratch which does not rely on any of the five intuitive foundations and then get people to really care about it? (An example might be the judgment we have seen in some academic circles that groups, teams, or clubs that happen to be ethnically homogeneous are bad, while ethnic diversity is, in and of itself, good.)

4. *Is there a sensitive period for learning moral virtues?* Haidt (2001) suggested that the period when the frontal cortex is myelinating, from roughly ages 7 through 15 or so, might be a sensitive period when a culture's morality is most easily learned. At present there is only one study available on this question (Minoura, 1992).

5. *Can people improve their moral reasoning?* And if they did, would it matter? It is undoubtedly true that children can be taught to think better about any domain in which they are given new tools and months of practice using those tools. However, programs that teach thinking usually find little or no transfer outside of the classroom (Nickerson, 1994). And even if transfer were found for some thinking skills, the SIM predicts that such improvements would wither away when faced with self-interest and strong gut feelings. (It might even be the case that improved reasoning skills improve people's ability to justify whatever they want to do.) A good test of rationalist models versus the SIM would be to design a character education program in which one group receives training in moral reasoning, and the other receives emotional experiences that tune up moral sensitivity and intuition, with guidance from a teacher or older student. Which program would have a greater impact on subsequent behavior?

Philosophical Implications

The SIM draws heavily on the work of philosophers (Hume, Gibbard, Aristotle), and we think it can give back to philosophy as well. There is an increasing recognition among philosophers that there is no firewall between philosophy and psychology and that philosophical work is often improved when it is based on psychologically realistic assumptions (Flanagan, 1991). The SIM is intended to be a statement of the most important facts about moral psychology. Here we list six implications that this model may have for moral philosophy.

1. *Moral truths are anthropocentric truths* On the story we have told, all cultures create virtues constrained by the five foundations of intuitive ethics.

Moral facts are evaluated with respect to the virtues based on these underlying intuitions. When people make moral claims, they are pointing to moral facts outside of themselves—they intend to say that an act *is in fact wrong*, not just that they disapprove of it. If there is a nontrivial sense in which acts are *in fact* wrong, then subjectivist theories are wrong too. On our account, moral facts exist, but not as objective facts which would be true for any rational creature anywhere in the universe. Moral facts are facts only with respect to a community of human beings that have created them, a community of creatures that share a *"particular fabric and constitution,"* as Hume said. We believe that moral truths are what David Wiggins (1987a) calls "anthropocentric truths," for they are true only with respect to the kinds of creatures that human beings happen to be. Judgments about morality have the same status as judgments about humor, beauty, and good writing. Some people really are funnier, more beautiful, and more talented than others, and we expect to find some agreement within our culture, or at least our parish, on such judgments. We expect less agreement (but still more than chance) with people in other cultures, who have a slightly different fabric and constitution. We would expect intelligent creatures from another planet to show little agreement with us on questions of humor, beauty, good writing, or morality. (However, to the extent that their evolutionary history was similar to our own, including processes of kin selection and reciprocal altruism, we would expect to find at least some similarity on some moral values and intuitions.)

2. *The naturalistic imperative: All ought statements must be grounded, eventually, in an is statement* If moral facts are anthropocentric facts, then it follows that normative ethics cannot be done in a vacuum, applicable to any rational creature anywhere in the universe. All ethical statements should be marked with an asterisk, and the asterisk refers down to a statement of the speaker's implicit understanding of human nature as it is developed within his culture. Of course, the kind of is-to-ought statements that Hume and Moore warned against are still problematic (e.g., "men *are* bigger than women, so men *ought* to rule women"). But there is another class of is-to-ought statements that works, for example, "Sheila *is* the mother of a 4-year-old boy, so Sheila *ought**[3] to keep her guns out of his reach." This conclusion does not follow logically from its premise, but it is instantly understood (and probably endorsed) by any human being who is in full possession of the anthropocentric moral facts of our culture. If Greene (volume 3 of this collection) is correct in his analysis of the psychological origins of deontological statements, then even metaethical work must be marked with an asterisk, referring down to a particular understanding of

human nature and moral psychology. When not properly grounded, entire schools of metaethics can be invalidated by empirical discoveries, as Greene may have done.

3. *Monistic theories are likely to be wrong*   If there are many independent sources of moral value (i.e., the five foundations), then moral theories that value only one source and set to zero all others are likely to produce psychologically unrealistic systems that most people will reject. Traditional utilitarianism, for example, does an admirable job of maximizing moral goods derived from the harm/care foundation. However, it often runs afoul of moral goods derived from the fairness/reciprocity foundation (e.g., rights), to say nothing of its violations of the in-group/loyalty foundation (why treat outsiders equal to insiders?), the authority/respect foundation (it respects no tradition or authority that demands anti-utilitarian practices), and the purity/sanctity foundation (spiritual pollution is discounted as superstition). A Kantian or Rawlsian approach might do an admirable job of developing intuitions about fairness and justice, but each would violate many other virtues and ignore many other moral goods. An adequate normative ethical theory should be pluralistic, even if that introduces endless difficulties in reconciling conflicting sources of value. (Remember, we are antiparsimonists. We do not believe there is any particular honor in creating a one-principle moral system.) Of course, a broad enough consequentialism can acknowledge the plurality of sources of value within a particular culture and then set about maximizing the total. Our approach may be useful to such consequentialists, who generally seem to focus on goods derived from the first two foundations only (i.e., the "liberal" foundations of harm and fairness).

4. *Relativistic and skeptical theories go too far*   Metaethical moral relativists say that "there are no objectively sound procedures for justifying one moral code or one set of moral judgments as against another"(Neilsen, 1967, 125). If relativism is taken as a claim that no one code can be proven superior to *all* others, then it is correct, for given the variation in human minds and cultures, there can be no one moral code that is right for all people, places, and times. A good moral theory should therefore be pluralistic in a second sense in stating that there are multiple valid moral systems (Shweder & Haidt, 1993; Shweder et al., 1997). Relativists and skeptics sometimes go further, however, and say that no one code can be judged superior to *any other* code, but we think this is wrong. If moral truths are anthropocentric truths, then moral systems can be judged on the degree to which they violate important moral truths held by members of that society. For example, the moral system of Southern White slaveholders

radically violated the values and wants of a large proportion of the people involved. The system was imposed by force, against the victims' will. In contrast, many Muslim societies place women in roles that outrage some egalitarian Westerners, but that the great majority within the culture—including the majority of women—endorse. A well-formed moral system is one that is endorsed by the great majority of its members, even those who appear, from the outside, to be its victims. An additional test would be to see how robust the endorsement is. If Muslim women quickly reject their society when they learn of alternatives, the system is not well formed. If they pity women in America or think that American ways are immoral, then their system is robust against the presentation of alternatives.

5. *The methods of philosophical inquiry may be tainted* If the SIM is right and moral reasoning is usually post hoc rationalization, then moral philosophers who think they are reasoning their way impartially to conclusions may often be incorrect. Even if philosophers are better than most people at reasoning, a moment's reflection by practicing philosophers should bring to mind many cases where another philosopher was clearly motivated to reach a conclusion and was just being clever in making up reasons to support her already-made-up mind. A further moment of reflection should point out the hypocrisy in assuming that it is only other philosophers who do this, not oneself. The practice of moral philosophy may be improved by an explicit acknowledgment of the difficulties and biases involved in moral reasoning. As Greene (volume 3 of this collection) has shown, flashes of emotion followed by post hoc reasoning about rights may be the unrecognized basis of deontological approaches to moral philosophy.

Conclusion

When the SIM was first published (Haidt, 2001), some people thought the model had threatening implications for human dignity. They thought the model implied that people are dumb and morality is fixed by genes, so there is no possibility of moral progress. The model does state that moral reasoning is less trustworthy than many people think, so reasoning is not a firm enough foundation upon which to ground a theory—normative or descriptive—of human morality. However, the alternative to reason is not chaos, it is intuition. Intuitive and automatic processes are much smarter than many people realize (Bargh & Chartrand, 1999; Gladwell, 2005). Intuitions guide the development of culture-specific virtues. A fully enculturated person is a virtuous person. A virtuous person really *cares* about things that happen in the world, even when they do not affect her directly, and she will sometimes take action, even when it does not seem rational to do so, to make the world a better place. We believe that social intuitionism offers a portrait of human morality that is just as flattering as that offered by rationalism, yet much more true to life.

Notes

We thank Cate, Birtley, Josh Greene, Ben Shear, and Walter Sinnott-Armstrong for helpful comments on earlier drafts.

1. Haidt (2001) had defined moral intuition as "the sudden appearance in consciousness of a moral judgment," (p. 818) thereby conflating the intuition, the judgment, and Link 1 into a single psychological event, obviating any need for the link. We thank Walter Sinnott-Armstrong for pointing out this error and its solution.

2. Haidt and Joseph (2004) talked about only the first four moral modules, referring to the in-group module only in a footnote stating that there were likely to be many more than four moral modules. In a subsequent publication (Haidt & Joseph, in press), we realized that in-group concerns were not just a branch of authority concerns and had to be considered equivalent to the first four.

3. It is an anthropocentric fact that motherhood requires loving and caring for one's children. There could be intelligent species for whom this is not true.

Does Social Intuitionism Flatter Morality or Challenge It?

Daniel Jacobson

"Morality dignifies and elevates," Jonathan Haidt has written (2003b, p. 852), and in their paper for this volume Haidt and Fredrik Bjorklund claim that their social intuitionism "offers a portrait of human morality that is just as flattering as that offered by rationalism" (p. 217). I can understand the social intuitionists' desire to insist that their theory does not cast morality in an unflattering light. No doubt they have gotten some grief from my fellow moral philosophers on this score. Hutcheson famously remarked that Hume's *Treatise* lacked "a certain warmth in the cause of virtue" (Darwall, 1995, p. 211, footnote 8), to which Hume responded by contrasting the aim of the anatomist, who seeks to "discover [the mind's] secret springs," with that of the painter, who seeks to "describe the grace and beauty of its actions" (Greig, 1983, p. 32). While Haidt and Bjorklund characterize their program as fundamentally descriptive, like the anatomist's, they clearly indulge in some painterly rhetoric as well. Indeed, I will suggest that the authors may go further in this direction than they realize, by engaging in some questionable ad hoc moralizing. However that may be, their flattering rhetoric seems odd. If social intuitionism provides an accurate theory of morality, then surely no apology is needed for any undignified conclusions; and if alternative theories elevate morality only by misrepresenting its nature, then that is just one more pretty illusion we are better off without.

A psychological "theory of morality," such as social intuitionism, is a fundamentally descriptive project; it thus differs essentially from a philosophical moral theory, whether normative or metaethical. This difference can easily cause confusion. Some mostly superficial difficulties arise from Haidt and Bjorklund's use of certain philosophers' terms of art (such as "intuitionism" and "rationalism") in ways that differ from their most familiar philosophical usage. Though the authors use these terms to refer to descriptive claims about the *origin* of moral beliefs, for philosophers they name views about their *justification*. Intuitionists hold that (some) evaluative beliefs are self-evident and therefore self-justifying, while rationalists hold that evaluative beliefs can be justified by reason alone, like (certain) necessary truths. Thus, many intuitionists are rationalists, in this sense. Yet Haidt and Bjorklund take rationalism as their primary foil, because they understand it as the causal claim that moral judgments arise from a process of reasoning. Similarly, by "intuitionism" they mean the thesis that moral judgments arise instead from some noninferential, quasiperceptual process involving the sentiments. To put it most crudely, social intuitionism holds that we arrive at moral judgments by feeling rather than thinking. Sometimes Haidt and Bjorklund go beyond this psychological claim about the etiology of moral judgment, however, to imply that these intuitions constitute moral knowledge, as philosophical intuitionists assert.

I suggest that social intuitionism, considered as a thesis of moral psychology, best coheres with a *sentimentalist* metaethical theory, which holds that (many) evaluative concepts must be understood by way of human emotional response.[1] According to Haidt and Bjorklund, moral beliefs and motivations "come from *sentiments* which give us an immediate feeling of right or wrong, and which are built into the fabric of human nature" (p. 185). The authors are right to adduce Hume as a predecessor, but a more apposite remark than the famous one they quote repeatedly—about reason being the slave of the passions—is his claim that morality "is more properly felt than judged of" (Hume, 1978, p. 470).[2] Yet Hume's sentimentalism was more nuanced than this slogan suggests. Even the earliest sentimentalists gave deliberation, whether manifested in reasoning or imagination, a crucial role in evaluation as well. Hume thus claimed the following about the moral sentiments:

But in order to pave the way for such a sentiment, and give a proper discernment of its object, *it is often necessary . . . that much reasoning should precede*, that nice distinctions should be made, just conclusions drawn, distant comparisons formed, complicated relations examined, and general facts fixed and ascertained. (1975, pp. 172–173; emphasis added)

On the account that emerges from these two contrasting but compatible ideas, which is developed in the most sophisticated forms of contemporary sentimentalism, certain evaluative concepts essentially involve specific emotional responses. (For something to be shameful, say, is for it not just to cause but to merit shame.) Such evaluative concepts as the shameful presuppose that the associated sentiments can either be fitting or unfitting responses to their objects, since not everything that people are ashamed of is genuinely shameful, and likewise for other sentiments (D'Arms & Jacobson, 2000a).

While some philosophers dismiss or minimize the relevance of an empirical approach to morality, more naturalistically inclined philosophers will agree with Haidt and Bjorklund that ethics must cohere with a realistic moral psychology. This is especially true of sentimentalists, who hold that some of our central evaluative concepts can be understood only by way of certain pan-cultural emotions—which are truly part of the "fabric of human nature"—such as guilt and anger, amusement and disgust. As I have been collaboratively developing such a sentimentalist theory of value, broadly in the tradition of Hume and Adam Smith (see D'Arms & Jacobson, 2000b, 2003, 2006a), the authors will get no objection from me on this score. Indeed, I can accept their primary empirical claims, suitably understood. Yet I also have some significant worries about social intuitionism, especially with what the authors take to be its philosophical implications. Since disagreement tends to be both more interesting and, one hopes, more fruitful than agreement, I beg their pardon for focusing in what follows on what I find problematic about the social intuitionist program.

My strategy here will be to grant both the main empirical claims of the social intuitionist model (SIM) of morality, albeit with some caveats, while calling into question its explicit and implicit philosophical implications. What then does the theory claim? First, the SIM claims that *moral reasoning is typically post hoc rationalization* for judgments already made on other, less deliberative grounds. This is the intuitionist aspect of social intuitionism: the claim that moral intuition, understood as an "instant flash of evaluation" (p. 188) grounded in the sentiments, plays the primary causal role in moral judgment. The social aspect of the view is its second principal claim: that *social influence also plays a crucial role in the development and explanation of people's moral beliefs*. "We have an intense need to belong and to fit in," Haidt and Bjorklund write, "and our moral judgments are strongly shaped by what others in our 'parish' believe, even when they don't give us any reasons for their beliefs" (pp. 192–193).[3] However, there is also a crucial negative thesis to social intuitionism, implied by its almost exclusive emphasis on immediate emotional response and nonrational forms of persuasion. According to the SIM, the role of reasoning—at least private reasoning—is both minor and, in an important sense, fraudulent. What passes for intrapersonal moral reasoning is instead, much more typically, a highly biased search for arguments in support of an already-made judgment. Thus, the "core of the SIM. . . . gives moral reasoning a causal role in moral judgment, but only when reasoning runs through other people" (p. 193).

This dictum brings me to my first caveat. In order to be made tenable, the negative thesis must be restated more modestly; and in order to be made substantive, it must be stated more precisely, so that exceptions cannot simply be shunted from the "core" of the model to its periphery. While so reckless a claim can be expected to irk philosophers, I would urge against the easy tendency to disciplinary chauvinism and suggest that we read such claims as charitably as possible. Two paragraphs later, Haidt and Bjorklund allow: "People may at times reason their way to a judgment by sheer force of logic, overriding their initial intuition. In such cases reasoning truly is causal and cannot be said to be the 'slave of the passions.' However, such reasoning is hypothesized to be rare . . ." (p. 193).[4] Despite their occasional suggestion that intrapersonal reasoning never occurs, is causally impotent, or must be preceded by an intuition, elsewhere Haidt and Bjorklund frame their claims as being about what is *typically* or *normally* true, and surely that is the best way to read them.[5] However, this tendency to vagueness and exaggeration masks a potentially deeper problem.[6] Moral reasoning need not involve the "sheer force of logic," since even universalization—a crucial tool of moral reasoning seriously underestimated by the SIM—requires substantive judgments of relevant and irrelevant differences between cases, which are not settled by logic alone.

The second caveat I need to mention is that social intuitionism seems to me less a theory of specifically moral judgment than of evaluative judgment in general, though its proponents tend to blur this distinction. Thus Haidt claims that " 'eating a low fat diet' may not qualify as a moral virtue for most philosophers, yet in health-conscious subcultures, people who eat cheeseburgers and milkshakes are seen as morally inferior to those who eat salad and chicken" (2001, p. 817). But different subcultures condemn burger eaters on disparate grounds, not all of them moral, and I doubt that the "health conscious" often ascribe *moral* superiority to themselves. There seems to be a crucial and obvious difference between the attitude of the militant vegan (who is outraged by meat eating, which he considers tantamount to murder) and the uptown sophisticate (who holds burger eaters in contempt for their bad taste). Yet the social intuitionists have no good way of marking this distinction, in part because they have too capacious a notion of the moral emotions. "Any emotion that leads people to care about [the human social world] and to support, enforce, or improve its integrity should be considered a moral emotion," Haidt claims, "even when the actions taken are not 'nice'" (2003b, p. 855). This capacious notion threatens to make even amusement a moral emotion, since it can powerfully enforce social conformity—especially via ridicule. It is much more promising to distinguish the moral emotions by their content and intrinsic motivational function, rather than by their effects. In fact, I think sentimentalism has better prospects as a theory of evaluative judgment than specifically as a theory of morality, and that it works best with respect to a class of sentimental values most closely tied to specific emotional responses (such as the shameful, the fearsome, and the funny).[7]

Interdisciplinary work is perilous, and Haidt and Bjorklund occasionally and understandably go out of their way to mollify (not to say flatter) philosophers. Thus Haidt suggests that the ability to engage in reasoned moral judgment "may be common only among philosophers, who have been extensively trained and socialized to follow reasoning even to very disturbing conclusions" (2001, p. 829).[8] At the risk of biting the hand that pets me, however, I will declare my skepticism about the philosophers' exemption from the two main empirical claims of social intuitionism. Philosophers, even moral philosophers, are people too; as such, they are subject to normal human infirmities. Whatever brain scans may tell us about differences between how philosophers and ordinary folk approach fantastic thought experiments or stipulated-to-be-harmless taboo violations, these differences go out the window when live moral and political problems are at issue. Or so I confidently suspect. Furthermore, it is not at all clear that professional training in philosophy gives one any special expertise in moral judgment, let alone wisdom—except perhaps for the ability to bring consistency pressure to bear in novel and clever ways, a skill likely tainted by the same forces at work in the reasoning of other humans.

And "tainted" seems just the right word, as the authors acknowledge when they are not flattering morality. With regard to ordinary nonmoral reasoning, they write:

[E]veryday reasoning is *heavily marred by the biased search* only for reasons that support one's already-favored hypothesis. . . . In fact, this human tendency to search only for reasons and evidence on one side of a question is so strong and consistent in the research literature that it might be considered *the chief obstacle to good thinking.* (p. 190; emphasis added)

This seems exactly right, but it raises an obvious question for the social intuitionists. If good thinking about what to believe requires an unbiased appraisal of the evidence—as Haidt and Bjorklund seem to grant—then why should matters be different when it comes to moral reasoning? Why not conclude, analogously, that these all-too-human tendencies show ordinary moral judgment to be *bad thinking* on just the same grounds that so much everyday reasoning is claimed to be marred and biased and, therefore, unjustified? The intuitionist aspect of their view creates a heavy argumentative burden for the social intuitionists if they are to avoid the conclusion that the SIM portrays moral judgment as a paradigm of bad thinking. Although Haidt and Bjorklund expressly disavow the notion that there are "objective" moral facts, they need to explain why intuition should be considered a reliable sensitivity to the moral facts on *any* model of that notion. Surely they do not want to ratify every intuition of the disgustingness of certain habits, actions, and people—no matter how widespread those intuitions may be within some society.

The authors seem to think that the social aspect of the SIM rescues moral judgment. Thus we are warned that *if we forget the social part of the model*, we will "feel that . . . [their] theory is a threat to human dignity, to the possibility of moral change, or to the notion that philosophers have any useful role to play in our moral lives" (p. 181). These sound like three distinct worries which do not stand or fall together, but in any case none of them is mine. My main worry, simply put, is that the social part of the SIM fails to vindicate moral judgment as a form of good thinking, specifically about questions of what to do and how to live. It will not do simply to disavow the model of objective, primary-quality moral truth; we need an argument that intuition can reveal moral truth and ground moral knowledge even on a less objectivist model (perhaps analogous to secondary-quality facts about color). Otherwise there might be no such thing as moral truth, just disparate moral judgments, all of them equally unjustified or even false. This conclusion would not cast doubt on social intuitionism as a descriptive theory of moral judgment—unless of course we presuppose that such an unflattering result cannot possibly obtain.

This problem with justification infects the philosophical implications Haidt and Bjorklund draw from their theory, on which I will focus the rest of this discussion. "If moral truths are anthropocentric truths," they write, "then moral systems can be judged on the degree to which they violate important moral truths held by members of that society" (p. 215).[9] I find this claim puzzling and, in two related respects, problematic. First, does social intuitionism really hold that moral truths are anthropocentric, or would they be better classified as ethnographic—that is, concerned with the description of (the moral systems held by) specific human cultures? If they are anthropocentric facts, then the appeal to the views held by a *society* seems puzzling, but if they are more culturally specific, then it is unclear how the view can avoid embracing an untenable cultural relativism. Second, can the social intuitionists properly speak of moral truth and knowledge at all? Despite the explicit statement that the SIM offers "a descriptive claim, about how moral judgments are actually made . . . not a normative or prescriptive claim, about how moral judgments ought to be made" (Haidt, 2001, p. 815), the authors seem to draw normative conclusions from it. This tendency remains largely tacit, but occasionally, as in the suggestion above about *how to judge moral systems*, it issues in what seem to be prescriptions. These normative claims are dubious, and it is unclear how they are supposed to follow from the SIM—which was supposed to be an empirical theory of morality rather than a covert moral theory.[10]

Consider first the social intuitionists' claim that moral truths are anthropocentric. Haidt and Bjorklund write:

On our account, moral facts exist, but not as objective facts which would be true for any rational creature anywhere in the universe. Moral facts are facts only with respect to a community of human beings that have created them, a community of creatures that share a *"particular fabric and constitution,"* as Hume said. We believe that moral truths are what David Wiggins (1987a) calls "anthropocentric truths," for they are true only with respect to the kinds of creatures that human beings happen to be. (p. 214; emphasis in original)

It is worthwhile to note Hume's full phrase, which is "the particular fabric and constitution of the human species" (Hume, 1975, p. 170). Anthropocentric truths concern facts of human nature—such as our idiosyncratic form of color vision—not contingencies of human culture. Yet Haidt and Bjorklund claim, in this very passage, that "[m]oral facts are facts only with respect to a community of human beings that have created them"; and, in order to explain moral disagreement among humans, they say that people in other cultures than ours "have a slightly different fabric and constitution" than we do (p. 214). However, differences between the moral systems of communities cannot seriously be explained by appeal to their members' different "fabric and constitution." Moreover, if moral facts are facts only with respect to the community that holds them, then they are not anthropocentric but ethnographic truths. Rather than being true because of the kind of creatures human beings are, they would be true because of the way in which some culture happens to be.

I am not proposing any strict dichotomy between human nature and human culture. As a sentimentalist, I too think that at least certain values are *constrained* by human nature, despite varying in detail among different cultures. Such constraints obtain because our emotional responses, though malleable, are not entirely plastic. Anthropocentric facts can undermine utopian or theoretically driven ideals that fail adequately to cohere with a realistic moral psychology (D'Arms & Jacobson, 2006a). Nevertheless, whatever constraints human nature places on moral systems must be compatible with the actual moral systems human societies have successfully adopted.[11] Haidt and Bjorklund introduce five master values, which they call "five sets of intuitions [which] should be seen as the foundations of intuitive ethics" (p. 203): suffering, reciprocity, hierarchy, purity, and concern for the distinction between in-group and out-group.[12] At this level of abstraction, however, it is unclear what the payoff of this discovery might be. Any actual moral system, no matter how heinous, seems capable of being modeled by some weighting of these values; indeed, that seems to be the goal of the inquiry, as would befit a wholly descriptive project. If that is the nature of the inquiry, though, why should moral judgments grounded on these "intuitions" (or abstract values) deserve to be called moral facts or knowledge, rather than sociological facts about the anthropology of morals?

This brings us to my principal worry about the social intuitionist program, which concerns the implications of its social aspect in particular: the claim that "moral judgments are strongly shaped by what others in our 'parish' believe, even when they don't give us any reasons for their beliefs" (p. 193). I am not denying this claim, which seems to me correct, albeit less than novel. The emotivists famously stressed the dynamic function of moral language, for the purposes of persuasion and motivation, bolstered by what they termed its "emotive meaning" (Stevenson, 1937): the positive and negative connotations of such loaded words as "barbaric" and "sexist." Yet Richard Brandt (1950) trenchantly criticized emotivism for being unable to distinguish good from bad reasons, since the theory can only recognize the persuasive force of a consideration. Haidt and Bjorklund seem to embrace this problematic implication, claiming, "The reasons that people give to each other are best seen as attempts to trigger the right intuitions in others" (p. 191).[13] Their picture seems to equate reason giving with persuasion, as if there were no such thing as one reason being any better than another, except in the sense of being more rhetorically effective. However, even if the more modest statements of the SIM are correct, and *much* moral reasoning and discourse can be seen as mere rhetoric, it does not follow that *all* moral reasons simply serve to trigger emotional responses, much less that moral reasoning can only realistically serve that function. Some reasons that we give to ourselves and others purport to *justify* sentimental responses, and sometimes that purport can be vindicated. At any rate, this is the presupposition on which all talk of evaluative fact and knowledge rests, even on Hume's prototypical sentimentalism—whence his talk of nice distinctions and distant comparisons drawn by reasoning, necessary to pave the way for proper moral sentiment.

An example of this problem with social intuitionism can be found in Haidt and Bjorklund's discussion of moral argumentation, where they follow the strangely misguided tendency of too many social scientists to conflate clitoridectomy with circumcision, as merely different forms of genital "alteration." This conflation allows them to (rather misleadingly) claim the practice to be "common in many cultures" (p. 191).[14] They then treat a statement specifically condemning clitoridectomy as so much rhetoric, despite calling it an argument—or rather seven arguments. In fact, there isn't a single whole argument in the statement, notwithstanding the merits of the speaker's emotionally laden disparagement of the practice. However, Haidt and Bjorklund ask us to "note that each argument is really an attempt to frame the issue so as to push an emotional button, triggering seven different flashes of intuition in the listener" (p. 192). The trouble, of course, is that they have chosen as their example a polemical statement rather than an argument, despite the fact that there are a surfeit of *very good reasons* to draw a moral distinction between circumcision and clitoridectomy.[15]

Thus, I accept the empirical claim at the heart of the social aspect of the SIM, which is claimed to protect the theory against charges of indignity. As we humans have survived the assaults on our dignity meted out by the likes of Copernicus and Darwin, I'm not too worried about this one. My problem is rather with the mostly implicit suggestion that the social aspect of the SIM vindicates moral judgment and earns the social intuitionists the right to talk about moral truth and knowledge, as they repeatedly do. How exactly is the social aspect of the SIM—the recognition that we humans are deeply prone to conformism with respect to parochial norms—supposed to dignify and elevate morality? In particular, how does it justify (some) moral judgment as constituting moral knowledge? Haidt and Bjorklund write:

Reasoning, even good reasoning, can emerge from a . . . [pair of people discussing a moral issue] even when each member of the dyad is thinking intuitively and reasoning post hoc. As long as people are at least a little bit responsive to the reasons provided by their partners, there is the possibility that the pair will reach new and better conclusions than either could have on her own. People are very bad at questioning their own initial assumptions and judgments, but in moral discourse other people do this for us. (p. 193)

If they really mean to claim merely that it's possible for moral discussion to improve moral judgment, then that can hardly be doubted; but it's also possible for discussion to hinder moral judgment.[16]

Indeed, there is ample reason for pessimism. Even casual observation of group psychology suggests that moral discourse between like-minded individuals tends not merely to reinforce their judgments but to make them more radical. People who converse only with those who roughly share their ideological perspective tend to become both more confident and more extreme in their views. This explains the emergence of *bien pensant* opinion—that is, those opinions uncritically accepted by some parish and widely assumed to be shared by all its right-thinking members—whether in the culture at large or in subcultural cliques (such as academia). Furthermore, since it is flattering to have our opinions "confirmed" by others, however dubious this confirmation, we tend to seek out the like-minded rather than testing our views against the strongest opposing positions. But these observations suggest that perhaps the single best candidate for an anthropocentric truth in this neighborhood—namely, the observation that we humans are conformists in our thinking as much as in our other habits—serves to undermine the justification of much social reasoning about morality, notwithstanding the authors' claim that the social aspect of the SIM palliates its seemingly unflattering implications.

Yet the social intuitionists draw a considerably different conclusion, one that approaches cultural relativism while officially disavowing it. Recall that, according to Haidt and Bjorklund, "Moral facts are facts only with respect to a community of human beings that have created them" (p. 214). This slogan seems to imply that all moral facts are relativized to some community or culture, and that they are created by social facts about that culture—presumably facts about its actual norms. This suggests an entirely different view, on which the role of social persuasion in the production of moral knowledge would be straightforward. Persuasion functions to inculcate and enforce the mores of society. Right action conforms to those mores, and wrong action violates them. On this view, moral knowledge is simply the habituated ability to see things the way others see them in your parish: to have the same intuitions as others in your society. Something like this thought seems to lie behind Haidt and Bjorklund's slogan: "A fully enculturated person is a virtuous person" (p. 216). However, while such habituated skills can be considered a kind of knowledge—perhaps more like know-how than propositional knowledge—it is not at all clear why this should be deemed virtue, or why its possessors should be ascribed moral knowledge (Jacobson, 2005).

Haidt and Bjorklund expressly deny that social intuitionism entails cultural relativism, despite the passages that seem to embrace it. However, they draw this conclusion partly because they consider only the most extreme form of relativism, on which "no one code can be judged superior to *any other* code" (p. 215; emphasis in original). They then claim, to the contrary, that "moral systems can be judged on the degree to which they violate important moral truths held by members of that society" (p. 215). But this suggestion raises more questions than it answers. Can the social intuitionists mean anything by "moral truth" here other than moral belief, given their claims that moral facts are created by the community that holds them and that virtue is full enculturation?

The authors suggest very briefly that endorsement (or "robust" endorsement) by a majority (or supermajority) within the culture does the needed justificatory work. "A well-formed moral system is one that is endorsed by the great majority of its members," they write, "even those who appear, from the outside, to be its victims" (p. 216). Although endorsement is significant, to be sure, any adequate standard of it must be substantially more complex than Haidt and Bjorklund consider: It will require much more than mere knowledge of alternatives. (Moreover, we must look far more critically at the suggestion that those who look "from the outside" like victims—perhaps because they are the subjects of honor killing or rape in accordance with culturally accepted practice—really do endorse the relevant moral system; academic discussion of these issues often seems quite credulous in this regard.) The deep challenge for social intuitionism is not to develop a better notion of endorsement, however, but to explain how the theory motivates, or even coheres with, any such requirement. One wonders why the social intuitionist view isn't that those who fail to endorse the cultural norms are therefore less than virtuous, because less than fully enculturated.

There seem at least three outstanding problems with the implicit suggestion that "well-formed" moral systems issue in anything worth calling "moral truth" and "moral knowledge." First, moral codes don't just concern behavior within society but also how to treat out-group members. A moral system that allowed any treatment whatsoever of out-group members would count as well formed, on this view, so long as it secured sufficient support from within society. That is surely an unacceptable conclusion. Second, this standard allows for any treatment whatsoever of minorities or nonconformists within a society, so long as they are sufficiently few that a "great majority" supports their persecution. Finally, the endorsement standard of justification is in tension with the social intuitionists' suggestions that virtue is full enculturation, and that moral facts are created by specific cultures. It seems less motivated by their theory of morality than an ad hoc addition to it, designed to save the theory from some of its least palatable conclusions. Yet without some account of the justification of moral judgments tacked onto their descriptive theory of morality, the social intuitionists seem to lack any basis for talking about moral truth and knowledge. If so, then social intuitionism does indeed flatter morality, but only in the pejorative sense: "to compliment excessively and often insincerely, especially in order to win favor."[17]

Notes

1. For a catalogue of the diverse theories that can be seen as in this way sentimentalist (including emotivism and forms of expressivism and subjectivism, as well as sensibility theory), see D'Arms and Jacobson (2006b). Haidt and Bjorklund systematically underestimate this philosophical tradition—for instance, by claiming that "Kant has had a much larger impact than Hume on modern moral philosophy" (Haidt, 2001, p. 816). I mention this not to quibble over issues of philosophical taxonomy and influence, but because (as we shall see) the sentimentalist tradition, and emotivism in particular, anticipates several of the social intuitionists' main ideas.

2. Haidt and Bjorklund seem to read Hume's "slave of the passions" dictum as implying that reasoning can have no causal role in evaluative judgment, which was not his view (as the following quotation will amply demonstrate).

3. I have elided a citation from this passage.

4. Compare footnote 2.

5. I have some qualms about even the weaker formulations of these claims, but I will not press them here except to say that critics are right to note that the SIM "allows for virtually all conceivable relationships between environment stimuli, deliberative reasoning, moral intuitions, and moral judgments" (Pizarro & Bloom, 2003, p. 195). Indeed, the primary relationship it rules out is the possibility of reasoning preceding judgment, since there is no link between A's intuition or perception of the eliciting situation and A's reasoning about it; A can only get to reasoning by first making a judgment. But surely this is *possible*, so yet another conceivable relationship needs to be accounted for by the model. A similar point can be made about reasoning that proceeds directly from the perception of an eliciting situation without any intervening evaluative intuition.

6. Perhaps more than one problem. Consider that they characterize their dispute with rationalists as follows: "Rationalists say the real action is in reasoning; intuitionists say it's in quick intuitions, gut feelings, and moral emotions" (p. 186). But what sort of empirical claim is stated in terms of where "the real action" is, anyway?

This is not just quantitatively vague but theoretically inadequate. Perhaps most of the *causal* action is in the sentiments, while much of the *justificatory* action is in reasoning about the sentiments—in particular, about when they are and are not fitting.

7. See D'Arms and Jacobson (1994) for an argument specifically directed against what we take to be the best sentimentalist moral theory, given by Gibbard (1990); and D'Arms and Jacobson (2006a) for discussion of the prospects for a sentimentalist theory of (nonmoral) value.

8. Similarly, Haidt and Bjorklund write that philosophers "excel at examining ideas 'dispassionately'" (p. 196). But compare with their final philosophical implication (p. 216), which calls into question the sincerity of their flattery.

9. Of course, moral systems *can* be judged by any absurd measure at all, but presumably the suggestion here is that moral systems can *properly* be judged by the suggested measure. This claim would be better put in terms of "should" rather than "can," which would have the virtue of making explicit the prescriptive nature of the claim. Or, perhaps better, it should be jettisoned as adventitious to the psychological task of the SIM.

10. Of course, the normative claims need not follow from the SIM in order to be held along with it, though Haidt and Bjorklund call them "philosophical implications" of the theory. And by claiming that their theory is no less flattering to morality than are its competitors, they strongly suggest that they can vindicate moral truth and knowledge (locutions that they expressly use).

11. What counts as successful adoption is a nice question, which I cannot afford to consider except by example. The communal child-rearing practices adopted on moral grounds by American communes and Israeli kibbutzim were fated to failure, I contend, because of the anthropocentric fact that humans ineradicably—not to say without exception—care more for their own children than for those of others (especially those not related to them). There is, of course, an obvious explanation from evolutionary psychology for this fact of human nature.

12. It is mysterious to me why Haidt and Bjorklund refer to these values as "sets of intuitions." They typically use the term "intuition" in the familiar philosophical sense of a judgment made on noninferential grounds. However, suffering is not a judgment. "Suffering is bad" is a judgment—though it should be clear that human societies are capable of denying so strong a generalization and holding instead that deserved suffering is good, or that the suffering of out-group members doesn't matter one way or another.

13. They further this suggestion by quoting Robert Wright's claim that the brain is "a machine for winning arguments" (p. 191). But this claim might be more apt as a description of some people's brains—or, rather, their dogmatic argumentative style—than others.

14. It's interesting to note the exact formulation of their discussion. They write: "For example, here is a quotation from an activist arguing against the practice, common in many cultures, of altering the genitalia of both boys and girls either at birth or during initiation rites at puberty" (p. 191). In fact—though one has to go to the cited source to discover this—the activist quoted belongs to a group called Washington Metropolitan Alliance Against Ritualistic FGM. FGM stands for *female* genital mutilation. Moreover, her complaint in the passage they quote is specifically against clitoridectomy, whereas the observation that the genital alteration of both boys and girls is common in many cultures is gratuitously inserted by Haidt and Bjorklund. Why does this matter? For two reasons. First, it offers a nice object lesson in intellectual conformism. According to the ideology accepted more or less uncritically by *bien pensant* Western academics, all cultures are equal (although occasionally non-Western cultures turn out to be, as it were, more equal than others). Therefore, it can seem biased not to note, in any discussion critical of FGM, that we Westerners too mutilate the genitals of our young. Second, it shows how double-edged is the social aspect of the SIM, since the tendency to uncritically accept parochial judgments can lead even brilliant social scientists into moral obtuseness. For discussion of a considerably more egregious academic apologia for female genital mutilation, see Jacobson (2002).

15. I hope those reasons, which can be given in clinical and unemotional terms, need not be specified here, at least for those readers who still possess what Bishop Berkeley called "a mind not yet debauched by learning."

16. Although Haidt and Bjorklund do not provide it, I can think of one reason for optimism. If we focus on cases where two self-interested disputants both advocate for their own advantage, then there may be reason to hope that discussion will lead to a just compromise. However, that is by no means the only way moral discourse and persuasion works.

17. *American Heritage Dictionary of the English Language*, Fourth Edition (2000).

Darcia Narvaez

Haidt and Bjorklund offer two important correctives to the long-standing cognitive perspective of moral reasoning. As Haidt and Bjorklund point out, psychological science is in the process of abandoning the view that humans make decisions in the classical sense, as rational decision makers who reason deliberately under full conscious control. Instead, human cognition and decision making is influenced to a large degree by nonconscious systems. The second corrective endorsed by Haidt and Bjorklund is the fact that human cognition is a social phenomenon, highly influenced by one's social situation and community, and not the individualistic activity that Western tradition has emphasized. Although these are important and worthwhile correctives, the social intuitionist model has several worrisome elements that bear some reflection.

Only a Small Sample of Moral Judgment and Reasoning Processes Are Addressed

Haidt and Bjorklund limit their discussion of moral judgment to the cognitive appraisal of the action or character of a person. See Haidt, 2001: "Moral judgments are therefore defined as evaluations (good versus bad) of the actions or character of a person that are made with respect to a set of virtues held by a culture or subculture to be obligatory" (p. 817). The equally narrow definition of "moral reasoning" ("transforming given information about people in order to reach a moral judgment"; Haidt, 2001, p. 818) is again limited to processing information about others. It is not clear how social intuitionist theory addresses aspects of moral judgment and reasoning beyond such cognitive appraisals. For example, most philosophical discussion since Kant has addressed moral decision making. Moral decision making includes such things as ascertaining which personal goals and plans to set (Williams, 1973), determining what one's responsibilities are (Frankfurt, 1993), weighing which action choice among alternatives is best (Rawls, 1971), reconciling multiple considerations (Wallace, 1988), and evaluating the quality of moral decisions made and actions taken (Blum, 1994), as well as juggling metacognitive skills such as monitoring progress on a particular moral goal or controlling attention to fulfill moral goals (Kekes, 1988). It is not clear where these types of activities fit in the social intuitionist model despite the fact that Haidt and Bjorklund present a wide-ranging discussion (i.e., discussing learning moral emotions regarding bathroom hygiene, "morality as grounded in a set of innate moral modules" [p. 206], the construction of virtue, decision making differences between liberals and conservatives, and individual differences in moral personality) that makes the reader infer they are presenting a comprehensive moral psychology theory. Although intuitions may play a role in a broad range of morally relevant behaviors, I argue below that at least some of the time moral deliberation and conscious reasoning may be required.

Flashes of Affect and Intuition Are Overcredited While Deliberative Reasoning Is Undervalued

Haidt and Bjorklund propose that moral judgment is the result of quick intuitions that evaluate events according to good–bad categories, and that these intuitions drive moral judgment. While it may be true that individuals react to stimuli emotionally, with approach–avoidant reactions, a quick flash of affect is but *one* piece of information that humans use to make decisions about their goals and behaviors (Hogarth, 2001). A person may attend to physical reactions and interpret them (correctly or not) when making a decision (e.g., "My stomach is tight; I must not like x, so I won't do x"), but this is only one contributing factor among many factors. Numerous elements play a role in moral decisions along with gut feelings, such as current goals and preferences (Darley & Batson, 1973), mood and energy (Hornstein, LaKind, Frankel, & Manne, 1975; Isen, 1970; Isen & Levin, 1972), environmental affordances (Gibson, 1979), situational press (Fiske, 2004), contextual cue quality (Staub, 1978), social influence (Hornstein, 1976), and logical coherence with self-image (Colby & Damon, 1991) and with prior history (Grusec, 2002).

People wrestle with moral decisions, commitments, transgressions, and judgments in a more complex fashion (e.g., Gilligan, 1982; Klinger, 1978) than Haidt and Bjorklund allow ("People sometimes do look on both sides of an issue, thereby triggering intuitions on both sides . . . but it must be stressed that such deadlocks are fairly rare in our moral lives . . ."). Everyday moral decisions are not necessarily, as they say, "like aesthetic judgments . . . made quickly, effortlessly, and intuitively" (p. 7). In response to the authors' suggestion of a diary study to determine the nature of moral judgment, table 4.2.1 lists a sampling of thoughts/issues from two days in my life recently, which I think suggest that moral deliberation is not the rare event Haidt and Bjorklund assume.

Wrestling with these issues included a simultaneous assessment of multiple factors: certainly assessing my gut feelings, but also considering my principles (e.g., being a kind sister, being a fair child caregiver, doing excellent work, being a team player, etc.); weighing my goals/needs and the goals/needs of others in the circumstances; encouraging myself to be patient, loving and nonjudgmental; keeping track of reactions and outcomes (mine and others'); and consciously letting go of conflicting (sometimes moral) goals. Instead of intuition's dominating the process, intuition danced with conscious reasoning, taking turns doing the leading. At different times, one or the other provided energy and drive, or a moral compass. I played "moral musical chairs" in terms of "feeling out" consequences of different decisions. As Krebs and Denton (2005) point out, my deliberations did not necessarily require postconventional reasoning in making choices. Nevertheless, intuition and reasoning worked hand in hand as an iterative process (much like social information processing is an iterative process among conscious, preconscious, and postconscious processes—see Hassin, Uleman, & Bargh, 2005).

Table 4.2.1
Moral Issues that Involved Intuition and Deliberation

"He looks upset; what could it be; what should I say?"

"Did I handle the kids well enough? What would be better next time?"

"I don't want to hurt her feelings; what do I do?"

"I'm feeling anxious. How do I keep that from affecting my caregiving?"

"This meeting is a waste of time. What can I do to make it worthwhile for everyone?"

"Woops, I screwed that up. How do I make it up to them?"

"What's the fairest way to distribute my limited time today?"

"I suppose I should stop over there and say hi, but I don't feel like it."

"Oh dear, another person needs my help, but I have a deadline to meet."

"I'm really mad at her, but I promised I would call her."

"How do I tell my boss that the workload is unfair?"

"I can't believe I am expected to use my time this way. How can the system be changed?"

In fact, one might suggest that my reasoning process resembles something of an internalized "common morality" approach to decision making (Beauchamp & Childress, 1994; Gert, 2004) in which principles and intuitions are integrated with the history, needs, and goals of local circumstance. Particularities are taken into account in light of principled goals, providing a unique response to each situation. Whereas Haidt and Bjorklund say the real action lies in "gut feelings" and "moral emotions" (p. 186), I contend that the real action occurs in the iterative pattern among the feelings, thoughts, drives, and reactions in the particular circumstances. Perhaps it is more appropriate to name this process "practical wisdom," for it requires applying the appropriate virtues in the right way for the particular situation. Practical wisdom coordinates intuitions, reasoning, and action systems for the circumstances. These are applied automatically by those with more experience (experts) but more deliberately, if at all, by nonexperts. The real work of moral decision making is found in practical wisdom in action.

Human Moral Development Requires More Psychology

Haidt and Bjorklund's explanation of moral development in children can be criticized both from the perspective of developmental psychology and from the perspective of neuroscience. In the view of Haidt and Bjorklund, the child seems to be a relatively passive creature, subject to the timed maturation of moral modules and the shaping of the cultural environment ("morality . . . is better described as emerging from the child . . . on a particular developmental schedule" [p. 206]; "morality requires guidance and examples from the local culture to externalize and configure itself properly" [p. 206]; "Each of the . . . foundations matures and gets built upon at a different point in development" [p. 206]). Genetic constraints and subsequent maturation interact with cultural shaping to "externalize" moral modules with a set of socially constructed virtues, all of which apparently requires little self-construction on the part of the individual. Contemporary developmental psychologists emphasize ecological contextualism where active individuals play leading roles in shaping their own development within many arenas of interaction (e.g., Bransford, Brown, & Cocking, 1999; Lerner, 1998). Individuals interact with multiple social environments, constructing understanding, building schemas and operations at a far greater and faster pace than initially understood by the acknowledged progenitor of developmental psychology, Jean Piaget. Moreover, a developmental systems model accepts a *biopsychosocial* approach. The social intuitionist model seems to include the biological and the social, but not the psychological.

There is equal doubt from the perspective of affective neuroscience. To propose the existence of modules in the human brain is a common practice these days among evolutionary psychologists (e.g., Cosmides & Tooby, 2000). Unfortunately, such suggestions are more rooted in creative thinking than in empirical evidence (Panksepp & Panksepp, 2000). Although there is vast evidence for many specialized neurodynamic units in subcortical structures of the brain that humans share with other mammals, "there is no comparable evidence in support of highly resolved genetically dictated adaptations that produce socio-emotional cognitive strategies within the circuitry of the human neocortex" (Panksepp & Panksepp, 2000, p. 111). Indeed, Haidt and Bjorklund do not cite physiological evidence for their modularity theory. Nor does their theory appear to have roots in what is known about mammalian brain circuitry, which is hardwired with specialized functions.[1] In contrast to subcortical regions, the very plastic neocortex, rather than being set up with genetically wired adaptive functions, is specialized via experience (Panksepp, 2005). The propensities that Haidt and Bjorklund describe would better be described within the ecological contextualism of developmental systems theory (Lerner, 1998) as experience-based units formed as a result of the plasticity of the neocortex grounded at least within the limits and propensities of subcortical adaptations (Panksepp, 1998).

It may be better to frame the development of automaticity in moral judgment with the novice-to-expert paradigm, a paradigm nearly universally accepted among cognitive researchers. Individuals start as novices and develop toward expertise in most domains of life, including morality (Dreyfus & Dreyfus, 1990; Bransford et al., 1999; Varela, 1999). When there are no intuitions, as with a novice in a new domain, performance can be ineffective. Novices are typically overwhelmed with stimulation that they cannot sort out. In such situations, novices and children (as universal novices) can appear dumbfounded. Their intuitions are often wrong, demonstrating a lack of experience and inadequate conceptualization. Ask novices for their intuitions about a set of wines, poems, or paintings, and their answers will differ markedly from those of experts because they do not have the conceptual structures to perceive and interpret the affordances and variability that experts perceive. Novices do not have the sensibilities to notice excellence in the domain, for example, to appreciate exquisite brush strokes or feel the beauty in a sublime turn of phrase. Novices will focus on the most concrete and superficial elements and often not realize what they missed.

Dreyfus (2005) suggests at least six levels of expertise development. Novices initially memorize and follow rules. Only with extensive practice and development of competencies do rules become internalized and eventually surpassed in the expert. For example, the "interview" transcript Haidt and Bjorklund present could be interpreted as an attempt by the advanced beginner to figure out when and where the rules apply because the rules have not yet been fully internalized as intuitions. This intertwining of deliberative reasoning and intuition cultivation, with increasing reliance on intuition, is the hallmark of expertise development.

Expert education in a particular domain cultivates reasoning and intuitions simultaneously. Immersion in the domain and theory are presented together, to cultivate both intuitions and deliberative understanding (Abernathy & Hamm, 1995). Through the course of expertise training, perceptions are fine-tuned and developed into chronically accessed constructs; interpretive frameworks are learned and, with practice, applied automatically; action schemas are honed to high levels of automaticity (Hogarth, 2001). What is painfully rule-based as a novice becomes, with vast experience, automatic and quick for an expert (Dreyfus & Dreyfus, 1990).

Moral development occurs in a similar fashion (see Narvaez, 2006; Narvaez & Lapsley, 2005). Moral expertise requires a whole host of processes and action schemas most easily described using Rest's four component model (Narvaez & Rest, 1995; Rest, 1983). Those with more expertise have more and better organized knowledge (declarative, procedural, conditional) and are able to employ this knowledge more effortlessly and skillfully. The four components of the model are described in a logical order, although they may influence one another in an iterative fashion in any order. First, a person must notice a need or an opportunity for moral action and employ the skills of ethical sensitivity primarily through moral imagination (identifying key players, possible actions and outcomes, possible reactions and results). This requires the iterative back-and-forth interplay of intuition and other cognitions (e.g., perception, attention, motivation, reason). Second, once the array of possibilities are laid out, the actor must choose the most moral action by employing a set of principles or rules or, with extensive practice to tune up automaticity, by deciding intuitively which is the most moral choice. But this is not enough either. Third, the actor must focus attentional resources and energy to seek the goal, setting aside other concerns or interests. Chronic moral goal setting becomes automatic. Yet this is still not enough for moral behavior to take place. Fourth, the actor must implement the goal by taking the necessary steps to complete the task and persevere to the end. The successful completion of these four processes (ethical sensitivity, ethical judgment, ethical focus, ethical action) results in an ethical behavior. Failure is possible at any point due to weaknesses in particular skills and other factors such as competing moral goals. The mismatch between intuition and reason may thwart an ethical action, but so too may other misfirings or inadequate skill deployment.

In summary, moral development is an active process. The individual acts on the environment and responds to environmental influences based on cultural and psychological factors and biological propensities. Individuals build moral expertise through social experience, particularly peer relations and with guidance from the more experienced (Piaget, 1932/1965). Individuals construct cognitive-affective-action schemas that become more complex and sophisticated with more relevant experience (Rest, Narvaez, Bebeau, & Thoma, 1999) and are shaped by the particularities of their experience. Human moral development is proactive and autopoetic (Juarrero, 1999; Varela, 1999).

Enculturation and Moral Development Are Not Equivalent

The social intuitionist theory seems to operate outside of one of the most critical discussions in the history of moral development research. In the early years of the cognitive developmental tradition, there was a distinction made between social conformity and moral development (Kohlberg, 1969). This distinction was necessary in order to explain how in some situations (e.g., Germany in the 1930s) social conformity worked against moral development, and in others resisting social pressures (U.S. civil rights movement of the 1950s and 1960s) was the virtuous path. Thus, it is shocking to read Haidt and Bjorklund assert that "a fully enculturated person is a virtuous person" (p. 216). Apparently Hitler youth and Pol Pot's Khmer Rouge were virtuous and most moral exemplars are not. Much like the behaviorists and psychoanalysts did before the cognitive revolution and Kohlberg's achievements, Haidt and Bjorklund praise moral conventionality. Kohlberg's enterprise was to fight the acceptance of relativism that pervaded psychology from its inception. Although it may be an open question whether psychological theory should be judged on whether it gives aid or comfort to ethical relativism, it is startling to see mere conventionality held up as the goal of moral formation.

Haidt and Bjorklund give no indication that they believe that intuitions can be flawed or wrong. Samenow (1984) points out the distinctive intuitions of the criminal mind, which focus on finding personal advantage at the expense of others in every situation. The intuitions of the criminal mind are not "good" intuitions. But how does social intuitionist theory judge the goodness or badness of particular intuitions? Intuitions appear to be (equally) meritorious, as are all cultural practices, if they conform with the norms of one's social group ("full enculturation"). This is precisely the attitude that drove Kohlberg to mount his research program—how to support the law-breaking behavior of Martin Luther King, Jr., and condemn the law-abiding behavior of the Nazi soldier. If one understands cultural influences as those influences to which youth are most exposed, enculturation today means becoming a good consumer, a celebrity groupie, and a materialist. Self-interest is cultivated more than moral citizenship. This is a situation that many are beginning to lament because it does not lead to psychological or community flourishing (e.g., Kasser, 2002; Linn, 2004).

Conclusion

Haidt and Bjorklund have initiated a substantial and important conversation about the nature of moral development and decision making. They are to be commended for pushing us to incorporate recent data and insights into moral psychological theory in an effort to make theory more true to life. I agree with many of their points. For example, I concur that intuition and automaticity are more intelligent than they are credited for being and that a naturalized ethics is fundamental to moral philosophizing. We should appreciate their efforts at highlighting the role of intuition and affect but note that there may be better ways of incorporating such insights into a more theoretically robust moral psychology.

Notes

Thanks to Dennis Krebs, Dan Lapsley, Steve Thoma, and Larry Walker for comments on earlier drafts.

1. Panksepp and Panksepp (2000, p. 119) suggest that if evolutionary psychology wants to propose modules, it should start with the dedicated circuitry found in mammalian brains for care, fear, lust, panic, play, and rage.

4.3 | Social Intuitionists Reason, in Conversation

Jonathan Haidt and Fredrik Bjorklund

How easy it is to see your brother's faults, how hard to face your own. You winnow his in the wind like chaff, but yours you hide, like a cheat covering up an unlucky throw.

—Buddha (Dhammapada 67, in *Byrom*, 1993)

Sages have long noted how difficult it is for people to find flaws in themselves or in their own ideas. We need others to do the hard work of critique because most of us find it far easier to see the "speck" in our neighbor's eye than the "plank" in our own (Mathew, 7:4–5). This psychological Great Truth is consistent with the social intuitionist model's (SIM's) claim that people rarely engage in good, unbiased, balanced moral reasoning on their own, but in conversation, where people can point out each other's flaws and give each other reasons, good reasoning often emerges from the dyad. This psychological Great Truth is also a superb justification for a volume such as this one, where a debate between authors and commentators can help the participants to see faults they could not find for themselves. Debates can often descend into warfare when each side uses its rhetorical powers only to craft defenses of its positions and attacks on all others. But when a debate begins with a mutual appreciation of the partners' virtues, and when criticisms are offered constructively and with nuance and moderation, the debate becomes spirited conversation, which is one of the joys of academic life. We are therefore quite fortunate that the editor has found for us two such spirited conversation partners.

Narvaez and Jacobson both begin their commentaries by granting that the SIM (Haidt, 2001; Haidt & Joseph, 2004; Haidt & Bjorklund, this volume) is largely correct in its two most basic descriptive claims: (1) moral judgments are influenced by intuitive processes to a greater degree than most previous theories acknowledged, and (2) moral judgment is a social phenomenon, and should not be studied as the private act of a lone reasoner. Narvaez and Jacobson then each go on to express two kinds of concerns: (1) scientific concerns that we have taken these two claims further than the evidence warrants and (2) moral and philosophical concerns about the implications of the model, such as the fear that it opens the door to moral relativism and to the justification of any moral system, from rampant consumerism through Nazism.

In this round of the conversation, we'll do two things. First, we'll briefly address most of the scientific concerns by pointing out two ways in which we believe the SIM has been misconstrued—due in part to our own lack of clarity—and where disagreement may vanish once claims are made explicit. Next, we'll engage Narvaez and Jacobson on three topics about which we think disagreement is more substantive. Narvaez and Jacobson both point out concerns that we think are valid and that might even get us to change (slightly) our minds and our model.

Misconstrual 1: Moral Judgment Is the Same as Moral Decision Making

Narvaez's first of four points is that the SIM is limited to a "small sample" of the relevant processes of moral psychology: It is a theory about moral judgment, not moral decision making. Her second point is the related claim that when one examines moral decision making, one often find true moral deliberation—private, internal, conscious weighing of options and consequences. She offers us a snapshot of twelve such moments of deliberation that occurred to her over the course of two days. In other words, she claims, the SIM is not a good description of moral decision making.

We quite agree. The SIM was designed to capture the phenomenology and causal processes of moral *judgment*, not moral decision making, because in our opinion those two processes are not closely related, functionally speaking. It may be parsimonious to suppose that there exists a single moral faculty that handles both moral judgment and moral action and that plays a large role in the formation of one's moral identity. However, we take a functionalist, evolutionary approach in which judging others and choosing actions for oneself are very different processes. Sages and scientists have long marveled at the disconnect between our righteousness and strictness in judging others and our leniency and flexibility in choosing our own actions. Psychologists since Freud have explained this disconnect with some form of modularity theory: The mind is divided into parts that sometimes conflict, and each part does not have full access to the information or motivations of the other parts. Kurzban and Aktipis

(2006) recently challenged the very idea of studying the "self" in social psychology; their review of social cognitive phenomena (such as self-deception, hypocrisy, and self-presentation) strongly suggests the operation of multiple functionally specific modules, some of which were shaped by selection pressures for accuracy, others by selection pressures for reputation management or for material gain. And we have proposed that even moral judgment involves not one but several functional systems (the "five foundations") which evolved to make us emotionally responsive to five kinds of patterns in our social worlds.

We therefore stick to our analogy that moral judgments are like aesthetic judgments (made quickly and intuitively), but we extend the analogy to acknowledge what Narvaez is right about: Moral *decisions* are like aesthetic *decisions*. When a person must choose a paint color for his kitchen, a great many factors come into play. One's own gut feelings are quite important but one must also ask: Will the rest of my family like it? Will it match the floor color? Will this color make the kitchen look bright or sterile? What will people think of me if I pick this unusual color? There are many factors to consider besides one's first intuitive response.

Moral and aesthetic *judgments* are so quick and easy because so little is usually at stake for the self: We can make a hundred judgments each day and experience them as little more than a few words of praise or blame, linked to flashes of feeling, that dart through consciousness. But moral and aesthetic *decisions* are different: They have real consequences for the self and others, and these consequences can only be examined by running the simulation in one's head. "If I choose this action/color, what will happen? Oh, that would be terrible. How about that action/color? Yes, better." Narvaez captured the process perfectly when she described her own deliberations. It is noteworthy that all 12 of Narvaez's entries in her diary of "moral judgment" are actually deliberations about what she should *do*. Not a single one involves deliberations about whether another person did something right versus wrong.

We have focused our writings on moral judgment, but we have never before been explicit that the SIM as published applies only to moral judgment, not to choices about morally relevant actions. We suggest that the SIM can be altered slightly to become a model of moral choice: Just make links 5 (reasoned judgment) and 6 (private reflection) into solid lines and state that "when making real behavioral choices, people often do deliberate." They try to imagine what consequences would follow each choice, and they think about principles that would support or oppose each choice. Thus modified, the SIM still retains three advantages over a straight

244 Jonathan Haidt and Fredrik Bjorklund

rationalist approach to moral decision making: First, for most morally relevant actions, there is no deliberation; we all do the right thing most of the time without thinking about it. Even heroes who jump into rushing rivers to save people's lives generally state, when interviewed afterwards, that they didn't think about it; they just acted. The importance of automaticity in moral judgment can therefore be brought into moral action as well. Second, when deliberation does occur, it is often biased by desire and an uneven search for evidence. Who would deny that people are extremely good at finding reasons to do what they want to do? Third, the phenomenology of moral choice blends intuition and conscious deliberation. In Narvaez's metaphor for her own experience, "intuition danced with conscious reasoning, taking turns doing the leading" during her attempts at "'feeling out' consequences of different decisions" (p. 235). We find this an apt description of moral deliberation. It is also exactly how we described the loop that results from using the private reflection link, which we described as "having an inner dialogue with oneself" in which conscious deliberation helps us to "feel our way to the best answer using a combination of conscious and unconscious, affective and 'rational' processes" (p. 195).

Misconstrual 2: Modularity Is Phrenology

The nineteenth-century phrenologists were spectacularly wrong—the cerebral cortex is not divided up into discrete spots that happen to map onto our psychological words (e.g., "amorousness," "inquisitiveness," "acquisitiveness"). In discarding phrenology, however, some twentieth-century psychologists seem to have moved to an equally extreme view of the cortex—a blank slate view in which any part of the cortex could just as well take on any function, so to the extent that there is localization of function it must be a product of childhood learning. Narvaez appears to endorse such a view, suggesting that the psychological propensities we say are innate (the five foundations of morality) are better described through "ecological contextualism" in which brain specializations arise gradually in childhood when "experience-based units . . . [form] as a result of the plasticity of the neocortex grounded within the limits and propensities of subcortical adaptations" (p. 237). We do not believe Narvaez could be proposing that the *entire* cerebral cortex is a blank slate, constrained only by subcortical structures. We'll assume she means only that a substantial portion of the frontal cortex is blank in this way and that there are (therefore?) few if any innate ideas that would be relevant to moral psychology.

As we read the literature from neuroanatomy and behavioral genetics, blank-slate models of the brain are no longer tenable. Recent research on the relationship between genes and brain development (summarized in Marcus, 2004) indicates a new resolution of the nature/nurture dichotomy in which the brain is plastic yet full of innate structure. The old model was that genes are a *blueprint* for building a body (including a brain), and so parts of the mind that show variation across cultures must not have been specified in the blueprint. Furthermore, because there are so few genes (only around 20,000), they couldn't possibly specify very much of the blueprint for the entire body and its 20-billion-neuron brain. Experience must do most of the designing. However, the new understanding of the genome is that it is not at all like a blueprint; it is rather more like a *recipe* for building a person. Single genes don't code for specific neurons, brain regions, or modular functions (just as a single line in a recipe doesn't correspond to a spot in the final cake), yet a particular configuration of genes ends up building a brain with a particular structure, including a great deal of localized function. A single change in a single gene can have enormous transformational effects (which can't happen with blueprints but happens easily with recipes). However—and this is crucial for our present discussion—the genes themselves remain active throughout life, and the structures they build can be modified by environmental experience.

Marcus (2004) uses the metaphor that genes create the first draft of the brain, and experience edits it: "Nature bestows upon the newborn a considerably complex brain, but one that is best seen as prewired—flexible and subject to change—rather than hardwired, fixed, and immutable" (p. 12). That is exactly the balance of nativism and empiricism we strive for in our "five foundations" theory: Evolutionary forces have "prewired" human brains to readily develop concerns about harm/care, fairness/reciprocity, in-group/loyalty, authority/respect, and purity/sanctity. This prewiring explains the otherwise uncanny similarity in cultural practices such as initiation rites, or displays of deference, or rules about purity and pollution that regulate food, sexuality, and menstruation in so many cultures. Yet at the same time our theory requires that the first draft be heavily edited by each culture, which explains how modern secular and technologically oriented societies have managed to erase or ignore some (but not all!) of their prewired purity and authority concerns, while greatly elaborating upon their ability to think about harm, rights, and justice.

We therefore think it quite appropriate and consistent with current brain science to speak of mental modules, as long as our modules are not taken to be the phrenologists' specific spots on the brain. We use the term "modularity" as a functional claim, not an anatomical one (Haidt & Joseph, 2004, in press). Functional modularity (the tendency to make quick, automatic moral judgments using knowledge that is partially encapsulated and not fully open to revision by other knowledge) need not be present in the brain of a newborn, but by the time the child is a competent member of society, she will have a mind full of mental modules that assist her in making rapid intuitive judgments. The psychology of moving from novice to expert, which Narvaez discusses, surely plays a role in this development. We insist only that the novice-to-expert transition does not play out on a blank slate or open neural canvas; it plays out in a mind that was prepared and prewired, by evolution, for some kinds of expertise and not others.

Conversation Topic 1: How Broad Is the Moral Domain?

There are so many approaches to morality in modern psychology and philosophy, but there seems to be a general working consensus that morality is about protecting and/or helping individual human beings (and occasionally animals). Utilitarianism is based directly on the maximization of welfare across people, while Kantians use a language of respect for persons. Either way, moral discussions seem always to be about drowning children, runaway trolleys, lies told to save lives, and other dilemmas that force trade-offs between the rights and welfare of individuals. The debate in moral psychology between Carol Gilligan and Lawrence Kohlberg loosely mirrored the utilitarian/Kantian debate: Is morality about caring for people directly (Gilligan) or about more abstract principles of justice and rights which ultimately afford people the greatest protections (Kohlberg)? Whichever side psychologists took, everyone agreed about the borders of the moral domain and the moral entities within that domain. Elliot Turiel (1983) codified this individual-centered view of the moral domain as

prescriptive judgments of justice, rights, and welfare pertaining to how people ought to relate to each other. Moral prescriptions are not relative to the social context, nor are they defined by it. Correspondingly, children's moral judgments are not derived directly from social institutional systems but from features inherent to social relationships—including experiences involving harm to persons, violations of rights, and conflicts of competing claims. (p. 3)

From our perspective, the fields of moral psychology and philosophy both agreed long ago to limit discussion to issues related to the first two of our five intuitive foundations of morality: issues of harm and issues related to fairness (including reciprocity, justice, and rights). It is from this two-foundation perspective that Jacobson doubts that health-conscious eaters ascribe moral superiority to themselves. He grants that a militant vegan, who is outraged by *harm* to animals, is taking a moral position. But he claims that the "uptown sophisticate" (p. 222) who holds burger eaters in contempt makes a judgment of taste, not morality. On the standard definition (morality = harm, rights, justice), he is right.

However, we are not interested in the standard definition, handed down to psychologists from philosophy and then applied in a top-down and Procrustean way to real people. We are moral psychologists, interested in how people in diverse societies live their lives and regulate their own behaviors and those of others. We have studied moral judgments in several nations (Brazil, India, Japan, the United States, and Sweden) and read many religious texts and ethnographies of traditional societies. Taking a bottom-up approach, we ask: What is the moral domain as people actually create it? When we examine what people care about, gossip about, legislate, regulate, prohibit, and praise, we find only one culture on earth that limits the moral domain to issues of harm, rights, and justice: well-educated secular Westerners, particularly those who are political liberals. It is no coincidence that nearly all moral philosophers and moral psychologists belong to this group. Empirical research has now documented that this group limits its moral judgments to violations of Shweder's "ethics of autonomy," while the moral domain is much broader among those of low social class in the United States and Brazil (Haidt, Koller, & Dias, 1993), in India (Jensen, 1998), among religious Americans (Jensen, 1997), and among political conservatives compared to political liberals (Haidt & Graham, 2007; Haidt, 2007; Haidt & Hersh, 2001). Real people in most human cultures care about much more than the welfare of individuals: They care about the prestige, stability, and honor of their in-groups and institutions; they care about their traditions and symbols; they care about whether people are fulfilling the duties of their roles (vs. pursuing their own personal goals and need for self-expression); and they care about whether people are living in a holy and pure way, treating their bodies like temples, rather than like playgrounds. In other words, for most people in all historical eras, the moral domain is based on all five intuitive foundations, not just the first two.

From this five foundation perspective, the uptown sophisticate who looks down on those who eat junk food is in fact expressing moral concerns about purity versus pollution. She is, as we say, feeling "holier than thou." However, those who have a two-foundation morality are unskilled at seeing purity violations and uneasy with disgust-based judgments (see Nussbaum, 2004). They therefore misunderstand the sophisticate's judgment and dismiss it as mere snobbery, just as they misunderstand the conservative opposition to gay marriage and dismiss it as nonmoral/immoral homophobia (see Haidt & Graham, 2007, for a discussion of this issue). When Jacobson accuses us of having "too capacious a notion of the moral emotions" (p. 222) and of having a theory so broad that it is better described as a theory of "evaluative judgment" (p. 222) than a theory of morality, we respond by saying that our broad notions are appropriate for the breadth of the moral domain. Many emotions besides anger, guilt, and sympathy play an important role in moral judgment. Many evaluations besides those pertaining to harm, rights, and justice are moral evaluations.

We hope that Jacobson will continue his generous tendency to grant us our empirical claims (about cultural variation in descriptive accounts of the moral domain) and then engage us on normative questions such as whether the three "conservative" foundations (in-group, authority, and purity) can really be used to justify moral claims. Liberals can easily point to bad consequences that follow when societies are based on a strong sense of in-group, respect for authority, and concerns for purity. Such societies can be quite cruel to those within who are labeled as impure or dirty, and they can be aggressive and even genocidal toward neighboring groups. On the other hand, some are quite peaceful, such as Confucian China, and all are likely to provide the sort of rich cultural resources for the construction of meaning and identity that diverse modern democracies have trouble providing (see Appiah, 2005; Bellah, Madsen, Sullivan, Swidler, & Tipton, 1985; Hunter, 2000; Taylor, 1989). The larger challenge for philosophers is to move beyond an individualist-consequentialist framework and take conservative ideas seriously. Might there be a sense in which societies, tribes, families, teams, and institutions are moral entities with a moral worth above and beyond the sum of the individuals that compose them or benefit from them? (See Muller, 1997, for such an argument.)

Conversation Topic 2: Deliberation, Private versus Social

Jacobson and Narvaez both claim that the SIM gives too little role to conscious moral deliberation. Jacobson points out that Hume himself wrote that before moral sentiments can be felt, "it is often necessary . . . that much reasoning should precede, that nice distinctions should be made, just conclusions drawn, distant comparisons formed. . . ." (Hume 1975/ 1777, p. 173). Jacobson further claims that in the SIM, "the role of reasoning—at least private reasoning—is both minor and, in an important sense, fraudulent" (p. 221).

Jacobson is certainly correct that one of the six links in the model—the "post hoc reasoning" link—represents a kind of reasoning that is not good reasoning yet which we often claim as good reasoning when it is our own (but not, usually, when it is produced by someone we disagree with). It is not the reasoning that is fraudulent; it is we who are frauds in our frequent claims that bias and motivated reasoning are all around us, but not in us. The vast social psychological literature on bias agrees with the vast corpus of admonishment from the ancients about hypocrisy to support the claim that people are congenitally bad at overcoming their self-serving motivations when their interests conflict with those of others (see review in Haidt, 2006, chapter 4). We suggested that moral philosophers may be less biased (fraudulent, hypocritical) than others, but Jacobson refused to accept this exemption for his field, stating that any apparent differences between philosophers and others "go out the window when live moral and political problems are at issue" (p. 223). We believe, therefore (and Jacobson seems to agree), that in real-life judgments, where we generally care about the people and actions involved, private reasoning is better described as a post hoc search for justifications of one's initial intuition than as an honest and open search for truth.

The post hoc reasoning link, however, is just one of six links in the SIM. Four of these links (67%!) are reasoning links. We have already granted that the reasoned judgment link and the private reflection link may be used fairly often in the course of moral *decision making*, and this single admission may be enough to account for many of our critics' insistence that they themselves deliberate more than the SIM seems to allow. However, if we restrict ourselves to moral judgments—to evaluations of the actions or character of other people—then how much of a role does deliberation play? Our answer is that moral deliberation occurs quite frequently in conversation and that moral theorists should start looking more closely at emergent properties of dyads and groups.

In a recent article Neil Levy (2006) provides a better example than we have of how rationality can emerge from a group. He takes the example of academic fields such as social psychology and points out that "the epistemological project in these areas is a community-wide enterprise" (p. 102). Individual social psychologists don't need to work very hard to seek out challenges to their views; such challenges will be forthcoming. "Distributed cognition, in which argument takes place outside the heads of particular individuals, is much more effective at exposing weaknesses than is any kind of more isolated process, in part because it ensures that the biases to which Haidt points are canceled out" (p. 102). Of course, moral discussions within a society do not have the ruthless correctives of peer review and failed replications to weed out bad moral arguments, so we would not expect an emergent moral consensus to be as rational (justifiable by reasons and also coherent within itself) as an emergent scientific consensus. Nonetheless, Levy suggests that the past century did involve a great deal of moral progress driven by good arguments, many produced by moral experts (e.g., philosophers and religious leaders) that filtered through populations and changed consensual views (e.g., about civil rights, women's rights, and human rights).[1] We agree with Levy's analysis. We add only that moral progress was probably driven more by words and images that triggered affectively laden intuitions (such as Martin Luther King's highly metaphorical "I Have a Dream" speech, and the televised images of peaceful marchers being attacked by police dogs) than by well-reasoned arguments that convinced people to care about the violated rights of strangers to whom they had no emotional ties.

Conversation Topic 3: Implications of the SIM for Ethics

Cross-disciplinary work is always risky, and we plead guilty to the charge of recklessness in our first attempt to spell out the philosophical implications of the SIM. Narvaez and Jacobson both reject our claim that "[a] fully enculturated person is a virtuous person." Both accuse us of dignifying conformity and moving dangerously close to a relativism that would grant moral legitimacy to whatever most members of a moral parish, even a Nazi parish, happen to believe. We are neither relativists nor emotivists (at least, not on any simple version of those positions), but we understand why our writings have let some critics think that we are. So let us try to clarify three points.

First, the SIM is about intuition more than emotion. It's true that the title of the initial paper (Haidt, 2001) referred to the "emotional dog" rather than the "intuitive dog," but that small victory for euphony was perhaps a defeat for clarity. Many critics have assumed that the SIM is an emotivist theory because it talks about the importance of emotions. The text of the article, however, made it clear at several points that the psychological basis of the theory was not a contrast of "cognition" versus "emotion"; it was a contrast between *two types of cognition*—reasoned and intuitive. Intuitions are often accompanied by affect, and all emotions include an intuitive component (the automatic appraisal which launches the emotion; see Ortony, Clore, & Collins, 1988). Yet moral judgment is still a cognitive process—cognitive in the psychological sense that it involves information processing (mostly unconscious), and cognitive in the philosophical sense that moral judgments report beliefs that can be said to be better or worse, more or less accurate (with reference to anthropocentric truths, since there are not any transcendent or fully objective moral truths). Thus, when Jacobson says that "to put it most crudely, social intuitionism holds that we arrive at moral judgments by feeling rather than thinking" (p. 220), we protest that this portrait is indeed too crude. Social intuitionism holds that we arrive at moral judgments by *intuition*, which is a kind of thinking that is not reasoning, and in which emotion often plays a role.

Second, we would like to take Jacobson up on his suggestion that the SIM implies that moral truths are like the secondary quality facts of color. Jacobson writes that his main worry is "that the social part of the SIM fails to vindicate moral judgment as a form of good thinking, specifically about questions of what to do and how to live" (p. 224). He further fears that if intuition cannot reveal moral truth and ground moral knowledge in some way, then the SIM implies that "there might be no such thing as moral truth, just disparate moral judgments, all of them equally unjustified or even false" (p. 224). We understand this worry. The SIM makes the empirical claim that people are quite bad at the sort of moral reasoning upon which many moral philosophers have hung their hopes for moral justification and moral progress. The SIM makes the further claim that moral truths, to the extent that they have any kind of reality, gain this reality with respect to the "particular fabric and constitution of the human species" as Hume (1975/1777, p. 170) put it. The situation is analogous, as a first pass, to the reality of colors. The redness of an apple is a real property, but not a property that is fully inherent in the apple. Redness emerges only because evolutionary processes have given the human eye the ability to pick out certain wavelengths of light and to translate those wavelengths into a certain psychological experience. Similarly, with acts of harm, unfairness, betrayal, disobedience, or impurity, the wrongness of these acts is a real property, but not a property that is somehow inherent to the acts and independent of the minds construing these acts. The wrongness emerges only because evolutionary processes have given the human mind the ability to pick out certain patterns of actions, intentions, and relationships and to translate these patterns into certain psychological experiences.

But now for the disanologies to color. First, with color, we really can speak, as Hume did, of the particular fabric and constitution of the human *species*. Despite the sexiness of the original Sapir–Whorf hypothesis, it turns out that the experience of color is far more similar across cultures than cross-language differences in color terms might suggest. The first draft of the visual system provided by the genes is so little edited by cultural experience (barring extreme environments such as being raised in a cave or closet) that we can base our theories of color perception on the "taste buds" of the visual system: the red-, blue-, and green-responding cones and the light-responding rods. With morality, however, the first draft provided by the genes is always edited by cultural experience (we claim), so that people in different cultures really do have a "slightly different fabric and constitution" (Haidt & Bjorklund, this volume, p. 214). Jacobson asserts that cultural differences "cannot seriously be explained" by such differences, but we challenge him to offer an alternative explanation. Does he believe that identical twins raised in radically different cultures will end up with the same minds, just as they would end up with the same color vision systems? Does he believe that cultural learning leaves no mark on the brain?

The second major disanalogy between color vision and moral vision is that moral perceptions are used (and probably evolved in order) to coordinate groups of individuals (Wilson, 2002). Much hangs on whether one's own actions are perceived by others to be justified or unjustified, so we have a great deal of evolved and developed ability and motivation to spin our own actions, and those of others, in ways that are conducive to our self-interest (see Wright, 1994). This is simply not the case for color vision. Moral vision is therefore always more contested, more biased by self-interest, and more difficult to judge as accurate or inaccurate than is color vision. However, that does not mean that there is no truth to be found. Moral communities are created by shared moral visions and goals, woven into moral narratives that explain where the community came from and who its heroes and villains are (Smith, 2003). No one human community has the single correct narrative, but within any community it is possible to judge certain actions as right or wrong, and as deserving of praise or punishment (see Haidt & Kesebir, 2007). These narratives are built upon and constrained by the five foundations of morality, and they tend to incorporate ideas of past harms, rights trampled and regained, in-group boundaries, proper subordination to gods or leaders (or proper rejection of improper and oppressive authorities), and metaphors of purity and contamination.

A third clarification: We understand Jacobson's and Narvaez's fears that our moral pluralism (there are multiple valid moral worlds) opens the door to relativism and Nazism, and upon reflection we regret and retract our slogan "A fully enculturated person is a virtuous person" (p. 216). We meant that as a purely descriptive account about how people who think about morality in terms of virtues (which, we believe, is most people) then think about moral development. And we should have been more explicit that we meant the enculturation of *ideals*, not of whatever the reality happens to be (e.g., in Narvaez's example, crass consumerism). Finally, we grant Narvaez's point that "[e]nculturation and moral development are not equivalent" (p. 239). We note, however, that the fear of conformity and the idolization of those who challenge existing power structures or create their own morality is particularly common in politically liberal parishes, which are based on just the first two intuitive foundations (Haidt & Graham, 2007; Haidt, 2007). In the majority of human cultures, where traditions, institutions, and in-group loyalties are valued, "full enculturation" may not be so wide of the mark as a description of the virtuous person.

Conclusion

We concluded our target article with the claim that the SIM "offers a portrait of human morality that is just as flattering as that offered by rationalism, yet much more true to life" (p. 217). We never intended to flatter moral psychologists and moral philosophers, and judging by Narvaez's and Jacobson's comments, we succeeded. The SIM is a direct challenge to most of moral psychology. It claims that the moral psychology community has restricted itself to a small range of moral phenomena (harm, rights, and justice) and has been pursuing the wrong mechanism of judgment and development (moral reasoning). The SIM is an indirect (and not yet well-formulated) challenge to some moral philosophers—to those who believe that moral truths exist in some mind-independent or culture-independent way, and to those who place their hopes for moral progress in the human capacity for unbiased reasoning and for persuasion by reasoning that does not also involve intuitive appeals.

However, for those who do not sacralize moral reasoning, the SIM offers a hopeful portrait of human nature: We are inescapably moral beings, governed (imperfectly) by norms and committed to working out shared evaluations of people's actions with respect to those norms. Even if evolution followed a ruthless principle of genetic self-interest in shaping our moral nature, the ultrasocial creatures that resulted are (for the most part) cooperative, caring, and motivated to preserve or improve the moral communities in which we are embedded. As Thomas Jefferson wrote in 1814, "nature hath implanted in our breasts a love of others, a sense of duty to them, a moral instinct, in short, which prompts us irresistibly to feed and succor their distresses. . . ." Jefferson was an optimist about human nature, and he surely exaggerated in suggesting that our urge to care for people is "irresistible." But Jefferson was right that there are such urges, and the SIM is a theory about where those urges came from and the important role that they play in our moral lives.

Note

1. Levy intends this point to be a criticism of Haidt (2001), which, he says, did not pay sufficient attention to the social side of the SIM. Whether or not that is true, our paper in this volume is more explicit about emergent rationality: "Reasoning, even good reasoning, can emerge from a dyad even when each member of the dyad is thinking intuitively and reasoning post hoc" (p. 193).

5 Sentimentalism Naturalized

Shaun Nichols

Sentimentalism, the idea that the emotions or sentiments are crucial to moral judgment, has a long and distinguished history. Throughout this history, sentimentalists have often viewed themselves as offering a more naturalistically respectable account of moral judgment. In this paper, I'll argue that they have not been naturalistic enough. The early, simple versions of sentimentalism met with decisive objections. The contemporary sentimentalist accounts successfully dodge these objections, but only by promoting an account of moral judgment that is far too complex to be a plausible account of moral judgment on the ground. I argue that recent evidence on moral judgment indicates that emotional responses do indeed play a key role in everyday moral judgment. However, the emotions themselves are only one part of moral judgment; internally represented rules make an independent contribution to moral judgment. This account of moral judgment is grounded in the empirical evidence, but it can also handle a cluster of desiderata that concern philosophical sentimentalists. If emotions and rules do make independent contributions to moral judgment, this raises a puzzle, for our rules tend to be well coordinated with our emotions. In the final section, I'll argue that this coordination can be partly explained by appealing to the role of cultural evolution in the history of norms.

Sentimentalist Metaethics

The history of sentimentalist metaethics is a history of increasing sophistication. On perhaps the most prominent contemporary account, Allan Gibbard's, to judge an act morally wrong is to "accept norms that prescribe, for such a situation, guilt on the part of the agent and resentment on the part of others" (1990, p. 47). In the next section, I'll argue that the sophistication of the philosophical accounts is their undoing. However, it's worth reviewing a bit of the history to see how we ended up with such a dazzlingly complex theory of moral judgment. Along the way, we'll accumulate several desiderata for an adequate sentimentalist metaethics.

The early, relatively simple sentimentalist accounts were met with crushing counterexamples. On one prominent version of the history (e.g., Stevenson, 1937), Hobbes promoted a first-person subjectivism, according to which "X is bad" just means "I disapprove of X." This runs up against the familiar problem of disagreement—when one person says X is bad and another says X is not bad, according to first-person subjectivism there is typically no conflict since they are both reporting their own psychological states. Yet it's clear that typically people *are* disagreeing when one claims that X is morally bad and the other says that it isn't. Hume is sometimes viewed as offering a community-based subjectivism according to which "X is bad" just means "Most people in my community disapprove of X." This allows for the possibility of *some* disagreement, since we can disagree about which views prevail in our community. However, as Stevenson points out, this account doesn't allow for disagreement between communities. And it seems implausible that the very meaning of the term "bad" should exclude the possibility of intercommunity moral disagreement (Stevenson, 1937). Thus, an adequate sentimentalist account must be able to accommodate the possibility of moral disagreement.

"Emotivism" emerged as the prevailing view that offered a solution to this problem. According to emotivism, in giving voice to a moral commitment, one is not merely reporting one's feelings, but *expressing* them. Thus, when we say that it's wrong to steal, what we are really saying is something like "I disapprove of stealing; do so as well" (see e.g., Stevenson, 1944). This account can more easily accommodate disagreement—if you and I express different attitudes about an action, we are promoting conflicting agendas.

Although emotivism was widely viewed as a major improvement on subjectivism, emotivism was beset by problems too. One problem that arose early in the discourse focused on the fact that emotivists maintained that a person must actually have the emotion that he is expressing when he utters a moral condemnation. However, as Darwall, Gibbard, and Railton (1992) put the problem, "it seems . . . that a person can judge something wrong even if he has lost all disposition to feelings about it" (pp. 17–18). Again, sentimentalists took this problem to provide a constraint on future theorizing—an adequate sentimentalist account must allow for the possibility that a person can still judge an action wrong even if he has lost all the relevant feelings about the action.

The final problem posed against the early sentimentalist theories concerns the role of reasoning in moral judgment (e.g., Toulmin, 1950; Brandt, 1950; Falk, 1953; Baier, 1958; Geach, 1965). Moral reasoning seems to play an important part in our moral lives, and if moral judgment is simply reporting or expressing one's feeling, it's unclear how the reasoning could proceed as it does. Even simple examples of moral reasoning served to make the point. For instance, Toulmin (1950) offers the following bit of ordinary moral reasoning from principles:

[S]uppose that I say, "I feel that I ought to take this book and give it back to Jones." . . . You may ask me, "But ought you really to do so?" . . . and it is up to me to produce my "reasons". . . . I may reply . . . "I ought to, because I promised to let him have it back." And if you continue to ask, "But why ought you really?", I can answer . . . "Because anyone ought to do whatever he promises anyone else that he will do" or "Because it was a promise." (p. 146)

If moral judgments merely express feelings, it is hard to see how to explain these apparently rational transitions from general principles to specific judgments. Geach (1965) presents a more direct attack on emotivism. Emotivists will have difficulty explaining the fact that we accept conditionals with embedded moral statements. People can accept the conditional "If spanking your own children is wrong, then spanking other people's children is wrong" without ever feeling or reporting any disapproval for spanking one's own children. This means, according to Geach (1965), that emotivists cannot accommodate simple instances of moral reasoning like the following:

If doing a thing is bad, getting your little brother to do it is bad.
Tormenting the cat is bad.
Ergo, getting your little brother to torment the cat is bad. (p. 463)

An adequate sentimentalist account must be able to accommodate the manifest role of moral reasoning.

We now have quite a diverse list of desiderata. An adequate sentimentalist account needs to accommodate the following:

1. *Sentimentalism* Emotion plays a crucial role in moral judgment.
2. *Moral disagreement* Individuals and communities sometimes have moral disagreements.
3. *Absent feeling* A person can judge something wrong even if he has lost all feelings about it.
4. *Moral reasoning* Reasoning plays a crucial role in moral judgment.

Given the disparate nature of these constraints, a sentimentalist theory that manages to meet all the constraints would be an impressive achievement indeed.

There is a basic move that manages to solve all these problems at once. Rather than identify moral judgment with the expression or reportage of emotions, contemporary "neosentimentalist" accounts identify moral judgment with the judgment that it is normatively appropriate to feel a certain emotion in response to the action (D'Arms & Jacobson, 2000, p. 729; see also Blackburn, 1998; Gibbard, 1990; Wiggins, 1987b). Although contemporary sentimentalists widely agree on this move, few sentimentalists provide an account that is sufficiently clear and detailed to permit thorough evaluation. In particular, few sentimentalists provide a detailed account of *which* emotion is at the heart of moral judgment. Gibbard (1990) is the most obvious and visible exception. As noted at the beginning of the section, Gibbard maintains that to judge an action morally wrong is to judge that it would be warranted to feel guilty for performing the action. He writes, "what a person does is *morally wrong* if and only if it is rational for him to feel guilty for doing it, and for others to resent him for doing it" (Gibbard, 1990, p. 42). The subsequent discussion will focus on Gibbard, since his theory is rich and detailed enough to evaluate systematically.

The striking feature about neosentimentalism is that it satisfies *all* of the desiderata. Sentiments are integral to moral judgment; indeed, emotions are part of the *meaning* of moral judgments. However, even if one has lost any disposition to feel guilty about a certain action, one can still think that feeling guilt is *warranted*. Thus the problem of absent feeling is addressed as well. Furthermore, the problem of moral disagreement is met handily— moral disagreement is really disagreement about whether it is appropriate to feel guilt for doing a certain action. Obviously that kind of disagreement is possible, indeed actual. Finally, the account can accommodate moral reasoning. When we argue about moral matters, we are arguing about the appropriateness of feeling guilt in response to doing certain actions.

This brief review of twentieth-century metaethics is intended both to show up the relevant constraints on an adequate account and to illustrate why the history of metaethics led us to such a complex account of moral judgment. The simpler stories ran into major difficulties. The neosentimentalist approach provides ingenious solutions to the diverse array of problems and constraints that emerged over the century. Indeed, I'll argue that the problem with the most prominent version of neosentimentalism is that it is *too* ingenious to be a plausible account of normal moral judgment.

Core Moral Judgment and the Dissociation Problem

At least since Hume, sentimentalists have often self-identified as naturalists. Sentimental accounts are supposed to give a more accurate rendering of moral judgment on the ground, as opposed to the disconnected, emaciated characterization of moral judgment promoted by some in the rationalist tradition (e.g., Cudworth, Locke; see Gill, 2006). Many contemporary sentimentalists continue to embrace naturalistic strictures. Gibbard (1990) again provides a prominent example: "The ways we see norms should cohere with our best naturalistic accounts of normative life" (p. 8).

Although sentimentalists often side with naturalism, it has been notoriously difficult to evaluate sentimentalism empirically, and neosentimentalists have rarely suggested experimental evidence that might confirm or undermine their theory. There is, however, one crucial place where the theory seems to have an empirical commitment. If moral judgments are judgments of the normative appropriateness of certain emotions, then the capacity for moral judgment should not be dissociable from the capacity to make judgments about the normative appropriateness of those emotions. More specifically, if moral judgments are judgments of the appropriateness of guilt, then *an individual cannot have the capacity to make moral judgments unless she also has the capacity to make judgments about the appropriateness of guilt.*

In due course, I'll argue that there *are* such dissociations between the capacity for moral judgment and the capacity for normative assessment of the appropriateness of guilt. This, I will argue, presents a serious problem for naturalistic neosentimentalism. But first, I need to say a bit about the empirical investigation of the capacity for moral judgment.

In the psychological literature, the capacity for moral judgment has perhaps been most directly and extensively approached empirically by exploring the basic capacity to distinguish moral violations from conventional violations (for reviews, see Smetana, 1993; Tisak, 1995). Turiel explicitly draws on the writings of several philosophers, including Searle, Brandt, and Rawls to draw the moral/conventional distinction (Turiel, 1983). But the attempt to draw a categorical distinction between morality and convention has been notoriously controversial. We needn't take sides in the controversy, for we can see the import of the evidence just by considering how people distinguish between canonical examples of moral violations and canonical examples of conventional violations. Canonical moral violations include pulling hair, pushing, and hitting. Canonical examples of conventional violations include violations of school rules (e.g., talking out of turn) and violations of etiquette (e.g., drinking soup out of a bowl). From a young age, children distinguish canonical moral violations from canonical conventional violations on a number of dimensions. For instance, children tend to think that moral transgressions are generally less permissible and more serious than conventional transgressions. Children are also more likely to maintain that the moral violations are "generalizably" wrong, for example, that pulling hair is wrong in other countries too. And the explanations for why moral transgressions are wrong are given in terms of fairness and harm to victims. For example, children will say that pulling hair is wrong because it hurts the person. By contrast, the explanation for why conventional transgressions are wrong is given in terms of social acceptability—talking out of turn is wrong because it's rude or impolite, or because "you're not supposed to." Further, conventional rules, unlike moral rules, are viewed as dependent on authority. For instance, if at another school the teacher has no rule against talking during story time, children will judge that it's not wrong to talk during story time at that school, but even if the teacher at another school has no rule against hitting, children claim that it's still wrong to hit.

These findings on the moral/conventional distinction are neither fragile nor superficial. They have been replicated numerous times using a wide variety of stimuli. Furthermore, the research apparently plumbs a fairly deep feature of moral judgment. For, as recounted above, moral violations are treated as distinctive along several quite different dimensions. Finally, this turns out to be a persistent feature of moral judgment. It's found in young and old alike. Thus, we might think of this as reflecting a kind of *core moral judgment*.[1]

Children begin to display a capacity for core moral judgment surprisingly early. Smetana and Braeges (1990) found that at 2 years and 10 months, children already tended to think that moral violations (but not conventional violations) generalized across contexts when asked, "At another school, is it OK (or not OK) to X?" (p. 336). Shortly after the 3rd birthday, children recognize that conventional violations but not moral violations are contingent on authority (Smetana & Braeges, 1990; Blair, 1993). Thus, the evidence suggests that from a very young age, children can make these distinctions in controlled experimental settings. In addition, studies of children in their normal interactions suggest that from a young age, they respond differentially to moral violations and social-conventional violations (e.g., Dunn & Munn, 1987; Smetana, 1989).

Although children have a strikingly early grasp of core moral judgment, their understanding of guilt seems to emerge significantly later. According to developmental psychologists, children don't understand complex emotions like guilt, pride, and shame until around age 7 (Harris, 1989, 1993; Harris, Olthof, Terwogt, & Hardman, 1987; Nunner-Winkler & Sodian, 1988; see also Thompson & Hoffman, 1980). Gertrude Nunner-Winkler and Beate Sodian asked children to predict how someone would feel after intentionally pushing another child off of a swing. Children under the age of 6 tended to say that the pusher would feel happy. Children over the age of 6, on the other hand, tended to say that the pusher would have some negative feelings. In another study, the experimenters showed children images of two individuals, each of whom had committed a moral violation. One of the children had a happy expression, and the other had a sad expression. The subjects were asked to rate how "bad" the children were. While most 4-year-old children judged the happy and sad transgressors as equally bad, "the majority of 6-year-olds and almost all 8-year-olds judged the person who displayed joy to be worse than the one who displayed remorse" (1988, p. 1329). Thus, between the ages of 4 and 8, children are gradually developing the idea that moral transgressions are and *should be* accompanied by some negative affect. However, the findings make it seem quite unlikely that 3- and 4-year-old children are capable of making a normative evaluation of whether guilt is an appropriate response to a situation.

Thus, it seems like young children have the capacity for core moral judgment while lacking the capacity to judge when it is appropriate to feel guilt. This dissociation seriously threatens the neosentimentalist view that for S to think that X is morally wrong is for S to think that it would be appropriate to feel guilty for having done X—for young children apparently make moral judgments but lack the capacity to judge whether guilt is normatively appropriate for a situation. In this light, the developmental sequence that neosentimentalism suggests begins to look implausibly demanding. To make moral judgments, one must be able to

1. Attribute guilt.
2. Evaluate the normative appropriateness of emotions.
3. Combine these two capacities to judge whether guilt is a normatively appropriate response to a situation.

This seems seriously overintellectualized as an account of children's moral judgments. Perhaps older children and adults do come to see that the actions that they judge as morally wrong are those for which guilt is appropriate, but the dissociation argument suggests that this is likely a peripheral feature, not a necessary component of moral judgment.

Of course, a natural response to this is to maintain that children don't understand morality after all. What I've called "core moral judgment" is better labeled "*ersatz* moral judgment." However, this move carries a number of dangers. First, neosentimentalism is supposed to capture everyday normative life (Gibbard, 1990, p. 26; Blackburn, 1998, p. 13), and it's an *empirical assumption* that most adult moral judgment is radically different from core moral judgment. The basic kind of moral judgment we see in children might be preserved without revision into adulthood, and it might well guide a great deal of adult moral judgment. As a result, if neosentimentalists cede core moral judgment, they risk neglecting a central part of our everyday normative lives.

Furthermore, several of the conditions set out above on an adequate sentimentalism apply to children's core moral judgment as well. Children enter into disagreements with each other and with their parents over matters in the moral domain. The emotions seem to figure importantly in children's moral judgment. It's likely that the emotions play a key role in leading children to regard moral violations as especially serious and authority independent; the emotions also seem to play a role in subserving a connection between moral judgment and motivation—children find rule violations to be emotionally upsetting, and they find it especially upsetting to witness another being harmed.[2] Finally, and as we will see in more detail in the next section, from a young age, children engage in moral reasoning of the sort appealed to by moral philosophers like Toulmin and Geach. Thus, many of the central constraints for an adequate sentimentalist account must be addressed by an account of core moral judgment, and the dissociation problem suggests that the most prominent neosentimentalist solution is unavailable for young children. It's plausible that whatever the right account *is* for moral judgment in young children, that account will also apply to adults, with no radical changes along neosentimentalist lines.[3]

Toward a Naturalistic Sentimentalism

Thus far I've argued that the most prominent neosentimentalist view is an implausible account of moral judgment. Although this neosentimentalist account falls prey to its own sophistication, the dissociation problem cannot dislodge neosentimentalism unless there is a plausible alternative to take its place. I would hardly urge that we resuscitate the less sophisticated accounts like emotivism or subjectivism. Philosophers rightly abandoned those theories, and for the right reasons. However, I think that an approach that leans more heavily on psychology will give us a more promising account.

Philosophical sentimentalists in the twentieth-century tended to maintain that emotions are part of the *content* of a moral judgment. This isn't all that surprising really, since philosophy of language reigned supreme. What else is there to do but give an account in terms of the content of moral terms? However, if we approach this question with an eye to psychology rather than semantics, we will find a different way that emotion comes into play in moral judgment. Emotion concepts do not figure into the content of a moral judgment; rather, emotions play a role in leading us to treat as distinctive certain violations, including many of those we consider "moral," like violations of harming others.

The basic idea is that core moral judgment depends on two mechanisms, a body of information prohibiting harmful actions and an affective mechanism that is activated by suffering in others. After sketching this approach, I'll argue that the account might deliver the explanatory goods promised by neosentimentalism without falling victim to the dissociation problem.

Core Moral Judgment Depends on an Affect-Backed Normative Theory

The empirical research on moral judgment indicates, in line with sentimentalism, that core moral judgment is mediated by affective response. In a series of provocative experiments, James Blair found that psychopaths do not perform the way normal people do on the moral/conventional task (Blair, 1995). Psychopaths, unlike normal adults, young children, autistic children, and nonpsychopathic criminals, failed to draw a significant moral/conventional distinction in Blair's experiments. In addition, children with psychopathic tendencies were more likely to regard moral violations as *authority contingent* than were other children with behavioral problems (Blair, 1997). Furthermore, psychopaths were less likely than nonpsychopathic criminals to appeal to the victim's welfare when explaining why the moral violations were wrong. Rather, psychopaths typically gave conventional-type justifications (e.g., "It's not the done thing") for all transgressions. Blair and colleagues also found that psychopaths have a distinctive deficit to their capacity to respond to the distress cues of other people (Blair, Jones, Clark, Smith, & Jones, 1997). This affective deficit is not found in nonpsychopathic criminals or in autistic children (Blair, 1999). Thus, apparently the one population with a deficit in moral judgment also has a deficit in affective response. This provides evidence that emotional response somehow mediates performance on the moral/conventional task.[4] It's not yet clear which affective mechanism is implicated in core moral judgment, but it is presumably some mechanism that responds to harm or distress in others. Two such mechanisms have been identified, one subserving "personal distress" (see, e.g., Batson, 1991) and another subserving "concern" (see, e.g., Nichols, 2001). Both of these mechanisms emerge quite early in development, well before the 2nd birthday. Thus, Blair's evidence on the psychopath's response to distress cues suggests that psychopaths have a deficit to either the personal distress mechanism or the concern mechanism (or both). And it is this affective deficit that explains their deficit in core moral judgment.

Although core moral judgment seems to be mediated by affective response, the affective response alone does not capture core moral judgment. For there are many cases in which another person's harm or distress has considerable affective consequences for a witness, but in which one does not make a corresponding moral judgment. For instance, victims of natural disasters often lead us to feel both personal distress and concern without also leading us to judge that a transgression has occurred. We also respond to other people's suffering when the suffering is a result of an accident or when the suffering is inflicted for some greater benefit (as in inoculations). In these cases too, we often respond affectively without drawing any moral judgment.

Appeal to an affective response like personal distress or concern does not suffice, then, to explain moral judgment. One natural way to fill out the account is to maintain that core moral judgment also depends on a body of information that specifies a class of transgressions. For present purposes, the important prohibitions are those that focus on harmful actions. We can think of this as a "normative theory," a body of mental representations proscribing harmful transgressions that is present in individuals who are capable of core moral judgment. Among other things, this normative theory provides the basis for distinguishing wrongful harm from acceptable harm.

Although core moral judgment plausibly depends on both an affective mechanism and a normative theory, these two mechanisms are at least partly independent. The affective mechanisms responsive to others' suffering emerge very early, before the 2nd birthday, but few, if any, researchers would maintain that children make core moral judgment before the age of 2. This is plausibly because they haven't yet developed the normative theory. More interestingly, it's likely that much of the normative theory can be preserved even when the affective system is damaged. Despite their deficits in core moral judgment, psychopaths are, in a sense, perfectly fluent with normative argument—they are quite capable of identifying which actions are proscribed, and they can marshal reasons for why certain actions count as violations and other, superficially similar, actions don't count as violations. The problem with psychopaths seems to be that the affective contribution to moral judgment is seriously diminished, and this shows up in their deficit at making the distinction that is at the heart of core moral judgment.

The proposal, then, is that there are two mechanisms underlying the capacity for drawing the moral/conventional distinction. One of these mechanisms is an affective mechanism, responsive to others' harms; the other mechanism is a body of information, a normative theory, proscribing a set of harmful actions. On this account, core moral judgment derives from an affect-backed normative theory. This quick sketch leaves open a number of important questions about the nature of the normative theory, the nature of the affective mechanism, and how these two mechanisms conspire to produce the distinctive pattern of moral judgment that we see in the experimental work. However, the sketch does suffice, I hope, to gesture toward a broadly sentimentalist account of moral judgment.

Meeting the Constraints

We began by considering the constraints on an adequate sentimentalism. Moral judgments typically involve the emotions, but online emotional processing isn't required to make a moral judgment. Furthermore, moral disagreement and moral reasoning play important roles in our normative lives. Neosentimentalism offers a sophisticated account that meets these constraints, but the very sophistication of the account leads to the dissociation problem. The account of core moral judgment outlined in the previous section is obviously underdescribed. However, it will be worth taking a brief look at how the account compares with neosentimentalism.

First, to return to the dissociation problem, the affect-backed-theory account is perfectly consistent with the evidence on young children. The affective mechanism that plausibly underwrites core moral judgment is present early in children. And the normative theory containing information about harm violations is also present in young children (see below). Therefore, the fact that core moral judgment emerges when it does poses no problem. Unlike neosentimentalism, the affect-backed-theory account makes no commitments about the child's *understanding* of emotions. But can the account address the constraints that neosentimentalism handles so impressively? I'll suggest the affect-backed-normative-theory account does indeed provide the beginnings of an account that can meet the constraints.

On the affect-backed-theory account, an affective mechanism plays a crucial role in moral judgment. Sentiments play a key role in leading us to treat norms prohibiting harmful actions differently from other norms. This fits. We care more about harm norms, we are more upset when they are flouted, and our emotions are more closely attuned to these kinds of transgressions.[5] The emotional mechanisms that give harm norms this distinctive status are defective in psychopathy, and as a result, the capacity for core moral judgment is seriously compromised in psychopaths. Psychopaths also, famously, seem to lack the normal motivation associated with prohibitions against harming others. That is, these prohibitions seem to carry less motivational weight for them than they do for the rest of us. On the account I've sketched, it's plausible that the affective deficit is responsible both for the deficit in moral judgment and for the deficit in moral motivation. Thus, the account of core moral judgment falls comfortably in line with the sentimentalist claim that emotions play a crucial role in moral judgment.

The affective mechanism is thus crucial to core moral judgment. To explain how the theory accommodates the other constraints, I will appeal to the role of the normative theory. To explain this, it will be useful to consider cases that involve a body of information specifying a set of transgressions that *don't* involve emotions in the way that core moral judgment does. Once again, evidence on children provides an instructive starting point.

Young children have an impressive facility with normative violations in general. As most parents of young children can testify, children often disagree with each other about what the rules in a given domain are and how those rules apply. This is most apparent when children dispute rules of games. However, it emerges in many other domains as well, including etiquette, school rules, and rules of the house. Moreover, even 3-year-olds are quite good at detecting transgressions of familiar rules as well as arbitrary novel transgressions. For instance, in one experiment on 3- and 4-year-olds, the experimenter said, "One day Carol wants to do some painting. Her Mum says if she does some painting she should put her helmet on" (Harris & Núñez 1996, p. 1581). Children were shown four pictures: Two pictures depicted Carol painting, one with and one without a helmet; in the other two pictures, Carol is not painting, but in one of these pictures she has a helmet on. Children were asked, "Show me the picture where Carol is being naughty and not doing what her Mum told her?" The children tended to get the right answer. In addition to children's success in identifying transgressions, children are also able to give some justification for their choice. For instance, in the task described above, after they answer the question about which picture depicts a transgression, the children are asked, "What is Carol doing in that picture which is naughty?" (p. 1581). The children in these experiments tended to give the right answer even here—they invoked the feature of the situation that was not present, for example, they noted that Carol isn't wearing her helmet. So, children are good at detecting violations of unfamiliar and arbitrary rules as well as violations of familiar rules (Harris & Núñez, 1996).

In earlier work on the moral/conventional distinction, Judith Smetana (1985) presented preschool children with transgression scenarios in which the actual transgression is not specified. Rather, in lieu of transgression terms, she used nonsense words. Some transgressions were modeled on the criteria associated with conventional transgressions (context specific, explicit appeal to rules), other transgressions were modeled on criteria associated with moral transgressions (generalizable, child cries). For instance, in one "conventional" scenario, children are told that Mary shouldn't piggle at school, but it is okay for her to piggle at home. For this scenario, children tend to infer that in another country, it's okay to piggle. Now, in order to move from the information to the conclusion, the child presumably relies on some inductive premise of the sort, "If an action is okay at home but not at school, it is likely that the action is okay in another country." That is, children seem to do something very like the reasoning in Geach's example:

If an action is okay at home but not at school, then it's probably okay in another country.
Piggling is okay at home but not at school.
Ergo, piggling is okay in another country.

Indeed, what is especially striking about Smetana's finding is that children undertake this reasoning without knowing what piggling is!

If we return to the remaining constraints—disagreement, absent feeling, and reasoning—the above evidence suggests that children can treat nonmoral rules in ways that answer to all these constraints. Children can disagree about what the rules are, they can recognize the rules without having distinctive affect, and they can reason about the rules. The reasoning here is not about feelings, of course. Rather, children accept certain rules and they reason about their application.

In the case of moral judgment, I've argued that core moral judgment depends on a body of rules, a normative theory. That is, rules make an independent contribution to moral judgment. And it is the rules, on this account, that allow us to explain disagreement, absent feeling, and reasoning.[6] Just as children can disagree and reason over rules that don't excite emotion, so too can we all disagree and reason about rules that prohibit harming others. Toulmin gives the example of reasoning that I should return a book because I promised to return it and I should keep my promises. Young children do something that seems quite analogous when they judge that it's wrong to pull hair because it *hurts* the other person. Presumably the child reasons that it's wrong to pull hair because pulling hair hurts the person and hurting people is prohibited. Thus, while emotions play a key role in moral judgment, the emotions are not invoked to solve this range of constraints. Disagreement and reasoning are features that moral judgment shares with the vast array of normative thinking that we find in children—it's driven by internalized rules.[7]

Obviously, this brief sketch of a theory of moral judgment leaves open a huge range of questions. However, we don't need to await the answers to these questions to see a stark difference between this relatively simple account and the spectacularly intellectualized account proffered by neosentimentalism. According to neosentimentalism, in moral discourse, we are arguing about the appropriateness of feeling some emotion. No doubt we sometimes do engage in such discussions over when emotions are appropriate. But much of the disagreement and argument we find in moral discourse can be accounted for more simply by adverting to the content of the normative theory. Of course, this would also allow us to explain why it is that when we disagree and argue about moral issues, it doesn't *seem* like we're talking about emotions at all. That's because typically we're *not* talking about emotions. We're talking about the content and implications of a largely shared normative theory.

Sentimentalism and the Evolution of Norms

Philosophers in the sentimentalist tradition are fond of pointing out that there is a striking connection between our emotions and our norms. We have norms prohibiting harming others, and these norms are closely connected to our responses to suffering; we have norms against the gratuitous display of bodily fluids, and these norms are closely connected to our disgust responses.

Part of the story here, of course, is that there is a *consequent* connection between emotions and norms. Once a rule is established, we often find it upsetting to see the rule broken, even when the rule bears no direct relation to our emotional repertoire. For instance, if the school rule is that you can't have snack until you've finished your picture, and children see

Johnny starting his snack without finishing his picture, this would upset the children. And children tend to say that people should be punished for violating conventional rules. Thus, there might be some emotional response that is easily elicited by rule breaking. However, this is something that the affect-backed-theory account can easily take on board. For what the affect-backed theory says is that harm norms get a special status because of their connections with specific kinds of emotions.

On the above issue, the view of traditional sentimentalists has no particular advantage over the theory I've been promoting. However, there is a different connection between emotions and norms as well. The kinds of things that we are independently likely to find upsetting (e.g., disgusting actions, harmful actions) also happen to be the kinds of actions that are proscribed. Traditional sentimentalists had an independently motivated answer to this—the norms just *are* the relevant emotions. On the early sentimentalist accounts, subjectivism and emotivism, moral judgment is just reporting or expressing the feelings that you have. Thus, since we have feelings of revulsion at harmful actions and at disgusting actions, it follows that we would have norms against these kinds of actions. The norms just are the emotions. In the more sophisticated neosentimentalist account, emotional activation isn't required, but the emotion concepts are still part of the very semantics of moral concepts. Either way, for philosophical sentimentalists, emotions are deeply, inextricably embedded in moral concepts.

On my view the norms are *not* the emotions. Nor are emotion concepts implicated in the semantics of moral judgment. Rather, norms make an independent contribution to moral judgment. However, now this leaves a bit of a puzzle. If the rules are independent of the emotions, why is it that the rules happen to fit so well with our emotional endowment? Why do we have rules that prohibit actions that we are independently likely to find emotionally aversive? Call this the "coordination problem." To address the problem, I want to look away from semantics, to history.

To explain the coordination between emotions and norms, I'll appeal to the role of cultural evolution. The hypothesis I want to promote is that emotions played a role in determining which norms survived throughout our cultural history. In particular, norms prohibiting actions likely to elicit *negative* affect will have enhanced cultural fitness. We can put this as an "affective resonance" hypothesis:

Norms that prohibit actions to which we are predisposed to be emotionally averse will enjoy enhanced cultural fitness over other norms.

It's worth emphasizing that *obviously* there are other important factors in cultural evolution. The hypothesis is only that affective resonance will be one of the factors that influence cultural evolution.

There are general theoretical reasons to favor the affective resonance hypothesis. For instance, emotionally salient cultural items will be attention grabbing and memorable, which are obvious boons to cultural fitness. In the case of norms, we also know that affect-backed norms, like the norms prohibiting disgusting actions, are regarded as more serious than other norms (Nichols, 2002a). Again, the fact that we take these norms more seriously provides reason to think they would be more robust across the ages.

Despite these general theoretical virtues, the affective resonance hypothesis would be much more compelling if we had evidence for it. Ideally, we want *historical* evidence, since the hypothesis is that norms that are affect-backed will be more likely to survive throughout the changes wrought through history. The affective resonance hypothesis predicts that, ceteris paribus, norms that prohibit actions that are independently likely to excite negative emotion should be more likely to survive than norms that are not connected to emotions.

The cultural evolution of etiquette bears out the prediction. Disgust is widely regarded as a basic emotion (Ekman, 1994; Izard, 1991; Rozin, Haidt, & McCauley, 2000, pp. 638–639), and, while there is cultural variation in the things that provoke disgust, bodily fluids are very common elicitors for disgust responses across cultures (Rozin et al., 2000, p. 647). Indeed, Haidt and colleagues maintain that it's useful to recognize "core disgust," which is elicited by body products, food, and animals (especially animals associated with body products or spoiled food; Haidt, McCauley, & Rozin, 1994).

Given this view of core disgust, the affective resonance hypothesis generates a specific prediction about the evolution of norms. Norms that prohibit core disgusting actions should be more likely to succeed than norms that are not connected to affective response. This prediction is impressively confirmed by a glance at the history of etiquette. In *The Civilizing Process*, Norbert Elias charts the history of etiquette in the West by reviewing etiquette manuals from the Middle Ages through the nineteenth century (Elias, 1939/2000). He reports numerous instances in which the culture came to have prohibitions against some action involving bodily fluids (e.g., norms involving spitting and nose blowing), and in each case these norms were preserved in the culture. A closer look at the most important manual, Erasmus's *On Good Manners for Boys*, corroborates our prediction more effectively. In Erasmus we find several norms that are not connected to core disgust and that did not survive:

When sitting down [at a banquet] have both hands on the table, not clasped together, nor on the plate. (p. 281)

If given a napkin, put it over either the left shoulder or the left forearm. (p. 281)

On the other hand, most of the norms in Erasmus's manual that prohibit core disgust actions are now so deeply entrenched that they seem too obvious to mention. Consider, for example, the following:

It is boorish to wipe one's nose on one's cap or clothing, and it is not much better to wipe it with one's hand, if you then smear the discharge on your clothing. (p. 274)

Withdraw when you are going to vomit. (p. 276)

Reswallowing spittle is uncouth as is the practice we observe in some people of spitting after every third word. (p. 276)

I had independent coders evaluate a representative sampling of norms from Erasmus's book, and their responses confirmed that the norms prohibiting disgusting actions were much more likely to survive than the other norms found in Erasmus (Nichols, 2002b).

We can turn now to the norms at the center of our moral worldview, norms prohibiting harming others. The affective resonance hypothesis would predict that harm norms should have an advantage in cultural evolution, for normal humans have strongly aversive emotional responses to suffering in others. These responses show quick onset, and they emerge quite early in development. Indeed, even newborn infants respond aversively to some cues of suffering (e.g., Simner, 1971). As with "basic emotions" like sadness, anger, disgust, and fear, there is good reason to suppose that the emotional response to suffering in others is universal and innately specified. As a result, we should expect that in all cultures, harming people will tend to produce seriously aversive affect. Thus, harmful actions themselves will be likely to arouse negative affect, all else being equal.

Just as we've seen that norms prohibiting disgusting actions have been extremely successful, so too have harm norms done well historically. It has become a commonplace in discussions of moral evolution that, in the long run, moral norms exhibit a characteristic pattern of development. First, harm norms tend to evolve from being restricted to a small group of individuals to encompassing an increasingly larger group. That is, the moral community expands. Second, harm norms come to apply to a wider range of harms among those who are already part of the moral community—

that is, there is less tolerance of pain and suffering of others. The trends are bumpy and irregular, but this kind of characteristic normative evolution is affirmed by a fairly wide range of contemporary moral philosophers (e.g., Brink, 1989; Nagel, 1986; Railton, 1986; Reiman, 1985; Smith, 1994).[8] Since we are disposed to respond aversively to even low-level signs of distress, the trend in moral evolution further confirms the affective resonance hypothesis that norms will have enhanced cultural fitness when they prohibit actions which we're predisposed to find emotionally aversive.

Thus, it seems that we can explain the impressive coordination between emotions and norms by appealing to history rather than semantics. Emotional mechanisms prove to be a potent factor in the cultural evolution of norms. Norms are more likely to be preserved in the culture if the norms resonate with our affective systems by prohibiting actions that are likely to elicit negative affect. We find confirmation for this both in the history of etiquette norms and in the history of norms prohibiting harming others. Norms prohibiting disgusting and harmful actions seem to have thrived in our culture, whereas affect-neutral norms have proved much more feeble.

Conclusion

Emotions do make vital contributions to moral judgment as sentimentalists have always maintained. However, the contribution of emotions isn't something that can be adequately gleaned from philosophical analyses. Rather, the case for the role of emotion is best made by looking at psychological evidence on moral judgment. Emotions drive a wedge between two different classes of normative judgment. Affect-backed normative judgment shows systematic differences from other kinds of normative judgment. However, the basic capacity for moral judgment cannot be explained solely in terms of emotional responses. Internally represented rules make an independent contribution to moral judgment. The emotions play a crucial role in making some of these rules psychologically distinctive. Furthermore, emotion plays an important historical role in the fixing of norms in the culture. Norms that fit with our emotions have a greater cultural resilience.

The naturalized sentimentalism promoted here does not look much like the earlier philosophical accounts. Nonetheless, it's clear that Hutcheson, Hume, and subsequent sentimentalists were right to think that emotions are at the heart of moral judgment. Our normative lives would be radically different if we had a different emotional repertoire.

Notes

This paper is a précis of the case for a naturalistic sentimentalism presented in Nichols (2004b). I'm grateful to Walter Sinnott-Armstrong for very helpful suggestions on a previous version.

1. Most of the research on the moral/conventional distinction has focused on moral violations that involve harming others. It's clear, however, that harm-centered violations do not exhaust the moral domain. To take one obvious example, adults in our society make moral judgments about distributive justice that have little direct bearing on harm. Nonetheless, it's plausible that judgments about harm-based violations constitute an important core of moral judgment. For the appreciation of harm-based violations shows up early ontogenetically (as we will see below), and it seems to be cross-culturally universal. The capacity to recognize that harm-based violations have a special status (as compared to conventional violations) is a crucial part of this core moral judgment.

2. The situation with motivation and moral judgment is rather complicated, as evidenced by the debate over internalism. For present purposes it's important to note that there are at least two different ways in which moral judgment is connected with motivation. First, moral violations fall into the class of rule violations, and people are generally motivated not to violate rules. Secondly, moral rules often prohibit actions that are inherently upsetting and hence to be avoided. Most saliently in the present context, suffering in others generates considerable negative affect, and so people are motivated not to do those things. This complication doesn't affect the present point though, since both of these strands of motivation—rule based and emotion based—seem to be present in young children.

3. Of course, it's possible that a neosentimentalist might maintain that the relevant emotion is something other than guilt. However, there remains a serious challenge for this approach. Neosentimentalists would need to show that there is some emotion that fits into the neosentimentalist schema and which is sufficient to exclude nonmoral cases. Further, in order to address the dissociation problem, the neosentimentalist would need to provide evidence that children have an early understanding of this emotion and of when the emotion is normatively appropriate. The difficulty of this project provides good reason to look elsewhere for a theory of moral judgment.

4. The claim that affect mediates performance on the moral/conventional task is corroborated by research on transgressions that are not moral but are affectively charged. In one experiment, a standard moral/conventional task was carried out in which the moral transgressions were replaced with disgusting transgressions (e.g., spitting in one's glass before drinking from it). The disgusting transgressions were distinguished from affectively neutral conventional transgressions on all the classic dimensions—disgusting transgressions were judged to be less permissible, more serious, and less authority contingent than conventional transgressions (Nichols,

2002a). In normal people, then, affect seems to infuse normative judgments with a special authority.

5. There are other rules, like the rules prohibiting disgusting actions, that also seem to share these features with harm norms (Nichols 2002a).

6. Actually, the situation with absent feeling is a bit more complex, for it's not yet clear whether core moral judgment really is preserved in the absence of all dispositions to feel. However, in any case, just as one can embrace etiquette norms in the absence of all dispositions to feel, so too can one continue to embrace the harm norms in the absence of all dispositions to feel.

7. Note that the kind of reasoning considered here, the kind that has been important to many metaethicists, is actually consistent with Jonathan Haidt's recent attack on moral reasoning (Haidt, 2001). Haidt's claim is that moral judgment typically doesn't depend on *conscious deliberate* reasoning. That's consistent with the possibility that in some key cases, moral judgment *does* depend on conscious deliberate reasoning. More importantly, Haidt's claim is consistent with the possibility that a great deal of moral judgment depends on quick, nondeliberative reasoning over rules. And in the examples from Toulmin and Geach, it's plausible that this kind of reasoning is not typically a deliberative conscious process. Indeed, it would be a bad thing for Haidt's theory if it did exclude the possibility of the kind of reasoning promoted by Toulmin and Geach, for the evidence indicates that even children engage in this kind of moral reasoning.

8. Even Nietzsche (1956) makes a (rather wittier) observation in this spirit: "in those days, pain did not hurt as much as it does today" (p. 199). Thanks to Walter Sinnott-Armstrong for reminding me of this line.

James Blair

In this extremely interesting chapter, Shaun Nichols makes four main points. I will consider each in term.

The first point is that the neosentimantalist account is "an implausible account of moral judgment" (p. 262). This appears such a reasonable position and the arguments that Shaun lays down are so clear that I can do nothing but agree with him. I will consider this issue no further.

Second, Shaun makes the point that core moral judgment appears to be mediated by affective response but that the affective response does not capture the core moral judgment. This was the most serious of the critiques that Shaun (Nichols, 2002a) aimed at the early "affective process" violence inhibition mechanism (VIM) model of moral development that I proposed some time ago (Blair, 1995). The VIM was a putative cognitive system that, when activated by distress cues (the sadness/fear of others) or representations of actions associated with those distress cues, engendered aversive affect. It was proposed that this aversive affect guided the individual away from the action that had elicited the affect.

The VIM model suggested that actions/events paired with the distress of others would come to be regarded as aversive. However, as Shaun points out here the class of actions considered to be morally "wrong" is only a subset of those that would be considered aversive on the basis of VIM activation; natural disasters causing harm to people are considered bad but not morally wrong.

In some respects, Shaun's argument is a knockdown against a unitary "affective process" position. Such positions cannot account for judgments of "wrong." However, how much of moral judgment is a judgment of "wrong"? Individuals with psychopathy know that it is "wrong," or at least not permissible, to hit others. Given this, does making a judgment of an action's "wrongness" even require an affective response? This does not imply that most healthy people do not have an affective response and use this response when making their "wrongness" judgments. The claim only is that the affective response may not be *necessary* for some "moral" judgments. Indeed, there are reasons to believe that psychopathy has no impact on your moral reasoning level as indexed by Kohlberg's assessment techniques (Colby & Kohlberg, 1987), although this remains an equivocal issue (Blasi, 1980).

However, other aspects of moral reasoning do require an affective response, the moral/conventional distinction described in Shaun's chapter for example and, I would argue, real-world decision making ("Do I rob that person or not?"). Moreover, do these forms of reasoning *necessarily* require anything else other than an affective response? The moral/conventional distinction does not require knowledge of rules. While our judgments of the nonpermissibility of a conventional transgression require knowledge of the existence of a rule and, presumably, consequent social punishment, this is not the case for judgments of moral transgressions; take away the rule and these actions are still regarded as nonpermissible.

In short, a complete theory of moral reasoning requires specification regarding under what moral reasoning conditions what forms of cognitive system are recruited and how they function.

Shaun's third point is that moral judgment depends on a body of rules, a normative theory. Shaun has argued that this normative theory does not "consist of a single simple rule. For instance, at least among adults, the normative theory allows that it is sometimes acceptable to harm a child for her long-term benefit" (Nichols, 2002a, p. 226). However, it remains unclear what this normative theory does consist of. How precise do the specified conditions have to be? Is it ever acceptable to harm a child? Is it acceptable to harm a child to improve her table manners? Or is it only acceptable to harm a child to prevent her engaging in life-threatening activities? Moreover, it remains unclear how this normative theory develops. Should there be individual differences in this normative theory? If there should be, why should there be?

I remain unconvinced that it is necessary to propose the existence of a normative theory for the purposes that Shaun wishes to propose it. I believe that it is only necessary to consider the interaction of the neural systems involved in the emotional response to the transgression situation with those involved in theory of mind. "Theory of mind" refers to the ability to represent the mental states of others, that is, their thoughts, desires, beliefs, intentions and knowledge (Frith, 1989; Leslie, 1987; Premack & Woodruff, 1978). I would argue that actions are considered "wrong" rather than merely "bad" when there is intent to cause harm. The actions of an intentional agent that cause harm to others are "wrong." The actions of an unintentional agent (including natural disasters unless these are attributed to a divine intent) are "bad." As the level of victim distress increases, the act is regarded as more "wrong"/"bad" depending on the intention associated with the action (this is the emotional component of the reasoning process). As it becomes clearer that the intent of the transgressor was to cause harm, the act becomes progressively more likely to be regarded as "wrong" rather than "bad" (this is the theory of mind component of the reasoning process).

There are some situations that might appear contradictory to this proposal—for example, drinking-and-driving fatalities or situations of child punishment such as that briefly mentioned above. A drunk driver who backs into five people and kills them is likely to be regarded as "wrong" rather than merely "bad." However, the driver clearly did not harm the five intentionally. But this situation can be accounted for if we consider a simulation view of theory of mind (this issue is considered in detail in Blair, Marsh, Finger, Blair, & Luo, submitted).

At a general level, simulation accounts of theory of mind suggest that the observation of another individual's action leads to the activation of parts of the same cortical neural network that is active during its execution. The observer understands the action because "he knows its outcomes when he does it" (Gallese, Keysers, & Rizzolatti, 2004, p. 396). The execution of an action involves an expectation of the action's consequences, such as whether the action will gain a reward or avoid a specific punishment.

Returning to the drunk driver, if we represent that the driver had the intent to become drunk, we, as part of the affective theory of mind process outlined above, generate expectations of likely reinforcements associated with this action—a state of happy well-being with respect to the drunkenness but also, especially when primed by the presented story (and cultured prior expectations), an aversive expectation generated by the victims. In other words, when we calculate the drunk driver's internal mental state, we calculate two valenced goals as a function of the automatic operation of the system: the appetitive reinforcement of the drunkenness and the aversive reinforcement of the victim's distress. Because these are expected outcomes of the behavior, they are considered the goals of the behavior. In short, the operation of the system implies that the drunk driver intended to take an action that could be expected to harm the victims and therefore should be considered "wrong" rather than "bad."

With respect to the individual punishing the child "for her own good," we again, according to this suggestion, represent the punisher's internal state and represent two valenced goals, the aversive reinforcement of the child's distress as well as the appetitive reinforcement of the child's future well-being. In this situation, the judgment becomes not whether we regard the punisher as "wrong" or "bad" but "wrong" or "right." According to the model, this judgment is determined according to whether or not the aversive reinforcement of the child's distress outweighs the appetitive reinforcement of the child's future well-being.

Shaun's fourth point is that norms are not the emotions but instead emotional reactions play a role in determining which norms survived throughout our cultural history. Shaun makes reference to cultural fitness and cultural evolution. I wish he had made reference to memetic fitness (Dawkins, 1989)! Dawkins proposed memes as the basic building blocks of our knowledge and culture and considered them analogous to genes. To survive, a meme, like a gene, needs to propagate. The easier a meme is to understand and remember, the easier that meme will propagate. Shaun's position here is that norms memes tied to emotional reactions will survive. Shaun provides historical data that this is the case. In additional support of his position, there is a considerable literature to demonstrate that emotional stimuli (memes) are remembered better than nonemotional stimuli (Cahill & McGaugh, 1998).

In summary, Shaun makes two claims that fit very well with the data and make perfect sense: The neosentimantalist account is an implausible account of moral judgment, and norms (memes) survive most successfully if they are tied to emotion. The basic suggestion that an affective process cannot explain all aspects of moral reasoning is also a solid one. However, it is difficult to know what to make of the notion of the normative theory. It is true that we do have rules available to us that we can verbalize. But it is unclear what purpose these have in moral reasoning, and it is also unclear to what extent such verbally accessible rules are part of Shaun's theory. I would suggest that the normative theory is in need of greater specification. I would also suggest on the basis of the theory-of-mind-grounded suggestion above that it may not be necessary.

5.2 Sentimental Rules and Moral Disagreement: Comment on Nichols

Justin D'Arms

Shaun Nichols's (2004b) fascinating book proposes a distinctive account of moral judgment and of the role of the emotions therein. Nichols rejects the contemporary neosentimentalist account of the relation between morality and emotion, while nonetheless embracing what he takes to be the central sentimentalist idea: that "emotions or sentiments are crucial to moral judgment" (this volume, p. 255). He therefore characterizes his theory as a new version of sentimentalism.[1] In his précis, which summarizes many of the central arguments from the book, Nichols argues (1) that there are empirical grounds for thinking that neosentimentalism is inconsistent with attributing the capacity for moral judgment to young children, (2) that this is a significant cost of the theory, (3) that his own preferred theory, the sentimental rules account, avoids this difficulty, and (4) that his theory meets the list of desiderata that motivate the move to neosentimentalism in the first place. I will grant (1) and (3) for purposes of this discussion and focus my critical remarks on (2) and (4). My aim is to provide a partial defense of neosentimentalism against the proffered alternative.

Nevertheless, I think Nichols has done sentimentalism a real service. There is some justice in his remark (2004b) that "For all the naturalistic enthusiasm surrounding neosentimentalism . . . researchers in this tradition seldom consider what empirical evidence could confirm or disconfirm sentimentalism" (p. 89). I admire the work Nichols does in pursuit of this question, bringing a wealth of empirical information to bear in new ways on the sentimentalist enterprise. Moreover, I am convinced that progress in moral philosophy, and in sentimentalist theorizing in particular, demands a realistic account of moral psychology. The studies that Nichols reports upon and himself conducts are a valuable contribution to the construction of such an account.

"Neosentimentalism" names a family of theories holding that various evaluative or normative judgments are judgments about the appropriateness of sentimental responses. Allan Gibbard's norm expressivism, for instance, is a form of neosentimentalism about moral judgments according to which to judge an act wrong is (roughly) to think it rational for the agent to feel guilty, and rational for others to be angry with him for doing it. I myself have some misgivings about neosentimentalism as an account of moral judgment in particular (D'Arms & Jacobson, 1994). However, I defend a version of neosentimentalism about some other evaluative concepts in collaborative work with Daniel Jacobson (2000b, 2006a), so I am more sympathetic to the program than Nichols is. For this reason, and because my qualms about the moral case are quite different from Nichols's, I will not rehearse them here. Instead I'll argue that Nichols's primary argument against neosentimentalism is not decisive, and, moreover, that it is not at all clear that his account can capture the desiderata he himself embraces for a viable sentimentalism. I will follow Nichols in using Gibbard's account as the test case and will therefore assume (what I think is plausible anyway) that the most promising sentiments for a neosentimentalist account of moral judgment are guilt and anger.

The central argument against neosentimentalism is the "dissociation problem," running roughly as follows. "If moral judgments are judgments of the appropriateness of guilt, then *an individual cannot have the capacity to make moral judgments unless she also has the capacity to make judgments about the appropriateness of guilt*" (Nichols, this volume, p. 259). However, various studies suggest that young children (ages 3–4) do have the capacity to make moral judgments, and others suggest that these children do not understand complex social emotions such as guilt. Surely, in order to make judgments about the appropriateness of guilt, one must have some understanding of the nature of this emotion (Nichols, this volume, pp. 260–261). Thus, these studies show that at least some moral judgments (the ones made by young children) are not judgments about the appropriateness of guilt.

Nichols's argument is a little more complicated than this, because the capacity that he actually claims for the children is a capacity for *core moral judgment* (CMJ). I am uncertain what exactly CMJ is supposed to be.[2] However, since children's capacity for CMJ is meant to constitute an empirical disproof of neosentimentalist accounts of judgments of right and wrong, I take it that CMJ must at least involve making some judgments of right and wrong ("moral judgments"). Thus, the challenge depends upon the plausibility of the claim that children who lack any understanding of guilt do indeed make moral judgments.

No doubt children use the words "right" and "wrong" and various other terms by which moral judgments are conventionally expressed. I assume, however, that in order to make moral judgments it is not sufficient to use moral terms in well-formed sentences. In order to make a moral judgment, I assume that it is necessary to have moral thoughts.[3] And in order to have moral thoughts, I assume that one must possess moral concepts. But children use many terms before they can plausibly be credited with possession of the concepts those terms express. For instance, shortly after turning 3, my daughter Katrina started saying that something is "not fair" just because it involves her not getting what she wants. I don't think she is insincere—it's just that her understanding of fairness at this point is exhausted by the idea that to call something not fair is to register a complaint.[4] I think it's clear that she hasn't got the concept of fairness yet. Thus, the neosentimentalist can question whether children's use of moral terms illustrates competence with moral concepts or not.[5]

The considerations Nichols offers to suggest that children are indeed competent with moral concepts are that they make the moral/conventional distinction, that they see moral infractions as especially serious, authority independent, and generalizable across contexts, that they offer harm-based considerations as their rationale for moral judgments, and that they "enter into disagreements with each other and with their parents over matters in the moral domain" (this volume, p. 262). I have doubts about how often young children engage in moral disagreements with their parents (absent special circumstances, where they are relying on someone else to teach them moral language), and this is one point on which Nichols cites no evidence. However, the rest of these claims do seem to be supported by the evidence he cites, and I will grant them in what follows.[6]

I take it that the neosentimentalist's answer will be roughly the one that Nichols anticipates: Children's CMJ is ersatz moral judgment. More specifically, it will be granted to be a kind of precursor to moral thinking, one that involves some sophisticated trappings of moral judgment but lacks certain commitments that are essential to the real thing. It is a familiar fact that along the way to acquiring a concept, children begin to use the term for that concept in phrases and contexts that they pick up from their parents and others. Sometimes they say seemingly quite sophisticated things and then go on to reveal their incomprehension in hilarious ways. Even in the evidence Nichols considers, there are some striking lacunae in children's understanding of morality. For instance, their exclusive focus on harms, and their failure to appreciate considerations of desert and reciprocal justice, should give anyone pause about whether to accord these children an adequate grasp of moral concepts. The moral neosentimentalist takes these doubts a step further, claiming that failure to appreciate the connection of moral claims to the appropriateness of emotional sanctions of guilt and anger renders the children's understanding of morality defective in a crucial way—one that makes it unclear what they can *mean* in calling an act wrong.

Until this response is assessed, the dissociation problem is not decisive. And I think Nichols grants as much.[7] The real question, he and I agree, should be what account best satisfies relevant desiderata for a theory of moral judgment. Nichols has made a prima facie case for the claim that children do make genuine moral judgments, and it should perhaps be counted as a cost of neosentimentalism that it must deny this.[8] In light of all the sophistication that some young children display in distinguishing wrongs from other sorts of rule violations, and their ability to adduce some of the right considerations in support of their claims, why think an understanding of the moral sentiments is needed for moral judgment? The response I have offered on behalf of neosentimentalism so far is partly theory driven. It relies on the plausibility of the neosentimentalist account of moral judgment that makes norms for guilt and anger crucial to moral judgment. Gibbard (1990) argues for this view at length, and I don't propose to rehearse all the motivations for neosentimentalist theories of moral judgment here. However, I will argue briefly that the neosentimentalist account of the meaning of moral claims makes sense of familiar moral disagreements in ways that the sentimental rules theory cannot, within constraints Nichols seems to embrace. Moreover, it does so in a way that helps to motivate the refusal to treat young children's judgments as moral ones.

First, though, I want briefly to consider the rejoinder Nichols offers when he anticipates the neosentimentalist reply above.[9] Against the suggestion that children who lack the concept of guilt cannot make moral judgments, Nichols says

... neosentimentalism is supposed to capture everyday normative life . . . , and it's an *empirical assumption* that most adult moral judgment is radically different from core moral judgment. The basic kind of moral judgment we see in children might be preserved without revision into adulthood, and it might well guide a great deal of adult moral judgment. As a result, if neosentimentalists cede core moral judgment, they risk neglecting a central part of our everyday normative lives. (p. 262)

I find this passage puzzling. In light of the surrounding context, the point seems to be that, for all we know, the same psychological mechanisms and states that are actively involved when children make their (pre-?) moral judgments are also involved when adults make moral judgments. According to Nichols, these include some sort of affective mechanism that responds to harm or distress in others and some kind of access to a "normative theory" that prohibits certain conduct. But why must the neosentimentalist deny any of this? Certainly Gibbard's norm-expressivist theory supposes that participants in moral discourse accept some body of norms, and it is not clear how this differs from their having a normative theory in Nichols's sense—a body of internally represented rules.[10] Moreover, I see no reason why Gibbard should be troubled were it to turn out that, in typical cases of harm-based wrongs, we are prompted to make moral judgments after reacting affectively to harms or distress. This response might be what induces us to attend to the action that brought about the distress, and once we do that we may well find that it violates norms we accept.

Of course, not everything that causes distress or harm violates a rule. And some acts that both cause distress and violate a rule are not moral infractions. Some violations of etiquette, for instance, cause distress without being wrongs. Thus, both Nichols and the neosentimentalist must suppose that we have some way of recognizing which harms are prohibited and of coding those prohibitions that we regard as moral. And of course the neosentimentalist will take it that the latter coding reflects one's attitudes toward feeling guilt and anger over the action—indeed, he will take it that this connection is what makes it a moral coding at all (whereas I am not sure what distinguishes moral prohibitions from other prohibitions on the sentimental rules account—which I take to be an important problem). However, this last commitment of neosentimentalism seems compatible with allowing a good deal of commonality between adults and children in the psychological processes underlying everyday moral and premoral judgment.

Perhaps the reason why Nichols thinks that neosentimentalism demands that adult moral judgment must look psychologically different from what children do is because he supposes that the theory is committed to there being some further psychological moment or process that is part of making a moral judgment. Presumably, this would be the moment at which the judge goes beyond being bothered and noticing that an action on which he is focused is in contravention of some internally represented (moral?) rules, to take a further step of deciding or noticing that it is an action that it would be appropriate for the agent to feel guilty for, and for others to be angry over. I don't see that any such step is needed. Yet the supposition that some such explicit reflection on the appropriateness of guilt is required seems to be behind Nichols's accusation that neosentimentalism is a "spectacularly intellectualized" (p. 268) account of moral judgment.

I would find it helpful to see this supposition fleshed out and defended, since it seems crucial to Nichols's criticism and important more generally for thinking about how the sorts of studies Nichols explores make contact with traditional metaethics. Neosentimentalism is a pattern of analysis or elucidation of the content of certain concepts. And there are many different ways of understanding what it is to give an analysis or elucidation of a given concept, few of which involve any obvious appeal to claims about the psychological mechanisms underlying deployment of the concept, or about what an agent must be aware of (i.e., consciously attending to) in order to count as deploying that concept. So what is it about the general shape of the neosentimentalist theory, or the specific claims of its various defenders, that Nichols thinks commits the theory to an implausibly intellectualist picture of moral judgment?

According to the neosentimentalist view I am exploring here, what makes it true that a moral thinker regards something as a *moral* infraction is that the infraction possesses the right kind of tie in his thinking to guilt (and anger). But it does not follow that this tie must be recognized expressly by the agent every time a transgression is coded as moral. For instance, the connection might instead be said to reside in such things as various inferences the moral thinker would make under relevant circumstances that are themselves best explained by attributing views about guilt and anger to him. It might involve such things as what he would avow about emotions if prompted; aspects of his own propensities to feel; attitudes he would have toward various ways he might feel; a tendency to take umbrage if others feel or fail to feel as (he thinks) they ought; a disposition to offer certain sorts of reasons (not) to feel to others, in the right context, and so on. I don't see why some set of dispositional truths along these lines should not suffice for the claim that our moral thinker has a view about the appropriateness of guilt and anger in a given case, without requiring any explicit reflection on these emotions to arise in that case.

That said, however, it is also worth noting that when normal adults are in real-life situations where an occurrent moral judgment would be apposite, they commonly experience guilt or indignation. (This is, admittedly, an empirical claim, but I don't think it is just an assumption, since it is based upon my own—admittedly fallible—observations of myself and others.) Such feelings are strictly neither necessary nor sufficient for moral judgment, according to neosentimentalism. However, when they do arise, along with attention to considerations that seem to justify them, or in the absence of anything that suggests the agent repudiates the emotion, it seems reasonable to take this as evidence for attributing to the agent the view that his emotions are appropriate. And this same pattern of evidence might suffice for attributing a moral judgment to the agent.

Let us turn now to one of the desiderata that Nichols mentions: explaining disagreement. Sentimentalists have historically been impressed by the significance of moral and evaluative disagreement—so much so that much of sentimentalism's development can be read as a series of increasingly sophisticated attempts to understand and explain such disagreement. Nichols recognizes this, and he takes it as a constraint on any adequate sentimentalist account that it must be able to "accommodate the possibility of moral disagreement" (p. 256). Moreover, he seems to accept that the arguments Charles Stevenson (1937) offered against first-person and community subjectivism (CS) are compelling. Stevenson argued that moral judgments should not be understood as judgments about what the speaker disapproves of, nor about what her community disapproves of.[11] First-person subjectivism makes apparent moral disagreements between speakers senseless. Parties would each be correctly reporting their own (patterns of) approval and disapproval, and the appearance of disagreement would be misleading. CS has two problems, according to Stevenson, of which Nichols notes only one. The one Nichols notes is that it seems to make disagreements between speakers from different communities senseless for reasons parallel to those afflicting first-person subjectivism.

The second problem Stevenson raises is that CS fails to make adequate sense of intracommunity disagreement. According to CS, when two speakers from the same community disagree about whether an action is wrong, their disagreement is about whether this act is such that it is disapproved of in their community. This turns their disagreement into a matter of sociology, over what acts are in fact disapproved of by some (typically unspecified) proportion of the population. This fails to capture what Stevenson called their disagreement in "interest," and what contemporary philosophers might call the "normative" character of their disagreement. When we disagree with members of our community over moral questions, we do not seem to be arguing about something that could be settled decisively by taking a poll. The argument seems to be about what people should disapprove of, not what they do in fact disapprove of. This, one might say (albeit somewhat tendentiously), is what makes it a genuinely moral disagreement.

Against this dialectical backdrop, though, how are we to understand Nichols's own proposal about disagreement? He tells us that "Children can disagree about what the rules are . . ." (p. 267). But when two young children have acquired different views about what is morally permissible—for instance, about whether suicide bombers are admirable martyrs or wicked terrorists—it is unclear what they disagree about on the sentimental rules account. Each might be correct about what is proscribed by his own normative theory. What we seem to need is a way of putting these two theories into conflict, as different answers to some shared question. But the question "What are the rules?" needs some explication if it is to serve in this context. "Whose rules?" it seems natural to ask.

A bit later Nichols says, "when we disagree and argue about moral issues. . . . We're talking about the content and implications of a largely shared normative theory" (p. 268). Perhaps, then, he only aspires to account for disagreements when parties largely share a normative theory. If so, there are two difficulties about this. One difficulty is that it apparently provides no resources for making sense of disagreements between communities with competing normative theories.[12] I am not sure how to reconcile that with Nichols's endorsement of Stevenson's first argument against CS above.

The other difficulty concerns intracommunity moral disagreement. No doubt some cases of moral dispute within a group with a largely shared normative theory can be understood as disagreements over the implications of some set of prohibitions for a concrete case, where both parties accept the same relevant prohibitions and the dispute is over what precisely they rule out. Sometimes these sorts of disputes will be resolvable by better reasoning or by getting clear about the nonmoral facts of the case. However, problems arise when that is not the situation, over cases where (as Nichols might put it) the parties differ over the content as opposed to the implications of their largely shared normative theory.

When disagreements about the content of this theory arise, what kind of disagreement are we dealing with, and what would settle it according to the sentimental rules approach? Do we revert to the CS answer to this question and ask which candidate rule has the right level of support in the community? If so, it is true that we have preserved a kind of disagreement here. But we face the second of the problems Stevenson raised above: We turn what looked like a normative disagreement (at the unsettled edges of the largely shared theory) into a sociological disagreement.

Much of the attraction of the neosentimentalist position, as I understand it, stems from this idea: that tying moral judgments semantically to specific sentimental responses gives them a subject matter that allows for the right kind of disagreement.[13] Moral prohibitions are those that call for anger and guilt, on the analysis we are considering. The analysis thereby gives us an account of what is at issue when two parties disagree about whether some kind of act is wrong—that is, when they differ in the normative theories they accept. What is at issue between them is, roughly, whether to feel guilt and anger for doing this sort of thing. More specifically, it is whether these emotions are appropriate. On Gibbard's analysis, this comes down to a disagreement in attitude: Their attitudes are in conflict because they endorse different norms for when guilt and anger are warranted. On other neosentimentalist accounts, such as those of McDowell and Wiggins, moral judgments will be beliefs about a normative subjective matter: about the existence of certain sorts of reason to respond with moral sentiments toward the act in question. However, what these views have in common is the idea that what makes moral disputes univocal, despite dramatic differences in the substantive convictions of the parties, is that they concern the appropriateness of responses to which all parties to the dispute are susceptible. This would provide one important motivation for excluding the children. If they aren't disagreeing about what to feel guilt and anger toward, it is not clear that the differences between the normative theories they accept are properly understood as rival answers to a shared question—which is to say that they may be talking past one another, and not really disagreeing at all.

In light of some things Nichols says about the vain quest for moral objectivity later in his book, he might be prepared to accept some of these consequences. Perhaps what I have been calling cases of "genuine moral disagreement" are really just exercises in talking past one another, as some relativists are content to assert. And perhaps the aspiration to provide an account of moral discourse that makes sense of such disputes (i.e., renders them univocal and substantive) is ultimately doomed to failure. But this, it seems to me, is both what Stevenson wanted from an account of moral disagreement and what neosentimentalism attempts to provide. In contrast, I think it is not yet clear in what sense the sentimental rules account even aspires to "accommodate the possibility of evaluative disagreement" (p. 256), much less that it succeeds.

Notes

I am grateful to Daniel Jacobson and Makoto Suzuki for extremely helpful comments on a draft of this paper.

1. Depending upon what is meant by "crucial," Nichols's characterization of sentimentalism may have the consequence that any view which holds as a psychological thesis that emotions are centrally implicated in most moral judgment will count

as sentimentalist. I prefer a more restrictive characterization, according to which, for a theory to be sentimentalist, it is required that the theory hold that the concepts or properties it treats be *response invoking*: They can only be explicated through some appeal to emotions or sentiments (see D'Arms & Jacobson, 2006a). This puts sentimentalism more squarely into dispute with other accounts of normative concepts and properties, such as those defended by naturalistic moral realists and analytic functionalists, who might well accept the psychological thesis that emotions are centrally implicated in most actual human practices of moral judgment. However, Nichols makes no claims about the nature of moral or evaluative properties and expressly disavows the idea that emotions figure in the content of moral claims. Having registered this taxonomic disagreement, I will set it aside and adopt Nichols's terminology for the present discussion. Perhaps no one but a sentimentalist could care about what this position gets called.

2. In both the book and the précis, this term is introduced in summary of a discussion that points to a number of different tendencies in moral thought, and it is not specified which or which combination of these are supposed to be definitive of CMJ. Indeed, it is not clear to me whether Nichols thinks CMJ is the kind of thing that can be defined, or whether it is intended to name some sort of natural syndrome, the characteristics of which are to be discovered empirically rather than stipulated. (I find some evidence for the latter hypothesis in précis footnote 6, where the question whether CMJ requires dispositions to feel is apparently left to future empirical inquiry.)

3. I think of a moral judgment as an inner act, of reaching some moral verdict, rather than as a speech act of announcing a moral claim. However, even if one adopts the latter use of "moral judgment," in order for an utterance like "That is wrong" to qualify as a moral judgment, surely it must express a thought comprised in part by a moral concept.

4. My main point here is simply the obvious one that using a moral word is not sufficient for making a moral judgment. I don't mean to be offering Katrina's case as a refutation of the thesis that many young children do make moral judgments. Katrina cannot yet make the distinctions that the children in the studies make. (Lest the reader leap to the conclusion that Katrina is obtuse, or the recipient of an unusually shoddy moral education, I hasten to note that the children in most of the studies are a bit older.) But I do want to suggest that if other children her age are to be credited with making moral judgments, they had better not be doing merely what she is doing with her talk of fairness.

5. In his survey of the developmental literature, Larry Nucci (2001) notes that many young children use "fair" in just the way Katrina does, and he claims that "Young children's morality . . . is not yet structured by understandings of fairness as reciprocity" (p. 86). He cites Davidson, Turiel, and Black (1983) for the finding that in children up to age 7, moral judgment is primarily regulated by concerns for maintaining welfare and avoiding harm.

6. Full disclosure: I have not checked all these sources myself. I am relying on Nichols's reports except where noted.

7. He says ". . . the dissociation problem cannot dislodge neosentimentalism unless there is a plausible alternative to take its place" (p. 262).

8. At least, it must deny it pending some revision to the account that fixes on different emotions—ones that are plausibly understood by young children. One possibility for such a revision would be to drop guilt and focus on anger. Children surely understand anger, so perhaps a neosentimentalist who was eager to accommodate children's moral judgment could treat it as about the appropriateness of (the right kind of?) anger. I have doubts about this strategy myself (see D'Arms & Jacobson, 1994). However, I am also less troubled than some may be about biting the bullet and insisting that young children are not really competent with moral concepts.

9. Here I consider the rejoinder he offers in the précis. Other lines of response are raised in his book at pp. 93–94, but adequate discussion of these would take me too far afield.

10. There is perhaps this difference: Gibbard insists that the norms accepted by actual agents form a highly incomplete system and that often when we make a moral judgment we commit ourselves to new norms that do not follow from what we had accepted before, rather than simply consulting a set of rules we had already accepted. However, this seems only reasonable, and I assume that Nichols would not want his talk of a child's "normative theory" to commit him to attributing *more* internally represented rules to children than Gibbard attributes to adults.

11. Actually, Stevenson's arguments were focused on the term "good," not on moral judgments per se. However, I will follow Nichols in applying them to moral matters, which I think is quite compatible with Stevenson's ultimate views about their significance.

12. Nichols seems to grant that there are some such cases in his book (Nichols, 2004b). See, for instance, the discussion of cross-cultural normative disagreement at pp. 147–149.

13. This is claimed as an advantage of sentimentalism by both Gibbard (1990) and Wiggins (1987b). I explicate this argument further in D'Arms (2005).

5.3 Sentiment, Intention, and Disagreement: Replies to Blair and D'Arms

Shaun Nichols

I am most grateful to James Blair and Justin D'Arms for commenting on my work. I would be hard put to name two other moral psychologists whose reactions I'd be so keen to hear. There is a striking asymmetry in their commentaries. Blair prefers a minimalist story about moral judgment, maintaining that the appeal to rules is unnecessary. D'Arms, by contrast, maintains that the account I offer is overly simple and that children lack moral concepts despite their partial facility with moral language. It is tempting to treat my account as achieving the golden mean between Blair's austerity and D'Arms's extravagance. But it would be unfair to both. Blair is attracted to the sparse account for empirical reasons, and D'Arms is attracted to a richer account for philosophical reasons. Nonetheless, I still think that the account I offer is preferable to Blair's minimalism and to D'Arms's neosentimentalism. Rather than give a point-by-point reply, which would likely be tedious, I'll try to say why I think that my account is still more plausible than the alternatives proffered by Blair and D'Arms.

The Necessity of Rules

In an earlier paper (Nichols, 2002a), I argued against Blair's account of moral judgment. Blair maintains that normal (i.e., nonpsychopathic) humans have a violence inhibition mechanism (VIM) which is activated by cues of distress or suffering. To simplify his account somewhat, Blair suggested that moral judgment occurs when the VIM generates an emotional reaction. The gist of my objection was that Blair's account leads to the awkward conclusion that we make moral judgments when we witness accident victims. For in those cases, the VIM will generate emotional responses to the distress cues. As a result, I argued, Blair's VIM mechanism might lead to judgments that something is *bad,* but it doesn't get us all the way to judgments that something is *wrong.*

Blair is extremely gracious about my previous objection, and he now allows that VIM alone isn't sufficient for moral judgment. On his new proposal, VIM activation is still essential to moral judgment, but so is the judgment that there was intent to cause harm. He writes, "actions are considered 'wrong' rather than merely 'bad' when there is intent to cause harm" (p. 276).

Blair recognizes two prima facie objections to his proposal. First, many clear cases of moral violations don't seem to count as moral violations on Blair's proposal. Sometimes an agent can lack the intent to cause harm but be just as much the target of moral condemnation. In his commentary, Blair discusses the case of a drunk driver causing fatalities, and Blair ultimately suggests that the drunk driver who kills receives our moral condemnation because he "intended to take an action that could be expected to harm the victims" (p. 277). That response works, but notice that Blair has now introduced a crucial change to his account. It isn't just "intent to cause harm"; moral judgment is also generated when there is *intent to act in a way that can (or should) be expected to cause harm*.

Now that Blair has expanded the range in this way, the other prima facie problem becomes clear. There will be many cases of actions that are not judged morally wrong but in which the agent expects that the action will cause harm or suffering. Consider first a delightful example from Alan Leslie and Ron Mallon: crybabies. Two children, James and Tammy, are eating their lunch, and each has one cookie. But James wants to eat both cookies, and it's clear that he'll be very upset if he doesn't get his way. When Tammy eats her cookie, this makes James cry. Tammy might have known that James would be distressed, but her action isn't regarded as morally wrong (Leslie et al., forthcoming). For a second example, take boxing—a sport in which participants have the intent to hurt the opponent badly enough to render him unconscious. Most people, at least in many cultures, do not regard the boxer as committing a moral violation when he punches his opponent. Finally, consider punishment—we often engage in or endorse punishment of others, with the express intent to inflict suffering on the target.

Blair acknowledges the problem punishment might pose. And he tries to solve the problem by invoking competing factors in the judge. When we consider the propriety of an agent punishing a child, we "represent the punisher's internal state and represent two valenced goals, the aversive reinforcement of the child's distress as well as the appetitive reinforcement of the child's future well-being. . . . According to the model, this judgment is determined according to whether or not the aversive reinforcement of the child's distress outweighs the appetitive reinforcement of the child's future well-being" (pp. 277–278). Thus, when the appetitive reinforcement outweighs the aversive reinforcement, we judge that the action is permissible.

Blair's presentation of the appetitive/aversive model is very brief, but it seems to run into a serious problem, for sometimes appetitive reinforcement outweighs *moral judgment*. A child's desire for candy can be so great that the child decides to steal in the face of a countervailing moral judgment. In such a case, and many more like it, the individual will often say something like "I know I shouldn't have done that, but I just wanted candy so badly that I went ahead anyway." In short, the problem for Blair's proposal is that our appetites sometimes win out over our moral judgments. Thus, it seems that Blair cannot account for the problematic cases of moral judgment simply by appealing to the victor of the competition between appetitive and aversive influences on our judgment.

The problem for Blair, then, is that often it is not a moral violation to intend to perform an action that is expected to cause harm. Crybabies, boxing, and punishment are the three examples that I suggested, though many more could be provided, of course. It will be no trivial matter to fix the account in a way that matches up with our everyday practices of moral judgment. In contrast to Blair's proposed competition between aversion and appetite, I would again invoke moral rules to explain the complex pattern of moral judgment that we see surrounding permissible harmful actions. Harmful actions can be permissible because our rules are a complex lot, involving such considerations as fairness, consent, and retributive justice.

Concepts, Content, and Moral Psychology: A Prelude to Disagreement

In the metaethical tradition that places emotions at the center of moral judgment, "neosentimentalism" is perhaps the major account on the contemporary scene. According to neosentimentalism, to judge that an action is morally wrong is to judge that it would be appropriate to feel guilt on doing the action.[1] In my paper, I argue that neosentimentalism is threatened by the fact that we find a dissociation in children between the capacity for moral judgment and the capacity to judge the appropriateness of guilt. D'Arms offers a defense of neosentimentalism against this dissociation argument. One of the themes in D'Arms's response is that neosentimentalism is an account of the *content* of moral concepts, so I want to say something about the relationship between theories of content and neosentimentalism before proceeding to his main argument.

Issues about content are complex in ways that bear on the viability of neosentimentalism. Let's consider two extremely prominent approaches to content: informational accounts and functional role accounts. For present purposes, we can be very crude about what these stories say. On prominent informational accounts, the content of a concept is characteristically determined by properties in the external world that cause the concept (Dretske, 1981; Fodor, 1990). So, familiarly, the concept WET refers to the property in the world that causes the tokening of that concept. If such an informational account is the globally correct theory of content, things don't look so good for neosentimentalism, for the typical external cause for the tokening of moral concepts is an *action*, not the appropriateness of an emotion. By contrast, if the informational account were globally true, that would weigh in favor of certain moral realist accounts, like Sturgeon (1988) and Brink (1989). On those views, the content of WRONG is indeed the property in the world that causes the tokening of that concept.

Let's turn to the most important rival to informational accounts of content, functional role accounts. According to some prominent versions of the functional role approach, the content of a concept is given by the overall functional or causal role it plays in the psychology of the agent (e.g., Block, 1986). Of course, when we look across individuals, there will be differences in the functional roles of the concepts, so the theorist needs some account of how much (or what part) of the functional role has to be the same in order for two people each to have a token of a concept with the same content. If we think that even small differences in functional roles mean a difference in content, then it will turn out that people rarely use the same concepts, and we typically talk past each other. Such fine-grained functional role theories would certainly give us reason to say that a young child and I do not share a common concept of morality. But those theories would also lead us to say that it would be exceedingly rare for any two adults to have the same concept of morality. At the other end of the spectrum, one might take a very coarse-grained functional role approach, on which two people have the same concept so long as there is some significant overlap in functional role. At least prima facie, that approach would favor the view that a young child and I have the same concept MORALLY WRONG, since there is significant overlap in the functional roles of our concept tokens (as indicated, say, by performance on the moral/conventional task). Neither of these outcomes would be favorable to D'Arms's neosentimentalism. D'Arms wants to maintain that people typically don't talk past each other in moral conversation, but also that children do not have the same concepts as adults. Fine-grained and coarse-grained accounts wouldn't let him have it both ways.

Thus, if we approach the issue of the content of moral concepts by considering different theories of content, there is no reason to think that neosentimentalism gives us the right semantics for moral concepts. My own suspicion is that there is no single correct theory of content, even for a given class of concepts, like proper name concepts or natural kind concepts (see, e.g., Machery, Mallon, Nichols, & Stich, 2004; Mallon, Machery, Nichols, & Stich, forthcoming). If that's right, then we need to be very cautious about claims like that of neosentimentalism, for neosentimentalists are promoting a univocal account of content for moral terms, and that might be a fundamentally misguided undertaking. It might turn out that *there is no* univocal account of content for moral terms.[2]

However, what I suspect is really going on is that D'Arms thinks that by looking at various facts about moral judgment, we can glean constraints on the semantics that push in favor of neosentimentalism. Thus, while D'Arms's neosentimentalism would be doomed if it turned out one of the above theories is the universally correct theory of content, D'Arms will presumably say that these cannot be globally correct theories of content, because, at least for evaluative concepts, the neosentimentalist account is right. The informational theories are incorrect as accounts of the content of moral concepts. For functional role accounts, when we individuate evaluative concepts, the grain is neither very fine nor very coarse. Rather, the grain must be neosentimentalist. Similarly, if D'Arms's argument succeeds, it will relieve my skepticism about the univocality of content, at least for moral terms. The arguments in favor of neosentimentalism will not only tell us something important about moral judgment but also inform the theory of content itself. That is, of course, a bold thesis, so let's look at the argument.

Disagreements

According to neosentimentalism, to judge that it is morally wrong to *A* is to judge that it is appropriate to feel guilty for doing the action. As D'Arms notes, this judgment of appropriateness needn't be occurrent whenever one makes a moral judgment. Rather, the key point is that people who make moral judgments have the *disposition* to judge that it's appropriate to feel guilty for doing the action. It is that disposition that makes a given judgment an instance of moral judgment.

Obviously there is a huge set of dispositions surrounding occurrent moral judgment. For instance, when people judge that it is wrong to *A*, they have dispositions like the following:

- The disposition to be attentive to such actions.
- The disposition to think that it is appropriate to be so attentive.
- The disposition to show high galvanic skin response (GSR).
- The disposition to respond more quickly in recognizing moral vocabulary in word/nonword tasks.

In addition, of course, when people judge that it is wrong to *A*, they have the disposition to make judgments about the appropriateness of guilt. Some of these dispositions are likely present in children, for example, GSR response, and some are likely absent in children, for example, dispositions to make judgments about the appropriateness of attentiveness or guilt. Why do neosentimentalists insist that the key disposition, the one that makes or breaks moral judgment, is the disposition to judge that guilt (or some other emotion) is appropriate? Apart from neosentimentalism, presumably the standard view is that judgments about the appropriateness of guilt are *consequences* of moral judgment. So why opt for the complex neosentimentalism view?

The answer is disagreement. According to D'Arms, we need a neosentimentalist account to accommodate moral disagreement. D'Arms is committed to the superiority of neosentimentalism here generally (see D'Arms, 2005), but for present purposes all D'Arms needs to argue is that neosentimentalism offers a better explanation of moral disagreement than the affect-backed-normative-theory account that I've proposed, so I'll restrict the discussion to these two accounts.

As I say in my paper, on the affect-backed-theory account, much of the moral disagreement that we see in everyday life can be explained by adverting to the content of a widely shared normative theory, for in most moral disagreements the disputants share certain basic moral principles that guide their judgments. Some philosophers suggest that once we clear away all the diversity in factual judgments, there will be no remaining cases of moral diversity (e.g., Boyd, 1988). I'm unwilling to take *that* strong a line. It seems likely that there are some cases of "fundamental" moral disagreement that would remain even after all factual disagreements are resolved. For instance, I think it quite possible that Brandt was right that there was fundamental moral disagreement between his Hopi informants and suburbanites on whether it's okay to harm animals for sport (Brandt, 1954). In addition, I think that Doris and Stich make a good case that there is fundamental moral disagreement in the United States between Southerners and Northerners on the moral propriety of violent reprisals for insults (Doris & Stich, 2005). And Doris and Plakias (this volume) make a nice case that there are fundamental disagreements between East Asians and Westerners on familiar cases like the magistrate and the mob. Nonetheless, I do think it's important to recognize that fundamental moral disagreement might be a comparatively rare form of moral diversity.

To see whether neosentimentalism provides a better account of fundamental moral disagreement than the account I've offered, I would like to begin by noting two central *apparent facts* about moral disagreement. The point here is not to insist that moral disagreement really has these characteristics but merely that this is how, at first glance, moral disagreement seems:

1. Many people *seem* to treat some moral transgressions as objectively wrong. They say things like "Ethnic cleansing is wrong even if another culture thinks something else" and "Ethnic cleansing would be wrong even if we didn't have the emotions we do."
2. Moral disagreements *seem* to be fundamentally about right and wrong, and not fundamentally about emotion.

On the neosentimentalist account of moral disagreement, things are not as they seem. According to neosentimentalism, moral disagreements are fundamentally about the appropriateness of certain emotions. D'Arms writes, "what makes moral disputes univocal . . . is that they concern the appropriateness of responses to which all parties to the dispute are susceptible" (p. 287). As far as I can tell, no one innocent of sentimentalist metaethics has ever thought that the content of their moral disagreements with others about, say, abortion, animal experimentation, circumcision, corporal discipline, or capital punishment were, most fundamentally, about the appropriateness of feeling various emotions. Although moral disagreements don't seem fundamentally to be about emotions, neosentimentalists would maintain that this superficial feature of moral disagreement doesn't reflect the deep truth about moral disagreement. The deep truth is that, despite appearances to the contrary, moral disagreements are really about the appropriateness of feeling certain emotions. As a result, the other apparent fact about moral disagreement is also false. Although it seems like some people are objectivists, this appearance is misleading. People don't really think that moral claims are true in some objective way. Rather, moral claims are about which emotional responses are appropriate, given the emotional repertoires that we have.

Now, of course, even if it's true that we don't think of our moral claims as having a certain content, it's possible that they do have that content nonetheless. Many philosophers think that sometimes we don't know the contents of our concepts. For instance, if we focus on the *extensional content* of our thoughts, then many would say that important elements of the extensional content of WATER were missed by ancient thinkers. They didn't realize that water is a combination of hydrogen and oxygen. But it's crucial to note that the neosentimentalist is not merely saying that judgments of appropriateness of emotions capture the *extensions* of moral concepts. Rather, as D'Arms (2005) writes, "A shared sentiment supplies a shared element in the *intensions* of our evaluative thoughts" (p. 17, emphasis added). Although it's a familiar claim that we often lack access to the *extensional content* of our concepts, it's quite controversial to maintain that we sometimes don't even know the *intensional* content of our everyday concepts.[3] Even a slave to Nisbett and Wilson (1977) like me thinks that we typically do have access to the intensional contents of our thoughts. As a result, I submit that the neosentimentalist needs a very good argument that the intensional contents of people's moral concepts and moral disagreements are not accessible to them.

How does my theory fare with respect to the apparent facts about moral disagreement listed above? On the account I've proposed, moral judgment derives from an affect-backed normative theory. On that approach, we can easily allow that things are as they seem. Many people seem committed to moral objectivism. To accommodate this, we can simply allow that one feature of the normative theory (at least for many people) is that it carries the presupposition that moral claims like "It's wrong to force sex on a stranger" are true *simpliciter*. Given the background of assumed moral objectivity, it's easy to accommodate these as disagreements about right and wrong rather than about emotions. The problem of capturing moral disagreement only emerges when we deny that people are moral objectivists. Now, I also doubt, as do many neosentimentalists, that morality really is objective. However, that does nothing to undermine the claim that lay moral disagreements are crucially underwritten by the presumption of objectivity.

Thus, the affect-backed-theory account can easily accommodate the two apparent facts about moral disagreement. What my theory *cannot* easily accommodate is fundamental ethical disagreement between individuals who fully reject moral objectivism about the target action. That is, if Mark thinks that it is wrong to *A* and Eric thinks that it's not wrong to *A*, and if both of them reject that idea that it is *objectively wrong (or not wrong)* to *A*, then my account has no obvious story to tell on which Mark and Eric are locked in fundamental ethical disagreement. However, it's not clear to me that this is much of a cost, for it's not clear to me that in such cases there *is* fundamental ethical disagreement.

There's another obvious gloss available, and it's one that D'Arms acknowledges at the end of his response. I can maintain that those who reject moral objectivism treat moral claims as true only relative to some community, culture, or arbitrary feature of human constitution. In fact, this seems fairly plausible to me. Many people seem to treat some moral transgressions as wrong in a relativistic way. They say things like "Unprovoked hitting is wrong in our culture, but it's not wrong in other cultures." These cases are somewhat controversial, but it is worth noting that there are utterly clear cases of normative relativism if we look to nonmoral transgressions. Consider the following scenario (from Nichols, 2002a): "Bill is sitting at a dinner party and he snorts loudly and then spits into his water before drinking it." The vast majority of subjects said that this was not okay and would not have been okay even if the host had said that such actions were permissible. However, Western undergraduates also say that the disgusting violations that are wrong for us need not be wrong *simpliciter* (Nichols, 2004a). In these cases, we find normative diversity without fundamental evaluative disagreement. Although I wouldn't count these judgments about disgusting transgressions as cases of *moral* diversity, the evaluative diversity surrounding disgusting violations can serve as canonical cases of relativism about norms. This gives us a natural place to fit our moral nonobjectivists—they treat moral transgressions the way most people (in our culture) treat disgusting violations.

In summary, the one thing that neosentimentalism can do that I can't is explain fundamental moral disagreement among nonobjectivists. However, this does not seem a sufficient advantage to favor the neosentimentalist approach to moral disagreement. First, in order to explain the disagreement, the neosentimentalist needs to claim that the appearances of moral disagreement are quite misleading—that people don't really understand what their moral disagreements are about. And second, it is independently dubious that moral nonobjectivists typically do engage in fundamental moral disagreement with each other. Neither of these reasons counts as a refutation of neosentimentalism. But they do, I think, suffice to show that the neosentimentalist lacks any powerful advantage over my theory when it comes to the phenomena of moral diversity.

What Is Moral?

Both Blair and D'Arms have a tidy story that picks out the moral domain. For Blair, the moral domain is given by his VIM mechanism. For D'Arms, the moral domain is carved out by the appropriateness of guilt or anger. I don't have any comparable proposal, as D'Arms notes: "I am not sure what distinguishes moral prohibitions from other prohibitions on the sentimental rules account—which I take to be an important problem" (p. 283).

My failure to give an account of the moral domain wasn't just an oversight on my part. One of the few things I recall from graduate school is that proposing definitions is not for the risk averse. Rather, definitions are for those willing to philosophize dangerously. Most proposed definitions in philosophy have been manifest failures. Indeed, it's hard to come up with any examples of successful definitions, despite the considerable energy philosophers have exerted. When chemists meet with so little success, their jobs are in jeopardy.

As with other philosophically important concepts, I think it unlikely that MORAL will have a nicely delineated definition. Although it might seem tempting to claim that the moral/conventional distinction provides a crisp line for characterizing the moral domain, the temptation should be resisted. The different factors in the moral/conventional task (e.g., generalizability, authority contingence, seriousness) have been shown to come apart in various ways (e.g., Kelly, Stich, Haley, Eng, & Fessler, forthcoming).[4]

Even though I refuse to adopt an account of the moral domain, this does not present an insurmountable problem for investigating moral psychology, for we can recognize obvious cases that fall in the domain of moral prohibitions (e.g., rape, murder) and obvious cases that fall outside the domain of moral prohibition (e.g., table settings). By coming to understand the clear cases, we can at least get the beginnings of an account of the nature of moral judgment, even if that account will not deliver anything like a sharp delineation of the moral domain.

Notes

Thanks to John Doris, Ron Mallon, and Walter Sinnott-Armstrong for many helpful suggestions.

1. I will focus here, following my paper and D'Arms's reply, on guilt as the crucial emotion for neosentimentalism. However, I should note that D'Arms's own view is more complex. He has argued against the view that an adequate neosentimentalist account of moral judgment can be provided by appealing to guilt alone (see D'Arms

& Jacobson, 1994). None of the discussion in D'Arms's commentary or in this reply, though, hangs on the additional complexities.

2. See the contributions by Gill (this volume) and Loeb (this volume) for arguments that moral semantics will not be univocal.

3. There are some approaches to intensional content on which we might lack such access. For instance, on a possible worlds semantics approach to intensions, an intension is just the extension of an expression across all possible worlds. However, I should think that neosentimentalists would not want to tie their fate to a particular approach to intensions. And, in any case, it would seem ad hoc to cast about for an approach to intensions that will assist the neosentimentalist in avoiding this problem.

4. These results pose a problem for trying to use the moral/conventional test to define the moral domain. However, the results do not, in my view, undermine the interest of the basic finding that there are important differences in judgments about intuitively immoral actions and judgments about intuitively convention-defying actions.

6 How to Argue about Disagreement: Evaluative Diversity and Moral Realism

John M. Doris and Alexandra Plakias

Given that moral disagreement so often seems intractable, is there any reason to think that moral problems admit objective resolutions? Such questions are among the most awkward for those philosophers—*moral realists* in the contemporary register—defending the objectivity of morality. Like others posed in the present volume, this pointed query has substantial empirical elements: It presupposes anthropological observations about how moral disagreements proceed—or fail to proceed. As commentators with both realist (Sturgeon, 1988, p. 230) and antirealist (Loeb, 1998, p. 284) sympathies acknowledge, evaluating the anthropological observations requires careful inquiry into real-world—as opposed to philosophically imagined—evaluative diversity. We quite agree, and we'll be doing some of this here. But the empirical issues are, inevitably, philosophically situated: The alleged incompatibility between intractable disagreement—if it exists—and moral realism can only be established—if it can be established—through philosophical investigation, so we'll be doing some of that, too. Like many central issues in ethics, the philosophical and empirical are here mutually insinuated, and deeply so; progress requires advances on both fronts.

Unlike some philosophers who are impressed with the empirical record (e.g., Harman, 1996), we will not go so far as to claim that evaluative diversity compels rejection of moral realism. Instead, we argue that moral realism suffers a pair of interacting pressures: On the one hand, there are good *philosophical* reasons to think realism would be undermined by the existence of intractable disagreement; on the other, there are good *empirical* reasons to suppose that such disagreement does in fact exist. Accordingly, the moral realist must either pull the philosophical duty of showing her position to be untroubled by disagreement or endure the empirical toil of establishing that the troubling disagreement does not exist. Neither job, we contend, makes easy work.

The provenance of the difficulty runs as follows. In 1977, Mackie argued that the apparent intractability of moral disagreement is best explained on the hypothesis that there are no "objective moral facts" undergirding moral judgment.[1] Realists have traditionally disputed the intractability claim, insisting that moral disagreements *are* rationally resolvable when disputants occupy optimal conditions (Boyd, 1988; Brink, 1984, 1989; Sturgeon, 1988; Smith, 1994). Lately, some realists have departed tradition and accepted Mackie's judgment that many serious moral disagreements may be insoluble; their response is simply to deny that disagreement unsettles realism (Bloomfield, 2001; Shafer-Landau, 1994, 1995, 2003). We will argue that there are good philosophical reasons to adopt the traditional response; disagreement does, we think, unsettle realism. At the same time, reflection on the empirical record indicates that the dissenters have good reason for wishing to avoid Mackie's challenge: The traditional response entails conjectures about the resolution of disagreement which will be difficult to substantiate. We do not claim that this difficulty dooms moral realism, but it does suggest that if the aspirations of moral realism are to be sustained, it will be by pressing an uphill fight over complex and varied empirical terrain. In what follows, we articulate some of the contours and indicate what would be required for a successful traverse.

The Philosophical Terrain

Two Moral Realisms: Convergentism and Divergentism

There are many species in the genus, but we expect that many moral realists (more or less) share this core commitment of Michael Smith's (1994, p. 9; cf. p. 13) realism: "Moral questions have correct answers, . . . made correct by objective moral facts." Mackie's (1977, pp. 36–37) abductive "argument from disagreement" purports to vitiate such positions: The phenomenon of moral disagreement, Mackie argued, is "more readily explained by the hypothesis that [moral judgments] reflect ways of life" than by the hypothesis that moral judgments reflect adherents' apprehension of moral facts (cf. Harman, 1977, chapter 1).[2]

So understood, the bone of contention is broadly *ontological*: Moral realists posit *moral facts* in the explanation of moral experience, while antirealists deny the existence of such facts, insisting that moral factualism represents an impotent explanatory strategy. As with any characterization of a philosophical problematic, one might have misgivings here, and indeed we have some ourselves. Important variants of moral realism (e.g., Smith, 1994, p. 9) evince *epistemological* as well as ontological commitments, holding not only that moral facts exist, but that they are discoverable or "epistemically accessible."[3] Moreover, a clearly demarcated epistemological/ontological distinction may be somewhat artificial in the context; indeed, it is tempting to think that antirealist ontological claims draw credibility from the (alleged) difficulty of articulating how epistemic access to moral facts may obtain.[4] Finally, variants of moral realism may eschew factualism and develop understandings of objectivity that do not proceed by reference to "moral facts" (see Sayre-McCord, 1988, p. 5). Cautions notwithstanding, factualist formulations are prominent in the literature,[5] as is couching the issues in explanatory terms.[6] Our demarcation of the rhetorical space is not eccentric and should allow an entrée into the problem of disagreement—and the kind of empirical work needed to responsibly address it—that is of general resonance.

Realists often respond to the problem by observing that actual moral disputants suffer epistemic disadvantages that are implicated in disagreement. If so, Mackie's antirealism doesn't enjoy a decisive explanatory edge—so much the worse for disputants, not so much the worse for morality. Accordingly, later writers (Loeb, 1998; Tolhurst, 1987) have focused on counterfactual rather than actual moral disagreement. What is philosophically threatening about moral disagreement, they claim, is that it may remain unresolved after all rational means of adjudication have been deployed. That is, even in *ideal* conditions, among fully informed, fully rational discussants, moral disagreement may persist.[7] Such *fundamental* disagreement, the worry goes, undermines the prospects for moral realism.[8] Firstly, it makes moral inquiry look importantly different from inquiries that seem to readily admit of realist treatments, such as natural science. Secondly, the existence of fundamental disagreement appears to buttress the abductive argument for moral antirealism: The most obvious explanation of such disagreement may be that there are, pace Smith, no moral facts to "make" our moral judgments correct.

Many realists—call them *convergentist* moral realists—deny that fundamental disagreement is a pervasive phenomenon; they maintain that the preponderance of actual moral disagreement is due to limitations of disputants or their circumstances and insist that (very substantial, if not unanimous)[9] agreement *would* emerge on most important moral questions, were the disagreement addressed in ideal conditions. To be a bit more precise, convergentist realism entails two commitments: (1) a philosophical observation to the effect that realism is troubled by fundamental disagreement and (2) an empirical conjecture to the effect that such disagreement will not widely obtain in appropriate discursive conditions.

Other realists—call them *divergentist* moral realists—have lately rejected the idea that fundamental disagreement counts against moral realism and have distanced themselves from empirical conjectures about convergence.[10] Accordingly, we here divide moral realism into two camps—convergentists, who are committed to the "convergence conjecture," and divergentists, who are not. Obviously, convergentist realism will be undermined if the convergence conjecture cannot be made good. Less obviously, divergentist realism cannot evade the difficulty posed by fundamental disagreement; divergentism occupies philosophically troubled ground. Or so we will argue.

Divergentism

The attraction of divergentism is immediate and obvious. In the first instance, its appeal rests on a venerable backwoodsism: *That everyone thinks something, sonny-boy, don't make it so.* Unlike some folk wisdoms, this one has a bit of philosophical bite: Agreement does not entail objectivity, and oftentimes should not be counted as even prima facie evidence for it. Depending on one's methodological predilections, divergentism also offers another benefit: If issues about disagreement are unrelated to the prospects of realism, it saves philosophers the trouble of examining an uncertain empirical record. Would that it were so easy. While we doubt that the connection between agreement and objectivity is of the watertight sort some philosophers like to think of as conceptual, we believe the issues are, nevertheless, intimately associated.

To see why, it will help to consider a familiar analogical argument for moral realism:

(1) Ethical theorizing is relevantly similar to theorizing in science.
(2) We should be realists about science.
(3) Therefore, we should be realists about ethical theorizing.

If we find no philosophically significant differences between moral inquiry and scientific inquiry, then there is no principled reason to maintain scientific realism while rejecting moral realism. And happily, scientific realism seems to require less Herculean philosophical ambition than moral realism; as Railton (2003, pp. 3, 5), a self-described defender of "stark, raving moral realism" acknowledges, "[a]mong contemporary philosophers, even those who have not found skepticism about empirical science at all compelling have tended to find skepticism about morality irresistible." So if morality can be made to look more like science than this (possibly invidious) way of making the comparison suggests, moral realism may start to look pretty good.

Paul Bloomfield (2001) has recently run an analogical argument advert-ing not to scientific inquiry, narrowly construed, but to inquiry about health. Bloomfield (2001) contends that "moral goodness has the same status as physical healthiness, so that if we are realists about the latter, then we ought to be also about the former" (p. 28). According to Bloomfield (2001, p. 32), "no properties are more deserving of realism than those of being alive and being dead, and the difference between them is one of healthiness"; therefore, we "cannot be other than realists about health without also denying that life differs from death." Perhaps surprisingly, Bloomfield takes this analogy to tell for divergentism. While medical experts tend to agree on the "easy cases," there are substantial "differences of opinion in the face of all the uncertainty that surrounds difficult cases"; these disagreements do not undermine realism about health, and "[m]oral realism should not be held to a higher standard" (Bloomfield, 2001, pp. 89–92).

A natural way for the moral antirealist to respond to this "companions-in-guilt argument" is to resist the analogy and insist that health discourse, unlike moral discourse, is not afflicted with fundamental disagreement. On this line, disagreement in health care is largely attributable to factors like the imprecision of prognosis; such disagreement is plausibly thought to be ameliorable by the resolution of epistemic disadvantages in ideal circum-stances, but there are not compelling reasons to expect similar ameliora-tion in the case of morality. There may be much to be said for this response, but we will not pursue it here. Rather, we are inclined to *accept* Bloom-field's analogy but *reject* his understanding of health care. While we are mindful that the philosophical issues afflicting discussions of health are no less tangled than those surrounding morality, we will argue for the fol-lowing: To the extent that fundamental disagreement obtains in health care, there is a strong case for antirealism about health.

Mental health care presents the obvious difficulty. Consider the ques-tion of whether a person afflicted with "extreme shyness" should be under-stood as exhibiting normal behavioral variation or suffering from treatable mental illness. This is not an ivory tower quibble; at issue is whether or not interventions directed at the amelioration of extreme shyness will be covered by health insurance. Both positions have defenders, with some commentators denying that insurance providers are obligated to provide such coverage (e.g., Sabin & Daniels, 1994, pp. 9–13) and others favoring the contrary view (e.g., Woolfolk & Doris, 2002, pp. 482–484). We've no need to take sides here; the important point is that such disputes are not easily managed. Familiar theoretical expedients, such as Bloomfield's

(2001, pp. 32, 134–137; cf. Daniels, 2001) understanding of health in terms of "proper functioning," are unlikely likely to be of much help. While functionalist constructions of health are bedeviled with complexities, not least those having to do with the uncertainty—and controversy—afflicting proposed standards of "normalcy" (see Murphy & Woolfolk, 2000; Murphy, 2005), extreme shyness quite arguably *is* an impediment to "normal" or "proper" functioning (Woolfolk & Doris, 2002, p. 471). Inevitably, mental health diagnoses (like other medical diagnoses) involve evaluative judgments, such as those regarding patient "quality of life" and the "moral hazard"[11] facing third-party payers, which can be expected to persist even after all the facts of the case are agreed upon (see Woolfolk, 1999). Insofar as disagreements about mental health depend on such judgments, there is reason to think they are fundamental.

Bloomfield (2001, pp. 28, 31) might avoid these difficulties by limiting his analogy to "physical health," which he construes as a "biological property." Discourses trading in such properties, one might be tempted to suppose, are more liable to realist interpretations than the messy and impressionistic discourse of mental health. But as Bloomfield (2001, p. 5) recognizes, the distinction between mental and physical health is at best a wobbly one (Murphy, 2005, chapters. 2–3). Consider the psychopathology currently understood as somatization disorder, where afflicted individuals suffer persistent pain, incur health care costs 6 to 14 times higher than average, and may be bedridden 2 to 7 days a month. These are physical manifestations, no doubt, yet the syndrome is responsive to cognitive–behavioral therapy—that is, good old "talk therapy" (see Allen, Woolfolk, Lehrer, Gara, & Escobar, 2001). Examples of "mental" illnesses with "physical" manifestations are legion, the currently endemic anorexia and bulimia being but two of the most obvious.[12] There are, of course, those who would impose order on the clinical understanding of psychopathology by reference to the "biological substrate" of mental illness. But adherents of this faith do well to remind themselves that there is at this time no clinically accepted biological test for *any* mental illness, including those, such as depression, which are responsive to pharmacological intervention (Woolfolk & Doris, 2002, pp. 476–478; cf. Slater, 2004, p. 79)—a state of affairs that would seem a little surprising, if mental illnesses were readily taxonomized in biological terms.

While we are struck by the extent to which health care is fraught with disagreement that is plausibly thought to be fundamental, we've no wish to deny that there are relatively clear cases of injury and ill health, such as fractured limbs, high fevers, and severe malnutrition, where realist treatments look apt (see Bloomfield, 2001, pp. 32–33)—if ever they do. We suspect that a "patchy" realism is most plausible here: Some areas of health discourse demand, and others resist, a realist treatment. The same may hold for morality, and it is an interesting—though underexplored—question whether this patchiness is a comfort to the realist or the antirealist: How much in the way of realism-apt areas of moral discourse must be confidently identified before the realist can declare victory? And how are the boundaries of these patches to be demarcated?[13] This question will recur—too briefly—later on. Our present point is this: *One is tempted to antirealism about health in just those cases where disagreement is plausibly construed as fundamental.* We won't opine on the prospects for Bloomfield's moral realism. What we do insist on is that the health analogy gives the realist little reason, so far as we can see, to be sanguine about the implications of fundamental disagreement.

Divergentism need not be associated with analogical arguments of the sort we've considered. In contrast to Bloomfield's naturalistic realism, Russ Shafer-Landau's (2003) rationalist moral realism construes ethical theorizing as an endeavor markedly *unlike* theorizing in science and medicine, since ethical reasoning may involve self-evident ethical beliefs.[14] According to Shafer-Landau, a belief *p* is self-evident just in case "adequately understanding and attentively considering just *p* is sufficient to justify believing that *p*"; among his candidates for self-evident moral beliefs are "it is wrong . . . to taunt and threaten the vulnerable, to prosecute and punish those known to be innocent, and to sell another's secrets solely for personal gain" (Shafer-Landau, 2003, p. 248).

Shafer-Landau claims that his realism is not committed to convergence, because "disagreement poses no threat to realism of any stripe, and so, a fortiori, poses no threat to moral realism in particular" (2003, p. 228; cf. Moody-Adams, 1997, p. 109). However, this divergentism may be in tension with his views on self-evidence; as Sinnott-Armstrong (2002, p. 313; cf. Tolhurst, 1987) argues, if a belief is subject to disagreement, then being justified in *maintaining* that belief apparently requires inferential justification, even if the belief itself is "self-evident" or "noninferentially justified." Borrowing Sinnott-Armstrong's example, suppose Jerry and Bob are riding in a car and Jerry expresses a belief that Tom Cruise is walking in front of them. In some circumstances, this belief may be noninferentially justified, but if Bob denies that it's Cruise gracing the crosswalk, Jerry now apparently owes some justification for his belief—he needs to do more than repeat himself. For Sinnott-Armstrong (2002, p. 313), an expression of disagreement changes the epistemic status of that belief; moral beliefs that are the subject of disagreement will require inferential justification.

Shafer-Landau (2003, p. 245) will respond that not just *any* disagreement—such as a disagreement where one disputant is seriously deranged—taints self-evident belief; he allows that agents may consider and understand a self-evident belief and yet fail to believe it, perhaps because "other beliefs of theirs . . . may stand in the way." For instance, you may fail to believe a self-evident proposition because you also believe that you should believe only what your guru tells you, and the great man has not yet issued a proclamation on the proposition. In this case, your failure to believe the self-evident proposition should not undermine the status of the belief as self-evident, since a centrally implicated ancillary belief is irrational.

However, *fundamental* disagreement regarding a putatively self-evident moral belief would be problematic, since no epistemic disadvantage would, ex hypothesi, be implicated in the disagreement. To put it another way, dissent on the part of an epistemically respectable interlocutor should unsettle the confidence with which one holds a belief. Shafer-Landau (2003, p. 262) seems to think such prospects empirically unlikely, for he thinks that disagreement over self-evident propositions "will occur just in situations the proponent of self-evidence would predict, namely, those in which the agent's associated beliefs are very badly off-target, or those in which the agent's belief-forming mechanisms are badly damaged." In other words, disagreement over self-evident propositions will not be fundamental, but attributable to a disputant's epistemic disadvantage. While we are generally hesitant in imputing to authors views they explicitly reject, Shafer-Landau's skepticism about the possibility of fundamental disagreement seems to us a tacit acknowledgement of our point: If fundamental disagreement is a central feature of moral experience, this problematizes realism. Indeed, Shafer-Landau offers convergence conjectures; as a realist, we suspect he must.

Convergentism

According to Richard Boyd (1988, p. 183), resistance to moral realism is fueled by a "presumed epistemological contrast between ethics, on the one hand, and the sciences, on the other," specifically insofar as "the methods of science (and of everyday empirical knowledge) seem apt for the *discovery* of facts while the 'methods' of moral reasoning seem, at best, to be appropriate for the rationalization . . . of preexisting social conventions or individual preferences." Boyd's problem, as with naturalistic moral realisms more generally, is to vitiate this allegedly invidious contrast; to do so, he develops an analogical argument that models moral realism on scientific realism.[15]

Boyd adopts what Railton (2003, p. 9) calls "the generic stratagem of naturalistic realism," which is to "postulate a realm of facts in virtue of the contribution they would make to the *a posteriori* explanation of certain features of our experience." A familiar argument for scientific realism argues that certain features of our scientific practice—typically, its successes—are best explained by invoking a realist understanding of this practice. Whether this strategy can be adopted by *moral* realists depends, first, on how closely moral practice resembles scientific practice and, second, on whether the postulation of moral facts can make a significant contribution to the explanation of experience.

Moral disagreement makes trouble on both scores. First, as Boyd (1988, p. 186) acknowledges, it makes moral inquiry—at least initially—look importantly different from scientific inquiry, insofar as "hard scientific questions are only temporarily rather than permanently unanswerable" whereas "hard ethical questions seem often to be permanent rather than temporary." Moreover, as Boyd (1988, p. 185) observes, "scientists with quite different cultural backgrounds can typically agree in assessing scientific evidence"; unlike aesthetic judgments, for example, scientific judgments seem to be relatively free from cultural variation or, in Boyd's terminology, "distortions." The putative lack of cultural variation provides the basis for an abductive argument to a realist interpretation of scientific inquiry: The best explanation of the apparent agreement is that scientific inquiry tends to converge, over time, on access to a culture-independent realm of fact.[16] In the case of moral inquiry, however, cross-cultural disagreement is substantial (as we argue below). This returns us to Mackie's argument: Variations in moral judgment are "more readily explained by the hypothesis that they reflect ways of life than by the hypothesis that they express perceptions . . . of objective values" (Mackie, 1977, p. 37).

Unlike divergentist realists, who deny that the onus exists, convergentist moral realists have typically tried to dispense with the explanatory burden that emerges from the (putative) contrast with science. Such realists attempt to "explain away" apparently fundamental moral disagreements with explanations—we'll call them *defusing explanations*—adverting to various sorts of epistemic disadvantage, such as incomplete information or imperfect rationality.[17] Further indulging the philosophical proliferation of terminology, we'll call disagreements where defusing explanations apply *superficial* disagreements. The ubiquity of defusing explanations in the literature, even in expositions such as Shafer-Landau's (2003), which officially reject convergentism, suggest that the problem of disagreement strikes a deep philosophical nerve. In any event, if the generic stratagem of naturalistic realism is to be successful in the moral case, it must provide compelling explanations of the actual disagreement that figures in our moral experience. In other words, it must explain why this disagreement is superficial rather than fundamental.

This challenge is not unique to adherents of scientific naturalism such as Boyd; it is also taken up in Michael Smith's (1994, p. 187) abductive argument for moral realism: "the empirical fact that moral argument tends to elicit the agreement of our fellows gives us reason to believe that there will be a convergence in our desires under conditions of full rationality. For the best explanation of that tendency is our convergence upon a set of extremely unobvious *a priori* moral truths." Smith's "rationalist" realism departs from scientific naturalism in positing a priori moral truths, but it makes the same bet: In optimal conditions—for Smith, in "conditions of full rationality"—moral judgment will converge. If we have good reason to believe that fundamental disagreement is widespread, the bet looks an imprudent one.[18]

Scorecard

Discourses where the prospects for convergence appear most troubled are typically the discourses where realist treatments seem least plausible; the existence of fundamental moral disagreement, if it exists, places a heavy rhetorical burden on the moral realist. First, the abductive argument for antirealism is most potent on the postulation of fundamental disagreement, for it is regards fundamental disagreement that antirealism enjoys a substantial prima facie explanatory advantage. Second, fundamental moral disagreement motivates unfavorable comparisons with paradigmatically realism-apt scientific inquiries. In response, divergentist moral realists may take a "companions-in-guilt" approach and argue that moral disagreement is neither quantitatively nor qualitatively different from disagreement in other, realism-apt, discourses. We have argued that this strategy is unpersuasive. Either the extent and nature of the disagreement in the target discourse is similar to the moral case, in which case both poles of the comparison are plausibly thought to resist realist treatments, or it is not, in which case the prima facie case for moral realism looks, by contrast, less compelling. Of course, we don't expect the divergentist to concede our way of depicting things without a fight, but we think it fair to say that it is unsurprising, in light of our depiction, to find familiar moral realisms committed to convergentism. It is our impression that convergentism has been the industry standard in contemporary moral realism; that is why the literature is studded with attempts at defusing explanations, and a committed realist like Sturgeon (1988, p. 229) singles out the argument from disagreement as especially worthy of respect. We agree that moral realism needs to take the bull by the horns and cannot be sanguine about disagreement; we will now, finally, take a look at actual moral disagreement and attempt to empirically enrich speculations about convergence.

The Empirical Terrain

As noted at the outset, both realists and antirealists have observed that philosophical disagreements about disagreement are very substantially empirical. Sturgeon (1988, p. 230) insists that it is "impossible to settle them . . . in any a priori way"; what's needed, as Loeb (1998, p. 284) observes, is "a great deal of further empirical research into the circumstances and beliefs of various cultures." In what follows we will attempt, in preliminary fashion, to carry forward this bipartisan agenda. As elsewhere in philosophical ethics, the empirical issues are unlikely to be resolved by armchair speculation, so we'll now be taking some pains over evidence from the human sciences. A proper treatment requires much more space than is available to us here; the best we can presently offer is some indication of what an appropriately developed discussion might show.

The Hazards of Ethnography

Some philosophers have voiced skepticism about the application of empirical literatures to the problem of disagreement; in an unusually detailed philosophical interrogation of the anthropological record, Michelle Moody-Adams (1997) goes so far as to claim that "it is difficult (at best) to establish that one has indeed *found* a genuine instance of fundamental disagreement" (p. 36; cf. Brink, 1984, 1989). One source of difficulty in establishing the existence of fundamental moral disagreement is a shortage of *philosophically relevant* details in the empirical record: Ethnographers, despite all they have taught us, don't always ask the questions philosophers want answered. Perhaps surprisingly, then, Moody-Adams directs some of her most pointed criticisms at the philosopher Richard Brandt, who in his remarkable *Hopi Ethics* (1954) made a concerted attempt at philosophically sophisticated ethnography.

As Brandt (1959, pp. 102, 283–284) recognized, classic ethnographies such as Westermarck's (1906) and Sumner's (1934), although documenting remarkable evaluative diversity, do not support confident inferences about moral disagreement under *ideal* conditions, in large measure because they often give limited guidance regarding how much of the moral disagreement can be traced to disagreement about factual matters that are not moral in nature, such as those having to do with religious or cosmological views. With this sort of difficulty in mind, Brandt (1954) undertook his own anthropological study of Hopi peoples in the American Southwest. His best known examples concern Hopi attitudes toward animals suffering:

[Hopi c]hildren sometimes catch birds and make "pets" of them. They may be tied to a string, to be taken out and "played" with. This play is rough, and birds seldom survive long. [According to one informant:] "Sometimes they get tired and die. Nobody objects to this." (Brandt, 1954, p. 213)

Brandt (1959, p. 103) attempted to determine whether this difference in moral outlook could be traced to disagreement about nonmoral facts, but he could find no plausible explanation of this kind; his Hopi informants didn't deny that animals so treated experience pain, say, nor did they believe that animals are rewarded for martyrdom in the afterlife. According to Brandt (1954, p. 245), the Hopi do not regard animals as mechanical or insensible; indeed, they apparently regard animals as "closer to the human species than does the average white man." The best explanation of the divergent moral judgments, Brandt (1954, p. 245) concluded, is a "basic difference of attitude." In our lexicon, this evaluative difference has the look of a fundamental moral disagreement.

Moody-Adams argues that little of philosophical import can be concluded from Brandt's—and indeed from much—ethnographic work.[19] Deploying Gestalt psychology's doctrine of "situational meaning" (e.g., Dunker, 1939), Moody-Adams (1997, pp. 34–43) contends that all institutions, utterances, and behaviors have meanings that are peculiar to their cultural milieu, so that we cannot be certain that participants in cross-cultural disagreements are talking about the same thing.[20] For example, infanticide or parricide in conditions of scarcity does not represent what it does in affluent circumstances, so differing norms regarding homicide, when situated in different material circumstances, cannot be assumed to indicate moral disagreement. Brandt's mistake with the Hopi, according to Moody-Adams (1997, p. 42), was thinking he could "read off . . . unstated moral beliefs and attitudes . . . from behavior."

Now Brandt *did* directly question his informants about their moral beliefs and attitudes, but Moody-Adams (1997, p. 42) also voices skepticism about self-reports in ethnography. With this skepticism, Moody-Adams may risk showing more than she intends. The problem of situational meaning, she (1997, p. 36) thinks, threatens "insuperable" methodological difficulty for those seeking to establish the truth of descriptive cultural relativism. Relativists will respond—not unreasonably, we think—that judicious observation and interview, such as that to which Brandt aspired, *can* motivate confident assessments of evaluative diversity. Suppose, however, that Moody-Adams is right, and the methodological difficulties are insurmountable. The shoes now pinch on *both* feet, for the methodological difficulty looks to undermine assertions regarding the existence of cross-cultural moral *agreement*—of the sort Moody-Adams (1997, p. 16) herself wants to make[21]—no less than it undermines assertions of disagreement. What is it about evidence of agreement that makes it more confidently interpretable than evidence of disagreement? If observation and interview are really as problematic as Moody-Adams suggests, aren't the convergence conjecture and its rejection *equally* undermotivated by the evidence? The appropriate position, given Moody-Adams's pessimism, would be agnosticism.

We do not endorse this agnosticism, because we think the implicated methodological pessimism excessive. Serious empirical work can, we think, tell us a lot about cultures—and the differences between them. The appropriate way of proceeding is with close attention to particular studies and what they show and fail to show; general methodological edicts, be they pessimistic or optimistic, do not make for informative readings of social science, or empirically responsible developments of ethical theory.[22] In a moment, we'll try to concretize our optimism with attention to cases. But we first need to consider another objection to the ethnographic project.

According to Moody-Adams (1997, p. 44), much ethnography is committed to "the doctrine of cultural integration"—the notion that the various elements of a culture "can always be understood to form a generally coherent whole." Against this, she (1997, p. 44) insists that "the moral practices of particular cultures are, in general, simply resistant to the kinds of generalizations needed to figure in the contrastive judgments implied by descriptive relativism." Apparently, cultures are so heterogeneous as to resist generalizations like "The Hopi are more tolerant of children's cruelty to animals than are White Americans." In short, it is near impossible to confidently establish the existence of intercultural moral disagreement because there is so much intracultural moral disagreement. We sense a tension here: How can Moody Adams be so confident about the existence of *intra*cultural disagreement, if she is right about the elusiveness of *inter*cultural disagreement? Why think the methodological situation is more congenial in the intracultural case? We won't pursue these questions, however; for us, the more important issue is that Moody-Adams may have again shown too much: If sustainable, her critique threatens to obviate the possibility of substantive generalizations about peoples and cultures. Certainly it is useful to remember that generalizations about a culture are just that—generalizations. When we claim that the Dutch are generally taller than the Japanese, we don't want to be understood as implying that this comparison holds for every Dutch person and every Japanese person. Does this undermine the possibility of *all* generalizations along the lines of "The Dutch are generally taller than the Japanese"?[23]

Without doubt, when we attempt to generalize on topics like American attitudes toward animal cruelty, we will find the record uneven; as Moody-Adams (1997, pp. 40–41) observes in commenting on Brandt, American attitudes toward the permissibility of causing animal suffering are extremely varied—the bestiary of vegans, vegetarians, pescatarians, fruitarians, and carnivores grows wilder by the hour. (It is less obvious that there is as much variation regarding the permissibility of allowing one's children to torture animals, and that may be the norm most vividly present in Brandt's case.) We agree with Moody-Adams that Brandt, the considerable merits of his philosophical ethnography notwithstanding, is rather too glib with generalizations like "the average white man"; unfortunately, he appears to take more care over Hopi culture than his own. However, we do not think the difficulty with Brandt's work need generally infect the study of culture. We'll now explain why.

Culture, Honor, and Defusing Explanations

The closing decades of the twentieth century witnessed an explosion of "cultural psychology" investigating the cognitive and emotional processes of different cultures (Shweder & Bourne, 1982; Markus & Kitayama, 1991; Ellsworth, 1994; Nisbett & Cohen, 1996; Nisbett, 1998; Kitayama & Markus, 1999). To get a feel for this research, and how it might address concerns like those voiced by Moody-Adams, consider cultural differences discovered by Nisbett and his colleagues while investigating regional patterns of violence in the American North and South.[24]

The Nisbett group applied the tools of cognitive social psychology to the "culture of honor," a phenomenon that anthropologists have documented in a variety of geographic and social settings. Although such cultures differ in many respects, they manifest important commonalities, particularly regarding the importance of male reputations for strength and decisive retaliation against insult or other trespass (Nisbett & Cohen, 1996, p. 5; cf.

Wyatt-Brown, 1982). According to Nisbett and Cohen (1996, pp. 5–9), an important factor in the genesis of honor culture in the American South was the presence of a herding economy. Apparently, honor cultures are particularly likely to develop where resources are liable to theft and where the state's coercive apparatus cannot be relied upon to prevent or punish pilfering. These conditions often occur in relatively remote areas where herding is a main form of subsistence; the "portability" of herd animals makes them prone to theft. In areas where farming rather than herding is the principal form of subsistence, cooperation among neighbors is more important, stronger government infrastructures are more common, and resources—like decidedly unportable farmland—are harder to steal. In such agrarian social economies, cultures of honor tend not to develop. The American South was originally settled primarily by herding peoples from remote areas of Britain; when these peoples emigrated from Britain to America, they initially sought out remote regions suitable for herding, and in such climes the culture of honor flourished.

In the contemporary South, police and other government services are widely available and the herding life has disappeared, but certain sorts of violence continue to be more common than they are in the North.[25] Nisbett and Cohen (1996) maintain that patterns of violence in the South, as well as attitudes toward violence, insults, and affronts to honor, are best explained by the hypothesis that a culture of honor persists among contemporary White non-Hispanic Southerners. In support of this hypothesis, they offer a compelling array of evidence:

• White males in the South are much more likely than White males in other regions to be involved in homicides resulting from arguments, although they are not more likely to be involved in homicides that occur in the course of a robbery or other felony (Nisbett & Cohen, 1996, chapter 2).
• Survey data indicates that White Southerners are more likely than Northerners to believe that violence would be "extremely justified" in response to a variety of affronts and that, if a man fails to respond violently to such provocation, he is "not much of a man" (Nisbett & Cohen, 1996, chapter 3).
• Legal scholarship has found that Southern states allow greater freedom to use violence in defense of self and property than do Northern states (Nisbett & Cohen, chapter 5, p. 63).

This multipronged methodology helpfully augments the more traditional ethnography pursued by Brandt. Cultural psychologists employ statistical techniques that allow more confident generalizations than those licensed by impressionistic speculation on entities like "the average White man," and supplementing demographic data with surveys and legal scholarship can help us to recover "situational meaning" that cannot be read off of behavior and interview alone.

The Nisbett group did experimental work that adds further texture to this sociological picture. In a field study (Nisbett & Cohen, 1996, pp. 73–75), letters of inquiry were sent to hundreds of employers around the United States. The letters purported to be from a hardworking 27-year-old Michigan man who had a single blemish on his otherwise solid record. In one version, the "applicant" revealed that he had been convicted for manslaughter; he had accidentally killed a rival in a barroom brawl after the rival had publicly boasted of sleeping with the applicant's fiancée and challenged the applicant to "step outside." In the other version of the letter, the applicant admitted that he had been convicted of motor vehicle theft perpetrated at a time when his family was short of money. Nisbett and his colleagues assessed 112 letters of response, and found that Southern employers were significantly more likely to respond sympathetically in response to the manslaughter letter than were Northern employers, while no regional differences were found in responses to the theft letter. One Southern employer replied to the manslaughter letter as follows:

As for your problems of the past, anyone could probably be in the situation you were in. It was just an unfortunate incident that shouldn't be held against you. . . . Once you are settled, if you are near here, please stop in and see us. (Nisbett & Cohen, 1996, p. 75)

No letters from Northern employers were comparably sympathetic.

In a laboratory study (Nisbett & Cohen, 1996, pp. 45–48) subjects— White males from both Northern and Southern states attending the University of Michigan—were told that saliva samples would be collected to measure blood sugar as they performed various tasks. After an initial sample was collected, each unsuspecting subject walked down a narrow corridor where he was bumped by an experimental confederate who called him an "asshole." A few minutes after the incident, saliva samples were collected and analyzed to determine the level of cortisol—a hormone associated with high levels of stress, anxiety, and arousal—and testosterone— a hormone associated with aggression and dominance behavior. Southern subjects showed dramatic increases in cortisol and testosterone levels, while Northerners exhibited much smaller changes (figure 6.1).

The two studies just described suggest that Southerners respond more strongly to insult than do Northerners and take a more sympathetic view

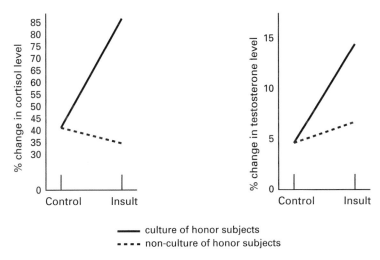

—— culture of honor subjects
- - - non-culture of honor subjects

Figure 6.1
The results of an experiment reported by Nisbett and Cohen in which levels of cortisol and testosterone increased much more substantially in culture of honor subjects who were insulted by a confederate.

of others who do so. We think that the data assembled by Nisbett and colleagues make a persuasive case that a culture of honor persists in the American South. Apparently, this culture affects people's judgments, attitudes, emotion, and behavior—down, as the hormone study might have us saying—"to the bone." In short, it seems that a culture of honor is deeply entrenched in contemporary Southern culture, despite the fact that many of the material and economic conditions giving rise to it no longer widely obtain.[26] We are therefore inclined to postulate the existence of a fundamental disagreement between (many) Northerners and (many) Southerners regarding the permissibility of interpersonal violence.

The argument is just beginning, however. To establish the existence of *fundamental* moral disagreement, the antirealist needs to establish that no "defusing explanations" apply. If one or more of these defusing explanations is applicable, the disagreement is plausibly thought to be superficial, rather than fundamental, and poses no threat to the convergence conjecture. We can now see how an empirically informed argument about moral disagreement might take shape: Find a case of actual moral disagreement and determine whether any defusing explanations are applicable. If any are, conclude that the disagreement would disappear under ideal circumstances and is not fundamental. If none apply, conclude that a fundamental disagreement has been identified.

Among the standard examples of defusing explanations are the following:[27]

1. *Disagreement about relevant nonmoral facts*   According to Boyd (1988, p. 213; cf. Brink, 1989, pp. 202–203; Sturgeon, 1988, p. 229), "careful philosophical examination will reveal ... that agreement on nonmoral issues would eliminate *almost all* disagreement about the sorts of moral issues which arise in ordinary moral practice."

2. *Partiality*   As Truman Capote (1994) reports the murderer Dick Hickock saying, "I believe in hanging, just so long as I'm not the one being hanged"; some moral disagreements don't so much betray deep features of moral discourse as they do the doggedness with which individuals pursue their perceived advantage (see Sturgeon, 1988, pp. 229–230).

3. *Irrationality*   According to Shafer-Landau (1994, p. 331; 2003, p. 218; cf. Brink, 1989, pp. 199–200), realists may say that "disagreement suggests a fault of at least one of the interlocutors [such as] ... some irrational emotional response that stands as a barrier to moral convergence."

4. *Background theory*   As Daniels (1979, p. 262) puts it, "[I]f ... moral disagreements can be traced to disagreements about [background] theory, greater moral agreement may result."

Let us see, briefly, how these explanations may apply to the North/South differences we've observed.

To begin, it is rather implausible to suggest that North/South disagreements as to when violence is justified stem from *partiality*; for example, is there reason to think that Southerners' economic interests are served by being quick on the draw, while Northerners' economic interests are served by turning the other cheek? At least, there do not seem to be such explanations ready to hand, as there are when timber barons disagree with the rest of us about the permissibility logging in the last remaining primeval forests.

We also find it hard to imagine what agreement on *nonmoral facts* could defuse the disagreement, for we can readily imagine that Northerners and Southerners could be in full agreement on the relevant nonmoral facts in the cases described. Members of both groups would presumably concur that the job applicant was cuckolded, for example, or that calling someone an "asshole" is an insult. We think it much more plausible to suppose that the disagreement resides in differing and deeply entrenched evaluative attitudes regarding appropriate responses to cuckolding, challenge, and insult.[28] It is of course possible that full and vivid awareness of the nonmoral facts might motivate the evaluative transformation envisaged by the moral realist; for example, were Southerners to become vividly aware that their culture of honor was implicated in elevated levels of avoidable lethal violence, they might be moved to change their moral outlook. (As conflict-averse Northerners, we take this way of putting the example to be the most natural one, but nothing philosophical turns on it. If you like, substitute the possibility of Northerners endorsing honor values after exposure to the facts.) On the other hand, Southerners might insist that the values of honor should be nurtured even at the cost of promoting violence; even if living by "Death before dishonor" is a mistake, it is not obviously a mistake of fact.

Nor does it seem plausible that Southerners' more lenient attitudes toward certain forms of violence are readily attributed to widespread *irrationality*. To make this work, one would have to identify a cognitive deficiency such that this fault is implicated in the disputed values, and this deficiency would have to be specifiable independently of adherence to the disputed value. This last may be a tall order; here, as elsewhere, we have difficulty seeing how charges of irrationality can be made without one side begging the question against the other.

We do find it plausible to suppose that the differences regarding violence may be embedded in differences in *background theory*—say, those having to do with masculinity and social status. This is a delicate issue, about which we will have a bit more to say later on, but for the moment notice that situating particular moral disagreements in broader theoretical disagreements doesn't always look like a *defusing* explanation; if our disagreement with the Nazis about the merits of genocide is a function of a disagreement about the plausibility of constructing our world in terms of pan-Aryan destiny, does it look more superficial for that?

We are therefore inclined to think that Nisbett and colleagues' work represents one potent counterexample to the convergence conjecture; the evidence suggests that the North/South differences in attitudes toward violence and honor might well persist in ideal discursive conditions. Admittedly, our conclusions must be tentative; we have not considered every defusing explanation that might plausibly be offered[29] and have not exhaustively surveyed the empirical issues.[30] Further, and of considerable theoretical interest, is the question of what establishing fundamental disagreement in this, or some limited set of cases, might show. One case is not an induction base. And even if fundamental disagreement could be shown in a variety of cases, there remains the intriguing possibility of "patchy realism" discussed above: Perhaps some areas of moral discourse are realism-apt, even if others are not.

How happy should the philosophical disputants be about the prospect of a patchy realism? (One is of course struck by the seemingly interminable disagreement that typifies research in ethics: Are moral philosophers epistemically disadvantaged, or are their disagreements fundamental?)[31] The moral realist might be content with a "core cases patchy realism" where some central swath of moral discourse admits of realist treatment; perhaps there is fundamental disagreement at the periphery but convergence at the center. Reverting (in a regrettably breezy fashion) to the political case, this suggests a realist reconstruction of morality in liberalism. There might be disagreement about pornography, say, but agreement about basic rights or the value of mutual respect among citizens (see Gutmann & Thompson, 1996, pp. 79–81)—recent U.S. developments regarding torture and habeas corpus (one hopes) notwithstanding. The overlapping regions of the "overlapping consensus" (Rawls, 1993, p. 15), the liberal moral realist might say, is where we should expect to find realism-apt stretches of moral discourse (here prescinding from Rawls's perhaps vexed relation to the realism/antirealism debate). The theoretical issues about patchy realism are important ones and are deserving of fuller treatment than they have, so far as we are aware, to date received. Unfortunately, we here lack the resources for fuller development of these issues. Instead, we finish with a provocation by presenting some empirical work on a philosophically suggestive case.

Toward a Geography of Morals: The Magistrate and the Mob

It is often claimed that utilitarian prescriptions for particular cases will conflict with the ethical responses many people have to those cases—to the detriment of the theory (e.g., Williams, 1973).[32] The case of "the magistrate and the mob" is a famous example of this kind:[33] Should the police prosecute and punish a single innocent scapegoat to prevent rioting that will lead to substantial destruction of property and loss of life? Utilitarians, so the story goes, are bound to say yes, and this result is widely believed to be seriously unpalatable. Neophytes are justly amazed at how little in the way of differing concrete prescriptions flows from ardently opposed positions in ethical theory, but philosophers have opined on the magistrate scenario with unusual confidence. Thus Bloomfield (2001 p. 86): "judges ought not find the innocent guilty to prevent riots in the street, period." And Shafer-Landau (2003, p. 248): "it seems to me self-evident that . . . it is wrong to prosecute and punish those known to be innocent." The thought that someone would so much as *consider* doing something like this finds Anscombe (1958) in high dudgeon: "I do not want to argue with him; he shows a corrupt mind."[34] Even Smart (1973, p. 71), a utilitarian of cheerfully bullet-biting disposition, was apologetic: "Even in my most utilitarian moods I am not *happy* about this consequence of utilitarianism." While philosophers may sometimes be quite mistaken about folk intuitions (see Doris & Stich, 2005), in this case they apparently have their fingers on the pulse of their client populations. In a pilot study on the magistrate case, Doris, Nichols, and Woolfolk (unpublished data) found a very strong tendency for their subjects to condemn the utilitarian expedient. This response is typical: "Falsely implicating a person is never justified. The individual's right to liberty outweighs the prevention of property damage, riots, and even the prevention of injury or death that would likely result from the riot." It's tempting to think the magistrate and the mob scenario is a candidate core case, an instance where it is plausible to expect convergence and, perhaps, to explain this convergence by reference to moral fact.

However, recent work in cultural psychology indicates the "standard" response to the scenario, together with the ideology that grounds it, may be parochial. Summarizing a burgeoning research tradition documenting East/West cognitive differences in *The Geography of Thought*—required reading for anyone interested in the present topics—Nisbett (2003, p. 50) remarks that "the Western-style self is virtually a figment of the imagination to the East Asian." In contrast to the Western independent or *individualist* conception of self, which focuses on personal attributes that may be characterized with limited reference to social context, the Eastern interdependent or *collectivist* conception of self understands persons in relation to group affiliations and social roles. Although we are inclined to think that this contrast enjoys enviable empirical support (see Doris, 2002, pp. 105–106), our present concern is not to defend our inclination. Instead, notice that this contrast, if it is a legitimate one, suggests the following prediction: East Asians should be more tolerant of utilitarian expediencies—sacrificing individual interests "for the good of the group"—in a magistrate and mob case than are Westerners.

Peng, Doris, Nichols, and Stich (n.d.) put this conjecture to the test. Their subjects—Americans of predominantly European descent and Chinese living in the People's Republic of China—were presented with the following vignette:

An unidentified member of an ethnic group is known to be responsible for a murder that occurred in a town. . . . Because the town has a history of severe ethnic conflict and rioting, the town's Police Chief and Judge know that if they do not immediately identify and punish a culprit, the townspeople will start anti-ethnic rioting that will cause great damage to property owned by members of the ethnic group, and a considerable number of serious injuries and deaths in the ethnic population. . . . The Police Chief and Judge are faced with a dilemma. They can falsely accuse, convict, and imprison Mr. Smith, an innocent member of the ethnic group, in order to prevent the riots. Or they can continue hunting for the guilty man, thereby allowing the anti-ethnic riots to occur, and do the best they can to combat the riots until the guilty man is apprehended. . . . the Police Chief and Judge decide to falsely accuse, convict, and imprison Mr. Smith, the innocent member of the ethnic group, in order to prevent the riots. They do so, thereby preventing the riots and preventing a considerable number of ethnic group deaths and serious injuries.[35]

American subjects were significantly more likely to think that the Police Chief and Judge were morally wrong to do as they did and significantly more likely to think that they should be punished for doing so. Additionally, Chinese subjects were significantly more likely to hold the potential rioters responsible for the scapegoating—suggesting that they attributed more responsibility at the level of the collective than did their more individualist counterparts.[36] This looks like evidence of moral disagreement—interestingly, disagreement about a candidate core case. By now, you know the drill: To determine whether the purported disagreement is superficial or fundamental, canvass defusing explanations.

Peng et al. (n.d.) did a bit of this. They asked subjects whether the false imprisonment would cause the scapegoat and his intimates to suffer, and they asked whether the riots, if they occurred, would cause members of the ethnic group to suffer. They did not find significant differences on these items, suggesting that the differences are not readily to be attributed to differences in conceptions of the *nonmoral facts*. Of course, there might be less obvious factual disagreements implicated in the moral difference, such as the probabilities assigned various outcomes, but it is not clear why there should be cultural differences on this dimension. Certainly, more detailed examination of how the different subject groups construe the facts of the case would ground more confident assessment of this explanatory strategy, but, as we shall argue in a moment, the literature favors another alternative.

Partiality does not seem a promising defusing explanation; it seems to us unlikely that the differences in moral judgment are attributable to differences in perceived self-interest, since all the subjects are plausibly construed as disinterested third-party observers when filling out their questionnaires. Nor does there seem much to recommend defusing explanations attributing *irrationality* to the philosophically deviant Eastern subjects: Would Anscombe have been willing to say that 1.2 billion Chinese are "corrupt of mind"? It is true that Easterners exhibit a substantially different cognitive style than do Westerners; for example, their "dialectical" reasoning style appears to be more tolerant of apparent contradiction (Nisbett, 2003, pp. 165–190). But to deploy such observations as defusing explanations, one would need to show that such differences are plausibly thought of as *deficiencies* and are plausibly thought to be *implicated* in the disagreement in question. Regards the first issue, as we said for the culture of honor studies, it is always going to be difficult to lodge such a complaint, especially cross culturally, without begging the question. But suppose the charge could be made with suitable delicacy. It will then be necessary to show that the established deficiency is implicated in the disagreement. This may not be easy. Suppose, important Eastern philosophical traditions notwithstanding, toleration of contradiction does represent a deficiency in rationality. Why does that make one more likely to countenance the utilitarian expedient in magistrate and the mob cases?

It is certainly true that the putative East/West disagreement here is enmeshed in large and striking differences in *background theory*; it is entirely plausible that those with a more contextualized view of the person and a more collectivist view of society would countenance a "one for many" approach to the magistrate and mob case. Doubtless, this difference in background theory can help explain why Eastern subjects respond as they do. But is the explanation a *defusing* explanation?

Everyone should accept a "The more we agree, the more we agree" principle: The more beliefs groups share, the more likely they are, ceteris paribus, to agree on moral matters. But this does not suggest that moral disagreements are superficial; the principle is easily swallowed precisely *because* it cuts so little philosophical ice. Larmore (1987) is helpful here:

> If we imagine that under ideal conditions others continue to hold their own view of the world, and that view is significantly different from our own (imagine them to be Bororo, or Tutankhamen and Li Po), we cannot expect that they could come to agree with us about the justification of some substantial claims of ours. And if . . . we imagine the supposedly ideal conditions as detached from our general view of the world as well as from theirs, we have no good notion of what would take place, if anything, and it is certainly unclear what sense there would be to saying that it is with the Bororo that we would be conversing. (pp. 57–58)

The role of background theories in moral disagreement presses a dilemma for the convergentist. Either ideal conditions require that discussants agree on all relevant background theories, in which case it is not clear to what extent the disagreement can be understood as between *different* cultures, or ideal conditions do not require agreement in background theory, in which case there is *relatively little reason to expect agreement* "lower down" at the level of particular cases. If the "ideal conditions" having to do with background theory are specified in such a way as to make fundamental disagreement look unlikely, the convergence conjecture risks degenerating into a philosophically empty "The more we agree . . ." principle.[37]

Further reflection on background theory indicates that the realists' situation may be more difficult than we have so far intimated. Up to now, we have been assuming (more or less) that moral disagreements proceed in surroundings typified by substantial *methodological agreement*. That is, defusing explanations often appear to assume that there are unproblematic standards for, say, rationality or impartiality that "ideal" disputants could be assumed to acknowledge. On this construction, the problem of disagreement is that application of the same method may, for different individuals or cultures, yield divergent moral judgments that are equally acceptable by the lights of the method, even in reflective conditions that the method countenances as ideal. Seen in this light, disputing the convergence conjecture may seem contentious, since a background of methodological agreement appears to make it more likely that moral argument could end in substantive moral agreement. However, this light itself burns with contention, because different cultures' encounters with the world are likely mediated, as they are in the East/West case, by divergent epistemic methodologies, meaning that the posited methodological agreement is sharply contrary to fact. Thus, the methodological restriction is in want of an argument—an argument that does not beg substantive methodological questions (see Stich, 1988).

We do not take the preceding example to be decisive. Let us emphasize that the empirical research just recounted is *preliminary*. The record is not as developed as one would hope, and further empirical research aimed explicitly at establishing fundamental disagreement may not substantiate what seems indicated by Peng and colleagues' initial work. Even if the empirical evidence were both voluminous and unassailable, there would remain the theoretical exercise of canvassing likely defusing explanations, and we do not pretend to have done that exhaustively here. Indeed, this exercise may never be absolutely decisive. Here, as elsewhere, negative existential propositions cannot be definitively established, and while considerations of plausibility may limit the space of candidate defusing explanations, philosophical ingenuity may not. What we do hope to have done here is motivate the suspicion that oftentimes, defusing explanations are much more appealing in principle than they are in respect to concrete cases of serious moral disagreement (cf. Snare, 1980, pp. 355–356). The explanatory burden, we think, will often fall most heavily on moral realism. But wherever the burden falls, we must remember that it can only be honorably borne through close, empirically informed discussion of concrete cases. Here, as elsewhere, the fight will be decided by boots on the battlefield, not by speculations launched from empirically thin air.

Conclusion

We have argued that moral realism is subject to a set of conflicting pressures: Philosophical reflection indicates that there are powerful reasons to embrace the convergence conjecture, and empirical investigation motivates confident speculation to the effect that conjecture is unlikely to be satisfied. To put it another way, there is—just as a tourist's view of a world fraught with conflict suggests—empirical reason to believe that fundamental disagreement is a substantial feature of morality, and philosophical reason to believe that this phenomenon should be troubling to the moral realist. If so, we have provided further reason—if further reason is still needed—to embrace the methodological conviction that informs this volume: Making progress with hard questions in ethical theory very often requires a prolonged encounter with the empirical human sciences.

Notes

Authors are listed alphabetically. We are grateful to Walter Sinnott-Armstrong for hosting, in Spring 2004, an exceptional conference on the biology and psychology of morality, which was the initial forum for the ideas presented here, and also for his editorial work, including much helpful discussion of our penultimate version. Many thanks to Paul Bloomfield, Cate Birtley, Shaun Nichols, Ben Shear, Steve Stich, and especially Don Loeb for valuable comments on earlier versions. Doris was most fortunate to begin his thinking on the present issues as an undergraduate in Nick Sturgeon's Moral Realism class; he hopes Sturgeon can approve of the method, if not the substance, advanced here.

1. As Brink (1989, p. 198n5) observes, the argument has origins in antiquity, but Mackie's (1977, pp. 36–38) argument, coinciding roughly with the recent "revival of metaethics" (Darwall, Gibbard, & Railton, 1992, p. 125) in moral philosophy, has been a focal point in contemporary debate.

2. Mackie (1977, pp. 36–38) called his argument "the argument from relativity"; later writers (e. g., Brink, 1989, p. 198; Loeb, 1998) have tended to the terminology we adopt here.

3. There may be versions of moral realism manifesting the ontological commitment without the epistemological commitment, but we suspect many would find such "epistemically impotent" moral realisms unattractive.

4. See Boyd (1988) and Loeb (1998) on "epistemic access."

5. In addition to Smith, see Brink (1984b, p. 116): "Moral realism claims that there are objective moral facts. . . ."

6. Like Mackie, Harman (1977, chapter 1) argued that moral realism bears a heavy explanatory burden; however, Harman's formulation is general and not limited to the phenomenon of disagreement. Incredibly, Harman's much-discussed argument occupied but a few paragraphs of an *introductory textbook*. For an important realist response, see Sturgeon (1988). For iterations of the debate, see Harman (1986) and Sturgeon (1986a).

7. We stipulate: An agent being "fully informed" does not require knowledge of any *moral* facts. Matters are delicate, for this exclusion risks begging the question. But so, it seems to us, does the contrary inclusion, which insists that full information requires knowledge of moral facts. Fortunately, we needn't be detained by these difficulties; this stipulation does not appear to prejudice the present discussion in any substantive way.

8. For a related understanding of "fundamental disagreement," see Moody-Adams (1997, p. 34; cf. Brink, 1989, p. 198). Compare Brandt (1959, pp. 99–101) on "ultimate disagreement."

9. It is plausible to suppose that convergence does not require unanimity. However, this plausible qualification raises hard questions: How much dissent can obtain in ideal conditions before "substantial disagreement" is a more apt characterization than "less-than-unanimous convergence"? As is usual in philosophy, we can't be very precise about the percentages, but we suspect that the relevant notion of convergence—always remembering that we are discussing *ideal* conditions—should be thought to allow only minimal dissent.

10. However, see the remarks on Shafer-Landau below (pp. 309–310); evidently, the idea of convergence is attractive even to realisms who deny that their realism is committed to it.

11. While the most obvious moral issues surrounding health insurance may seem to be the problem of uninsured poor and obstructionist corporate practices designed to deny legitimate benefits, "moral hazard" is here a term of art referring to insurer costs caused by patient malingering.

12. There are, of course, numerous examples, such as Alzheimer's, suggesting the converse. Both types of cases are awkward for the distinction in question.

13. Wiggins (1987a, p. 95 ff.), in the happy event that we understand him aright, may be offering something like a patchy moral realism; he appears to favor a (broadly) realist account of "evaluations" such as "x is good," and a (broadly) non-realist account of "directive judgments" such as "I ought to *phi*." The patchiness we have in mind is rather patchier than that suggested by this dualistic picture, but we cannot—and thankfully need not—argue the point here.

14. Boyd (1988, pp. 192, 207) claims that intuition plays a significant role in scientific theorizing; however, this role is explanatory and not justificatory—on a natural understanding of the practice, appeal to scientific intuition can explain how a theory was arrived at but can't justify the theory.

15. According to Boyd (1988, p. 181; cf. Boyd, 1983), scientific realism can be understood as "the doctrine that scientific theories should be understood as putative descriptions of real phenomena, that ordinary scientific methods constitute a reliable procedure for obtaining and improving (approximate) knowledge of the real phenomena which scientific theories describe, and that the reality described by scientific theories is largely independent of our theorizing." For some critical discussion, see Laudan (1981) and Fine (1984).

16. Of course, one might disagree with Boyd on either the extent of agreement in science, or the best explanation regarding whatever agreement exists, or both. Arguments from disagreement may also be deployed against scientific realism; if these arguments go through, the problem of disagreement may threaten a general antirealism. We acknowledge, with Sturgeon (1988, p. 230), that it may hard for the moral antirealist to limit her antirealism to morality; while we here leave the question open, it may be that our approach will ultimately leave us with a generally skeptical bullet to bite.

17. Even if some moral disagreements do turn out to be irresolvable under ideal conditions—that is, fundamental—naturalistic moral realists believe they can explain why. Given that moral properties supervene upon or are reducible to a whole cluster of natural properties, these realists claim, it is to be expected that there will be borderline cases of moral properties and that statements asserting these borderline cases may be statements for which bivalence fails. Therefore, we should expect that for some moral questions such as "Is X good?" there will be no uniquely correct answer, because it may be indeterminate whether X is good. And therefore, even under ideal conditions, it may be impossible to resolve the dispute between the agent who believes "X is good" and the agent who believes "X is not good." Thus, for some X, we should expect fundamental disagreement over whether or not X is good (see Shafer-Landau, 1994, 1995, 2003; Brink, 1984, 1989; Boyd 1988; Railton, 1992; see also Schiffer, 2002). The appeal of this response depends on whether or not most instances of fundamental disagreement look like disagreements over borderline cases of goodness or some other relevant moral property. Some moral disputes may look like this—the debate over whether a fetus is a person, perhaps—but others do not, such as the debate over capital punishment (cf. Loeb, 1998, pp. 287–288). If the appeal to indeterminacy is too widespread, it becomes unclear how appealing a moral realism we are dealing with; as Loeb (1998, p. 290) puts it, "an account of morality that allowed for a great deal of indeterminacy would be both disappointing and suspect."

18. Smith takes convergence as evidence of objectivity, but he also appears to define objectivity in terms of convergence; for Smith (1994, p. 6), objectivity "signifies the

possibility of a convergence in moral views." The second sort of claim seems to us stronger, and more difficult to defend, than the explanatory claim discussed in the text, but we lack the space to address it here.

19. Interestingly, Brandt is not the only philosopher working in the Anglo-American "analytic" tradition to produce ethnography. Ladd (1957) reports field work with the Navaho; his conclusions (e.g., 1957, p. 328) about the difficulties posed by disagreement seem somewhat more sanguine than, though perhaps not radically at odds with, Brandt's.

20. For remarks on situational meaning with affinities to what follows, see Snare (1980, pp. 356–362). We are grateful to the editor for drawing our attention to Snare's valuable discussion.

21. We take Moody-Adams (1997, p. 1), who seeks to "provide a plausible conception of moral objectivity," to defend a version of moral realism. In terms of the taxonomy offered here, she probably counts as a divergentist, but, since our present interest is in her criticism of the anthropological record, we will not consider whether moral disagreement presents difficulty for her positive view.

22. One of us, at least, thinks this point cannot be made often enough (see Doris, 2002, pp. 9–10, 114; Doris, 2005; Doris and Stich, 2005).

23. For empirical research on height and culture, see Komlos and Baten (2004).

24. Our treatment of the Nisbett research builds on that of Doris and Stich (2005).

25. As Nisbett and Cohen (1996, p. 97) acknowledge, the taxonomic issues are not without delicacy. For our purposes, Southern states can be thought of as former confederate states.

26. The last clause is important, since realists (e.g., Brink, 1989, p. 200) sometimes argue that apparent moral disagreement may result from cultures' applying similar moral values to different economic conditions (e.g., differences in attitudes toward the sick and elderly between poor and rich cultures). However, this explanation seems of dubious relevance to the described differences between *contemporary* Northerners and Southerners, who are plausibly interpreted as applying *different values* to *similar economic conditions*.

27. For a development of defusing explanations that prefigures some of the strategies cited here, see Ewing (1953, pp. 126–129).

28. As philosophers observe, terms like "challenge" and "insult" look like "thick" ethical terms, where the evaluative and descriptive are commingled (see Williams, 1985, pp. 128–130); therefore, it is very difficult to say what the extent of the factual disagreement is. But this is of little help for the expedient under consideration, since the disagreement-in-nonmoral-fact response apparently *requires* that one *can* disentangle factual and moral disagreement.

29. Brink (1989, pp. 197–210) and Loeb (1998) offer valuable discussions of explanatory strategies other than those we have discussed here, Brink manifesting realist sympathies, and Loeb, antirealist.

30. We have reported on but a few studies, and those we do consider here, like any empirical work, might be criticized on either conceptual or methodological grounds, but we think Nisbett and Cohen will fare pretty well under such scrutiny. See Tetlock's (1999) favorable review.

31. Loeb (1998) and Shafer-Landau (2003) raise the problem of *philosophical* disagreement in the context of present concerns. One is here reminded of Baier's (1985, pp. 207–208) pointed observation that introductory ethics courses, steeped as they are in theoretical controversy, serve as finishing schools for moral skepticism.

32. For appeals to intuitions in ethics and moral psychology, see Blum (1994, p. 179), Fischer and Ravizza (1998, pp. 10–11, *passim*), Strawson (1986, pp. 87–89), Strawson (1982, p. 68), Wallace (1994, pp. 81–82), and Williams (1973, pp. 99–100; 1981, p. 22). For criticism of "intuition pumps" in philosophical ethics, see Doris and Stich (2005).

33. Perhaps due to McClosky (1963) and made prominent by Smart (1973).

34. The case Anscombe directly considers involves execution rather than imprisonment, but there is no evidence to suggest that her impressive moral confidence would diminish in the latter case.

35. Chinese subjects read the stimulus materials in Chinese translation.

36. Dependent variables were measured on a 7-point Likert scale (1 = Completely Disagree, 7 = Completely Agree). The American/Chinese means for the reported items are as follows: morally wrong, 5.5/4.9; punishment, 5.5/5.0; rioters responsible, 4.2/5.6 (all differences significant at the .05 level or greater). For those unfamiliar with this experimental tradition: (1) The effect sizes are typical of those reported in the social psychology literature; (2) The Likert scale as used here is a *comparative* measure and does not allow inferences regarding "absolute" agreement, such as "American subjects agreed with the statement."

37. A related question looms: Does the background theory in question include *moral* theory? If it does, moral agreement "in the foreground" appears more likely, but again, the explanatory strategy begins to risk looking empty, since it is not clear how there could obtain much substantive foreground disagreement to be explained away, against such a background.

6.1 | Against Convergent Moral Realism: The Respective Roles of Philosophical Argument and Empirical Evidence

Brian Leiter

I share the skepticism of Doris and Plakias about the view they dub "convergent moral realism" which consists of

> a philosophical observation to the effect that realism is troubled by fundamental disagreement and . . . an empirical conjecture to the effect that such disagreement will not widely obtain in appropriate discursive conditions. (pp. 305–306)

Since my space is limited and divergent moral realism strikes me as incredible (in part for reasons Doris and Plakias ably adduce), I am going to concentrate on the case against convergent moral realism. In particular, I want to raise some questions about the respective contribution of empirical and philosophical considerations to the refutation of convergent realism.

Those of us who are relaxed Quineans—who are skeptical about intuition-driven methods of philosophy and conceptual analysis, who think that the facts matter for philosophy, who take philosophy to be continuous with empirical science, and who take a far more Quinean (i.e., pragmatic) view of both ontology and what counts as science than Quine (the arch-behaviorist-and-physicalist!) himself—should, at least, agree with Frank Jackson (1998) about philosophical method this far: We need to have a handle on "the folk theory" (1998, p. 32) of the concepts we use to frame philosophical problems, even when the problems posed have an empirical answer.[1] As Jackson (1998) puts it:

> [T]he *questions* we ask when we do metaphysics are framed in a language, and thus we need to attend to what the users of the language mean by the words they employ to ask their questions. When bounty hunters go searching, they are searching for a person and not a handbill. But they will not get very far if they fail to attend to the representational property of the handbill on the wanted person. These properties give them their target, or, if you like, define the subject of their search. (p. 30)

To be sure, it is an open question whether what is required to figure out the representational property of the handbill are intuitions about possible cases or simply a dictionary. But whatever the case, one possible role for philosophical inquiry is to figure out what kinds of empirical evidence will matter given the conceptual question at stake.

A generation ago, Larry Laudan (1977) documented another important role that "conceptual analysis"—in a more capacious sense than Jackson's—played in the development of science. For the history of science is replete with examples of debates about *conceptual* problems, either "internal" to a theory—for example, the theory "exhibits certain internal inconsistencies . . . or its basic categories of analysis are vague and unclear" (Laudan, 1977, p. 49)—or "external" to the theory, but related to how the theory comports with other theories that are already viewed as rationally vindicated. However, in both cases, conceptual problems are not resolved by appeal to intuitions about the extension of the concepts á la Jackson but rather by reliance on standards of clarity and logical entailment.

Thus, Quinean skeptics about conceptual analysis as a tool for discovering truths can agree that (1) we need to know what our concepts mean when doing empirical science and (2) clarity about those concepts, and appreciation of their logical entailments, can affect the conclusions of empirical science.

I don't read Doris and Plakias as having a *principled* disagreement with any of the preceding points. I worry, instead, a bit about their practice. Whether there is fundamental moral disagreement is, in some sense, an empirical question, but also a conceptual one, as they recognize. However, they are, I fear, sometimes a bit loose with the relevant concepts. Consider the empirical literature on the "honor culture" in the American South, which documents the greater tolerance of violence as a response to insults and arguments than in the American North. The fascinating empirical results adduced, however, don't obviously support the interpretation of "moral disagreement" that Doris and Plakias offer: "We are . . . inclined to postulate the existence of a fundamental disagreement between (many) Northerners and (many) Southerners regarding the permissibility of interpersonal violence" (p. 319). The concept of "permissibility," however, cannot be read off the empirical data described by Doris and Plakias.[2] That Southern employers are more likely to *forgive* criminal malfeasance by a betrayed lover hardly shows they think it is *permissible*, unless we conflate a variety of concepts which can be distinguished. Consider the differences between, for example, "It is O.K., that is, morally justified or defensible, that he did that" versus "It is O.K., although not morally justified, that he did that" versus "He really should not have done that, though it is explicable and perhaps excusable that he did so" versus "He really should not have done that, though I can understand what drove him to it, and it's sufficiently far in the past that we should no longer hold it against him." Only the first of these four analyses strikes me as expressing the concept of "permissibility," but the empirical evidence adduced seems compatible with any of the other three (perhaps especially the last two). So, yes, whether there is moral disagreement is, in some sense, an empirical question, but what the empirical evidence shows will depend on understanding the concepts in play. A disagreement about, for example, when certain conduct is excusable may still be a moral disagreement, but it is not a disagreement about the permissibility of violence.

Among the useful *conceptual* points Doris and Plakias make in their essay is that defenders of convergent moral realism employ a strategy of explaining away "apparently fundamental moral disagreements" (p. 311) with four kinds of "defusing explanations" (p. 320): that such disagreement is *really* about "nonmoral facts"; that it betrays *partiality*; that it reflect *irrationality*; and that it reflects what is really a dispute about "*background theory*" rather than morality. Doris and Plakias do a nice job of explaining why disagreements about "background theory" are likely to do little to defuse cases of fundamental moral disagreement (pp. 321 ff.), but "partiality" and "irrationality" deserve equally skeptical treatment. Toward the end, Doris and Plakias note that "defusing explanations often appear to assume that there are unproblematic standards for, say, rationality or impartiality that 'ideal' disputants could be assumed to acknowledge" (p. 326), but this assumption is, itself, contentious and may be belied by cross-cultural empirical studies.

Yet even without empirical studies, we have grounds to resist the idea that moral disagreement can be explained away by appeal to "partiality" and "irrationality." Consider, to start, *partiality*. If what is really at issue is *normative* or *evaluative* realism—that is, whether there are objective facts about what ought to be done or valued—then it just begs the question against certain kinds of normative or evaluative views that give primacy to partiality (to oneself, to family, to one's clan, to one's nation, to one's coreligionists, etc.) to treat them as not really *disagreeing* with normative views that treat impartiality as central: They may be disagreeing *precisely* about the normative import of impartiality in deciding what one ought to do and value.

Given that "rationality" itself admits of antirealist treatment (e.g., Gibbard, 1990), it should also not be surprising that some attempts to "explain away" moral disagreement as reflecting one party's "irrationality" are nothing more than expressions of meta-evaluative judgments about a particular disfavored first-order moral judgment, as opposed to diagnoses of a cognitive failing. This may also be terrain where Doris and Plakias's worry about whether there are shared epistemic standards is especially important. Failures to draw logical inferences may seem to be paradigmatic cases of failures of rationality, but most moral disagreements that purport to fall prey to defusing explanations will involve the failure to adhere to contestable standards of "rational warrant" or, more problematically, failures of "practical reason"—which, one suspects, is the "special kind of reason for cases in which one need not bother about reason," as Nietzsche scathingly put it (1895/1999, section 12).

Nietzsche, in fact, presents a fine armchair test case for any thesis about moral disagreement, since he so clearly repudiates "the egalitarian premise of all contemporary moral and political theory—the premise, in one form or another, of the equal worth and dignity of each person" (Leiter, 2002, p. 290). As Doris and Plakias note briefly in passing (p. 322 and note 31), the history of moral philosophy itself is the history of moral disagreements—disagreements, moreover, under what often seem to be ideal epistemic conditions of discursive freedom. Even the last hundred years of *intensive* systematic theorizing about ethics has done essentially nothing to resolve fundamental disagreements between, for example, deontological and consequentialist moral theories.[3] For this observation, we do not need empirical studies; we just need to know the history of philosophy.

However, with Nietzsche we take this moral disagreement to a whole new level, since we here have a thinker who is not only quite prepared, like any consequentialist, to sacrifice the well-being of some for others, but ready to sacrifice the well-being of *the majority* for the sake of the flourishing of his favored examples of human excellence like Goethe (Leiter, 2002, pp. 113–136)—a view presumably uncongenial to the vast majority of academic moral theorists! Here, then, is a stark philosophical challenge for convergent moral realists: "defuse" Nietzsche's disagreement by reference to a failure to appreciate nonmoral facts or norms of rationality.[4] If the realist faithful can discharge this straightforward philosophical task, we may well need to turn to empirical studies to defeat moral realism. Until then, careful attention to the profound moral disagreements among the great philosophers will suffice, I suspect, to doom convergent moral realism.

Notes

Thanks to John Doris and Walter Sinnott-Armstrong for some helpful feedback on a draft.

1. The contours of the folk theory itself constitute a fertile subject for empirical investigation, as Jackson admits when he endorses "doing serious opinion polls on people's responses to various cases" (1998, p. 36).

2. Perhaps it is warranted by the underlying details of the studies they reference; I am relying on what Doris and Plakias describe.

3. Note that it is not even plausible to try to "defuse" these disagreements by appeal to differing "background theories," since the moral disagreement is precisely at this level already: There is, in most instances, *no background* to appeal to in order to defuse the disagreement. Of course, as noted, I am sympathetic to Doris and Plakias's response to the general strategy of trying to defuse disagreement by appeal to background theories.

4. I have expressed skepticism that it can be done: see Leiter (2001, pp. 90–91).

6.2 | Disagreement about Disagreement

Paul Bloomfield

It is a pleasure to have the opportunity to comment both on John Doris and Alexandra Plakias's paper and on the topic as a whole: The former because I so strongly approve of their attention to empirical data and the latter because the topic is so philosophically rich and intrinsically important. I'll drive straight to some nonpolemical comment, to be followed by more polemical responses, without stopping any more to praise what is so obviously of merit. To coin their phrase, let's get the "boots on the battlefield."

Doris and Plakias do a good job at characterizing the take on disagreement that falls out of accepting a form of moral realism that ontically and epistemically models moral goodness on physical health. A form of what they call "divergentism" is the result, wherein it is unrealistic, as it were, ever to expect to get full consensus or convergence on moral issues. The remainder of this lack of consensus is what they call "fundamental disagreement."

I do not intend to engage any of their particular arguments when I point out that I think that the situation would be clearer if we had a better understanding of "fundamental disagreement" (not to mention "convergence"). Fundamental disagreement is disagreement that persists "even in *ideal* conditions, among fully informed, fully rational discussants" (Doris & Plakias, p. 305). Of course, the same philosophical worries here attend the specification of such ideal conditions as attend the similar move in debate about the metaphysics of, say, redness: How does one specify "ideal observers" and "ideal conditions"? In particular, in the moral case, are these discussants human beings? We cannot be asked to imagine "infallible human beings"; this is an oxymoron at best and a contradiction in terms at worst. And we should not expect that all the fallibility of which we are capable is due to our (necessarily?) having incomplete information, for being infallibly rational is no more comprehensible for creatures like us than having infallible information. One wonders what possible bearing any empirical evidence might have on a discussion of fundamental disagreement that involves beings capable of being so much more well-informed and rational than any actual member of *Homo sapiens* could ever possibly be. We have no empirical data, for example, nor will we ever get it, about whether or not such perfectly rational and fully informed beings would have "fundamental disagreement." Thus, I assume that Doris and Plakias are talking about actual, merely fallible human beings here, and then we are being asked to consider the most fully informed real-life humans we can imagine, who will nevertheless always fail to be perfectly rational. If there were a moral disagreement among such actually possible people, they might not ever be able to detect among themselves who is being irrational and who is not. Clearly, we could not conclude in a situation such as this that there is no right answer or that opposing views are somehow equally correct, since the disagreement is attributable to cognitive mistakes due to our ultimately fallible human nature.

From a purely dialectical standpoint, it is also worth noting that while some, like Doris and Plakias, criticize moral realism for not being able to adequately account for moral disagreement, others, such as Sharon Street (2006), criticize moral realism for not being able to adequately account for moral agreement. Street points out a variety of ways in which moral agreement seems cross-culturally universal, for example: Ceteris paribus, (1) the fact that something would promote one's survival is a reason in favor of doing it, (2) the fact that something would promote the interests of a family member is a reason to do it, (3) we have greater obligations to help our children than we do to help complete strangers, and so forth. She goes on to argue that moral realists cannot explain this convergence of our evaluative practices with the independent moral facts of the matter to which moral realists are committed. Taken in conjunction with Doris and Plakias, one wonders both about the standard moral realism is being held to ("Damned if we do, damned if we don't"), and what to say about this apparent disagreement about disagreement between the critics of moral realism. Perhaps the existence of moral realism cannot explain either moral agreement or disagreement (or anything at all), but this is not the tone the critics take: Doris and Plakias think that fundamental disagreement is one of the strongest arguments against moral realism, implying that it would be that much more plausible if there weren't any.[1]

The degree of (fundamental?) agreement is part of the empirical evidence that should be noted when weighing the importance of "fundamental disagreement." Let us assume that the cultures of the American South, the

nineteenth-century Austro-Hungarian, and the medieval Japanese samurai are all examples of "cultures of honor."[2] The evidence seems to indicate that they have different conceptions of honor, but they all, presumably, have the same concept of honor.[3] Perhaps, however, it should not be surprising that we do not find a "culture of honor" where people there think that the honorable thing to do is to abandon one's friends in danger, run away and hide from one's enemies, and, in general, avoid conflict by engaging in obsequious behavior toward those who appear threatening. *That*, one might say, would imply a truly "fundamental disagreement" between these cultures of honor.

Again, as a dialectical question, should we think of fundamental disagreement as disagreement about what to do in particular moral circumstances or disagreement about moral principles in the abstract? Doris and Plakias write as if the problem for moral realism is located in what to do in particular circumstances, but disagreements such as this are consistent with agreements across wide ranges of particular circumstances, as well as agreements in moral principle. Southerners, duelists, and samurai might disagree with each other about whether or not ϕ-ing counts as an insult, though they might agree that many sorts of behavior are insulting, as well as agreeing in principle that, ceteris paribus, one ought not to "accept" an insult without responding somehow. They might also agree about what counts as an appropriate response. (I think these comments also bear on the relevance of the research on the "magistrate and the mob" case by Peng et al., (n.d.).) The threat to moral realism from "fundamental disagreement" is not as clear when viewed in a context that includes extant moral agreement as well. Doris and Plakias consider how difficult it is to be precise about how much agreement is needed for "convergence" (note 9, p. 328), but focusing exclusively on disagreement and ignoring agreement will not give us a balanced picture against which we may evaluate moral realism.

It should not be forgotten that moral realism is consistent with the idea of actual global moral error. For a realist, convergence in moral matters is far from a guarantee of the moral truth: If Hitler had won World War II, there is no telling what moral opinions human beings would all have converged upon by now. We should also keep in mind the epistemic possibility that in 100 years, teaching evolution in schools might be banned everywhere in the world as pernicious, given an overwhelmingly religious and possibly tyrannical majority convergence of the human population on a creationist theory of the universe.

Moral realists like myself fall under Doris and Plakias's heading of "divergentism," because we say that we should not expect complete moral

convergence, even among humans in circumstances as much idealized as we can realistically imagine. Furthermore, we do not take this to be a strike against moral realism in the least, since we see so-called "fundamental disagreement" in the sciences. For example, imagine a scientist who disagrees with Einstein over the existence of absolute simultaneity across vast distances and sees the special theory of relativity as being infected with an overweening verificationism that comes from Einstein's reading too much Ernst Mach. How would such a disagreement be settled? It would certainly not be by empirical means—as the logical positivists found out (the thesis of verificationism itself can't be verified). Or perhaps reading Lawrence Sklar (1993) has convinced one that there are good theoretical reasons to doubt the reduction of thermodynamics to statistical mechanics. Or one may note that the debate over the proper interpretation of quantum physics does not seem as if it will be settled any time soon, empirically or otherwise, especially since some pragmatically minded scientists think that we should not bother to interpret it, since it works perfectly well in its uninterpreted form (Feynman, 1985). Contra the quotation from Boyd on p. 311 of Doris and Plakias's paper, there is no reason to assume that all hard scientific questions are only temporarily unanswerable.

How much realism in morality is required for moral realists to be vindicated? Well, if the metaphysical debate is founded upon the fact/value distinction, then, seemingly, a single moral (evaluative) fact should carry the ontological day for moral realism. In fact, while ontically significant, one moral fact probably would not be enough, since we are looking for the foundations of humanity's manifold moral practices. Nevertheless, neither does it seem reasonable to say that moral realism is false unless *every* aspect of our moral practice and every particular moral judgment that is made has determinate truth conditions fixed by mind-independent moral facts. Moral realism is consistent with some degree of conventional difference between cultures. If we assume that there are reasons for morality, or we understand moral practices as having some goal, point, or purpose (be it either deontic, consequential, or based on virtue or care), then we should acknowledge the possibility that there may be functionally equivalent ways of attaining this goal. The now impolitic phrase is that "there are many ways to skin a cat." These may seem "divergent" from one another, especially when considering judgments about particular moral situations. There may also, of course, be outright error, endemic practices which fail to attain or perhaps even lead away from the point of being moral. Far from being inconsistent with moral realism, these "divergences" are to be expected.

Also, different moral practices have arisen in different contexts and these should be taken into account in weighing the relevance of divergence. It is commonplace to note that conditions of extreme scarcity may make some actions morally permissible that would otherwise be proscribed. Members of herding cultures, or any culture in which people are required to defend themselves as if they were in something similar to a "state of nature," will be required to resort to violence much quicker than most of us today. However, this does not inveigh against moral realism in the least. This sort of "relativism" is consistent with the idea that there are facts about when violence is morally permissible and these facts will be aptly contextual. In nutrition, humans require a different diet than, say, cows, and different humans, based on gender, age, general physical condition, and so forth, will need different diets. None of this contextualization inveighs against the idea that nutrition deserves a realist's treatment. Importantly, the violent tendencies of those living in herding cultures may have been justified while those people were actually herding, but the descendents of those cultures, whose lifestyles have long left herding behind, are not justified if they have retained violent tendencies despite their living in a culture in which violence is not required.[4]

I would like to close with a final thought about my own view of moral realism. In my work, I deliberately model the property of moral goodness on physical health, not psychological health. The reason for this is that the ontological status of psychological properties is itself so contentiously suspect that these properties does not seem to me to be able to provide a helpful model by which to understand moral properties. While in fact I am personally most tempted to accept a nonreductive materialism as the correct account of the mind, my view of moral realism does not require me to take a stand on the relationship between physical and psychological health (or on the philosophy of mind more generally). I do not, however, think there will be a sharp dividing line between physical and psychological health. It seems much more likely that there will be a vague distinction between them, like the distinction between night and day. Such distinctions are not, as Doris and Plakias suggest, "wobbly" (p. 308), any more than the distinction between night and day is wobbly. Physical health, as such, provides a perfectly adequate model of a property that deserves a realist's treatment: There are any number of purely physical ailments that have nothing to do with psychology, and a trip to any medical hospital will confirm that, if one's childhood memory of chicken pox is not sufficient. Concluding, as Doris and Plakias do, that there is no real distinction between physical and psychological health is, to break out an old philosophical saw, the same as concluding that there is no difference between noon and midnight because twilight makes the day/night distinction a vague one.

Notes

1. Doris and Plakias do emphasize that the empirical research they discuss is preliminary (p. 326). Given that, it bears note that there is a new and growing literature in empirical psychology called "positive psychology," wherein psychologists are attempting to identify a cross-culturally applicable model of psychological health, in contrast to traditional clinical psychology that has focused on pathology. These psychologists find large amounts of cross-cultural moral agreement. See, for example, Peterson and Seligman (2004). One wonders how those like Doris and Plakias would interpret this data.

2. In trying to discern the origins of cultures of honor, it bears note that many do not seem to emerge from herding cultures.

3. I use the concept/conception distinction as it is found in Hart (1961), Rawls (1971), and Dworkin (1978) in their discussions of law and justice.

4. The ideas in this paragraph and the previous one are discussed in greater length in chapter 1 of Bloomfield (2001).

6.3 How to Find a Disagreement: Philosophical Diversity and Moral Realism

Alexandra Plakias and John M. Doris[1]

Famously, moral philosophers disagree, and just as famously, the vats of ink spilt in professional journals and scholarly monographs show little sign of resolving these differences. Indeed, as Baier (1985, pp. 207–208) laments, this threatens to reduce introductory courses in philosophy to "finishing schools in moral skepticism": If the professional philosophers are unable to quiet their bickering, what's a college sophomore to think? According to Leiter's commentary on our paper, the problem of disagreement is amply on display when one considers "the last hundred years of *intensive* systematic theorizing about ethics" (p. 336); to feel the problem's bite, he thinks, "we do not need empirical studies; we just need to know the history of philosophy" (p. 336).[2] As Leiter notes, our paper mentions this problem of *philosophical* disagreement, but the difficulty raises suggestive issues we did not take up, and it is here we will focus our response to the challenging critiques of Leiter and Bloomfield.

The problem seems especially acute because moral discussion in philosophical settings might be thought to better approximate "ideal conditions" for moral inquiry. First, academic philosophers (the population we will here reference with "philosophers") often enjoy the leisure to pursue *prolonged* discussion. Second, philosophical training in the evaluation of argument and evidence might be thought to facilitate discussion better approximating cannons of *rationality* than discussions pursued by untrained individuals. Third, the academic character of much philosophical discussion may reduce the considerations of *self-interest* on which nonacademic moral discussion often founders; when philosophers are fighting, they often don't have a dog in the fight. Fourth, academicians have ready access to an enormous body of factual knowledge, which presents the hope that their discussions may be less impeded by ignorance of, or disagreement about, *nonmoral fact*. Finally, philosophers are typically laboring in a substantially shared intellectual tradition invoking considerable commonalities in *background theory*: Their moral confrontations do not take place in the circumstances conjured from the anthropological literature, where disputants may often be supposed to regard their opposite numbers as (more or less distasteful) exotics. For example, philosophers in the United Kingdom, United States, and Australia no doubt represent different "intellectual cultures," but their conferences present little of the diversity that would be found at a conference attended by Yanamani, Nuer, Saudis, Serbs, and Maori. Yet even in the relatively homogeneous environs of English-speaking philosophy, disagreement persists. Is this especially awkward for the convergentist moral realist's assertion that moral disagreement is typically "rationally resolvable"?

Of course, it should be evident, even to outsiders, that the above characterization of academic philosophical inquiry as approximating ideal discursive conditions is more than a little Panglossian; those who hang around philosophy departments were probably smirking by the middle of the paragraph. Indeed, there is a more cynical characterization of academic philosophy ready to hand, and it presents the possibility of a defusing explanation for philosophical disagreement. The explanation is simple: Academic philosophers get *paid* to disagree. Academic culture rewards novelty (or apparent novelty), not joining a consensus. Indeed, even when a philosopher records *agreement* with a colleague, she often does so by marking *disagreement* with that colleague's critics. This might tempt us to say that philosophical disagreement is a species of "motivated cognition" (e.g., Murray, Holmes, Dolderman, & Griffin, 2000; Jost, Glaser, Kruglanski, & Sulloway, 2003) driven more by the demands of careerism than by the cannons of argument and evidence. This worry gets magnified by empirical work on "attitude polarization," the tendency for exposure of evidence for an alternative view to strengthen the commitment people have to their own views (e.g., Lord, Ross, & Lepper, 1979); the main impact of a lively seminar, then, may be the ossification of participants' philosophical commitments! Also in the neighborhood is a disconcerting genetic story: While philosophers may get paid to disagree, there's heavy incentive to agree, in broad outlines, with the views of one's mentors, but what mentors one ends up with often looks to be determined by quite arbitrary factors. Then it is plausible to suppose that philosophical disputants fail epistemic standards of impartiality or rationality: Their disagreements, one might then suppose, are not fundamental disagreements, but disagreements driven by professional self-preservation. If so, philosophical moral disagreement shouldn't trouble the moral realist—at least so long as she has reason to believe that her arguments are not similarly tainted!

Is there a way to decide between our two stories? Maybe not, given the material at hand: We've been indulging in (gleefully) speculative armchair anthropology, of just the sort we've been at pains to caution against. However, there's a question here that may be helpfully, and perhaps less speculatively, asked: *What do philosophers disagree about, when they disagree about morality?* Leiter (this volume) contrasts empirical studies with the history of philosophy, and he seems to think that properly pursuing the latter renders the former otiose in this context. But historians of philosophy do ask empirical questions, even if they are sometimes asking especially vexing ones.[3] After all, "What did Nietzsche believe about agency?"—a question dear to Leiter's (2002, pp. 73–112) own heart—is not obviously different than "What did the president believe about economics?" Nor is "What do Kantians think about suicide?" so obviously different than "What do Catholics think about abortion?" Historical questions such as these can be vexing, but they are not obviously the less empirical for that.

Indeed, the difficulties faced by historians of philosophy and anthropologists exhibit striking similarities. As we've noted, the study of culture is afflicted by the problem of "situational meaning," the difficulty of interpreting behavior and language with appropriate sensitivity to cultural context. And similarly for the history of philosophy: How closely does the Greeks' notion of the ethical correspond to our own?[4] So too, the history of philosophy is complicated by something like intracultural diversity; just as it is not clear what sense can be given "the average Greek," it is unclear what sense can be given "the average Nietzschean." And the same, of course, for most any philosophical creed one cares to mention. If we could be forgiven for waxing postmodern, we'd say anthropology and exegesis face analogous hazards.

One particularly salient possibility this suggests is that much philosophical moral disagreement is more apparent than actual. More than occasionally, the fullness of time engenders such suspicions: What is it, in a few words—or a few thousand—that realists and quasirealists are disagreeing about? When the verbiage clears, we often seem to find not disagreements, but (as we might call them) *misagreements*: Discussions framed in ways that preclude substantive disagreement. Protracted discussion may cast doubt on whether we and the Greeks—or the Yanomami, or the Kalahari—are talking about the same thing when we talk about "the ethical," and if we come to believe we are not, then "we fail to have disagreement on the very same propositions" (Sosa, forthcoming).

Misagreements, then, are instances of "talking past" one another; although they have the prima facie appearance of disagreement, this appearance is illusory. For example, we may argue over the maximum speed attainable by our Mustangs.[5] But when we discover that your Mustang has bucket seats and five speeds, and ours has four legs and a tail, we realize that we're not disagreeing, but misagreeing. So, for example, in response to claims by Weinberg, Nichols, and Stich (2001, 2003) to have located cross-cultural disagreements in epistemic intuitions, Sosa (forthcoming) has argued that putative disagreements between East Asians and Westerners about what counts as knowledge are in fact misagreements, since Easterners reference communitarian standards of justification and Westerners individualistic ones. We needn't take sides here; our point is simply that if an apparent disagreement dissolves into misagreement, it is not philosophically telling. At the same time, it is worth noting that misagreements may also disguise themselves as agreements; we may appear to agree that Mustangs are expensive to maintain, but again, when we come to realize the differences in the Mustangs we're talking about, this no longer looks like a genuine agreement but rather a misagreement engendered by confusion. The appearance of agreement, no less than disagreement, may turn out to be misleading—agreement may also be merely verbal.

To get clear on the status of philosophical moral disagreement (or agreement) we need to be clear, as moral realists have repeatedly emphasized, on the *level* at which it obtains. There may be disagreement/agreement at the level of *metaethics*, or the nature of justification of ethical claims—for example, our disagreement between realists, like Bloomfield, and antirealists, such as Leiter. There may also be disagreement/agreement at the level of *normative ethics*, concerning the appropriate principles (or absence of principles) to govern ethical thought. Finally, there may be disagreement at the level of *particular judgments*, as to whether a given action or state of affairs is prohibited or permissible. We don't wish to give the impression that this taxonomy can be neatly constructed; for example, we, like others (e.g., Darwall, 1998, p. 12; Kagan, 1998, pp. 4–6), doubt that the metaethics/normative ethics distinction can be stably drawn. Still, it can be helpful to situate different disagreements in these strata.

The first thing to see is that disagreements/agreements may decompose across levels. For example, the realist and antirealist (or quasirealist) are, let's stipulate, in metaethical disagreement. But this does not commit them to disagreement at the level of normative theory: There may be both realist (Boyd, 1988; Sturgeon, 1988; Railton, 2003) and less than realist (Gibbard, 1990; Blackburn, 1993, 1998) consequentialists. Still less must metaethical disagreement be implicated in disagreement at the level of particular ethical judgments (Loeb, 1998, p. 291); antirealists are often at pains to insist that the appropriate particular judgments, about something the Nazis did, for example, are open to them (e.g., Blackburn, 1984, pp. 189–223).

Suppose we have metaethical disagreement backdropping agreement about particulars. Do the disputants mostly agree or disagree? Such cases tempt us to suggest that metaethical disagreement isn't very ethically substantial: Who cares if we disagree at some highly abstract theoretical level, as long as we agree, so to speak, where the bullet meets the bone?[6] Now some moral realists insist that the metaethical differences *do* matter substantively (e.g., Sturgeon, 1986b: e.g., pp. 125–126). The question here, however, is whether disagreements at one or another level are more *metaethically telling*; should the realist be reassured by particular agreements or dismayed by theoretical disagreements? And what if the situation is reversed?

According to Bloomfield's commentary, "Doris and Plakias write as if the problem for moral realism is located in what to do in particular circumstances, but disagreements such as this are consistent with agreements across wide ranges of particular circumstances, as well as agreements in moral principle" (p. 341). He further asserts that "it should not be surprising that we do not find a 'culture of honor' where people think that the honorable thing to do is to abandon one's friends in danger, run away and hide from one's enemies, and, in general, avoid conflict by engaging in obsequious behavior toward those who appear threatening" (p. 341). That is what it would take to have a fundamental disagreement between cultures of honor, and that, Bloomfield thinks, is what the anthropological record will not reveal. Now, we confess to some uncertainty about whether feudal Japan counts as an honor culture in the sense at issue here, as Bloomfield thinks it must. Must the samurai avenge a disgrace visited on him by his Lord, or does he not count such disgraces as insults? While we cannot here canvass a historical record well-shrouded in legend, it is perhaps worth noting that accounts of Miyamoto Musashi, perhaps the most fearsome of Japanese swordsmen, indicate that he had little hesitation about running and hiding; his legendary prowess in mortal combat notwithstanding, he appears to have been a rather sneaky sort (see Harris, 1974; Sugawara, 1985).

But that is not the main point. It's that Bloomfield doesn't have us quite right. We don't think that disagreement about particulars is *the* problem for moral disagreement, but we certainly think it is *a* problem. And why shouldn't we? Is there reason for thinking that (putative) agreement on some (yet to be specified) insult/revenge honor principle is more metaethically telling than (putative) disagreement about what sort of conduct counts as insult in the ways covered by the principle? Bloomfield (cf. Brink, 1984, p. 116) seems to think that disagreement at the level of principles is more metaethically telling, but why think that is the case? Disagreement about whether our gazing lasciviously at your lover *in this instance* merits violent response doesn't look inconsequential, especially if your sticks and stones are breaking our bones. Bloomfield apparently manifests a familiar philosophical tendency to suppose that the real ethical action goes on at the level of principle, but we're not sure exactly what the argument is supposed to be, and "ethical particularists" (see Hooker & Little, 2000) have certainly—here we go again—disagreed with it. It may be tempting to suppose that many particular disagreements are not genuinely *moral* disagreements at all but reflect differences regarding inference and treatment of evidence, but even if the philosophical project of "defining morality" had borne more fruit than it appears to have (see Stich, forthcoming), it is not obvious that disagreements about whether to perpetrate violence against that individual, at this time, for that transgression, can be readily divested of moral content.

The levels game, it seems to us, is a game readily played—perhaps too readily. To use Leiter's central example, Nietzsche and Aristotle might both be called "perfectionists": Both agree, as a general theoretical commitment, that the realization of human excellence is the practically paramount end, or summum bonum.[7] But they are plausibly supposed to disagree, and rather starkly, as to what human excellence consists in: At one approximation, Aristotle much more the communitarian, and Nietzsche more the individualist. Is this disagreement unimportant, because it is associated with a more general theoretical agreement? Sometimes, of course, disagreement (or agreement) may seem to infect more than one level, and indeed, disagreement (or agreement) "higher up" may be thought implicated in disagreement (or agreement) lower down. That's one reading of the magistrate and the mob case, involving judicial imprisonment (or execution) of the innocent. Utilitarians and Kantians may disagree about the relative ethical importance of aggregate welfare and respect for persons, and that is perhaps why utilitarians are more comfortable hanging the patsy than are Kantians.[8] Of course, actual utilitarians may not be that happy to do so—even the cheerfully bullet-biting utilitarian Jack Smart (1973, pp. 69–71) admitted as much—but they may be forced to, in light of their theoretical commitments. We've no stake in denying that such disagreements may in some sense be "deeper" than disagreements about "mere particulars," but we see no reason to suppose that particular disagreements don't make trouble for moral realism. The fundamental/superficial distinction, so far as we can see, cuts across levels, and there's no obvious reason to suppose that there aren't fundamental philosophical disagreements to be found at all levels—of course, pending the requisite exegetical work.

We don't mean to deny that many philosophical disagreements will turn out to be superficial in the harsh light of exegesis. Indeed, we've intimated as much. (N.B.: The same may be true for philosophical *agreements*.) But here we are inclined to agree with Leiter that fundamental disagreement will remain; our casual reading finds us concurring with historians of moral philosophy like Leiter. How *much* disagreement remains matters, of course. We agree with Bloomfield that a *single* fundamental moral agreement that licensed inference to a single "moral fact" would not, however "ontically significant," be enough to satisfy the realist, since "we are looking for the foundations of humanity's manifold moral practices" (p. 342). If the sort of fundamental disagreement that blocks inferences to moral facts were widespread enough, the most reasonable "default perspective" on any of those practices would be that they are not grounded in realist foundations.[9] Of course, we, like Bloomfield, have not done the counting, so our argument is limited, in effect, to an inductive skepticism based on the small proportion of cases we do have reasonably full information about. This looks to us like a safe bet, but we of course welcome further empirical and exegetical study.

We should note that Bloomfield has kindly suspended disbelief in his comments: He's a "divergentist" moral realist, and so is officially untroubled by failures to find fundamental disagreement. Like Leiter, we are suspicious of divergentism, but we've nothing more to say about why this is so than we've already said. However, there's another way in which Bloomfield appears to find our approach wrongheaded, and we should say something about that. On our story, fundamental disagreement is disagreement that would obtain in "ideal conditions," and as Bloomfield notes, there's notorious difficulty in specifying such states. In particular, Bloomfield seems to find unintelligible the notion of the "infallible human beings" that we might expect to be the discussants in ideal conditions: This is, he thinks, "an oxymoron at best and a contradiction in terms at worst" (p. 339). We're not sure the notion is really incoherent: Take any person, and start subtracting reasoning errors, and see what you finish with. Hard to imagine?—obviously. Incoherent?—less obviously. But let us grant the point and move on.

In the first instance, notice the shape of the debate. The antirealist starts by noticing the extent of actual disagreement and wonders how this could be so, if moral realism is true. It is the convergentist moral *realist* who needs to introduce a notion like "ideal conditions" as a way of explaining away the actual disagreement. It is the notion of defusing explanations that invokes ideal conditions, and it's the realist who requires such explanations; the antirealist who agrees to consider ideal conditions, instead of insisting on life as we find it, is allowing the convergentist realist her best hope.

The convergentist moral realist, when faced with Bloomfield's concerns about idealization, may quite reasonably advert to a notion of *improved* conditions. Her argument does not require the possibly hopeless labor of specifying ideal conditions, but only observing that some conditions better enable reasonable moral discourse than others. If we do see, or can expect to see, moral disagreement—important moral disagreement, anyway—reduced as conditions improve in this way, we start to have reason for faith in at least a limited convergentism. How to specify the relevant improvements is both a familiar problem and a difficult one. On one reading, it is the project of "deliberative democrats" working in the Rawlsian liberal tradition (e.g., Gutmann & Thompson, 1996). Of course, deliberative democrats do not expect to see all moral disagreement resolved; a large part of their project concerns how liberal polities may peacefully navigate disagreement (e.g., Gutmann, 1999). But their work certainly presents material for the liberal who is—perhaps unlike many liberal theorists—a moral realist: The improvement of conditions for moral discussion is not something, it seems to us, about which we are completely in the dark.

We cannot here explore the relevant regions of political philosophy and science, but the above discussion of philosophical moral disagreement might gives us some clues, by way of closing, about how to evaluate the discursive condition of moral discussants. Remember that we told two stories about "the philosophical condition." In the cynical version, we noted that the pressures of professionalism might actually encourage moral disagreement. In the Pollyannaish version, we observed that academic philosophers have relevant training, the leisure to pursue prolonged discussion, and so on, advantages that might be thought conducive to reasonable moral discussion of the sort convergentists think will facilitate agreement. It would require a detailed and delicate sociological story to help us decide which story is right—or which parts of each story are right. Hard work this, and at least partly empirical work. But what makes it hard, we submit, is not that we've no idea what makes some conditions more conducive to reasoned moral discussion than others. And this remains true when we abandon, with Bloomfield, the hope of fully specifying ideal conditions.

Although we are not without hesitation, we are strongly tempted to conclude by sharing in the suspicion driving Leiter's remarks and say that the problem of philosophical disagreement presents especially acute difficulty for moral realism, because philosophical contexts should be thought conducive to fundamental agreement. However, it is also arguable that the problem of disagreement is *not* more acute in philosophical contexts, because a defusing explanation like our cynical story is available.[10] A third possibility, suggested by a pessimistic reading of Bloomfield's skepticism about idealization, is that we have no clear idea what makes some conditions more conducive to fundamental agreement than others and can therefore never ascertain whether defusing explanations are, or are not, appropriate. But if this is the case, there's more trouble for moral realism than disagreement, for it becomes quite unclear how we are to evaluate *any* moral considerations. And that's a moral skepticism that moral realists are compelled to reject.

Notes

1. The order in which co-authors are listed was determined randomly.

2. For a related argument, see Loeb (1998).

3. For a compelling application of empirical techniques to the history of philosophy, see Nichols (forthcoming).

4. For some discussion of this question, see White (2002).

5. For discussion of some related points, and a similar example, see Loeb (1998, pp. 294–295).

6. For articulation of a related perspective in political theory, see Herzog (1985).

7. For a note of caution on the comparison, see Leiter (2002, p. 121).

8. It may well be, as a matter of psychological fact, that the particular judgment more often motivates the commitment to principle than the other way round, but that's another story.

9. For simplicity's sake, we here equate realism and factualism. The distinction may be important in some contexts, but it needn't trouble us here.

10. Of course, in this instance the difficulty pressed by the anthropology and cultural psychology literatures remains.

7 Moral Incoherentism: How to Pull a Metaphysical Rabbit out of a Semantic Hat[1]

Don Loeb

Come, let us go down, and there confound their language, that they may not understand one another's speech.
—Genesis 11:7[2]

It seems a truism that the way we think and talk can have no bearing on the metaphysical structure of the world. In particular, whether there are or fail to be any real moral properties would seem to have nothing to do with the semantics of moral language. However, like many apparent truisms, the one about moral semantics contains only part of the truth. It is true that whatever properties exist do so whether we talk about them or not. But those properties are indeed the *moral* properties if and only if they are the properties we are talking about when we talk about morality. This is not to say that if we were to change the way we talk, we would thereby change the metaphysical structure of the universe. If we decided to call chairs "tables," they would still be chairs. But the truth of the previous sentence depends on what we use the words "chair" and "table" to talk about *now*. Similarly, whether there is such a thing as, for example, moral rightness depends upon whether there is any of whatever it is (if anything) we use the *word* "rightness" to talk about now. Thus, an investigation into the semantics of moral language (construed broadly to mean questions of meaning and/or reference) is a crucial element in our search for a resolution of one of the central issues of metaethics—whether or not *moral* properties are real.

The claim that moral language is relevant to metaethical inquiry is not new. What is not often appreciated, however, is that the matter to be investigated consists largely of *empirical* questions. In saying this I do not mean to claim that empirical science can easily discover the answers, or even to presuppose that the answers can be uncovered at all. That remains to be seen. However, an inquiry into what, if anything, we are talking about when we employ the moral vocabulary must at least begin with an inquiry into the intuitions, patterns of thinking and speaking, semantic commitments, and other internal states (conscious or not) of those who employ it. Although not everyone would be comfortable with the phrase, I'll loosely refer to these internal states as our "linguistic dispositions."[3] In the metaethical context, we must begin with the linguistic dispositions, including dispositions to revise our linguistic practices upon reflection, that are relevant to fixing the reference (if any) of the terms in the moral vocabulary. Philosophers' a priori speculations (doubtless heavily influenced by philosophical theory) or a posteriori generalization (based mostly upon encounters with undergraduates) might be relevant to such an inquiry, but they cannot be the whole of it. Such speculation and unscientific sampling are no substitute for careful and philosophically informed intrapersonal, interpersonal, and cross-cultural anthropological and psychological inquiry.

One dispute especially in need of settling involves two prominent hypotheses, each of which claims to capture the essential features of moral thought and discourse. Moral *cognitivism* holds that moral sentences make factual claims—or, slightly more formally, that they express propositions, the bearers of truth value. Moral *noncognitivism*, at least in its traditional forms, holds that moral sentences do not make factual claims; instead they express something other than propositions—emotions, imperatives, attitudes, or the acceptance of norms, for example.[4] A cognitivist need not deny that moral utterances serve these expressive functions *in addition to* making factual claims. However, the views are still in conflict, since noncognitivists (traditionally, at least) deny that moral sentences make factual assertions at all. A proposal along either of these lines is not an invitation *to use* moral language in the specified way but rather a hypothesis about the way moral language *is* used by people in general. It is this feature that makes resolution of the dispute in principle subject to philosophically informed empirical investigation.

No account can expect to capture everyone's linguistic dispositions for all cases, of course. An account of moral semantics is meant to represent what is being thought and said in *ordinary* circumstances by ordinary thinkers and speakers. But ordinary people can be confused, and where they are, we might want to tidy things up a bit. For these reasons, both cognitivists and noncognitivists are often prepared to recognize that any account of moral thought and language will involve some degree of idealization. Some would even go so far as to follow what Richard Brandt (1979) called "the method of reforming definitions" (pp. 3–23). However, although idealization is a matter of degree, there is a crucial difference between an appropriate idealization and a reform. The former seeks to find the analysis that best explains our linguistic behavior, despite the idiosyncrasies of our actual speech and thought. The latter merely changes the subject.

Brandt (1979) himself rejected what he called the "appeal to linguistic intuitions" to answer questions in moral philosophy, on the grounds that normative terms are too vague, that "there is no reason to think there is any language-wide single meaning for these terms," that "they may well embody confusing distinctions, or fail to make distinctions it is important to make," and that "the locutions of ordinary language are not always well adapted to say what on reflection we want to say, or to raise questions which on reflection we want to raise" (pp. 6, 7, and 9).[5] But the fact that an appeal to linguistic intuitions would show vagueness, confusion, conflict, and flawed thinking *supports* the hypothesis that our ordinary moral talk is confused, and it is evidence that on reflection we would *not* all want to raise the same questions. However confused our current moral language is, reforming it simply changes the subject, if there was ever even a subject to begin with. Indeed, the move to a reforming definition often presupposes irrealism with respect to the referents of the original terms.

However, recognizing that a reforming definition is changing the subject raises an important worry. Suppose no *coherent* account would fit our linguistic dispositions well enough to count as giving the real meanings of the terms in the moral vocabulary. Suppose, that is, that any coherent account would involve changing the subject in some important way or ways. If so, then it seems to follow that there are no particular things (properties, etc.) we are referring to when we employ the terms of that vocabulary. A simple analogy can help us to see one way in which such semantic incoherence can lead to irrealism. Both roundness and squareness are central to any proper understanding of the phrase "round square." An analysis that left either element out would amount to a serious reform. But given that both are present in any proper analysis, there can be no such thing as a round square. Semantic analysis (together with an uncontroversial logical premise) has led us to conclude that nothing in the world could actually *be* a round square.

Moral semantics is, of course, much more complicated than this. The debate between cognitivists and noncognitivists is one example of the ways in which it is less tractable than the analysis of "round square." Nevertheless, I will argue, the persistence of such a fundamental dispute about moral semantics is evidence that inconsistent elements—in particular, commitments both to and against objectivity—may be part of any accurate understanding of the central moral terms as well. Alternatively, it could be that there is incoherence at a higher level, that there is so much confusion and diversity with respect to the linguistic dispositions surrounding our use of the moral vocabulary that it does not make sense to think of our moral sentences as making any particular assertions or expressing any particular attitudes. If the moral vocabulary is best understood as semantically incoherent, the metaphysical implication is that with respect to that vocabulary there is nothing in particular to be a realist *about*—no properties, that is, that count as the referents of the moral terms. I call the hypothesis that the moral vocabulary contains enough semantic incoherence to undermine moral realism in this way "moral incoherentism." If moral incoherentism is correct, then we can indeed pull a metaphysical rabbit out of a semantic hat.

In what follows, I argue that there is reason to take this odd possibility seriously, and that the only way to see whether it is correct will require sophisticated, philosophically informed, empirical research. In "Moral Incoherentism," I offer an explanation and partial defense of moral incoherentism. In the two sections following that one, I turn to Frank Jackson's recent work on the connections between semantics, metaphysics, and ethics. While sympathetic with much of what Jackson has to say, I argue that he fails to take the importance of systematic empirical research sufficiently seriously and that he fails to take the possibility of (moral) semantic incoherence sufficiently seriously as well. Next, in "Semantic Approaches More Generally," I argue that little actually depends on whether we accept Jackson's controversial approach to semantics. The empirical issues are roughly the same on *any* reasonable approach. I close by pointing out some of the pitfalls presented by the sort of research I claim is necessary.

First, however, I turn to the recent history of metaethics, in order to further illustrate what I mean by "pulling a metaphysical rabbit out of a semantic hat."[6]

Moore and Ayer: A Lesson from the Recent History of Philosophy

G. E. Moore began his great work, *Principia Ethica*, with a stern and seemingly sensible warning:

It appears to me that in Ethics, as in all other philosophical studies, the difficulties and disagreements, of which its history is so full, are mainly due to a very simple cause: namely to the attempt to answer questions, without first discovering precisely *what* question it is which you desire to answer. . . . At all events, philosophers . . . are constantly endeavouring to prove that 'Yes' or 'No' will answer questions, as to which *neither* answer is correct, owing to the fact that what they have before their minds is not one question, but several, to some of which the true answer is 'No,' to others 'Yes.' (1903, p. vii)

Ironically, Moore seems to have committed the very error he warned against, when he put forward his famous open-question argument. Take any property we might be tempted to identify with moral goodness—pleasure, for example.[7] Still, the question can reasonably be asked whether something having that property (something pleasurable, in our example) is indeed good. Thus, pleasure and goodness must not be the same thing. In contrast, it is not an open question whether something that is a three-sided, enclosed, two-dimensional figure is a triangle. Thus, such figures are triangles.

Moore is widely thought to have conflated two questions, one semantic and one metaphysical. Asking which questions appear open *might* be a way of testing to see whether the word "goodness" means the same thing as the word "pleasure" (though most of us would agree that it's not a very good test). But even if it were a perfect test, it couldn't tell us anything about the nature of goodness itself. Famously, it could be (and at one time, at least, was) an open question in the relevant sense whether water is H_2O, but water itself is H_2O in any event. By looking into the *meaning* of "goodness," Moore tried to support the claim that the *property* of goodness is not identical to any natural property. In running semantic and metaphysical questions together in this way, we might say, Moore tried unsuccessfully to pull a metaphysical rabbit out of a semantic hat.

But now consider A. J. Ayer's (1952) noncognitivist account of moral semantics (chapter IV, pp. 102–113). The analysis is doubtless incorrect as it stands, but let us suppose, for argument's sake, that it *is* correct. Moral sentences, we are assuming, do not make factual claims at all and, thus, do not express propositions, the bearers of truth values.[8] Instead, they are used *merely* to express emotions or to issue commands.[9] If this is so, then statements like "It is wrong to cheat in school" simply do not make factual claims—they *cannot* be true *or* false. They are, on Ayer's view, cognitively meaningless.

It seems reasonable to treat anyone who denies that sentences like "It is wrong to cheat in school" are ever true as a moral irrealist, even if he also denies that such statements are ever false. However, we needn't get into the taxonomical issue here. The important point is that on the assumption that Ayer's moral semantics *is* correct, he has managed to do exactly what Moore failed to do. He *has* pulled a metaphysical rabbit out of a semantic hat, for he has shown that a correct understanding of the meaning of moral sentences shows moral realism to be untenable.

Moral Incoherentism

Although almost no one takes Ayer's arguments for noncognitivism seriously these days, noncognitivist approaches to moral semantics have remained well represented.[10] These approaches typically emphasize the endorsing, commending, or (as I shall call them) "prescriptive" function of moral statements. However, despite this focus on the prescriptive features, there is often a significant effort among noncognitivists to capture certain objective-seeming features of our moral thought, discourse, practice, and experience, as well. Thus, for example, Allan Gibbard (1990, pp. 164–166) claims that we take our moral statements to involve a commitment to what he calls "standpoint independent validity." Roughly, when I make moral statements, I express my acceptance of norms that I take to apply even in circumstances in which those subject to my moral appraisals do not themselves accept the norms I'm expressing, including hypothetical cases in which I myself am being appraised! "If I were to change my mind," I think, "I would be making a mistake." But to think this is (merely) to accept a norm whose application has broad scope in the way just described.[11]

In contrast, cognitivists understand moral statements to be straightforward statements of fact. They point out that this seems to fit nicely with the surface grammar of those statements and to capture in a more natural way the objective-seeming features contemporary noncognitivists are at such pains to accommodate, such as the possibility of erroneous moral beliefs, our seeming recognition of moral demands, and the existence of moral disagreement. It is often thought that cognitivist theories have trouble accommodating the prescriptive, commending, or motivational features of moral thought and language, and that noncognitivist theories have a leg up in this regard. However, cognitivists will often try to show that their approaches can indeed accommodate the most important aspects of this family of features. "We're fresh out of *necessary* connections between moral considerations and reasons or motives for action," the cognitivist often seems to be saying, "but we're running a special on strong *contingent* connections of that sort."

Cognitivism and noncognitivism, as I have characterized them, are in direct conflict with one another.[12] The persistence of this conflict requires explanation. Why hasn't one view of moral language come to dominate? An obvious answer is that each of these theories captures something important about our moral thought and language; we are committed to *both* objectivity *and* prescriptivity. Thus, each side begins with a certain advantage, owing to its apparent facility for accommodating either the objectivity or the prescriptivity commitment, and then does what it can to address the other. The top contenders among current theories do a good job of accommodating our concerns about both objectivity and prescriptivity.

The claim that both objectivity and prescriptivity are essential features of moral thought, and therefore of moral language, was central to (one version of) J. L. Mackie's (1977) famous argument from queerness (pp. 38–42).[13] Mackie thought that no moral theory could adequately accommodate both elements. That is one reason why he held an error theory of morality. A proper *analysis* of moral sentences incorporates both elements, he thought, but nothing in the world could correspond to what that analysis says we should be looking for. Moral statements are indeed factual assertions, he claimed, but statements like "Abortion is permissible" or "Abortion is morally wrong" are always false.

Mackie was surely correct in thinking that some sort of commitment to both objectivity and prescriptivity is built into our moral thought and talk. But the appeal of noncognitivism is not fully explained by its allegedly greater facility with the prescriptive elements of moral thought and language. If paradigmatic forms of noncognitivism are incompatible with moral realism, then it is reasonable to think that this incompatibility, far from being seen as a problem, was and is welcome in at least some noncognitivist quarters, for a theory according to which moral language is not used to make factual assertions is plausible only if we assume that ordinary people do not think the realm they are talking about is a realm of fact. As Mackie (1977) himself argued regarding subjectivism (according to which moral sentences state facts about the speaker):

It is because [subjectivists] have assumed that there are no objective values that they have looked elsewhere for an analysis of what moral statements might mean, and have settled upon subjective reports. Indeed, if all our moral statements were such subjective reports, it would follow that, at least so far as we were aware, there are no objective values. *If we were aware of them, we would say something about them.* (p. 18; emphasis added)

As is true for subjectivism, noncognitivism's anti-objectivist implications explain much of its appeal, at least for those who find it appealing.

Mackie (1977) himself took the anti-objectivist implications of subjectivism and noncognitivism as evidence that these theories were inadequate accounts of the meaning of moral statements, since those implications seemed incompatible with the objectivist strand in ordinary moral thought (pp. 32–35). However, in doing so, he overlooked a possibility even more radical than the one envisioned by his argument from queerness. Perhaps side by side with the objectivist strand in ordinary moral thought is a more broadly *anti*-objectivist strand. On this hypothesis, one important reason for the continued appeal of core forms of noncognitivism—those according to which moral language is *not* used to make factual assertions—is that there is a powerful strand of everyday moral thought according to which morality is *not* a realm of fact.

The objectivist/anti-objectivist distinction cuts across the more familiar realist/irrealist and cognitivist/noncognitivist divides. On the objectivist side are moral realism, Kantianism, most forms of constructivism, and perhaps even certain sophisticated forms of noncognitivism.[14] On the anti-objectivist side are the error theory and traditional emotivism like Ayer's. There is a sense in which relativism and subjectivism do acknowledge the existence of moral facts—facts about what is morally permissible and so on *around here*, or about what any given individual happens to approve of. However, both theories are inconsistent with the more robustly objectivist strand in ordinary thought that holds that there is a *nonrelative* set of moral facts, a strand whose widespread appeal is not in question.[15] Because relativism and subjectivism assume that there are no nonrelative moral facts, I will treat them as anti-objectivist, reserving the term "objectivist" for views according to which there are (only) nonrelative moral facts, albeit facts having different applications for different circumstances.

No doubt the anti-objectivist strand does not typically reflect any well-worked-out metaethical position on the part of nonphilosophers. However, most people do recognize a distinction between realms of fact and realms in which there are no facts. "Is there more than one inhabited planet?" asks a question of fact; "Which is better, chocolate or vanilla?" does not. The former concerns a realm about which ordinary people are (at least implicitly) objectivists, and the latter a realm about which they are anti-objectivists.

It is reasonable to suppose that we use our words to make factual assertions (perhaps among other things) in roughly those cases in which we believe that we are talking about a realm of fact, and to do something *inconsistent* with the making of factual assertions when we think that we are not talking about a realm of fact. Mackie was right to say that if ordinary people see morality as a realm of fact, then it would be surprising for them not to use the moral words to make claims about that supposed realm. However, the converse is also true. If ordinary people see morality as something *other* than a realm of fact, it would be surprising to see them using their moral words to talk about such a realm. Indeed, it is unlikely that they would be using their moral words to talk *about* anything.

There is certainly no consensus among *philosophers* about whether morality is a realm of fact. However, philosophers' views on hotly disputed metaethical questions are hardly dispositive concerning what ordinary people are using their words to do. But what if ordinary people are themselves often deeply conflicted (both interpersonally and *intra*personally) on the question of moral objectivity? Again, it is reasonable to suppose that moral language would reflect that division.

Theories like cognitivism and noncognitivism attempt to force our moral thought and language into one or the other box, with noncognitivism typically pushing it into the anti-objectivist box and cognitivism pushing it into the objectivist box. However, the truth may be much more messy and complicated than either theory is capable of handling, at least without violating the constraint against changing the subject. It may be that ordinary people use the moral words *both* to make factual assertions *and* to do something incompatible with the making of such assertions, because ordinary people are at bottom widely and irremediably, if perhaps only implicitly, conflicted about questions of moral objectivity.[16]

That there is indeed a strong objectivist strand in the way ordinary people think about morality is virtually uncontroversial. However, although it is often downplayed or treated as merely superficial, there is evidence of a fairly robust *anti*-objectivist strand as well. Almost anyone who has taught philosophy has encountered this anti-objectivist strand frequently among students. When asked about metaethics, a number of them say things that suggest a commitment either to moral relativism or to the view that morality is not a realm of fact at all.[17] I will have more to say soon about whether we should take this strand in ordinary thought seriously. But prima facie, at least, we seem to be presented with commitments *both* to *and* against moral objectivity. And again, it would be surprising if these apparently powerful strands in ordinary moral thought were not reflected in the meanings of our moral words.

But how *could* they be? An account according to which we use moral language both to make (nonrelative) factual assertions *and* to talk in a way that assumes there to be no such facts (or only relative facts) would reveal incoherence in our moral talk. Isn't that in itself grounds for rejecting any such analysis? I see no reason to think that it must be. We are trying to discover what it is people are actually using (or trying to use) the moral words to do. The answer depends on people's actual linguistic dispositions and not on what makes things look uncomplicated. As we saw, an analysis of the phrase "round square" would be incomplete if it didn't reveal incoherence. It is worth knowing whether our moral terms build in incoherence of this or any other form as well, however concealed from us it is in ordinary contexts.

Certainly, *interpersonal* and *cross-cultural* incoherence present no objection, since it may be that we are using our words at cross-purposes (or not talking to one another at all). The former is possible if there is enough overlap among our linguistic dispositions for it to be useful to employ the moral vocabulary *even if* in important respects we are not all talking about the same thing. But surely there is enough overlap. Imagine a die-hard voluntarist arguing with a committed atheist. It is at least possible that, when talking about morality, the voluntarist is talking about the will of God and the atheist is using the same vocabulary to talk about something else. Even if, unbeknownst to them, the two are really using the words at cross-purposes, it is still easy to see how they could continue to talk to one another, and to find the language of morality useful in communicating about what to do and coordinating their behavior. Some of the reasoning tools they employ (such as analogy and clarification of the nonmoral facts) would undoubtedly be similar enough for something very much like an argument to take place. Both may be committed to trying to do whatever it is that morality turns out to require, and, more generally, morality as each understands it may play a very similar role in their lives. Given these commonalities, moral talk would be useful to these individuals, even against a backdrop of substantial interpersonal semantic conflict. That it is useful to them, however, does not establish that they are, in the end, talking about the same thing.

However, even *intra*personal conflict is possible. Admittedly, it is hard to imagine an ordinary person having in her vocabulary a word like "squound" (meaning both square and round at the same place and time). But just as it is possible for a person to have inconsistent beliefs, it seems possible for a person to have inconsistent linguistic dispositions as well.[18] As long as our inconsistent beliefs are sufficiently isolated from one another and we aren't made aware of their contradictory nature (and even sometimes when we are), we can and indeed do hold them. The same may be true of our linguistic dispositions.

If both objectivity and its denial really are central and persistent features of our moral thought and talk, that would have profound implications for the debate over moral realism. Specifically, a form of irrealism would emerge. For if no adequate, coherent moral semantics can be found, then once again there doesn't seem to be anything (anything logically possible, anyway) to be a realist *about*. More precisely, nothing we can be realists about would be entitled to unqualifiedly go by the name "morality," and so with at least many other terms in the moral vocabulary, at least insofar as they build in this incoherence. Perhaps we *can* pull a metaphysical rabbit out of a semantic hat in something like the way Ayer tried to.[19]

It might be objected that as long as *some* people have a realm of objective fact in mind, morality (and the various associated moral properties) in *one* sense of the word could still exist. Perhaps there are simply two different senses of the word "morality," one of which, M_1, presupposes a realm of moral fact and the other of which, M_2, presupposes that there is no such realm. On this view we might expect to find that some of us are always using M_1, others are always using M_2, others are using M_1 sometimes and M_2 other times, some have linguistic dispositions that suggest that they are somehow trying to use both at once, and sometimes it is indeterminate which vocabulary a person is using. No doubt people typically haven't noticed that the two meanings exist side by side, so, as before, they talk and act as if there is only one. However, when people *are* employing the M_1 sense of the term, nothing in the argument I've made undermines realism about morality *in that sense*.[20]

Something like the situation just imagined could perhaps be the case. However, even if so, it would still be true that much of our moral talk is at cross-purposes and that the moral words do not have unqualified meanings. Questions like whether moral properties are real or whether a certain action is morally permissible would be ambiguous at best. More importantly, the more semantic disarray there is (of either the incoherence or the ambiguity variety), the less plausible it is to claim that any particular usage represents the meaning of a given term in the moral vocabulary *in any important sense*.

We can learn how much disarray there is, if at all, only through empirical inquiry. However, there is at least some reason to think that there *is* a good deal of disarray when it comes to the moral vocabulary. Philosophers sometimes dismiss inconvenient features of ordinary people's views as not just erroneous but as the sorts of things the hapless folk wouldn't be caught dead with if they saw things properly. Thus, to return to our previous example, they assume that if people who think that morality just *is* what God tells us to do came to believe that there is no God (or came deeply to appreciate the Euthyphro arguments), they'd continue to believe in an objective morality—just a morality divorced from God.

However, we have no convincing evidence that this is true. Admittedly, the fact that we appear to believe we are all talking about the same thing is some evidence that we are. But the claim that God is the author of morality is undoubtedly so central to *some* people's use of the term "morality" as to be *nonnegotiable*, in the sense that those people would stop using the term rather than give up their disposition to use it in this way.[21] If so, and if those people became convinced that there is no God, such people would have to abandon moral realism. (Indeed, I have witnessed people asking atheists like me why we refrain from behavior such as stealing and cheating, or asserting that they themselves would have no reason for avoiding such conduct if it were not for God's commands.)

Furthermore, it is not just the disputes among the various forms of objectivism and anti-objectivism that should worry those who assume that the moral words have definitive, coherent meanings. Other terms in the moral vocabulary proper might present problems similar to those encountered in metaethical contexts. "Right" might simply (and nonnegotiably) *mean* different things to those with consequentialist leanings than to those with deontological, virtue theoretical, or feminist ones. In fact, *any* irresolvable (apparent) moral disagreement would be *some* evidence that those appearing to disagree are not talking about the same thing.[22] Again, the fact that we often seem to think we *are* talking about the same thing is some evidence that we are. However, nonnegotiable conflict of the sort I have described here is evidence that we are not. Just how much conflict of this nonnegotiable sort exists is still an open question. But if there is enough of it, then even the limited sort of realism described above is in trouble.

Would a metaethical stance resting on a claim of incoherence (or multiple incompatible meanings) be an error theory like Mackie's? Perhaps, in an attenuated sense, it would, since there is something erroneous in being confused over what we are talking about when we speak about morality. But moral incoherentism is in a crucial respect very much *unlike* the error theory, for it denies that moral utterances are factual assertions. Thus, it makes more sense to treat it as an entirely new variety of moral irrealism. Traditionally, moral irrealists have been forced to choose between noncognitivism and the error theory (leaving aside relativism and subjectivism, anti-objectivist theories which may or may not be thought of as versions of moral realism). Moral incoherentism is a form of moral irrealism that denies the semantic assumptions behind *both* of the traditional forms. Whether or not it is correct remains to be seen. And, as I have suggested, philosophically informed empirical study of people's metaethical views and linguistic dispositions is necessary if we are to uncover the truth.[23]

Most philosophers, Mackie included, have based their claims about moral thought and language on thought experiments and introspection (though Mackie also made reference to the history of philosophical thought and to the thinking of "ordinary people"). It is rare, however, to see any *serious* empirical inquiry into these questions. One philosopher who claims to recognize the importance of empirical inquiry to moral semantics, however, is Frank Jackson. However, although I am sympathetic with many features of Jackson's approach, I think he is wrong to ignore evidence supporting moral incoherentism. In the next two sections, I explore his position and ask why he does so. Part of the answer, I'll argue, is that he has not taken the empirical nature of these issues seriously enough.

Jackson's Marriage of Metaphysics and Semantics

Although in many ways far apart in substance, *From Metaphysics to Ethics* (Jackson, 1998) is a manifesto of what is sometimes called "the Canberra Plan" (or sometimes just "the Plan") in much that same way that *Language, Truth, and Logic* was a manifesto of logical positivism. A central element of the Plan's approach involves conceptual analysis, the purpose of which is to define the subject—to discover what it is we are talking about when we use a given vocabulary:

[M]etaphysicians will not get very far with questions like: Are there Ks? Are Ks nothing over and above Js? and, Is the K way the world is fully determined by the J way the world is? in the absence of some conception of what counts as a K, and what counts as a J. (Jackson, 1998, pp. 30–31)

Although metaphysics is concerned with figuring out what there is, we must *first* figure out what it is we are *looking* for when we ask our questions in the terms given by a particular vocabulary. To do that, we must come to understand the concepts behind our words. If we do not understand these concepts, Jackson argues, we risk talking past one another, or simply changing the subject.[24]

Our concepts, then, are what guide us in using our words to cover certain cases and not others. They are not tied to any particular language. While "Schnee" and "snow" almost certainly stand for the same concept, a word like "socialism" may stand for one thing in the mouth of a typical

American but stand for something very different when uttered by a typical British voter (Jackson, 1998, p. 35). How we use our language is, in a sense, up to us, Jackson thinks. Indeed, he refers approvingly to Humpty Dumpty's dictum that words can mean whatever we wish for them to mean (Jackson, 1998, p. 118).[25]

The pretty clear implication, I think, is a kind of semantic individualism. You've got your concepts, and I've got mine. But Jackson doesn't think that is such bad news, because he believes that there is actually a good deal of overlap among our concepts. As we saw, this shouldn't be surprising, given the way we use our words to communicate with one another. There is your concept of rightness and my concept of rightness, Jackson thinks, but there is also a *common* concept of rightness, a *folk* concept shared by most users of any given language (and perhaps others as well). It is folk concepts like these that we are often interested in when we ask the sorts of questions philosophers ask, Jackson says. More generally, there is folk *morality*, "the network of moral opinions, intuitions, principles and concepts whose mastery is part and parcel of having a sense of what is right and wrong, and being able to engage in meaningful debate about what ought to be done" (Jackson, 1998, p. 130).

Clearly, we do not simply make moral judgments at random. There is some pattern, often largely unknown to us, to the moral judgments we make. Thus, there must be something, no matter how hard to identify, guiding our use of words. And just as a grammarian might uncover the hidden, but principled, structure of classificatory practices that do not often involve the conscious application of known rules, we might hope to uncover, through conceptual analysis, the implicit theory behind our use of any given term.

Jackson is not using the word "theory" in any *ordinary* sense. (Humpty Dumpty was right, remember?) What *he* means by "theory," he tells us, is simply "a commonality or a projectible pattern to the cases where [a given term] applies" (Jackson, 2001, p. 659).[26] A theory needn't be conscious, accessible, explanatory, or anything beyond what is needed to account for a person's use of a given vocabulary. It will almost surely involve some borderline cases. And there is nothing in this notion of a theory, he says, that is incompatible with a causal or historical approach to reference for some terms or with our being committed to using a word in a way that defers to whatever the best *scientific* theory would say or to divisions in nature "worth marking."

The task of discovering the theories or concepts behind our words is an empirical one, Jackson notes. The *method* of discovery is the "method of possible cases," wherein we consult people's intuitions about what would count as appropriate uses of the terms whose concepts we are seeking to understand:

Intuitions about how various cases, including various merely possible cases, are correctly described in terms of free action, determinism, and belief, are precisely what reveal our ordinary conceptions of free action, determinism, and belief. . . . For what guides me in describing an action as free is revealed by my intuitions about what various possible cases are or are not cases of free action. (Jackson, 1998, pp. 31–32)

If we want to know what a person using a particular term is talking about, we need to understand the concept behind her use of the term. To find out, we must ask the person questions about whether the term is correctly applied in a range of possible cases.

However, we can't simply accept people's initial answers to those questions. We need to correct for any distortions caused by confused thinking and the like:

A person's first-up response as to whether something counts as a K may well need to be discounted. One or more of: the theoretical role they give K-hood, evidence concerning other cases they count as instances of K, signs of confused thinking on their part, cases where the classification is, on examination, a derivative one (they say it's a K because it is very obviously a J, and they think, defeasibly, that any J is a K), their readiness to back off under questioning, and the like, can justify rejecting a subject's first-up classifications as revealing their concept of K-hood. (Jackson, 1998, p. 35)[27]

We want to know what really *is* within the scope of people's concepts, and not merely what they *treat* as within their concepts' scope at first blush.

Interestingly, just as we refine our "first-up" responses to questions aimed at eliciting the scope of our concepts, we also subject our initial responses to questions about *morality* to a similar process of refinement. "Folk morality," we are told, "is currently under negotiation: its basic principles, and even many of its derived ones, are a matter of debate and are evolving as we argue about what to do" (Jackson, 1998, p. 132). Through such evolution, we hope to move from our current moral theory to our *mature* one. Mature folk morality is "the best we can do by way of making good sense of the raft of sometimes conflicting intuitions about particular cases and general principles that make up current folk morality" (Jackson, 1998, p. 132). If Rawls was right, it is the morality that would emerge in what we might call *ideal* reflective equilibrium. Jackson himself believes that at the limit of moral inquiry there would be widespread convergence, so that it makes sense to talk of mature folk morality *simpliciter*, rather than of this or that community's mature folk morality. Indeed, he tells us, "it is part of current folk morality that convergence will or would occur" (Jackson, 1998, p. 137).[28] However, he recognizes that both he and current folk morality could be wrong about this, and if so, he is prepared to accept the relativistic implications (Jackson, 1998, p. 137).

Although Jackson's description of the way those seeking to clarify people's concepts must correct for people's initial responses is somewhat vague, it seems clear that many aspects of the correction process will coincide with those involved in the correcting of our moral beliefs—the ordinary methods of moral reasoning (minimizing the impact of confused thinking and testing to see how firmly intuitions are held, e.g.). Both processes involve refining people's intuitions about whether a range of possible cases involves morally right action and the like. Indeed, some of the negotiation toward mature folk morality Jackson has in mind can reasonably be understood to involve debates over the correct application of terms like "right," "virtuous," or "blameworthy."

Furthermore, the motivations for understanding our concepts and for getting into ideal reflective equilibrium have at least one common thread. For, even now, we often use our words to talk about things some of whose contours are not yet clear to us. Thus, when a person attributes a property like rightness to something (in this case an act), the person is typically saying that the act has the property of rightness, not as she currently *believes* it to be, but as it really is—or at least as she *would* see it if she were thinking without any error or confusion. In many cases, our concepts already commit us to some form of idealization or correction of our initial intuitive responses.

However, if the distinction between current and mature folk morality is to be maintained, it seems that there must be two *different* sorts of correction processes, or at least significant differences of degree. Jackson has not told us how to differentiate between the sorts of corrections or changes to our intuitive responses needed to understand current folk morality and the sorts needed to arrive at mature folk morality. Until he does so, it is not clear what, according to his theory, people are talking about when they use the moral vocabulary *now*. And unless he can find some reasonably *principled* way of drawing the line, his distinction between current and mature folk morality appears to collapse.

More generally, and perhaps more importantly, Jackson hasn't given us a way to distinguish between refining our understanding of a concept (by adjusting our understanding of that concept's scope to better reflect people's actual linguistic dispositions) and changing the subject. With regard to morality, he hasn't given us a way to distinguish between refining our understanding of our moral concepts and changing our concepts, in the manner of reforming definitions. We'll see in the next section that there are other serious problems associated with Jackson's claims about the need for correction of our initial intuitions.

More Worries about Jackson's Methodology as Applied to Ethics

I agree that semantics is highly relevant to metaphysics and, in particular, to metaethics: Moore was right. If we want to know the answers to our metaethical questions, we had better figure out what it is we are asking, and doing so requires understanding what it is ordinary people are using the moral vocabulary to do. I also agree that this is largely an empirical task and that it is likely that we will find a good deal of interpersonal overlap among our semantic intuitions (or, as I have been saying, our linguistic dispositions)—enough, at least, to make using the moral vocabulary the helpful tool that it is for communicating with one another about what to do, and for coordinating our behavior.

However, I do not believe that Jackson has taken the empirical nature of semantic inquiry seriously enough. His failure to do so may help to explain both his optimism about convergence and his inattention to the possibility that the moral words are semantically incoherent. One reason for thinking that Jackson has not taken the empirical nature of semantic inquiry seriously enough, suggested by Stephen Stich and Jonathan M. Weinberg, is based in Jackson's confidence in our ability to know what other people's linguistic intuitions are, and in particular to know that they match our own. "[O]ften," he says, "we know that our own case is typical and so can generalize from it to others. It was surely not a surprise to Gettier that many people agreed about his cases" (Jackson, 1998, p. 37). In a symposium on Jackson's book, Stich and Weinberg take issue with Jackson over the Gettier case, but I do not wish to enter into that dispute. Instead, I want to consider another case they bring up.

Stich and Weinberg are *astounded* to hear Jackson say the following of students and of the folk in general: "We have some kind of commitment to the idea that moral disagreements can be resolved by critical reflection— which is why we bother to engage in moral debate. To that extent objectivism is part of current folk morality" (Jackson, 1998, p. 137).[29] In *their* experience, we are told, a significant number of undergraduates show an inclination toward moral *relativism*. Stich and Weinberg suspect that Jackson is treating moral relativists as mere outliers. (Jackson does acknowledge that some people might use words in unconventional ways and thus could be asking different questions than the rest of us.) Stich and Weinberg don't know *why* Jackson treats the putative relativists as outliers, but their best guess is that Jackson is overconfident about his own ability to tell when his intuitions are typical.

As I have suggested, my own impression about students' reactions is much closer to Stich and Weinberg's, though I would have pointed to forms of anti-objectivism other than relativism as well. However, I don't want to put too much weight on *anybody's* impressions. For one thing, the fact that Jackson and his critics have such different impressions of their students' reactions is itself evidence precisely that we, sometimes at least, are *not* very good at knowing when our own intuitive responses can be trusted to be sufficiently typical to warrant our treating them as standard. It seems clear that at least one side has misunderstood the situation. It is of course *possible* that Jackson's students (and his acquaintances among the folk) just happen to be different than the crowd Stich and Weinberg associate with. But surely this is unlikely. And even if it is the case, widespread disagreement over moral objectivity is as much of a problem for Jackson as is widespread anti-objectivism.

However, perhaps it is unfair of Stich and Weinberg to hypothesize that Jackson's claims about folk objectivism rely primarily on confidence in his ability to tell when his intuitions are typical, for presumably Jackson has *asked* some people whether their intuitions agree with his. He is, after all, in favor of empirical research on such matters. Indeed, he thinks such research is going on all the time:

> I am sometimes asked—in a tone that suggests that the question is a major objection—why, if conceptual analysis is concerned to elucidate what governs our classificatory practice, don't I advocate doing serious opinion polls on people's responses to various cases? My answer is that I do—when it is necessary. Everyone who presents the Gettier cases to a class of students is doing their own bit of fieldwork, and we all know the answer they get in the vast majority of cases. (Jackson, 1998, pp. 36–37)

Jackson may have missed the point of the "major objection" implicit in the question about opinion polls, however. The problem is not that opinion polls are a bad idea; the problem is that Jackson is far too cavalier about the methodological standards for satisfactorily *conducting* such polls. As Stich and Weinberg point out, Jacksonian classroom "fieldwork" is a travesty of social scientific rigor. Classroom polls sample only "students at elite universities" and of those only the group choosing to take philosophy courses (usually advanced ones), run the risk of experimenter bias, and overlook the proven tendency to "suppress dissenting opinions" when people are asked to state their opinions by some public gesture such as a showing of hands (Stich & Weinberg, 2001, p. 642).

In addition to the complaints Stich and Weinberg make about Jackson's methodology, we can add a few others. It is not as though anyone is compiling all of this "fieldwork" in an effort to produce greater accuracy through a larger sample. Furthermore, I don't think we should trust our own impressions and memories as accurately representing what went on in the classroom. Most of us haven't counted or kept records. From time to time we have asked for a show of hands and gotten an impression, but it is not at all clear that our impressions were uninformed by our expectations.[30] Moreover, one thing we have learned from recent work in psychology is that how a question is framed can have an enormous impact on how it is answered.[31] For example, I strongly suspect that I get a higher proportion of my students saying yes to relativism when I first mention abortion as an example of a moral question than when I begin with parricide. But I have made no careful attempt to systematically remove any such framing biases from my fieldwork, if indeed that can even be done.

The worst feature of Jacksonian fieldwork, however, is that it systematically ignores much of the data with which it is presented. It does this for two reasons. First, Jackson's methodology takes as its starting point the *common* features of our moral thought and thus turns our attention away from what is controversial:

We can think of the rather general principles that we share as the commonplaces or platitudes or constitutive principles that make up the core we need to share in order to count as speaking a common moral language. What we disagree about are the fundamental underpinnings of these generally agreed principles, and, accordingly, we disagree about the nature and frequency of the exceptions to them. (Jackson, 1998, p. 132)[32]

This makes it look as though anything we do not currently agree upon is in principle expendable, if abandoning it is necessary for reaching agreement. However, as we have seen, certain controversial platitudes (such as that morality is what God wishes for us to do, or even that it is *not* a realm of fact), may be nonnegotiable for some people. And mature folk morality itself may be unable to eliminate a great deal of residual conflict. If so, then according to Jackson's account, we do *not* share a common set of concepts after all.

In fact, some of the "platitudes" Jackson himself mentions are themselves quite controversial, at least among philosophers. One example is "that people who claim to believe that something is very wrong but show not the slightest inclination to refrain from doing it are in some sense insincere" (Jackson, 1998, p. 132). Externalists about morality such as Richard Boyd (1988), David Brink (1989, especially pp. 37–80), and Peter Railton (1986) deny that sincere moral beliefs require motivational impacts. Another is that "what we should aim at is not doing what is right *qua* what is right. I should rescue someone from a fire because if I don't they will die, not because that is the right thing to do" (Jackson, 1998, p. 141). The claim that we should do what is right *because* it is right and *not* for some other reason is fundamental to Kantianism (Kant, 1785/1969, pp. 16–19).[33]

One might think that philosophers' quarrels over such matters aren't really very interesting, as our training has led us far away from the folk concepts. However, we should remember that the concepts we are typically looking for are those we would employ if we were freed from confusion and other sorts of epistemic misfortune. It is reasonable to think (or at least hope!) that "the folk" would wind up sounding *more* like philosophers, the more their epistemic positions improved.[34]

But perhaps Jackson thinks people like Stich and Weinberg would share his impressions of what students are like if only they were to look at the evidence *properly*. And this brings me to the second and more important reason why much of the data is systematically ignored in Jackson-style fieldwork. Remember that simply looking at what we say offhand does not reveal our moral concepts. Our answers have to be corrected, at least to some high degree, to remove the influence of confused thinking and the like. However, this raises a serious concern. To put it perhaps a bit too crudely, the risk is that answers that don't agree with the observer's own favored interpretation of folk morality will be rejected because they will be viewed as the products of confused thinking.

For example, in response to Stich and Weinberg's claims about their students' apparent relativism, Jackson (2001) says:

What is relevant is not whether the students use the words "moral relativism" to describe their position. It is what they do when they debate moral issues which is relevant. In my experience, the actions of students, and of the folk in general, reveal that they have "some kind of commitment" to the idea that moral disagreements can be resolved by sufficient critical reflection. . . . (p. 662)

Now in fairness, I think Jackson would admit that no one is relying on the mere fact that the students *use the words* "moral relativism" to describe their positions. The point is that a very plausible explanation for their having the tendency to use these words is that they believe them to be true. Perhaps, that is, a number of them say that they are moral relativists because they *do* have "some kind of commitment" to moral relativism.

There is no reason to believe that theoretical intuitions like those behind moral relativism are, *in general*, irrelevant to the question of what people are doing when they employ the terms of the moral vocabulary. Perhaps Jackson thinks that insofar as the intuitions tend toward relativism or irrealism, they are the products of confusion, as evidenced by the fact that would-be relativist students continue to debate moral issues. However, the fact that they engage in moral reasoning does not establish that they are committed to moral objectivity, much less that they are committed to it at the expense of their anti-objectivist leanings. They might reason in the *hope* of reaching agreement. But neither hoping for agreement nor agreement itself presupposes that we are discussing a realm of fact.

Indeed, most irrealist views make room for moral reasoning. If Gibbard's sophisticated noncognitivism were correct, for example, the students would still be saying many of the things that sound to an objectivist like expressions of a commitment to objectivity. They'd still disagree with one another at times, and when they did, they'd think their interlocutors wrong, recognize that *they* could be wrong instead, and believe that they have been wrong in the past. Gibbard thinks these and other putative indicia of objectivity are quite compatible with his expressivist analysis of moral language. If irrealist theories can make sense of moral reasoning, then people who engage in moral reasoning can, without confusion, be irrealists.

More generally, what *counts* as confused thinking is itself a matter of some dispute. Both the standards for theory evaluation and their applications are frequently controversial. For example, some philosophers believe that we should discount our intuitions about particular cases in favor of more general intuitions about matters of principle or theory, thereby rejecting the more widely accepted reflective equilibrium approach.[35] Indeed, attempting to carry out the empirical research properly would be likely to reveal just how little has actually been settled concerning the appropriate standards for correcting our initial intuitive responses.

Admittedly, we can all agree that an internally inconsistent concept is confused in the relevant sense. However, we may disagree about what would happen if the confusion were to be removed. How can anyone claim to *know* that when confronted with the alleged inconsistency between their putative relativism and their actual practice in debating moral issues, students would agree that these are indeed inconsistent and, even if so, that they would choose to become objectivists or realists rather than to reform their practices (or their understanding of these practices)? How can we know that instead of adopting moral realism and abandoning their anti-objectivist leanings, the students would not choose instead to say, as some error theorists do, that morality is a useful fiction (Joyce); that it is a horrible institution that we are lucky to be rid of (Joshua Greene); or that the institutions of morality are distinct from morality itself, and that many of these institutions are enormously useful, given our often-common concerns (as I believe).[36] It is sheer dogmatism (and an insult to moral irrealists!) to claim, without having done the necessary empirical and philosophical legwork, to know that unconfused people would be committed to moral objectivity.

My own impression, again, is that once they learn some metaethics, some of these self-proclaimed anti-objectivists do indeed move over to the objectivist camp. But many do not. Some are not sure where to come out, even after lots of reflection. However, even when they are willing to plunk for one side or the other, there still seem to be plenty plunking for the opposite side. If so, then even when intrapersonal conflict can be eliminated, interpersonal and cross-cultural conflict remain. In light of the kinds of considerations I've mentioned, I do not think it reasonable to put *too* much trust in that impression. But there is at least good prima facie reason to take moral incoherentism seriously. To test it, we must do the "serious opinion polls on people's responses to various cases" that Jackson pooh-poohs for this area of inquiry.

Jackson's confidence in folk moral objectivism may help to explain his failure to take the possibility of moral semantic incoherence seriously. Although many of the folk *do* have some sort of commitment to moral objectivity, it seems likely that many *also* (and many others) have some sort of commitment *against* it. Indeed, there is a hidden assumption in Jackson's position (and perhaps even in the strong opposition to it we saw in Stich and Weinberg): that because the intuitions conflict, they can't *both* be central, nonnegotiable elements in our implicit "theory" of morality.[37] However, that assumption has not been defended. If, in the end, conflicting elements do turn out to be nonnegotiable, we have nonnegotiable conceptual incoherence, and moral incoherentism is vindicated.

Now Jackson admits that it is at least possible that he is wrong about there being a unique mature folk morality. And he might even admit that the publicly available moral concepts contain some contradictions that would not disappear in ideal reflective equilibrium. Even if so, on his view, all need not be lost. For there might well be concepts in the neighborhood of the confused ones that would serve as useful alternatives. In discussing compatibilism, he offers a suggestion of just this sort, insisting that if a revised account of free action is changing the subject, it is doing so only in "a strictly limited sense":

> For compatibilists do, it seems to me, show, first, that the folk conception of free action involves a potentially unstable attempt to find a middle way between the random and the determined, second, that the folk conception is nowhere instantiated, and third, that a compatibilist substitute does all we legitimately require of the concept of free action. (Jackson, 1998, p. 45)

However, we must remember that even on Jackson's view, an idealization can only go so far. And we might reasonably worry that the "all we legitimately require" clause represents a form of sour grapes. More importantly, irrealists need not fear this sort of idealization, for it is consistent with their views about the nonexistence of morality and the associated moral properties. Indeed, although Jackson doesn't mention Brandt, changing the subject, even if only in "a strictly limited sense," is just what the method of reforming definitions recommends. And as we saw, that method often *presupposes* irrealism with respect to the referents of the original terms.

Although Jackson claims that his approach is neutral with respect to certain theories of reference, his semantic theory is far from universally accepted. In the next section, I argue that this isn't a serious problem for empirical moral semantics. Regardless of which approach we take, the information to be sought by the would-be moral semanticist is largely the same. What is needed is an investigation into our (moral) linguistic dispositions, as reflected both in our metaethical and ethical views and in our moral practice.

Semantic Approaches More Generally

What counts as a correct semantics of morality seems to depend on what counts as a correct *approach* to semantics at a much more general level. Thus, although questions about moral language are largely empirical, this is another respect in which they cannot be wholly so. How can we know what to look for if we have not settled the question of whether a broadly internalist (or descriptivist) approach or a broadly externalist (or causal) approach to reference is correct? Indeed, don't we need to decide on a particular version of any of these approaches before we can figure out how to see whether moral incoherentism is correct?

Unfortunately, there is no consensus on which, if any, of the many going approaches to semantics is right, and even less consensus about how to put these approaches into practice in any but the simplest of cases. However, that doesn't mean that the project of reaching empirically sound conclusions about moral semantics is doomed until we have made a good deal more progress in the philosophy of language. In fact, I think, we needn't be so fine grained to start off. Roughly the same information will be relevant no matter which semantic approach we decide to take. To see why, we need to take a brief look at the most prominent of the available options.

The more traditional philosophical approach to questions of semantics looks a lot like Jackson's. It is internalist or descriptivist. On this view, very roughly, meaning and reference are at first a personal matter. What a person is talking about, according to this approach, is whatever corresponds to the speaker's own understanding of the term. Thus, each of us can ask a question like "Is moral rightness real?" in his or her own personal idiolect. If by "moral rightness" I mean the property of maximizing the overall net expected ratio of pleasure over suffering, given the alternatives open to an agent, then there is moral rightness just in case there is something corresponding to that particular description. How then is communication possible? It is possible, as we have seen, if we share definitions that are more or less equivalent.

So is there a common question we are all asking when we ask whether there are facts about moral rightness? That depends on whether our conceptions of moral rightness agree, at least in their essential features. However, while some would argue that each individual can know his or her own conception of rightness (or of any other property or entity) by introspection, whether there is agreement among any number of us is an empirical matter, one that can be addressed only by investigating the linguistic dispositions of those engaged in the discussion.

More recently, externalist semantic theories have gained wide, though by no means universal, acceptance. One family of such theories focuses on the causal histories underlying our use of the words in question. On one prominent version, when we talk about water, we are talking about the stuff causal contact with which (by seeing, tasting, etc.) is responsible for our use of the word "water." Likewise, rightness is whatever it is that is "causally regulating" our use of the *term* "rightness."[38] On this approach, semantic questions do not reduce to what individual language users believe about the nature of moral rightness—nor even to what they *would* believe if free from error. Indeed, one of the advertised advantages of the causal approach is its ability to accommodate widespread and serious disagreement about the nature of the entities or properties that any number of people are nevertheless all talking about in common.

Causal regulation chains are not always straightforward, according to the theory. Sometimes, for example, coreference is said to be achieved by way of deference to experts, in what Hilary Putnam (1975) has called the "linguistic division of labor" (pp. 227–229). But whether there is such deference is revealed by our linguistic dispositions. Thus, one set of questions to ask has to do with whether people believe that there are any such experts with respect to morality.[39] These questions could take one of two forms. We might ask people directly whether they believe that there are any such experts and, if so, who the experts are. Or we might ask them questions closer to the normative end of the spectrum, such as whether abortion would be wrong if there were wide agreement among certain specified people (like religious leaders) that it was not wrong.

Not all reference can involve deference to experts, however, for among other things, the experts cannot be deferring to themselves. Instead, they are often said to be deferring to nature, referring to whatever things have the true nature, whatever it might be, of the thing they intend to talk about. Cases in which ordinary speakers are *not* deferring to experts may have something like this structure as well. In other cases (or on other versions of the theory), it is thought that we defer to those initially choosing to adopt a word to stand for a certain thing. It is hard to believe that this latter sort of deference is involved in regard to the central words in the moral vocabulary. But even if it were, linguistic dispositions of the sort we have been discussing would matter, in this case both the dispositions of those responsible for the initial dubbings and our dispositions to defer (or not) to *their* decisions. In all of these cases, we can discover the relevant dispositions, if at all, only with empirical research of roughly the sort I have described here.

A final approach in the broadly externalist camp involves deference of yet another sort, to the linguistic community as a whole. One version, sometimes called the *consensus* view, involves a combination of the internalist view with a kind of linguistic democracy. No individual's understanding of what a word means is definitive, but those of the community in general are, and we use words incorrectly when we deviate too far from community usage. Whether we are disposed to defer to communities in this way, and what those communities on the whole believe, are once again empirical questions.

On all of these approaches, internalist and externalist, what we are using our moral language to do is in large part revealed by our linguistic dispositions, collective or individual. Of course, the route from these data to semantic incoherence is likely to vary from theory to theory, and it is possible that the road will be rougher on some theories than it is on others. However, in all cases, we must ask questions designed to elicit a family of related linguistic dispositions. To discover what these dispositions are, if it is possible at all, will require more than introspection and projection or hasty generalization. It will demand careful empirical study involving a great deal of philosophical sophistication, subtlety, and ingenuity. In the next section, I point to some of the challenges that such an inquiry presents.

Problems for Empirical Moral Semantics

Cognitive psychologists and other social scientists (and, for that matter, some philosophers) have devised empirical tests that are nothing short of ingenious. Even so, there are special difficulties for anyone contemplating such an enterprise here. To begin, both metaethical and normative dispositions are relevant to moral semantics. Thus, we could ask people whether they believe that there are moral facts or whether moral truths are independent of what people believe about them. Or we could ask more indirect questions, designed to elicit people's metaethical views, for example, "Would it still be wrong to commit adultery even if God said it was ok?" We could also ask straightforwardly normative questions and try to figure out what would have to be true in order for people's answers to be correct. Presumably all of these data are relevant to the dispute between cognitivism and noncognitivism.

If moral incoherentism is correct, we can expect to see (intrapersonal and interpersonal) conflicts, both within and across all of these areas. However, since our linguistic dispositions are hardly transparent to us, it is likely that the answers people give will not always accurately reflect their actual psychologies. For example, we might find someone saying that morality is all a matter of taste and not a matter of fact but then treating many of his or her moral views as if they are factual all the same. But such conflicts, even if widespread, would not be dispositive. For one thing, as we saw in our discussion of Jackson, people are sometimes disposed to defer to their less confused selves. To find out how people would respond if they were thinking as clearly and as thoroughly as possible, however, would *itself* involve clear and thorough thinking, much of which, we can safely assume, has not yet been done.

Furthermore, given the ingenuity of both cognitivist and noncognitivist attempts to shore up their theories' apparent weaknesses in accommodating what are thought to be the linguistic dispositions built into ordinary moral talk, it is difficult to imagine an instrument capable of giving us the sort of information we need. Suppose, for example, that we want to know whether someone uses statements like "It is wrong to kill your children for fun" to express propositions. Simply asking whether such statements are true is insufficient, since it makes perfect sense to say that they are true, according to recent noncognitivist theories like those put forward by Gibbard, Blackburn, and Timmons. The investigator might try to push deeper, asking whether the statement is true simply because the agent believes it to be true or whether instead its truth is independent of its being believed. However, as we have seen, an account like Gibbard's, in spite of its noncognitivism, claims to have room for the latter thought.

We might make limited attempts at educating the subject about metaethics. In this vein, I sometimes offer my students a contrast between questions of fact and questions of taste (with examples like the inhabited planets and the chocolate) and then ask them whether moral questions are more like the former or more like the latter. However, it isn't always easy to get people to understand these issues, and the more explaining we have to do, the less confident we should be that the answers reflect the subjects' own views. As seen earlier, this susceptibility to framing and other forms of influence itself illustrates the fragility and inchoate nature of people's linguistic dispositions.

Finally, when we start to think about cross-cultural investigations involving speakers of different languages, the difficulties of rendering adequate translations loom large. We can't assume that people using terms *treated* as synonymous with terms in our moral vocabulary are indeed using them for the same purposes we are. For all of these reasons, it is no wonder that philosophers have relied on more informal methods of semantic analysis. But like the drunk searching for his wallet under a streetlight because the light is better there than it was where he dropped it, we cannot expect to succeed if we don't look in the right place.

Conclusion

I have argued that empirical semantics is crucial to assessing one of the fundamental issues in metaethics, the debate between cognitivism and noncognitivism. And I've suggested that resolving this debate might lead to some surprising results. In particular, if moral incoherentism—the hypothesis that because of fundamental and irreconcilable inconsistencies in our dispositions with regard to moral discourse, no adequate, coherent moral semantics can be formulated—is correct, then moral realism is in serious trouble. In this way it might indeed be possible to pull a meta-physical rabbit out of a semantic hat. Whether or not that is the case remains to be established, and I've suggested that it won't be easy. But figuring out how to do it and conducting the relevant research are necessary if we are to discover whether the trick will actually work.

Notes

This paper was conceived and an initial draft was prepared when I was a fellow at Dartmouth College's Institute on the Psychology and Biology of Morality. I thank those responsible, especially Walter Sinnott-Armstrong, for their generous support. I'd also like to thank the many people who helped me by providing comments on various drafts and much helpful discussion. Among these are David Barnett, David Christensen, Tyler Doggett, Owen Flanagan, Richard Joyce, Arthur Kuflik, Mark Moyer, Derk Pereboom, Walter Sinnott-Armstrong (again), Barbara Rachelson, Chandra Sripada, and Steven Stich. The paper is dedicated to the ordinary person.

1. Nathan Salmon had the unbridled temerity to think of (and publish) the meta-physical rabbit/semantic hat phrase before I had a chance to come up with it on my own, and he even graced the dust jacket of his book, *Reference and Essence* (1981), with a hat and rabbit illustration. Salmon takes a dim view of semantics-to-metaphysics prestidigitation.

2. Philadelphia: Jewish Publication Society of America, 1955. Somebody else has probably cited this verse before I did, too.

3. For example, most of us are disposed to use the word "donkey" to refer to certain quadruped animals, and not to refer to abstract things like love or humility. We are also disposed to refrain from applying the term to mules, at least once we learn about the species-crossing provenance of the latter. These dispositions are strong evidence that the word does indeed refer to animals of a particular sort.

4. Some, such as Mark Timmons, prefer the less fashionable but etymologically more revealing "descriptivism/nondescriptivism" terminology (1999, p. 19, footnote 15).

5. Brandt was a pioneer in the movement to bring empirical science to bear on ethical theory. See Brandt (1954).

6. I have recently come across two excellent unpublished manuscripts that move from moral semantics to moral irrealism (or skepticism) in ways that bear some similarity to the approach I take here. They are David Merli's (1990) "Moral Realism's Semantic Problem" and Adam Pautz's (n.d.) "From Moral Semantics to Moral Skepticism." For a related, but importantly different view, see Stephen Schiffer (1990).

7. Moore himself asked about the meaning of "good," but he meant by it something like goodness.

8. There are noncentral cases, like "You acted wrongly in stealing," which does express the proposition that you stole, on Ayer's (1952) view (pp. 107–108).

9. The label "emotivist" is a bit misleading in suggesting only the emotion-expressing function. Ayer (1952) all along acknowledged a prescriptive or hortatory function as well (p. 108).

10. Blackburn (1984), Dreier (1990, 1999), Gibbard (1990), Hare (1952, 1981), Silverstein (1983), Stevenson (1944), and Timmons (1999).

11. Likewise, Mark Timmons (1999) discusses (what he takes to be) the importance of *accommodating* the "commonsense assumptions of ordinary moral discourse," within a "nondescriptivist" (as he calls it) framework (pp. 11–12). In particular, Timmons (1999) focuses on what Gibbard called the "objective pretensions" of moral discourse (pp. 71–76, 158–177, and 224–226).

12. There are other ways to define things, but this is a standard way. There is an excellent treatment of these issues by Mark van Roojen (2005).

13. There are several other versions. For a thorough review of the variations, see Doggett (n.d.).

14. Arguably, some of the most recent versions of noncognitivism, such as Gibbard's, Blackburn's, and Timmons's, have gone so far in the direction of accommodating objectivity that they are no longer consistent with the anti-objectivist strand I have been discussing.

15. Most moral relativists think that facts about morality are like facts about legality; they differ from place to place and from one time to another. (Some would even go so far as to say that the moral facts differ from person to person.)

16. There is also the possibility of borderline cases. It may simply be vague whether or not our moral terms are such that we can employ them to make factual assertions. If so, then it is vague whether or not cognitivism is correct. If it is correct, then moral realism is still a possibility; if not, then it is not a possibility. But even here the possibility that cognitivism, and hence moral realism, is so precarious is not a happy one for the would-be moral realist.

17. For a discussion of this, see Nichols (2004b).

18. It is widely agreed that most of us *do* have at least some inconsistent beliefs. See Sorensen (2001).

19. Approaches bearing *some* resemblance to mine have been gaining ground with respect to a number of other philosophically important terms. See, for example, Double (1991, especially chapter 5), Eklund, (2004), Nichols and Knobe (forthcoming), Sider (2001).

20. Walter Sinnott-Armstrong got me thinking about this objection.

21. I owe this use of "nonnegotiable" to Steven Stich and Jonathan Weinberg.

22. I discuss this at greater length in "Moral Realism and the Argument from Moral Disagreement" (1998, pp. 281–303, especially section III).

23. In some cases, presumably (as with words like "heat"), the relevant linguistic dispositions involve deference to the way things are, as discovered by nonpsychological scientific inquiry.

24. Jackson, of course, is not the first to make this point. In many ways, he is defending a sophisticated version of the *traditional* rationale for conceptual analysis, the very rationale Moore was appealing to in the passage quoted earlier. More recently, Richard Hare (1981) has said, "I am not suggesting that we are tied to using words in the way that we do, or to having the conceptual scheme we have. But if we were to alter the meanings of our words, we should be altering the questions we were asking. . . . If we go on trying to answer *those* questions, we are stuck with those concepts" (p. 18).

25. " 'When *I* use a word,' Humpty Dumpty said in a rather scornful tone, 'it means just what I choose it to mean—neither more nor less' " (Carroll, 1946, p. 238).

26. Jackson does not fully articulate the relationship among our *concepts* (or sometimes, our *conceptions*) and our explicit or implicit *theories*, but it's obvious that he intends for them to be fairly tightly connected, and he sometimes appears to be using the terms interchangeably. The example of grammar is offered at a point in which he is mostly talking in terms of theory. Jackson says that grammar is an area in which our folk theory represents only part of the truth. For the rest of the truth (about our own grammatical practices), we must turn to grammarians. The claim that our folk theory of grammar contains part of the truth suggests that by "theory," Jackson has in mind neither the underlying psychological mechanism that causes us to speak the way we do nor the usage pattern itself, but some more or less conscious or accessible view *about* the contours of that mechanism or pattern. However, that seems inconsistent with his talk of our theories as "the patterns that guide us in classifying the various possible cases" (Jackson, 1998, p. 130). Perhaps he is using the word in two senses.

27. Also see Jackson's (1998) discussion of the Gettier cases, where he notes that we are typically prepared to set aside intuitive reactions that are due to confusion, not as a reform, but in order "to make explicit what had been implicit in our classificatory practice all along" (p. 36).

28. This raises the possibility of another argument against moral realism for a theory like Jackson's. If it *is* a (nonnegotiable) conceptual truth that morality is something we would converge upon, but there is nothing on which we would after all converge, then there is no such thing as morality.

29. Stich and Weinberg's (2001) comment is in "Jackson's Empirical Assumptions." They are astounded on p. 641. Jackson's (2001) reply is in the same issue (pp. 656–662).

30. Perhaps some of these concerns are encompassed in Stich and Weinberg's vague "experimenter bias."

31. Tversky and Kahneman (1981). In this connection, Walter Sinnott-Armstrong has reminded me that the polls are also being conducted by a teacher who has the power to issue grades. It wouldn't be surprising if students were sometimes influenced by their beliefs about what would please a teacher. Presumably, an objectivist like Jackson is pleased to find a commitment to objectivity.

32. Jackson says here that actual moral disagreement "requires a background of shared opinion to fix a common, or near enough common, set of meanings for our moral terms" (1998, p. 132). But, as I argued above, the minimum overlap needed to support the *activity* of disagreeing (which we see all the time) may not be sufficient to support the claim that we are using the words in the same way—or as I have been saying, that we are all talking about the same things.

33. Indeed, most consequentialists would claim that a person's motivations for doing the right thing are only of interest morally insofar as they are *instrumentally* relevant.

34. To some degree this may count against Stich and Weinberg's (2001) claim that the intuitions of Jackson and some of his colleagues are suspect guides to folk theory, since most of these people are "high socio-economic status males ... *who have advanced degrees in philosophy* and whose cultural background is Western European" (p. 642; emphasis added). My point, however, is that after considerable reflection, even *these* people cannot agree on many fundamental questions about when the terms in the moral vocabulary are correctly applied.

35. See Singer (1974, 2005) and Unger (1996). In contrast, Baruch Brody (1979) once claimed that *only* intuitions about particular cases have justificatory force. Others, like Brandt (1979, pp. 16–23) and Hare (1981, pp. 10–12), reject any appeal to moral intuitions at all.

36. Joyce (2001) and Greene (2002).

37. I doubt that this actually represents Stich's considered view.

38. Boyd (1988, pp. 195, 200–202, 209–212). As we've seen, Jackson claims that his approach is compatible with the causal theory.

39. It would be surprising if at least some people didn't think of God *not* as the author of morality but (merely) as a "super expert" on the subject.

bear in direct and uncontroversial ways on certain metaethical debates (such as the debate between cognitivists and noncognitivists; see pp. 380–381). But I think he is absolutely right in his contention that metaethicists ought to make a much more determined and thorough attempt than they have traditionally done to ground their positions in systematic observations of the phenomena they are trying to give an account of.

Of course, we cannot say in advance that empirical investigation will confirm or disconfirm the variability thesis, just as we cannot say in advance that it will confirm or disconfirm cognitivism or noncognitivism, internalism or externalism, objectivism or relativism, or any other metaethical position. If we heed Loeb's call for a new, more serious empirical grounding for metaethics, all of these positions have to be taken, at this stage, to be merely hypotheses in need of testing. Let us consider nonetheless what the implications would be if the variability thesis were vindicated. If we were to find that ordinary moral thought and language contain both cognitivist and noncognitivist aspects—and if there could be found no principled way of granting conceptual priority to, or of dismissing as conceptually aberrant, one of these aspects—what conclusions would we be compelled to draw about our concept of morality?

According to Loeb, the variability thesis implies or at least strongly suggests that our moral thought and language embody incompatible commitments, that participants in moral discourse are engaged in an activity that harbors internal contradictions, that incoherence infects the very semantics of moral terms. If the variability thesis is true, according to Loeb, it would not simply be the case that people who use moral terms are trying to refer to something that does not exist, which is the kind of error made by nineteenth-century adherents to the theory of phlogiston, an entity that scientific investigation revealed did not exist but at least could have existed. Participants in moral discourse would, rather, be like people discussing the characteristics of a round square, an activity we know to be mistaken without having to do any scientific investigation at all.

I do not think, however, that the variability thesis leads as directly to the conclusion that moral thought and language are as pervasively incoherent as Loeb suggests. That we can find in our uses of moral terms both cognitivist and noncognitivist (as well as internalist and externalist, and objectivist and relativist) aspects might signal ineluctable incoherence, but then again it might not. It all depends on where those different aspects are located, on how they're distributed in our thought and language. If the different aspects are implicated by each and every use of moral terms, then Loeb's diagnosis of incoherence will be apt. But if one of the aspects is implicated within one pocket of moral thought and language and the other aspect is implicated within a different pocket of moral thought and language, then Loeb's moral incoherentism might be a misdiagnosis. For it might be perfectly sensible to use a moral term in a way that involves one commitment, and also to use a moral term in a way that eschews that commitment, just so long as the first use occurs in a situation that is semantically[3] insulated from the situation in which the second use occurs. Two things that cannot both be coherently asserted at the same time might each be coherently asserted at different times.

To illustrate this possibility, we can point to our uses of "happy" and its cognates. Sometimes "happy" is used noncognitively. If a person says, "I'm happy," she may be expressing an attitude rather than trying to describe anything about herself. Sometimes, however, "happy" is used cognitively. If a person says of someone else, "He's happy," she may be trying to describe something about the other person. And among cognitive uses of "happy," there are also variations. Sometimes "happy" is used to refer exclusively to occurrent feelings. Sometimes it is used to refer to dispositions. Sometimes it is used to refer to a condition that is necessarily connected to objective (nonaffective) features of a person's situation. Now if we were to gather up all the commitments implicated by all our different uses of "happy" and take each of them to be implicated by every use of "happy," then our thought and language about happiness would look to be inexorably confused, akin to discussion of a round square. There would be something ineluctably incoherent about a mode of discourse that commits us to holding that one and the same person, at a single time and in a uniform way, is both happy and not happy. But our happiness discourse is not that confused or incoherent. It is perfectly sensible, when describing a person's life as a whole, to use "happy" in a way that involves a commitment that, were one seeking to express gratitude to another for a recent act of kindness, one would eschew. What would be erroneous would be an analysis that fails to take into account the differences between the various contexts in which "happy" is used.

It seems to me that just as we can give a reconciling pluralist account of "happy," so too might we be able to give a reconciling pluralist account of moral terms. And the possibility of such an account opens up the conceptual space to accept the variabilist thesis while rejecting Loeb's moral incoherentism. For if such a pluralist account were at hand, we could hold that some pockets of ordinary moral discourse really are best analyzed as thoroughly cognitivist (or objectivist, or externalist), and some pockets really are best analyzed as thoroughly noncognitivist (or relativist, or internalist). The existence of such variability would not, however, necessarily reveal that ordinary moral thought and language are incoherent or confused. It may reveal, rather, that our moral terms are flexible enough to be put to numerous different kinds of uses. Moral terms, according to this possibility, can be used cognitively and noncognitively, relativistically and objectively, externally and internally—even if they cannot coherently be used in all these different ways at the same time. Thus, ordinary folk do not necessarily make any mistake when they put moral terms to these different uses, so long as they do not try to use them in too many different ways simultaneously. If there is a mistake that requires diagnosing here, it is that of metaethicists who have assumed that if a certain feature (such as a commitment to cognitivism, or to objectivism, or to a necessary connection between moral judgment and motivation) is implicated by the use of moral terms in one pocket of discourse, it must also be implicated by the use of moral terms in every other pocket.

Let me fill in a bit this notion of pockets of moral discourse. What I have in mind are two types of cases. The first type of case is that in which some people use a moral term in one way while other people always use the moral term in a different way. The second type of case is that in which some people use a moral term in one way in certain situations and the same people use the moral term in another way in other situations. There may, for instance, be some people—say, some college sophomores—who always use a moral term in a relativistic way, while there may be others—say, some priests or rabbis—who always use the moral term in an objectivist way. And there also may be some people who use moral terms relativistically in certain situations—say, when discussing the moral status of individuals in distant times or places or when conversing with other people who themselves use moral terms in a predominantly relativistic way—and who use moral terms objectively in other situations—say, when assessing the laws, policies, or customs of their own country or when conversing with other people who themselves use moral terms in a predominantly objectivist way. Metaethical objectivists typically begin their accounts by focusing on the pockets of moral discourse that truly are objectivist. They then try to show that, despite the appearance of relativistic commitments in some other pockets, everyone's uses of moral terms are fundamentally objectivist—that the seemingly relativistic uses are parasitic on objectivist uses, or insincere, or implicitly placed in inverted commas, or otherwise conceptually aberrant. Metaethical relativists typically do the same sort of thing, although they of course begin with uses of moral terms in relativistic pockets and then try somehow to dismiss or accommodate the seemingly objectivist uses. Metaethical objectivists and metaethical relativists, in other words, both begin by pointing to uses of moral terms that really do fit very well with their own analyses, and then both have to fight like hell to explain away the uses that look not to fit.

Loeb rightly raises the possibility that when we pay sufficiently close attention to how moral terms are actually used in ordinary discourse, we will find that there truly are both objectivist and relativistic commitments—and that neither sort of commitment can be convincingly explained away. But it seems to me that Loeb does not give sufficient consideration to the possibility that the objectivist and relativistic uses may be semantically insulated from each other. He seems to share with metaethical objectivists and relativists what I call the "uniformity assumption"—namely, that if a metaethical commitment is implicated in one pocket of ordinary moral discourse, then it must also be implicated in every other pocket. This is the assumption I want to question. The possibility I want to raise is that some pockets of moral discourse are consistently objectivist, that other pockets are consistently relativistic, and that the uses of moral terms in each of these types of pockets is completely coherent. That we can find in ordinary moral discourse as a whole both objectivist and relativistic commitments does not imply that both of these different commitments are implicated in every pocket of ordinary moral discourse—just as that we can find in ordinary "happiness" discourse as a whole a good reason to say that one and the same person is happy (in one sense) and not happy (in another sense) does not imply that our thought and language about happiness suffer from any ineluctable incoherence.[4]

But let us now consider how this idea that ordinary discourse involves variable metaethical commitments that are semantically insulated from each other might apply to the debate between cognitivist and noncognitivists. According to the variabilist–insulationist hypothesis, there may be some people who use moral terms in a way that is best analyzed as noncognitivist and other people who use moral terms in a way that is best analyzed as cognitivist. Examples of the first sort might be Beavis and Butthead, who use value terms in ways that seem to be most accurately analyzed as nonfactual, as expressing attitudes rather than propositions. Examples of the second sort might be certain evangelicals, who claim that they use value terms to represent God's will and whose use of value terms turns out to track perfectly factual claims they hold about God's will; or hard-core utilitarians, who claim that they use value terms to represent certain facts about the production of happiness and whose use of moral terms turns out to track perfectly factual claims they hold about the production of happiness. Noncognitivists have developed impressive, sophisticated ways of accounting for the seemingly cognitivist character of the uses to which certain evangelicals and hard-core utilitarians put moral terms. And cognitivists would surely have ways of accommodating or dismissing the thought and language of people like Beavis and Butthead. But why think that either of these uniformist, one-size-fits-all positions captures all the phenomena of the uses of moral terms better than a variabilist–insulationist account? Why think that the moral discourses of priests, rabbis, evangelicals, utilitarians, and Beavis and Butthead all share the same metaethical commitments? The possibility I want to raise is that the phenomena can be better captured—accounted for in a way that is explanatorily more virtuous than either cognitivism or noncognitivism—by the view that Beavis and Butthead really do use moral terms thoroughly noncognitively and that certain evangelicals and utilitarians really do use moral terms thoroughly cognitively. Loeb criticizes cognitivists and noncognitivists for failing to consider the possibility that ordinary moral thought and language contains both cognitivist and noncognitivist features. With this criticism I completely agree. It seems to me, however, that Loeb's moral incoherentism is based on the idea that cognitivist and noncognitivist features are both implicated by all, or at least by most, ordinary uses of moral terms. But I think we should at least take to be a live option the possibility that these features are usually insulated from each other—that our moral discourse rarely implicates both kinds of features simultaneously.

Indeed, as I noted in my discussion of objectivism and relativism, it seems to me plausible that even the uses to which a single person puts moral terms might be variable and insulated in this way. Some of us might spend time in both the noncognitivist camp (in which Beavis and Butthead can be found) and in the cognitivist camp (in which certain evangelicals and utilitarians can be found) but not reside permanently in either. Some person may, for instance, use moral terms in a way that is best analyzed cognitively when she is discussing policy choices in a professional setting (let us say, when, in her capacity as a physician, she is serving on an ethics committee that is trying to decide whether to alter the hospital's do-not-resuscitate [DNR] policies) and yet also use moral terms in a way that is best analyzed noncognitively when she is discussing personal issues in a nonprofessional setting (let us say, when she is talking with a close friend about how a mutual acquaintance of theirs went about ending a romantic relationship). But such a person would not necessarily be guilty of any incoherence or confusion. She could very well be applying moral terms effectively and appropriately in both the professional and personal situations. The metaethical commitments it would be fair to attribute to her in one situation would be different from the metaethical commitments it would be fair to attribute to her in the other situation, but, because the two situations are insulated from each other, she may have no problem using moral terms in completely sensible ways on both occasions. Moreover, there may be no principled reason to hold that her use of moral terms in one of the situations is conceptually more central or aberrant than her use of moral terms in the other situation. Even though there are metaethical differences between them, both kinds of uses may be orderly, sincere, clear—and completely ordinary—cases of moral thought and language.

Some might continue to insist, however, that certain uses of moral terms just must be conceptually superior to other kinds. All the different uses, some might hold, cannot be equally copacetic. In responding to this way of thinking, variabilist–insulationists should start by drawing a distinction between the attempt to analyze ordinary uses of moral terms—which we can call "descriptivist metaethics"—and the attempt to articulate the way of using moral terms that is normatively the best—which we can call "prescriptivist metaethics." The variability thesis, as Loeb points out very clearly, is entirely on the descriptivist side (pp. 356, 364), and I intend the variabilist–insulationist hypothesis to be entirely on that side as well. However, even if this hypothesis turns out to be an accurate account of how people actually use moral terms, there may still be excellent normative reasons to prefer one, uniform way of using moral terms to any other. One can be a variabilist in descriptive metaethics (holding that cognitivist and noncognitivist, and relativist and objectivist, and internalist and externalist commitments are all present in ordinary moral thought and language) and still contend that one set of metaethical commitments is normatively superior to any other set (holding that everyone should always use moral terms only in ways that involve, say, cognitivist, objectivist, and externalist commitments). Indeed, it seems to me rather unlikely that the particular set of metaethical commitments that any of us comes to think are normatively the best will also turn out to be exactly the same ones that characterize all ordinary uses of moral terms.

Some might hold, however, that even within descriptive metaethics there are principled reasons to reject a variabilist account even before delving into the details of lots of particular examples of ordinary usage. One of the reasons that might be offered for this position is that there must be some uniform commitments that characterize all ordinary uses of moral terms because we do in fact classify all these uses as *moral*. When we classify some bit of thought or language as moral, we do not mean to say merely that words like "moral," "right," or "virtuous" have been used. We mean to say, rather, that a certain concept is in play, and that concept must have some more or less determinate shape in order to serve the function it does in fact serve. But morality could not serve this function if it were taken to cover bits of thought and language with as widely disparate features as a variabilist account implies. In response, variabilists should, I think, accept that their account implies that our concept of morality is something of a hodgepodge—more of a miscellany than a system. But the hodgepodge–miscellany picture may very well fit the phenomena better than the uniformist accounts that metaethicists have traditionally offered. The many bits of thought and language we classify as moral may bear only a family resemblance to each other. That we can give nothing more precise than a family resemblance account of morality does not, however, imply that the concept is unusable. Our uses of "game" bear only a family resemblance to each other. But the concept of a game is perfectly usable nonetheless. Perhaps it's not the most orderly concept we possess. Some of our "game" talk may be imprecise, and that imprecision may at times produce confusion and miscommunication. Yet most of the time our "game" talk works quite well. Most of the time, when people use "game," all the participants in the conversation know what is being talked about to an extent clearly sufficient for a coherent, sensible, useful application of the term. Similarly, morality may not be our most orderly concept. Some uses of moral terms may produce confusion and miscommunication. Consider the potential pitfalls of a conversation between an evangelical and an undergraduate cultural relativist, or between Beavis and a rabbi. But such confusion and miscommunication does not occur in all our moral conversations. Often enough, we manage to use moral terms coherently and effectively. And we manage this even though the way we use moral terms in one situation may differ from the way we use them in another situation. Ordinary users of moral terms usually find it relatively easy to pick up on the conversational clues that signal the metaethical parameters of any particular moral discussion. It's only traditional metaethics that, in this regard, may have been a bit clueless.

Let me now briefly discuss the relationship between the variabilist–insulationist view I've sketched and several kinds of metaethical error.

First, there is what we can call "the uniformist error." The possibility of a variabilist–insulationist account implies that it is a mistake to assume that just because a metaethical commitment is implicated by one bit of moral thought and language it is also implicated by every bit of moral thought and language. I attribute this uniformist error to many of the twentieth-century descriptive metaethicists who argued that our moral discourse as a whole is thoroughly absolutist or relativist, externalist or internalist, cognitivist or noncognitivist.

I do not think, however, that the uniformist error infects most of ordinary moral thought and language. When ordinary people think or talk about specific moral matters, they are usually engaged in an activity that does not commit them to views on whether moral discourse as a whole is uniformly absolutist, externalist, cognitivist, or whatever. When a physician in a hospital ethics committee meeting is considering changes to DNR policy, for instance, it may be fair to attribute to her metaethical commitments about how to think and talk about matters of professional ethics in official settings. But that does not mean it is fair to attribute those same metaethical commitments to her when she is talking with a close friend about how a fraught personal issue ought to be dealt with. The metaethical commitments this second, personal conversation involves her in may be specific to matters and settings quite different from the matters and settings of conversations about professional ethics in official committees. Thought and language directed at specific, local moral matters need not—and typically do not—implicate global positions on moral discourse as a whole.

That is not to say that all ordinary users of moral terms consciously reject the uniformity assumption and embrace the variabilist–insulationist hypothesis. I suspect that if asked, some people would say that all moral thought and language does involve certain uniform metaethical commitments, and others would give a more variabilist answer. But however that may be, I don't think there is good reason to attribute to most instances of ordinary moral thought and language a commitment to the uniformist assumption. The analogy to our concept of a game is once again instructive. Most ordinary people have probably given little or no thought to the question of whether all the things we call a "game" share some robust conceptual characteristics or bear only a family resemblance to each other. Probably, if asked, some people would give one answer and other people would give the other. However, now consider those people who say that all the things we call a "game" do share some robust conceptual characteristics (metagame uniformists). Do we have any reason to think that a commitment to the conceptual uniformity of game discourse as a whole has infected all of their particular first-order discussions of football, poker, duck-duck-goose, and so on? I think it's clear we do not. That a person gives a uniformist answer to the metalevel question about the concept of a game does not give us reason to think that her ordinary thought and language about particular games has involved any uniformist commitments. Similarly, that a person gives a uniformist answer to a metalevel question about the concept of morality does not constitute strong evidence that all of her ordinary moral thought and language has involved a commitment to robust metaethical uniformity.

A second kind of metaethical error is what Loeb identifies as "moral incoherentism." According to Loeb's moral incoherentism, ordinary people "use the moral words *both* to make factual assertions *and* to do something incompatible with the making of such assertions" (p. 363). This is Loeb's "attenuated" error theory, according to which internal inconsistency ineluctably afflicts moral discourse (p. 366).

While I agree with Loeb that we can find in ordinary discourse cases in which moral words are used to make factual assertions and cases in which moral words are used to do something incompatible with the making of such assertions, I do not think that there are good grounds for holding that the error of internal inconsistency is as pervasive as his moral incoherentism implies. This is because I think it likely that the cases in which moral terms are used one way are usually semantically insulated from the cases in which moral terms are used the other way. My hypothesis is that within some particular conversations, moral terms are used in a coherently cognitivist (or objectivist or externalist) way; within other conversations, moral terms are used in a coherently noncognitivist (or relativist or internalist) way, and most ordinary people are fairly adept at semantically navigating between and within the two different types of conversations.

At the same time, I also think some people fail at this navigational task, and perhaps most of us fail at least some of the time. At least some of the time, the semantic variability of our moral terms can cause our moral discourse to flounder or founder. I suspect these kinds of problems occur at the interpersonal level more often than at the intrapersonal level. This kind of interpersonal problem arises when one person in a conversation uses moral terms in a way that is semantically different from the way the other person uses them. It might be the case that the first person always uses moral terms in a certain way and the second person always uses them in another, incompatible way, as, for instance, in conversations between diehard relativists and evangelicals, or between Beavis and a rabbi. Or it might be the case that for various reasons the first person, when discussing a particular moral issue, happens to use moral terms in a way that is incompatible with how the second person happens to use moral terms when discussing that issue, even if the two of them may use moral terms consonantly when discussing many other issues. Two people may be able to discuss the ethics of famine relief in a perfectly coherent manner but then encounter formidable semantic obstacles when the conversation turns to gay marriage. In such cases, moral communication can become very difficult, like trying to hold a serious conversation over a bad cell phone connection, or it may break down altogether, reducing the parties to hurling verbal clods at each other. I imagine we can all recall some situations, personal and societal, in which moral conversation seems to have degenerated in this way.

Even if these interpersonal cases are more common, however, I think Loeb is right that profound semantic confusion can also occur intrapersonally. A single person's thought and language might involve metaethical commitments that really do conflict with each other, and this might make it impossible for her to use moral terms coherently. And perhaps most of us have been afflicted by this kind of confusion at one time or another. Perhaps most of us have at one time or another been in a state not merely of moral perplexity (unclear about the right thing to do in a particular situation) but of metamoral perplexity (unclear about what would even constitute being right in a particular situation). I don't think ordinary people end up in this state every time they use moral terms, but it seems reasonable to me to hold that some of us are in this state at least some of the time. In certain situations or in the face of certain issues, the semantic insulation that separates one set of our metaethical commitments from another set may break down.

Now, what I've said in the preceding two paragraphs may make my disagreement with Loeb seem to be slighter than it might have first appeared. I think Loeb is right that some uses of moral terms suffer from incoherence. And perhaps there is no obstacle to his holding, as I do, that some uses of moral terms are coherent. Our disagreement may thus seem to be only about the frequency of these types of cases: I think coherence is more common than he does. And my challenge to Loeb may, then, simply be to give us reasons to think that breakdowns in our uses of moral terms are typical rather than atypical.

It seems to me, however, that a number of Loeb's claims suggest not merely that *some* uses of moral terms are incoherent but that incoherence clings to *every* use of moral terms—that the error of holding incompatible metaethical commitments infects the semantics of moral thought and language as whole (pp. 357–358, 363, 365–366, and 380). And if Loeb holds that incoherence pervades all our moral thought and language, then the difference between us is not simply about the frequency of breakdowns.

For I think that some uses of moral terms are free of incoherence altogether. I think that, even though serious metaethical mistakes of the kind Loeb describes do sometimes occur, there is no insurmountable semantic barrier to our using our moral terms in a completely coherent way.

In addition to thinking that the kind of incoherence on which Loeb focuses afflicts some (but not all) of our moral thought and language, I also believe that some instances of ordinary moral thought and language commit a third kind of error and that this third kind of error is what Mackie's cognitivist error theory describes. Mackie claimed that our moral discourse, while not internally logically inconsistent, commits us to the existence of entities that in fact do not exist—that our moral thought and language presuppose false views of what the world is like. And it seems to me likely that at least some of the time some people do think and talk in ways that make it fair to attribute to them this kind of error. There may, for instance, be people who hold certain theological views about the origin of morality, and these views may permeate their moral thought and language to such an extent that an accurate analysis of their moral thought and language would have to include them. Their theological views may be so entrenched in their moral thought and language that the latter could not be maintained without the former; if they were ever to abandon their theological views, their moral discourse would undergo a drastic change or they would abandon thinking and talking in moral terms altogether (p. 366). But these persons' theological views, which an accurate analysis will have to include as integral to their moral discourse, may be false. And if views inextricably built into persons' moral thought and language are false, then it seems to me just to convict their moral discourse as a whole of the kind of error on which Mackie focused. Or, to take another example, consider self-professed relativists who hold certain views about the causal role culture plays in the development of morals, and whose moral thought and language are so embedded in those views that an accurate analysis of their moral discourse will have to include them. Such people, we can imagine, could not give up their views about the cultural origins of morality and still engage in the kind of moral thinking and talking that they currently do engage in. However, these people's views about the causal role culture plays in the development of morals may be false. And in such a case, once again, it seems to me just to hold that their moral discourse as a whole is erroneous, and erroneous in roughly the way Mackie describes. In some cases, a person's metatheory may so saturate her practice that we will be able to discern simply by observing her practice what metatheory she holds; in some cases, persons' metatheories about morality may infect their first-order moral practices. And if in such cases the metatheory is erroneous, then the first-order practice will be erroneous as well.

I do not think, however, that there are good grounds to hold, as Mackie did, that everyone's first-order moral practice is inextricably linked to an erroneous metatheory. For one thing, some people may hold metatheories that are not erroneous, and their first-order moral practice may reflect their nonerroneous understanding. And for another thing, many people much of the time may use moral terms in ways that do not embody any very specific metatheory at all, erroneous or otherwise.[5] Many people much of the time may use moral terms in ways that do not contain observable evidence of the robust kinds of metaethical commitment that characterize the uses of moral terms of the theologians and relativists I described in the previous paragraph. Indeed, even some people who say they hold to certain metaethical claims (say, that morality is determined by God's will or that morality is nothing but cultural norms) may use moral terms in ways that indicate that they would continue to think and talk about particular moral matters in pretty much the same way even if they were to abandon those metaethical claims, and this gives us good reason to think that their first-order moral practices are not infected by their metaethical views. As Blackburn (1993) has put it, their uses of moral terms may be capable of being "clipped onto" a nonerroneous metaphysic as easily as they can be clipped onto an erroneous one (p. 151). And so it's just to hold, in such cases, that even if the metaethical claims they say they hold are false, their ethical thought and language do not embody error.

Parts of ordinary moral thought and language embody error. But the kinds of error some parts embody differ from the kinds of error other parts embody. And still other parts of ordinary moral thought and language do not embody error at all. A blanket error theory will not capture all the phenomena any more than a blanket nonerror theory will. A successful theory will have to distinguish what is erroneous in our moral discourse from what is not, and between different kinds of error. Such a theory will be richly multifarious, complicated, and messy. But that is just what we should expect of any account that is true to what human beings actually think, say, and do.

Notes

1. See Loeb, p. 358. I discuss the variability thesis in more detail in my "Meta-ethical Variability and our Miscellaneous Moral Discourse" (forthcoming).

2. For a full treatment of this empirical approach to metaethics, see Nichols (2004b).

3. Throughout my discussion, I follow Loeb in taking the metaethical issues to involve the semantics of moral terms. It's not clear to me, however, that these issues really are about semantics rather than pragmatics. I am not sure, that is, whether all the metaethical commitments Loeb and I discuss are part of the semantics of moral terms or some of the commitments are merely pragmatically implicated by moral terms. Thus, while I say throughout my discussion that the metaethical commitments in one situation can be *semantically* insulated from the metaethical commitments in another situation, it could be the case that what I should be saying is that the metaethical commitments in one situation can be *pragmatically* insulated from the metaethical commitments in another situation.

4. However, the following objection might be raised to my attempt to analogize our moral terms to "happiness." If I say that a person is happy, and mean by it that she is experiencing a pleasurable occurrent emotion, and you say that the same person is not happy, and mean by it that her life as a whole is not going well, we will probably be able to quickly disambiguate our uses of the term "happy" and thus dissolve any disagreement there might have seemed to be between us. But if I say that some action is wrong and you say that the same action is not wrong, then even if we are using the term "wrong" in different ways (say, I am using it objectively and you are using it relativistically), it seems likely that there will still be some kind of conflict between us that will not be as easily dissolvable as was the apparent disagreement between us about whether a person is happy. I cannot address this objection fully here, but I would respond to it, first of all, by claiming that a lot of apparent moral disagreements *can* be dissolved by disambiguating between the different senses in which moral terms are being used and, secondly, by claiming that people using moral terms in metaethically different ways can nonetheless disagree (or at least come into conflict) with each other about some first-order moral issues (see Loeb, p. 364).

5. The possibility I raise but do not develop here is that moral terms are often used in ways that are indeterminate with regard to the questions separating cognitivists and noncognitivists, internalists and externalists, objectivists and relativists. There may be nothing in some uses of moral terms that gives us any principled reason for taking them to implicate one kind of metaethical commitment rather than the other. I discuss this possibility—which I call the indeterminacy thesis—in some detail in "Meta-ethical Variability and our Miscellaneous Moral Discourse."

| **Moral Semantics and Empirical Inquiry**

Geoffrey Sayre-McCord

People working in metaethics regularly take a stand as to what we are doing in claiming that some action is wrong, another right, that some characters are virtuous, others vicious, and that some institutional structures are just, others not.

Cognitivists argue that in making such claims we are expressing beliefs that have a moral content and that might be true or false. And then they go on to advance one or another account of what that content is, and so the conditions under which the beliefs expressed might be true. Thus, for instance, some argue that in claiming that an action is morally right we are saying that no alternative act has better consequences, others argue that we are saying that the action conforms with norms currently in force, while still others hold that we are saying the action has some *sui generis* property that is objectively prescriptive.

Alternatively, noncognitivists argue that in making such claims we are not expressing beliefs but are instead expressing a noncognitive state of some sort. And then they go on to advance one or another account of what that distinctive state is, and the conditions under which someone might count as holding a moral view about some matter. Thus, for instance, some argue that in claiming an action is morally right we are voicing our approval of its being done, others argue that we are advancing a universal prescription that it be done, while still others hold that we are expressing our acceptance of a system of norms that require the action.

Curiously, when one or another of these views is embraced, very little time and attention is given to gathering empirical evidence concerning what people are actually doing when they use moral terms. Even as metaethicists do regularly focus on the semantics of moral language, they do so (as Don Loeb notes) without systematically studying "what it is ordinary people are using the moral vocabulary to do" (p. 371). In fact, metaethicists often treat such evidence as largely irrelevant. Don Loeb thinks that they are making a serious mistake.

Loeb's own guess is that once we study people's actual "linguistic dispositions" we will discover that no theory that offers a coherent semantic account of moral language will capture peoples' actual use of terms like "right," "wrong," "moral," and "immoral." We surely cannot simply assume otherwise. For all we know, these words might well genuinely mean different things in different peoples' mouths and mean nothing at all in the mouths of others. In particular, Loeb suspects that a cognitivist semantics will account for some people's use of moral terms and not others, and he suggests that a correct semantic theory will have to recognize that at least some people use moral terms in a way that commits them simultaneously to thinking that there are objective moral facts and that there are no such facts.

It is worth noting too, though this is a different point, that there is no doubt that people would, if pressed, give different, often incompatible, accounts of what makes something right or wrong, moral or immoral. Deep disagreements about the nature of morality are commonplace. The sharp divide between consequentialists and deontologists is enough to establish the point.

Moreover, as Kant noted, if we consult honestly what people think and say, what we will find "in an amazing mixture, is at one time the particular constitution of human nature (but along with this also the idea of a rational nature in general), at another time perfection, at another happiness; here moral feeling, and there the fear of God; something of this, and also something of that" (1785/1993, p. 21). Such confusion is as likely to be found intrapersonally as interpersonally.

All told, however harmonious moral discussion might appear to be, a clear-eyed appraisal of moral discourse—one that takes proper account of what ordinary people are actually doing when they use moral terms—is likely to reveal serious semantic and cognitive cacophony.

Against the background of this possibility, Loeb defends two claims: (i) that the acceptability of one or another of the standard metaethical views turns crucially on the results of empirical investigation of what ordinary people are thinking and saying and (ii) that due attention to what the evidence *might* show reveals an important, yet overlooked, metaethical position: moral incoherentism. As he sees it, the cognitive and semantic cacophony he suspects we would discover, were we to pay proper attention to empirical evidence, would undermine metaethical cognitivism and noncognitivism alike, since no version of either could legitimately claim to capture what we all are doing in using moral language, and it would also recommend seeing moral thought and talk as genuinely incoherent.

The right view would then be, he thinks, that in using moral language we are not actually talking about anything, with the result that this semantic discovery would be grounds for accepting antirealism when it comes to moral metaphysics.

In what follows, I will focus on the first of these two claims.[1] I am unsure whether, in what I argue, I will be disagreeing with Loeb or just working to moderate the impression his arguments might give. Either way, I have no doubt that the issues Loeb has raised are of central importance, and figuring out where one should stand with respect to them is crucial to having a well-worked-out position in metaethics.

What Ordinary People Think and Say

According to Loeb, an "account of moral semantics is meant to represent what is being thought and said in *ordinary* circumstances by ordinary thinkers and speakers" (p. 356). No doubt, he acknowledges, developing such a semantics will "involve some degree of idealization" (p. 356) since ordinary people can be confused in various ways. However, he points out that there is a crucial difference between mere idealization and actually changing the subject. To offer a semantics that leaves behind pretty much entirely what ordinary people think and say is, he thinks, to change the subject. As long as we are considering cognitivism and noncognitivism as accounts of what we are talking about (if anything) in using moral language, we are, Loeb insists, committed to defending the accounts as capturing what "ordinary thinkers and speakers" are thinking and saying. For that reason, he maintains, these metaethical positions are answerable to the results of "careful and philosophically informed intrapersonal, interpersonal, and cross-cultural anthropological and psychological inquiry" (p. 356) into the linguistic behavior of ordinary people.

For reasons I will turn to shortly, I think Loeb's focus on "ordinary thinkers and speakers" is misguided. Before highlighting what I take to be the problem, though, let me register that Loeb is rightly careful to resist the idea that the empirical research would properly be primarily a matter of questionnaires or surveys seeking the ordinary person's views about metaethics or moral theory. Instead, he has in mind studies that would work to tease out "the intuitions, patterns of thinking and speaking, semantic commitments, and other internal states (conscious or not)" (p. 356) of ordinary speakers. These are what would underwrite adopting one or another semantic theory to interpret what they say.

To bring out what strikes me as wrong about focusing on "ordinary thinkers and speakers," let me briefly develop an analogy. Suppose you were wondering whether God exists. You would no doubt consider the familiar arguments that appeal, for instance, to the need for a first cause, to apparent design, and to Pascal's famous suggestion that betting on God makes sense. Suppose that, in light of equally familiar replies, you remain agnostic. Now imagine that someone comes along and offers the following less familiar argument: "You believe in love, don't you? Can you explain love? Do you have a full theory of love? Of course not. Love is a mystery. Right? Well, if you grant me that, you must grant as well that God exists, for God *is* love and mystery."

What should you make of that argument? First off, while you would likely admit that there is love and mystery, you might well resist the claim that believing in love and mystery is the same as believing in God. After all, the existence of love and mystery is compatible with there being no Creator and no Supreme Being, and with there being nothing even close to an omnipotent, omniscient, and all good Being of the sort that seems to figure prominently in many religions. If, in wondering whether God exists, you were wondering whether there was such a Being, registering the existence of love and mystery will not address your problem.

When someone claims that God exists, you might point out, they don't mean that love and mystery exist; and when you wonder whether God exists, you are not wondering whether there is love and mystery. In fact, as a claim about what people have meant in saying that they do, or don't, believe in God, the suggestion that they were talking (merely) of love and mystery is not very plausible, to say the least. Thus, you might reasonably reply to the argument saying that it depends on changing the subject.

Suppose, though, that your interlocutor counters your skepticism by mobilizing carefully collected empirical evidence that nowadays what *ordinary* people mean when they say that "God exists" really is that "there is love and mystery." What would be the appropriate response? Well, if the evidence really is compelling, it would mean that you should find a new way to express your doubts, at least when you are talking with such people. Yet you would not then have also found any grounds for believing in what you had originally doubted. You would need to express the doubts differently, but they would not have been allayed at all,[2] nor would the evidence have shown that your doubts were incoherent or confused.

Empirical evidence about what ordinary people nowadays mean when they make various claims *is* relevant to how we should express our views (and, of course, it is relevant to how we should understand their claims).

However, if the concerns and questions we have were intelligible in the first place, discovering that the terms one was disposed to use to express those concerns and questions are not suitable does nothing to address, nor to discredit, the concerns and questions themselves.

What if Most People Meant . . .

So imagine, as Loeb thinks might happen, that empirical evidence shows that, nowadays, what ordinary people mean in saying that something is moral is simply that it accords with social norms that are being enforced; or suppose the evidence shows that different people mean different things; or (most likely) that while some mean one thing, and others something else, still others use the terms with no specific meaning at all. This evidence would certainly be relevant to deciding how to express your own concerns and questions about the nature of morality. Nonetheless, if those concerns and questions were intelligible in the first place, discovering that the terms one was disposed to use to express them are not suitable does nothing address the concerns and questions. Nor does it, taken alone, give any reason to doubt the intelligibility of those concerns and questions. Perhaps most significantly for our purposes, the evidence would have no particular implications when it comes to determining whether cognitivism or noncognitivism captures what you are thinking and talking about in raising your concerns and questions.

Of course, we need to be careful here. Whether one is wondering about the existence of God or the nature of morality, one normally takes oneself to be addressing issues of common concern. The more idiosyncratic your concerns and questions, the less likely they are to have the significance you supposed. Moreover, the more one is convinced that, in talking of God, people have been talking merely of love and mystery, or that, in talking of right and wrong, they have been talking merely about social norms or expressing their tastes, the more reason one will have to think that the concerns that come with thinking something more is at issue may themselves be confused. Thus, in considering empirical evidence about what others are doing in making claims about God or morality, one is presented with evidence about what one might, oneself, intelligibly be taken to be claiming. Our own capacities to think and speak about various things do not develop in isolation.

Still, it is no news to metaethicists that their semantic theories won't capture all the ways in which ordinary people might actually be using moral language. After all, people regularly misuse language, and even when misuse is not at issue, there is no reason to suppose that different people won't use the same terms with significantly different meanings. None of the metaethical positions that Loeb is challenging are committed otherwise. What metaethicists are commonly claiming, however, is that their preferred account captures the important core of what *we* are doing in thinking and talking about what *we* characterize as morality. Of course, who the "we" are is regularly left unspecified. The "we" is not so capacious as to include all who use the terms "right," "wrong," "moral," and "immoral," yet it is supposed to include those who speak languages other than English (in cases where they have terms that are properly translated by *our* terms "right," "wrong," "moral," "immoral," etc.), and it is meant as well to identify a group of people who can properly be seen as all thinking and talking about (as we would put it) what is right and wrong, moral or immoral.

This means that the various versions of cognitivism and noncognitivism face two constraints: To be plausible (i) they need to be bringing within their sweep all whom we would recognize as thinking and talking about what is right or wrong, moral or immoral, in whatever terms, and in whatever language, they happen to be using, and (ii) they need to be capturing accurately the semantic commitments of *these* people (when they are thinking and talking about morality). The two constraints are not, in practice, independent. The fact that someone differs apparently in their semantic commitments will be grounds for treating them as thinking and talking about something different, and the fact that we see them as sharing our semantic commitments will be grounds for seeing them as thinking and talking about what we are thinking and talking about.[3] Still, each of the constraints works to limit the class of people for whom the moral semantics is being offered. And together they may well rule out a number of people whom we recognize as using moral terms in other ways.

Us and Them

Emphasizing a distinction between what ordinary people might be saying and doing and what *we* are saying and doing carries three risks.

First, it might suggest that metaethicists are giving competing accounts of something esoteric. But this would be a mistake. While neither cognitivists nor noncognitivists are trying to account for all the ways in which people might well be using moral words, they do usually assume that the use they hope to capture is fairly widespread and important to many people. Consider here the questions you might raise about God's existence.

In wondering whether there is a God—that is (as you think of it), a Supreme Being who is omnipotent, omniscient, and all good—you would understandably see yourself as wondering about something that figures prominently in the thought and talk of others. To think and talk about whether there is a God, in this sense, is not (it seems) to be engaging in anything especially esoteric. At the same time, though, your own account of what you are thinking and talking about is not answerable, in any serious way, to the discovery (should it be made) that a lot of people mean something utterly different when they speak of God.

Second, it might suggest that cognitivism and noncognitivism are immune from refutation, since (one worries) defenders of each can simply reject as not among the relevant "we" anyone whose use of moral terms does not conform to the theory in question. But this would be a mistake as well. While cognitivists and noncognitivists are (if I am right) trying to capture only how *we* are thinking and talking about morality, they share a fairly robust sense of the phenomenon in question, with both sides recognizing that an acceptable metaethical view needs to do justice to that phenomenon. Although they disagree with each other, as well as among themselves, as to which account best captures what is going on when we are thinking and talking about morality, there is remarkable agreement about what needs to be explained or explained away. Thus, while these views would not be seriously challenged by the discovery that ordinary people use terms such as "right" and "wrong," "moral" and "immoral" in variety of incompatible ways, the theories do stand or fall with their ability to capture accurately "the intuitions, patterns of thinking and speaking, semantic commitments, and other internal states (conscious or not)" (p. 356) not of all ordinary speakers but of those whom cognitivists and noncognitivists alike recognize as engaged in the sort of thought and talk at issue.

Third, and finally, there is a risk that stressing that the metaethical accounts are trying to capture what *we* are thinking and saying may misleadingly suggest that in taking up a metaethical position, one must oneself be a participant in moral thought and talk and see oneself as among those whose participation is being explained. There has got to be room to distance oneself from the practice one hopes to explain, as an atheist might, for instance, hope to explain what other people are thinking and saying in speaking of God even as she herself does not engage in such talk. I suspect there is no way to understand appropriately what needs to be explained without being able oneself to think and talk in the ways in question, but one may have that ability without being disposed to put it to use.

Genuine Instances of Moral Thought and Talk

In any case, and especially in light of these risks, it might be better to characterize the relevant contrast differently: Loeb supposes that cognitivists and noncognitivists are offering accounts of how ordinary people happen to use certain words, where the target population—ordinary people—is set without relying on *ex ante* substantive criteria for who counts as engaging in moral thought and talk. In contrast, I am suggesting, metaethicists commonly and rightly discriminate among the various ways people might use the terms in question, counting only some as genuine instances of moral thought and talk. Cognitivists and noncognitivists should be seen as offering accounts of what those who are genuinely engaging in moral thought and talk are doing. Such accounts are answerable to what such people are in fact doing, but discovering what *they* are doing is not the same as discovering how *ordinary people* happen to use certain terms.

The substantive criteria that are relied on in identifying genuine instances of moral thought and talk are themselves open to dispute, of course. Moreover, at the margins different metaethical positions will guard their flanks by identifying certain uses as relying on inverted commas or on disingenuousness and rejecting those as not having to be accounted for within the theory. Still, the central cases of competent engagement in moral thought and talk are widely acknowledged and work well to fix in our sights what needs to be explained.

Conclusion

Whether Loeb would disagree with what I have claimed is a bit unclear to me. It may well be that the "ordinary people" he had in mind are just the people I am singling out as those who are engaging in genuine instances of moral thought and talk. If so, though, it is worth noting that focusing on this group is fully compatible with thinking that the evidence Loeb imagines would establish moral incoherentism works instead to establish that fewer people than we assumed are actually engaging in moral thought and talk.

At the same time, though, it is important to recognize that, even supposing I am right about the aims of metaethics, the evidence might well end up supporting some version of what Loeb calls "moral incoherentism."

Notes

Thanks are due to Walter Sinnott-Armstrong and Joshua Knobe for helpful comments and discussion of the argument in this paper.

1. When it comes to the second of Loeb's claims, my sense is that the positions he counts as instances of incoherentism fall into two (apparently incompatible) kinds: (1) those that see moral terms as expressing a concept, albeit an incoherent concept (on analogy with the concept of a "round square") that could never be satisfied and (2) those that see the incoherence of linguistic practice as showing that moral terms fail to express concepts altogether. Views of the first kind are, in effect, error theories, while views of the second kind are versions of noncognitivism. However, the possibilities Loeb identifies differ in interesting ways from more familiar error theories and noncognitivist positions. Unlike familiar error theories, incoherentist error theories find the error not in the metaphysics the concepts require, but in the concepts themselves; and unlike most versions of noncognitivism, incoherentist noncognitivism seems to reject the idea that there is any interestingly systematic (albeit noncognitive) role played by moral terms. These differences raise a number of interesting issues that, unfortunately, I do not have space to explore here.

2. And the situation would be materially the same if the evidence showed instead that different people meant different things by "God" and that some (perhaps many) really meant nothing in particular. Such evidence leaves the original questions and puzzles untouched and unanswered.

3. Putting things this way is a little misleading, since noncognitivists standardly recognize the constraints I am identifying even though it is a stretch to say that, on their view, people who are engaged in moral thought and talk are, in any interesting sense, talking about anything. Thus, perhaps the better way to describe the first constraint would be: They need to be bringing within their sweep all who we would recognize as genuinely engaging in moral thought and talk concerning what is right or wrong, moral or immoral, in whatever terms, and in whatever language, they happen to be using. Even noncognitivists, though, are concerned to make sense of how it is people so engaged seem to be talking *about* something (even if, on their view, the appearances are, in a sense, misleading).

7.3 | Reply to Gill and Sayre-McCord

Don Loeb

I am grateful to Michael Gill and Geoffrey Sayre-McCord for their thoughtful and provocative comments. I'm also gratified that we don't appear to disagree about much, at least not if we all remain as tentative and open to a variety of possibilities as we seem to be. In what follows, I'll try to explain where I think the central points of agreement and disagreement are located. Where there's disagreement, I'll explain why I am not ready to concede.

Before turning to the individual comments, however, I want to set aside a possible confusion that sometimes seems to be suggested by both, but which I do not believe either commentator actually intends to rely on. Nothing I have said in support of the moral incoherentist hypothesis requires that a proper analysis of a given vocabulary cover *every* instance of people using that vocabulary. Yet at times both Gill and Sayre-McCord appear to be hinting that this *is* (or should be) the basis for my claims: "[As Loeb sees it, neither cognitivism nor noncognitivism] could legitimately claim to capture what we *all* are doing in using moral language . . ." (Sayre-McCord, p. 404; emphasis added), and, "If the different aspects are implicated by *each and every* use of the moral terms, then Loeb's diagnosis of incoherence will be apt" (Gill, p. 389; emphasis added).

As I said in my paper, "No account can expect to capture everyone's linguistic dispositions for all cases. . . ." (p. 356) Any proper account will be to some degree an idealization. What is important, however, is that "although idealization is a matter of degree, there is a crucial difference between an appropriate idealization and a reform. The former seeks to find the analysis that best explains our linguistic behavior, despite the idiosyncrasies of our actual speech and thought. The latter merely changes the subject" (p. 357). Thus, while I agree that no analysis can capture all talk that employs the moral vocabulary, I do think that paring off a great deal of it for the sake of a clean analysis can distort what people using that vocabulary are actually doing.

Gill

Michael Gill agrees with me that moral semantics (or perhaps, as he suggests, pragmatics) is both of central importance to metaethical inquiry and consists of questions whose resolution, if possible at all, will require philosophically informed empirical investigation. Still, he seems very sympathetic to the hypothesis that neither cognitivism nor noncognitivism contains the whole truth about our semantic (let's assume) commitments, and that, more generally, a variety of related but incompatible and yet ineliminable elements may well be present both across and even within individuals and cultures. He calls this hypothesis "the variability thesis."

I hope my paper made clear that my suspicions about these conflicts are not confined to the debate between cognitivists and noncognitivists. Gill and I agree that it is reasonable to take seriously the suspicion that our linguistic (to use a less precise term) differences extend over a broad range of issues—from matters of moral substance (Does "right" refer to what utilitarians have in mind, or what Kantians, virtue theorists, or feminist ethicists point to?) to more metaethical questions (Does "goodness" refer to the property of being approved by God, to something relative to cultures or individuals, or to some other natural or nonnatural property? Do terms in the moral vocabulary contain implicit internalist commitments, or are they compatible with completely externalist uses?).[1] And Gill agrees with me that moral incoherentism is a real possibility and that it represents a novel form of moral irrealism, one qualifying as neither noncognitivism nor the error theory. In these respects, then, we seem not to be far apart at all.

Is there something about which we disagree? Well, yes and no. Gill suggests that I have overlooked an important possibility, one that is compatible with the variability thesis but does not support moral incoherentism:

> I do not think, however, that the variability thesis leads as directly to the conclusion that moral thought and language are as pervasively incoherent as Loeb suggests. . . . If the different aspects are implicated by each and every use of moral terms, then Loeb's diagnosis of incoherence will be apt. However, if one of the aspects is implicated within one pocket of moral thought and language and the other aspect is implicated within a different pocket of moral thought and language, then Loeb's moral incoherentism might be a misdiagnosis. (pp. 389–390)

We do not disagree that this is a possibility. In fact I acknowledge something similar when I say:

> Perhaps there are simply two different senses of the word "morality," one of which, M_1, presupposes a realm of moral fact and the other of which, M_2, presupposes that

there is no such realm. On this view we might expect to find that some of us are always using M_1, others are always using M_2, others are using M_1 sometimes and M_2 other times, some have linguistic dispositions that suggest that they are somehow trying to use both at once, and sometimes it is indeterminate which vocabulary a person is using. (p. 365)

What is different about Gill's proposal is that he imagines the disparate uses of the terms in the moral vocabulary to be (largely, at least) "semantically insulated" from one another, so that it is not true, as I suggested, that "much of our moral talk is at cross-purposes" (p. 365). Although I did not originally have this situation in mind, I should not deny that it is a possibility. And if it is indeed the case that our moral thought and language is (usually or often) packaged into neat "pockets," as this picture suggests, then "moral incoherentism" may be a misleading way to characterize it. Within these pockets, there would be no incoherence, and cross-pocket incoherence might not trouble us in the way that unbounded cacophony (to use Sayre McCord's nicely chosen term) would.

But *should* it trouble us after all? Recall that talking past one another was only one of my concerns regarding this sort of situation. Would it still be true, as I suggested, "that the moral words do not have unqualified meanings," and that "[q]uestions like whether moral properties are real or whether a certain action is morally permissible would be ambiguous at best" (p. 365)? The answer depends on whether or not the words are used and the questions are asked from standpoints that presuppose a fairly well-defined context. If we all understand that someone (or some group) is using moral terms noncognitively when discussing personal matters but cognitively when discussing professional ones, then, at least within those contexts and for those people, the words would be unambiguous. Still, there would be no standpoint-neutral position from which to ask questions and make claims employing the moral vocabulary, because there would really be a variety of very different kinds of questions and claims, even if they are mostly held together by the sort of Wittgensteinian family resemblance Gill suggests.

I concede, then, that something like what Gill describes (though presumably much more complex) is a possibility. And, since we both acknowledge that questions about moral (or any other) semantics are largely empirical, I don't wish to make too strong a claim about how likely it is that this is in fact the case. Perhaps what we have is merely a disagreement in conjectures about how that investigation would turn out. Still, I can't help suspecting that things aren't very likely to be as neat as Gill sometimes seems to suggest. The fact that some terms, like "happiness," have a variety of related but different and incompatible context-bound senses opens up the *possibility* that moral terms do as well. However, much more would be needed in order to make that plausible.

For example, the scenario involving a doctor who uses moral words cognitivistically when serving on an ethics committee but noncognitivistically when speaking about personal matters is described in so little detail as to make it hard to see what is going on. Does she really presuppose (even if only unconsciously) that when it comes to personal issues, moral rightness is never a matter of fact, but that when it comes to the issues taken up by the ethics committee, they always are? It would be surprising, to say the least, for her to overlook the immense overlap among the sorts of issues that come up in these two contexts, where the lines between personal and public are blurry at best.

Furthermore, it does not seem implausible that people typically presuppose (though again, perhaps, not in any conscious way) that the moral words are used to talk about the very *same* things in all or at least many of the contexts in which we use them. On the face of it, I see no reason to assume that when a person says that it was wrong for your husband to dump you without warning just because you cut your hair, she means something different by "wrong" than when she says that it was wrong for that doctor to fail adequately to warn his patient of the risks of the operation. What's wrong in both of these cases, I suspect most people would think, is in some respects the same thing.

Suppose, for example, that I have trouble telling which of the various semantically insulated pockets I am in at any given time. When asked whether John is happy, I answer that if you mean to ask about how he is feeling at the moment, he certainly seems to be happy, but if you mean to ask whether he is a happy person in general, the answer, sadly, seems to be that he is not. Although few people would be this self-conscious and most of us can tell from various conversational (and other) cues what is being asked in a case like this, my answer does not strike me as *otherwise* odd. However, suppose instead that you ask me whether it is morally wrong to hit one's children. Perhaps I would say that although I myself can't stomach it, I don't believe that it is really wrong. But I think it would be *extremely* odd for me to reply, "If you are using 'wrong' in a way that presupposes moral objectivity, the answer is no, but if you are using it in a way that seeks only an expression of my attitudes, then, 'Boo to hitting one's children.'" Similarly, it would be bizarre for me to ask whether you have in mind wrongness according to utilitarianism, Kantianism, or some version of virtue or feminist ethics; or whether it is wrong on the assumption that something is wrong if and only if it violates the will of God, or on the assumption that right and wrong are relative to a given culture. These all appear to be answers to the *same* question, and not to a variety of *different* questions (typically recognized, however, by their contexts). In this way, the claim that there are semantically insulated pockets of coherent discourse seems to face a serious obstacle.[2]

However, even if the claims about semantically insulated pockets of moral talk and thought *were* correct, that would not be a happy result for moral objectivists or realists. For they believe that there is some core group of people who are using the moral vocabulary to think and talk about, as Sayre-McCord says, "what is right and wrong, moral or immoral," in some fairly uniform sense (p. 408). And, as I suggested in my paper, the more the various senses of the moral terms are multiplied, the less claim any one of them has to grounding *the* correct analysis of some *core* use of the moral vocabulary.

In saying this, I don't think I am committing myself to what Gill calls the "uniformist error," the "mistake [of assuming] that just because a metaethical commitment is implicated by one bit of moral thought and language it is also implicated by every bit of moral thought and language" (pp. 395–396). However, moral realists and objectivists (and if I am right, ordinary people, at least implicitly) do seem to presuppose that there is a common subject matter that all who use the moral vocabulary—or at least all those using it to talk about morality (and its constituents)—are talking about. If that assumption is undermined, then so are realism and objectivism about morality. Facts about "type-12 wrongness" are, according to these views, a poor substitute for facts about wrongness (etc.) simpliciter.

Sayre-McCord

This, of course, brings me to Geoffrey Sayre-McCord's challenge, which holds that even if there is substantial semantic disarray, there is some group, "we," who are all talking about the same thing—a thing appropriately characterized as morality (and similarly for the various moral properties such as rightness and virtue). He argues that I am mistaken in focusing on the semantic commitments of "ordinary people" and should instead focus on the commitments of "those who are genuinely engaging in moral thought and talk . . ." (p. 410).

In the paper I use "we" and "ordinary people" pretty much interchangeably. And I don't think Sayre-McCord intends for the difference between these groups to be apparent merely from what they are called—

as if *we* are the experts on how to use moral language, and ordinary people are, well, you know, . . . *ordinary*, and thus more liable than us to *misuse* the moral vocabulary. If someone uses "moral rightness" to refer to a certain color, for example, I think Sayre-McCord and I would both agree that he is *not* at all ordinary and that metaethics needn't be at all concerned with his semantic dispositions.

Rather, Sayre-McCord is clear that by "we" he means those people who are using the moral vocabulary *correctly*, "those whom cognitivists and noncognitivists alike recognize as engaged in the sort of thought and talk at issue" (p. 409)—genuine *moral* thought and talk:

> Of course, who the "we" are is regularly left unspecified. The "we" is not so capacious as to include all who use the terms "right," "wrong," "moral," and "immoral," yet it is supposed to include those who speak languages other than English (in cases where they have terms that are properly translated by *our* terms "right," "wrong," "moral," "immoral," etc.), and it is meant as well to identify a group of people who can properly be seen as all thinking and talking about (as we would put it) what is right and wrong, moral or immoral. (p. 408)

If there indeed *is* such a group, I'd agree with Sayre-McCord that these are the people whose semantic dispositions metaethics should be looking at. And again, I think this to be largely an empirical question, so I don't want to rule out the possibility that there is enough of a coherent core usage to support the claim that there is such a group. But I do think there is reason to worry that this may not be the case, and Sayre-McCord has to (and I think does) acknowledge this possibility as well.

Suppose that the variability with which Gill and I are concerned is in fact present. As I argued in my paper, some (but nowhere near all) of the basis for my suspicion that this is so comes from the evidence surrounding the debate between cognitivism and noncognitivism. To the extent that these are inconsistent and each has its appeal in large part because of its ability to track a central commitment (to or against moral objectivity) of some very substantial (though in some cases, perhaps, overlapping) subset of the users of the moral vocabulary, then we have a potential for incoherence. We could just *say* that one side isn't using that vocabulary "properly" to talk about morality, but what *nonarbitrary* way of deciding could we appeal to?

Sayre-McCord does not want to treat his thesis that there is a common and uniform subject matter as unfalsifiable or true by fiat, or only to count people as using the moral vocabulary to talk about morality if they use it in a particular way, no matter what others are doing. But then what does "those who are genuinely engaging in moral thought and talk" (p. 410) mean? That locution itself uses the phrase "moral thought and talk," and part of what is at issue here is whether there is some uniform referent of that phrase.

In this connection, Sayre-McCord's God analogy seems misleading. I do not wish to deny that one can ask whether an all-powerful, benevolent creator of the universe exists, no matter what people now use (or ever used) the word "God" to signify. However, the force of this example lies in the fact that questions about God in our *actual* language do in fact have a clear and coherent meaning. As things stand, "God" does *not* mean love and mystery, and as far as I know it never has. Thus, the coherent question is in reality the very question we *do* ask when we ask the question about God in today's sense. The example trades on the fact that people using "God" to mean love and mystery *would* in fact be misusing the term—or at a minimum changing the subject.

Suppose, as Sayre-McCord asks us to, that our current talk about God really *did* turn out to be best understood as talk about love and mystery. As he acknowledges, that would at least give us reason to rephrase our question about the creator of the universe. We would be asking about God (in today's sense) only if we were asking about whatever it is people now use the word "God" to signify. And if "God" had all along meant love and mystery, then we couldn't even ask about a creator by asking whether God (in the *original* sense) exists. Although there would indeed be other clear, coherent questions to ask, it wouldn't in any sense be proper for us to treat them as questions about God.

Still, Sayre-McCord points out, none of this would give us reason to think that the original questions were incoherent or confused. I agree. Likewise the moral incoherentist should not deny that there are clear and consistent questions we can ask about what would maximize utility, what sorts of norms are taken as central to governing the relationships among people in this or that society, and any number of other matters. What the moral incoherentist *does* deny is that there are clear and coherent questions we can ask in the *moral* vocabulary. There are questions about moral rightness (e.g.) only if there is something that users of that phrase are, in general, committed to talking about.

Sayre-McCord's talk about the cogency of our "original questions" (p. 411) suggests that there has been or might have been a shift from some clear, coherent original usage to some confused or incoherent current usage, as he seems to have in mind for the God example. However, if moral language is indeed confused or incoherent now, then it may well have been confused or incoherent all along. Sayre-McCord needs to tell us why he thinks there was an original, coherent, clear usage of the moral words, what it was, and why we should think questions phrased in those terms to be of interest to people asking different questions in the newer senses of the words.

Alternatively, if Sayre-McCord does not think that there has been such a change, then what is he saying? Is he saying that if moral language is severely confused there are nevertheless clear, coherent questions that some of us might want to use the moral vocabulary to ask (even though they are not questions about morality, since that is whatever people using the moral vocabulary are talking about)? I don't want to deny this possibility. However, if the incoherentist is right, then the clear, coherent questions would be the ones that involve misuse of terminology or changing the subject.

As I said, Sayre-McCord does not want his claim to be unfalsifiable, and he does admit that moral incoherentism is a real possibility. However, he also thinks that both cognitivists and noncognitivists "share a fairly robust sense of the phenomenon in question" and recognize "that an acceptable metaethical view needs to do justice to that phenomenon" (p. 409). Metaethicists are interested in the thought and talk of those whom both sides "recognize as engaged in the sort of talk at issue" (p. 409). I am not convinced that there really is as much agreement as Sayre-McCord assumes over whose thought and talk needs explaining. But even if we have a clear fix on that, Sayre-McCord has not shown that the (provisional) evidence I have put forward of diverse and conflicting semantic commitments involves people *outside* of this group. Instead, the evidence concerned people who at least appear to be "genuinely engaging in moral thought and talk" (p. 410), even though their use of the moral vocabulary suggests commitments both to and against objectivity, to and against an identity between morality and the will of God, and to and against utilitarianism, Kantianism, and many other matters.

Sayre-McCord's focus on *we* who are using the moral vocabulary genuinely to talk about morality assumes something that has not been established, that even if there is the sort of semantic cacophony the incoherentist hypothesizes, there is still some nonarbitrary classification according to which *certain* people's use of the moral vocabulary constitutes genuine moral talk. If he is not to rule out some people by mere fiat, then he must show not simply that they are ordinary people but that some of their commitments are not very deep after all and that they would be disposed to resolve conflicts among those commitments rather than to give up on using the vocabulary to talk about a common subject matter.

Alternatively, he could try to show that, despite appearances, "fewer people than we assumed are actually engaging in moral thought and talk" (p. 410). However, the more we decide that our original assumptions about who is actually engaging in moral talk were wrong, the more doubt is cast on the claim that there *was* a robust and recognizable phenomenon to be explained in the first place, and the more suspicious we should be that any account of the "we" in question *is* arbitrary. If I am right, we are not in a position now to say whether there is a nonarbitrary "we," but there is at least some serious reason for doubting it as things stand.

All of this having been said, however, I remain convinced that the disagreements between me and both Gill and Sayre-McCord are relatively minor. And although such disagreements, small as they are, do persist, I thank them both for forcing me to think more carefully about these important issues.

Notes

1. Perhaps in many cases these are not questions about language at all. Sometimes, for example, we want to know whether goodness *itself* is the property of being approved of by God. Still, people's linguistic dispositions alone may often commit them to answers to these questions. For some people, I suspect, an opinion about goodness just *is* an opinion about what God approves of, for example.

2. If I am right that people typically presuppose a *common* context for moral discourse, that presupposition is some evidence for a disposition to resolve our semantic differences in a way that leads ultimately to coherence. However, as I've suggested, there may well be deeply entrenched dispositions that push in the other direction, too.

8 | Attributions of Causation and Moral Responsibility

Julia Driver

The notion of causation is important to moral responsibility since most people think that someone is morally responsible for an event only when that person has caused the event. This is referred to as the entailment claim—that moral responsibility *entails* causal responsibility (MC). Note that it does not work the other way around: Causal responsibility is (generally) *not* taken to entail moral responsibility. We can formulate (MC) as follows:

(MC)   If an agent A is morally responsible for event *e*, then A performed an action or an omission that caused *e*.[1]

(MC) is a thesis that seems extremely intuitively plausible. A commitment to (MC) not only has the obvious implications for accounts of moral responsibility and blame/praise, it also has implications for the viability of other philosophical views. For example, fatalists were often criticized for holding views that would undermine the practice of praise and blame. Fatalists believe that our choices make no difference at all to what happens in the world. If one is fated to meet death in Smyrna, then, whatever one chooses to do, that is what will happen. Given the impotence of our choices, we do not cause events to occur.[2] Thus, we cannot be held responsible for what occurs. And this was seen as a vile, corrupting doctrine leading to moral chaos. However, what underlies the argument is a commitment to (MC). A fatalist who rejected (MC) would not be faced with this problem.

Some philosophers have rejected (MC) due to the metaphysical commitments of the philosophical systems they have adopted. For example, one could read David Hume as rejecting it insofar as one reads him as a causal eliminativist who still believes that we are morally responsible for our actions. Hume's empiricism seemed to lead him down this road. There are events we call "causes" and events we call "effects." However, there is nothing underlying the relation between them in any deep metaphysical sense. Another philosopher who can be read as rejecting (MC) is Gottfried Leibniz. He was not a causal eliminativist, since God, at least, had genuine causal powers, but Leibniz did ascribe to the doctrine of parallelism. God has established a "preexisting harmony" between human wills and events in the world. Thus, when one acts, one does not cause—rather, God has set up a perfect correlation between what is willed and occurrences in the world. Yet Leibniz did not reject the view that we are morally responsible for our actions.

More recently, this entailment claim has been attacked by philosophers who believe it to be false, but not for reasons having to do with the metaphysical commitments of the systems of philosophy they adopt. Rather, they believe that common sense counterexamples can be offered to (MC), ones that don't depend upon robust empiricism or notions of how God must have configured the universe. First of all, some philosophers hold that omissions are not causes and yet we can still be morally responsible for what we *fail* to do. They believe that absences or omissions lack power and thus cannot by their very nature *produce* effects. We might also note that one can "make a difference" and thus be responsible for something, without, strictly speaking, causing it. For example, one could imagine situations in which a judge declared a dead man "innocent" without causing anything to occur in the world. He's just created an institutional fact that did not exist before. In a similar spirit, some philosophers have discussed so-called "Cambridge" changes—when I leave the room it may be the case that Samantha then becomes the shortest person in the room, but it seems odd indeed to say that I have caused her to be shorter than anyone else in the room (Sosa, 1993).

Another philosopher, John Leslie (1991) holds that we can be responsible for outcomes that we don't cause but that would not have occurred but for our own actions, via what he terms "quasi-causation." And, more recently, Carolina Sartorio (2004) also attacks the entailment claim by appealing to disjunctive causation. Both Leslie and Sartorio offer novel cases to motivate their claims, and we will be looking at them later in the paper. What I would like to do in this paper is draw upon findings in social psychology, as well as some of the philosophical literature on causation and moral responsibility, to help develop a strategy to defend (MC) against some of the challenges raised. This is not a strategy to show that (MC) must be true. Rather, it is a strategy that questions the methodology of some of the challenges to (MC). I will return to the counterexamples to (MC) later in the paper and review them in more detail in light of the empirical findings.

When we make attributions of primary causation, that is, when we pick out *the* cause of an event among a nest of causal factors, it is quite true that we often rely on *pragmatic* and *contextual* considerations. Here's an example of this practice discussed by Hart and Honoré (1959).

First, when causal language is used of the provision or failure to provide another with an opportunity, it is implied that this is a deviation from a standard practice or expected procedure; the notions of what is unusual and what is reprehensible by accepted standards both influence the use of causal language in such cases. Hence the case of a house-holder whose prudential storing of firewood in the cellar gave a pyromaniac his opportunity to burn it down would be distinguished from that of the careless friend who left the house unlocked: the fire would not be naturally described as a consequence of the storing of the wood though the loss of the spoons was a consequence of leaving the house unlocked. (p. 56)

This example is one where one figures out who is blameworthy, or responsible, and then assigns causation. We have a sea of causation, and in assigning praise and blame we need to be able to make selections among the respective causal factors. Not all causal factors are blameworthy or praiseworthy, or indicate moral responsibility for the causing agent. This is why (MC) entails only in one direction. The identification in judgment of something's being *the* cause depends upon pragmatic factors and may well include moral judgments—Hart and Honoré's cases support this. The householder was not negligent, so his actions were not the cause of the fire, even though it is true that there would have been no fire if he had not been so prudent. Similarly, the careless friend is failing in his responsibilities, so he is identified as the cause, or part of the cause, when the spoons go missing. However, these cases are in no way a threat to (MC) since one, of course, says that there is still a causal connection between what the householder did and the fire. We just don't *attribute* causation to him since we don't view him as morally responsible *at all* for what happened. Neither case shows we would attribute this moral responsibility in the absence of any actual causal connection. Nor do such cases show that if pressed one would actually deny any causation—rather, the correct thing to say would be something like—"well, of course, the homeowner's actions were a causal factor, but not the primary cause since he didn't do anything wrong or unusual." What we call a "cause" or "causal factor" in many cases depends on what we relegate to the background conditions of the event in question. In the case of the householder, since he behaved normally, we don't single his actions out. Similarly—in the context as described by Hart and Honoré—we wouldn't say that oxygen caused the fire. But, again, when pressed, we of course acknowledge that it was one of the many causal factors. Oxygen was not sufficient, but the fire would not have occurred without it. This is some evidence that we regard the friend's negligence as more of a cause than oxygen in the air.

However, as we shall see, other cases purport to show that we assign, or would assign, moral responsibility for something in the complete and total absence of causal connection. For example, in the case offered by John Leslie, there is no causal connection, but there is a counterfactual connection, and that is the true necessary (though not sufficient) condition for attributing moral responsibility. Evidence from omissions purport to show us this as well. And what other writers have shown (like Hart and Honoré) is that when it comes to isolating out which counterfactual connections are relevant for the purposes of blame (there are so, so many), we rely on pragmatic features, and one of those features may be the extent to which it pays to attribute the responsibility—what difference would the attribution itself make, if any?

There has been some empirical research conducted on the question of how we assign causation and blame, and this research may shed some light on these questions. The reason is that this research can tell us the sorts of factors that we do tend to focus on—not the factors, perhaps, that we ought to focus on. However, I will also be noting that thought experiments, so-called "armchair" methods, are often useful as well, and just as useful, in clarifying our attributions of causation and moral responsibility.

Alicke's Research on Causal Attribution

Again, our task is not to come up with an account of causation but to look at ordinary, or common sense, ascriptions of causation with respect to attributions of moral responsibility. The claim is that these are what inform our intuitions about fixing both causation and moral responsibility.

Empirical studies have supported the view that people are reluctant to call a person p's action a the cause of an event e when e is bad and p is not blameworthy in any way in performing a. M. D. Alicke (1992), for example, has made an intriguing study along these lines. Alicke (1992) asked subjects to consider the following options and then assign primary causation:

John was driving over the speed limit (about 40 mph in a 30 mph zone) in order to get home in time to . . .

Socially desirable motive
. . . hide an anniversary present for his parents that he had left out in the open before they could see it.

Socially undesirable motive

... hide a vial of cocaine he had left out in the open before his parents could see it.

Other cause

Oil spill   As John came to an intersection, he applied his brakes, but was unable to stop as quickly as usual because of some oil that had spilled on the road. As a result, John hit a car that was coming from the other direction.

Tree branch   As John came to an intersection, he failed to see a stop sign that was covered by a large tree branch. As a result, John hit a car that was coming in the other direction.

Other car   As John came to an intersection, he applied his brakes, but was unable to avoid a car that ran through a stop sign without making any attempt to slow down. As a result, John hit the car that was coming from the other direction.

Consequence of accident

John hit the driver on the driver's side, causing him multiple lacerations, a broken collarbone, and a fractured arm. John was uninjured in the accident.

Complete the following sentence: The primary cause of this accident was ••. (p. 369)

What Alicke discovered is quite interesting. When John's motive is the socially undesirable one—the "culpable" one—he is far more likely to be identified as the primary cause of the accident. As Alicke (1992) himself put it, "With causal necessity, sufficiency, and proximity held constant, the more culpable act was deemed by subjects to have exerted a larger causal influence" (p. 370).

Thus, we have two accidents, let's say, both completely the same except the motive of the driver in question is different. His causal responsibility is deemed much greater when the motive is bad as opposed to when the motive is good. This looks similar to the Hart and Honoré thought experiment, but the result is empirically substantiated by looking at the reactions of 174 people.

Further, subjects tended to identify John as a cause more frequently when John was the only agent involved. This was because he "... was viewed as less responsible when another driver contributed to the accident" (Alicke, 1992, p. 370). This factor will be very relevant when we look at the counterexamples again.

Joshua Knobe has recently written a paper in which he is critical of how Alicke models the data. Like Alicke, he believes that moral considerations are crucial to the application of our concept of causation. He argues that "causal attributions are not purely descriptive judgments. Rather, people's willingness to say that a given behavior caused a given outcome depends in part on whether they regard the behavior as morally wrong" (Knobe, 2005a, p. 2). A folk psychological account of these attributions has to address the issue of what work they do for us, "what sort of question a causal attribution is supposed to be answering" (Knobe, 2005a, p. 4). His idea is to use evidence to come to an understanding of our competencies that underlie causal attributions (on analogy with linguistics), and he thinks this is where some normative considerations are to be found.

The sorts of cases he asks us to consider are very similar to the sorts of cases presented by Hart and Honoré—for example, cases where someone fails to live up to a responsibility and thus creates an opportunity for something bad to happen. He also presents a vignette that does not involve omission:

Lauren and Jane work for the same company. They each need to use a computer for work sometimes.

Unfortunately, the computer isn't very powerful. If two people are logged on at the same time, it usually crashes.

So the company decided to institute an official policy. It declared that Lauren would be the only one permitted to use the computer in the mornings and that Jane would be the only one permitted to use the computer in the afternoons.

As expected, Lauren logged on the computer the next day at 9:00 am.

But Jane decided to disobey the official policy. She also logged on at 9:00 am.

The computer crashed immediately. (Knobe, 2005a, p. 6)

Knobe points out that in this case we seem to think that Jane caused the computer to crash, even though it is also true that if Lauren had not logged on, it would not have crashed. To spell out how these attributions work, Knobe discusses the role of contrast cases; these contrasts are often very subtly signaled in ordinary language—often the speaker relies on features of the context and various inflections and emphases to indicate what the appropriate or intended contrast is. Further, picking out the appropriate contrast is a pragmatic issue, highly contextual. To use a familiar case, if Sally starts a fire that burns down her house, then we would normally attribute the cause of the fire to Sally's irresponsible behavior, but not to the fact that there is oxygen in the air that fed the fire.[3] This is not to deny that the presence of oxygen in the air is a cause. However, we may more easily say that Sally's irresponsibility is more of a cause than oxygen because it obtrudes more, or strikes one as more salient. It is not relegated to the background conditions.

Knobe uses the word "obtrude" to indicate that one contrast is more salient or more relevant. He also goes over various considerations people use to determine degrees of salience. However, for our purposes here, I simply want to focus on the normative factors—most specifically, the moral factors. So, when—as in Hart and Honoré's case—one's friend fails to lock the door behind him, which he ought to have done, then we attribute, at least in part, the cause of the burglary to him, since the normative consideration of his moral failing has more salience than other causal factors. One of Knobe's aims is to show that attributions can work somewhat differently than most social scientists believe; they are not merely descriptive but also responsive to normative considerations—like who we think ought to be blamed for something. We attribute causation to Jane in the above case, and not Lauren, because Jane is the one who should be blamed even though both actions were necessary for the computer to crash.

Thus, Knobe does agree with Alicke that normative factors play a crucial role in these attributions—though he disagrees on Alicke's model for how this works. Alicke's model moves from (1) the judgment of an agent's having acted wrongly to (2) the agent's being blamed to (3) causation's being attributed to the agent. Knobe (2005a) argues this is not entirely accurate. He believes instead that we move from (1) the judgment of an agent's having acted wrongly to (2) the attribution of causation to the agent to (3) blaming the agent. We attribute causation prior to the blaming step, at least in some cases—thus, he argues, Alicke's failure to accurately model the competency. His main case for illustrating this is the following:

George and Harry both work in a large office building. George is the janitor; Harry takes care of the mail.

Every day, George goes through the entire building and empties all of the garbage baskets. Since the building is large, this task normally takes him about one half hour.

One day, George is feeling tired and decides not to take out the garbage.

Harry sees that the garbage hasn't been taken out. He doesn't go to take it out himself, since that is not his job.

But it turns out the company is extremely lucky. An accountant had accidentally thrown out an important document, and everyone is overjoyed to find that the trash hadn't been taken out and hence that the document is still there.

The idea is that we attribute causation to George because it was his failure to act as he ought to have acted that caused the letter to be saved. However, we do not blame him for saving the letter. Thus, attribution of causation must precede the blame step. If this were not the case, then we would need to blame George for saving the letter before holding his failure to be the cause of the letter's being saved. And we need to be clear about this. Someone might try to argue that George is blameworthy, and we do in fact blame him for his failure to take out the garbage. But

Knobe's point is that even though we do think he did something wrong by not taking the garbage out, and I might blame him for the resulting stinky hallways in the building, I would not blame him *for the letter's being saved*. Technically, we might note that attribution of causation is *independent* of the blame step.

Knobe has picked up on the fact that we tend not to blame people for good outcomes, even when the outcomes are the result of something bad that they have done. We tend to blame only for bad outcomes. Someone—let's say a competitor of George's bosses—might blame George for doing something that resulted in the document's being saved, but that's because he would regard the outcome as a bad one.

A critic could respond by claiming that the case has not been accurately described. What George has done wrong is fail to take out the garbage, and we do blame him for *that*. His saving of the letter wasn't wrong. However, Knobe could respond to this by just slightly changing the case description so that George has spitefully failed to take out the garbage because he thinks the document would be harmful to the company. We still don't blame him *for saving the document*. Of course, we wouldn't praise him either.

I agree with Knobe that Alicke's analysis doesn't properly accommodate this case. For my purposes I'd like to focus on what they do agree on, which is the fact that normative considerations influence causal attributions—and one of those normative considerations is the consideration that the agent has acted wrongly. However, we might ask whether or not it was that the agent acted wrongly or, rather, somehow "out of the norm"? Consider a slight modification of the George case, one where George does not take out the garbage, though it is his job to do so, but also where George very rarely takes it out even though it is his job. The idea is that this failure to act is normal for George, not unusual at all. On the other hand, Harry's happening to walk down the hall and see the document poking out of the garbage bag was unusual. In this case, I think, we'd probably attribute primary causation to Harry rather than George (another way to put this is that we might say that Harry is more of a cause than George here). This observation is in keeping with some of Joel Feinberg's work on attributing causation. In discussing Bertrand Russell's views on the Cuban Missile Crisis, for example, Feinberg (1970) notes: "Common sense, I would submit, would not necessarily select the last active intervention, in seeking the cause of the crisis, but rather that act or event that was a radical deviation from routine, which was clearly the Soviet construction of missile bases in Cuba" (p. 165, footnote 15). Likewise, he argues that when someone is stabbed to death at a dinner table the cause is not that the table had been laid for dinner with the knife on it. Everybody agrees with this, but Feinberg's explanation is that this is not the cause because ". . . it is the abnormal deviation that distinguishes the whole incident from other dinners where diners are *not* killed" (p. 166).

It may be that the hypothesis that judgments of the unusualness of an event or action affecting causal attribution and judgments of normativity affecting causal attribution are not in conflict. However, it may also be that the unusualness hypothesis can account not only for Alicke and Knobe's cases but also nonnormative ones, in which case it would offer a more general explanation, or a more general model. In any case, it is a hypothesis that would be interesting to test more carefully. It would still allow for the contrastivism that Knobe discusses. Whether or not an action or event is "unusual" is relative to a contrast class.

What relevance does the work of Alicke and Knobe have for the sorts of cases we started discussing? Let's look at the counterexamples to (MC) in more detail.

Counterexamples to the Entailment Claim

Again, some philosophers have argued that we need to give up the idea that moral responsibility rests, *necessarily*, on causal responsibility. For example, some do so out of concerns about being able to spell out coherently what something like "negative" causation consists in. The idea is that an absence cannot have causal influence. For example, David Armstrong (1999) writes that "Omissions and so forth are not part of the real driving force in nature. Every causal situation develops as it does as a result of the presence of positive factors alone" (p. 177). There are two reasons why some find this view attractive. The first is that many regard causation as a kind of power in the world. Absences are not powers at all—thus the oddity of viewing them as causes. The second reason is a concern for simplicity. Allowing for negative causation will multiply the numbers of causes astronomically. Just think about how many things we are causing to happen right now by our failures to act.

In the moral case, then, if I hold Constance responsible for failing to reach over and flip a switch that would save Bella's life, I am holding her responsible for an omission. It would then follow, if omissions are not actual causes, that she is responsible for Bella's death even though she did not cause it. Thus, we would have moral responsibility without causal responsibility.

Thus, given their concerns about the metaphysical shakiness of negative causation, there are some ethicists who are prepared to give up the view that moral responsibility entails causal responsibility (Harris et al., 1987). Others, such as John Leslie, seem to agree that the entailment claim is false, but for a very different reason, suggesting that we attribute moral responsibility in the absence of causal responsibility when someone does something that, for example, constitutes incredibly strong evidence that the event in question will happen or is happening. What this involves, more specifically, is that subjunctive conditionals track the quasi-effect. He calls this "quasi-causation." To illustrate, Leslie (1991) asks us to imagine the following fascinating case:

> Crossing a plain, I come to what looks like a gigantic mirror. But pushing a hand against it, I feel flesh and not glass. The universe must be symmetric, the flesh that of my double—left-right reversed but otherwise a perfect replica.
>
> The universe must also be fully deterministic, for how else could my double have moved exactly as I did? But never having seen freedom and determinism as incompatible I find this untroubling. . . .
>
> Do I not actually have twice the power I earlier seemed to have? (p. 73)

Suppose that a woman, Melissa, finds herself in this situation. Of course, there will be Melissa 1 and Melissa 2, a Melissa for each of the universes. Leslie asks us to consider what would happen if one agent picks up a rock and throws it at a bird. The other agent would do the same, given the symmetry. Thus, it is true that were Melissa 1 to throw rock 1 Melissa 2 would throw rock 2, and it is true that were Melissa 2 to throw rock 2 Melissa 1 would throw rock 1. Both Melissa 1 and Melissa 2 would have the feeling of making double the difference. And we get tracking when these sorts of conditionals hold up, so the occurrence doesn't seem as though it is a freak occurrence. The idea Leslie is employing is this: Even though there is no causal connection between what I do and what my double does, what I do still makes a difference to what she does, and thus my power to bring things about, to make a difference, has doubled. This power relies on the symmetry between these universes. But Leslie goes on to show that symmetry can exist outside of science fiction thought experiments. He notes that two balls may bounce exactly the same height, and that is explainable not by one ball's affecting the other but by the fact that they are structurally the same and the other background conditions are the same. He terms this not "causation," but "quasi-causation." As he notes, fish will respond the same way to the same stimulus, and act identically, though there is no causal interaction *between them*.[4] There is no causal *oomph*, so to speak. What we have is a correlation between behaviors that is explainable in terms of structural similarities. In the twin universe cases, the intuition is that Melissa 1's action can make even more of a difference. This, in turn, might be explainable by the fact that her action generates bad news about how Melissa 2 acts, or by the fact of a (suitably qualified) counterfactual dependence between the two. If this intuition bears scrutiny, then we have another way in which someone could be morally responsible for an outcome even though not causally responsible for it.[5]

Leslie's case is a stipulation of a Leibniz-like scenario in that there is a perfect correlation between one's willings and agency and what happens in the world. The parallelism has not been set up by God but exists independently. Given parallelism, had Melissa not thrown the rock, the bird would not have died, in the same way that had Melissa 1 not thrown rock 1, bird 2 would not have died. One might claim that once we get these sorts of robust, tracking, conditional relationships that's just all there is to causation. However, numerous counterexamples call this claim into question.[6]

Leslie then goes on to apply his findings on quasi-causation to the problem of voting—his view is that if one person fails to vote for the good candidate, then she is responsible, at least partly responsible, for the loss if that candidate loses the election. That is because—in virtue of the symmetry claim—she could have generated the good news but did not; her not voting "meant that" others like her did not vote. Of course, these others share the responsibility for the same reason. Her failure to vote did make an enormous difference even if it lacked the requisite causal power to generate the effect of a loss.

However, another, rather deflationary tack to take is this: There is the illusion of power based on features this case has in common with cases where we ascribe causation to the agent. In the absence of causation, this feeling of power or of "making a difference" is simply an illusion. This is supported by the fact that our intuitions are heavily influenced by the temporal sequence of events—the evidence approach is a counterintuitive basis for "making a difference" when we look at counterfactuals involving past events—for example, either I have spent 1,000 years in hell or not, and if I have, I do not remember it (this is all true). Suppose that the following is true: If I tell a lie to my Mom, then it is likely that I spent a thousand years in hell. Does my telling the lie make a difference—even if "Were I to tell a lie to my Mom, I would have spent 1,000 years in hell already"? Intuitively, not, even though it would be good evidence that I spent 1,000 years in hell, which is a pretty terrible fate.[7] But perhaps this simply means that we need an evidentialist account with some other constraints.

While Leslie's case seems to rely on imputing some sort of magical power (he denies this), we can find analogies to the case that Leslie is concerned with in the psychology literature on rationality and game theory.[8] However, this line of thought leads us to adopt an evidentialist decision procedure, which, as already noted, leads to very odd results. In Leslie's case it seems odd for someone to think he ought to vote because that means that others will vote, *in the absence of a causal connection* (or, more precisely, his voting constitutes extremely good evidence that others will vote). This seems analogous to opting for the one-box in Newcomb's problem.[9]

Another writer who has recently argued against the entailment claim is Carolina Sartorio. Her argument rests on a consideration of two cases to be contrasted:

> Imagine the following situation. There was an accidental leak of a dangerous chemical at a high-risk chemical plant, which is on the verge of causing an explosion. The explosion will occur unless the room containing the chemical is immediately sealed. Suppose that sealing the room requires that two buttons—call them "A" and "B"—be depressed at the same time t (say, two seconds from now). You and I work at the plant, in different rooms, and we are in charge of accident prevention. Button A is in my room, and button B is in yours. We don't have time to get in touch with each other to find out what the other is going to do; however, we are both aware of what we are supposed to do. As it turns out, each of us independently decides to keep reading his magazine instead of depressing his button. The explosion ensues. (Sartorio, 2004, p. 317)

She will argue that here you are morally responsible for the explosion though you didn't cause it, by contrasting this case with the following:

> Again, button A is in my room, and I fail to depress it. This time, however, there is no one in the room containing button B; instead, a safety mechanism has been automatically set to depress B at t. When the time comes, however, B becomes stuck while being up. Just as in the original case, then, neither button is depressed and the explosion occurs. Call the two cases "Two Buttons" and "Two Buttons—One Stuck" respectively. The cases differ in the respect that, in Two Buttons, B isn't depressed because you decided not to depress it, whereas in Two Buttons-One Stuck, it isn't depressed because it got stuck. (Sartorio, 2004, p. 318)

Sartorio claims that the Two Buttons case is a counterexample to the entailment claim. It is a case where one has moral responsibility but the responsible agent has not caused the explosion. The core of her argument rests on our intuitive view that in the Two-Buttons case we think that the agent is morally responsible for not pressing the button, and that in the Two Buttons—One Stuck case we judge lack of causation. Since the omissions are the same in both cases, we must then think that in Two Buttons there is no causation between the failure to depress the button by the single agent and the explosion. Therefore, there is moral responsibility without causation.

Her diagnosis is to suggest the following alternative to the entailment claim: "If an agent is responsible for an outcome, then it is in virtue of the fact that agent is responsible for something that caused the outcome" (Sartorio, 2004, p. 329). One is morally responsible if one causes what in turn causes the outcome in question. Thus, causation is transmissible on her view.

Needless to say, these cases are controversial—Leslie's in particular. Leslie seems to be arguing for—or perhaps just assuming—evidential decision theory. One ought to do what will generate good evidence that the desired event will occur. Controversial indeed.

Sartorio, on the other hand, is arguing, in effect, that the two acts are causally the same since their intrinsic properties are the same. The failure to press the button is the same in both cases. Thus, if the two acts are the same and one is a cause, then the other is a cause as well. However, the claim they are relevantly the same would be controversial since one could argue that acts are differentiated in terms of relational features as well. Intrinsic features may not be sufficient. She is also, in her analysis, relying on disjunctive causes. These are some very interesting features of her argument which deserve further attention, but I will be focusing on her claim that "I am responsible for the explosion in Two Buttons." Remember that in this case her action was necessary but *not sufficient* for the explosion to have been prevented. The other person failed to act, and their conjoined failure to prevent the explosion is what caused it. Thus, if Sartorio is right about her claim, then she does have a case of moral responsibility without causation. However, my claim is that—as in Leslie's counterexample—we are responding to cues that are associated with causation to assign moral responsibility. We should not deny that she is a cause of the explosion. For example, one factor is that Sartorio has put the case in terms of omissions, which we seem to have some difficulty in regarding as causes to begin with (as the quote from Armstrong indicates).

Interestingly, both Leslie and Sartorio apply their analyses to the voting problem. I've already mentioned that Leslie views the responsibility to vote as based on generating evidence that others will too—and all those votes will make a difference. Sartorio's analysis is that if an agent fails to vote for the good candidate, along with a number of other agents who would have voted for the good candidate as well, then she is responsible when the good candidate fails to win even though she did not cause it—rather, her failure to vote is part of a *disjunctive cause* for the failure of the good candidate to win. Her omission is a cause of that disjunctive omission, and it is that disjunctive omission that is the cause of the good candidate's failure to win.

Applying this certainly does not commit one to anything like evidentialism, since one really does view one's actions in causal terms, but just as part of a disjunctive cause for a particular event. However, one factor that affects Sartorio's analysis is that we may be influenced by the intuition of irresponsibility when someone fails to vote. This makes it seem like we are precommitted to moral responsibility in these sorts of cases, and it explains why we think Sartorio is right. But this by itself would do nothing to distinguish the case from Leslie's. For Sartorio then, imagine a case where—for example—a famine caused by drought decimates a population in a far-off land. Suppose also that my driving my car and contributing to global warming was part—a small part—of a huge disjunctive cause leading up to the drought and famine. Am I morally responsible for the deaths? It doesn't seem so. The larger the disjunction, the less one's feeling of responsibility. This tracks the lessening contribution to the causal disjunction. But is one morally responsible for the disaster, or morally responsible for simply *contributing to* the cause of the disaster? Of course, Sartorio is just concerned with presenting a counterexample to the entailment claim, and in doing this she isn't committed to holding that all cases where one of my actions is part of a disjunctive cause of *x* are cases where I am morally responsible for *x*—and I don't mean to claim that she is doing this. However, what is doing the work in considering these cases—where there is moral responsibility and where there isn't—seems to depend on preexisting intuitions about moral responsibility. One doesn't first try to figure out the disjunctive cause issue and then figure out moral responsibility.

What Does the Psychology Research Indicate about How We Fix Moral Responsibility and Causation?

Causation by omission, and thus moral responsibility for failures, can be handled by allowing for negative causation. The previously mentioned objections can be handled by allowing that causes are not powers and by noting that even with positive causation we need to use pragmatic considerations to narrow down the range of relevant alternative causes. Some of these pragmatic considerations, as we've discussed, are amply illustrated by some empirical research on how people attribute causation.

However, the other cases will be handled somewhat differently. The Leslie case trades on our intuitions that intending to harm is blameworthy. That is, these sorts of intentions qualify as socially undesirable. Further, even though we have stipulated in the Leslie case that there is no causation at work, these are cases where we have some counterfactual dependence. We are greatly influenced by this connection to feel that there is moral responsibility and, thus, blame is warranted. Even without causation, it is true that but for Melissa 1's action bird 2 would still be alive. But the psychology of attributions of moral responsibility can explain this misleading intuition. In the case of Melissa 1 we have a perception of very poor motivation and character on her part along with the strong counterfactual connection between her actions and those of Melissa 2, and this makes it more likely for us to attribute to her moral responsibility for bird 2's death. At least it explains why we have this feeling. The case meets the cues we pick up for attributing both causation and moral responsibility. Even though we have stipulated lack of causation, this cue is still responsible for why we have the feeling of moral responsibility. Of course, relying simply on a counterfactual connection does not stand up to reflection. When we tinker with another cue, like temporal ordering, the feeling of responsibility will diminish. Of course, we could do another study to test whether or not this is so—how much does temporal ordering affect our intuitions about moral responsibility? I suspect, however, that thought experiments are sufficient to show that we will not be willing to say that *a* is responsible for *b* when *a* comes after *b*.

In Sartorio's case, again, the fact that the agent has failed to live up to a responsibility affects our intuitions in the way described by Alicke. Sartorio is discussing moral responsibility without causation, and Alicke is discussing our attributions of causation in light of our feelings of moral responsibility. However, Alicke's research isolates factors that we pick up on in judging, or making attributions of, moral responsibility. He notes that when John acts alone, for example, people tend to judge him as being much more responsible than when it was the case that a nonactor contributed to the accident. The evidence that Alicke has gathered gives us a good indication of how people tend to assign moral responsibility—more agents, less responsibility; bad intentions or motives, more responsibility; and so on. These are the sorts of factors that have a high degree of salience, or, in Knobe's terminology, "obtrudeness."

Much will hinge on how the case is described. The agent in Two Buttons contributes to the disjunctive cause, but so do a lot of other factors. Maybe her mom gave her a particularly interesting magazine to read, for example, thus making her want to continue reading rather than press the button. Sartorio's analysis in terms of disjunctive causation doesn't show that we aren't just responding first to our view that the agent's failure—itself—is bad and she is morally responsible for *that*. Very many philosophers have held the view that we have an obligation to vote independent of the expectation that a single vote will decide an election. The thinking is: Yes, my one single vote does not make a difference, and thus my failure to vote does not cause the good candidate to lose, but I have a responsibility to vote nevertheless, and when I fail to vote I am morally responsible for that failure and should be blamed for *that*. Thus, it is true that one has moral responsibility without causal responsibility *in a sense*, but it is moral responsibility for failure to vote with respect to lack of causal responsibility for failure to win an election. However, it's not moral responsibility for *x* without causation for *x*.

Conclusion

I have had two goals in this paper. The first has been to provide a limited defense of (MC)—limited, because I believe that there will be some odd, Cambridge-change cases that are problematic for (MC). In offering the defense, I have drawn on material in philosophy of law and normative ethics, as well as empirical data from psychological studies by M. D. Alicke—all of which show that many pragmatic factors influence how we make attributions of moral responsibility in situations where a variety of causal factors (or counterfactual ones) obtain.

I have also wanted to show that, though psychological research into these issues of normative significance is very interesting, it should not be seen either as a replacement for, or superior to, traditional "armchair" methods in philosophy. Thought experiments employed by philosophers such as Hart and Honoré, Feinberg, and many, many others have shown that these methods are used to develop extremely nuanced and sophisticated accounts of the sorts of factors that influence our intuitions in normative cases. I have suggested that some factors discussed by Hart and Honoré as well as Feinberg even suggest a more general account of our attributions of causation than the account offered by Alicke and Knobe.

Notes

Earlier versions of this paper were read at Union College, Boston University, and the Conference on Morality and the Brain at Dartmouth College. I would like to thank the members of those audiences for their very helpful comments. Research for this paper was supported by the Leslie Humanities Center at Dartmouth College as part of a workshop on "Morality and the Brain." I would like to thank the Leslie Humanities Center for its support. The paper has also benefited from conversations with Walter Sinnott-Armstrong and Roy Sorensen.

1. Versions of this thesis appear in various places throughout the literature. Sartorio (2004) explicitly discusses a version in her paper. The force of the thesis resides in the fact that it is generally taken to be sufficient for moral innocence with respect to a given event that one did not *cause* the event in question to occur. Thus, many discussions of moral fault and responsibility assume the thesis.

It is worth noting that the intuition behind the thesis can sometimes be tricky to spell out. For example, we need to note a distinction between someone's being morally responsible for an event and the appropriateness of holding someone morally responsible for an event, which some scholars argue may be done even absent a causal connection between the agent and the event. If someone has a strict instrumental account of the appropriateness of praise and blame, this would be a possibility. An investigation into this wrinkle, however, is beyond the scope of this paper.

2. This depends on treating causes as difference makers.

3. This case is frequently used in the literature. For example, see Hart and Honoré (1959), p. 32.

4. In making this point, Leslie draws on the work of Lewis (1979). There Lewis notes that replicas can provide the basis for great predictive success. "To predict whether I will take my thousand, make a replica of me, put my replica in a replica of my predicament, and see whether my replica takes *his* thousand" (p. 237).

5. Note that even though it is true that one hand moving would not have happened but for the other, this is not an example of causation even on a counterfactual dependence account simply in virtue of this claim's being true—other conditions are often inserted.

6. Ned Hall (2004) argues that we basically have two fundamentally different concepts of causation. They are (1) what we standardly think of as the production view that holds that causes generate their effects, and then, as well, (2) the counterfactual view that holds that causation can be characterized in terms of counterfactual dependence.

7. I thank Roy Sorensen for this case.

8. Andrew Colman and Michael Bacharach (1997) argue that the "Stackleberg heuristic" in games offers the best payoff strategy, and that this heuristic is "justified by evidentialist reasoning." (p. 1).

9. And Leslie actually does this.

8.1 Causal Judgment and Moral Judgment: Two Experiments

Joshua Knobe and Ben Fraser

It has long been known that people's causal judgments can have an impact on their moral judgments. To take a simple example, if people conclude that a behavior caused the death of ten innocent children, they will therefore be inclined to regard the behavior itself as morally wrong. So far, none of this should come as any surprise.

But recent experimental work points to the existence of a second, and more surprising, aspect of the relationship between causal judgment and moral judgment. It appears that the relationship can sometimes go *in the opposite direction*. That is, it appears that our moral judgments can sometimes impact our causal judgments. (Hence, we might first determine that a behavior is morally wrong and then, on that basis, arrive at the conclusion that it was the cause of various outcomes.)

There is still a certain amount of debate about how these results should be interpreted. Some researchers argue that the surprising results obtained in recent studies are showing us something important about people's concept of causation; others suggest that all of the results can be understood in terms of straightforward performance errors.

Driver provides an excellent summary of the existing literature on this issue,[1] but she also offers a number of alternative hypotheses that threaten to dissolve the debate entirely. These hypotheses offer ways of explaining all of the experimental data without supposing that moral judgments play any real role in the process that generates causal judgments. If her alternative hypotheses turn out to be correct, we will be left with no real reason to suppose that moral judgments can have an impact on causal judgments.

We think that Driver's hypotheses are both cogent and plausible. The only way to know whether they are actually correct is to subject them to systematic experimental tests. That is precisely the approach we have adopted here.

The Problem

Driver introduces the basic problem by discussing a few cases from the existing literature. Here is one of the cases she discusses:

Lauren and Jane work for the same company. They each need to use a computer for work sometimes.

Unfortunately, the computer isn't very powerful. If two people are logged on at the same time, it usually crashes.

So the company decided to institute an official policy. It declared that Lauren would be the only one permitted to use the computer in the mornings and that Jane would be the only one permitted to use the computer in the afternoons.

As expected, Lauren logged on the computer the next day at 9:00 am.

But Jane decided to disobey the official policy. She also logged on at 9:00 am.

The computer crashed immediately. (Knobe, 2005a; discussed in Driver, p. 428)

In this case, people seem more inclined to say that Jane caused the computer crash than they are to say that Lauren caused the computer crash. Yet Jane's behavior resembles Lauren's in almost every way. The key difference between them is a purely normative one: Jane violated one of her obligations, whereas Lauren did not. Thus, it appears that people's normative judgments may be having some influence on their causal judgments.[2]

Driver's question is about how to understand what is going on in cases like this one. Do people's judgments about obligations, rights, etc. actually serve as input to their judgments about causal relations?

Morality and Atypicality

Driver's first suggestion is that it might be possible to explain all of the puzzling results by appealing to the concept of *atypicality*. Some behaviors are fairly common or ordinary; others are more atypical. Perhaps we can explain the results of existing experiments if we simply assume that people have a general tendency to pick out atypical behaviors and classify them as causes.

With this thought in mind, we can revisit the story of Jane and Lauren. We noted above that Jane's behavior differs from Lauren's in its moral status, but it seems that we can also identify a second difference between the two behaviors. Jane's behavior seems quite atypical for a person in her position, whereas Lauren's behavior seems perfectly common and ordinary. So perhaps people's tendency to pick out Jane's behavior and classify it as a cause has nothing to do with its distinctive moral status. It might be that people simply classify Jane's behavior as a cause because they regard it as atypical.

This point is well-taken. The immoral behaviors in existing experiments were always atypical. Thus, Driver's hypothesis explains all of the existing results just as well as the hypothesis that moral judgments really do have an impact on causal judgments. To decide between the competing hypotheses, we will therefore need to conduct an additional experiment.

What we need now is a case in which two behaviors are equally typical but one is morally worse than the other. Here is one such case:

The receptionist in the philosophy department keeps her desk stocked with pens. The administrative assistants are allowed to take the pens, but faculty members are supposed to buy their own.

The administrative assistants typically do take the pens. Unfortunately, so do the faculty members. The receptionist has repeatedly e-mailed them reminders that only administrative assistants are allowed to take the pens.

On Monday morning, one of the administrative assistants encounters Professor Smith walking past the receptionist's desk. Both take pens. Later that day, the receptionist needs to take an important message . . . but she has a problem. There are no pens left on her desk.

In this case, the professor's action and the administrative assistant's action are both typical, but only the professor's action is in any way reprehensible. What we want to know is whether this small difference in perceived moral status can—all by itself, with no help from typicality judgments—have any impact on people's causal judgments.

To address this question, we ran a simple experiment. All subjects were given the story of the professor and the administrative assistant. They were then asked to indicate whether they agreed or disagreed with the following two statements:

- Professor Smith caused the problem.
- The administrative assistant caused the problem.

The results showed a dramatic difference. People agreed with the statement that Professor Smith caused the problem but disagreed with the statement that the administrative assistant caused the problem.[3] Yet the two behaviors seem not to differ in their typicality; the principal difference lies in their differing moral statuses. The results therefore suggest that moral judgments actually do play a direct role in the process by which causal judgments are generated.

Conversational Pragmatics

When researchers want to understand people's concept of causation, the usual approach is to look at how people apply the English word "cause."

But it should be clear that this method is a fallible one. There are certainly cases in which people's use of words in conversation can diverge from their application of concepts in private thought. After all, the point of conversation is not simply to utter sentences that correspond to one's beliefs. People are also concerned in an essential way with the effort to provide information that is relevant and helpful to their audience members. Thus, if people think that using the word "cause" in a given case might end up giving audience members the wrong impression, they might refuse to use that word for reasons that have nothing to do with a reluctance to apply the corresponding concept in their own private thoughts. Here we enter the domain of *conversational pragmatics*.[4]

Driver's second major suggestion is that it might be possible to account for the apparent role of moral considerations in causal judgments simply by appealing to the pragmatics of conversation. The basic idea here is simple and quite plausible. When we offer causal explanations, our aim is not simply to utter sentences that express true propositions; we are also engaged in an effort to say things that prove relevant and helpful to our audience. It seems clear, moreover, that moral considerations will often play an important role in this pragmatic aspect of conversation. When a person's house has just been burned down, it won't do to give him just any cause of the fire. He will want a causal explanation that helps him to figure out who is morally responsible for what happened. In this way, moral considerations can affect the *speech act* of offering a causal explanation even if they play no role in people's underlying *concept* of causation.

We certainly agree that conversational pragmatics can have an impact on people's use of causal language. The only question is whether the apparent connection between moral judgments and causal judgments is due to pragmatics alone. In other words, the question is whether this connection is due *entirely* to pragmatics (so that it would simply disappear if we eliminated the relevant pragmatic pressures) or whether the connection is also due in part to *other processes* (so that it would persist even if we could somehow eliminate the pragmatics entirely).

One way to investigate this issue is to construct a case in which conversational pragmatics alone gives us no reason to specifically pick out the morally bad behavior and classify it as a cause. Here is one such case:

Claire's parents bought her an old computer. Claire uses it for schoolwork, but her brother Daniel sometimes logs on to play games. Claire has told Daniel, "Please don't log on to my computer. If we are both logged on at the same time, it will crash." One day, Claire and Daniel logged on to the computer at the same time. The computer crashed. Later that day, Claire's mother is talking with the computer repairman. The repairman says, "I see that Daniel was logged on, but this computer will only crash if two people are logged on at the same time. So, I still don't see quite why the computer crashed."

The morally bad behavior in this case is Daniel's act of logging on, but the conversational context is constructed in such a way that there are no pragmatic pressures to perform the speech act of asserting that this morally bad behavior was the cause. In fact, all of the pragmatic pressures go in the opposite direction. Even though Daniel's act of logging on is a morally bad behavior, it would be inappropriate in this conversation to mention it in a causal explanation. The key question now is how a speaker would react in such a case.

If the entire connection between moral judgments and causal judgments were due to conversational pragmatics, the connection should simply disappear in cases like this one. That is, the speaker should be left with no inclination at all to specifically pick out the immoral behavior and classify it as a cause.

But there is another possible way of understanding what is going on here. Perhaps the connection between moral judgments and causal judgments is not merely a matter of pragmatics but actually reflects something fundamental about the way people ordinarily think about causation. On this hypothesis, some connection should persist even in cases like the one under discussion here. Even when it seems pragmatically inappropriate to *say* that the immoral behavior was the principal cause, people should still *think* that the immoral behavior was the principal cause. Thus, the mother should think: "Daniel's act of logging on truly was the cause of the computer crash; it just wouldn't be appropriate to mention that in this conversation."

To decide between these hypotheses, we ran a second experiment. All subjects were given the story of Claire and Daniel. Each subject was then asked two questions. One question was about what explanation would be most *appropriate in the conversation*; the other was about what the mother *actually believes*.[5]

The results were simple and striking. The vast majority of subjects (85%) responded that it would be most appropriate in the conversation to explain the crash by saying that Claire was logged on.[6] But intuitions about what the mother actually believed did not correspond to intuitions about what it would be most appropriate to say. Instead, subjects responded that the mother would believe that Claire *did not* cause the crash but that Daniel *did* cause the crash.[7]

Ultimately, then, it seems that there is more going on here than can be explained by pragmatics alone. Pragmatics can determine what would be appropriate to say in a given conversation. But even in conversations where it would clearly be inappropriate to mention the morally bad behavior, people insist that an observer would specifically pick out that behavior and regard it as a cause. This result suggests that moral considerations are not merely relevant to the pragmatics of conversation but actually play a fundamental role in the way people think about causation.

Notes

We are grateful to Christopher Hitchcock for many hours of valuable conversation on these issues.

1. Driver's summary focuses especially on the competing theories of Alicke (1992) and Knobe (2005a). For further experimental evidence, see Alicke (2000), Alicke, Davis, and Pezzo (1994), Knobe (2005b), and Solan and Darley (2001). For philosophical discussions, see Beebee (2004), Gert (1988), Hart and Honoré (1959), Hitchcock (2005), McGrath (2005), Thomson (2003), and Woodward (2003).

2. This point has occasionally been made with regard to causation by omission (Beebee, 2004; McGrath, 2005; Thomson, 2003; Woodward, 2003). But the effect does not appear to have anything to do with omissions specifically. Normative judgments appear to affect causal judgments even in cases like this one where we are not concerned with omissions in any way.

3. Subjects were 18 students in an introductory philosophy class at the University of North Carolina—Chapel Hill. The order of questions was counterbalanced, but there were no significant order effects. Each subject rated both statements on a scale ranging from –3 ("not at all") to +3 ("fully"), with the 0 point marked "somewhat." The mean rating for the statement that the professor caused the problem was 2.2; the mean for the statement that the assistant caused the problem was –1.2. This difference is statistically significant, $t(17) = 5.5$, $p < .001$.

4. Note that our concern in this section is only with the pragmatics of *conversation*. Even if the effect under discussion here has nothing to do with conversational pragmatics, one might still argue that it is "pragmatic" in a broader sense, i.e., that it arose because it enables us to achieve certain practical purposes.

5. Subjects were first asked to say which of two replies would be more appropriate in the conversation. The two options given were "Daniel was logged on" and "Claire was logged on." Subjects were then asked to rate the degree to which the mother actually believes each of two sentences. The two sentences were "Daniel caused the computer crash" and "Claire caused the computer crash."

6. This percentage is significantly greater than what would be expected by chance alone, $\chi^2(1, 47) = 24.1$, $p < .001$.

7. Subjects rated each statement on a scale ranging from -3 ("not at all") to $+3$ ("fully"), with the 0 point marked "somewhat." The order of questions was counterbalanced, but there were no significant order effects. The mean rating for the statement that Claire caused the computer crash was -1.3; the mean for the statement that Daniel caused the computer crash was 1.6. This difference is statistically significant, $t(40) = 6.2$, $p < .001$.

8.2   Can You Be Morally Responsible for Someone's Death If Nothing You Did Caused It?

John Deigh

Lately, I've been watching reruns of the popular TV crime drama *Law &
Order*. These episodes contain useful illustrations of the issues of causation
and responsibility that Julia Driver's paper raises. They also contain some
pointers. The issues the paper raises are thorny, and these pointers should
help us avoid their snags. The main issue is whether a person's being
morally responsible for some event entails that he caused that event.
Driver, with some qualification, holds that it does. I don't think her view
can be sustained, however. Once one takes account of the different circumstances that warrant attributing moral responsibility for some event,
it should be clear that they do not support her view. They do not support
the converse view either. Driver, to be sure, does not maintain the converse view. Indeed, she expressly denies it. Nevertheless, it will be useful
to see why it would be hard to maintain that either entailment relation
holds.

First, a *caveat*. In using episodes from a TV crime drama, I will be considering the relation between criminal responsibility for an event and causation of that event, and criminal responsibility for an event is not the
same thing as moral responsibility for it. For one thing, the criminal law
must, of necessity, apply more exact standards of responsibility than we
look to in attributing moral responsibility. For another, for reasons of social
policy, the criminal law includes some limitations on attributing responsibility for certain harms that we do not observe in attributing moral
responsibility for those harms. One can, for example, be relieved of criminal responsibility for someone's death, even though it is due to injuries
one inflicted on the deceased, if the death occurs many years after one
inflicted them, whereas one's moral responsibility for the death is never
subject to such statutes of limitation. Finally, the criminal law defines a
few offenses, the so-called "strict liability offenses," as not requiring that
the offender be morally responsible for the harm he caused in order to be

criminally responsible for it. So, plainly, criminal responsibility for the harms people cause in committing these offenses is not the same thing as moral responsibility for those harms. These differences between criminal and moral responsibility should remind us, then, that the correspondence between the concept of responsibility used in criminal law and that used in everyday morality is not exact. Still, the correspondence is close enough to allow use of legal examples from a crime drama for discussing the issues at hand.

A typical episode of *Law & Order* opens with some innocuous person or couple finding a dead body in circumstances suggesting foul play. The second scene cuts in immediately. The police have arrived and begun their investigation. One of the first things they want to know is the cause of death. The detectives look to the medical examiner for the answer, and she offers a preliminary one. Later, the detectives visit the medical examiner in her lab, where she has performed the autopsy, and she now gives them a definite answer. Death, she announces, was the result of . . . , which is almost always some internal event and its immediate cause like the brain's hemorrhaging behind the right temporal lobe due to the skull's being crushed or asphyxiation due to strangulation or smoke inhalation. The medical examiner may then go on to describe the instrument that was used: the victim's skull was crushed by a blow from a mechanic's wrench, or strangulation resulted from a woman's stocking being wrapped around the throat and pulled tight. She may even, on the basis of a reconstruction of these events, be able to describe some of the physical features of the person who wielded the instrument: that he is left-handed, say, or over six feet tall. She never, however, speculates as to who the culprit is. That question is left to the detectives.

It is a question of a different order. The detectives must determine who, if anyone, is criminally responsible for the death, and this question is not reducible to who, if anyone, caused that death. At the same time, in seeking the person who is responsible for the death, the detectives naturally trace back along the chain of causes, whose last links the medical examiner has described, to the person whose wielding of the instrument is the next link. This person is usually the culprit. But not always. Sometimes the culprit has acted at several removes. If the instrument of death is a bomb, for example, delivered to the victim by mail in a package designed so that opening it detonates the bomb, then the next link is the act of opening the package. And typically, as was the case in the episode in which the estranged wife of a distinguished physicist is killed by a bomb she receives in the mail, the person who performs this act is not the culprit.

Nor is the postman, even though his putting the package in the victim's mailbox was the next obvious link in the chain of causes leading to the victim's death. For while the postman's act of delivering the package to the victim was voluntary and did cause the subsequent events that were the death's proximate cause, it did not, on those grounds, make him criminally responsible for the death. To be criminally responsible for someone's death on account of a voluntary act that causes it, one's act must issue from a guilty mind, and the postman's act—for he had no idea that the package contained a bomb—did not issue from such a mind. Not all voluntary acts that cause someone's death are blameworthy, and only those that are render their agents criminally responsible for that death. The detectives therefore, in their investigation of the bombing, had to go further back in the chain of causes in order to find one on the basis of which they could identify someone whose blameworthy action made him criminally responsible for the victim's demise.

Did that action have to be a link in this chain? Or could a person be criminally responsible for someone's death even though nothing he did was a cause of that death? These questions bring us to the main issue of Driver's paper. We have seen that not every voluntary action that causes a death renders the person who did the action criminally responsible. If we also determine that not every action that renders its agent criminally responsible for someone's death need be a cause of that death, then we will have shown that the object of the detectives' investigation into who is responsible for the death is wholly distinct from the object of the medical examiner's investigation into the cause of death. Accordingly, it should then be clear that the question of criminal responsibility is not even partly a question about causation (and conversely), though of course the answer to it is often based on causal connections to the death, and to determine its answer invariably requires examining the causal connections that link the death to events for which someone is responsible.

To see how a person could be criminally responsible for another's death despite doing nothing that is a cause of that death, let us consider another *Law & Order* episode. In this episode, the detectives investigate the death of a pizza deliveryman. Their investigation leads them to a group of youths who are the culprits. Like many such groups, this one contains ringleaders and followers. On the night of the murder, the youths found themselves short of cash and decided to rob someone. The idea of a robbery was the ringleaders', and the followers went along with the plan, though they did nothing materially to forward it. The plan was to order a pizza and ask that it be delivered to an address where the youths knew they could easily ambush the deliveryman and overpower him. Part of their plan was to throw a tarp over him so that he couldn't identify any of them, but it was understood that if he did catch a glimpse of any of them, he would have to be silenced. When the deliveryman arrived, a tarp was thrown over him but not before he eyeballed one of them. One of the ringleaders noticed this, or so he claimed. He then began beating the deliveryman brutally. Others joined in, though not all. One or two, who were among the followers, hung back. The beating was severe, causing the deliveryman to suffer multiple internal injuries, from which he died. The youths then relieved the dead man of his cash, divided it among themselves, and disposed of his body.

In this example, all of the youths share responsibility for the victim's death. This is so, even though the death may have resulted from the actions of only some. In particular, any one of the followers might have kept clear of the beating, and before it occurred his participation in the crime may have consisted in little more than tacit agreement and bodily presence. It may have consisted, for instance, in his being a lookout whose signal to the others that the deliveryman was approaching was preempted by a second lookout who spotted the deliveryman first. Such participation in the robbery would still be sufficient to make him responsible for its lethal consequence, despite its being caused by the actions of the others. That he acted jointly with those who caused the death in a criminal enterprise and that his so acting was blameworthy is sufficient for him to share in the responsibility for this consequence. Accordingly, the detectives, once they determine that the deliveryman's death occurred in the course of a robbery carried out by several people and at the hands of at least some of them, turn their attention from identifying the person or persons whose voluntary actions were a cause of the death to identifying who participated in the robbery. For they recognize that responsibility for the death attaches to every participant, regardless of the causal connection between his participation and the death, as long as that participation is blameworthy.

The principle they apply is that of complicity.[1] When one joins with others in a criminal enterprise, one becomes responsible for the harmful consequences of that enterprise regardless of whether one's own actions or the actions of one's accomplices cause those harms. The principle is open to interpretation, and in particular there is disagreement among philosophers and legal theorists over what constitutes joint action with others. Some think it consists in cooperative action that is done from an intention so to act that one shares with those with whom one cooperates (Kutz, 2000, pp. 66–112). Others believe that to act jointly with others requires forming with them a joint intention to act cooperatively (Gilbert, 1996, pp. 177–194 and 281–311). The difference between these two views may affect who counts as an accomplice, and if it does, then the scope of the principle of complicity is open to dispute. But the principle itself is not. And its soundness is sufficient to refute the thesis that one's being criminally responsible for an event entails that one's actions are a cause of that event.

Driver, I should note, does not distinguish cases in which responsibility for an event is shared from those in which it is not. She bases the defense of her view, which she expresses in the thesis (MC) that a person's being morally responsible for an event entails that an action he did is a cause of that event, largely on consideration of cases of individual responsibility. One might be tempted, then, to suppose that the entailment relation belief in which Driver defends is at least true of these cases. That is, one might be tempted to hold a restricted version of (MC)—call it (MC′)—that a person's being morally responsible for an event by virtue of an action that is not joint with others entails that his action is a cause of that event. But once one recognizes that (MC) is not a universal truth, it is hard to see why one should think that (MC′) is true. What could be the basis for so thinking? It can't be something about the concept of moral responsibility, since (MC) would then have to be universally true. After all, the concept doesn't change when one reformulates (MC) as (MC′). And for similar reasons, it can't be something about the very nature of being morally responsible for some event, as if being morally responsible for an event were a real relation like being someone's forebearer. Perhaps, the basis for affirming (MC′) is that it serves justice to hold people morally responsible for an event only when some action they do is a cause of that event. But no one questions whether the principle of complicity is consistent with justice, so why think, in cases of individual responsibility, justice requires that we hold people responsible for an event only if actions they do are a cause of that event?

Driver's defense of (MC) consists of rebutting objections to it and eliminating threats to its soundness that putative counterexamples from the philosophical literature pose. She does not offer a positive argument for it. She does not advance reasons that would supply a sufficient basis for affirming it. What she says by way of motivating its affirmation is that it "seems extremely intuitively plausible" (p. 423). This suggests that she thinks the thesis is close to being a self-evident truth or a piece of common sense that, as such, carries a strong presumption of truth. Cases of shared responsibility in which the principle of complicity applies show that it is neither. Perhaps, though, Driver would want to defend (MC′) as close to being a self-evident truth or as a piece of common sense that, as such, carries a strong presumption of truth. It is difficult, as I've just observed, to find a basis for (MC'), but of course if it were self-evident or a piece of common sense that as such carried a strong presumption of truth, it would not need one.

Driver identifies as the most troublesome type of case for (MC) that of individual responsibility in which a person's responsibility for another's being harmed is due to his having omitted doing something that, had he done it, would have prevented the harm from occurring. She thinks cases of this type, which I'll call "cases of omission," are the most troublesome for (MC) because they require conceiving of an omission as a cause, and an omission, because it consists essentially in something's not being done, would seem to have no causal power. Driver, however, does not think we are required to understand causes as active forces in the world. Such an understanding may fall out of some philosopher's metaphysical views, but ordinary thought and talk about causation does not require it. In this regard, she agrees with Hart and Honoré (1959), who observe that we commonly cite omissions as causes in our everyday explanations of events (pp. 35–38). Their stock example is the death of a plant in some garden that occurs because the gardener fails to water it. Hence, Driver clears (MC) from the threat it faces from cases of omission. As long as the attributions of moral responsibility in question are understood as the common attributions of everyday life, then there can be no objection to regarding omissions as causes.

Her point is well taken. Absences are regularly cited as causes of events, and an omission is a kind of absence. Thus when the medical examiner tells the detectives that the victim bled to death, she in effect says that the victim's vital organs failed as a result of the absence of blood necessary to their operation. And if the victim bled to death because he was a hemophiliac, then a cause of his death was the absence of the genes in virtue of which blood clots. Similarly, in an episode in which a baby died because its teenage mother found breast-feeding frustrating and ultimately failed either to nurse it properly or bottle-feed it, the medical examiner determined that the baby had starved to death. Hence, in this episode, the failure to feed the baby and the lack of nourishment could each be cited as causes of its death. And criminal responsibility for the baby's death would then be attributable to the mother on account of her having caused it, provided, of course, that her failure to feed her baby was blameworthy.

But not all cases of criminal responsibility for harm where responsibility for the harm is attributed on account of a blameworthy omission are like this. In some cases, the omission does not occur in the kind of context that supports citing an omission as a cause of an event, and consequently Driver's clearance of (MC) from the threat of cases of omission does not cover these cases. When we cite an omission as a cause of an event E, the omission represents a deviation from what normally goes on in situations like the one in which the omission occurs. The omission is seen as a cause of E because E too is a change from what is normal in that situation. Thus the gardener's omission, in Hart and Honoré's example, is a cause of the plant's death because the gardener normally waters the plant, and his watering it was the source of the nourishment by virtue of which it had continued to live. This context is necessary to picking out the gardener's omission as a cause, for it explains why the death of the plant is due to *his* not watering it. After all, indefinitely many other people didn't water it, the housekeeper, the next-door neighbor, the homeowner's 6-year-old child, Queen Elizabeth II, etc., yet in no case is their not watering the plant a cause of its death. For none of them normally watered it. The gardener's not watering the plant is a cause of its death, by contrast, because it is the change in the normal situation that explains the change in the plant's well-being (1959, p. 36). Some omissions, however, do not occur in contexts in which the action omitted is of a kind on which someone's or something's continued well-being has depended, yet we nonetheless blame the agent of the omission, on account of what he failed to do, for harm that another has suffered. We need, then, to consider whether omissions of this sort create trouble for (MC) and, particularly, (MC′). I think they do.

Let me, in drawing out why I think so, again use examples from episodes of *Law & Order*. These are examples of one person's killing another in a violent fit brought on by psychotic delusions. In one episode, the killer knew of his illness, having been treated for it off and on since college. It became manifest in college when, under the delusion that his then girl-friend was a biblical siren from whom he had to protect himself, he viciously attacked her. Subsequently, he had kept his illness in check by taking antipsychotic drugs. But periodically, because of the drugs' side effects, he would stop taking them, whereupon his delusional behavior would return and he would eventually have to be institutionalized. During a period when he had stopped taking the drugs, he again became delu-sional and attacked several store clerks with a sword, killing three and seri-ously injuring a fourth. In the other episode the killer was unaware of the nature of his illness, having never been properly treated for it. Shortly after being released from county jail, where he had served a short sentence for a minor offense, he bashed in the head of a young woman with a paving stone, thus killing her. The killing was completely random.

The first episode illustrates responsibility for someone's death owing to a blameworthy omission that was a cause of the death. This should be clear. As long as the killer took the antipsychotic drugs prescribed for his illness, he could keep his illness in check. His not taking those drugs is thus a cause of his becoming violent and of the effects of that violence. And because he knew that he became prone to violence when he stopped taking the drugs, his failure to take them is blameworthy. So attributing criminal responsibility to him for the deaths of the three people he killed is warranted. Being responsible for the omission, he is responsible for its reasonably foreseeable consequences.

The second episode is more complicated. The killer's psychosis, given his history, excuses him from responsibility for the death of the woman he killed. The question, however, is whether someone else is responsible, particularly, the medical personnel at the county jail who signed off on releasing him into the general population. The district attorney handling the case looked into the matter and discovered that, though one of the physicians assigned to care for the jail's inmates saw the man, the examination he gave him was cursory and the treatment inadequate.[2] The physician, it turned out, worked for a private HMO with which the county had recently contracted for delivery of medical services to the jail's inmates. In the interest of keeping costs down, the HMO's chief executive had instructed the physicians assigned to the jail to provide the inmates with only the most minimal care and to avoid costly tests and treatment regimes. The case for holding the HMO and its chief executive, along with the physician, responsible for the woman's death was then clinched when the district attorney learned from the physician that the executive had threatened him with termination if he did not follow these instructions.

Like the first episode, this one too illustrates responsibility for someone's death owing to a blameworthy omission. But unlike the first episode, the omission's being a cause of the death is not a factor in determining responsibility. For responsibility for the death attaches to the physician and the HMO he works for even though one cannot say that their omitting properly to examine and treat the killer was a cause of the death. What one can say is that their omission put people at substantial risk of being fatally attacked by a psychotic offender and this risk was realized. Since the omission was blameworthy—since, in the statutory language the district attorney likes to use, it displayed depraved indifference to human life, these factors are enough to warrant attributing responsibility to those responsible for the omission.

The reason one cannot say that their omission is a cause of the death is that one cannot say that the killer would not have bashed the woman's head with a paving stone if the physician had properly examined and treated him for his illness. Unlike Hart and Honoré's example, proper treatment of mentally ill inmates at a county jail does not normally lead to the inmates' continuing that treatment once they are released from jail. Some will; others won't. Consequently, one cannot say that the killer's bashing the woman's head with a paving stone deviates from what normally would happen if he had been properly treated for his illness.

Still, one might think that even though it is distinctly possible that the death did not result from the failure to provide the offender with proper treatment, we must nonetheless be assuming that it did if we hold the physician and the HMO he works for responsible for it. For surely we recognize that they would not be responsible for the death if additional evidence established that their omission could not have been among its causes.[3] But the reason we would not attribute to them responsibility for the death, should there be such evidence, is that the evidence would also show that the death would have occurred despite their providing the offender with proper treatment, which is to say that the treatment, had they provided it, would not have helped to prevent the death. What is important is that the risk to which people were exposed when the offender was released into the general population would not, in this case, have been due to their failure to provide him with proper treatment. That their omission would also not have been a cause of the death is therefore not a factor in the determination of responsibility.

Finally, one might wonder whether the kind of research in social psychology that Driver discusses could yield results that supported taking the omission of the physician and the HMO he worked for to be a cause of the woman's death. If it did, then there would be reason to question my argument for holding that their responsibility for the death is independent of their omission's being among its causes, that the latter is not a factor in determining the former. But the research, at least as it is described in Driver's paper, could not yield such results. A comment of Hart and Honoré (1959) about the different things people could mean when they say that someone caused harm shows why:

Much modern thought on causation in the law rests on the contention that the statement that someone has caused harm either means no more than that the harm would not have happened without ('but for') his action or where (as in normal legal usage and in all ordinary speech) it apparently means more than this, it is a disguised way of asserting the 'normative judgment' that he is responsible in the first sense, i.e., that it is proper or just to blame or punish him or make him pay. On this view, to say that a person caused harm is not really, though ostensibly it is, to give a *ground* or *reason* for holding him responsible in [this] sense; for we are only in a position to say that he has caused harm when we have decided that he is responsible. (pp. 61–62, italics in the original)

If the subjects in the research Driver discusses understood 'cause' as having the second of the two meanings Hart and Honoré distinguish (i.e., as affording a disguised way of attributing responsibility of the kind that justifies blame, punishment, or compensation), then obviously one cannot use the results of the research to establish that the omission was a cause of the death. Indeed, unless the researchers designed their studies so that they could be confident that the subjects, when asked to identify the cause of an event, understood 'cause' to express a concept independent of that of moral responsibility, unless they could be confident that the subjects understood the question as like the one the medical examiner investigates and not like the one the detectives investigate, one cannot use their studies' results to settle the dispute over the truth of (MC').

Notes

1. See Fletcher (1978, pp. 634–640) and Kutz (2000, pp. 115–124). This principle, it is important to note, is distinct from another principle, the principle of vicarious responsibility, by which one member of a group may be responsible for the action of another and so of its consequences. Vicarious responsibility attaches when one member or several members collectively are agents or representatives of another so that the latter is responsible for the acts of the former. Whether harm for which one is vicariously responsible must result from actions one did that are among its causes is a separate matter from the question as it is applied to shared responsibility among partners in crime, and my argument concerns the latter only. For the distinction between shared and vicarious responsibility see Fletcher (1978, pp. 647–649).

2. Specifically, to suppress the inmate's tendencies to violence, the nurses, following the physician's instructions, kept the inmate sedated during his time in jail.

3. Suppose, for instance, it emerged on further investigation that the offender, after being released from jail, sought and received treatment for his illness from a local clinic, that the clinic physician, having properly diagnosed the illness, prescribed the antipsychotic drugs that the offender needed to keep his illness in check, but that after taking these drugs and suffering their side effects, he stopped taking them. In this case, the physician and his HMO, while still responsible for their failure to provide the offender with proper treatment, would not be responsible for the woman's death.

Kinds of Norms and Legal Causation: Reply to
Knobe and Fraser and Deigh

Julia Driver

Knobe and Fraser

I would like to thank Joshua Knobe and Ben Fraser for their comments, which have made me clarify the position that I advocate in my paper. They have done an excellent job of responding to me in kind. They meet the challenge empirically, and I certainly do not find fault with their results. However, what I was suggesting in my paper is not incompatible with what they have found.

Knobe and Fraser are responding to one interpretation of the abnormality hypothesis—that it is *atypicality*, in the statistical sense of what is unusual, that affects our attributions of causation. They then, very nicely, construct an experiment to test this claim. In the case of Professor Smith and the administrative assistant, the actions in question are both typical in the statistical sense. As with the Lauren and Jane case, they again obtained the result that moral judgments still ". . . play a direct role in the process by which causal judgments are generated" (p. 443).

This is not incompatible with my suggestion, because I argued that we are more likely to make attributions of causation to events that do not conform to norms. Norms can be understood in a variety of ways—as statistical, where what is abnormal is what is unusual, or as deviating from some idealization, which need not be statistical at all. Some norms then, are statistical, and some are evaluative. Moral judgments—such as the judgment in Knobe and Fraser's paper that Jane violated an obligation—are judgments of just such a deviation. This means that there is a more general hypothesis that explains the data in terms of these sorts of norm deviations.

Knobe and Fraser also argue that conversational pragmatics alone cannot account for the tendency to allow moral judgments to influence causal attributions. I agree with them that what it would be appropriate to say, in conversation with another, can be different from what it is reasonable or appropriate to believe privately. The case of Claire and Daniel, however, may simply display warring pragmatic concerns. There is conversational pragmatics, which influences how we pick out relevant details to mention in our conversational utterances. Then there are other pragmatic factors that influence how we pick out details as relevant, even when we aren't going to talk about them or express them in any way to others. For example, in one standard example that I discussed in the paper, a fire sheriff might not believe that the presence of oxygen in the atmosphere is causally relevant to the fire's occurring, regardless of whether or not he is going to talk about it to others or mention it in conversation. This is because we tend to factor out background conditions in thought as well as conversation.

I am in agreement with Knobe and Fraser's findings. Moral judgments affect causal attributions. However, this is consistent with the more general claim that we are sensitive to norm deviations in making causal attributions.

Deigh

I would also like to thank John Deigh for his very interesting and helpful comments. Deigh attacks (MC) using a different strategy than the ones I looked at in my paper. As I noted, there may be other ways to argue that (MC) is flawed. Deigh's strategy is to hold that it cannot adequately account for *criminal* responsibility, particularly in cases where some agents are complicit with others in a collective enterprise that leads to harmful consequences.

(MC) is not claiming that all cases of causal responsibility for an event make the agent morally responsible. Deigh mentions one such case— clearly the postman who unknowingly delivers a bomb is not morally responsible for the death caused by the bomb even though he is part of the causal chain leading up to the death. (MC) merely states that if he is morally responsible, he must have been a cause of the event. Thus, to question (MC), Deigh needs to establish that someone can be criminally responsible for something that he did not cause. He must also show that moral responsibility is relevantly like criminal responsibility. I share Deigh's misgivings about (MC) when it is understood in terms of criminal responsibility. Nevertheless, I also believe that someone who would like to maintain (MC) with respect to moral responsibility has resources to mount a compelling defense.

The case of complicity that Deigh discusses is the case of a pizza deliveryman who is killed in an ambush by some thieves. Only some of the thieves actually beat him to death. Others are compliant, however, and watch, though they do not actually beat him. Deigh's claim is that all of the thieves are morally and criminally responsible for the death of the deliveryman, even though only some of them caused it.

This case is not a counterexample to (MC). For example, allowing for negative causation, if the complicit thieves could have stopped the beating, or at least mitigated its severity or lowered the probability of its occurrence, and did not, then they can be deemed causally responsible. In having planned the robbery with the others, a plan that included the possibility of killing the deliveryman, they are also causally responsible. They may not be the primary cause, but (MC) is not committed to that.

What of members of a collective who do not know that some of its members are planning a murder? Suppose that some of those who knowingly participated in the robbery had no clue that a murder was even being contemplated and were not close enough to the murder to do anything to affect the outcome? This sort of case, I believe, highlights one of the crucial differences between legal responsibility and moral responsibility. Legally, they are responsible for the death in that we have compelling reasons to hold them responsible since we cannot distinguish those who didn't know what was going to happen from those who did. But morally, if someone in the collective had no idea of what was happening, what other parts of the collective were doing, and had no reason to know either, then he is not morally responsible.

Lastly, Deigh discusses how Hart and Honoré explicitly note that often when people make attributions of causation they are really just "asserting the 'normative judgment' that . . . it is proper or just to blame or punish him . . ." (p. 457; Deigh quoting Hart and Honoré, 1959, pp. 61–62). As I hope my paper and the above discussion have made clear, I am in complete agreement with this.

References

Abernathy, C. M., & Hamm, R. M. (1995). *Surgical intuition.* Philadelphia: Hanley & Belfus.

Abu-Lughod, L. (1986). *Veiled sentiments: Honor and poetry in a Bedouin society.* Berkeley: University of California Press.

Alicke, M. D. (1992). Culpable causation. *Journal of Personality and Social Psychology, 63,* 368–378.

Alicke, M. D. (2000). Culpable control and the psychology of blame. *Psychological Bulletin, 126,* 556–574.

Alicke, M. D., Davis, T. L., & Pezzo, M. V. (1994). A posteriori adjustment of a priori decision criteria. *Social Cognition, 12,* 281–308.

Allen, L. A., Woolfolk, R. L., Lehrer, P. M., Gara, M. A., & Escobar, J. I. (2001). Cognitive behavior therapy for somatization disorder: A preliminary investigation. *Journal of Behavior Therapy and Experimental Psychiatry, 32,* 53–62.

Anderson, S. R., & Lightfoot, D. (2000). The human language faculty as an organ. *Annual Review of Physiology, 62,* 697–722.

Anderson, S. W., Bechara, A., Damasio, H., Tranel, D., & Damasio, A. R. (1999). Impairment of social and moral behavior related to early damage in human prefrontal cortex. *Nature Neuroscience, 2,* 1032–1037.

Anscombe, G. E. M. (1958). Modern moral philosophy. *Philosophy, 33,* 1–19.

Appiah, K. A. (2005). *The ethics of identity.* Princeton, NJ: Princeton University Press.

Ariew, A. (1996). Innateness and canalization. *Philosophy of Science, 63*(Supp.), S19–S27.

Ariew, A. (1999). Innateness is canalization: In defense of a developmental account of innateness. In V. Hardcastle (Ed.), *Where biology meets psychology: Philosophical essays* (pp. 117–139). Cambridge: MIT Press.

Armstrong, D. (1999). The open door. In H. Sankey (Ed.), *Causation and laws of nature* (pp. 175–185). Dordrechts, The Netherlands: Kluwer Academic Publishers.

Armstrong, K., Schwartz, J. S., Fitzgerald, G., Putt, M., & Ubel, P. A. (2002). Effect of framing as gain versus loss on understanding and hypothetical treatment choices: Survival and mortality curves. *Medical Decision Making, 22*(1), 76–83.

Asch, S. E. (1956). Studies of independence and conformity: A minority of one against a unanimous majority. *Psychological Monographs, 70,* 1–70.

Audi, R. (2004). *The good in the right: A theory of intuition and intrinsic value.* Princeton, NJ: Princeton University Press.

Ayer, A. J. (1952). *Language, truth and logic.* New York: Dover Publications.

Baier, A. (1985). *Postures of the mind: Essays on mind and morals.* Minneapolis: University of Minnesota Press.

Baier, K. (1958). *The moral point of view.* Ithaca, NY: Cornell University Press.

Bargh, J. A. (1994). The four horsemen of automaticity: Awareness, efficiency, intention, and control in social cognition. In J. R. S. Wyer & T. K. Srull (Eds.), *Handbook of social cognition* (2nd ed., pp. 1–40). Hillsdale, NJ: Erlbaum.

Bargh, J. A., & Chartrand, T. L. (1999). The unbearable automaticity of being. *American Psychologist, 54,* 462–479.

Bargh, J. A., & Ferguson, M. J. (2000). Beyond behaviorism: On the automaticity of higher mental processes. *Psychological Bulletin, 126,* 925–945.

Baron, J. (1994) Nonconsequentialist decisions. *Behavioral and Brain Sciences, 17,* 1–10.

Baron, J. (1998). *Judgment misguided: Intuition and error in public decision making.* New York: Oxford University Press.

Baron, J., & Siepmann, M. (2000). Using Web questionnaires for judgment and decision making research. In M. H. Birnbaum (Ed.), *Psychological experiments on the Internet* (pp. 235–265). New York: Academic Press.

Batson, C. (1991). *The altruism question.* Hillsdale, NJ: Erlbaum.

Baumeister, R. F., & Leary, M. R. (1995). The need to belong: Desire for interpersonal attachments as a fundamental human motivation. *Psychological Bulletin, 117,* 497–529.

Baumol, W. J. (2004). On rational satisficing. In M. Augier & J. G. March (Eds.), *Models of a man: Essays in the memory of Herbert A. Simon* (pp. 57–66). Cambridge: MIT Press.

Beauchamp, T. L., & Childress, J. F. (1994). *Principles of biomedical ethics* (4th ed.). New York: Oxford University Press.

Bechara, A., Damasio, H., Tranel, D., & Damasio, A. R. (1997). Deciding advantageously before knowing the advantageous strategy. *Science, 275,* 1293–1295.

Beebee, H. (2004). Causing and nothingness. In J. Collins, E. J. Hall, & L. A. Paul (Eds.), *Causation and counterfactuals* (pp. 291–308). Cambridge, Mass.: MIT Press.

Bellah, R., Madsen, R., Sullivan, W. M., Swidler, A., & Tipton, S. (1985). *Habits of the heart.* New York: Harper & Row.

Bentham, J. (1907). *An introduction to the principles of morals and legislation.* Oxford: Clarendon Press. (Original work published 1789)

Bishop, M. A. (2000). In praise of epistemic irresponsibility: How lazy and ignorant can you be? *Synthese, 122,* 179–208.

Bjorklund, F., & Haidt, J. (In preparation). *Vivid violations are morally worse.* Unpublished manuscript, University of Lund.

Blackburn, S. (1984). *Spreading the word: Groundings in the philosophy of language.* Oxford: Oxford University Press.

Blackburn, S. (1993). *Essays in quasi-realism.* Oxford: Oxford University Press.

Blackburn, S. (1998). *Ruling passions: A theory of practical reason.* Oxford: Oxford University Press.

Blair, R. J. R. (1993). *The development of morality.* Unpublished doctoral dissertation, University of London.

Blair, R. J. R. (1995). A cognitive developmental approach to morality: Investigating the psychopath. *Cognition, 57,* 1–29.

Blair, R. J. R. (1997). Moral reasoning and the child with psychopathic tendencies. *Personality & Individual Differences, 26,* 731–739.

Blair, R. J. R. (1999). Psychophysiological responsiveness to the distress of others in children with autism. *Personality & Individual Differences, 26,* 477–485.

Blair, R. J. R., & Cipolotti, L. (2000). Impaired social response reversal: A case of "acquired sociopathy." *Brain, 123,* 1122–1141.

Blair, R. J. R., Marsh, A. A., Finger, E., Blair, K. S., & Luo, Q. (Submitted). *Neurocognitive systems involved in morality.*

Blair, R. J. R., Mitchell, D. G. V., Richell, R. A., Kelly, S., Leonard, A., Newman, C., & Scott, S. K. (2002). Turning a deaf ear to fear: Impaired recognition of vocal affect in psychopathic individuals. *Journal of Abnormal Psychology, 111,* 682–686.

Blair, R., Jones, L., Clark, F., Smith, M., & Jones, L. N. (1997). The psychopathic individual: A lack of responsiveness to distress cues? *Psychophysiology, 34,* 192–198.

Blasi, A. (1980). Bridging moral cognition and moral action: A critical review of the literature. *Psychological Bulletin, 88,* 1–45.

Block, N. (1986). Advertisement for a semantics for psychology. In P. A. French, T. E. Uehling, & H. K. Wettstein (Eds.), *Midwest studies in philosophy* (Vol. 10, pp. 615–678). Minneapolis: University of Minnesota Press.

Bloom, P. (2004). *Descartes' baby.* New York: Basic Books.

Bloomfield, P. (2001). *Moral reality.* New York: Oxford University Press.

Blum, L. A. (1994). *Moral perception and particularity.* Cambridge: Cambridge University Press.

Boorse, C., & Sorensen, R. (1988). Ducking harm. *Journal of Philosophy, 85*(3), 115–134.

Bouchard, T. J. J. (2004). Genetic influence on human psychological traits: A survey. *Current Directions in Psychological Science, 13,* 148–151.

Boyd, R. (1983). On the current status of scientific realism. In R. Boyd, P. Gasper, & J. D. Trout (Eds.), *The philosophy of science* (pp. 195–222). Cambridge: MIT Press.

Boyd, R. (1988). How to be a moral realist. In G. Sayre-McCord (Ed.), *Essays in moral realism* (pp. 181–228). Ithaca and London: Cornell University Press.

Boyd, R., & Richerson, P. J. (2005). *The origin and evolution of cultures.* New York: Oxford University Press.

Boyer, P. (2001). *Religion explained: The evolutionary origins of religious thought.* New York: Basic Books.

Brandt, R. B. (1950). The emotive theory of ethics. *Philosophical Review, 59,* 305–318.

Brandt, R. B. (1954). *Hopi ethics: A theoretical analysis.* Chicago: University of Chicago Press.

Brandt, R. B. (1959). *Ethical theory: The problems of normative and critical ethics.* Englewood Cliffs, NJ: Prentice-Hall.

Brandt, R. B. (1979). *A theory of the good and the right.* New York: Oxford University Press.

Bransford, J. D., Brown, A. L., & Cocking, R. R. (Eds.). (1999). *How people learn: Brain, mind, experience, and school.* Washington, DC: National Academy Press.

Brighton, H. (2006). Robust inference with simple cognitive models. In C. Lebiere & B. Wray (Eds.), Between a rock and a hard place: Cognitive science meets AI-hard problems. Papers from the AAAI Spring Symposium. (AAAI Tech. Rep. No. 55-06-03, pp. 17–22.) Menlo Park, CA: AAAI Press.

Brink, D. (1984). Moral realism and the skeptical arguments from disagreement and queerness. *Australasian Journal of Philosophy, 62*, 111–125.

Brink, D. (1989). *Moral realism and the foundations of ethics.* Cambridge: Cambridge University Press.

Brody, B. (1979). Intuitions and objective moral knowledge. *The Monist, 62*, 446–456.

Brown, D. E. (1991). *Human universals.* Philadelphia: Temple University Press.

Browning, C. R. (1993). *Ordinary men: Reserve Police Battalion 101 and the final solution in Poland.* New York: Harper.

Burstyn, L. (1995). Female circumcision comes to America. *The Atlantic Monthly, 275-4*, 28–35.

Byrom, T. (Ed.). (1993). *Dhammapada: The sayings of the Buddha.* Boston: Shambhala.

Cacioppo, J. T., & Petty, R. E. (1982). The need for cognition. *Journal of Personality and Social Psychology, 42*, 116–131.

Cahill, L., & McGaugh, J. L. (1998). Mechanisms of emotional arousal and lasting declarative memory. *Trends in Neuroscience, 21*, 294–299.

Camerer, C. (2003). *Behavioral game theory: Experiments in strategic interaction.* Hillsdale, NJ: Erlbaum.

Camille, N., Coricelli, G., Sallet, J., Pradat-Diehl, P., Duhamel, J., & Sirigu, A. (2004). The involvement of orbitofrontal cortex in the experience of regret. *Science, 303*, 1167–1170.

Capote, T. (1994). *In cold blood.* New York: Vintage.

Carroll, L. (1946). *Through the looking glass.* Kingsport, TN: Grosset & Dunlap.

Chaiken, S., & Trope, Y. (Eds.). (1999). *Dual process theories in social psychology.* New York: Guilford Press.

Chan, W.-T. (1963). *A source book in Chinese philosophy.* Princeton, NJ: Princeton University Press.

Chartrand, T. L., & Bargh, J. A. (1999). The chameleon effect: The perception–behavior link and social interaction. *Journal of Personality and Social Psychology, 76*, 893–910.

Chater, N., Oaksford, M., Nakisa, R., & Redington, M. (2003). Fast, frugal and rational: How rational norms explain behavior. *Organizational Behavior & Human Decision Processes, 90*, 63–86.

Chomsky, N. (1986). *Knowledge of language: Its nature, origin, and use.* New York: Praeger.

Chomsky, N. (1988). *Language and problems of knowledge*. Cambridge: MIT Press.

Chomsky, N. (1995). *The minimalist program*. Cambridge: MIT Press.

Chomsky, N. (2000). *On nature and language*. New York: Cambridge University Press.

Churchland, P. M. (1998). Toward a cognitive neurobiology of the moral virtues. *Topoi, 17*, 83–96.

Colby, A., & Damon, W. (1991). *Some do care*. New York: Free Press.

Colby, A., & Kohlberg, L. (1987). *The measurement of moral judgement*. New York: Cambridge University Press.

Colman, A., & Bacharach, M. (1997). Payoff dominance and the Stackelberg heuristic. *Theory and Decision, 43*, 1–19.

Cosmides, L., & Tooby, J. (1994). Origins of domain specificity: The evolution of functional organization. In L. A. Hirschfeld & S. A. Gelman (Eds.), *Mapping the mind: Domain specificity in cognition and culture* (pp. 85–116). Cambridge: Cambridge University Press.

Cosmides, L., & Tooby, J. (2000). Evolutionary psychology and the emotions. In M. Lewis & J. Haviland (Eds.), *The handbook of emotions* (2nd ed., pp. 91–116). New York: Guilford Press.

Cosmides, L., & Tooby, J. (2004). *Knowing thyself: The evolutionary psychology of moral reasoning and moral sentiments*. Unpublished manuscript.

Cushman, F., Young, L., & Hauser, M. D. (2006). The role of conscious reasoning and intuition in moral judgments: Testing three principles of harm. *Psychological Science, 17*, 1082–1089.

Czerlinski, J., Gigerenzer, G., & Goldstein, D. G. (1999). How good are simple heuristics? In G. Gigerenzer, P. M. Todd, & the ABC Research Group, *Simple heuristics that make us smart* (pp. 97–118). New York: Oxford University Press.

D'Arms, J. (2005). Two arguments for sentimentalism. *Philosophical Issues, 15*, 1–21.

D'Arms, J., & Jacobson, D. (1994). Expressivism, morality, and the emotions. *Ethics, 104*, 739–763.

D'Arms, J., & Jacobson, D. (2000a). The moralistic fallacy: On the "appropriateness" of emotions. *Philosophy and Phenomenological Research, 61*, 65–90.

D'Arms, J., & Jacobson, D. (2000b). Sentiment and value. *Ethics, 110*, 722–748.

D'Arms, J., & Jacobson, D. (2003). The significance of recalcitrant emotion (or, anti-quasijudgmentalism). In A. Hatzimoysis (Ed.), *Philosophy and the emotions* (pp. 127–146). Cambridge: Cambridge University Press.

D'Arms, J., & Jacobson, D. (2006a). Anthropocentric constraints on human value. In R. Shafer-Landau (Ed.), *Oxford studies in metaethics* (Vol. 1, pp. 99–126). New York: Oxford University Press.

D'Arms, J., & Jacobson, D. (2006b). Sensibility theory and projectivism. In D. Copp (Ed.), *The Oxford handbook of moral theory* (pp. 186–218). Oxford: Oxford University Press.

Damasio, A. (1994). *Descartes' error: Emotion, reason, and the human brain*. New York: Putnam/Boston: Norton.

Damasio, A. (2000). *The feeling of what happens*. New York: Basic Books.

Damasio, A., Tranel, D., & Damasio, H. (1990). Individuals with sociopathic behavior caused by frontal damage fail to respond autonomically to social stimuli. *Behavioral Brain Research, 41*, 81–94.

Daniels, N. (1979). Wide reflective equilibrium and theory acceptance in ethics. *The Journal of Philosophy, 76*, 256–282.

Daniels, N. (2001). Justice, health, and healthcare. *American Journal of Bioethics, 1*, 2–16.

Darley, J. M., & Berscheid, E. (1967). Increased liking as a result of anticipation of personal contact. *Human Relations, 20*, 29–40.

Darley, J., & Batson, C. D. (1973). From Jerusalem to Jericho: A study of situational and dispositional variables in helping behavior. *Journal of Personality and Social Psychology, 27*, 100–108.

Darwall, S. (1995). *The British moralists and the internal "ought": 1640–1740*. Cambridge: Cambridge University Press.

Darwall, S. (1998). *Philosophical ethics*. Boulder, CO: Westview Press.

Darwall, S., Gibbard, A., & Railton, P. (1992). Toward *fin de siècle* ethics: Some trends. *Philosophical Review, 101*, 115–189. Reprinted in S. Darwall, P. Railton, & A. Gibbard (Eds.), *Moral discourse and practice: Some philosophical approaches* (1997, pp. 3–50). New York: Oxford University Press.

Daston, L. (1988). *Classical probability in the Enlightenment*. Princeton, NJ: Princeton University Press.

Davidson, P., Turiel, E., & Black, A. (1983). The effect of stimulus familiarity on the use of criteria and justifications in children's social reasoning. *British Journal of Developmental Psychology, 1*, 46–65.

Dawes, R. M. (1979). The robust beauty of improper linear models in decision making. *American Psychologist, 34*, 571–582.

Dawkins, R. (1989). *The selfish gene* (2nd ed.). Oxford: Oxford University Press.

De Waal, F. (1996). *Good natured: The origins of right and wrong in humans and other animals*. Cambridge: Harvard University Press.

Dehaene, S. (1997). *The number sense*. Oxford: Oxford University Press.

DeMiguel, V., Garlappi, L., & Uppal, R. (2006). *1/N*. EFA 2006 Zurich Meetings. Available at SSRN: http://ssrn.com/abstract=911512.

Dhami, M. K. (2001). *Bailing and jailing the fast and frugal way: An application of social judgement theory and simple heuristics to English magistrates' remand decisions*. Unpublished doctoral thesis, City University, London.

Dhami, M. K. (2003). Psychological models of professional decision-making. *Psychological Science, 14*, 175–180.

Dhami, M. K., & Ayton, P. (2001). Bailing and jailing the fast and frugal way. *Journal of Behavioral Decision Making, 14*, 141–168.

Doggett, T. (n.d.). *The arguments from queerness*. Unpublished manuscript.

Doris, J. M. (2002). *Lack of character: Personality and moral behavior*. New York: Cambridge University Press.

Doris, J. M. (2005). Replies: Evidence and sensibility. *Philosophy and Phenomenological Research, 71*, 656–677.

Doris, J., & Stich, S. (2005). As a matter of fact: Empirical perspectives on ethics. In F. Jackson & M. Smith (Eds.), *The Oxford handbook of contemporary analytic philosophy*. Oxford: Oxford University Press.

Double, R. (1991). *The non-reality of free will*. New York: Oxford University Press.

Downie, R. S. (1991). Moral philosophy. In J. Eatwell, M. Milgate, & P. Newman (Eds.), *The new Palgrave: A dictionary of economics*. (Vol. 3, pp. 551–556). London: Macmillan.

Dreier, J. (1990). Internalism and speaker relativism. *Ethics, 101*, 6–26.

Dreier, J. (1999). Transforming expressivism. *Noûs, 33*, 558–572.

Dretske, F. (1981). *Knowledge and the flow of information*. Cambridge: MIT Press.

Dreyfus, H. L. (2005). *Six stages of skill acquisition: Novice to mastery*. Conference on Philosophical Anthropology: Reviewed and Renewed, University of Notre Dame.

Dreyfus, H. L., & Dreyfus, S. E. (1990). What is moral maturity? A phenomenological account of the development of ethical expertise. In D. Rasmussen (Ed.), *Universalism vs. communitarianism* (pp. 237–266). Cambridge: MIT Press.

Driver, J. (2001). *Uneasy virtue*. New York: Cambridge University Press.

Druckman, J. N. (2001). Evaluating framing effects. *Journal of Economic Psychology, 22*(1), 91–101.

Dunbar, R. (1996). *Grooming, gossip, and the evolution of language*. Cambridge: Harvard University Press.

Dunker, K. (1939). Ethical relativity (an enquiry into the psychology of ethics). *Mind, 48*, 39–53.

Dunn, J., & Munn, P. (1987). Development of justification in disputes with mother and sibling. *Developmental Psychology, 23*, 791–798.

Dworkin, R. (1978). *Taking rights seriously*. Cambridge: Harvard University Press.

Dwyer, S. (1999). Moral competence. In K. Murasugi & R. Stainton (Eds.), *Philosophy and linguistics* (pp. 169–190). Boulder, CO: Westview Press.

Dwyer, S. (2004). *How good is the linguistic analogy?* Retrieved February 25, 2004, from www.umbc.edu/philosophy/dwyer

Eklund, M. (2004). Personal identity, concerns, and indeterminacy. *The Monist, 87*, 489–511.

Ekman, P. (1994). All emotions are basic. In P. Ekman & R. Davidson (Eds.), *The nature of emotion* (pp. 15–19). New York: Oxford University Press.

Elias, N. (2000). *The civilizing process* (E. Jephcott, Trans.). Malden, MA: Blackwell. (Original work published 1939)

Ellman, J. L. (1993). Learning and development in neural networks: The importance of starting small. *Cognition, 48*, 71–99.

Ellsworth, P. C. (1994). Sense, culture, and sensibility. In S. Kitayama & H. Markus (Eds.), *Emotion and culture: Empirical studies in mutual influence* (pp. 23–50). Washington, DC: American Psychological Association.

Erasmus, D. (1985). *On good manners for boys* (B. McGregor, Trans.). In J. Sowards (Ed.), *Collected works of Erasmus* (Vol. 25). Toronto, Ontario, Canada: University of Toronto Press. (Original work published 1530)

Ewing, A. C. (1953). *Ethics*. New York: Macmillan.

Fagley, N. S., & Miller, P. M. (1990). The effect of framing on choice: Interactions with risk-taking propensity, cognitive style, and sex. *Personality and Social Psychology Bulletin, 16*, 496–510.

Falk, W. (1953). Goading and guiding. *Mind, 53*, 145–171.

Feinberg, J. (1970). Causing voluntary actions. In his *Doing and deserving: Essays in the theory of responsibility* (pp. 152–186). Princeton, NJ: Princeton University Press.

Feynman, R. P. (1985). *QED: The strange theory of light and matter*. Princeton, NJ: Princeton University Press.

Fine, A. (1984). The natural ontological attitude. In R. Boyd, P. Gasper, & J. D. Trout (Eds.), *The philosophy of science* (pp. 261–278). Cambridge: MIT Press.

Fischer, J. E., Steiner, F., Zucol, F., Berger, C., Martignon, L., Bossart, W., et al. (2002). Use of simple heuristics to target macrolide prescription in children with community-acquired pneumonia. *Archives of Pediatrics and Adolescent Medicine, 156,* 1005–1008.

Fischer, J. M., & Ravizza, M. (1992). *Ethics: Problems and principles.* New York: Holt, Rinehart & Winston.

Fischer, J. M., & Ravizza, M. (1998). *Responsibility and control: A theory of moral responsibility.* New York: Cambridge University Press.

Fiske, A. P. (1991). *Structures of social life.* New York: Free Press.

Fiske, A. P. (1992). Four elementary forms of sociality: Framework for a unified theory of social relations. *Psychological Review, 99,* 689–723.

Fiske, S. T. (2004). *Social beings: A core motives approach to social psychology.* New York: Wiley.

Fitch, W. T., Hauser, M. D., & Chomsky, N. (2005). The evolution of the language faculty: Clarifications and implications. *Cognition, 97,* 179–210.

Flanagan, O. (1991). *Varieties of moral personality: Ethics and psychological realism.* Cambridge: Harvard University Press.

Fletcher, G. (1978). *Rethinking criminal law.* Boston: Little, Brown.

Fodor, J. (1981). Introduction: Some notes on what linguistics is about. In N. Block (Ed.), *Readings in the philosophy of psychology* (Vol. 2, pp. 197–207). Cambridge: Harvard University Press.

Fodor, J. (1983). *Modularity of mind.* Cambridge: MIT Press.

Fodor, J. (1990). *A theory of content and other essays.* Cambridge: MIT Press.

Foot, P. (1967). The problem of abortion and the doctrine of double effect. *Oxford Review, 5,* 5–15.

Foot, P. (1984). Killing and letting die. In J. Garfield & P. Hennessey (Eds.), *Abortion: Moral and legal perspectives* (pp. 177–183). Amherst: University of Massachusetts Press.

Frank, R. (1988). *Passions within reason: The strategic role of the emotions.* New York: Norton.

Frankfurt, H. (1993). What we are morally responsible for. In J. M. Fischer & M. Ravizza (Eds.), *Perspectives on moral responsibility* (pp. 286–294). Ithaca, NY: Cornell University Press.

Franklin, B. (1987). *Writings*. New York: The Library of America. (Original letter written September 19, 1772)

Freud, S. (1976). *The interpretation of dreams*. New York: Norton. (Original work published 1900)

Frisch, D. (1993). Reasons for framing effects. *Organizational Behavior & Human Decision Processes, 54*, 399–429.

Frith, U. (1989). *Autism: Explaining the enigma*. Oxford: Blackwell.

Frohlich, N., & Oppenheimer, J. A. (1993). *Choosing justice: An experimental approach to ethical theory*. Berkeley: University of California Press.

Gallese, V., Keysers, C., & Rizzolatti, G. (2004). A unifying view of the basis of social cognition. *Trends in Cognitive Sciences, 8*, 396–403.

Galotti, K. M. (1989). Approaches to studying formal and everyday reasoning. *Psychological Bulletin, 105*, 331–351.

Garcia, J., & Koelling, R. (1966). Relation of cue to consequence in avoidance learning. *Psychonomic Science, 4*, 123–124.

Gazzaniga, M. S. (1985). *The social brain: Discovering the networks of the mind*. New York: Basic Books.

Geach, P. (1965). Assertion. *The Philosophical Review, 74*, 449–465.

Gert, B. (1988). *Morality: A new justification of the moral rules*. New York: Oxford University Press.

Gert, B. (1998). *Morality: Its nature and justification*. New York: Oxford University Press.

Gert, B. (2004). *Common morality*. New York: Oxford University Press.

Gibbard, A. (1990). *Wise choices, apt feelings: A theory of normative judgment*. Cambridge: Harvard University Press.

Gibson, J. (1979). *The ecological approach to perception*. Hillsdale, NJ: Erlbaum.

Gigerenzer, G. (1996). On narrow norms and vague heuristics: A reply to Kahneman and Tversky (1996). *Psychological Review, 103*, 592–596.

Gigerenzer, G. (1998). Surrogates for theories. *Theory and Psychology, 8*, 195–204.

Gigerenzer, G. (2000). *Adaptive thinking: Rationality in the real world*. New York: Oxford University Press.

Gigerenzer, G. (2002). *Calculated risks: How to know when numbers deceive you*. New York: Simon & Schuster. (UK version: *Reckoning with risk*, London: Penguin, 2002).

Gigerenzer, G. (2004). Fast and frugal heuristics: The tools of bounded rationality. In D. Koehler & N. Harvey (Eds.), *Handbook of judgment and decision making* (pp. 62–88). Oxford: Blackwell.

Gigerenzer, G. (2007). *Gut feelings: The intelligence of the unconscious.* New York: Viking. (UK version: *Short cuts: The intelligence of the unconscious,* London: Penguin, 2007)

Gigerenzer, G., & Goldstein, D. G. (1996). Reasoning the fast and frugal way: Models of bounded rationality. *Psychological Review, 103,* 650–669.

Gigerenzer, G., & Hug, K. (1992). Domain-specific reasoning: Social contracts, cheating, and perspective change. *Cognition, 43,* 127–171.

Gigerenzer, G., & Regier, T. (1996). How do we tell an association from a rule? Comment on Sloman (1996). *Psychological Bulletin, 119,* 23–26.

Gigerenzer, G., & Selten, R. (Eds.). (2001). *Bounded rationality: The adaptive toolbox.* Cambridge, MA: MIT Press.

Gigerenzer, G., Todd, P. M., & the ABC Research Group. (1999). *Simple heuristics that make us smart.* New York: Oxford University Press.

Gilbert, M. (1996). *Living together.* Lanham, MD: Rowman & Littlefield Publishers, Inc.

Gill, M. B. (Forthcoming). Meta-ethical variability and our miscellaneous moral discourse.

Gill, M. B. (2006). The british moralists on human nature and the birth of secular ethics. Cambridge: Cambridge University Press.

Gilligan, C. (1982). *In a different voice.* Cambridge, Mass.: Harvard University Press.

Gladwell, M. (2005). *Blink: The power of thinking without thinking.* New York: Little, Brown.

Goldman, A. (1976). Discrimination and perceptual knowledge. *Journal of Philosophy, 73,* 771–791.

Goldman, A. (1986). *Epistemology and cognition.* Cambridge: Harvard University Press.

Goldstein, D. G., & Gigerenzer, G. (2002). Models of ecological rationality: The recognition heuristic. *Psychological Review, 109,* 75–90.

Green, L., & Mehr, D. R. (1997). What alters physicians' decisions to admit to the coronary care unit? *The Journal of Family Practice, 45,* 219–226.

Greene, J. (2002). *The terrible, horrible, no good, very bad truth about morality and what to do about it.* Doctoral dissertation, Department of Philosophy, Princeton University (and forthcoming, revised and expanded, Penguin Press).

Greene, J., & Haidt, J. (2002). How (and where) does moral judgment work? *Trends in Cognitive Sciences, 6*, 517–523.

Greene, J. D., Nystrom, L. E., Engell, A. D., Darley, J. M., & Cohen, J. D. (2004). The neural bases of cognitive conflict and control in moral judgment. *Neuron, 44*, 389–400.

Greene, J. D., Sommerville, R. B., Nystrom, L. E., Darley, J. M., & Cohen, J. D. (2001). An fMRI study of emotional engagement in moral judgment. *Science, 293*, 2105–2108.

Greenwald, A. G., McGhee, D. E., & Schwartz, J. L. (1998). Measuring individual differences in implicit cognition: The implicit association test. *Journal of Personality and Social Psychology, 74*, 1464–1480.

Greenwald, A. G., Nosek, B., & Banaji, M. R. (2003). Understanding and using the Implicit Association Test: I. An improved scoring algorithm. *Journal of Personality and Social Psychology, 85*, 197–216.

Greig, J. Y. T. (Ed.). (1983). *The letters of David Hume.* New York: Garland.

Grusec, J. E. (2002). Parenting and the socialization of values. In M. Bornstein (Ed.), *Handbook of parenting* (pp. 143–168). Mahwah, NJ: Erlbaum.

Gutmann, A. (1999). How not to resolve moral conflicts in politics. *Ohio State Journal on Dispute Resolution, 15*, 1–18.

Gutmann, A., & Thompson, D. (1996). *Democracy and disagreement.* Cambridge Mass.: Belknap Press.

Haidt, J. (2001). The emotional dog and its rational tail: A social intuitionist approach to moral judgment. *Psychological Review, 108*, 814–834.

Haidt, J. (2003a). The emotional dog does learn new tricks: A reply to Pizarro and Bloom (2003). *Psychological Review, 100*, 197–198.

Haidt, J. (2003b). The moral emotions. In R. J. Davidson, K. R. Scherer, & H. H. Goldsmith (Eds.), *Handbook of affective sciences* (pp. 852–870). Oxford: Oxford University Press.

Haidt, J. (2004). The emotional dog gets mistaken for a possum. *Review of General Psychology, 8*, 283–290.

Haidt, J. (2006). *The happiness hypothesis: Finding modern truth in ancient wisdom.* New York: Basic Books.

Haidt, J. (2007). The new synthesis in moral psychology. *Science, 316*, 998–1002.

Haidt, J., & Baron, J. (1996). Social roles and the moral judgement of acts and omissions. *European Journal of Social Psychology, 26*, 201–218.

Haidt, J., & Graham, J. (2007). When morality opposes justice: Conservatives have moral intuitions that liberals may not recognize. *Social Justice Research.*

Haidt, J., & Hersh, M. A. (2001). Sexual morality: The cultures and reasons of liberals and conservatives. *Journal of Applied Social Psychology, 31*, 191–221.

Haidt, J., & Joseph, C. (2004). Intuitive ethics: How innately prepared intuitions generate culturally variable virtues. *Daedalus, 133*(44), 55–66.

Haidt, J., & Joseph, C. (In press). The moral mind: How five sets of innate intuitions guide the development of many culture-specific virtues, and perhaps even modules. In P. Carruthers, S. Laurence, & S. Stich (Eds.), *The innate mind* (Vol. 3). New York: Oxford University Press.

Haidt, J., & Kesebir, S. (2007). In the forest of value: Why moral intuitions are different from other kinds. In H. Plessner, C. Betsch, & T. Betsch (Eds.), *Intuition in judgment and decision making*. Mahwah, NJ: Erlbaum.

Haidt, J., Algoe, S., Meijer, Z., Tam, A., & Chandler, E. C. (2000). *The elevation-altruism hypothesis: Evidence for a new prosocial emotion*. Unpublished manuscript, University of Virginia, Charlottesville.

Haidt, J., Bjorklund, F., & Murphy, S. (2000). *Moral dumbfounding: When intuition finds no reason*. Unpublished manuscript, University of Virginia.

Haidt, J., Koller, S., & Dias, M. (1993). Affect, culture, and morality, or is it wrong to eat your dog? *Journal of Personality and Social Psychology, 65*, 613–628.

Haidt, J., Lobue, V., Chiong, C., Nishida, T., & DeLoache, J. (2007). When getting something good is bad: Young children's reactions to inequity. University of Virginia.

Haidt, J., McCauley, C., & Rozin, P. (1994). Individual differences in sensitivity to disgust: A scale sampling seven domains of disgust elicitors. *Personality & Individual Differences, 16*, 701–713.

Hall, N. (2004). Two concepts of causation. In J. Collins, E. J. Hall, & L. A. Paul (Eds.), *Causation and counterfactuals* (pp. 225–276). Cambridge: MIT Press.

Hare, R. M. (1952). *The language of morals*. Oxford: Clarendon Press.

Hare, R. M. (1981). *Moral thinking: Its levels, method, and point*. Oxford: Oxford University Press.

Harman, G. (1977). *The nature of morality: An introduction to ethics*. New York: Oxford University Press.

Harman, G. (1986). Moral explanations of natural facts: Can moral claims be tested against moral reality? *Southern Journal of Philosophy, 24*(Supp.), 57–68.

Harman, G. (1996). Moral relativism. In G. Harman & J. J. Thomson (Eds.), *Moral relativism and moral objectivity* (pp. 3–19). Oxford: Blackwell.

Harman, G. (1999). Moral philosophy and linguistics. In K. Brinkmann (Ed.), *Proceedings of the 20th World Congress of Philosophy: Vol. 1. Ethics* (pp. 107–115). Bowling Green, OH: Philosophy Documentation Center.

Harris, J. R. (1995). Where is the child's environment? A group socialization theory of development. *Psychological Review, 102,* 458–489.

Harris, P. (1989). *Children and emotion: The development of psychological understanding.* Oxford: Blackwell.

Harris, P. (1993). Understanding emotion. In M. Lewis & J. Haviland (Eds.), *Handbook of emotions* (pp. 237–246). New York: Guilford Press.

Harris, P., & Núñez, M. (1996). Understanding of permission rules by preschool children. *Child Development, 67,* 1572–1591.

Harris, P. L., Olthof, T., Terwogt, M. M., & Hardman, C. (1987). Children's knowledge of the situations that provoke emotions. *International Journal of Behavioral Development, 10,* 319–344.

Harris, V. (1974). Translator's introduction. In M. Musashi (Ed.), *Book of five rings: The classic guide to strategy* (V. Harris, Trans., pp. 1–32). New York: Overlook Press.

Harrison, J. (1967). Ethical objectivism. In P. Edwards (Ed.), *The encyclopedia of philosophy* (Vols. 3–4, pp. 71–75). New York: Macmillan.

Hart, H. L. A. (1961). *The concept of law.* Oxford: Clarendon Press.

Hart, H. L. A., & Honoré, T. (1959). *Causation in the law.* Oxford: Clarendon Press.

Hassin, R. R., Uleman, J. S., & Bargh, J. A. (Eds.). (2005). *The new unconscious.* New York: Oxford University Press.

Hauser, M. D. (2006). *Moral minds: How nature designed a universal sense of right and wrong.* New York: Ecco Press/HarperCollins.

Hauser, M. D., Chomsky, N., & Fitch, W. T. (2002). The faculty of language: What is it, who has it, and how did it evolve? *Science, 298,* 1569–1579.

Hauser, M. D., Cushman, F., Young, L., Jin, R. K.-X., & Mikhail, J. (2006). A dissociation between moral judgment and justifications. *Mind & Language, 22,* 1–21.

Hauser, M. D., Newport, E. L., & Aslin, R. N. (2001). Segmenting a continuous acoustic speech stream: Serial learning in cotton-top tamarin monkeys. *Cognition, 78,* B53–B64.

Henrich, J., Boyd, R., Bowles, S., Camerer, C., Fehr, E., & Gintis, H. (2004). *Foundations of human sociality: Economic experiments and ethnographic evidence from fifteen small-scale societies.* New York: Oxford University Press.

Hertwig, R., & Todd, P. M. (2003). More is not always better: The benefits of cognitive limits. In L. M. D. Hardman (Ed.), *The psychology of reasoning and decision making: A handbook* (pp. 213–231). Chichester, England: Wiley.

Herzog, D. (1985). *Without foundations: Justification in political theory.* Ithaca and London: Cornell University Press.

Hirschfeld, L. A. (2002). Why don't anthropologists like children? *American Anthropology, 104*, 611–627.

Hitchcock, C. (2005). *Token causation.* Unpublished manuscript, California Institute of Technology.

Hoffman, M. L. (1983). Affective and cognitive processes in moral internalization. In E. T. Higgins, D. N. Ruble, & W. W. Hartup (Eds.), *Social cognition and social development: A sociocultural perspective* (pp. 236–274). Cambridge: Cambridge University Press.

Hoffrage, U., Hertwig, R., & Gigerenzer, G. (2000). Hindsight bias: A by-product of knowledge updating? *Journal of Experimental Psychology: Learning, Memory, and Cognition, 26*, 566–581.

Hogarth, R. M. (2001). *Educating intuition.* Chicago: University of Chicago Press.

Hogarth, R. M. (in press). When simple is hard to accept. In P. M. Todd, G. Gigerenzer, & the ABC Research Group, *Ecological rationality: Intelligence in the world.* New York: Oxford University Press.

Hogarth, R. M., & Karelaia, N. (2005). Ignoring information in binary choice with continuous variables: When is less "more"? *Journal of Mathematical Psychology, 49*, 115–124.

Hogarth, R. M., & Karelaia, N. (2006). "Take-the-best" and other simple strategies: Why and when they work "well" with binary cues. *Theory and Decision, 61*, 205–249.

Holland, J. H., Holyoak, K. J., Nisbett, R. E., & Thagard, P. R. (1986). *Induction: Processes of inference, learning and discovery.* Cambridge: MIT Press.

Hom, H., & Haidt, J. (in preparation). *The bonding and norming functions of gossip.* Unpublished manuscript, University of Virginia.

Hooker, B. (2000). *Ideal code, real world: A rule-consequentialist theory of morality.* Oxford: Oxford University Press.

Hooker, B., & Little, M. (Eds). (2000). *Moral particularism.* Oxford: Oxford University Press.

Hornstein, H. (1976). *Cruelty and kindness: A new look at aggression and altruism.* Englewood Cliffs, NJ: Prentice-Hall.

Hornstein, H., LaKind, E., Frankel, G., & Manne, S. (1975). The effects of knowledge about remote social events on prosocial behavior, social conception, and mood. *Journal of Personality and Social Psychology, 32,* 1038–1046.

Horowitz, T. (1998). Philosophical intuitions and psychological theory. *Ethics, 108,* 367–385.

Hume, D. (1969). *A treatise of human nature.* London: Penguin. (Original work published 1739–1740)

Hume, D. (1975). *Enquiry concerning human understanding and concerning the principles of morals* (3rd ed., L. A. Selby-Bigge & P. H. Niddich, Eds.). Oxford: Clarendon Press. (Original work published 1777)

Hume, D. (1978). *A treatise of human nature* (2nd ed., L. A. Selby-Bigge & P. H. Niddich, Eds.). Oxford: Clarendon Press. (Original work published 1739–1740)

Hunter, J. D. (2000). *The death of character: Moral education in an age without good and evil.* New York: Basic Books.

Isen, A. M. (1970). Success, failure, attention, and reaction to others: The warm glow of success. *Journal of Personality and Social Psychology, 6,* 400–407.

Isen, A. M., & Levin, P. F. (1972). Effect of feeling good on helping: Cookies and kindness. *Journal of Personality and Social Psychology, 21,* 384–388.

Izard, C. (1991). *The psychology of emotions.* New York: Plenum Press.

Jackendoff, R. (2002). *Foundations of language.* New York: Oxford University Press.

Jackendoff, R. (2005). *Language, culture, consciousness: Essays on mental structure.* Cambridge, Mass.: MIT Press.

Jackson, F. (1998). *From metaphysics to ethics: A defense of conceptual analysis.* Oxford: Clarendon Press.

Jackson, F. (2001). Responses. *Philosophy and Phenomenological Research, 62,* 653–664.

Jacobson, D. (2002). Review of Robert Hinde, *Why good is good: The sources of morality. Notre Dame Philosophical Reviews.* Retrieved from http://ndpr.nd.edu/review.cfm?id=1095

Jacobson, D. (2005). Seeing by feeling: Virtues, skills, and moral perception. *Ethical Theory and Moral Practice, 8,* 387–409.

Jaffe, E. (2004). What was I thinking? Kahneman explains how intuition leads us astray. *American Psychological Society Observer, 17,* May.

Jefferson, T. (1975). Letter to Thomas Law. In M. D. Peterson (Ed.), *The portable Thomas Jefferson* (pp. 540–544). New York: Penguin. (Original work published 1814)

Jensen, L. A. (1997). Culture wars: American moral divisions across the adult lifespan. *Journal of Adult Development, 4*, 107–121.

Jensen, L. A. (1998). Moral divisions within countries between orthodoxy and progressivism: India and the United States. *Journal for the Scientific Study of Religion, 37*, 90–107.

Johnson, E. J., & Goldstein, D. G. (2003). Do defaults save lives? *Science, 302*, 1338–1339.

Jost, J. T., Glaser, J., Kruglanski, A. W., & Sulloway, F. J. (2003). Political conservatism as motivated social cognition. *Psychological Bulletin, 129*, 339–375.

Joyce, R. (2001). *The myth of morality*. Cambridge: Cambridge University Press.

Juarrero, A. (1999). *Dynamics in action: Intentional behavior as a complex system*. Cambridge: MIT Press.

Kagan, J. (1984). *The nature of the child*. New York: Basic Books.

Kagan, S. (1988). The additive fallacy. *Ethics, 90*, 5–31.

Kagan, S. (1998). *Normative ethics*. Boulder, CO: Westview Press.

Kahneman, D. (1999). Objective happiness. In D. Kahneman, E. Diener, & N. Schwarz (Eds.), *Well-being: The foundations of hedonic psychology* (pp. 3–25). New York: Russell Sage.

Kahneman, D., & Tversky, A. (1979). Prospect theory: An analysis of decision under risk. *Econometrica, 47*, 263–291.

Kahneman, D., & Tversky, A. (1996). On the reality of cognitive illusions. A reply to Gigerenzer's critique. *Psychological Review, 103*, 582–591.

Kahneman, D., & Tversky, A. (Eds.). (2000). *Choices, values, and frames*. Cambridge: Cambridge University Press.

Kahneman, D., Knetsch, J. L., & Thaler, R. H. (1986). Fairness as a constraint on profit-seeking: Entitlements in the market. *American Economic Review, 76*, 728–741.

Kahneman, D., Slovic, P., & Tversky, A. (Eds.). (1982). *Judgment under uncertainty: Heuristics and biases*. Cambridge: Cambridge University Press.

Kamm, F. M. (1998a). Moral intuitions, cognitive psychology, and the harming-versus-not-aiding distinction. *Ethics, 108*, 463–488.

Kamm, F. M. (1998b). *Morality, mortality: Death and whom to save from it*. New York: Oxford University Press.

Kant, I. (1969). *Foundations of the metaphysics of morals* (L. W. Beck, Trans.). Indianapolis: Bobbs-Merrill. (Original work published 1785)

Kant, I. (1993). *Grounding for the metaphysics of morals* (J. Ellington, Trans.). Indianapolis: Hackett. (Original work published 1785)

Kareev, Y. (2000). Seven (indeed, plus or minus two) and the detection of correlations. *Psychological Review, 107,* 397–402.

Kasser, T. (2002). *The high price of materialism.* Cambridge: MIT Press.

Katsikopoulos, K., & Martignon, L. (2004). *Which is more accurate for paired comparisons: Ordering or adding cues?* Manuscript submitted for publication.

Kekes, J. (1988). *The examined life.* University Park: Pennsylvania University Press.

Kelly, D., Stich, S., Haley, K., Eng, S., & Fessler, D. (Forthcoming). Harm, affect and the moral/conventional distinction. *Mind and Language.*

Kitayama, S., & Markus, H. R. (1999). *Yin* and *yang* of the Japanese self: The cultural psychology of personality coherence. In D. Cervone & Y. Shoda (Eds.), *The coherence of personality: Social-cognitive bases of consistency, variability, and organization* (pp. 242–302). New York and London: Guilford Press.

Klein, G. (2001). The fiction of optimization. In G. Gigerenzer & R. Selten (Eds.), *Bounded rationality: The adaptive toolbox* (pp. 103–121). Cambridge, Mass.: MIT Press.

Klinger, E. (1978). Modes of normal conscious flow. In K. S. Pope & J. L. Singer (Eds.), *The stream of consciousness: Scientific investigations into the flow of human experience* (pp. 225–258). New York: Plenum.

Knobe, J. (2005a). *Attribution and normativity: A problem in the philosophy of social psychology.* Unpublished manuscript, University of North Carolina—Chapel Hill.

Knobe, J. (2005b). Cognitive processes shaped by the impulse to blame. *Brooklyn Law Review, 71,* 929–937.

Knobe, J., & Doris, J. (Forthcoming). Strawsonian variations: Folk morality and the search for a unified theory. *Rethinking Moral Psychology.*

Kochanska, G. (1997). Multiple pathways to conscience for children with different temperaments: From toddlerhood to age 5. *Developmental Psychology, 33,* 228–240.

Koenigs, M., Young, L., Adolphs, R., Tranel, D., Cushman, F., Hanser, M., & Damasio, A. (2007). Damage to the prefrontal cortex increases utilitarian moral judgments. *Nature,* online.

Kohlberg, L. (1969). Stage and sequence: The cognitive-developmental approach to socialization. In D. A. Goslin (Ed.), *Handbook of socialization theory and research* (pp. 347–380). Chicago: Rand McNally.

Kohlberg, L. (1971). From is to ought: How to commit the naturalistic fallacy and get away with it in the study of moral development. In T. Mischel (Ed.), *Cognitive development and epistemology* (pp. 151–235). New York: Academic Press.

Komlos, J., & Baten, J. (2004). Looking backward and looking forward: Anthropometric research and the development of social science history. *Social Science History, 28*, 191–210.

Konecni, V. J., & Ebbesen, E. B. (1984). The mythology of legal decision making. *International Journal of Law and Psychiatry, 7*, 5–18.

Kraut, R., Olson, J., Banaji, M. R., Bruckman, A., Cohen, J., & Cooper, M. (2004). Psychological research online. *American Psychologist, 59*, 105–117.

Krebs, D. L., & Denton, K. (2005). Toward a more pragmatic approach to morality: A critical evaluation of Kohlberg's model. *Psychological Review, 112*, 629–649.

Kühberger, A. (1995). The framing of decisions: A new look at old problems. *Organizational Behavior & Human Decision Processes, 62*, 230–240.

Kühberger, A. (1998). The influence of framing on risky decisions: A meta-analysis. *Organizational Behavior & Human Decision Processes, 75*, 23–55.

Kühberger, A., Schulte-Mecklenbeck, M., & Perner, J. (1999). The effects of framing, reflection, probability, and payoff on risk preference in choice tasks. *Organizational Behavior & Human Decision Processes, 78*, 204–231.

Kuhn, D. (1989). Children and adults as intuitive scientists. *Psychological Review, 96*, 674–689.

Kuhn, D. (1991). *The skills of argument.* Cambridge: Cambridge University Press.

Kuhn, K. M. (1997). Communicating uncertainty: Framing effects on responses to vague probabilities. *Organizational Behavior & Human Decision Processes, 71*, 55–83.

Kunda, Z. (1990). The case for motivated reasoning. *Psychological Bulletin, 108*, 480–498.

Kurtines, W. M., & Gewirtz, J. L. (Eds.). (1995). *Moral development: An introduction.* Boston: Allyn & Bacon.

Kurzban, R., & Aktipis, C. A. (2006). Modularity and the social mind: Why social psychologists should be less self-ish. In M. Schaller, J. Simpson, & D. Kenrick (Eds.), *Evolution and social psychology* (pp. 39–54). New York: Psychology Press.

Kutz, C. (2000). *Complicity: Ethics and law for a collective age.* Cambridge: Cambridge University Press.

Kysar, D., Ayton, P., Frank, R. H., Frey, B. S., Gigerenzer, G., & Glimcher, P. W. (2006). Are heuristics a problem or a solution? In C. Engel & G. Gigerenzer (Eds.), *Heuristics and the law* (pp. 103–140). Cambridge, MA: MIT Press.

Ladd, J. (1957). *The structure of a moral code: A philosophical analysis of ethical discourse applied to the ethics of the Navaho Indians.* Cambridge: Harvard University Press.

Laland, K. (2001). Imitation, social learning, and preparedness as mechanisms of bounded rationality. In G. Gigerenzer & R. Selten (Eds.), *Bounded rationality: The adaptive toolbox* (pp. 233–247). Cambridge: MIT Press.

Lapsley, D. K. (1996). *Moral psychology.* Boulder, CO: Westview.

Larmore, C. E. (1987). *Patterns of moral complexity.* Cambridge: Cambridge University Press.

Latane, B., & Darley, J. M. (1970). *The unresponsive bystander.* Englewood Cliffs, NJ: Prentice-Hall.

Laudan, L. (1977). *Progress and its problems: Toward a theory of scientific growth.* Berkeley: University of California Press.

Laudan, L. (1981). A confutation of convergent realism. *Philosophy of Science, 48,* 19–49. (Reprinted in R. Boyd, P. Gasper, & J. D. Trout (Eds.), *The philosophy of science* (1991, pp. 223–246). Cambridge: MIT Press.)

LeBoeuf, R. A., & Shafir, E. (2003). Deep thoughts and shallow frames: On the susceptibility to framing effects. *Journal of Behavioral Decision Making, 16,* 77–92.

Leiter, B. (2001). Objectivity, morality, and adjudication. In B. Leiter (Ed.), *Objectivity in law and morals* (pp. 66–98). Cambridge: Cambridge University Press.

Leiter, B. (2002). *Nietzsche on morality.* London and New York: Routledge.

Lerdahl, F., & Jackendoff, R. (1996). *A generative theory of tonal music.* Cambridge: MIT Press.

Lerner, R. (1998). Theories of human development: Contemporary perspectives. In W. Damon (Ed.), *Handbook of child psychology* (Vol. 1, pp. 1–24). New York: Wiley.

Leslie, A. M. (1987). Pretense and representation: The origins of "theory of mind". *Psychological Review, 94,* 412–426.

Leslie, A., Mallon, R., & Dicorcia, J. (Forthcoming). Transgressors, victims, and cry babies: Is basic moral judgment spared in autism? *Social Neuroscience.*

Leslie, J. (1991). Ensuring two bird deaths with one throw. *Mind, 100,* 73–86.

Levin, I. P., Schneider, S. L., & Gaeth, G. J. (1998). All frames are not created equal: A typology and critical analysis of framing effects. *Organizational Behavior & Human Decision Processes, 76,* 149–188.

Levy, N. (2006). The wisdom of the pack. *Philosophical Explorations, 9,* 99–103.

Levy, N. (Forthcoming). Deflating morality?

Lewicki, P., Czyzewska, M., & Hill, T. (1997). Nonconscious information, processing and personality. In D. Berry (Ed.) *How Implicit is Implicit Learning? Debates in Psychology* (pp. 48–72). New York: Oxford University Press.

Lewis, D. (1979). Prisoners' dilemma is a Newcomb problem. *Philosophy & Public Affairs, 8*, 235–240.

Linn, S. (2004). *Consuming kids*. New York: New Press.

Loeb, D. (1995). Full-information theories of individual good. *Social Theory and Practice, 21*(1), 1–30. Reprinted in G. Sher (Ed.), *Moral philosophy: Selected readings* (2nd ed., pp. 637–658). Fort Worth, TX: Harcourt Brace College Publishers.

Loeb, D. (1998). Moral realism and the argument from disagreement. *Philosophical Studies, 90*, 281–303.

Lord, C. G., Ross, L., & Lepper, M. R. (1979). Biased assimilation and attitude polarization: The effects of prior theories on subsequently considered evidence. *Journal of Personality and Social Psychology, 37*, 2098–2109.

Machery, E., Mallon, R., Nichols, S., & Stich, S. (2004). Semantics, cross-cultural style. *Cognition, 92*, B1–B12.

Mackie, J. L. (1977). *Ethics: Inventing right and wrong*. New York: Penguin Books.

Macnamara, J. (1990). The development of moral reasoning and the foundations of geometry. *Journal for the Theory of Social Behavior, 21*, 125–150.

Mallon, R., & Weinberg, J. M. (2006). Innateness as closed process invariance. *Philosophy of Science, 73*, 323–344.

Mallon, R., Machery, E., Nichols, S., & Stich, S. (Forthcoming). Against arguments from reference.

Marcus, G. (2004). *The birth of the mind*. New York: Basic Books.

Markus, H. R., & Kitayama, S. (1991). Culture and the self: Implications for cognition, emotion, and motivation. *Psychological Review, 98*, 224–253.

Marr, D. (1982). *Vision: A computational investigation into the human representation and processing of visual information*. San Francisco: Freeman.

Martignon, L., & Hoffrage, U. (1999). Why does one-reason decision making work? A case study in ecological rationality. In G. Gigerenzer, P. M. Todd, & the ABC Research Group, *Simple heuristics that make us smart* (pp. 119–140). New York: Oxford University Press.

Martignon, L., & Hoffrage, U. (2002). Fast, frugal and fit: Lexicographic heuristics for paired comparison. *Theory and Decision, 52*, 29–71.

McClosky, H. J. (1963). A note on utilitarian punishment. *Mind, 72*, 599.

McCrae, R. R. (1996). Social consequences of experiential openness. *Psychological Bulletin, 120*, 323–337.

McElroy, T., & Seta, J. J. (2003). Framing effects: An analytic–holistic perspective. *Journal of Experimental Social Psychology, 39*, 610–617.

McGrath, S. (2005). Causation by omission. *Philosophical Studies, 123*, 125–148.

Merenstein, D. (2004). Winners and losers. *Journal of the American Medical Association, 7*, 15–16.

Merli, D. (1990). Moral realism's semantic problem. Unpublished manuscript.

Messick, D. M. (1993). Equality as a decision heuristic. In B. A. Mellers & J. Baron (Eds.), *Psychological perspectives on justice* (pp. 11–31). New York: Cambridge University Press.

Miceli, G., Capasso, R., Banvegnu, B., & Caramazza, A. (2004). The categorical distinction of vowel and consonant representations: Evidence from dysgraphia. *Neurocase, 10*, 109–121.

Mikhail, J. (2000). Rawls' linguistic analogy: A study of the "generative grammar" model of moral theory described by John Rawls in "A theory of justice." Doctoral dissertation, Cornell University.

Mikhail, J. (In press). *Rawls' linguistic analogy*. New York: Cambridge University Press.

Mikhail, J., Sorrentino, C., & Spelke, E. S. (1998). *Toward a universal moral grammar*. Paper presented at the Proceedings of the Cognitive Science Society.

Milgram, S. (1963). Behavioral study of obedience. *Journal of Abnormal and Social Psychology, 67*, 371–378.

Mineka, S., & Cook, M. (1988). Social learning and the acquisition of snake fear in monkeys. In T. R. Zentall & J. B. G. Galef (Eds.), *Social learning: Psychological and biological perspectives* (pp. 51–74). Hillsdale, NJ: Erlbaum.

Minoura, Y. (1992). A sensitive period for the incorporation of a cultural meaning system: A study of Japanese children growing up in the United States. *Ethos, 20*, 304–339.

Mischel, W. (1968). *Personality and assessment*. New York: Wiley.

Moody-Adams, M. (1997). *Fieldwork in familiar places*. Cambridge: Harvard University Press.

Moore, G. E. (1903). *Principia ethica*. Cambridge: Cambridge University Press.

Muller, J. Z. (1997). What is conservative social and political thought? In J. Z. Muller (Ed.), *Conservatism: An anthology of social and political thought from David Hume to the present* (pp. 3–31). Princeton, NJ: Princeton University Press.

Murphy, D. (2005). *Psychiatry in the scientific image*. Cambridge: MIT Press.

Murphy, D., & Woolfolk, R. L. (2000). The harmful dysfunction analysis of mental disorder. *Philosophy, Psychiatry, Psychology, 7*, 241–252.

Murray, S. L., Holmes, J. G., Dolderman, D., & Griffin, D. W. (2000). What the motivated mind sees: Comparing friends' perspectives to married partners' views of each other. *Journal of Experimental Social Psychology, 36*, 600–620.

Nagel, T. (1986). *The view from nowhere*. Oxford: Oxford University Press.

Narvaez, D. (2005). The neo-Kohlbergian tradition and beyond: Schemas, expertise and character. In G. Carlo & C. Pope-Edwards (Eds.), *Nebraska symposium on motivation: Vol. 51. Moral motivation through the lifespan* (pp. 119–163). Lincoln: University of Nebraska Press.

Narvaez, D. (2006). Integrative ethical education. In M. Killen & J. Smetana (Eds.), *Handbook of moral development* (pp. 703–733). Mahwah, NJ: Erlbaum.

Narvaez, D., & Lapsley, D. (2005). The psychological foundations of everyday morality and moral expertise. In D. Lapsley & C. Power (Eds.), *Character psychology and character education* (pp. 140–165). Notre Dame, IN: University of Notre Dame Press.

Narvaez, D., & Rest, J. (1995). The four components of acting morally. In W. Kurtines & J. Gewirtz (Eds.), *Moral behavior and moral development: An introduction* (pp. 385–400). New York: McGraw-Hill.

Neilsen, K. (1967). Ethics, problems of. In P. Edwards (Ed.), *The encyclopedia of philosophy* (Vol. 3, pp. 117–134). New York: Macmillan.

Newell, A. (1982). The knowledge level. *Artificial Intelligence, 18*, 87–127.

Nichols, S. (2001). Mindreading and the cognitive architecture underlying altruistic motivation. *Mind & Language, 16*, 425–455.

Nichols, S. (2002a). Norms with feeling: Towards a psychological account of moral judgment. *Cognition, 84*, 221–236.

Nichols, S. (2002b). On the genealogy of norms: A case for the role of emotion in cultural evolution. *Philosophy of Science, 69*, 234–255.

Nichols, S. (2004a). After objectivity: An empirical study of moral judgment. *Philosophical Psychology, 17*, 5–28.

Nichols, S. (2004b). *Sentimental rules: On the natural foundations of moral judgment*. New York: Oxford University Press.

Nichols, S. (2005). Innateness and moral psychology. In P. Carruthers, S. Laurence, & S. Stich (Eds.), *The innate mind: Structure and content* (pp. 353–370). New York: Oxford University Press.

Nichols, S. (Forthcoming). The rise of compatibilism: A case study in the quantitative history of philosophy.

Nichols, S., & Knobe, J. (Forthcoming). Moral responsibility and determinism: The cognitive science of folk intuitions. *Noûs*.

Nichols, S., Stich, S., & Weinberg, J. (2003). Metaskepticism: Meditations in ethno-epistemology. In S. Luper (Ed.), *The skeptics* (pp. 227–247). Burlington, VT: Ashgate.

Nickerson, R. S. (1994). The teaching of thinking and problem solving. In R. J. Sternberg (Ed.), *Thinking and problem solving* (pp. 409–449). San Diego, CA: Academic Press.

Nietzsche, F. (1956). *The birth of tragedy and the genealogy of morals* (F. Golffing, Trans.). New York: Doubleday.

Nietzsche, F. (1999). *The anti-Christ* (H. L. Mencken, Trans.). Tucson, AZ: Sharp Press. (Original work published 1895)

Nisbett, R. E. (1998). Essence and accident. In J. M. Darley & J. Cooper (Eds.), *Attribution and social interaction: The legacy of Edward E. Jones* (pp. 169–200). Washington, DC: American Psychological Association.

Nisbett, R. E. (2003). *The geography of thought: How Asians and Westerners think differently . . . and why*. New York: Free Press.

Nisbett, R. E., & Cohen, D. (1996). *Culture of honor: The psychology of violence in the South*. Boulder, CO: Westview Press.

Nisbett, R. E., & Ross, L. (1980). *Human inference: Strategies and shortcomings of social judgment*. Englewood Cliffs, NJ: Prentice-Hall.

Nisbett, R. E., & Wilson, T. D. (1977). Telling more than we can know: Verbal reports on mental processes. *Psychological Review, 84*, 231–259.

Nucci, L. (2001). *Education in the moral domain*. New York: Cambridge University Press.

Nunner-Winkler, G., & Sodian, B. (1988). Children's understanding of moral emotions. *Child Development, 59*, 1323–1338.

Nussbaum, M. C. (2003). *The fragility of goodness: Luck and ethics in Greek tragedy and philosophy*. Cambridge: Cambridge University Press.

Nussbaum, M. C. (2004). *Hiding from humanity*. Princeton, NJ: Princeton University Press.

O'Neill, P., & Petrinovich, L. (1998). A preliminary cross cultural study of moral intuitions. *Evolution and Human Behavior, 19*, 349–367.

Opie, I., & Opie, P. (1969). *Children's games in street and playground*. Oxford: Clarendon Press.

Ortony, A., Clore, G. L., & Collins, A. (1988). *The cognitive structure of the emotions.* Cambridge: Cambridge University Press.

Osgood, C. E. (1962). Studies on the generality of affective meaning systems. *American Psychologist, 17,* 10–28.

Panksepp, J. (1998). *Affective neuroscience: The foundations of human and animal emotions.* New York: Oxford University Press.

Panksepp, J. (2005, October 28). *Affective neuroscience: The ancestral sources of human feelings.* Colloquium, Department of Psychology, University of Notre Dame.

Panksepp, J., & Panksepp, J. B. (2000). The seven sins of evolutionary psychology. *Evolution and Cognition, 6,* 108–131.

Parfit, D. (1984). *Reasons and persons.* New York: Oxford University Press.

Pautz, A. (n.d.). *From moral semantics to moral skepticism.* Unpublished manuscript.

Payne, J. W., Bettman, J. R., & Johnson, E. J. (1993). *The adaptive decision maker.* Cambridge: Cambridge University Press.

Pelham, B. W., Mirenberg, M. C., & Jones, J. K. (2002). Why Susie sells seashells by the seashore: Implicit egotism and major life decisions. *Journal of Personality and Social Psychology, 82,* 469–487.

Peng, K., Doris, J. M., Nichols, & Stich, S. (n.d.). Unpublished data.

Perkins, D. N., Farady, M., & Bushey, B. (1991). Everyday reasoning and the roots of intelligence. In J. F. Voss, D. N. Perkins, & J. W. Segal (Eds.), *Informal reasoning and education* (pp. 83–105). Hillsdale, NJ: Erlbaum.

Peterson, C., & Seligman, M. E. P. (2004). *Character strengths and virtues: A handbook and classification.* Washington, DC: American Psychological Association; New York: Oxford University Press.

Petrinovich, L., & O'Neill, P. (1996). Influence of wording and framing effects on moral intuitions. *Ethology and Sociobiology, 17,* 145–171.

Petrinovich, L., O'Neill, P., & Jorgensen, M. (1993). An empirical study of moral intuitions: Toward an evolutionary ethics. *Journal of Personality and Social Psychology, 64,* 467–478.

Petty, R. E., & Cacioppo, J. T. (1986). The elaboration likelihood model of persuasion. In L. Berkowitz (Ed.), *Advances in experimental social psychology* (Vol. 19, pp. 123–205). New York: Academic Press.

Piaget, J. (1965). *The moral judgment of the child* (M. Gabain, Trans.). New York: Free Press. (Original work published 1932)

Pinker, S. (1994). *The language instinct.* New York: Morrow.

Pinker, S. (1997). *How the mind works*. New York: Norton.

Pinker, S. (2002). *The blank slate: The modern denial of human nature*. New York: Viking.

Pizarro, D. A., & Bloom, P. (2003). The intelligence of the moral intuitions: Comment on Haidt (2001). *Psychological Review, 110*, 193–196.

Posner, R. A. (1972). A theory of negligence. *Journal of Legal Studies, 1*, 29–96.

Pratto, F., Sidanius, J., Stallworth, L. M., & Malle, B. F. (1994). Social dominance orientation: A personality variable predicting social and political attitudes. *Journal of Personality and Social Psychology, 67*, 741–763.

Premack, D., & Woodruff, G. (1978). Does the chimpanzee have a theory of mind? *Behavioral and Brain Sciences, 1*, 515–526.

Prinz, J. J. (Forthcoming, a). *The emotional construction of morals*. Oxford: Oxford University Press.

Prinz, J. J. (Forthcoming, b). Against moral nativism. In M. Bishop & D. Murphy (Eds.), *Stich and his critics*. Malden, MA: Blackwell.

Putnam, H. (1960). Minds and machines. In S. Hook (Ed.), *Dimensions of mind* (pp. 138–164). New York: New York University Press.

Putnam, H. (1975). The meaning of meaning. Reprinted in his *Mind, language and reality* (pp. 215–271). Cambridge: Cambridge University Press.

Pylyshyn, Z. (1984). *Computation and cognition: Toward a foundation for cognitive science*. Cambridge: MIT Press.

Quinn, W. (1993). *Morality and action*. New York: Cambridge University Press.

Rachels, J. (1975). Active and passive euthanasia. *New England Journal of Medicine, 292*, 78–80.

Railton, P. (1986). Moral realism. *Philosophical Review, 95*, 163–207.

Railton, P. (1992). Pluralism, determinacy, and dilemma. *Ethics, 102*, 720–742.

Railton, P. (2003). *Facts, values, and norms: Essays toward a morality of consequence*. Cambridge: Cambridge University Press.

Rawls, J. (1971). *A theory of justice*. Cambridge: Harvard University Press.

Rawls, J. (1993). *Political liberalism*. New York: Columbia University Press.

Rawls, J. (1998). *Justice as Fairness*. Cambridge: Harvard University Press.

Reiman, J. (1985). Justice, civilization, and the death penalty. *Philosophy & Public Affairs, 14*, 115–148.

Rest, J. (1983). Morality. In P. H. Mussen (Series Ed.) & J. Flavell & E. Markman (Vol. Eds.), *Handbook of child psychology: Vol. 3. Cognitive development* (4th ed., pp. 556–629). New York: Wiley.

Rest, J., Narvaez, D., Bebeau, M. J., & Thoma, S. J. (1999). *Postconventional moral thinking: A neo-Kohlbergian approach.* Mahwah, NJ: Erlbaum.

Richerson, P. J., & Boyd, R. (1998). The evolution of human ultra-sociality. In I. Eibl-Eibesfeldt & F. K. Salter (Eds.), *Indoctrinability, ideology, and warfare: Evolutionary perspectives* (pp. 71–95). New York: Berghahn.

Ridley, M. (2004). *Nature via nurture: Genes, experience, and what makes us human.* New York: HarperCollins.

Rosander, K., & von Hofsten, C. (2002). Development of gaze tracking of small and large objects. *Experimental Brain Research, 146,* 257–264.

Ross, L., & Nisbett, R. E. (1991). *The person and the situation.* New York: McGraw-Hill.

Ross, W. D. (1939). *Foundations of ethics.* Oxford: Clarendon Press.

Rozin, P. (1982). Human food selection: The interaction of biology, culture and individual experience. In L. M. Barker (Ed.), *The psychobiology of human food selection* (pp. 225–254). Westport, CT: AVI.

Rozin, P., Fallon, A. E., & Augustoni-Ziskind, M. (1985). The child's conception of food: The development of contamination sensitivity to "disgusting" substances. *Developmental Psychology, 21,* 1075–1079.

Rozin, P., Fallon, A., & Augustoni-Ziskind, M. L. (1986). The child's conception of food: The development of categories of acceptable and rejected substances. *Journal of Nutrition Education, 18,* 75–81.

Rozin, P., Lowery, L., Imada, S., & Haidt, J. (1999). The CAD triad hypothesis: A mapping between three moral emotions (contempt, anger, disgust) and three moral codes (community, autonomy, divinity). *Journal of Personality and Social Psychology, 76,* 574–586.

Rozin, P., Haidt, J., & McCauley, C. (2000). Disgust. In M. Lewis & J. Havilland-Jones (Eds.), *Handbook of emotions* (2nd ed., 637–653). New York: Guilford Press.

Sabin, J. E., & Daniels, N. (1994). Determining "medical necessity" in mental health practice. *Hastings Center Report, 24,* 5–13.

Salmon, N. (1981). *Reference and essence.* Princeton, NJ: Princeton University Press.

Saltzstein, H. D., & Kasachkoff, T. (2004). Haidt's moral intuitionist theory. *Review of General Psychology, 8,* 273–282.

Samenow, S. E. (1984). *Inside the criminal mind.* New York: Times Books.

Samuels, R. (2002). Innateness in cognitive science. *Mind and Language, 17*, 233–265.

Samuels, R., Stich, S., & Bishop, M. (2002). Ending the rationality wars: How to make disputes about human rationality disappear. In R. Elio (Ed.), *Common sense, reasoning and rationality* (pp. 236–268). New York: Oxford University Press.

Saporta, S. (1978). An interview with Noam Chomsky. *Linguistic Analysis, 4*, 301–319.

Sartorio, C. (2004). How to be responsible for something without causing it. *Philosophical Perspectives, 18*, 315–336.

Sayre-McCord, G. (1988). The many moral realisms. In G. Sayre-McCord (Ed.), *Essays in moral realism* (pp. 1–26). Ithaca and London: Cornell University Press.

Scheffler, S. (1994). *The rejection of consequentialism: A philosophical investigation of the considerations underlying rival moral conceptions.* New York: Oxford University Press.

Schiffer, S. (1990). Meaning and value. *The Journal of Philosophy, 87*, 602–614.

Schiffer, S. (2002). Moral realism and indeterminacy. *Philosophical Issues, 12*, 287–304.

Schmidt, W. C. (1997). World-Wide-Web survey research: Benefits, potential problems, and solutions. *Behavior Research Methods and Computers, 29*, 274–279.

Schnall, S., Haidt, J., Clore, G. L., & Jordan, A. H. (2007). *Irrelevant disgust makes moral judgments more severe, for those who listen to their bodies.* Unpublished manuscript, University of Virginia.

Schwartz, S. H., & Bilsky, W. (1990). Toward a theory of the universal content and structure of values: Extensions and cross-cultural replications. *Journal of Personality and Social Psychology, 58*, 878–891.

Seligman, M. E. P. (1971). Phobias and preparedness. *Behavior Therapy, 2*, 307–320.

Selman, R. (1971). The relation of role taking to the development of moral judgment in children. *Child Development, 42*, 79–91.

Selten, R. (2001). What is bounded rationality? In G. Gigerenzer & R. Selten (Eds.), *Bounded rationality: The adaptive toolbox* (pp. 13–36). Cambridge, Mass.: MIT Press.

Sen, A. (1982). Rights and agency. *Philosophy and Public Affairs, 11*, 3–39.

Shafer-Landau, R. (1994). Ethical disagreement, ethical objectivism and moral indeterminacy. *Philosophy and Phenomenological Research, 54*, 331–344.

Shafer-Landau, R. (1995). Vagueness, borderline cases and moral realism. *American Philosophical Quarterly, 32*, 83–96.

Shafer-Landau, R. (2003). *Moral realism: A defense.* Oxford: Clarendon Press.

Shaffer, D. M., Krauchunas, S. M., Eddy, M., & McBeath, M. K. (2004). How dogs navigate to catch Frisbees. *Psychological Science, 15*, 437–441.

Sherif, M. (1935). A study of some social factors in perception. *Archives of Psychology, 27*(187), 1–60.

Shiloh, S., Salton, E., & Sharabi, D. (2002). Individual differences in rational and intuitive thinking styles as predictors of heuristic responses and framing effects. *Personality & Individual Differences, 32*, 415–429.

Shweder, R. A., & Bourne, E. J. (1982). Does the concept of the person vary cross-culturally? In A. J. Marsella & G. M. White (Eds.), *Cultural conceptions of mental health and therapy* (pp. 97–137). Boston: Reidel.

Shweder, R. A., & Haidt, J. (1993). The future of moral psychology: Truth, intuition, and the pluralist way. *Psychological Science, 4*, 360–365.

Shweder, R. A., Mahapatra, M., & Miller, J. (1987). Culture and moral development. In J. Kagan & S. Lamb (Eds.), *The emergence of morality in young children* (pp. 1–83). Chicago: University of Chicago Press.

Shweder, R. A., Much, N. C., Mahapatra, M., & Park, L. (1997). The "Big Three" of morality (autonomy, community, and divinity), and the "Big Three" explanations of suffering. In A. Brandt & P. Rozin (Eds.), *Morality and health* (pp. 119–169). New York: Routledge.

Sider, T. (2001). Criteria of personal identity and the limits of conceptual analysis. In J. Tomberlin (Ed.), *Metaphysics: Philosophical perspectives* (Vol. 15, 189–209). Cambridge: Blackwell Press.

Silverstein, H. (1983). Assenting to "ought" judgments. *Noûs, 17*, 159–182.

Simner, M. (1971). Newborn's response to the cry of another infant. *Developmental Psychology, 5*, 136–150.

Simon, H. A. (1955). A behavioral model of rational choice. *Quarterly Journal of Economics, 69*, 99–118.

Singer, P. (1974). Sidgwick and reflective equilibrium. *The Monist, 58*, 490–517.

Singer, P. (1979). *Practical ethics*. Cambridge: Cambridge University Press.

Singer, P. (1994). *Rethinking life and death*. New York: St. Martin's Press.

Singer, P. (2005). Ethics and intuitions. *The Journal of Ethics, 9*, 331–352.

Sinnott-Armstrong, W. (2000). From "is" to "ought" in moral epistemology. *Argumentation, 14*, 159–174.

Sinnott-Armstrong, W. (2002). Moral relativity and intuitionism. *Philosophical Issues, 12* (*Realism and Relativism*), 305–328.

Sinnott-Armstrong, W. (2006). *Moral skepticisms*. New York: Oxford University Press.

Sinnott-Armstrong, W. (Forthcoming). Reflections on reflection in Audi's moral intuitionism. In M. Timmons, J. Greco, & A. Mele (Eds.), *Rationality and the good*. New York: Oxford University Press.

Skinner, B. F. (1971). *Beyond freedom and dignity*. New York: Knopf.

Skitka, L. J. (2002). Do the means always justify the ends, or do the ends sometimes justify the means? A value protection model of justice reasoning. *Personality and Social Psychology Bulletin, 28*, 588–597.

Sklar, L. (1993). *Physics and chance*. Cambridge: Cambridge University Press.

Slater, L. (2004). *Opening Skinner's box: Great psychological experiments of the twentieth century*. New York and London: Norton.

Smart, J. J. C. (1967). Utilitarianism. In P. Edwards (Ed.), *The encyclopedia of philosophy* (Vol. 8, pp. 206–212). New York: Macmillan.

Smart, J. J. C. (1973). An outline of a system of utilitarian ethics. In J. J. C. Smart & B. A. O. Williams (Eds.), *Utilitarianism: For and against* (pp. 3–74). Cambridge: Cambridge University Press.

Smetana, J. (1985). Preschool children's conceptions of transgressions: Effects of varying moral and conventional domain-related attributes. *Developmental Psychology, 21*, 18–29.

Smetana, J. (1989). Toddler's social interactions in the context of moral and conventional transgressions in the home. *Developmental Psychology, 25*, 499–508.

Smetana, J. (1993). Understanding of social rules. In M. Bennett (Ed.), *The development of social cognition: The child as psychologist* (pp. 111–141). New York: Guilford Press.

Smetana, J., & Braeges, J. (1990). The development of toddlers' moral and conventional judgements. *Merrill-Palmer Quarterly, 36*, 329–346.

Smith, A. (1976). *The theory of the moral sentiments*. Oxford: Clarendon Press. (Original work published 1759)

Smith, C. (2003). *Moral, believing animals: Human personhood and culture*. Oxford: Oxford University Press.

Smith, M. (1994). *The moral problem*. Cambridge: Basil Blackwell.

Smith, S. M., & Levin, I. P. (1996). Need for cognition and choice framing effects. *Journal of Behavioral Decision Making, 9*, 283–290.

Snare, F. E. (1980). The diversity of morals. *Mind, 89*, 353–369.

Sober, E. (1998). Innate knowledge. In E. Craig (Ed.), *The Routledge encyclopedia of philosophy* (Vol. 4, pp. 794–797). London: Routledge.

Solan, L. M., & Darley, J. M. (2001). Causation, contribution, and legal liability: An empirical study. *Law and Contemporary Problems, 64,* 265–298.

Sorensen, R. (2001). *Vagueness and contradiction.* Oxford: Clarendon Press.

Sosa, D. (1993). Consequences of consequentialism. *Mind, 102,* 101–122.

Sosa, E. (Forthcoming). A defense of the use of intuitions in philosophy. In M. Bishop & D. Murphy (Eds.), *Stich and his critics.* Malden, MA: Blackwell.

Spelke, E. S. (1994). Initial knowledge: Six suggestions. *Cognition, 50,* 431–445.

Sperber, D. (1994). The modularity of thought and the epidemiology of representations. In L. A. Hirschfeld & S. A. Gelman (Eds.), *Mapping the mind: Domain specificity in cognition and culture* (pp. 39–67). Cambridge: Cambridge University Press.

Sperber, D. (2005). Modularity and relevance: How can a massively modular mind be flexible and context-sensitive? In P. Carruthers, S. Laurence, & S. Stich (Eds.), *The innate mind: Structure and contents* (pp. 53–68). New York: Oxford.

Sperber, D., & Hirschfeld, L. A. (2004). The cognitive foundations of cultural stability and diversity. *Trends in Cognitive Sciences, 8,* 40–46.

Staub, E. (1978). *Positive social behavior and morality: Vol. 1. Social and personal influences.* New York: Academic Press.

Stevenson, C. (1937). The emotive meaning of ethical terms. *Mind, 46,* 14–31.

Stevenson, C. (1944). *Ethics and language.* New Haven and London: Yale University Press.

Stich, S. (1972). Grammar, psychology, and indeterminacy. *Journal of Philosophy, 69,* 799–818.

Stich, S. (1975). Introduction: The idea of innateness. In his *Innate ideas* (pp. 1–22). Berkeley: University of California Press.

Stich, S. (1988). Reflective equilibrium, analytic epistemology, and the problem of cognitive diversity. *Synthese, 74,* 391–413.

Stich, S. P. (2006). Is morality an elegant machine or kludge? *Journal of Cognition and Culture, 6,* 181–189.

Stich, S., & Weinberg, J. (2001). Jackson's empirical assumptions. *Philosophy and Phenomenological Research, 62,* 637–643.

Strawson, G. (1986). *Freedom and belief.* Oxford: Oxford University Press.

Strawson, P. (1982). Freedom and resentment. In G. Watson (Ed.), *Free will* (pp. 59–80). New York: Oxford University Press. (Original work published 1962)

Street, S. (2006). A Darwinian dilemma for realist theories of value. *Philosophical Studies, 127*, 109–166.

Sturgeon, N. (1986a). Harman on moral explanations of natural facts. *Southern Journal of Philosophy, 24*(Supp.), 69–78.

Sturgeon, N. (1986b). What difference does it make whether moral realism is true? *The Southern Journal of Philosophy, 24*(Supp.), 115–141.

Sturgeon, N. (1988). Moral explanations. In G. Sayre-McCord (Ed.), *Essays in moral realism* (pp. 229–255). Ithaca and London: Cornell University Press.

Sugawara, M. (1985). *Lives of master swordsmen.* Tokyo, Japan: East Publications.

Sumner, W. G. (1934). *Folkways.* Boston: Ginn.

Sunstein, C. R. (2003). *Why societies need dissent.* Cambridge: Harvard University Press.

Sunstein, C. R. (2004). Lives, life-years, and willingness to pay. *Columbia Law Review, 104*, 205–252.

Sunstein, C. R. (2005). Moral heuristics. *Brain and Behavioral Sciences, 28*, 531–573.

Sutker, P. B., Moan, C. E., & Swanson, W. C. (1972). Porteus Maze test qualitative performance in pure sociopaths, prison normals, and antisocial psychotics. *Journal of Clinical Psychology, 28*, 349–353.

Takemura, K. (1994). Influence of elaboration on the framing of decision. *The Journal of Psychology, 128*, 33–39.

Tappan, M. (1997). Language, culture, and moral development: A Vygotskian perspective. *Developmental Review, 17*, 78–100.

Taylor, C. (1989). *Sources of the self: The making of the modern identity.* Cambridge: Harvard University Press.

Terkel, S. (1997). *My American century.* New York: New Press.

Tetlock, P. E. (1999). Review of *Culture of honor: The psychology of violence in the South. Political Psychology, 20*, 211–213.

Tetlock, P. E. (2003). Thinking the unthinkable: Sacred values and taboo cognitions. *Trends in Cognitive Sciences, 7*, 320–324.

Thompson, R., & Hoffman, M. (1980). Empathy and the arousal of guilt in children. *Developmental Psychology, 15*, 155–156.

Thomson, J. J. (1970). Individuating actions. *Journal of Philosophy, 68*, 774–781.

Thomson, J. J. (2003). Causation: Omissions. *Philosophy and Phenomenological Research, 66*, 81.

Timmons, M. (1999). *Morality without foundations*. New York: Oxford University Press.

Tisak, M. (1995). Domains of social reasoning and beyond. In R. Vasta (Ed.), *Annals of child development* (Vol. 11, pp. 95–130). London: Jessica Kingsley.

Todd, P. M., & Miller, G. F. (1999). From pride to prejudice to persuasion: Satisficing in mate search. In G. Gigerenzer, P. M. Todd, & the ABC Research Group, *Simple heuristics that make us smart* (pp. 287–308). New York: Oxford University Press.

Tolhurst, W. (1987). The argument from moral disagreement. *Ethics, 97*, 610–621.

Tolhurst, W. (1990). On the epistemic value of moral experience. *Southern Journal of Philosophy, 29*(Supp.), 67–87.

Tolhurst, W. (1998). Seemings. *American Philosophical Quarterly, 35*, 293–302.

Tooby, J., Cosmides, L., & Barrett, C. (2005). Resolving the debate on innate ideas: Learnability constraints and the evolved interpenetration of motivational and conceptual functions. In P. Carruthers, S. Laurence, & S. Stich (Eds.), *The innate mind: Structure and contents* (pp. 305–337). New York: Oxford University Press.

Toulmin, S. (1950). *An examination of the place of reason in ethics*. Cambridge: Cambridge University Press.

Tranel, D., Bechara, A., & Damasio, A. (2000). Decision making and the somatic marker hypothesis. In M. Gazzaniga (Ed.), *The new cognitive neurosciences* (pp. 1047–1061). Cambridge: MIT Press.

Tranel, D., Bechara, A., Damasio, H., & Damasio, A. (1998). Neural correlates of emotional imagery. *International Journal of Psychophysiology, 30*, 107.

Turiel, E. (1983). *The development of social knowledge: Morality and convention*. Cambridge: Cambridge University Press.

Turiel, E., Killen, M., & Helwig, C. C. (1987). Morality: Its structure, function, and vagaries. In J. Kagan & S. Lamb (Eds.), *The emergence of morality in young children* (pp. 155–243). Chicago: University of Chicago Press.

Turkheimer, E. (2000). Three laws of behavior genetics and what they mean. *Current Directions in Psychological Science, 9*, 160–164.

Tversky, A., & Kahneman, D. (1974). Judgment under uncertainty: Heuristics and biases. *Science, 185*, 1124–1131.

Tversky, A., & Kahneman, D. (1981). The framing of decisions and the psychology of choice. *Science, 211*, 453–458.

Unger, P. (1996). *Living high and letting die: Our illusion of innocence*. New York: Oxford University Press.

Van Roojen, M. (1999). Reflective moral equilibrium and psychological theory. *Ethics, 109*, 846–857.

van Roojen, M. (2005). Moral cognitivism vs. non-cognitivism. In E. N. Zalta (Ed.), *The Stanford encyclopedia of philosophy*. Stanford, CA: The Metaphysics Research Lab, Center for the Study of Language and Information, Stanford University. Retrieved from http://plato.stanford.edu/archives/win2005/entries/moral-cognitivism/

Varela, F. (1999). *Ethical know-how: Action, wisdom, and cognition*. Stanford, CA: Stanford University Press.

Vouloumanos, A., Hauser, M. D., & Werker, J. (Unpublished). Human infants do not show an innate preference for speech over other biological sounds.

Wallace, J. D. (1988). *Moral relevance and moral conflict*. Ithaca, NY: Cornell University Press.

Wallace, R. J. (1994). *Responsibility and the moral sentiments*. Cambridge: Harvard University Press.

Wegner, D., & Bargh, J. (1998). Control and automaticity in social life. In D. T. Gilbert, S. T. Fiske, & G. Lindzey (Eds.), *Handbook of social psychology* (4th ed., pp. 446–496). New York: McGraw-Hill.

Weinberg, N., Nichols, S., & Stich, S. (2001). Normativity and epistemic intuitions. *Philosophical Topics, 29*, 429–460.

Westermark, E. (1906). *Origin and Development of the Moral Ideas*, 2 vols. New York: Macmillan.

Wheatley, T., & Haidt, J. (2005). Hypnotic disgust makes moral judgments more severe. *Psychological Science, 16*, 780–784.

White, N. (2002). *Individual and conflict in Greek ethics*. Oxford: Oxford University Press.

Wiggins, D. (1987a). *Needs, values, truth*. Oxford: Blackwell.

Wiggins, D. (1987b). A sensible subjectivism? In his *Needs, values, truth* (pp. 185–214). Oxford: Blackwell.

Williams, B. (1973). A critique of utilitarianism. In J. J. C. Smart & B. Williams (Eds.), *Utilitarianism: For and against* (pp. 77–150). New York: Cambridge University Press.

Williams, B. (1981). *Moral luck*. Cambridge: Cambridge University Press.

Williams, B. (1985). *Ethics and the limits of philosophy*. Cambridge, Mass: Harvard University Press.

Williams, B. (1988). Consequentialism and integrity. In S. Scheffler (Ed.), *Consequentialism and its critics* (pp. 20–50). New York: Oxford University Press. Reprinted from B. Williams & J. J. C. Smart (Eds.), *Utilitarianism: For and against* (1973, pp. 82–118). Cambridge: Cambridge University Press.

Wilson, D. S. (2002). *Darwin's cathedral: Evolution, religion, and the nature of society.* Chicago: University of Chicago Press.

Wilson, E. O. (1975). *Sociobiology: A new synthesis.* Cambridge: Harvard University Press.

Wilson, E. O. (1998). The biological basis of morality. *The Atlantic Monthly, 281,* 53–70.

Wilson, J. Q. (1993). *The moral sense.* New York: Free Press.

Wilson, T. D. (2002). *Strangers to ourselves: Discovering the adaptive unconscious.* Cambridge: Belknap Press.

Wilson, T. D., Lindsey, S., & Schooler, T. (2000). A model of dual attitudes. *Psychological Review, 107,* 101–126.

Woodward, J. (2003). *Making things happen.* Oxford: Oxford University Press.

Woolfolk, R. L. (1999). Malfunction and mental illness. *Monist, 82,* 658–670.

Woolfolk, R. L., & Doris, J. M. (2002). Rationing mental health care: Parity, disparity, and justice. *Bioethics, 16,* 469–485.

Wright, R. (1994). *The moral animal: Why we are the way we are.* New York: Pantheon.

Wyatt-Brown, B. (1982). *Southern honor: Ethics and behavior in the old South.* New York: Oxford University Press.

Zahn-Waxler, C., & Radke-Yarrow, M. (1982). The development of altruism: Alternative research strategies. In N. Eisenberg (Ed.), *The development of pro-social behavior* (pp. 109–137). New York: Academic Press.

Zajonc, R. B. (1980). Feeling and thinking: Preferences need no inferences. *American Psychologist, 35,* 151–175.

Zweig, J. (1998, January). Five investing lessons from America's top pension fund. *Money,* 115–118.

Contributors

Fredrik Bjorklund
University of Lund

James Blair
National Institute of Mental Health

Paul Bloomfield
University of Connecticut

Fiery Cushman
Harvard University

Justin D'Arms
Ohio State University

John Deigh
University of Texas at Austin

John M. Doris
Washington University

Julia Driver
Dartmouth College

Ben Fraser
Australian National University

Gerd Gigerenzer
Max Plank Institute

Michael B. Gill
University of Arizona

Jonathan Haidt
University of Virginia

Marc D. Hauser
Harvard University

Daniel Jacobson
Bowling Green State University

Joshua Knobe
University of North Carolina at Chapel Hill

Brian Leiter
University of Texas at Austin

Don Loeb
University of Vermont

Ron Mallon
University of Utah

Darcia Narvaez
University of Notre Dame

Shaun Nichols
University of Arizona

Alexandra Plakias
University of Michigan

Jesse J. Prinz
University of North Carolina at Chapel Hill

Geoffrey Sayre-McCord
University of North Carolina at Chapel Hill

Russ Shafer-Landau
University of Wisconsin

Walter Sinnott-Armstrong
Dartmouth College

Cass R. Sunstein
University of Chicago

William Tolhurst
University of Northern Illinois

Liane Young
Harvard University

Index to Volume 1

Note: Figures are indicated by "f"; tables are indicated by "t," and footnotes by "n."

abstraction, xv, 283–285, 287, 303
action, theory of, 321, 362, 363, 365
acts, 215, 231, 294, 308
adaptation(s)
  as constant, 43
  versus creation, 437
  and incest, 177–182, 185–188, 197, 200
  and kin-directed altruism, 175
  moral virtues as, 251–258
  and sexual selection, 212–215, 223, 233–235
  and social behavior, 69–71, 286
  and third-parties, 167–169, 206
  values as, 437
  See also fitness consequences
adaptive problems
  domain differences, 58, 77, 115
  and ecological rationality, 65–69, 82
  and inbreeding, 178–182, 205–207
  and social exchange, 65–69, 77, 82, 115
addictions, 212
adolescents, 221, 238, 322
advantage, 5, 52n
  See also benefit
aesthetics, 232, 253, 257, 282
  See also physical appearance

Affective Resonance Account, 339
age, 221, 236, 238
agency
  and cheating detection, 157
  harm infliction, 329, 346, 363
  and inference, 66–69
  and moral norms, 362
  and nativism, 321, 362, 363
  non-naturalist view, 7
  and social contracts, 74n, 108, 149, 151–155
  symbolic thought, 287, 310
aggression
  and conflict resolution, 251–258
  and domain specificity, 58
  lack of, 294
  and sexual selection, 223
  symbolic extention, 288
  and vicarious distress, 374
agnosticism, 21n7
agreeableness, 224, 227, 229, 239
altruism
  and aesthetics, 233
  and animals, 254, 400–402
  genetic transmission, 224
  kin-directed, 175, 179, 190n6, 214
  and sexual selection, 233, 235, 254
  and status, 257

altruistic punishment, 235
ambition, 256
amygdala, 291, 389, 390, 391
analogy, 280–282
See also linguistic analogy
analysis/synthesis, 27–28, 46
anger
  and blame, 368
  versus disapproval, 193
  innateness, 382
  as moral response, 198, 241
  and parenting, 431
  and psychopaths, 390
  and third-parties, 198
  for victim, 404
  and violations, 380, 393
animal rights, 242, 312n6, 340
animals
  aesthetic displays, 232, 253
  altruism in, 254, 400–402
  causality, 283
  cognition, 275
  conditioning, 371, 401, 404
  conflict, 252
  courtship, 219, 253–254
  display-defer strategy, 253, 255
  domain generality, 296n4
  empathy, 221
  fairness, 399
  group-level equilibrium selection, 234
  innate traits, 370–372
  kin detection, 175
  kindness, 294
  lek paradox, 224
  morality, 221, 286, 287, 304, 307, 313n17
  sharing, 400, 402
  signaling theory, 215, 233, 249–250, 273
  symbolic thought, 269, 271, 279, 282, 285, 286, 290
  and third-party behavior, 404
  vicarious distress, 398

anthropocentrism, 226
approval
  and childhood, 395
  in courtship, 212
  emotions of, 368
  third-party behavior, 166, 193, 199
Aquinas, Thomas, 350
Arendt, H., 292
Aristotle
  and acts, 211
  virtues, 231, 422, 435
  and will, 9
artifact theory, 106–109
artistic virtuosity, 229
asceticism, 255
assassination, 242
associative learning, 269–271, 273, 282, 386
attachment security, 227
attention, 273, 276, 282, 291, 296n3
Augustine, 3
Australian ethical naturalism, 1
authoritarianism, 224, 226
authority
  and conventions *versus* morality, 392, 430, 432
  dependence on, 385
  and permission rules, 96, 99
autism, 66, 117n4
aversions, 335
  See also inbreeding avoidance

Bain, A., 193
bald naturalism, 12, 20n1, 24n24
bargaining, 103, 376
Baron-Cohen, S., 66, 111
Barrett, H. C., 56, 67, 99, 102, 115
Beaman, C. P., 139, 149, 150–151t, 152, 157, 163n2, 163n3
beauty, 253
  See also aesthetics; physical appearance

behavior
  adaptive social, 69–71, 286
  and moral competence, 418n1
  of others (*see* third-party behavior)
  tendencies, 405
behavioral conditioning. *See*
  conditioning
behavioral outcomes, 23n14, 282, 294,
  362
beliefs
  and conscience, 23n19
  false, 23n14
  in just world, 230
  versus logic, 64
  and naturalistic ethics, 7
  of others, 12, 288
benefit
  and cheater detection, 78–86, 89f,
    98–102, 106–109, 156–158
  contingency, 71, 100, 118n8
  and drinking age law, 108, 152–155
  and entitlement, 79f
  and obligation, 100
  and performance, 159
  and permission rules, 100, 104
  and precautionary rules, 100
  and social contracts, 75t, 79f, 81, 89f,
    147
  and third-party behavior, 166, 206
  withholding, 207
  See also cost-benefit analysis
Berlin, I., 259
biases
  cultural factors, 332, 336–343, 428
  about food, 338
  innateness, xv, 332–336, 340–343, 365
  Sperberian, 332–337
  See also inbreeding avoidance
bioethics, 241–242
bipolar disorder, 228
Bjorklund, F., 428
Blackburn, S., 38, 52n7, 423
Blair, R. J. R., 369, 374, 390

blame, 368, 382–383, 402
body
  and capitalism, 293
  and Christianity, 288, 290, 309
body language, 278, 285
Booth, A., 257
Bowles, S., 215
Boyd, R., 342
Boyer, P., 127
brain
  and hazards, 95
  modules, 279, 387–391
  of psychopaths, 390
  and reasoning, 60–66, 111–113, 112f
  and social exchange, 110–113, 112f
  and tokenization, 291, 312n9
  and vices, 237
  See also neuroimaging
brain damage, 110, 157, 226, 389
Bramati, I., 391
British moralists, 368
Brosnan, S. F., 399
Buddha, 4
Buller, D., 68, 139, 162n1
Buss, D., 221
by-products, 82, 97, 118, 165, 168–170,
  174, 177, 182–183, 185–186, 189,
  192, 197–201, 203, 206–208, 281,
  368, 371, 375, 382, 386, 398, 400,
  403, 406–407, 420

cannibalism, 373, 405, 429
capacity nativism, 321, 361–364
capitalism, 293
Cara, F., 118n9
Casebeer, W., xii, 30n1, 46
Castañeda, H.-N., 56, 117n1
categoricity, 25n30, 42, 45
categorization, xv, 291, 303, 305
  See also symbolic thought
causation, 7, 283, 362
certainty, 288
Chandler, M., 364

charisma, 238

Charlie task, 66

cheating

as artifact theory, 106–109

and decision rules, 70

definition, 81, 114

detection (*see* cheating detection)

and intelligence, 405

and nativism, 409

and permission schema, 97

sexual infidelity, 168, 228, 239

See also violations

cheating detection

and benefit, 78–86, 89f, 98–102, 106–109, 156–158

and brain damage, 157, 389

and content *versus* logic, 84, 88, 90, 94, 118n11, 158

as ESS, 54, 71, 102

mistakes, 157 (*see also* intentionality)

and perspective, 157

and Wason selection task, 69, 388

Cheng, P., 65, 77, 95, 96, 119n14

childhood

and conventions, 392, 414, 416, 430–433

emotions, 434

inbreeding avoidance, xiii, 170–177, 180–182, 190n6

moral development, 393, 395–397, 407–409, 414, 430

natural jurisprudence, 354, 355, 364

punishment, 354, 373, 387, 392, 404, 416, 431

stories and myths, 414

children

and harm norms, 329

infanticide, 429

marriages, 176

number of, 342

peer pressure, 393

raised by wolves, 394

social response to, 391

Chisholm, R., 7

choice. *See* decision rules; intentionality

Chomsky, N., xv, 277, 319, 325, 331, 355, 359n1, 367, 371, 409

Christianity

on cousin marriage, 378

for Nietzsche, 436

and physical body, 288, 290, 309

virtues, xiv, 211, 251, 252, 254, 256, 259, 266

Church, R. M., 398

Churchland, P., 29

classical conditioning. *See* conditioning

Cleckley, H. M., 369

cognition

abstraction, xv, 283–285, 287, 303

analogy, 280–282

concept, 130n1

content generality, 84, 88, 90, 94, 106

content specificity, 137, 160

cross-modular binding, 273–280

in dogs, 275

and emotion, 29, 196

epistemic conscientiousness, 231

and inbreeding avoidance, 188, 189

and kin detection, 190n6

least effort, 291, 312n9

library model, 124, 133–135

and moral competence, 418n1

and moral virtues, 225

multiple grammars, 164n6

about social events, 389, 391

tokenization, xv, 291, 303, 305

See also inference(s); mental representations; reasoning; symbolic thought

cognitive control, 29

cognitive disorders, 85

cognitive nativism, 321

cognitivism, 22n9

Cohen, D., 330

Collins, J., 410, 415
commerce, 377
  See also capitalism
commitment, 234
common sense, 72–76, 114
compassion, 294, 306, 317, 380, 382
  See also empathy; vicarious distress
compatibilism, 8, 29
competition
  natural selection impact, 253
  sexual, 222, 239, 253
  and testosterone, 258
compliance, 144, 159, 162
conditional helping, 71, 81, 102
conditional reasoning
  and cheater detection, 83–87,
    106–109, 388
  evolution of, 164n5
  and obligation, 139
  and specialization, 94, 157, 388
  See also Wason selection task
conditional rules, 62–64, 69, 84, 118n9,
  145
conditioning
  and domain-specificity, 397
  of emotions, 386, 404, 431
  operant conditioning, 371, 400–402,
    406
  and psychopaths, 390
conflict
  and moral norms, 330
  of self-interests, 48–49
  tolerance of, 51
  between two "oughts," 125–127, 129,
    131–133
conflict resolution, 251–258, 260n2,
  267
Confucianism, 4, 49–50
Confucius, 9
connectionism, 24n23
conscience
  in children, 396
  evolution of, 9

conscientiousness, 226, 229, 239
  epistemic, 231
consequences. *See* behavioral outcomes;
  fitness consequences
consequentialism, 117, 426n2
considered judgments, 354, 358n1
constraints, 52n9, 413, 415, 418n3, 429
  See also universal grammar
content
  and inference, 67, 137, 145
  and logical form, 137, 146–155,
    150–151t, 154f, 158–162
  of social contracts, 90
content-general reasoning
  and cheater detection, 84, 88, 90, 94
  and cues, 115
  and switched contracts, 106, 118n9,
    160
content nativism
  versus capacity nativism, 321, 362–365
  and cultural factors, 332, 336–343
  innate biases model, xv, 332–336,
    340–343, 365
  principles and parameters model,
    324–332, 346–351, 403
  simple innateness model, 322–324,
    345
context, 44n1, 48–49
  and cheating, 102
  and deontology, 56–59
  of harm infliction, 329
  and moral judgment, 38–42, 44n1,
    47–49
contingency
  advantages, 19
  on authority, 392
  of benefit, 71, 118n8
  and cultural factors, 46
  of moral judgments, 40–42
  and moral language, 47
  of moral norms and rules, 411, 412,
    429, 432
  and naturalistic model, 48

contingency (cont.)
and social contracts, 72, 74*n*, 100,
118*n*8
and truth, 28
control, 29
See also self-regulation
conventions
versus moral rules, 384–386, 392–395,
416, 430–433
and psychopaths, 369
cooperation
and benefit, 70
and cheater detection, 81, 102
conflict resolution theory, 251–258
reciprocity, 58, 377
and sexual selection, 226, 227, 254
Cosmides, L., xiii, 53, 55, 56, 58, 62,
64, 65, 66, 67, 68, 69, 70, 71, 72, 75,
81, 82, 84, 85, 90, 91, 94, 95, 99,
100, 104, 113, 114, 116, 118*n*5,
118*n*8, 118*n*11, 119*n*4, 119*n*17,
121–129, 132, 137–141, 143, 144,
145, 146, 147, 154, 165, 176, 181,
187, 190*n*7, 199, 299, 387, 389
cost-benefit analysis
inbreeding, 173, 186–188
mate selection, 237
social contracts, 75t, 81, 118*n*8, 147
third-party behavior, 167–169, 189,
206
costly signaling
and Darwinian aesthetics, 232
description, 215–217
moral virtues as, 219, 246–250, 265
counterfactuals, 56
counterintuitivity, 128
courage. *See* heroism
courtship
displays, 221, 238, 257
as domain, 58
dominance and submission, 267
generosity in, 219
lek paradox, 224

and moral virtues, 210–212
as obstacle course, 258
See also costly signaling; sexual
selection
cousins, 378
Cowie, F., 370
Cox, J., 64
creationism, 21*n*6
creativity
versus adaptation, 437
and doubt, 289
imagination, 274
and sexual selection, 221, 257
criminal justice system, 230, 233, 306,
357, 359*n*4
cross-dressing, 431
cross-modular binding, 273–285,
296*n*2, 299–300, 303
cruelty, 429
cues
and deontic conditionals, 115
dominance relationships, 253, 255,
257
for kin detection, 172, 174, 179–182,
188, 190*n*6
and sexual aversion, 176, 180–182,
185
for social contract, 76, 113, 148
of submission, 258, 260*n*1
and third-party behavior, 167,
169
cultural change, xv, 340–343, 405
cultural creativity, 257
cultural factors
biases, 332, 336–343, 428
and contingency, 46
cooperation, 377
courtship, 211, 267
divorce, 212
evil, 293, 295
fairness, 376
harm, 373, 381, 385
inbreeding, 165, 171, 176, 179, 185

incest, 183–185, 200, 332, 337, 378
individualism, 412
and language, 325
mate traits, 221–223
moral constraints, 429
moral development, 397
moral norms, 322–324, 329–331, 337,
  357, 426n5, 435
rape, 381
relativism, 16, 50
sexual infidelity, 239
sharing, 377
and social exchange reasoning, 85, 91,
  115, 135
symbolic thought, 277, 303, 310
third-party behavior, 214, 303
values, 436, 439
Curry, O., xiv, 266, 267
Cushman, F., 413, 428

Daly, M., 340–341
dancing, 277
danger, 77, 94, 374, 398
  See also precautionary rules
Darley, J., 350
Darwin, C.
  on aesthetics, 232
  on conscience, 9
  and costly signaling, 216
  and God, 20n4
  on moral sense, 198
  on religion, 23n19
  on submission, 255
Darwinian naturalism, 33–36
Dawkins, R., 70, 128
death, 116, 284, 288
decision rules, 70, 86, 87f
de Oliveira-Souza, R., 391
deontic logic
  and content (see content; content-
    general reasoning)
  domain-specificity, 59, 109, 114 (see
    also domains)

entitlement and obligation, 72–76 (see
  also entitlement; obligation)
  and ethics, 117
  neurological basis, xiii, 109–113
  operators, 56–58
  practicality, 59–60
deontic rules
  compliance with, 144–145, 159, 162
  without benefit or hazard, 97f,
    98–100, 156
  See also permission schema;
    precautionary rules; social contracts
DePaul, M., 231
dependability, 226, 227, 229
depression, 228
Descartes, R., 7
descriptive adequacy, 353–356
de Wahl, F. B. M., 399, 402
Dewey, J., 8–9, 17
Dias, M., 381
Dietrich, M., xv, 315
dilemmas, 125–127, 131–133
disapproval
  versus anger, 193
  in courtship, 212
  emotions of, 368
  of third-party behavior, 166–169, 193,
    199
disgust
  and blame, 368
  and death, 116
  and etiquette violations, 333, 430
  extension, 382
  and food, 336, 337
  and inbreeding, 179, 181, 197, 206,
    208, 333
  and moralization, 196, 241, 320, 369,
    379
  and power, 336
  and psychopaths, 390
display-defer strategy, 253, 255
dispositionalism, 309, 313n14, 313n15,
  332, 375, 383–385

diversity
  and ecological perspective, 43
  of individual interests, 48–49
  and language, 325
  and moral norms, 329, 355
  respect for, 19
divorce, 212, 219
domain generality
  in animals, 296n4
  in deontic logic, 105–109, 125–129,
    131–133, 158, 160
  nonmodular, 276, 296n2
  and symbolic thought, 125, 283
domains
  differences, 58–60, 85
  innateness, 380–383, 403
  interaction, 58, 77
  immoral, 383–385
  prioritization, 77
  and reasoning, 66–69, 76–78, 389
domain specificity
  versus conditioning, 397
  evolution view, 58–60
  and inference, 67, 76–78, 114, 124,
    139–141
  and native peoples, 85
  and "ought," 56–59, 101, 122–125, 133
  and schizophrenia, 85
  and social contracts, 58–60, 76–78, 85,
    109, 114, 125, 145, 148
domestic violence, 223
dominance
  and aggression, 374
  and courtship, 267
  cues, 253, 255, 257, 260n1
  domain specificity, 58
  and etiquette, 258
  hierarchy, 380
  See also Pareto dominance
Donald, M., 285
double dissociation, 110
double effect, 346, 348, 350, 364
  See also intentionality

double standards, 439
doubt, 289
Down's syndrome, 249, 264
drinking age, 107–108, 119n20, 139,
  150–153, 154f, 163n3
Driscoll, C., xiv, 263–266
Duke naturalism, xii, 20n1
Dummett, M., 415
Durkheim, E., 321
Dworkin, R. M., 349, 350
Dwyer, S., xvi, 326, 354, 367, 392, 393,
  408, 411, 414, 422, 427, 428–433

ecological rationality, 65–69
education, 394, 396–397
  See also learning
Edwards, C. P., 328
E-language, 411
E-morality, 411
emotional stability, 227
emotions
  and children, 434
  and cognition, 29, 196
  conditioning, 386, 404, 431
  in courtship, 212, 267
  versus desires, 202n4
  for good or evil, 294
  and inbreeding, 179, 181, 190n8, 196,
    208
  incest taboo, 192–194, 196–200
  innateness, 382
  meta-emotions, 404
  and moral competence, 418n1
  and moral domains, 380–382
  and moral judgments, 241, 304, 369,
    370
  and moral norms, 339, 368–370, 387,
    404, 423
  and psychopaths, 390
  self- and other-directed, 369, 402
  versus sentiment, 168, 196, 202n1,
    207
  and social exchanges, 101

and third-party actions, 168, 192–194,
198
See also anger; disgust; guilt; vicarious
distress
emotivism, 36, 304
empathy
in animals, 221
genetics, 224
and psychopathy, 292
selection for, 235
sexual selection, 222
See also vicarious distress
empiricism, 5, 407, 434
Enlightenment, 367
entitlement
and benefit, 79f
meanings, 56–58
and precaution rules, 78
and social contracts, 72–77, 74t, 81,
114
Wason selection task, 64, 79f
See also benefit
entrainment, 271, 277–281
epidemiology of representations, 116,
128–129, 135–136
epistemology, 4, 10–11, 23n20, 24n25,
27, 231
Ermer, E., 111, 157
ethical naturalism, 2–9, 12–19, 20n3,
33–36, 45, 424
ethical skepticism, 34–36, 45
ethics
Aristotelian, 435
consequentialism, 117
and deontic logic, 117
and empiricism, 434
and God, 2–4
human ecology, 18, 42–44
human nature, 15–17, 36, 310
Kantian view, 6
naturalist view, 2–9, 12–19, 33–36,
424
normativism, 10–15

reciprocation, 35
relativism, xii, 15–17, 19
sexual selection, 231–233, 240–243
thick concepts, 414
virtue ethics, 231–233
ethnicity, 230, 428
etiquette
and courtship, 258
and disgust, 333, 430
and dominance, 255, 258
permission rules, 96
See also conventions
euthanasia, 242
evil
body as, 288
definition, 290, 316
from good intentions, 294
killing as, 36
and moral philosophy, 22n11
particularist view, 304
recognition of, 19
relativism, 317
and responsibility, 292, 306, 308
sadism as (*see* sadism)
symbolism, xv, 286, 290–295, 303
tokenization, 290, 305, 307, 311
evolution
conflict resolution theory, 251–258
and game theory, 70
and inbreeding, 178–182
of morality, xvi, 52, 166–169, 249,
286–290
progressive nature, 35
of reasoning, 65–69, 118n7, 146,
164n5, 295n1
of social interaction, 58, 166–169
of symbolic thought, 276–283, 300
and third-party behavior, 166–169
See also adaptation(s); fitness
consequences; natural selection;
sexual selection
evolutionarily stable strategy (ESS), 70,
81, 102, 118n7, 253

expectations
  of others, 214, 395
  of reward, 395
experience, 436
explicit change rule, 100
exploitation, 246, 248, 293
expressivism, 38, 423
extraversion, 227, 229

facial expressions, 101, 390
faculty, 409–415
fairness, 355, 376, 394, 398–402
faith, loss of, 17, 20n4
family values, 259
fear, 390
feasibility, 52n9
Feldman, F., 57
fertility rates, 342
Fessler, D., 338–339
fetuses, 349
fiber tract tracing, 279
Fiddick, L., 58, 68, 72, 77, 78, 84, 85,
  95, 99, 100, 101, 103, 115, 118n9,
  118n11, 119n17, 159
Fiske, A. P., 380
Fitch, T., 277
fitness consequences
  and costly signaling, 215–217,
    246–248
  and inbreeding, 167, 173, 175, 178,
    186, 191, 199
  and morality, 242, 247, 265
  and sexual selection, 214, 220, 234,
    237, 239, 249, 265
  and values, 437
Flanagan, O., xii, 8, 13, 27–30, 37–44,
  52n9
Fodor, J., xiii, 106–109, 119n17, 138,
  140, 144–164, 150, 155, 161, 270,
  296n2, 296n4, 358, 387
folk naturalism, 3, 4
food
  conditional reasoning, 388

religious laws, 385
sharing, 376, 400–402
taboos, 338, 380
Frazer, J. G., 172, 203n9
freedom
  and belief, 289
  of individual, 425
  for Kant, 6, 7
free will, xii, 8–9
  See also neocompatibilism
Freud, S., 173, 190n5, 211
friendship, 58
functional naturalism, 30
fundamentalism, 289

Gainer, P., 398
Gallistel, C. R., 118n5
games, 103, 376
game theory, 70, 215, 235, 252, 377
Gangestad, S. W., 239–240
Garcia effect, 269
Geertz, C. J., 383
gender
  attitudes toward women, 288, 322,
    329, 340
  and culture, 257
  and innate biases model, 365
  and sexual selection, 218, 223, 237,
    238, 257
  testosterone effect, 223, 257, 258
  and virtue, 259
Gendler, T., 56
generalization, xv, 393, 416
  See also domain generality
generosity
  and bipolar disorder, 228
  and dominance, 259
  sexual, 220
  and sexual selection, 219, 222, 257
  and status, 254, 257
  superogatory acts, 259, 261n7, 266
genetics
  and beauty, 232

and cross-modular binding, 279, 281, 299–300

and inbreeding, 178, 236

and innate moral norms, 323

and moral virtues, 223–225, 236, 248

and personality traits, 227

and sexual infidelity, 240

and sexual selection, 217, 223–225, 236–238, 248

genocide, 242, 290

gesticulation, 278

Gibbard, A., 38, 52n7, 423

Gibbs, B. J., 272

Gigerenzer, G., 81, 86, 90, 118n5

Gintis, H., 215, 235, 376

Girotto, V., 118n9

glory, 256

God

  deist view, 20n4

  and ethics, 2–4

  for Kant, 6, 22n2

  loss of faith in, 17, 20n4

Golden Rule, 4

Goldman, A., 24n21, 431

good

  definition, 15, 28, 290

  and moral philosophy, 22n11

  noncognitive view, 309

  particularist view, 304

  symbolic thought, 286, 294, 303

Goodnow, J. J., 393

gossip, 239, 263

Gould, S. J., 34, 299

Grafman, J., 391

greater good, 346

greed, 292

  See also selfishness

gregariousness, 375, 420

Gregersen, E., 257–258

Griggs, R., 64

group-level equilibrium, 234, 246

groups

  ethnic base, 230, 428

and harm norms (see harm norms, distributional patterns)

hierarchy, 260n2, 365, 380, 403

  versus individualism, 412, 425

moral and nonmoral, 246, 249

similarity recognition, 284

size, 168

group selection, 234, 246

Grusec, J. E., 393

guilt

  conditioning, 404

  and convention violations, 385

  as domain, 380

  as moral sentiment, 196

  and responsibility, 308

  and self-regard, 197

  of survivors, 202n2

Haidt, J., 56, 369, 380–381, 384–385, 396, 413, 428

Haig, D., 173

halo effect, 230, 238

hallucination, 275

Hamilton, W., 175, 190n6

Harman, G., xv, 228, 326, 329, 353, 355, 365, 426n5, 428

harm norms

  versus conventions, 384, 385

  cultural factors, 381–382

  distributional patterns, 326, 329, 348, 362, 373–375, 381, 385

  and emotions, 339

  and greater good, 346

  and own young, 429

  training children, 393, 431

hatred, 287

Hauser, M. D., 277, 321, 367, 378, 380, 392, 400, 413, 421, 428

Hawkes, K., 257

hazard management

  as domain, 58

  and evolution, 162

  and logical form, 161

hazard management (cont.)
 reasoning, 113
 theory of, 95, 100
headhunters, 381
health, 226, 237
helping, 71, 81, 102
Hempel, C., 354
Henrich, J., 376, 399
heredity. *See* genetics
heroism
 for Hume, 256
 and sexual selection, 219, 221, 228,
  242
 superogatory acts, 259, 261*n*7, 266
hierarchies, 260*n*2, 365, 380, 403
Holyoak, K., 65, 77, 95, 96, 119*n*14
homosexuality, 171
honesty, 222, 226
honor, 330, 381
Hubbard, E. M., 279
Hug, K., 81, 86, 90
human ecology, 18, 42–44
human nature
 and certainty, 289
 dispositions, 23*n*19
 and ethics, 15–17, 36, 310
 hawks and doves, 256–258
 least effort, 291, 312*n*9
 morality objectification, 52*n*5
 moral standards, 310
 natural selection, 55–58
human rights, 357, 363
Hume, D.
 on human nature, 256, 260*n*3
 and justification, 34
 and motivation, 421
 on normativism, 13
 on religion, 23*n*3
 on vice, 359*n*3
 on virtues, 436
humility, 255, 256
hunter-gatherers, 72, 216, 322, 377
hunting, 44, 216, 257, 377

Hutcheson, F., 367, 406, 423, 426*n*4
hypothesizing, 38–41, 315, 325

ideology, 221, 226, 228
illness, 311
imagination, 274
imitation, 416, 431
I-moralities, 411–412
imperatives, 414
Implicit Association Test, 228, 230
improvement criteria, 438
inbreeding avoidance
 cousins, 378
 cultural factors, 165, 171, 176, 179,
  185
 emotions, 179, 181, 190*n*8, 196, 208
 and evolution, 178–182
 and innateness, 334
 moralization of, 405
 and natural selection, 178–182, 194,
  198
 as taboo (*see* incest)
 Westermarck studies, 170–177, 182,
  185, 188, 192–194, 334–338
inbreeding genetics, 178, 236
incest
 cultural factors, 183–185, 200, 332,
  337, 378
 dyad types, 188
 and emotions, 192–194, 196–200
 and kin selection, 259
 and moral nativism, 323, 379
 between siblings, 168, 332, 428
 as taboo, 177, 182–185, 199–201,
  334–336
individual
 versus act, 231
 versus group, 246, 425
 and morality, 215, 246, 306
 versus situation, 228
 tokenization of (*see* tokenization)
individualism, 49, 412, 425
inductive learning, 327, 393

infanticide, 242, 429

inferences
about others, 111–113, 117n4,
213–215, 285

inference(s)
of causality, 283
Charlie task, 66
by children, 393
cognitive architecture, 147, 160
and content, 67, 137, 145
and counterfactuals, 56
domain specificity, 67, 76–78, 114,
124–125, 139–141, 145, 148
about emotions, 101
about intentions, 101–103, 111
interactions between, 77
and logic, 57, 145, 161
about mental states, 66–69, 321
about moral character, 104
and moral preferences, 241
about others, 111–113, 117n4, 167,
169, 213–215, 285
about "oughts," 133
perceptual *versus* cognitive, 297n5
and permission schema, 96
and precautionary rules, 95, 100,
124
religion role, 115–116
and sexual selection, 213, 241
and social exchange, 54–59, 69,
72–77, 74t, 79f, 94, 114–116
Wason selection task, 63, 65, 79f
See also symbolic thought
inference systems, 164n6
infidelity, 168, 228, 239
innate biases model, xv, 332–336,
340–343, 365
innateness
defined, 370–372
of emotions, 382
gregariousness, 375
and justification, 422–425, 437–439
of language, 410

of moral disposition, 383–385
of morality, xv–xvi, 387–391 (*see also*
nativism)
of moral norms, 335, 411
of moral principles, 435
of moral rules, 412
and motivation, 419–422
intelligence
and free rider, 405
and moral virtues, 265
and quasi-moral traits, 231
and sexual selection, 226, 236, 237,
249
and status, 257
intentionality
and cheater detection, 80, 98, 102,
108
and children, 354, 364
and compliance, 159–160
and good or evil, 290, 294, 308, 317
inference about, 101–103, 111, 112
and killing, 357
lack of, 157
mental representation, 118n10
and nativism, 321, 362
and permission schema, 101
and symbolic thought, 275, 284
of violations, 101–106, 119n15, 156,
159, 354
and virtue epistemology, 232
See also double effect
internalism, 434
internalization, 431
interpretation, 68, 105, 119n16, 138
intuition
and belief system, 289
cognitive architecture, 55
conflicts, 135
of morality, 241–243, 356
violation of, 117, 127
and Wason selection task, 163n5
See also inference(s)
island constraints, 413, 418n3

Israeli kibbutz, 176, 334
Itard, J.-M.-G., 394

Jackendoff, R., 415
James, W., 288
jealousy, 239
Johnson, M., 280
Joseph, C., 380–381
Joyce, R., xiv, 202*n*2, 203*n*9, 205,
  207
judgmentiveness
  of acts *versus* person, 213
  in courtship, 212
  and emotions, 304
  halo effect, 230, 238
  hierarchical inferences, 213
  Implicit Association Test, 228, 230
  of incest, 193, 198, 200
  and intuition, 241
  about moral norms, 423
  and physical appearance, 233
  of third-party behavior, 166–169,
    196–199, 205–207
juries, 306
justice, 365, 394
  See also criminal justice system;
  fairness
justification, 34–36, 289, 422–425,
  437–439
just world belief, 230

Kahneman, D., 272
Kant, I.
  categorical imperative, 226
  and ethical (non)naturalism, 38–39
  on ethics, 6, 22*n*13
  and God, 22*n*12
  and moral philosophy, 22*n*11
  on reciprocation, 35
Kelly, D., 384, 430
killing
  and criminal justice system, 359*n*4
  as evil, 36

justifications, 354, 357
  and theory of action, 321, 362
  vocabulary for, 323, 358
Kim, J., 10–11
Kim, S. Y., 383
kin detection, 172, 174, 179–182,
  190*n*6
kin-directed altruism, 175, 179, 190*n*6,
  214
kindness, 222, 229, 249, 294
kin selection, 233, 259
Kitcher, P., 20*n*5
Knight, R., 389
Kohlberg, L., 395–397
Koller, S., 381
Kroll, N., 389
Kvanvig, J., 232

Lakoff, G., 280
language
  acquisition paradox, 415
  commonality and diversity, 324–326,
    331
  and context, 38–42
  of deontology, 56–58
  gesticulation, 278
  kinship terms, 179
  and mental representation, 130*n*3
  and morality (*see* language analogy)
  moral sentiments, 168, 196, 201
  and motivation, 47–48
  "must" and "may," 164*n*7
  and ownership, 287
  poverty-of-stimulus, 355
  and psychology, 206–207
  of requirement, 149–153, 154f
  slander, 287
  and social exchange, 73
  and symbols, 270, 276, 287
  universal grammar, 325, 331, 348,
    371, 410
  writing, 287
Laurence, S., 130*n*1

learning
 and beliefs *versus* logic, 64
 of disgust, 382
 good and evil, 295
 by induction, 327, 393
 of language, 325–327, 327, 356f, 361,
  396, 415
 of morality, 384, 395–397, 416
 of moral norms, 326–328, 333, 347,
  353–355, 356f, 361
 and social exchange, 86
 and tokenization, 291
 See also associative learning
legal processes, 287, 306, 320
 See also criminal justice system
lek paradox, 224
Lewis, D., 426n4
Lewontin, R., 299
Li, N. P., 187
library model, 124, 133–135
Lieberman, D., xiii, 165, 170, 176, 177,
  178, 179, 180, 181, 182, 183, 185,
  187, 188, 190n6, 190n7, 191–194,
  195–202
likeability, 230
linguistic analogy
 acquisition, 356f, 408, 428
 as byproduct, 372
 constraints, 413, 415, 418n3, 429
 ideal speaker-listener, 359n1
 innateness, 346, 349–351, 408–410
 poverty-of-stimulus, xv–xvi, 326, 361,
  391, 417, 430
 principles and parameters, 325, 331
Locke, J., 357, 359n2
logic
 adaptive *versus* first-order, 88–90
 and cognitive architecture, 67, 161
 and content, 137, 145, 146–155,
  150–151t, 154f, 158–162
 Wason selection task, 60–65, 79f
Lombroso, C., 233
longevity, 226, 237, 239

love
 excess, 294
 withdrawal, 404, 431
 "love your neighbor," 35

MacIntyre, A., 20n5
Mackie, J. L., 22n9, 34, 51n1
magnetic resonance imaging, 111–113,
  112f, 157, 350
Maljkovic, V., 85
Mallon, R., xiii, 126, 131–136
Manktelow, K., 91
Margolis, E., 130n1
marriage, of minors, 176
mate selection. *See* sexual selection
Maynard Smith, J., 70, 252, 253
Mazur, A., 257
McAdams, R. H., 321
McAndrew, F. T., 215
McDowell, J., 12, 20n1
McNamara, P., 59–60, 128
meekness, 255
memory, 29, 272–276, 284, 295n1
mental representations
 and abstraction, 283, 287
 concept as, 130n1
 of intentionality, 118n10
 and language, 130n3
 object files, 272–275
 and "ought," 122–127, 130n3, 133
 of ownership, 287
 symbols, 271–277
mental retardation, 249
mental states
 inferences about, 66–69
 of others, 118n10, 390, 416, 433
 theory of action, 321, 362, 363, 365
merit, 229
meta-emotions, 404
Michigan naturalism, 20n1
Mikhail, J., xv–xvi, 326, 353, 354, 355,
  356, 358, 359n4, 363–365, 367, 392,
  413, 428

Mill, J. S., 421

Miller, G., xiv, 209, 213, 218, 220, 221, 222, 223, 225, 227, 228, 229, 232, 233, 234, 235, 236, 238, 240, 242, 245–250, 251, 257, 260, 265

Millikan, R. G., 30

mimesis, 285

mind, theory of, 29, 321, 362, 365, 404

mistakes. *See* intentionality

modularity, 279, 387–391

  See also cross-modular binding

Moll, J., 391

monitoring, 166–169

Montaldi, A., 104

Montmarquet, J., 231

Moore, G. E., xi, 3, 14, 45, 46

moral character, 104, 221–224, 230, 233

moral claims, 22*n*9, 135

moral competence

  acquisition of, 393, 407–409, 414, 430

  and cognitive architecture, 354, 418*n*1

  and universals, 380

moral development

  and intentionality, 354, 364

  natural jurisprudence, 355

  and punishment, 387, 392

  stages, 395–397

moral disputes, 44

moral emotions, 193, 196–197, 368–370, 382, 386, 404, 421, 423

moral dumbfounding, 56, 428

moral imperatives, 16, 46, 50

morality

  and actions, 215, 231, 294

  of act *versus* person, 215

  breakdowns, 13

  as by-product, 397–406

  definitions, 46

  disposition toward, 383–387

  E-morality, 411

  evaluation criteria, 52*n*9, 438

  evolution of, xvi, 52, 166–169, 249, 286–290

fitness consequences, 242, 247, 265

I-moralities, 411–412

imposition, 288

innateness (*see under* innateness; nativism)

Kantian view, 6

language analogy (*see* language analogy)

learning, 384, 395–397

motivation, 419–422

and psychology, 404–406 (*see also* moral psychology; psychology)

rationality, 289, 309, 437

and religion, 2–4, 37

and social contract, 100

and symbolic thought, 286–290, 304

moral judgments

  considered judgments, 354, 358*n*1

  and context, 38–42, 44*n*1, 47–49

  contingency, 40–42

  descriptive *versus* normative, 424

  and emotions, 241, 304, 369, 370

  and moral dumbfounding, 428

  and motivation, 38, 41, 44*n*2, 47, 434

  and nativism, 321, 362

  neuroimaging, 350

  and perception, 358

  and physical appearance, 230, 232

  practical clout, 47

  prescriptive force, 5, 46–47, 52*n*

  rationality, 46–48

  systematicity, 413

  about torture, 310

  underlying norms, 346

  See also judgmentiveness

moral naturalism, 45

moral norms

  behavioral outcomes, 362

  versus conventions, 384, 392, 416

  and cultural change, xv, 340–343, 405

  cultural factors, 322–324, 329–331, 337, 357, 426*n*5, 435

  definition, 320

distributional pattern, 326, 329–332
diversity, 329, 355
emergence, 336–338
and emotions, 339, 368–370, 387, 404, 423
exceptionless, 331
about harm (*see* harm norms)
versus innate aversion, 335
innate biases model, xv, 332–336, 365
judgment of, 423
language analogy, 325, 331, 346, 349–351, 356f, 359n1, 361, 372, 391, 395, 408–410
learning, 326–328, 333, 347, 353–355, 356f, 361
versus moral rules, 412–414
nativist view, 321, 372–384
and others, 369, 404
and power, 336
principles and parameters model, 324–332, 346–351
psychological mechanisms, 424
rationality, 375
simple innateness model, 322–324, 345
themes, 330, 337, 380–383
violations, 320, 431
and women, 340
moral philosophy, 5, 22n11, 28, 228
moral principles, 409–415, 428–430, 435, 437–439
moral psychology
capacities, 407–409, 424
cultural change, 340–343
innate capacities, 404–406
innate moral norms, 322–324, 349–351
versus moral philosophy, 22n11
role, 358, 423, 425
See also psychology
moral rules
associative learning, 386–387
constraints on, 429

contingency, 412, 429
versus conventions, 384–386, 392–395, 416, 430–433
innateness, 412
versus moral norms, 412–414
and psychopaths, 369, 390
See also moral norms
moral sentiments, 168, 196–199, 201, 207
moral standards, 310
moral systems, 50, 335
moral theory, 126
moral virtues
as adaptations, 251–258
in Christianity (*see under* Christianity)
and cognition, 225
as costly signals, 219, 246–250, 265
fitness consequences, 265
and intelligence disorders, 265
pagan, 251–253, 259, 288
and sexual selection, xiv, 219–226, 230, 235–240, 246–248
See also virtue(s)
Morris, D., 258, 261n4
motivation
in animals, 401
behavioral outcomes, 294
and cheating detection, 108
and contingency, 40
by false beliefs, 23n14, 23n19
and inference systems, 66–69
and internalization, 432
for judging others, 166–169, 196–199, 205–207
and killing, 357
for morality, 419–422
and moral judgments, 38, 41, 44n2, 47, 434
and moral language, 47–48
and nativism, 409, 434
of nativists, 418
proximate *versus* evolutionary, 212
and sexual infidelity, 239

motivation (cont.)
  and social contract, 144, 159
  variability, 7, 17, 40, 436
  See also intentionality
murder. *See* killing
Murdock, G., 323
Murphy, S., 428
music, 282
mutualism, 259–260

naive realism, 138
Nash equilibria, 234
native peoples
  and harm norms, 330, 373, 381
  and incest, 378
  and sharing, 257, 376
  and social exchange, 85, 91
nativism
  capacity *versus* content, 321,
    361–365
  and conventions, 386
  and cultural factors, 332, 336–343
  empiricist attacks, 407
  faculty approach, 408–415
  and incest, 195, 378
  innate aversions, 335
  innate biases model, xv, 332–336,
    340–343, 365
  and internalism, 435
  moral development, 395–397
  and moral norms, 321, 329, 372–384
  on motivation, 409, 434
  motivation for, 418
  principles and parameters, 324–332,
    346–351, 403
  and sharing, 376
  simple innateness model, 322–324,
    345
  universal rules, 372–379
  and values, 436
  See also language analogy; poverty-of-
    stimulus
natural aversion, 203*n*9, 335

naturalism
  bald, 12, 20*n*1
  definition, 1
  and epistemology, 11
  and ethics, 2–9, 12–19, 33–36, 424
  functional, 30
  Moore view, 45
  ontological, 4, 21*n*6
  and science, 20*n*3, 33
  and supernatural, 22*n*9
  See also ethical naturalism
naturalistic fallacy, 423
natural selection
  of competition methods, 253
  and content sensitivity, 146
  and cross-modular binding, 279,
    282–283, 300
  and fairness, 377
  at group level, 234–235, 246
  and human nature, 55–58
  and inbreeding avoidance, 171,
    178–182, 194, 198
  lek paradox, 224
  Pareto dominance, 234
  social selection, 233–235
  See also sexual selection
nature, 4
Navarrete, C., 338–339
negligence, 354
neocompatibilism, 8
neuroimaging
  and conditionals, 157
  and moral appraisals, 350, 391
  of rule interpretation, 111–113, 112f
  and symbolic thought, 279
neuroscience
  cross-modular binding, 273–280, 300
  deontic reasoning, xiii, 109–114, 157,
    160
  executive control, xii, 29
  of inferential systems, 147, 160
  and permission schema theory, 97
  and responsibility, 29

of symbolic thought, 277–280, 299, 315
Nichols, S., 126, 333, 339, 368, 430
Nietzsche, F., 211, 216, 259, 436
nihilism, 17, 25n30
Nisbett, R. E., 330, 411–412
normative epistemology, 10, 23n20
normative ethics, 10, 240
normativism, 13, 316, 435, 438
See also moral norms
Nucci, L. P., 383, 385, 416
nurturance, 224

obedience, 255, 256, 292
object files, 272–276, 280, 281, 287
objective values, 49
obligation
and benefit, 79f, 100
and Darwinian naturalism, 36
and precautionary rules, 78, 100
prioritization, 125–127, 129, 131–133
and rationality, 25n30, 41, 56
requirement, 107, 149, 159
and social contract, 72–77, 74t, 81, 92, 114
and Wason selection task, 64, 79f, 139
See also deontic logic; "ought"
obsessive-compulsive disorder, 95
olfaction, 175, 176
ontological naturalism, 4, 21n6
openmindedness, 226
operant conditioning. See conditioning
optimism, 227
orgasm, 220
others
beliefs of, 12, 288–289
as commodities, 293
expectations of, 214, 395
inferences about, 111–113, 117n4, 213–215, 285 (see also intentionality)
mental state of, 118n10, 390, 416, 433 (see also theory of mind)
and moral norms, 369, 404

and self (see under self)
social reputation models, 235
See also third-party behavior
"ought"
and domain-specificity, 56–59, 101, 122–125, 133
mental representations, 122–127, 130n3
and parenting, 417
and physical disabilities, 214
trade-offs, 125–127, 129, 131–133
See also obligation
Over, D., 91
ownership, 287, 303
of women, 340

paganism, 251–253, 259, 288, 290
pain, 311, 329
See also harm norms; sadism
parenting
discipline, 373, 392, 416, 430–432
genetics, 224
and incest, 183–185
kin altruism, 214
love withdrawal, 404, 431
overprotectiveness, 294
and sexual selection, 217, 218–220, 227, 238
Pareto dominance, 215, 234
Parsons, T., 321
perception, 358
permissibility, 413
permission rules, 99–100, 104, 105
permission schema, 66, 95–101, 96t, 97f, 104
person. See self; individual
personal advantage, 5, 52n
personality disorders, 212, 228
perspective
and adaptation, 43
and cheating, 157
and moral variety, 48–49
perceptual integration, 358

perspective (cont.)
and sexual selection, 222
and social exchanges, 81, 93, 106, 118*n*9, 160
and third-party behavior, 167
of victims, 404
Pettit, P., 321
philosophical naturalism, 33
philosophy, xii, 5, 22*n*11, 28
physical appearance
and costly signaling, 232
and moral judgments, 230–231, 232–233
and sexual aversion, 176
and sexual selection, 213, 229, 237, 251, 253
physical disability, 214
physics, 21*n*6
Piaget, J., 396
Pierce, C. S., 288
Pigden, C. R., 22*n*9
Pittsburgh naturalism, 1
Plantinga, 3, 20*n*5
Plato, 3
play, 285, 374, 376
pleasantness, 230
pluralistic relationalism, 43, 51
pluralistic relativism, 17–19, 42–44, 51
pollution, 293
Popperian falsification, 147
poverty-of-stimulus
language analogy, 361, 391, 417, 430
in linguistics, 355
and perception, 358
and principles and parameters, 326–328, 347
and wolf-boy, 394
Povinelli, D. J., 285
power, 291, 336, 392, 431
practical significance, 127–129
pragmatism
and ethical naturalism, 17–19, 30
and morality imposition, 288–289

precautionary rules
and brain areas, 111–113, 112f, 389
and drinking age, 107–108, 119*n*20
and inference, 124
and social contracts, 78, 96t, 97f, 100, 126
violations, 95, 103
prejudice, 226
prescriptivism, 5, 46–47, 52*n*, 316
See also moral norms
pretending, 248, 285
Preuschoft, S., 260*n*1, 260*n*2
Price, G., 252, 253
Price, M., 58, 72, 113
pride, 256
principles and parameters, 324–332, 346–351, 403
Prinz, J., xv, xvi, 195, 200, 203*n*9, 329, 368, 373, 378, 387, 405, 411, 414, 415, 416, 418, 419, 420, 421, 424, 426*n*2, 434
prioritization
of conventions, 430–431
of domains, 77
and harm norms, 374
and killing, 359*n*4
of "oughts," 125–127, 129, 131–133
Prisoners' Dilemma, 53, 71
promiscuity, 220, 228, 239
property, 287, 303
women as, 340
proselytizing, 289
protected classes, 326, 329
protomoral appraisals, 402
psychological realism, 426*n*6
psychological realizability, 52*n*9
psychological selection, 128
psychology
inbreeding aversion, 184–186, 188
SSSM, 171
and third-party behavior, 166–169
and values, 439

of vicarious distress, 340
See also moral psychology
psychopathology, 85, 228, 275
psychopathy
  emotional deficit, 369
  genetics, 224
  and moral rules, 369, 390
  versus sadism, 306
  and sexual selection, 224
  and submission, 258
  and symbolic thought, 292, 306,
    312n12
punishment
  for accidental violations, 81
  altruistic, 235
  and children, 354, 373, 387, 392,
    416
  for convention violations, 385, 392,
    416, 430–433
  corporal, 340, 373
  and cost-benefit analysis, 206
  and incest, 198, 203n9
  love withdrawal, 404, 431
  moral justification, 203n9, 206, 320
  as retaliation, 329
  and sexual selection, 234, 249
purity, 380, 381, 382, 403
Putnam, H., 10

quietude, 255
Quine, W. V. O., 10, 23n20, 28, 107,
  163n5

race, 230, 428
racism, 226
Railton, P., xii, 25n30, 44n2, 47
Ramachandran, V. S., 279
rape, 358, 381
rationalism, 22n9
rationality
  ecological, 65–69
  and morality, 289, 309, 437
  of moral judgments, 46–48

and moral norms, 375
and obligation, 25n30, 41, 56
and social contract, 65
and Wason selection task, 60–65,
  79f
Rawls, J., 259, 289, 353–354, 358n1,
  428
Read, K. E., 381
realism, 22n9, 138, 426n6
realizability, 52n9
reason(s)
  abductive, 29, 51n2
  for cooperation, 81
  pure reason, 6
  See also "ought"
reasoning
  brain areas, 60–66, 111–113, 112f
  content-generality (*see* content-general
    reasoning)
  content specificity, 137, 160 (*see also*
    domain specificity)
  about danger (*see* hazard
    management)
  evolution of, 65–69, 118n7, 146,
    164n5, 295n1
  and free rider, 405
  least effort, 291, 312n9
  mechanisms, number of, 109–113,
    123–129
  modularity, 388 (*see also* cross-
    modular binding)
  and moral development, 396
  and moral judgments, 413
  and parenting, 392
  and social exchange, 65, 69–77,
    80–84, 162
  speed factor, 296n4
  syntactic, 276, 295n1
  about third-party behavior, 167
  Wason selection task, 60–65, 79f
  See also conditional reasoning; deontic
    logic; symbolic thought
reciprocal altruism, 233

reciprocity, 53
  in animals, 400
  versus ethics, 35, 41
  moralization of, 405
  versus parenting, 214
  and sharing, 377
  and social contracts, 53, 70–72, 81, 100
  as universal domain, 41, 380, 403
  See also mutualism
reflective equilibrium, xvii*n*6
Regan, T., 312*n*6
relationalism, xii, 43, 48–50, 51
relationships
  cause and effect, 283
  domain specificity, 58
  and good or evil, 294
  gregariousness, 375
  sadistic, 292
  See also inbreeding avoidance; sexual selection; tokenization
relativism
  context, 38–42, 44*n*1
  ecological niches, 19, 42–44
  and ethics, xii, 15–17, 19
  and evil definition, 317
  and expressionism, 424
  locale factor, xii, 16, 35, 50
  and moral norms, 426*n*5
  versus relationalism, 50
  and sadism, 317
religion
  and abstraction, 284, 288
  Buddhism, 4
  as by-product, 403, 406
  Confucianism, 4
  for Darwin, 23*n*19
  deities, 4, 230 (*see also* God)
  dietary laws, 385
  extreme views, 221
  and human nature, 289
  for Kant and Hume, 22*n*13
  and morality, 2–4, 37

  and purity, 380
  sacred texts, 3–4
  and social contracts, 116
  and submission, 256, 261*n*4, 266
  See also Christianity
religiosity, 23*n*19, 229, 284, 403
remorse, 404
reproduction, 54–55
reputation, 235
requirement, 149–153, 154f, 159, 161
resentment, 368, 380
respect, 4, 380, 382
responsibility
  and evil, 292, 306, 308
  and genes, 224
  and mate selection, 226
  neuroscience, 29
  tokenization, 308
restitution, 354
reward, 24*n*20, 235, 395
  See also benefit
Rice, G. E., Jr., 398
Richerson, P., 342
Rips, L., 147
risk
  and moral norms, 375
  sensation-seeking, 224
  and sexual selection, 234, 254
  superogatory acts, 259, 261*n*7, 266
rituals, 4, 116
Robarchek, C. A., 330
Robarchek, C. J., 330
romantic virtues, 210–212, 214
Rorty, R., 25*n*31
Ruse, M., xii, 31*n*2, 45–46, 51*n*5
Rushton, J. P., 224
Rutgers naturalism, 20*n*1

sadism
  and evil, 309–317
  individual focus, 306
  and power, 291
  versus psychopathy, 306

and restraint, 308
and theory of mind, 292, 303
safety, 77–78, 289
See also hazard management; risk
Samuels, R., xiii, 124, 133
San Diego naturalism, 31*n*1
Sarkissian, H., xii, 27–30, 37–44
scarification, 385
Schaik, C. P. van, 260*n*1, 260*n*2
schizophrenia, 85, 228, 275
Schmitt, D., 221
Schultz, T. R., 350
scientific naturalism, 2, 4, 20*n*3
selection tasks. *See* Wason selection
  task
self
  death of, 284
  for Kant, 6
  and others, 166–169, 189, 196–200,
    205–208, 369 (*see also* tokenization)
self-control. *See* self-regulation
self-interest, 250
selfishness, 228, 235, 292, 400
self-preservation, 5, 52*n*
self-regulation
  and inbreeding, 165, 188, 197
  and sadistic urges, 308
  and sexual selection, 219, 222, 226
  and temptation, 362
self-sacrifice. *See* sharing; superogatory
  acts
Sell, A., 104
Semai, 330
sexism, 226
sexual coercion, 238, 358, 381
sexual competition, 222, 239, 253
sexual fidelity
  and bipolarity, 228
  infidelity, 168, 239
  predictive traits, 227, 239
  signaling power, 220
sexual harassment, 238
sexuality, 288

sexual jealousy, 239
sexual promiscuity, 220, 228, 239
sexual purity, 380
sexual selection, 219–226
  as adaptation, 212–215, 223, 233–235
  and bipolar disorder, 228
  desirable traits, 225–232, 242, 249,
    254
  dominance/submission, 267
  and ethics, 231–233, 240–243
  and fidelity, 220, 227, 239
  fitness, 214, 220, 234, 239, 249, 265
  gender differences, 218, 223, 237, 257
  and genetics, 217, 223–225, 236–238,
    248
  group level equilibria, 234, 246
  immuno-compatibility, 251
  lek paradox, 224
  and moral virtues, xiv, 219–225,
    235–240, 246–248
  and orgasm, 220
  and parenting, 217–220, 227
  physical appearance, 213, 229, 237,
    251, 253
  predictions, 235–239, 260
  and psychopathology, 228
  and self-interest, 250
  self-restraint, 219, 222, 226
  social pressures, 233–235
  See also costly signaling; courtship;
    inbreeding avoidance
sexual selection theory, 245–246
shame, 241, 379, 385
sharing, 375–377, 400, 402
Shostak, M., 72
Shweder, R. A., 380
siblings
  adoptive, 183
  coresidence, 174, 190*n*6, 192
  cues, 179–182
  incest between, 168, 190*n*8, 332, 428
signaling. *See* costly signaling
simple innateness model, 322–324, 345

Simpson, J. A., 239–240

Singer, P., 242, 312*n*6

situation
 creation, 108
 versus individual, 228
 interpretation, 66, 72–78, 86
 and third-party behavior, 167–169

skepticism, 34–36, 45

Skinner, B. F., 401
 See also conditioning

slander, 287

Sloman, A., 29

Smetana, J., 383, 384, 385, 392, 416

Smith, E., 215

social attitudes, 224, 226

social contracts
 algorithms, 54–56, 60, 65, 72–77, 74t,
  80, 88, 114, 125, 148, 161
 and brain areas, 110–113, 112f
 and children, 396
 cognition library, 133–135
 cognitive architecture, 53, 160
 compliance, 100, 144, 155–159,
  162, 396 (*see also* cheating
  detection)
 cost-benefit analysis, 75t, 81, 147
 domain specificity, 58–60, 76–78, 85,
  109, 114, 125, 145, 148
 with gods, 116
 inference, 74t (*see also* inference(s))
 interpretation, 106, 138
 performance of, 144–145, 159, 162
 and permission rules, 96t, 97f, 98,
  104
 and precaution rules, 78, 96t, 97f,
  100, 110, 126
 reasoning, 65, 72–77, 80–84, 100, 138,
  162
 and requirement, 107, 149, 159
 social exchange definition, 72
 switched (*see* switched social
  contracts)
 unfamiliar rules, 86, 87f

violations, 155–158
 and Wason selection task, 65, 79f, 83,
  89f, 91, 119*n*17
 See also entitlement; obligation

social contract theory, 68–72, 145–152,
 160–162

social domain, 389

social exchange
 interpretation system, 68–72

social harmony, 49–50

social learning, 416

social reputation, 235

social reputation model, 235

societal needs, 373–375, 380, 396, 405,
 425

sociological constraints, 52*n*9

Sokol, B., 364

Song, M., 383

Sorce, J. F., 431

Sorrentino, C., 326

Spelke, E., 326

Sperber, D., 115, 118*n*9, 127, 332

Sperberian biases, 332–337

Sripada, C. S., xv, xvi, 321, 345–351,
 353–359, 431

SSSM. *See* Standard Social Science
 Model

Standard Social Science Model (SSSM),
 171–173, 183–185

status
 and fertility rate, 342, 343*n*1
 and generosity, 254, 257
 and merit, 229
 reputation, 235
 and sexual selection, 229, 230,
  237–238, 257
 and symbolism, 292
 See also dominance

stereotyping, 291

Stevenson, C. L., 42

Stich, S., 384

Stone, V., 68, 110, 389

Stroud, B., 1, 20*n*5

submission
  and conflict resolution, 253, 255,
    260n1
  and psychopathy, 258
  and religion, 256, 261n4, 266
  signals of, 255
  as universal domain, 380
  and vicarious distress, 374
  and withdrawal, 374
suffering, 381, 403, 431
  See also vicarious distress
Sugiyama, L. S., 91, 154
supernaturalism, 2–4, 22n9
superogatory acts, 259, 261n7, 266
switched social contracts, 88–94, 106,
    118n9, 154f, 158, 160
symbolic thought
  abstraction, xv, 283–285, 287, 303
  analogy, 280–282
  and attention, 273, 276, 282, 296n3
  domain generality, 125, 283
  evolution of, 276–283, 300
  good and evil, 286, 290–295, 303
  and morality, 286–290
  neuronal architecture, 277–280, 299,
    315
  and play, 285
  and psychopathy, 292, 306, 312n12
  referent mapping, 271, 273–276
  and religion, 284
  versus syntactic thought, 276, 295n1
  See also tokenization
symbols
  body as, 285, 288
  defining properties, 271
  and evil, 290–295
  of status, 292–293
  and violence, 287
sympathy, 380, 382, 384, 422
  See also compassion
synesthesia, 279
syntactic reasoning, 276, 295n1
syntax, 155, 157, 158, 164n6, 270

taboos
  food, 338
  incest, 177, 182–185, 192–194,
    199–201
  personal versus group, 202n8
  Taiwanese minor marriages, 176
taxation, 376
Taylor, C., 20n5
teleology, 435
territoriality, 287
testosterone, 223, 257, 258
theft
  child raised by wolves, 394
  innate wrongness, 324, 358
  and sharing, 377
  and symbolic thought, 286, 304
  and territoriality, 287
  vocabulary for, 323, 358
theory of action, 321, 362, 363, 365
theory of mind, 321, 362, 365, 404
  and sadism, 292, 303
third-party behavior
  and animals, 398, 402, 404
  concern for, 166–169, 196–202, 206,
    285
  and evolution, 166–169
  incest, 182–185, 191, 193, 198, 201,
    207, 428
  and moral norms, 369, 404
  and self, 189, 205, 208
  social reputation, 235
Thornhill, R., 379
Thrall, N., 104
threats. See danger; hazard
  management
Tiberius, V., xvi, 434–439
Tinklepaugh, O. L., 399
Todd, P. M., 238, 265
tokenization
  and evil, 290, 305, 307, 317
  and human brain, 291, 303, 317
  versus kindness, 294, 307
  right kind, 311

tolerance, 12, 19, 43–44, 51
Tooby, J., xiii, 53, 55, 56, 58, 62, 64, 65, 66, 67, 68, 69, 70, 71, 72, 75, 81, 82, 84, 85, 91, 94, 95, 99, 100, 104, 113, 114, 116, 118n5, 118n8, 118n11, 119n17, 121–129, 132, 137–141, 143, 145, 146, 147, 154, 165, 173, 176, 181, 187, 190n7, 199, 299, 387, 389
torture, 310, 317, 429
Tourette's syndrome, 214
trade-offs, 125–127, 129, 131–133
   See also reciprocity
transformation, 295
Treisman, A. M., 272
trolley problems, 350, 355, 364, 413
truth
   certainty versus doubt, 289
   and contingency, 28
   and morality, 46, 48, 232
   versus reason, 59
truth claims, 125
Tse, P., xiv–xv, 299–300, 303–314
Turiel, E., 383, 384, 385

ultimatum game, 235, 376–377
United States
   religious beliefs, 2
universal grammar, 325, 331, 348, 371, 410
   of morality, 355
universality
   moral domains, 380–383
   and moral judgments, 304
   of moral norms, 323, 331, 346, 372–379
   of moral principles, 438
universe governance, 21n6
utilitarianism, 22n9, 348

values
   as adaptation, 437
   contingency, 19

double standards, 439
family values, 259
moral dumbfounding, 429
(un)natural, 436
and relationalism, 49
universally-held, 438
Veblen, T., 216
vicarious distress
   and children, 431–433
   and danger, 374, 398
   and harm norms, 340
   innateness, 421
   and self, 404
vice(s)
   and courtship, 212
   genetic transmission, 224
   murder as, 359n3
   and physical appearance, 233
   and sexual competition, 222
   and sexual selection, 226, 237
victims, 381, 404, 433
violations
   accidental, 81
   and benefit, 156
   of conventions, 384–386, 392, 416, 430–433
   of etiquette rules, 333, 430
   Fodor view, 108
   of innate principles, 435
   intentionality, 101–106, 119n15, 156, 159, 354
   of intuition, 116, 127
   of linguistic rules, 413, 418n3
   and moral character, 104
   of moral norms, 320, 431
   of permission rules, 104
   of precautionary rules, 95, 103
   of regularities versus rules, 388
   of social contract, 155–158 (see also cheating)
   and Wason selection task, 60–65, 69
violence
   cultural variation, 373

domestic, 223
and honor, 330
and moral norms, 326, 329, 365,
  373–375
perception of, 358
in play, 374
sexual competition, 222–223
symbolic substitute, 287
and transformation, 295
virtue aesthetics, 232
virtue epistemology, 231
virtue ethics, 231–233
virtue(s)
  for Aristotle, 231, 422, 435
  for Christianity, xiv, 211, 251, 252,
    254, 256, 259, 266
  etymology, 259
  for Hume, 436
  See also moral virtues
virtuosity, 229

Waal, F. de, 254
Wainryb, C., 364
Wallace, K., xv, 316
war criminals, 242
Wason, P., 60–64
Wason selection task
  and brain damage, 110, 390
  and cheater detection, 69,
    388
  description, 60–65, 61f
  and domain specificity, 139
  Fodor view, 106–109, 119n17, 141,
    150
  and no benefit, 99, 158
  and schizophrenia, 85
  and social contracts, 65, 79f, 83, 89f,
    91, 119n17
waterboarding, 310
wealth, 229, 230
Westermarck, E., xiii, 170–177, 182,
  185, 188, 192–194, 198, 200, 203n9,
  334

Westermarck hypothesis (WH),
  170–171, 173–176, 180, 203
Wheatley, T., 369
Williams, G. C., 70, 186
Williams syndrome, 249, 264
Wilson, E. O., 35
Wilson, M., 340–341
witnesses. See vicarious distress
Wolf, A., xiv, 170, 176, 180, 181,
  194n1, 201, 207, 208
women
  attitude toward, 288, 322, 340
  and food, 376
  and harm infliction, 329, 330
  sexual selection, 223, 238, 257
Wong, D., xii, 27–30, 37–44
Wright, L., 30
writing, 287
Wynne, C. D. L., 399

Yanamomo, 330, 373
Young, L., 413, 428

Zagzebski, L., 231, 232
Zahavi, A., 216

Index to Volume 2

Figures are indicated by "f"; tables are indicated by "t," and footnotes by "*n.*"

absent feeling, 258, 267, 274*n*6
acquired sociopathy, 199–200
action analysis, 119f, 146, 161
actions
  brain site, 190
  chess analogy, 22
  competence, 125, 142*n*5, 151
  and consequentialism, 20–23, 35
  freedom, 369, 377
  harmless, 142*n*1, 198, 283
  and heuristics, 4, 8–11, 16, 28, 34, 41
  and impulse, 194
  and intuition, 140, 196, 238
  killing (*see* killing)
  lack of (*see* doing and allowing;
   omission)
  and moral decisions, 234–239, 243
  and moral faculty, 117f, 119, 146
  and moral judgment, 116
  morally repugnant, 1, 26*n*1
  and moral rules, 168
  phoneme analogy, 118
  and subconscious, 118
  unusualness, 431, 442, 455, 457, 459
  wrong-doing, 19
  See also behavior; moral actions
act utilitarianism, 5, 21
addition paradox, 75*n*9
adequate justification, 73–74

adolescence, 209
Adolphs, R., 137, 177
aesthetics, 243
affective primacy, 186
affective resonance, 269–272
age factors
  and brain damage, 199
  generation gap, 211
  and moral judgment(s), 264, 283
  and trolley problem, 131
  See also moral development
agency
  and context, 53
  doing *versus* allowing, 55–67, 63f, 65t,
   66t, 140
  and moral facts, 328*n*7
  and moral virtue, 34
  number of agents, 437
  and responsibility, 426–428, 430, 437,
   439*n*1, 458*n*1
Aktipis, C., 211, 242–243
Alicke, M. D., 426–429, 437
ambiguity, 192
  See also uncertainty
Anderson, S. R., 111
Anderson, S. W., 115
anger
  appropriateness, 287
  and children, 162–164, 166, 289*n*8

anger (cont.)
  and killing, 166
  and moral development, 183–185
  and moral judgment, 282
  neosentimentalist view, 280, 283–287
  nonmoral causes, 176
animals
  chimpanzee, 194
  and consequences, 123
  harming, 296, 314–316
  and intuitive values, 203
  ultrasocial species, 192
  vocal imitation, 112–113
Anscombe, G. E. M., 322–323, 331n34
anthropocentrism, 213, 215, 217n3,
  224–226, 228
appetites, 277, 293
Aristotle, 350
Armstrong, D., 431
as-if, 16, 21, 32, 46n1
Aslin, R. N., 172
as process
  perception(s), 116, 118–120
asset allocation, 37, 45
attachment, 163
attitudes, 163
atypicality, xvii, xviii, 431, 442,
  455–459
Audi, R., 50, 95n4, 104
authority
  contingency on, 263, 273n4
  and emotions, 274n4
  and honor, 207
  and in-groups, 217n2
  as intuitive value, 203, 245
  liberals and conservatives, 209,
  248
  and moral claims, 248
  and moral intuition, 51
  and morally repugnant act, 26n1
  obedience, 1, 26n1, 192
  as virtue, 208
  See also default

automaticity, 186, 212, 237–239, 244
  See also reaction time
Ayer, A. J., 359, 362, 365, 383n8, 383n9

background theory, 320, 325, 331n37,
  335, 337n3, 346
badness, 240, 276
  See also wrongness
Baier, A., 331n31, 345
bail decisions, 12–17, 32, 42
Banaji, M. R., 135
Baron, J., 57, 58, 62–67, 135, 140
Barrett, C., 201
Bechara, A., 115, 177
behavior
  as-if, 16, 21, 32, 46n1
  and beliefs, 211, 314
  complicit, 452–454, 461
  decision-making, 238–239
  and default, 3, 6, 28, 174
  and heuristics, 5
  innate versus coping, 163
  law-breaking, 240
  and moral beliefs, 314
  and moral character, 208
  and moral mandate, 212
  and natural selection, 123
  optimized, 23
  praiseworthy, 165
  self-reported, 11
  self-reports, 11
  situational nature, 211
  in social groups, 2, 4, 9, 33, 192,
  451–454
  social intuitionist view, 243
  societal norms, 190–192
  of soldiers, 4, 30
behavioral genetics, 210
beliefs
  versus behavior, 211, 314
  conceptions of, 369
  ethical, 309
  Gettier cases, 371, 384n27

and knowledge, 102
mistakenness, 89, 93, 105
and moral semantics, 399, 403
reliability, 97–99
scientific *versus* moral, 101
self-evident, 310
See also framing effects; moral beliefs;
  moral intuitions
Bentham, J., 20, 35
Berscheid, E., 192
bias
  and fieldwork, 375, 385*n*31, 388
  and heuristics, 4, 8
  and moral judgments, 174, 224
  and reasoning, 190, 224, 244, 249
Bilskey, W., 202
biopsychology, 237
Bjorklund, F., xv, 197, 199, 203,
  233–240, 241, 252
Black, A., 288*n*5
Blackburn, S., 381, 383*n*14, 400
Blair, R. J. R., xvi, 160, 263, 277,
  291–293, 300
blame
  and causal attribution, 425–431,
  437
  and complicity, 452, 461
  and omission, 455–457
Bloom, P., 120
Bloomfield, P., xvii, 307–309, 322,
  344n4, 349–353
bodily states, 199
Boorse, C., 48
boxing, 292
Boyd, R., 310–312, 320, 328*n*4, 329*n*15,
  329*n*16, 342, 374, 385*n*38
Braeges, J., 260
brain
  blank-slate models, 245
  and heuristics, 8
  and moral competence, 199
  and moral dilemmas, 195, 200
  and moral faculty, 124, 177

and moral judgments, 137, 150, 177,
  200
and moral reasoning, 213
neural plasticity, 244
and rationalization, 190
See also human mind
Brandt, R. B., 226, 259, 296, 314, 316,
  328*n*8, 356–357, 382*n*5, 385*n*35
breaking ranks, 2, 4, 9, 33, 192
  See also complicity; social interaction
Brink, D., 294, 320, 327*n*1, 328*n*5, 374
Brody, B., 385*n*35
Brown, D., 202
Browning, C., 1, 26*n*1
Bushey, B., 190

Cacioppo, J. T., 212
Cambridge changes, 423
Canberra Plan, 367–371
cannibalism, 198
capital punishment, 159
Capote, T., 320
caring, 203, 209, 217*n*3, 245, 253–254
causal attribution
  and atypicality, xvii, xviii, 431, 442,
  457, 459
  and moral judgments, 115–121,
  425–430, 441–446, 459
  and motivation, 266, 427, 437, 444
  and normativism, 426–430, 442,
  446*n*2, 459
  plant watering example, 455
  and punishment, 457, 461
  See also consequences
causation
  concepts of, 439*n*6
  descriptive *versus* normative, 426–430
  disjunction, 435–438
  evidence approach, 428, 432–437
  of harm, 266
  for Hume, 423
  and intuition, 433, 437, 439*n*1
  Law & Order examples, 450–456

causation (cont.)
and moral reasoning, 181, 193, 200
negative, 454–458 (*see also* omission)
parallelism, 433
quasi-causation, 432
single source, 215
voting example, 433, 435, 438
chameleon effect, 192
chastity, 203, 208
chess analogy, 22
children
and anger, 162–164, 166, 289*n*8
brain damage, 199
cognition and reasoning, 267, 281
and conventions, xvi, 184, 260, 267,
281
cultural factors, 206–207
and guilt, 261, 280, 282, 296
innate preparedness, 204
and intuitions, 201, 238
language acquisition, 111–113
moral development, 122, 163,
182–184, 206, 213, 236–239
moral disagreements, 262, 267, 281,
286
moral judgment, xvi, 260–262, 265,
280–282, 288*n*4, 288*n*5
and moral reasoning, 262, 274*n*7
motivation types, 273*n*2
own *versus* others, 340
punishment, 276–278, 292
and rule violations, 262, 266–269, 282
and shame, 261
torture example, 83, 85, 94, 97, 104
vicarious emotions, 183, 206, 264,
267
Chomsky, N., 108, 109, 143*n*10, 159,
171
Churchland, P., 207
Clore, G. L., 199
cognition
adaptational strategies, 237
versus affective primacy, 186

brain region, 200
in children, 281
(un)conscious, 10, 15, 21, 32, 233
distributed, 249
Eastern *versus* Western, 323–326,
331*n*36, 348
and emotions, 195, 199, 250
fast and slow, 200
and framing effects, 70
and language, 110
morality-specific (*see* moral faculty)
and moral judgments, 114, 250
novice-to-expert paradigm, 237
of perception, 116
for rationalists, 183–184
versus reasoning, 250
social impact, 233
social intuitionist view, 181, 200, 250
See also human mind; mental
representation; moral reasoning;
reflection
cognitive load, 198
cognitivism
and incoherentism, 366–367,
387–391, 411*n*1
versus noncognitivism, 356–363, 403,
408–410, 411*n*3, 418
and objectivity, 375
terminology, 401*n*5
Cohen, D., 317, 318, 330*n*25
Coleman, A., 439*n*8
collectivism, 169, 322–324, 348, 350
common morality, 236
common sense, 236
community(ies)
ethics, 197
moral, 252
subjectivism, 256, 285–287, 299
understanding, 379
community subjectivism, 256,
285–287, 299
complicity, 452–454, 461
See also breaking ranks

computer crash example, 428, 442
concept(s)
  of beliefs, 369
  of causation, 439n6, 444
  versus intuitions, 370
  morality as, 395
  and moral semantics, 411n1
  and neosentimentalism, 293–295,
    298, 301n3
  and theories, 384n26
  wrongness, 164
conceptual analysis, 334, 367–369, 372,
  384n24, 384n26, 396
conditionals, 257
conditioning, 163, 166, 182
confabulation, 190, 199
conflicts
  and brain regions, 200
  and folk morality, 373, 376
  heuristics, 5
  intrapersonal, 364, 376, 380, 398
  of intuitions, 193–196, 200–201 (*see
    also* moral dilemmas)
  and moral principles, 159
  and moral semantics, 378, 398,
    401n4, 421n2
  within self, 364, 376, 380, 398
  in values, 159, 166, 188
  See also moral disagreements
conformism, 28, 42, 192, 223, 228, 253
  See also breaking ranks; complicity
confusion, 369, 375, 380, 384n27, 390,
  398
consensus, 191, 228, 232n14, 249, 341
consequences
  and animals, 123
  anticipation of, 235, 244
  for child transgression, 163
  perception of, 119, 121, 146, 151
  and theory of mind, 277
consequentialism
  and atrocity, 31
  criteria, 23

cultural factors, 169
  and decision procedure, 35
  exceptional situations, 23–25
  and happiness, 37
  and heuristics, xiv, 5, 20–22, 29, 36
  interpretations, 39n4
  and massacre example, 29–30
  as maximization, 44
  and moral action, 20–23, 35
  and moral realism, 348
  and moral virtue, 34
  and motivation, 385n33
  and source plurality, 215
conservatives, 159, 209, 248
consistency
  belief and behavior, 211, 314
  judging self and others, 242
  of moral intuitions, 55, 375
  and moral judgments, 61, 127
consumerism, 240, 253
contagion, 206, 209
context
  of actions, 118
  and causal responsibility, 425
  child rapist example, 83, 85, 94, 97
  and heuristics, 5, 8, 11, 19, 26, 42
  and moral decisions, 234–236
  and moral development, 236
  and moral discourse, 193, 421n2
  and moral intuitions, 52–54, 79 (*see
    also* framing effects)
  and moral realism, 343
  and moral semantics, 390–396, 401n3,
    415, 421n2
  new situation, 121, 163
  nonverbal, 80
  order as, 53, 60–66, 62t, 75n9
  and parameterization, 169
  and virtues, 211
contingency, 263, 273n4
conventions
  versus harm-based violations, 273n1
  and moral realism, 342

conventions (cont.)
 taboo violations, 197
 universal, 203
 See also moral–convention distinction
conversational pragmatics, 443–446,
 459
Cooties game, 206–207
core disgust, xvi, 270
core moral judgment, xvi, 260–266,
 275, 280, 282, 288n2
cortisol, 318, 319f
Cosmides, L., 201, 204, 237
criminal behavior, 240
criminal justice
 bail decisions, 12–17, 32, 42
 and honor culture, 317
 legal responsibility, 449–458, 460
cuisine analogy, 202, 209
cultural evolution, 269–272
cultural factors
 and children, 206–207
 collectivism *versus* individualism, 169,
 322–324, 348, 350
 color analogy, 225, 251
 cross-cultural agreement (*see*
 universals)
 cuisine analogy, 202, 209
 default action, 3
 and disgust, 270, 299
 ethnography, 225, 296, 314–316,
 330n19
 and gender, 215
 genital alteration, 191, 227, 232n14
 and harm norms, 159, 169, 271
 and helping norms, 169
 heterogeneity, 315
 honor (*see* honor)
 and human nature, 225
 killing, 122, 169
 memes, 278
 and moral development, 207, 236,
 253
 and moral dilemmas, 169

 and moral disagreements, 313–316,
 323–326
 and moral facts, 228
 and moral grammar, 118
 and moral incoherence, 364
 and moral intuitions, 202
 and moral judgment, 133, 135, 193,
 214, 326
 and moral principles, 122
 and moral realism, 342
 and moral truths, 224
 relativism, 215, 225, 229, 239, 252,
 299
 rich and poor cultures, 330n26
 and scientific evidence, 311
 utilitarianism, 322–324, 331n36, 341
 and virtues, 208, 216, 229, 233, 239
cultural psychology, 316
Cushman, F., xv, 127–135, 145–155,
 157–170, 173, 177, 201

Damasio, A., 115–116, 137, 177, 195,
 199
Damasio, H., 115
Daniels, N., 320
Darley, J., 192
D'Arms, J., xvi, 221, 226, 230n1,
 231n7, 258, 280, 287n1, 289n8,
 289n13, 293–300, 300n1
Darwell, S., 256
Davidson, P., 288n5
Dawkins, R., 16, 278
decisions
 brain site, 137
 and consequentialism, 20, 35
 and emotions, 276
 influences, 1–6, 10, 28, 42, 174
 maximization, 45
 moral decisions, 233–238, 243, 249
 one-reason, 14, 19, 22, 33
default rule, 3, 6, 28, 174
 See also doing and allowing; omission
defeasible justification, 73, 90

defeaters, 73
Deigh, J., xviii, 460
deliberative democrats, 352
Denton, K., 235
deontology
  and ecological rationality, 34
  and moral judgments, 151
  and personal situations, 116
  and rationalization, 216
  and societal standards, 39n3
determinism, 369, 423
De Waal, F., 202
Dhami, M. K., 12–14
Dias, M., 196, 247
dignity, 181, 216, 224, 227
disapproval, 256, 285
disgust
  and bodily state, 199
  versus breaking rank, 1
  core disgust, xvi, 270
  cultural factors, 270, 299
  hypnotism example, 198
  and moral development, 183–185
  non-moral cause, 176
  and snobbery, 247
  and transgressions, 273n4
  and universalism, 203, 270
doing and allowing, 55–67, 65t, 66t,
  75n8, 140
  See also default; omission
domain competence, 152
domain-specificity, 163, 170–178,
  184
Doris, J., xvi, xvii, 211, 296–297, 323,
  330n22, 330n24, 331n32, 333–337,
  339–344
double effect, 134, 141, 150
Dreyfus, H. L., 238
drinking-and-driving, 277, 292
Driver, J., xvii, 34, 41, 42, 44, 441–447,
  449–458
Dunbar, R., 190
Dworkin, R., 344n3

Dwyer, S., 107, 138, 171
dyads, 149, 193, 227, 232n16, 254n1

ecological contextualism, 236, 244
ecological rationality
  and deontology, 34–35
  goals, 41
  and heuristics, 4, 8, 19, 33, 35
education level, 131, 132
Elias, N., 270
embodiment, 7
emotions
  affective primacy, 186
  and broken rules, 268
  and children, 183, 206, 263, 267
  and cognition, 195, 199, 250
  conditioned, 163, 166
  innateness, 163, 165
  and intuition, 250
  and killing norms, 165
  lack of, 258, 267, 274n6
  and memetic fitness, 278
  and mental representations, 176–178
  and moral claims, 282, 288n1, 297
  and moral dilemmas, 137, 143n8
  and moral faculty, 176
  and moral judgments, 115–117, 121,
    137, 162–166, 176–178, 268–272,
    274n4
  and (moral) norms, 268–272
  and moral reasoning, 226, 257
  neural systems, 276
  non-moral, 176
  and psychopathy, 161, 169
  and reasoning, 195, 199, 227
  and wrongness, 161, 176, 275
  See also moral emotions;
    sentimentalism; vicarious emotions
emotivism, 256
empirical psychology, 74, 82, 344n1
empiricism
  and metaethics, 388
  and moral development, 182

empiricism (cont.)
and moral disagreements, 313, 319,
323–327, 339, 344n1
and moral intuitions, 74, 82
and moral semantics, xvii, 355, 358,
365–367, 371–374, 380–382, 405–409
and neosentimentalism, 259
and responsibility, 423, 426–428
and science, 342
ends *versus* means, 132, 134
environment
and heuristics, 5, 11, 17, 19, 26, 42
and moral development, 122,
234–239, 245
and moral judgments, 116, 199
See also context
epistemology, 327n3, 336
equality, 24
equipotentiality, 182, 208
errors
on global scale, 341
and heuristics, xiv, 42
mistakeness, 89, 93, 105
and moral intuitions, 88, 89, 93
error theories, 361, 376, 400, 411n1
ethical focus, 238
ethical intuitionism, 81, 83, 86, 91, 94
ethical theorizing, 306–309
ethics
of community, 197
descriptive *versus* prescriptive,
139–140
disagreements, 348–349
and heuristics, 9, 12
intuitive, 226
moral psychology, 221
naturalistic imperative, 214
and reasoning, 309
and social intuitionism, 250–253
ethnic cleansing, 1, 297
ethnicity, 209, 213, 323
ethnography, 225, 313–318, 330n19
etiquette, 270, 283

euthanasia, 140
evaluative diversity, 303–315
evangelicals, 393
evil(s), 19, 36
lesser of, 131
evolution
cultural, 269–272
and helping norms, 166
and heuristics, 4, 8, 19, 32, 46
and human mind, 240n1, 244–246,
251
and killing norms, 166
and language, 112, 190
and master values, 203
and mate selection, 174
of moral faculty, 123–125, 155n5
and moral judgment, 152
of moral norms, 268–272, 278
and norm disposition, 190–191
evolutionary psychology, 190, 204,
231, 237, 240n1
expectations, 277, 292
experience
and brain, 244
and moral judgment, 133
nonverbal, 80
in novice-to-expert paradigm, 238,
246
experientialism, 49
experts, 379
externalism
and moral judgment, 149–153
and moral semantics, 378–380, 391,
401n5, 414
and motivation, 374
and thermometer example, 91
externalization, 206–209, 212, 236

facts
moral (*see* moral facts)
nonmoral, 314, 320, 330n28, 335, 345
factualism, 353n9
Fagley, N. S., 70

fairness
and children, 281, 288*n*4, 288*n*5
and framing effects, 58
as universal value, 203, 206–209, 245
Farady, M., 190
fatalism, 423
Feinberg, J., 430, 438
fetuses, 38
Fiske, A., 202, 206
Fletcher, G., 458*n*1
Fodor, J., 204–205
folk concepts, xvii–xviii, 368, 369, 374
folk morality, 368–376
folk theory, 333, 337*n*1, 384*n*26, 385*n*34
forgiveness, 319, 334
foundationalism, 87, 89
framing effects
and addition paradox, 75*n*9
definition, xiv, 52–54
epidemic example, 54
genital alteration, 192, 227, 232n14
and human mind, 191
invulnerability to, 85, 92
lack of, 70, 81, 84, 92
and moral dilemmas, 54–67, 143*n*6
and moral intuitions, 73
non-moral cases, 103
number of intuitions, 70, 100, 105
and reflection, 103
and risk, 58
See also wording
Franklin, B., 9
Fraser, B., xviii, 459
free action, 369, 377
free-riders, 166
free will, 423–424
Freud, S., 182, 242
friendship, 24, 62–67
See also peers
Frisch, D., 56

gains and losses, 56, 57
Galotti, K. M., 189
galvanic skin response, 296
games, 22, 207, 266, 395, 439*n*8
game theory, 166
Garcia, J., 182–183, 204
gaze heuristic, 7, 16, 19, 27
Gazzaniga, M. S., 190
Geach, P., 257
gender
and honor, 207
masculinity, 321
and moral dilemmas, 131, 155*n*5
in Muslim societies, 216
and virtues, 208
generation gap, 208
genetics, 210, 245, 251–252
genital alteration, 191, 227, 232n14
genocide, 321
Gert, B., 122, 138
Gettier cases, 371, 384*n*27
Gibbard, A., xvi, 190–191, 231*n*7, 255, 256, 258, 259, 280, 283, 287, 289*n*10, 289*n*13, 360, 375, 381, 383*n*14
Gigerenzer, G., xiv, 4–5, 9, 10, 14, 15, 26*n*2, 27–30, 31–39, 42
Gilbert, M., 453
Gill, M. B., xvii, 400*n*1, 401*n*5, 414–417
Gilligan, C., 246
God
and morality, 182, 185, 209, 366, 373, 385*n*39
and moral semantics, 406, 409, 411*n*2, 419, 421*n*1
for Pascal, 20
Goldman, A., 76*n*11, 91
Goldstein, D. G., 42
goodness
and fundamental disagreement, 329*n*17, 339
health analogy, 307, 328*n*11, 343, 344*n*1

goodness (cont.)
and moral semantics, 359, 414, 421n1
social intuitionism, 240
and social intuitionism, 240
Graham, J., 203, 209, 210, 247, 248,
253
greater good, 131, 264
Greene, J., 115, 116, 142n3, 177, 188,
195, 200, 216, 376
group psychology, 228
guilt
appropriateness of, 261, 265, 280–284,
287, 295–297, 300
and children, 261, 280, 282, 296
and core moral judgment, 261, 265,
280–282
and killing norms, 166
neosentimentalist view, 259, 261,
273n3, 280, 283–287, 293, 295–297,
300n1
versus sadness, 163
gut feelings, 200, 213, 234–236, 243

Haidt, J., xv, 9, 10, 15, 18, 50, 62–67,
120, 133, 154, 159, 161, 181, 185,
187, 188, 189, 190, 196, 197, 198,
199, 202, 203, 205, 206, 208, 209,
210, 213, 215, 216, 217n1, 217n2,
219–233, 230n1, 233–240, 241, 246,
247, 248, 249, 250, 252, 253, 254n1,
270, 274n7
Hall, N., 439n6
happiness
as-if maximizing, 16
as goal, 20, 24
and moral semantics, 390, 401n4, 416
variability, 24, 37, 40n8
Hare, R., 384n24
Harman, G., 107, 150, 328n6
harmless actions
and moral dumbfounding, 198
and Rawlsian analogy, 142n1
as violations, 283

harm norms
and absent feeling, 274n6
and affective resonance, 271
cultural factors, 159, 169, 271
doing versus allowing, 55–62, 63f, 140,
173
intentionality, 173, 276, 292
non-nativist view, 165
and parameterization, 159, 169
physical contact, 173
and sentimentalism, 266
for victim benefit, 276
violations, 273n1
Harris, P., 266
Harrison, J., 9
Hart, H. L. A., 344n3, 425, 438, 454,
455, 457
Hauser, M. D., xv, 107, 108, 116, 117,
125, 127, 145–155, 157–170, 171,
172, 173, 177, 201
health analogy, 307–309, 328n11, 343,
344n1
Heinz dilemma, 197
helping
and causal attribution, 444
cultural factors, 169
and evolution, 166
and trolley problems, 167–169
universalism, 203, 209
Helwig, C., 196
herding societies, 317, 343, 344n2
heroism, 244
Hersh, M. A., 197, 247
Hertwig, R., 5
heuristics
and actions, 4, 16, 28, 34, 41
asset allocation example, 37, 45
and bail decisions, 12–17, 32, 42
and biases, 4, 8
and brain, 8
conflicts, 5, 6
and consequentialism, xiv, 5, 20–22,
29, 36

and context, 5, 8, 11, 19, 26, 42
ecological rationality, 4, 8, 19, 33, 35
and errors, xiv, 42
and evolution, 4, 8, 19, 32, 46
fast *versus* frugal, 4, 7, 13f, 14
in games, 439n8
and information, 5–7, 19, 33, 45
majority, 2, 4, 10, 28, 42
maximization, 20–25, 29, 37, 42, 44–46
models, 15–17
and moral actions, 6, 8–11, 19
and moral intuitions, xiv, 9, 15, 41
and normativism, 5, 18, 20, 30, 34, 38
one-reason, 19
prescriptive, 19
and reaction time, 4, 6, 12, 33
reliability, 41
and social intuitionism, xiv, 9, 15
Stackleberg, 439n8
success criterion, 8
and trust, 25
and uncertainty, 19, 23–25, 45
underlying reasons, 42
and utilitarianism, 5, 21, 28
wrong-doing, 19
Hitler examples, 36, 195
Hobbes, T., 256
Hoffman, M. L., 164
Hoffrage, U., 5
Hom, H., 190
honesty, 208
See also lying
honor
in American South, 316–322, 330n25, 330n26, 334
and authority, 207
concepts *versus* conceptions, 341, 344n3
gender differences, 207
and herding economy, 317, 344n2
and killing, 122

and moral disagreements, 325, 341, 349
universals in, 341
See also insults
Honoré, T., 425, 438, 454, 455, 457
Hooker, B., 29
hormones, 318, 319f
Horowitz, T., 55–58, 75n4
Hug, K., 10
human mind
computational mechanisms, 151
evolution, 240n1, 244–246, 251
good–bad evaluations, 186, 188
intuitive moral values, 203, 226
lawyer analogy, 191, 231n13
modularity (see modularity)
and wrongness, 251
human nature
for Aristotle or Nietzsche, 350
conformism (see breaking ranks; conformism; default)
fallibility, 339
Hume view, 185, 189
and norms, 190–192
versus reasoning, 194
social intuitionist view, 253
See also anthropocentrism
Hume, D.
and causes and effects, 423
on human nature, 185, 189
and moral facts, 214
moral judgment, 115, 137, 188, 220, 230n2
on reason, 189, 220
hypnotism, 198
hypocrisy, 211, 249

ideal equilibrium, 369–371, 376
idealization, 356–357, 370, 376, 405
identity, 242, 248
See also self
imitation
chameleon effect, 192

imitation (cont.)
 in children, 122, 163
 and language acquisition, 112
 role models, 206
Implicit Association Test, 194
impulses, 194
incest, 174, 198, 205
indignation, 284
individualism
 versus collectivism, 169, 322–324, 348,
  350
 and conservativism, 248
 semantic, 368
individual(s)
 ecological contextualism, 236
 in moral domain, 246–248
 and moral judgments, 326
 moral reasoning by, 181
 moral responsibility, 46, 452–454, 461
inference
 and knowledge, 102
 and language acquisition, 112
 and moral disagreements, 309
 and moral intuition, 47–51, 70–74,
  77–81, 83–94, 98–104
in-groups
 and authority, 217*n*2
 and evolution, 245
 and moral claims, 248
 moral communities, 70, 191, 228, 252
 as universal, 203, 208, 215, 217*n*2,
  247
innateness
 and children, 204
 of helping norms, 166
 and language, 107–111, 117, 141
 and moral emotions, 163, 165
 of moral faculty, 164
 moral intuition, 210
 moral judgment, 161–164
 moral rules, 148, 155*n*3, 164
 and virtues, 210
 See also modularity

institutions, 17, 209, 376
insults, 297, 330*n*28
 See also honor
intelligence, 211, 217*n*3
intentionality
 and blameworthiness, 437
 and harm, 173, 276, 292
 knowledge of, 461
 and moral intuition, 174
 and morality, 160
 and moral judgments, 151, 292
 and moral virtue, 34
 and Rawlsian model, 117
internalism
 and moral semantics, 378–380, 391,
  401*n*5, 414
 and motivation, 273*n*2
 and Rawls model, 149–154
 and rules, 272, 283, 289*n*10
Internet, 127–137
intuitionism
 cons, 52–68, 78, 83–91, 95, 98–105
 definitions, 50, 220, 230*n*6
 emergence, 114
 and heuristics, xiv, 9, 15, 41
 on knowledge, 102
 and moral principles, 72, 92
 pros, 68–74, 79–82, 91–95, 206–210
 versus rationalism, 186
 and rationalization, 115
 reflection (*see under* reflection)
 reliabilists, 41, 49, 55, 75*n*2
 See also social intuitionism
intuitions
 about particular cases, 375, 385*n*35
 and authority, 51, 203, 245
 of causation, 433, 437, 439*n*1
 and children, 201, 238
 and conceptual analysis, 368–370
 conflicting, 193–196, 200
 and emotions, 250
 externalization, 212
 and framing effects, 70, 100, 105

initial responses, 369–372
linguistic, 357, 371
and metaphors, 250
novice-to-expert paradigm, 237
overriding, 193–196, 222
and reasoning, 141, 194, 235–239
and sequence, 433, 437
universal themes, 202–204, 245, 252
See also moral intuition(s)
iteration, 235–238, 244

Jackendoff, R., 116
Jackson, F., 333, 358, 367–377, 380,
   384n26, 384n27, 384n28, 385n32
Jacobson, D., xv, 221, 226, 228, 230n1,
   231n7, 232n14, 241, 246–253, 258,
   280, 287n1, 289n8, 301n1
James, W., 194
Japan, 341, 349
Jefferson, Thomas, 253
Jin, R. K.-X., 129
Jordan, A. H., 199
Jorgensen, M., 152
Joseph, C., 159, 202, 203, 205, 208,
   217n2, 219–232, 241, 246
Joyce, R., 376
justice
 and liberals, 209
 Rawls' work, 116, 138, 142n2, 149
 See also criminal justice
justification
 defeasible, 73, 90
 versus judgment, 133
 in moral dilemmas, 131, 133, 174,
   200
 of moral intuitions, 47–52, 55–58,
   67, 70–74, 75n2, 77–81, 83–94,
   98–104
 of moral judgments, 115, 136, 154,
   160, 230
 and moral mandate, 212
 and moral psychology, 115
 non-inferential, 83

and "ought," 75n3
rationalist view, 183
and reasoning skill, 213
social intuitionist view, 201

Kahneman, D., xiv, 19, 54, 56,
   188–189, 385n31
Kamm, F. M., 57, 126, 142n5
Kant, I.
 on lying, 194
 and morality, 246
 on moral judgment, 114, 133, 142n3
 on right action, 374
 on thought and speech, 404
Kasachkoff, T., 182
Katsikopoulos, K., 14
Kepler, J., 24, 39n6
Kesebir, S., 252
Killen, M., 196
killing
 action *versus* wrongness, 160
 versus breaking ranks, 2, 26n1, 29–30,
   33
 of child, 83, 85, 94, 97, 104
 cultural factors, 122
 doing *versus* allowing, 55–62, 63f, 140
 euthanasia, 140
 versus helping, 166
 and honor, 122 (*see also* honor)
 moral rules, 163
 non-nativist view, 165
 and pluralistic societies, 169
 and wording, 59, 60t
 See also trolley problems
kin, 340
kindness, 208
King, Martin Luther, Jr., 250
kinship, 24, 174, 340
Knobe, J., xviii, 427–430, 437, 446n1,
   459
knowledge
 Eastern and Western, 323–326,
   331n36, 348

knowledge (cont.)
 expressed or operative, 109, 117, 125, 173
 and inference, 102
 of intent, 461
 See also moral knowledge
Koelling, R., 182–183, 204
Koenigs, M., 137, 177
Kohlberg, L., 11, 15, 114–115, 178, 183–185, 194, 197, 239, 240, 246, 276
Koller, S., 196, 247
Krebs, D. L., 235
Kühberger, A., 68, 69
Kuhn, D., 67, 69, 75n5, 188, 190, 196
Kunda, Z., 190
Kurzban, R., 211, 242–243
Kutz, C., 452, 458n1

Ladd, J., 330n19
language
 causal, 425
 deep structures, 113
 evolution, 112, 190
 grammar, 108, 384n26
 linguistic intuitions, 357, 371
 linguistic judgments, 109
 understanding of, 333
 unique properties, 110
 See also language analogy; moral language; moral semantics; wording
language analogy
 actions and phonemes, 118
 and brain-damage, 178
 causes and consequences, 119, 121, 146
 competence and performance, 110, 121, 125, 142n5, 151
 and deficits, 120, 137, 153, 160
 disanalogies, 141, 158–161, 175–178
 faculties, 107–111, 117, 141
 grammar, 368, 384n26
 and inference, 112
 and moral semantics, 368
 parameterization, 159, 169

pidgin and Creole, 209
Rawls' work, 114, 116–117, 138
representation types, 137, 143n10, 147, 151, 175, 206
second-language, 175
speech perception, 172
strong and weak, 121, 139, 145, 153, 154n1
unconscious, role of, 111, 117, 133–135, 141, 174, 206–209
Lapsley, D., 238
Latane, B., 192
Laudan, L., 334
lawbreaking, 240
Law & Order, 450–456
Learned Hand formula, 21
least effort, 3, 6
LeBoeuf, R. A., 70
legal responsibility, 449–458, 460
Leibniz, G., 424
Leiter, B., xvii, 336, 337n4, 347, 350, 351, 353
Leslie, A., 292
Leslie, J., 424, 426, 432–434, 435, 437
Levin, I. P., 70
Levy, N., 249, 254n1
Lewis, D., 439n4
liability, 21, 43
liberals, 209, 248, 253, 322
Lieberman, D., 205
Lightfoot, D., 111
Loeb, D., xvii, 33, 39n1, 41, 42, 44, 303, 313, 328n4, 329n17, 331n31, 384n22, 387–401, 403–411
logic, 193, 222
love, withdrawal of, 163
loyalty, 203, 208, 245
 optimization impact, 25, 37, 40n7
lying, 62–67, 75n8, 433

Machery, E., 295
Mackie, J. L., 304, 305, 311, 327n2, 361, 367, 399

Macnamara, J., 115, 125

Mahapatra, M., 196, 197

majority
as endorsement, 216, 229
as heuristic, 2, 4, 10, 28, 42
sacrifice of, 336

Mallon, R., xv, 172, 173, 174, 292, 295

Marcus, G., 245

Markowitz, H., 45

Martignon, L., 14

mate selection, 24, 39n6, 174, 197

maximization, 20–25, 29, 37, 42, 44–46

McDowell, D., 287

meaningfulness, 248
See also situational meaning

means *versus* ends, 132, 134

media, 210, 250
Law & Order, 450–456

medicine
epidemic dilemma, 54–58
euthanasia, 140
testing and screening, 43–45, 60
transplant dilemma, 60, 72
wording effect, 69

memetic fitness, 278

memory, 125

Mencius, 202

mental health, 307, 343, 344n1

mental representation
and heuristics, 7
language analogy, 137, 143n10, 147, 151, 206
and moral judgments, 173–178

Merli, D., 382n6

metaethics
descriptive and prescriptive, 394
disagreements, 348–350
and empiricism, 388
and language, 355
and relativism, 215
research, 375, 385n31, 388
sentimentalist, 220, 255–259
See also moral semantics

metaphors, 250

metaphysics, 367, 371, 382

Mikhail, J., 107, 116, 125, 127, 129, 135, 138, 139–140, 141, 171

Milgram, S., 2, 6, 192

Miller, J., 196

Miller, P. M., 70

Minesweeper, 23

Mischel, W., 211

mistakenness, 89, 93, 105

modularity
discussion, 204–206, 217n2, 234, 237, 242–246
and evolution, 240n1
and inconsistency, 211, 242
interpreter module, 190
and moral development, 236

mood, 234

Moody-Adams, M., 313–316, 328n8, 330n21

Moore, G. E., 358, 371, 382n7, 384n24

moral actions, 8–11, 19–23, 26, 35
See also actions

moral agreement
and affect-backed norms, 270
and kinship, 340
master values, 203, 206–209, 226
and methodology, 315
and moral realism, 340, 351
positive psychology, 344n1
and reasoning, 336

moral beliefs
versus moral intuitions, 47, 86
and motivation, 374
and perception, 80
versus scientific, 101
social intuitionist view, 181–186, 221

moral character, 208

moral claims
and conservatives, 248
and emotions, 282, 288n1, 297
versus moral judgment, 288n3

moral claims (cont.)
  and moral semantics, 356–361, 366,
    403
  relativism, 299
moral cognitivism, 356–363, 375
  See also cognitivism
moral community, 70, 191, 228, 252
moral competence
  brain region, 199
  in children, 122
  future research, 179
  language analogy, 139, 141
  and moral judgments, 121
  versus performance, 125, 142*n*5, 151
  and (im)personality, 152
moral concepts, 281, 292–295, 298
moral–convention distinction
  and children, xvi, 184, 260, 267, 281
  factors, 300
  and moral domain, 301*n*4
  and psychopaths, 263–267
  and real-world decisions, 276
  underlying mechanisms, 265
  violations, 197, 259, 273*n*4
moral decisions, 233–238, 243, 249
moral development
  in children, 122, 182–184, 206, 213,
    236–239
  and context, 236
  cultural factors, 207, 236, 253
  empiricist approaches, 182
  and environment, 122, 234–239,
    245
  language analogy, 121–123, 158, 175
    (*see also* language analogy)
  and modularity, 236
  novice-to-expert, 237–239, 246
  Piaget-Kohlberg views, 114
  and punishment, 158, 163, 210
  role taking, 194–196
  of second moral system, 175
  social intuitionist view, 184–186,
    206–210

moral dilemmas
  arrow example, 48
  brain regions, 177, 195, 200
  car sale, 62–67
  chimpanzee *versus* acephalic human,
    194
  crying baby, 195, 200–201
  and cultural factors, 169
  and (in)direct harm, 200
  doing *versus* allowing, 55–67
  drownings, 55
  and emotions, 137, 143*n*8
  epidemic example, 54, 56, 57, 58
  experimental subjects, 86, 101,
    129–135, 130t, 137
  faulty crane, 65–67, 65t, 66t
  and framing effects, 54–67, 143*n*6
  justification, 131, 133, 174, 200
  lifesaving drug theft, 197
  and moral judgments, 165, 193
  and moral psychology, 153
  order factor, 60–66, 62t, 75*n*9
  organ transplant, 60, 72
  (im)personality, 132, 134, 152, 169,
    200
  and real-life situations, 87, 103, 126
  risk factor, 58
  for small-scale societies, 135–137
  social intuitionist view, 187f, 188,
    193–196, 200
  Web studies, 127–137
  See also trolley problems
moral disagreements
  and children, 262, 267, 281, 286
  cultural factors, 313–316, 323–326
  defusing, 320–327, 335, 337*n*3, 345,
    353
  and empiricism, 313, 319, 323–327,
    339, 344*n*1
  and first-person subjectivism, 285–287
  fundamental, xvii, 305–311, 319,
    321*n*17, 334, 339–341, 351
  versus misagreements, 348

and moral principles, 296
and moral semantics, 366, 385n32, 401n4
and neosentimentalism, 258, 265, 268, 295–298
and nonmoral facts, 314, 320, 330n28
and normativism, 286, 298, 335
particular cases, 348–350, 353n8
(anti)realist views, xvii, 304–313, 319, 323–327, 340
and real-life circumstances, 341
moral discourse
  Brandt view, 357
  and community norms, 191
  compromise, 232n16
  context, 193, 421n2
  criteria, 410
  inner dialogue, 194
  insulated pockets, 391, 414–417
  by moral philosophers, 249
  neosentimentalist view, 268
  and social intuitionism, 226
  uniformity assumption, 392, 395–397, 417
  See also moral semantics
moral domain, 246–248, 300, 301n4
moral dumbfounding, 197, 199
moral emotions
  anticipation of, 163, 165
  and children, 263
  for Hume, 185
  parenting example, 183–185
  social intuitionist scope, 222–223, 248
  See also anger; emotions; guilt; shame
moral facts
  and agency, 328n7
  and intuitions, 214, 224, 226
  and moral semantics, xvii, 356–362, 366, 380, 404
  and (anti)realists, 304, 328n5, 342, 351
  relativism, 228, 383n15

versus taste, 381
versus values, 342
moral faculty
  and actions, 117f, 119, 146
  brain regions, 124, 177
  combinatory role, 173
  and deficits, 120, 137, 153, 160
  description, 118–121
  development, 121–123
  evolution, 123–125, 155n5
  innateness, 164
  language analogy, 107–111, 117, 141
  and moral identity, 242
  and moral judgments, 173
  and moral principles, 122, 146–151, 155n2
  non-nativist view, 162–165
  and (im)personality, 151–153
  and real-world cases, 142n5
  strong and weak, 121, 139, 145, 154n1
  subsystems, 178
  and trolley problems, 126–135
  uniqueness, 141
  and wrongness, 164, 176
moral grammar, 107, 118, 125, 150
moral identity, 242
moral intuition(s)
  about incest, 205
  and action, 140, 196, 238
  and authority, 51
  confirmation, 50–52, 71, 84, 88, 92–94, 95n3, 105
  consistency, 55, 375
  and context, 52–54, 79
  and cultures, 202
  definition, 47, 75n2, 97, 188, 217n1
  and empiricism, 74, 82
  errors, 88, 93
  and framing effects, 52, 59, 60t, 73, 79, 80
  gains and losses, 56
  of general principles, 73, 206–209

moral intuition(s) (cont.)
and heuristics, xiv, 9, 15, 41
and individual responsibility, 46
and innateness, 210
and intentionality, 174
justification, 47–52, 55–58, 70–74,
  75n2, 77–81, 83–94, 98–104
and language analogy, 114
limitations, 18
versus moral beliefs, 47, 86
and moral dilemmas, 133
and moral facts, 214, 224, 226
and moral judgments, 186, 187f
and moral principles, 72, 212
and moral reasoning, 15, 26n2, 32,
  47, 194
and order, 53, 60–66, 62t, 75n9, 80
overriding, 193, 222
reliability, 67–74, 97–99, 105
underlying reasons, 16, 19, 88
widely-held, 105
See also intuitionism
morality
definition, 300
as expertise, 237
folk morality, 368–376
and God, 182, 185, 209, 366, 373,
  385n39
health analogy, 307–309, 328n11, 343,
  344n1
institutions of, 376
objectivity of (see objectivity)
rationalist view, 183
shared, 368–376, 385n32 (see also
  moral community)
for social intuitionists, 202–204, 245,
  252
variations, 365, 376, 395, 414
moral judgment(s)
and actions, 116
age factors, 264, 283
and appetites, 293
and bias, 174, 224

brain regions, 137, 150, 177, 200
capacity for, 259
and causal attribution, 115–121,
  425–430, 441–446, 459
and cognition, 114–117, 250
consistency, 61, 127
cultural factors, 133, 135, 193, 214,
  326
definition, 233
and emotions, 115–117, 121, 137,
  162–166, 176–178, 268–272, 274n4
experiential factor, 133
externalist and internalist, 147,
  151–154
first-person, 256, 285
in future, 135
and (im)personality, 116, 132, 134,
  169, 200
innateness, 161–164
intentionality, 151, 292
intuitionist view, 15
judgments about, 151, 155n5
justification, 115, 136, 154, 160, 230
and memory, 125
versus moral claim, 288n3
versus moral decisions, 243, 249
and moral dilemmas, 165, 193
and moral faculty, 173
of moralists, 210
by moral philosophers, 196, 223
and moral principles, 149, 173–175
and moral reasoning, 9, 233
and motivation, 273n2
neosentimentalist view, 261, 273n3,
  275, 280, 293, 295–297, 300n1
and normativism, 259, 276, 289n10
prescriptive account, 147
probability parallel, 69
process, 14–19, 114–119, 148, 152,
  162
psychology of, 149, 175
rationalization, 115, 133, 154, 181,
  189, 221

and reasoning, 15, 21, 32, 114–117, 120, 133, 230*n*5, 274*n*7
and representations, 173–178
and self-interest, 151
sentimentalist view, 258, 269
situatedness, 116, 199
and social intuitionism, 181, 186–196, 198, 221, 224, 242
subconscious level, xv, 250
type and frequency, 212, 222, 234
utilitarianism, 116, 151
variation, 169, 304, 311, 314
and wrongness, 275, 288*n*3
See also core moral judgment
moral knowledge
harm study, 174
language analogy, 107, 113–120
and moral intuitions, 220, 226, 251
moral language, 226, 357, 394
moral mandate, 212
moral norms
acquisition, 123
and evolution, 190, 268–272, 278
and moral judgments, 259, 276, 289*n*10
See also normativism
moral outrage
rationalism as, 24
moral philosophers
and moral disagreements, 345–348, 352
versus moral intuitions, 194
moral judgments, 196, 223
and real-life situations, 249
and virtue as skill, 207
moral philosophy
definitions, 300
disagreements, 336
empirical inquiry, 367
and equality, 24
Kant *versus* Hume, 230*n*1
and moral psychology, 46, 213–216
and social intuitionism, 213–216, 219

and trolley problem responders, 131
moral principles
conflicts, 159
(un)conscious, xv, 117, 133–135, 141, 174, 178, 206–209, 212
cultural factors, 122
in folk morality, 369
innateness, 155*n*3
and intuitions, 72, 92, 212
master themes, xv, 203, 206–209, 226, 245, 252
and moral disagreements, 296
and moral faculty, 122, 146–151, 155*n*2
and moral judgments, 149, 173–175
operative *versus* expressed, 173–174
versus particular cases, 350, 353*n*8
for Rawls, 142*n*2
moral psychology
blank slate theories, 183
competence and performance, 125, 142*n*5, 151
and ethics, 221
and justification, 115
labels, 15
and moral dilemmas, 153
and moral judgments, 149, 175
and moral philosophy, 46, 213–216
and nonconscious systems, 233
positive approach, 344*n*1
Rawls' work, 113
single source theories, 206, 215
social intuitionist view, 253
moral realism
and consequentialism, 348
and context, 343
convergentism, 310–313, 315, 321, 327, 328*n*9, 329*n*18, 333–336, 341, 352, 369
cultural factors, 342
divergentism, xvii, 306–310, 330*n*21, 333, 341–344, 351
and epistemology, 327*n*3, 336

moral realism (cont.)
honor, 316–322, 334, 341, 349
and indeterminacy, 329n17
and moral agreement, 340, 351
and moral disagreements, xvii,
304–313, 319, 323–327, 340
and moral facts, 304, 328n5, 342, 351
and moral reasoning, 375
and moral semantics, 356–358, 361,
365–367, 375–377, 381, 382n6,
383n16, 384n28, 417
and moral truths, 312
and objectivity, 303–306, 329n18,
330n21, 335
patchy realism, 322, 328n13
moral reasoning
and bias, 224, 244
in children, 262, 274n7
definition, 189, 194, 233
and emotions, 226, 257
improvement, 213
and intuitions, 15, 26n2, 194
and moral irrealism, 375
and moral judgment, 9, 233
and objectivity, 375
and psychopathy, 276
rationalist view, 212
social intuitionism, 189, 193, 200,
216, 221, 251
by two individuals, 181
moral repugnance
versus breaking ranks, 2, 26n1, 33
and Rawlsian analogy, 142n1
reasoning as, 24, 39n6
and Singer work, 194
and taboo violations, 197
moral responsibility
and causal attribution, 430, 441–446,
459
without causality, 434–438, 439n1
counterfactuals, 426, 431–437, 439n6
entailment claim, 423–436, 439n1,
453

individual versus complicit, 452–454,
461
inquiry mode, 438
versus legal responsibility, xviii,
449–456, 461
and pragmatics, 426, 428, 438,
443–446, 459
without unusualness, 443
moral rules
and action, 168
innateness, 148, 155n3, 164
and linguistic rules, 159, 160, 169
unconsciousness, 160
moral semantics
Canberra Plan, 367–371
and (non)cognitivism, 366–367,
387–391, 411n1
conceptual analysis, 334, 367–369,
372, 384n24, 384n26, 396
and conflicts, 364, 378, 380, 398,
401n4, 421n2
and context, 390–396, 401n3, 415,
421n2
empirical inquiry, xvii, 355, 358,
365–367, 371–374, 380–382, 405–409
error theories, 361, 366, 376, 400,
411n1
and (in)externalism, 377–380, 391,
401n5, 414
game example, 395
and God, 406, 409, 411n2, 419, 421n1
and goodness, 359, 414, 421n1
happiness example, 390, 401n4, 416
incoherentism, xvii, 363–367, 381,
397–400, 413–416, 419
insulated pockets, 391, 414–417
and moral claims, 356–361, 366, 403
and moral disagreements, 366,
385n32, 401n4
and moral facts, xvii, 356–362, 366,
380, 404
and moral realism, 356–358, 361,
365–367, 375–377, 381, 382n6

and moral truths, 381
ordinary speakers, xvii, 356, 361–363, 405–410, 417–421
and pragmatics, 401n3, 443–446
and underlying beliefs, 399, 403
uniformity assumption, 392, 395–399, 417
variability thesis, 390–395, 414
moral skepticism, 49, 74, 75n2, 215
moral systems, 216, 226, 229
second, 175
moral theories
and background theory, 331n37
metatheories, 399
Nietzsche view, 336
single-source, 215
moral truths
anthropocentrism, 213–215, 224–226
color analogy, 224, 251
cultural factors, 224
and global error, 341
and moral realism, 312
and moral semantics, 381
and neosentimentalism, 297
motivation
and causal attribution, 427, 437, 444
consequentialist view, 385n33
externalist view, 374
harm causation avoidance, 266
and moral judgment, 273n2
social intuitionist view, 181–186
Much, A., 197
Murphy, S., 197
Muslims, 216

Narvaez, D., xv, 238, 241–246, 248–253
natural disasters, 264, 275, 436
naturalism, 259
naturalistic imperative, 214
nature versus nurture, 245
negligence, 19, 21, 425
neosentimentalism
and absent feeling, 259

and concepts, 293–295, 298, 301n3
defense of, 279–287
and moral claims, 282, 288n1, 297
and moral disagreements, 258, 265, 268
and moral judgments, 261, 273n3, 275, 280, 293, 300n1
and norms, 280, 283, 289n10, 296–299
See also sentimentalism
neural systems, 276
Newcomb's problem, 434
Newport, E. L., 172
Nichols, S., xvi, 147, 150, 264, 270, 271, 274n5, 275–278, 279–289, 291, 295, 299, 323, 348
Nietzsche, F., 262, 274n8, 336, 347, 350
Nisbett, R. E., 189, 298, 316–322, 323, 330n25
noncognitivism. See under cognitivism
nonverbal situations, 80
normative theory
and core moral judgment, xvi, 264–268
individual differences, 276
and moral disagreements, 286, 298
and neosentimentalism, 283, 289n10, 296–299
and theory-of-mind, 278
normativism
and causal attribution, 426–430, 442, 446n2, 457, 459, 461
in children, 267
and core moral judgment, 264
and ethics, 348
and heuristics, 5, 18, 20, 30, 34, 38
and metaethics, 394
and moral disagreements, 286, 298, 335
and moral judgments, 259, 276, 289n10
and moral language, 357, 394
and moral semantics, 360

normativism (cont.)
and naturalism, 259
and psychopaths, 264
and (neo)sentimentalism, 266–268,
273n3, 280, 283
and social interaction, 190–192
and social intuitionism, 50, 225,
231n10, 248, 253
and utilitarianism, 21, 39n4
norm expressivism, 280, 283
norms, consensus on, 191
Northerners, 297, 316–321, 330n26,
334
novice-to-expert paradigm, 237–239,
246
Nucci, L., 288
Nuñez, M., 266–267
Nunner-Winkler, G., 261

obedience, 1, 192
objectivity
(non)cognitivism, 375
versus disagreements, 287, 297
and folk morality, 376
of moral facts, 214, 225
and moral realists, 303–306, 329n18,
330n21, 335
and moral semantics, 357–366, 375,
391, 401n5, 418
and moral truths, 224, 251
in reasoning, 195
omission
versus acting, 28, 65–67, 65t, 66t, 140,
173 (*See also* default rule; doing and
allowing)
and causal responsibility, xvii, 424,
428, 431, 434–436, 446n2, 454–458,
458n3
See also doing and allowing
O'Neill, P., 58–62, 85, 152
1/N rule, 45
open-question, 359
operative knowledge, 109, 117, 173

opinions
bien pensant, 228, 232n14
poll results, 372
optimization, 25, 44
See also maximization
order, 53, 60–66, 62t, 75n9, 80, 433,
437
Osgood, C. E., 186
others, 241–243, 276, 371, 407
See also dyads; vicarious emotions
"ought," 19, 30, 75n3, 214, 328n13

Panksepp, J., 237, 240n1
Panksepp, J. B., 237, 240n1
parameterization, 159, 169
parenting, 183–185, 209, 217n3, 281,
340
See also caring
Parfit, D., 75n9, 194
Park, L., 197
partiality, 320, 335
particular cases
and bail decisions, 14
moral disagreements, 348–350, 353n8
moral principles, 350, 353n8
and moral semantics, 375, 385n35,
396
Pascal, B., 20
patchy realism, 322, 328n13
patriotism, 203, 209
Pautz, A., 382n6
Payne, J. W., 5
peers, 4, 209
See also breaking ranks
Peng, K., 323, 324, 341
perception(s)
of consequences, 119, 121, 146, 151
and modularity, 205
and moral beliefs, 80
and moral judgments, 114
as process, 116, 118–120
of speech, 172
Perkins, D. N., 190

permissiblity, 34, 319, 334
Perner, J., 68
(im)personality
  and moral dilemma, 132, 134, 152,
    169, 200
  and moral faculty, 151–153
  moral judgments, 116
personality traits, 210
perspective, 162, 194–196
persuasion, 191–193, 210–212, 221,
  226, 232n16
Petrinovich, L., 58–62, 85, 152
Petty, R. E., 212
physical contact, 173
physical health, 307–309, 328n11, 343,
  344n1
physical response, 318, 319f
Piaget, J., 15, 114–115, 183, 194, 207,
  236
Pinker, S., 183, 204
Pizarro, D. A., 120
Plakias, A., xvi, xvii, 297, 333–337,
  339–344
The Plan, 367–371
pleasure, 359, 378
  childkiller example, 83, 85, 94, 97,
    104
pluralism, 169, 252
power, 341, 432–434
practical wisdom, 236
pragmatics, 401n3, 428, 438, 443–446,
  459
praiseworthiness, 165
prefrontal cortex. See brain
prescriptivism, 147, 231n9, 360
  See also normativism
pride, 261
Prinz, J., xv, 153, 161, 172, 175, 176
promises, 5, 53, 268
pros and cons, 159, 194–196
prospect theory, 56–58
psychopathology, 308, 455–457, 458n3
psychopathy

and emotions, 161, 169
and intentionality, 160
and moral–convention distinction,
  263–267
and moral reasoning, 276
and wrongness, 178
punishment
  capital punishment, 159
  and causal attribution, 457, 461
  of children, 276–278, 292
  of free-riders, 166
  and honor systems, 317
  of innocents, xvi, 309 (see also
    scapegoating)
  and moral development, 158, 163,
    210
purity, 203, 206–209, 245, 247
Putnam, H., 8, 379

Quine, W. V., 333
Quinn, W., 55

Rachels, J., 140
Railton, P., 256, 306, 310, 374
rape, 163
  of child (example), 83, 85, 94, 97, 104
rationalism
  definitions, 220, 230n6
  versus intuitionism, 186
  limitations, 215
  morality view, 183
  morally unacceptable, 24
  and moral reasoning, 212
rationality
  and disagreements, 311, 320,
    324–326, 335
  and heuristics, 4, 8, 29, 33, 35, 41
  and justification, 183
rationalization
  brain site, 190
  and intelligence, 211
  and intuitionism, 115
  moral dumbfounding, 197, 199

rationalization (cont.)
  for moral judgments, 115, 133, 154,
    181, 189, 221
  and reasoning, 193, 227
  and social intuitionism, 115, 154,
    216, 221
  and taboo violations, 197
Rawls, J., 113–114, 116–118, 121, 124,
    138, 142*n*2, 148, 151, 152, 259, 322,
    344n3
reaction time
  and heuristics, 4, 6, 12, 33
  and moral intuition, 47
  and operative knowledge, 109
  See also automaticity
reasoning
  bias impact, 190, 224, 244, 249
  brain site, 195
  in children, 267, 281
  versus cognition, 250 (*see also*
    cognition)
  definition, 189
  and dyads, 193, 227, 232*n*16, 249,
    254*n*1
  and emotions, 195, 199, 227
  ethical beliefs, 309
  versus human nature, 194
  and intuition, 141, 194, 235–239
  and justification, 213
  and moral agreements, 336
  and moral dilemmas, 194
  and moral judgments, 15, 21, 32,
    114–117, 120, 133, 230*n*5, 274*n*7 (*see
    also* moral reasoning)
  morally repugnant, 24, 39*n*6
  objectivity, 195
  one-sidedness, 191–192
  and self-interest, 213, 244, 249, 252
  and social intuitionism, 194–196, 198,
    200, 213
  timing, 230*n*5
reciprocity, 203, 208, 245, 281
reflection

critical, 371, 374
  and framing effects, 103
  ideal equilibrium, 369–371, 376
  and inference, 104
  and intuitionism, 49, 70, 75*n*4, 89,
    95*n*4
  social intuitionist view, 194–196, 201,
    244
reforming, 356–357, 371, 377
Regier, T., 15, 26*n*2
relativism
  and culture, 215, 225, 229, 252, 299
  and folk morality, 370
  and Kohlberg, 239
  on moral facts, 383*n*15
  and moral semantics, 362, 391, 401*n*5
  versus pluralism, 215, 252
  and semantics, 371–375
  and social intuitionism, 228, 250–252
  and violence, 343
religion, 131, 182
  See also God
replicas, 439*n*4
respect, 203, 208, 245
responsibility
  for harm, 457
  in legal system, 449–458, 460
  liability, 21, 43
  and moral intuition, 46
  vicarious, 458*n*1
  See also moral responsibility
Rest, J., 238
reward, 210, 277
rightness
  acquisition, 164
  and brain damage, 200
  and community, 252
  for Kant, 374
  and moral semantics, 366, 368, 370,
    378, 414, 419
  social intuitionist view, 188
risk, 58
Ross, W. D., 73, 92

rules
and children, 262, 266–269, 282
and disgust, 270
and emotions, 268
internal, 272, 283, 289n10
and language, 110
transparency, 20
rule utilitarianism, 5, 28

Salmon, N., 382n1
Salton, E., 70
Saltzwtein, H. D., 182
Samenow, S. E., 240
samurai, 341, 349
sanctity, 203, 209, 245
Sartorio, C., 424, 434–437, 439n1
satisficing, 21, 25, 29, 37
Sayre-McCord, G., xvii, 415, 417–421
scapegoating, xvi, 322–324, 336, 350
Schnall, S., 199
Schulte-Mecklenbeck, M., 68
Schwartz, S. H., 202
science, 309–311, 329n15, 329n16, 334,
342
See also medicine
selective deficits, 120, 137, 153, 160
self
conflicts within, 364, 376, 380, 398
as cultural factor, 323
modularity, 243
and strong beliefs, 399
as Western concept, 323
self-image, 234
self-interest
and compromise, 232n16
in current culture, 240
and reasoning, 213, 244, 249, 252
selfish genes, 123
self-judgment, 241–243
self-presentation, 211
self-reported behavior, 11
self-sacrifice, 208
self-survival, 340

Seligman, M. E. P., 204
Selten, R., 4
semantics. See conversational
pragmatics; moral semantics
sentimentalism
and children, xvi
definition, 287n1
and human nature, 225–226
and moral claims, 282, 288n1, 297
and naturalism, 259, 268–272
normative theory, 265–269
and reasoning, 227
and social intuitionism, 220
utility, 223
See also emotions; neosentimentalism
sentimentalist metaethics, 220,
255–259
September 11th, 195
sequence, 53, 60–66, 62t, 75n9, 80,
433, 437
sexual partner, 174, 197
See also mate selection
Shafer-Landau, R., xiv, 49, 101,
102–105, 309, 310, 312, 320, 322,
331n31
Shafir, E., 70
shame, 122, 261
shamefulness, 220
Sharabi, D., 70
Sherif, M., 192
Shiloh, S., 70
Shweder, R., 196, 197, 202, 215, 247
Simon, H., 4, 25
Singer, P., 194
Sinnott-Armstrong, W., 75n1, 75n3,
77–82, 83–95, 102, 143n8, 309,
383n20, 385n31
situatedness
of behavior, 211
and consequentialism, 23–25
of heuristics, 5, 8, 11, 19, 26, 42
of moral decisions, 234–236
and moral disagreement, 341

situatedness (cont.)
  and moral intuition, 73, 80, 87
  of moral judgments, 116, 199
  and moral semantics, 391–396, 401n3,
    415
  new situations, 121, 163
  uncertainty, 192
  See also particular cases
situational meaning, 314, 318, 330n20
skepticism, 215, 365–367, 375, 382,
  384n28
Skitka, L. J., 212
Sklar, L., 342
slavery, 195, 215
small-scale societies, 135–137, 165
Smart, J. J. C., 20, 21, 39n4, 323, 350
Smetana, J., 260, 267
Smith, Adam, 107
Smith, Michael, 304, 312, 329n18
Smith, S. M., 70
Snare, F. E., 330n20
social groups
  behavior in, 30, 33, 451–454
  collectivist *versus* individualist, 169,
    322–324, 348, 350
  consensus, 249–250, 341
  and deontology, 39n3
  group psychology, 228
  in-groups (*see* in-groups)
  and killing norms, 165, 169
  moral communities, 70, 191, 228,
    252
  moral disagreements, 285–287
  out-groups, 229
  shared opinions, 228, 232n14, 368
  small-scale societies, 135–137, 165
  stigmatized, 188
social interaction
  breaking ranks, 2, 4, 9, 33, 192
  chameleon effect, 192
  chess analogy, 22
  conditioning effect, 182
  conflicts, 364, 376, 380, 398

dyads, 193, 227, 232n16, 249, 254n1
game transmission, 207
and language, 190
and moral decisions, 234
and moral development, 236
and moral reasons, 181
norm generation, 190–192
persuasion, 191–193, 210–211, 212,
  221, 226, 232n16
and virtues, 207
social intuitionism
  and behavior, 243
  and biopsychology, 237
  and dignity, 181, 216, 224, 227
  and ethics, 250–253
  and goodness, 240
  and heuristics, xiv, 9, 15
  and justification, 201
  and moral decisions, 242
  on moral development, 184–186,
    206–210
  and moral dilemmas, 187f, 188,
    193–196, 200
  and moral discourse, 226
  versus moral intuitionism, 50
  on moral judgment, 181, 186–196,
    198, 221, 224, 242
  and moral philosophy, 213–216,
    219
  on moral psychology, 253
  and moral reasoning, 181, 193, 200,
    216, 221, 251
  and motivation, 181–186
  and normativism, 50, 225, 231n10,
    248, 253
  and obedience, 192
  and out-group members, 229
  and rationalization, 115, 154, 216,
    221
  and reasoning, 194–196, 198, 200
  and reflection, 194–196, 201, 244
  and relativism, 228, 250–252
  summary, 181

supporting studies, 196–199
unresolved issues, 212
See also moral intuitionism
social learning, 207
social psychology
 causal attribution, 426–431, 437
 distributed cognition, 249
 and honor, 316 (*see also* honor)
 modular self, 243
 and virtues, 211
sociobiology, 123
socioeconomic class, 197, 247, 321,
 385*n*34
sociopathy, 199
Sodian, B., 261
soldiers, 1–4, 30
Sorensen, R., 48, 439*n*7
Sosa, D., 424
Sosa, E., 347, 348
Southerners, 297, 316–321, 330*n*25,
 330*n*25, 330*n*26, 334, 341
speech, 172, 404
Sperber, D., 205
Stackleberg heuristic, 439*n*8
status quo, 56
See also default rule
stem cells, 120
Stevenson, C., 256, 285, 287, 289*n*11
Stich, S., 155*n*3, 155*n*5, 155*n*6, 295,
 296–297, 323, 330*n*24, 331*n*32, 348,
 350, 371–376, 384*n*21
stigmas, 188
Street, S., 340
Sturgeon, N., 294, 303, 304, 313, 320,
 328*n*6, 329*n*16
subconscious level
 and actions, 118
 and cognition, 10, 15, 21, 32, 233
 and harm norms, 173
 language, 111, 117, 133–135, 141,
 174, 206–209
 and moral decisions, 235t
 moral judgments, xv, 250

and moral principles, xv, 117,
 133–135, 141, 174, 178, 206–209,
 212
 and moral psychology, 233
 moral rules, 160
subjectivism, 256, 285–287, 299,
 361–363
suicide bombers, 286
Sunstein, C. R., xiv, 19, 27, 28, 41, 42,
 46, 58
survival, 340

taboos, 196–198, 203
Takemura, K., 70
taste, 381
 See also cuisine analogy
Terkel, S, 4
terrorism, 195, 286
testosterone, 318, 319f
Tetris, 23
theory of mind, xvi, 276–278
thermometer, 70–72, 76*n*11, 90–94, 105
threat, redirected, 132
Timmons, M., 381, 382*n*4, 383*n*11,
 383*n*14
Todd, P. M., 4
tolerance, 209
Tolhurst, W., xiv, 49, 100–102
Tooby, J., 201, 204, 237
Toulmin, S., 257, 268
Tranel, D., 115, 137, 177
trolley problems
 and double effect, 150
 emotion-based view, 167–169
 and framing effects, 58–62, 63f, 143*n*6
 and moral faculty, 126–135
 versus real-life, 11, 21, 38
trust
 and heuristics, 8, 25, 37, 40*n*7
 in moral intuitions, 70–74
truth(s)
 anthropocentricity, 213, 215,
 224–226, 228

truth(s) (cont.)
 and conceptual analysis, 334
 and heuristics, 28
 and moral intuitions, 75n2, 85, 224
 See also lying; moral truths
Turiel, E., 184, 196, 246, 259, 288n5
Turing, A., 8
Tversky, A., xiv, 19, 54, 56, 385n31
Two Buttons example, 434

uncertainty
 health analogy, 308
 and heuristics, 19, 23–25, 45
 and social interaction, 192
Unger, P., 75n9
uniformity assumption, 392, 395–397,
 417
universal grammar, 107, 118, 125, 150
universalization, 222
universals
 of affect-backed norms, 270
 and color, 251
 disgust, 203, 270
 versus ethnography, 315
 and harm, 173–175
 in honor codes, 341
 and human nature, 226
 and positive psychology, 344n1
 power effect, 341
 recurring themes, 203, 206–209, 226,
 246–248, 340
university students, 356, 363, 372,
 374–376, 385n31, 395
unusualness, xvii, xviii, 431, 442,
 455–459
utilitarianism
 and atrocity, 31
 and brain region, 138, 200
 cultural differences, 322–324, 331n36,
 341
 ends *versus* means, 132, 134
 focus, 246
 versus gut feelings, 200

and heuristics, 5, 21, 28
and massacre example, 29
and moral judgments, 116, 151
and moral semantics, 393
and Nietzsche, 336
normative, 21, 39n4
as single source theory, 215
and trolley problems, 131

values
 conflicts, 159, 166, 188
 versus moral facts, 342
 recurring themes, 203, 206–209, 226,
 246–248, 340
 terms for, 392
Van Roojen, M., 56, 75n4, 383n12
vicarious emotions
 and affective resonance, 272
 in children, 183, 206, 264, 267
 neural explanation, 277
 social intuitionist view, 194
 as universals, 203
 and violence, 264, 267, 275, 291
vicarious responsibility, 458n1
victims, 229
VIM. *See* violence inhibition
 mechanism
violations
 and brain region, 177
 convention *versus* moral, 197, 259,
 273n4
 harmless actions, 283
 harm norms, 273n1
 of rules (children), 262, 266–269, 282
 of taboos, 196–198
violence
 and herding cultures, 343
 and honor, 122, 316–322, 334, 341,
 349
 prevention, 455, 458n3
 sensitization, 26n1
violence inhibition mechanism (VIM),
 263, 275, 291, 300

virtue(s)
  and agency, 34
  cultural factors, 208, 216, 229, 233, 239
  definition, 207
  intention *versus* outcome, 34
  pluralism, 252
  variation, 210
Vouloumanos, A., 172

Web-based studies, 127–135
weighing pros and cons, 194–196
Weinberg, N., 348, 371–376, 384n21, 385n30, 385n34
welfare debate, 159
Werker, J., 172
Western culture, 247, 322–324, 331n36, 348
Wheatley, T., 198
Wiggins, D., 214, 287, 289n13, 328n13
Williams, B., 22
Wilson, E. O., 123–124
Wilson, T. D., 189, 298
women. *See* gender
Woolfolk, R. L., 323
wording
  child rapist example, 85
  of choices, 1–3
  and default, 6, 26
  and moral intuitions, 52, 59, 60t, 79, 80
  and nonverbal situations, 80
  and probability estimate, 69
  and trolley problems, 143n6
Wright, R., 191, 211, 231n13
wrongdoing, 19
wrongness
  as attribute, 160, 251
  and brain damage, 200
  and children, 260
  and community, 252
  as concept, 294
  and emotions, 161, 176, 275

and intent, 276, 292
and moral faculty, 164, 176
and moral judgments, 275, 288n3
and moral semantics, 401n4, 416
and promise, 53
and psychopathy, 178
social intuitionist view, 188
of taboo violations, 197
and VIM, 291
Wundt, W., 186

Young, L., xv, 127–135, 145–155, 157–170, 173, 177, 201

Zajonc, R. B., 186
Zumbardo, P., 6

Index to Volume 3

Figures are indicated by "f"; tables are indicated by "t," and footnotes by "*n*."

Abe, J. A. A., 347, 349

abortion, 160

abstraction
  and adolescents, 326, 331, 333, 339,
    355, 367
  brain region, 132, 201
  in children, 300–303, 330–331
  language, 131
  moral judgments, 222

Abu Ghraib, 369

accomplishment, 312

Acevedo, M. C., 348

acquired sociopathic personality, xv,
  124, 188–189, 383, 385

action
  altruistic, 308, 315
  brain sites, 160, 184, 204, 207
  and emotions, 246, 248–251
  harmless, and deontology, 57
  and moral standards, 298, 308
  and pain, 425
  and practical reasons, 413, 424
  and psychopaths, 124, 236
  See also agency; moral action;
    motivation

adaptations, 410

addictions, 415

adolescence
  abstraction, 333, 339, 355, 367

brain, 327–329, 332, 355, 365
cognition, 326–335
imaginary audience, 333–335, 355
and inference, 345
moral development, 302
personal fable, 333–335, 355
risk-taking, 334, 338, 353
as social category, 305

adolescents
  behavioral control, 353, 356, 367
  and belief conflict, 322
  and conventions, 316
  and criminal justice system,
    352–359
  and empathy, 335, 338, 348
  environment impact, 357
  fear, 369, 370
  and guilt, 331, 352
  and happiness, 307
  high-reactive, 310, 321
  moral reasoning, 336, 339, 347
  and peers, 333–338, 353, 355–357,
    367
  and prejudice, 301, 314, 316
  religiosity, 321
  right *versus* wrong, 357
  self-awareness, 333, 339, 346
  torture murder case, 323, 340, 343,
    346, 351, 366, 370

Adolphs, R., 194, 196, 345
adultery, 301
aesthetics, 263
affective-cognitive integration
  and agency, 251–254, 286–288
  atypical cases, 281–283
  and behavioral response, 367
  and compassion, 286
  and cosmic structure, 287
  and development stages, 349, 362
  and footbridge dilemma, 106–110
  and moral reasoning, 344
  and punishment, 286
affluence, 45–47, 76, 116, 306
age factors
  and amygdala, 365–366
  anterior cingular cortex, 328–329
  and autism, 279
  cognition and emotion, 324, 345, 348
  and criminal justice system, 352–354, 357
  and cultural factors, 315
  and false-belief task, 238
  and moral development, 299–305, 313, 322, 339, 347
  and moral emotions, 348
  and moral judgments, 56
  and psychopathy, 339
  and ventromedial frontal cortex, 186, 198
  See also adolescents; children
agency
  amoral and immoral, 272
  and autism (see under autism)
  brain regions, 10–12, 160, 204
  egocentrism versus allocentrism, 278, 290
  and emotions, 11t, 13, 246, 251
  good or bad, 289
  and guilt, 12
  interacting factors, 251–252
  and moral standards, 298, 308
  and pity/compassion, 12, 286

  and psychopathy, 254, 283
  and reason, 234–245, 261–263, 283, 289
  and social position, 251, 286
  unconscious inference, 91n4
  See also ends; moral action; motivation; reaction time
aggressiveness
  brain region, 124
  and child sexual abuse, 300
  child view, 301
  and disgust, 8
  and indignation, 15
  and monkeys, 315
  and moral behavior, 28
allocentrism, 277–280, 290
altruism, 60, 76, 308, 315
Alzheimer's patients, 110
Amish teenagers, 254, 255n5
amnesia, 61, 196
amoralism, 272, 398
amygdala
  and affect recognition, 365
  age at damage, 365–366
  and attachment, 7
  and emotions, 15, 41, 128
  and moral development, 363
  and moral judgment, 4
  and prefrontal cortex, 365
  and psychopathy, 126–128, 135, 143–145, 148, 151, 165, 339
  and reward processing, 21
  and temperament, 309–311, 318, 321
  and uncertainty, 309, 319
ancients, 287, 301
Anderson, S. W., 186, 189
anger
  brain regions, 15
  emotivist view, 376
  as moral emotion, 248
  and punishment, 54
  recognition, 8
  and social norm violations, 13

animals, 307, 315, 411
anterior cingulate
  and adolescence, 328
  age factors, 124, 329
  and anger/indignation, 15
  and disgust, 15, 128
  and gratitude, 16
  and guilt, 13
  and inhibition, 329
  and moral dilemmas, 45
  and oddball effect, 12
  and psychopathy, 126, 136, 143–145,
    165, 364
anthropocentricity, 74–77
antidepressants, 203
antisocial behavior disorder, 152–155,
  166
  See also true community antisocials
antisocial personality disorder
  as diagnostic category, 123, 154, 167,
    254, 255n3
  predators and parasites, 155, 167
  statistics, 366
  See also antisocial behavior disorder
anxiety
  and autism, 240, 244, 267
  and moral behavior, 304, 311
  and temperament, 309
apologies, 375, 386, 393n2, 393n6
appropriateness
  in children, 302, 304, 325
  versus permissibility, 90, 114
  of punishment, 276, 302
approval-seeking, 9, 338
  lack of, 307
arithmetic, 394n8, 405
Aron, A. P., 61
Asperger syndrome, 276, 278, 290
  See also autism
atheism, 422, 425
attachment
  and autism, 253
  and awe, 16
  brain region, 7

  and gratitude, 16, 28, 32
  and guilt, 8
  and immoral behavior, 29
  and pity/compassion, 15, 32
  and theory of mind, 28
attention, 6, 178, 182
Audi, R., 96, 97, 100
Aureli, F., 315
authority
  and children, 175, 189n3, 277, 335
  jurisdiction question, 189n3
  and moral error theory, 423
  obedience, 268–271, 295n1, 370
  and psychopaths, 174
  of reflective feelings, 285
  society as, 272
  and transgression type, 231, 254,
    255n5
  See also God
autism
  anxiety, 240, 244, 267
  description, 233, 242
  and empathy, 232–237, 252, 256n7,
    272n1, 274, 277, 290
  and fairness, 278
  and lying, 244
  and moral agency, 232, 244, 253, 279,
    291, 295
  moral reasoning, 234–244, 279
  versus psychopathy, 242, 259
  and rationalism, 234, 257n9
  and rules, 239–245, 256n8, 257n9,
    262, 266–268, 280, 290, 292–294
  and self, 238
  and social interaction, 235, 244, 246,
    267, 280
  and social position, 253
  systemizing, 253, 263, 279
  and vicarious distress, 253, 256n7,
    259, 266, 293–295
  See also Asperger syndrome
automaticity, 324, 345, 349
awe, 16, 49, 250
Ayer, A. J., 374

Baby Jessica, 48, 50
bad
  and children, 322
  definition, 300
  and moral error theory, 423
  and suffering, 410
  versus wrong, 276
  See also ethics
Baird, A. A., 343–349, 351–359, 364
Bandura, A., 368
Baron, J., 36, 51, 75
Baron-Cohen, S., 279
Barry, K. L., 157
basal ganglia, 15
Bearman, P. S., 369
Bechara, A., 188, 197, 225n5
behavior
  in adolescents, 353, 356, 367
  automaticity, 345
  brain region, 124, 184–188, 192, 221,
    329, 344, 362
  and children, 57, 325, 336, 365
  in community antisocials, 157
  emotions, 306–307
  factors, 368
  internal *versus* external, 173, 178–182
  and moral judgment, 173, 178–184,
    189, 193 (*see also* moral action)
  and psychopathology, 362
  in psychopaths, 159, 161, 165, 189
  of third-parties, 249
  and uncertainty, 304, 322
  See also impulses; inhibition
beliefs
  about value, 410
  and apologies, 393n6
  conflicting, 322
  emotivist view, 373–377
  false-belief task, 238
  moral cognitivist view, 190n5
  and moral judgments, 98, 104n14,
    182, 387–388, 392
  moral *versus* other types, 179–181, 193

Benson, D. F., 124
Bentham, J., 50
Berndt, T. J., 338
Berridge, K. C., 415
Berthoz, S., 274
Bihrle, S., 137, 166
Bisarya, D., 279
Bjorklund, F., 74, 411, 412
Blackburn, S., 205n1, 224n2, 389
Blair, R. J. R., 128, 148, 174, 183, 189,
    230, 253, 254, 256n6, 263, 266, 276,
    293, 339, 365, 403
blame, 54
Blumer, D., 124
body language, 178, 239
body state, 329–333
Bosnia, 368
brain
  and abstraction, 132, 201
  and adolescence, 327–329, 332, 355,
    365
  and agency, 10, 160, 204
  and attachment, 7
  and behavior, 184–188, 192, 221, 329,
    344–345, 362
  cognition sites, 40, 192, 327, 329
  and diachronicity, 318
  disgust sites, 15, 128, 330
  in early childhood, 327
  and emotions, 7–16, 41, 128, 329,
    332, 365
  and ethics, 178, 184–188, 198–201
  and fairness, 54
  fear sites, 363
  and future, 6
  and guilt, 13, 318, 364
  and ideal forms, 303
  incarceration effect, 166
  and intentionality, 10, 12, 160
  and learning, 319
  and lying, 364
  and moral development, 365
  and moral emotions, 7–16

and morality, 4, 183, 192, 201, 221, 313, 317
and motivation, 178, 182–189, 192, 196–201, 221
neural plasticity, 171
and oddball effect, 12
and other-critical emotions, 8
and outcome assessment, 10
paralimbic system, 146–149, 147f
of psychopaths (*see* psychopathic brain)
and remorse, 186, 364
reward processing, 10, 21
and shame, 14
and social cues, 7, 16, 222
and temperament, 309–311, 318, 321
See also electroencephalograms; magnetic resonance imaging; neuroimaging
Brazil, 55
Brink, D., 399
Brodmann, K., 147
Bugental, D. B., 348
bystander problem. *See* trolley problem

Cacioppo, J. T., 345
Camus, A., 266
CAPITAL, 213
Caramassa, A., 225n5
Carlsmith, K. M., 52, 78n7
Casebeer, W. D., 21, 31, 32, 33, 345
Casey, B. J., 328
Catastrophe case, 107
categorical imperative
and deontology, 65, 96, 100
as motivation, 272, 311
Catholic Church, 160
caudate nucleus, 21
Chandler, M., 176
change
and adolescents, 357
dealing with, 309, 319
in morality, 316

charitable donations, 50, 77n4
children
and authority, 175, 189n3, 277, 335
with autism, 238, 243, 245, 252, 263, 274, 276, 278
behavioral control, 57, 325, 336, 365
brain development, 327
cognition, 299–305, 325, 330–331
and conventions, 175, 231, 261–262, 275, 316
and criminal justice system, 352–359
and emotions, 57, 347
ethnicity, 303, 304
fairness, 302
and guilt, 301, 304, 318, 321, 325, 352
and inference, 299, 322
(un)inhibited, 309, 317
as killers, 359n3, 359n6
moral development (*see* moral development)
and moral *versus* conventional, 175, 231, 261–263
sexually-abused, 300
and social categories, 303, 322
social position, 303
temperament, 308–311, 317
choice
crying baby, 44–46
and practical reason, 413, 424
reasons for, 36
trolley problem, 39, 41–44
Chomsky, N., 83, 90
Churchland, Patricia, 21
Churchland, Paul, 21
cingulate, 143, 144, 145, 147f, 364
See also anterior cingulate; posterior cingulate
Cipolotti, L., 183, 189
Cleckley, H., 121, 136, 168, 189n1, 230
Clore, G., 58
coercive power, 338

cognition
  in adolescents, 326–335
  age factors, 324, 345, 348
  and autism, 253, 263, 279
  bad reasoning, 289
  and beliefs, 190n5
  brain regions, 40, 192, 327, 329
  in children, 299–305, 325
  and consequentialism, 41, 45, 56,
    63–65
  definition, 40
  and deontology, 65, 111, 113
  and emotion, 162, 254n1, 339, 345,
    348 (see also affective-cognitive
    integration)
  and moral judgment, 111, 113, 223,
    377
  normative thought, 262
  and psychopathy, 162, 170, 178
  versus reason, 199
  recognition of moral situations, 201
  second-order representations, 329–331
  social, 6, 277–280, 303
  and visceral information, 330, 339,
    345, 362
  and westernization, 56
  See also moral reasoning; social
    cognition
cognitive-affective integration. See
  affective-cognitive integration
cognitive dissonance, 89
cognitive load, 111
cognitivism, 190n5, 387, 393n3, 393n6,
  394n6
cognitivist expressivism, 104n14
Cohen, J., 77
colliculus, 310, 311
comedy, 111
compassion
  and attachment, 15, 32
  brain regions, 16
  and moral agency, 12, 286
  and moral emotions, 252

compensation
  in autism, 238
  in psychopaths, 145, 151, 165, 171
computational theory, 85–90, 106
conceptual rationalism, 380–388, 396–
  400, 419–422
conceptual truths, 382, 396, 398
conditioning
  and amygdala, 363
  and decision-making, 330
  and early childhood, 324, 331, 338,
    345
  and psychopathy, 136, 162
confabulation, 61–63
conflict resolution, 315, 337
conflicts
  of beliefs, 322
  of intuition, 89
  of moral judgments, 202
conscience, 347
consequentialism
  and age, 56
  and cognition, 41, 45, 56, 63–65
  definition, 37–39, 94, 159–160
  versus deontology, 37–46
  emotions, 42–46
  and harmless actions, 57, 78n10
  and heuristics, 36
  and intuition, 70, 74–77
  and psychopathy, 159–161
  and punishment, 50–55, 70–72
  and sentimentalism, 102
  and trolley/footbridge, 39, 42, 65
  See also utilitarianism
consonance, 309
  lack of, 309, 322
constructivism, 98, 102, 115–117
contempt, 8, 15
contingency
  and motivation, 203, 205, 210,
    224n1
  on pleasure, 426
contractualist theory, 97, 117

conventions
and adolescents, 316
and authority, 231
and autism, 243, 253, 280, 293
and children, 175, 231, 261, 276, 316
and history, 301
linguistic, 376, 393n6
and psychopaths, 159, 174, 183, 202,
219, 230, 256n6, 275
cooperation, 9, 59–60, 70
Cords, M., 315
core moral motive
and autism, 238, 244
reason as, 229, 237–246, 262, 271,
389
corporate liability, 51
cosmic concern, 250–253, 261, 266–
268, 287–289
Costa, M., 112
cost-benefit analysis, 45, 65
lack of (see disinterested concern)
criminal justice system, 352–359
Critchley, H. D., 329
cruelty, acts of, 289
crying baby dilemma, 44, 89, 111
Cuddy, A. J., 369, 370
cultural factors
and agency, 251–252
Brazil, 55–57
and children, 303
and individual differences, 363
and moral development, 315
and moral emotions, 5
and morality, 31, 252, 315
and norm violations, 12
westernization, 56–58
Cushman, F., 112

DAAD, 255n2
See also vicarious distress
Damasio, A. R., 111, 124, 183, 184,
185, 187, 188, 196, 197, 199, 225n5,
329, 345, 364, 365, 383

Damasio, H., 187, 188, 196, 197,
225n5, 383
Darwall, S., 205n1, 224n2
Darwin, C., 332
death penalty, 358n3
deception, 244, 301, 364
decision-making
and adolescents, 354, 356
and autism, 243, 279
brain site, 184–186, 196–199, 223, 345
and conditioning, 330
and consequentialism, 36
and criminal justice system, 352
and folk concepts, 421
moral decisions, 169, 308, 324, 349
and skin conductance, 188, 199
somatic marker hypothesis, 329
deity. See God
Deldin, P., 225n5
dementia, 110
De Oliveira-Souza, R., 151, 158, 165–
167, 374–375
deontology
and cognition, 65, 111, 113
as confabulation, 61–63
versus consequentialism, 37–46
definitions, 37–39, 72–74, 94
distant poverty versus own luxury,
45–47
and emotions, 39, 41, 59–64, 69–72,
115
and footbridge/trolley, 39, 42, 63, 74
and harmless actions, 57
and intuition, 91n3, 94–99, 116
and metaethics, 116
and punishment, 50, 70, 78n6, 98
rationalist, 69, 98–101, 117, 119
rationalization, 95
and self, 72–74
and sentimentalism, 102
depression, 152, 180, 203, 412
De Quervain, D. J.-F., 54
desires, 284, 412–417, 424

DeSteno, D., 111
De Vignemont, F., 278, 290–294
the devil, 398, 422
De Waal, F. B. M., 315
Dewey, J., 311
Dewey, M., 279
diachronic psychological rationalism, 378–380
diachronic view
  and agency, 261
  anticipation, 304, 312, 330, 331, 355, 367
  brain site, 318
  outcome assessment, 10
  past and present, 325, 327, 345, 354, 378, 406n2
  short- versus long-term, 354
  See also future; history
dignity, 95–97
discrepant events, 309, 322
disgust
  and aggressiveness, 8
  brain regions, 15, 128, 330
  and contempt, 15
  Kant view, 69
  posthypnotic suggestion, 58
  and psychopathy, 128
disinterested concern, 249, 251–254, 257n10, 268, 286
  See also impartiality
distance, 46–48, 76, 116
distress
  causing, 251
  of child's relative, 301
  gastric, 330, 331
  and psychopathy, 128
  See also vicarious distress
doing and allowing, 160–162
Dolan, R. J., 329
domain generality, 110
dominance
  and moral emotions, 2, 9, 11t, 14, 26
  neurotransmitters, 8–9

and primates, 315
and psychopathy, 254
  See also hierarchy
dopamine
  and aggressiveness, 8
  and dominance, 9
  and motivation, 415
  and reward processing, 21
dorsal lateral prefrontal cortex
  (DLPFC), 16, 40, 44–46, 65, 110, 129, 159–160
  See also prefrontal cortex
double effect (DDE), 160–162
drowning child, 46–48
DSM-III, 254
DSM-IV, 254
DSM-IV-TR, 254
Dutton, D. G., 61
duty, 68
  See also obligation

education, 56, 252, 305
EEG, see electroencephalograms
ego, observing, 334, 356
egocentrism, 278–280, 290
Eichler, M., 176
electroencephalograms (EEGs)
  and guilt, 318
  of high-reactive children, 310
  and inconsistency, 304
  and psychopathy, 129, 132–135, 133f, 138–142
Eliot, G., 289
Elkind, D., 333
Elliott, C., 235
embarrassment, 3, 13, 14, 27
emotions
  and action, 246, 248–251
  age factors, 324, 345, 348
  and agency, 11t, 13, 246, 251
  basic, 2, 26, 32
  and behavior, 306–307
  and body state, 329–333

brain sites, 7–16, 41, 128, 329, 332, 365
and children, 57, 347
and cognition, 162, 254n1, 343, 345, 348 (*see also* affective-cognitive integration)
and deontology, 39, 41, 59–64, 69–72, 115
and disinterest, 249, 252–254, 257n10, 286
gut feelings, 330, 339, 345, 362
and metaethics, 373–377
and moral judgments, 5, 37, 115, 223, 227, 392, 405
and motivation, 27, 37, 55, 228, 234–246
of others, 8, 228, 255, 411, 416
and (im)personality, 42–46, 53, 70, 76, 77n2, 106, 108, 112
projections of, 376
and psychopathy, 129, 134, 143–145, 162, 169, 203
and punishment, 71
and reason, 227, 234–246
recognition of, 8, 365
reflective feelings, 285
and right *versus* wrong, 36
self-conscious, 2, 3t, 331–333, 339, 346, 355
social, 32
and temperament, 309, 317
trigger mechanism, 114
See also moral emotions; sentimentalism; *specific* emotions
emotivism, 373–377
empathy
and adolescents, 335, 338, 348
and autism, 232–237, 252, 256n7, 272n1, 274, 277, 290
brain regions, 7–8, 128–129
definitions, 255n2, 285
Kantian and Humean views, 228
limitations, 248

and moral emotions, 248, 252
and moral judgments, 348
piano-smashing example, 263
and psychopathy, 229–231, 235, 274
versus reason, 232–238, 263
versus sympathy, 331
See also vicarious distress
empirical facts, 371–377, 400–405, 407n6, 421
empirical rationalism. *See* psychological rationalism
ends
and autistic rules, 236
and desires, 417
and emotion, 228, 260, 285
and footbridge dilemma, 85
happiness as, 307
and moral agency, 285–288
of others, 271
and psychopathy, 236
(ir)rationality, 420
and reason, 228, 248, 270
See also means and ends
environment, 357, 366–369
environmentalism, 51, 287
Epicureans, 416
epilepsy, 127, 171
Erb, M., 136
error theory, 422–425
Eslinger, P. J., 158, 183, 184, 185, 375
ethics
brain region, 178, 184–188, 198–201
and children, 303, 322
definition, 409
diverse standards, 305, 312
and evolution, 410, 412
and moral stage theory, 344
response-dependence, 75
and science, 67
and social categories, 303–307, 322 (*see also* social categories)
See also metaethics

ethnicity, 303, 306
ethnic slurs, 301, 316
euthanasia, 160
event-related potentials (ERPs)
  and guilt, 318
  and psychopathy, 129, 132–135, 133f,
    138–142
  See also electroencephalograms
evil, 398
evolution
  and arithmetic, 394n8
  and ethics, 410, 412
  and intuition, 60
  and moral judgments, 390, 392,
    394n9
  and personality, 108
  and psychological rationalism, 378
  and punishment, 70
  and self-conscious emotions, 332
  and social order, 250, 261, 286
  and third-party interests, 250
  and virtuous self, 312
evolutionary psychology, 180
expectations, 12, 270
  unexpected events, 309
experience
  and existing moral sense, 357
  and language, 416, 420
  learning from, 325–330, 345, 354
explanations, need for, 61–63
externalism, 204, 218–220
  versus internalism, 173, 189, 193

face recognition, 20
facial expressions, 170, 230, 239, 253
fairness, 54, 278, 302, 422
  See also justice
false-belief task, 238
falsehood, 244, 364
Farah, M. J., 223
faux pas, 276, 294, 296n2
fear
  in adolescents, 369, 370

brain site, 363
  as moral emotion, 248
  and moral values, 32
  of punishment, 28, 331
  and temperament, 309
  and young boys, 304
  See also anxiety
feedback, 367
Fellows, L. K., 223
Fessler, D., 9, 202
fights, 68
Fine, C., 191–206, 207, 208, 284
first-person, 181–183, 193, 220
Fischer, J. M., 42
Fiske, S. T., 369, 370
Fleming, M. F., 157
Flor, H., 136
fMRI, *see* magnetic resonance imaging
folk concepts
  about psychopaths, 381, 396
  and empirical facts, 405
  mastery limitations, 219, 399, 420
  and rationalism, 396–399, 406n6
footbridge dilemma
  and cognition, 109–110
  consequentialist view, 39, 42, 65
  and emotions, 68, 111
  and intuition, 70, 84–87, 86f, 99, 106,
    110
  means and ends, 74, 86f, 99
  neuroimaging study, 107
  and (im)personality, 42–44, 70
  and psychopatholgy, 110
  rationalist view, 68
  and right *versus* wrong, 63
  versus trolley problem, 84, 86f, 89,
    107
  unconscious inferences, 91n4
  variations, 82–83, 88, 108, 112
  See also reaction time
Forth, A. E., 139
Fowles, D. C., 146
Fox, N., 321

friendship
and children, 301, 303
and obligations, 304
as relational category, 321
See also peers; relational categories
Frith, U., 274, 278, 290–294
frontal cortex
and adolescence, 327, 355, 365
and emotion, 41
parents acting as, 335
and psychopathy, 145, 151, 165–166,
171, 364
and temporal projections, 365
See also prefrontal cortex;
ventromedial frontal cortex
frontotemporal dementia, 110
functional MRI, *see* magnetic resonance
imaging
future
anticipation, 304, 311, 325, 330 (*see
also* conditioning)
and brain regions, 6
and cosmic concern, 288
delight anticipation, 312
investment in, 284
See also diachronic view

gambling task, 187, 197
games, 278
game theory, 16
gastric distress, 331
Gazzaniga, M. S., 62
gender, 304, 311
generalization, 327, 335, 345
genes, 59
genocide, 368
Gewirth, A., 389
Gill, M., 103, 104n15
goals. *See* ends
God
and goodness, 254, 255n5, 267
and Kant, 69, 98
Goldberg, E., 157

golden rule, 231, 273, 401, 407n7
Goldman, A., 273
good
definition, 300
and God, 254, 255n5, 267
and pleasure, 410
self as (*see* self-characterization)
social *versus* individual, 63, 65
and survival, 412
Goodnow, J. J., 348
Good Samaritan laws, 160
Grafman, J., 151
Grafton, S., 159
Grandin, T., 232, 235, 239, 243, 244,
245, 266, 267, 292, 294
gratitude, 8, 16, 28, 32
grave, visiting promise, 56–58
greater good, 288
See also footbridge dilemma; social
good; trolley problem
Greene, J., 6, 21, 40, 43, 44, 45, 46,
48, 65, 77, 81, 84, 88–90, 91n2,
93–103, 105, 110, 113, 114,
160, 372, 373, 375, 378, 395, 410,
411
Greene, J. D., 313
guilt
in adolescents, 331, 352
and agency, 12
alleviation, 308
anticipation of, 304
and attachment, 8
brain regions, 13, 318, 364
in children, 301, 304, 318, 321, 325,
352
in criminal justice system, 352
and intentionality, 12
and outcome assessment, 10
and psychopathy, 120
and social norm violations, 13
and temperament, 309–311, 318
Gurunathan, N., 279
gut feelings, 330, 331, 339, 345

Haidt, J., 3, 36, 41, 48, 55, 58, 63, 74, 83, 85, 90n1, 91n5, 229, 248, 249, 268, 286, 372, 373, 375, 390, 395, 411, 412

Happé, F., 239, 245

happiness, 307, 410

Hare, R. D., 121–123, 134, 137, 139, 162, 165, 167, 170, 177, 189n1, 189n2, 230, 254, 255n3

Hare Psychopathy Checklist, 121–123, 122t, 148, 154, 157, 167, 168
  screening version (PCL-SV), 153–155, 168

harm
  and autism, 242, 266, 293–295
  harmless scenarios, 55, 57, 78n8
  versus obedience, 269
  (im)personal, 43
  probability of, 367, 370

Harman, G., 205n1, 224n2

Harpur, T. J., 134, 167, 170

Harris, L. T., 369, 370

Harsanyi, J., 117

Hart, S. D., 167

Hauser, M., 89, 161, 196, 225n5

hazardous waste, 51

hedonism, 410–415, 424
  See also luxuries; pleasure; suffering

Herman, B., 221, 261

Hermann, C., 136

Hershkowitz, N., 302

heuristics, 36

hierarchy, 8, 157, 370

Hill, E., 127, 274

Hinduism, 287

hippocampus, 136, 146, 148, 198

history, 301, 306, 308, 316

Hobbes, T., 412

Hobson, R. P., 234

Hoffman, M. L., 335, 344

Horgan, T., 104n14

Hornak, J., 126

Howard-Snyder, F., 160

humanity, respect for, 73, 95–97, 100

human nature
  and authority, 268–271, 295n1, 370
  cooperation, 59–60
  cosmic orientation, 250, 251, 266
  explanation-seeking, 61–63
  and inconsistency, 304

Hume, D.
  and autism, 234
  and consequentialism, 41, 64
  emotivism, 372, 374, 376
  and moral cognitivism, 394n6
  on motivation, 228, 231, 237, 247, 260, 274, 283
  and "ought," 72
  on science and morality, 66
  sympathy, 246, 255n2

humor, 111

Hynes, C. A., 32, 159

hypnosis, 58, 62

hypthalamus, 16

ideal forms, 298, 302

Ignácio, F. Azevedo de, 151, 158, 165–167, 166

imagined audience, 333, 355

immorality, 29, 272, 289

impartiality, 390, 400, 403
  See also disinterested concern

impulses
  and adolescents, 354
  control of, 236, 245, 270, 318, 364
    (see also inhibition)
  and psychopaths, 236

incarceration, 166, 256n6, 269, 288

incest taboo, 60

inconsistency, 304, 309, 322

indignation, 8, 12, 15, 249, 251

individual
  differences, 251, 363
  versus greater good, 288
  and intuition, 403
  versus social good, 63, 65

induction, 72
infanticide dilemmas, 44, 89
inference
  and adolescence, 345
  and allocentrism, 278
  in children, 299, 322
  and ideals, 303
  of mental state (*see* mental states, of
    others)
  and moral judgments, 84, 182
  unconscious, 91*n*4
inferior colliculus, 310, 311
information-processing, 81
inhibition
  and basic emotions, 27
  brain region, 7, 329
  and temperament, 309, 317
  of violence, 276
innateness, 392
  See also internalism
insula
  and agency/intentionality, 10
  anger/indignation, 15
  and compassion, 16
  and disgust, 15
  and fairness, 54
  and guilt, 13
  and oddball effect, 12
  and somatic marker hypothesis, 330
intellect
  definition, 162
  and psychopathy, 120, 162, 168
intentionality
  and altruism, 308, 315
  brain regions, 10, 12, 160
  and guilt, 12
  and hedonism, 415
  and internalism, 184, 196
  and moral standards, 298
  and pride, 14
  and trolley/footbridge, 42
  See also double effect; ends; planning
interactional-socialization theory, 314

interalism
  and practical rationality, 179, 193,
    211–215, 224*n*1, 225*n*6
internalism
  apology example, 393*n*6
  brain site, 178, 182–189, 192, 196–
    201, 221
  and ceteris paribus clause, 174, 179,
    192, 195, 208–210, 217
  and conceptual rationalism, 380–385
  descriptions, 191–195, 205*n*1
  versus externalism, 173, 189, 193
  and folk concepts, 397–399
  and intention, 184, 196
  and necessity, 192
  non-naturalist, 180, 205*n*2
  and psychopathy, 180, 201–205, 381,
    397
  simple motivational, 380, 382–385,
    392*n*5, 393n6
  Smith (weak) version, 211–215, 225*n*6
  strict-motive version, 179–181, 207–
    211, 223, 225*n*6
  See also practical rationality
intuition(s)
  and conceptual rationalism, 380, 382
  conflicts, 89
  versus consequentialism, 70, 74–77
  and deontology, 91*n*3, 94–99, 116
  and evolution, 60
  justification principle, 402–404,
    407*n*10, 421
  and moral judgment, 36, 67, 108, 396
  and psychopathy, 403–404
  and right *versus* wrong, 36, 63, 83
  source, 403, 407*n*10, 421
  and trolley/footbridge, 70, 84–87, 86f,
    99, 106, 110
  See also moral grammar
investment game, 53
Ishikawa, S. S., 137, 166
item response theory analyses, 167
Izard, C. E., 347, 349

Jackendoff, R., 81
James, W., 329
Joliffe, T., 240
joy, 248
Joyce, R., 176, 387, 392, 393*n*3, 395–406, 409–417, 421, 425
justice, 63, 65
    See also fairness
justification
    for choices, 36
    and deontology, 39, 61
    in footbridge dilemma, 42
    hedonism as, 415
    and human nature, 61–63
    of moral standards, 308
    See also rationalization
justification principle, 402–404, 407*n*10, 421
justificatory rationalism, 388–391, 394n8, 395, 400–405, 421–422
Jutai, J. W., 138

Kagan, J., 299, 302, 304, 309, 311, 313–316, 317–319
Kahneman, D., 52, 78*n*7
Kamm, F., 68, 108
Kant, I.
    categorical imperative, 65, 96, 100, 311
    and God, 69, 98
    on lying to murderer, 66
    on motivation, 37, 41, 221, 228, 234, 238, 246, 256*n*9, 259, 261
    on punishment, 50, 70, 78*n*6
    and reason, xiv, 260, 262, 271, 284
    respect for humanity, 73, 95–97, 100
    and sexual experimentation, 57, 66
Katz, L., 411, 414, 415–416, 422–426
Keel, J. H., 241
Kelly, D., 202
Kennett, J., 191–206, 207, 225*n*3, 229, 233, 234, 235, 236, 237, 242, 244, 246, 254, 256*n*8, 256*n*9, 265, 271, 272, 282–285, 288, 295

Kiehl, K. A., 131, 132, 133, 135, 138, 139, 141, 142, 143, 144, 151, 160, 162, 165, 169, 170
Killen, M., 314, 315, 321, 344
killing
    by adolescent girls, 323, 340, 343, 346, 351, 366, 370
    Catastrophe case, 107
    by children, 359*n*3, 359*n*6
    consequentialist view, 38
    contractualist view, 97
    deontological view, 38–39
    euthanasia, 160
    and self-defense, 29
    See also footbridge dilemma; trolley problem
kindness, 59
kin selection, 59
Kluever-Bucy syndrome, 126
Knight, R. T., 141
Kochanska, G., 308
Koenigs, M., 111, 196
Kohlberg, L., 41, 190*n*4, 227, 254*n*1, 325, 336, 343, 346, 348, 349, 377
Korsakoff's amnesia, 61
Korsgaard, C. M., 73, 75, 389
Krueger, F., 151

Laakso, M. P., 136
Lacasse, L., 137, 166
Lamb, S., 299
language
    concrete *versus* abstract, 131
    emotivist view, 373–377
    and experience, 416, 420
    grammar acquisition, 303
    of hedonism, 414, 416
    moral utterances, 373, 375, 385, 393*n*3, 393*n*6
    and psychopathy, 131–136, 138, 144–145, 170, 176, 219
Lapsley, D. K., 334, 335, 344, 349, 366
Lawson, W., 280

Lazy Susan case, 108
learning
 and amygdala, 319
 of grammar, 303
 from peers, 337, 367
 and psychopathology, 362
LeDoux, J. E., 62, 363
legal judgments, 181, 190n8
Lencz, T., 137, 166
Lennett, J., 191
Lewis, M., 331, 397
liability, 51
Loewenstein, G., 48, 49, 50, 53
Lorenz, A. R., 165
loyalty, 301, 305, 416
luxuries, 45–47, 76
lying, 244, 364
Lykken, D. T., 136

Maass, P., 368
Mackie, J., 180
magnetic resonance imaging (fMRI)
 and abstraction, 132
 and consequentialism, 160–161
 and emotional arousal, 378
 and moral judgments, 4, 160–162
 and psychopathy, 130, 142, 144
 result interpretation, 171
 and trolley/footbridge, 107
Maibom, H., 235, 285, 287, 288,
 295n1
Maier, N. R. F., 61
Mallon, R., 107, 108
Manstead, A. S. R., 27
Margie, N. G., 314
Marr, D., 81, 87, 90
masturbation, 68
materialism, 306
 See also affluence
mathematics, 394n8, 405
Mathias, C. J., 329
Maxwell, L. B., 157
McDowell, J., 179, 180, 190n6, 207,
 208, 393n6

McGeer, V., 260, 262, 264n1, 265–272,
 273–276
McGinn, C., 68
McIntyre, A., 160
McNaughton, D., 180
means and ends, 38–39, 42, 85–87,
 101, 112–113
 and agency, 245–247, 261
 trolley/footbridge, 74, 86f, 99
media, 305, 308, 368
Meltzoff, A., 231
memory
 and adolescence, 346
 amnesia, 61, 196
 and hippocampus, 198
 and moral judgments, 182
 in psychopaths, 129, 144–145, 162,
 169
 See also diachronic view
memory disorders, 61
Mendez, M., 110
mens rea, 160
mental representations, 298
mental states, of others, 7–10, 230,
 239, 253, 299
mesocortex, 146, 147f
Mesulam, M. M., 147
metaethics
 conceptual rationalism, 380–388
 and consequentialism, 102
 description, 371
 emotivism, 372
 justificatory rationalism, 388–391,
 394n8, 395, 400–405, 421–422
 and moral error theory, 423
 motivation internalism, 393n5
 and neuroscience, 372–374, 377–380,
 386, 388, 392, 400
 projectivism, 373–377, 393n3
 psychological rationalism, 377–380
 (see also psychological rationalism)
 and sentimentalism, 102
metaphors, and psychopaths, 177,
 203

Mikhail, J., 81, 82, 83, 87, 88–89, 91*n*2, 105–114

Milgram, S., 28, 268, 288, 368

military, 369

modus ponens, 422

Moll, J., 5, 6, 13, 19–22, 25–30, 31, 32, 151, 158, 165–167, 166, 374

mood, 111, 180, 203, 222

  See also depression

Moody, J., 369

Moore, G. E., 72, 300

Moore, K., 231

moral, defined, 298

moral action

  and conceptual rationalism, 380–385, 396

  and evolution, 180

  externalism, 173, 189, 193, 204, 218–220 (*see also* internalism)

  and moral understanding, 189

  and sociopathy, 385

  underlying theory, 272, 289

  See also action; agency; motivation

moral cognitivism, 190*n*5, 387, 393*n*3, 393*n*6, 394*n*6

moral competence, 346–347

moral decisions

  automatic response, 324, 349

  and psychopathy, 169

  and sociobiology, 308

  See also decision-making

moral development

  and adolescence, 302

  in children, 299–305, 313, 322, 336

  conditioning, 324, 331, 338, 345

  cultural factors, 315

  ethics, 344

  pathology, 339, 363–366

  temporal lobe role, 365–366

moral dumbfounding, 78*n*8

moral emotions

  age factors, 348

  anticipation of, 304, 312

  versus basic emotions, 2, 26, 32

  brain sites, 7–16

  cultural factors, 5

  definition, 286

  and deontology, 63

  emergence, 348

  and empathy, 248, 252

  examples, 2

  and genes, 59

  Haidt classification, 249

  impact on morality, 30, 36, 39

  and moral judgments, 5

  versus moral reasoning, 60

  neurocognitive components, 11t

  representational view, 22, 25, 32

  self- and other-conscious, 2f, 3, 3t, 8, 304

  and social norms, 13

  and social order, 252, 286

  and temperament, 309

  See also emotions; *specific* emotions

moral error theory, 422–425

moral grammar, xix*n*3, 85, 90, 109, 114

moral imperatives, 27

morality

  brain site, 201, 313, 317

  changing, 316

  components, 316

  cultural factors, 31, 252, 315

  definitions, 26, 31

  emotion role, 30, 36, 39 (*see also* emotions; moral emotions)

  propositional content, 29

  rational status, 405–406 (*see also* cognition; rationalism; reason)

  and social concern, 268–271 (*see also* social order)

moral judgment(s)

  and abstraction, 222

  acting on, 396 (*see also* action; agency; contingency; moral action; motivation)

and adolescents, 348
age factors, 56
and beliefs, 98, 104n14, 182, 387–388, 392
brain regions, 4
cognition role, 36, 65, 377
cognitive and emotional, 41–46, 218–220
and cognitive load, 111, 113, 223
conflicting, 202
consequentialist *versus* deontological, 37–46
definitions, 174, 218–220
domain description, 20
and emotions, 5, 37, 115, 223, 227, 392, 405
emotivist view, 371, 373–376
and empathy, 348
and evolution, 390, 392, 394n9
expanded perceptual model, 84f
first- *versus* third-person, 181–183, 193, 220
harmless scenarios, 55, 57, 78n8
in situ, 181, 194, 208–210, 222, 225n6
and intuition, 36, 67, 108, 396
versus legal judgments, 181, 190n8
and mood, 111, 180, 203, 222
moral philosophy debate, 173–174
and normative thought, 262
persistence, 186, 198
and psychological rationalism, 377–380, 406n2, 407n11
and psychopathy, 174–178, 204
quality, 289
for sensibility theorists, 190n6
and sentiment, 102, 104n13
source, 392
as speech act, 385, 393n6
universal nature, 189n2
moral norms
and autism, 266, 280, 294
and pain, 425
and psychopaths, 159, 174–178

moral philosophy, 61–63, 67, 74–77, 173–174
See also moral truths
moral principles, 75, 97, 99, 100
moral reasoning
and adolescents, 336, 339, 347
and autism, 234–244, 279
automatized, 345, 349
brain sites, 183, 192, 221, 313
and children, 324 (*see also* moral development)
emotional role, 60, 372, 392 (*see also* affective-cognitive integration)
Kohlberg tasks, 190n4
pathology, 339, 357
propaganda effect, 368
and psychopaths, 175, 203, 235
moral requirement, 396
moral sensibility, 5, 242, 275–277, 292–294, 354
See also sensibility theory
moral situations. *See* situations
moral standards, 298, 301, 308
moral truths
constructivist view, 98, 102, 115
and deontology, 69–74
and innate moral faculty, 392
and moral philosophy, 377
and natural selection, 410
philosopher views, 374
moral utterances, 373, 375, 385, 393n3, 393n6
Moran, T., 176
MORTAL, 212
motivation
for altruism, 76
and autism, 233, 236, 238, 244
core motive, 229, 237–246, 262, 271, 389
and decision-making, 188, 196
and dopamine, 415
and emotions, 27, 37, 55, 228, 234–246

motivation (cont.)
 individual differences, 251
 internalism *versus* externalism, 173
 and justificatory rationalism, 389
 lack of, 196, 214, 221, 225*n*5
 moral error theory, 423
 and moral judgment, 191–196, 205*n*1,
  207–215, 217–225, 386 (*see also*
  contingency)
 pleasure as, 306, 311–312
 practical reasons, 413–415, 424
 for punishment, 21, 51, 54, 70, 71
 reason as, 227–229, 234–246, 262,
  271, 389
 self-characterization, 297
 self-interest, 307 (*see also* self-interest)
 sense of duty, 37
 and skin conductance, 188, 198–200,
  199, 385
 social category, 303–307
 suffering as, 425
 types, 298
 well-being of another, 251, 256*n*6,
  307, 311–312
 See also action; agency; internalism
motivational states, 10
motor cortex, 10
murder. *See* killing
Murphy, M. N., 334, 335
myelination, 328

Nagel, T., 205*n*1, 224*n*2, 389, 410, 411,
  413, 415, 417, 426
narcissism, 312
Narvaez, D., 344, 349
natural selection. *See* evolution
necessity, 192
neuroimaging
 adequacy, 77*n*3
 and fairness, 54
 and metaethics, 378–380
 and moral dilemmas, 45, 106–112
 and (im)personality, 109

and psychopathy, 143, 148
 See also electroencephalograms;
  magnetic resonance imaging
neurons, 171, 327–329
neuroscience
 and hedonism, 415
 and metaethics, 372–374, 377–380,
  386, 388, 392, 400
neurotransmitters, 8, 9, 21, 415
Newman, J. P., 165
Nichols, S., 12, 107, 108, 230, 380–382,
  393*n*4, 393*n*5, 395, 399, 403, 409–
  410, 419–422
Nisbett, R. E., 61
nominal categories, 303–307, 321
normative motivation internalism,
  381–384
normative persistence, 206*n*4
normative practical reasons, 413, 416,
  424
normative thought, 262
normative values, 261
norms
 defined, 12
 and peers, 367
 permanent nature, 194, 203, 206*n*4,
  220
Nucci, L., 254, 255*n*5, 267
nurturance, 411

obedience, 268–271, 288, 295*n*1, 325,
  370
obligation
 and autism, 232
 in children, 304
 and social categories, 304–306, 312,
  314
 See also deontology
observing ego perspective, 334, 356
occipital cortex, 129, 143
occupation, 157
oddball stimuli, 12, 137, 140–143,
  141f

orbital frontal cortex
and awe, 16
and behavior change, 124
and compassion, 16
and disgust, 15
and embarrassment, 14
and gratitude, 16
and intentionality, 160
and moral judgment, 4
and oddball effect, 12
and psychopathy, 124–126, 136, 143, 146, 148, 364
and reward processing, 21
order
and autism, 239–245, 256n8, 262, 266–268, 279
in cosmos, 250–253, 261, 266–268, 287–289
maintenance of, 249
seeking *versus* creating, 266
and self-understanding, 261
ostracism, 369
other-conscious emotions, 2, 3t, 8
others
acknowledgment by, 297
and adolescents, 333–335
and autism, 235, 236, 263, 279
concern for, 307
and embarrassment, 27
emotions of, 8, 228, 255, 411, 416
ends of, 271
mental states, 7–10, 230, 239, 253, 299, 333
perspective, 334, 356, 389, 401–403
and pride, 14
and psychopaths, 236, 274
and self, 231, 234, 271, 312, 321, 416, 426
and uninhibited children, 318
well-being of, 251, 256n6, 307, 311–312
See also disinterested concern; empathy; third-party behavior

"ought"
versus "is," 72, 79n14, 371
metaethics view, 293n1
and moral error theory, 423
and obedience, 295n1
versus "want," 284
outcome assessment, 10, 11t, 13, 14, 15, 16
See also consequentialism; reward
outrage, 53, 55, 78n7, 358n3
oxytocin, 7

pain, 136
See also suffering
pantyhose experiment, 61
paralimbic system, 144–149, 147f, 160, 162, 165, 171
parasites, 155, 167
parents, 336
parietal lobes
and agency, 10
and cognition, 40
and emotion, 41
and moral dilemmas, 44–46
and psychopathy, 129, 141, 141f
and temperament, 311
peers
in adolescence, 333–338, 353, 355–357, 367
in military, 369
Peirce, C. S., 311
perfection, 298, 302
persistence
of moral judgments, 186, 198
and normativism, 206n4
personal fable, 333, 355
personality, 108
See also temperament
(im)personality
and charity, 47
and cognitive *versus* emotional, 106–108, 112
computer fairness study, 54

(im)personality (cont.)
  and harm, 43–49, 77n2
  and reaction time, 109
  and suffering, 45–48, 76
  teacup and lazy susan cases, 108
  and violations, 70
personality disorders, 123, 126
perspective
  and adolescents, 334, 346, 348, 356
  and autism, 234, 241, 291
  egocentric versus allocentric, 278
  and emotions, 376
  and empathy, 285
  and moral judgments, 179, 181–183
  of others, 334, 356, 389, 401–403
  phenomenalism, 349
  and psychopathy, 230
perspective taking, 9
phenomenalism, 349
Piaget, J., 302, 326, 336, 377
piano-smashing, 263
picture-viewing task, 187, 199, 200, 274
Pinel, P., 119
pity, 12, 16
planning
  long-term, 251, 261, 284
  and practical reasons, 413
Plato, 67
play
  and autism, 245, 263
  gambling task, 187, 197
  games, 278
pleasure, 306, 311–312, 329, 409–415
positron emission tomogrophy (PET), 148
posterior cingulate
  and psychopathy, 135–136, 143–145, 165, 364
  and second-order representations, 329
posthypnotic suggestion, 58, 62
poverty
  in American society, 306
  distance, 46–48, 76, 116

poverty of the stimulus, 87
power, 338
practicality requirement, 393n5, 406
practical rationality
  and conceptual rationalism, 380–389
  illness example, 224n1
  and internalism, 179, 193, 211–215, 224n1, 225n6
  and justificatory rationalism, 394n8
  and terminology, 393n5, 406
practical reason(s), 413, 416, 424
praise, 302
predators, 155, 167
prefrontal cortex
  and action, 10–12, 159–160
  and adolescence, 327–329, 344–347
  and amygdala, 365
  and anger/indignation, 15
  and awe, 16
  and cognition, 40
  and compassion, 16
  and embarrassment, 14
  and ideal forms, 303
  and inhibition, 7
  and intentionality, 12
  moral dilemmas, 45
  and moral judgment, 4
  and psychopathy, 129, 339, 364
  reward processing, 21
  and social knowledge, 6
  and temperament, 318, 321
  See also dorsal lateral prefrontal cortex; frontal cortex; ventromedial prefrontal cortex
prejudice, 301, 314, 316
Price, R., 379
Prichard, H. J., 94, 101
pride, 2, 9, 14, 355
Prinz, J., 395, 403
priorities, 321, 401
prison, 166, 256n6
prisoners, 269, 288, 369
process, defined, 32
projective error, 410

projectivism, 373–377, 393*n*3
promiscuity, 364
promises
  breaking, 57, 79*n*11, 182, 187, 197, 208–210, 220, 223
  contractualist view, 97
propaganda, 368
prosocial tendency, 249
prosopagnosia, 170, 230
proximity, 42–47, 76, 116
pseudopsychopathy, 124
psychological rationalism
  versus conceptual rationalism, 395
  versus justificatory rationalism, 389–391, 395, 400–404
  and moral judgments, 377–380, 406*n*2, 407*n*11
  terminology, 393*n*4, 406*n*1
psychology, 180, 377
psychopathic brain
  amygdala, 126–128, 135, 143–145, 165, 339, 363–365
  cingulate, 126, 136, 143–145, 165, 364
  compensatory activity, 145, 151, 165, 171
  EEGs, 129, 132–135, 133f, 138–142
  frontal cortex, 145, 171, 364
  hippocampus, 136, 146, 148
  neuroimaging, 129–136, 133f, 138–143, 144, 148
  orbital frontal cortex, 124–126, 136, 143, 146, 160, 364
  paralimbic system, 145–147, 147f, 160–162
  parietal lobes, 141, 141f
  prefrontal cortex, 129, 339, 364–366
  temporal lobes, 126–129, 135, 140–143, 141f, 145, 365
  ventral striatum, 144
  ventromedial prefrontal cortex, 364
psychopathology
  frontotemporal dementia, 110

  and moral development, 339, 346, 362–370
  schizophrenia, 120, 167
psychopathy
  in adolescent girl, 323, 340
  age factor, 339
  and attachment, 28
  and authority, 174
  versus autism, 242, 259
  behavioral control, 159, 161, 165, 189
  brain regions (*see* psychopathic brain)
  and cognition, 162, 170, 178
  and conditioning, 136, 162
  and conventions, 159, 174, 183, 202, 219, 230, 256*n*6, 275
  definitions, 189*n*1, 254, 255*n*3
  DSM classification, 254, 255*n*3
  and emotions, 129, 134, 143–145, 162, 169, 203
  and empathy, 229–231, 235, 274
  folk view study, 381, 396
  gestures, 178
  and guilt, 120
  incarceration impact, 166
  and intellect, 120, 162, 168
  and internalism, 180, 201–205, 381, 397
  and justification principle, 404
  and language, 131–136, 138, 144–145, 170, 176, 219
  memory, 129, 144–145, 162, 169
  and moral decisions, 169
  and moral judgments, 174–178, 204
  moral reasoning, 175, 203, 235
  and paralimbic system, 145–149, 160, 165
  and psychological rationalism, 380, 407*n*11
  psychometric assessment, 167
  and reason, 235, 254, 265
  and social position, 254, 270
  successful, 137, 152, 166

psychopathy (cont.)
traits, 120–123, 122t
and vicarious distress, 259
psychopathy (cont.)
and violent crime, 155
and voice emphasis, 177, 203
See also antisocial behavior disorder;
antisocial personality disorder
puberty, 336
See also adolescence
punishment
altruistic, 60
appropriateness, 276, 302
avoidance of, 325
consequentialist view, 50–55, 70–72
criminal justice system, 352–359
deontological view, 50, 70, 78n6, 98,
358n3
fear of, 28, 331
motivation, 21, 51, 54, 70
and natural selection, 70
by peers, 338
and social structure, 286
and temperament, 311
Pythagoras, 287

questionnaires, 382, 398, 420

Rabbitt, C. E., 364
racial slurs, 301, 316
Raine, A., 137, 146, 166
rational amoralism, 398
rationalism
and autism, 234, 257n9
core motive, 389
and deontology, 69, 98–101, 117, 119
empirical (*see* psychological
rationalism)
versus gut reaction, 345
and Kant, 228, 234
and order, 256n8
and perspective, 389, 401–403
and psychopaths, 235, 254, 265

versus sentimentalism, 259, 282,
403–405
See also conceptual rationalism;
justificatory rationalism;
practical rationality; psychological
rationalism
rationalization
and deontology, 95
post hoc, 61–63
of punishment, 71
and reason, 257n9
spotting, 67
See also justification
Ravizza, M., 42
Rawls, J., 63, 75, 85, 89, 116
reaction time
automaticity, 324, 345, 349
and moral dilemmas, 45, 89, 107,
109, 111
and psychopaths, 134, 138, 140
reason
and agency, 234–245, 261–263, 283,
289
versus cognition, 199
definition, 162
and emotions, 227, 234–246
and empathy, 232–238, 263
and ends, 248, 270
and moral judgments, 36, 406n2
as motivation, 227–229, 234–246, 262,
271, 389
and perspectives, 389
and psychopathy, 235, 254, 265
and rationalization, 257n9
and sentimentalism, 104n13, 406n2
See also moral reasoning
reciprocity, 16, 59
reflective equilibrium, 399
reflective feelings, 285
regret, 375, 386, 393n2
See also remorse
relational categories, 303–307, 312,
314, 321, 336

and perception, 403
and rationality, 389
relatives, 301, 303, 321
religion(s)
Catholicism, 160
and cosmic concern, 250, 287
and love, 73
and moral standards, 308
religiosity, 321
remorse
apologies, 375, 386, 393n2, 393n6
brain region, 186, 364
respect, 73, 95–97, 100
response-dependence, 75
responsibility, 364
retribution, 50, 70, 78n6, 98, 358n3
reward, 10, 21
Richler, J., 279
rightness, 357, 397
See also wrongness
rights, 68, 74
Rilling, J., 54
risk-taking, 334, 338, 353
Ritov, I., 51
rituals, 287
Robinson, J. L., 348
Rogan, M. T., 363
Roper v. Simmons, 358n3
Roskies, A., 178–189, 190n7, 192, 193, 207–215, 218, 220, 221, 224n2, 225n4, 225n5, 225n6, 383, 385, 386, 387
Ross, W. D., 94, 96, 101
Rozin, P., 56

sacrifice, 288
sadism, 269
See also torture
sadness, 248
Sanfey, A., 54
Satin, 396, 422
satisfaction, 311–312
Savin-Williams, R. C., 338

Scanlon, T. M., 97, 98, 99, 100, 116, 414, 415, 417n1
Schaich Borg, J., 159, 165–171, 166, 168–170, 169, 171
Schelling, T., 48
schizophrenia, 120, 167
Schnall, S., 58
science, 67, 250, 307
scientific methodology, 19–21
Scott, E., 353, 354, 356
second-order representations, 329
self
and agency, 245
and autism, 238
body state, 329–333
deontologic view, 72–74
diachronic awareness, 251, 261
and enlightenment, 267
and moral standards, 298
and others, 231, 234, 271, 312, 321, 416, 426
and psychopaths, 176, 203, 235
social position awareness, 303
third-party perspective, 334, 356
understanding, 261, 267, 288, 299–305
self-characterization, 72–74, 297, 300, 303–305, 312, 322
self-conscious emotions, 3t, 331–333, 339, 346, 355
self-control. *See* behavior; inhibition; self-regulation
self-defense, 29
self-enhancement, 312, 321, 338
self-esteem, 9, 13, 14, 26
self-interest, 249, 270, 289, 307, 416
selfishness, 157, 390
self-organization, 237
self-reactive attitudes, 249
self-regulation, 27
Selman, R. L., 334, 335, 346
Semin, G. R., 27
sensation-seeking, 354

sensibility theory, 75, 190*n*6
  See also moral sensibility
sentimentalism
  definition, 173
  and deontology, 102
  and justification principle, 407*n*10
  and psychopathy, 178, 219, 265
  versus rationalism, 259, 282, 403–405
  and reason, 104*n*13, 406*n*2
  See also emotions; intuition(s)
Serbs, 368
serotonin, 9
sexual abuse, 300
sexual experimentation, 57, 66
Shamay-Tsoory, S. G., 276, 294
shame
  and adolescents, 355
  brain region, 14
  in children, 300, 322
  and dominance, 9
  versus embarrassment, 3
  and moral behavior, 304
  and self-esteem, 14, 26
  and temperament, 309
Sidgwick, H., 417
Sifferd, K. L., 366
simple motivation internalism, 380,
    382–385, 392*n*5, 393n6
simulation theory, 9
Sinclair, J., 235
Singer, P., 46, 75, 116, 389, 390, 400–
    402, 413, 417
single photon-emission tomography
  (SPECT), 143
Sinno, S., 314
Sinnott-Armstrong, W., 103*n*5, 104*n*16,
    159, 160, 392, 406*n*2, 421
situations
  context, 222
  discrepant, 309, 322
  emotivist view, 376
  moral recognition, 181, 194, 201,
    208–210, 222, 225*n*6
  and response, 90*n*1

skin conductance
  and amygdala, 127
  and motivation, 188, 198–201, 221,
    225*n*5, 385
  and psychopaths, 136
  and ventromedial frontal cortex, 178,
    187, 200, 225*n*5
Small, D. A., 48, 49, 50, 53
Smetana, J. G., 315, 344
Smith, Adam, 1, 41, 307
Smith, M., 179, 190*n*7, 193, 218, 220,
    225*n*3, 225*n*6, 381–384, 389, 393*n*5,
    396, 397, 399, 404–405, 420
Snidman, N., 309, 311
Sobel, D., 413, 417*n*1
social categories, 303–307, 312, 314,
    322
social cognition, 6, 277–280, 303
social concern, 268–272
social cues
  and autism, 243, 244
  brain regions, 7, 16, 222
social-domain theory, 314
social emotions, 32
social good, 63, 65
social interaction
  and adolescents, 334
  and autism, 235, 244, 246, 267, 280
  egocentrism *versus* allocentrism,
    278
  feedback effect, 367
  and moral reasoning, 368
  nurturance model, 411
  and third-party behavior, 249
  See also obedience
social judgment, 222
social norms, 12–15, 21, 27, 251
social order
  and agency, 251–254
  and autism, 253
  and conventions, 276
  desire to conform, 268–271
  egalitarianism, 304, 306
  and evolution, 250, 261, 286

hierarchy, 8, 157, 370
and moral emotions, 252, 286
and punishment, 286
social position
and adolescents, 335–339, 367–368
and autism, 253
and awe, 16
and children, 303, 322
and contempt/disgust, 15
emerging awareness, 303
media effect, 305
and moral agency, 251, 286
and obedience, 268–271, 288
and psychopaths, 254, 270
See also dominance
sociobiology, 307
socioeconomic status, 57, 166
sociolinguistics, 376, 388, 416
sociopathy, xv, 124, 188, 383, 385
Sokolov, E. N., 137
somatic marker, 329, 345
spatial perception, 278, 290
Stalin, J., 43
Stanford prisoner experiment, 269, 288
startle response, 128, 143
Steinburg, L., 353, 354, 356
stereotypes, 6, 40, 314
Stich, S., 202
Strawson, P. F., 249
structured event complex (SEC), 10
Stuss, D. T., 183
submission, 8
suffering
and action, 425
distant, 46–48, 76
and ethics, 409–414
and justificatory rationalism, 401–403
and moral norms, 425
of others, 426
superior temporal sulcus (STS), 4, 10–12, 13, 14, 16
surveys, 382, 398, 420

Swick, D., 125
sympathy, 228, 255*n*2, 331
See also compassion; empathy; pity
systemizing, 279

Tangney, J. P., 2, 3
taste, 376
Taylor, J. H., 337
TCA. *See* true community antisocials
teacups case, 108
television, 305, 308
temperament, 308–311, 317, 321
temporal lobes
and adolescence, 365
and compassion, 16
and dementia, 110
and development, 365
and disgust, 15
and embarrassment, 14
and frontal cortex, 365
and intentionality, 160
and moral judgment, 4
and psychopathy, 126–129, 135, 140–142, 141f, 145
theft, 374
theory development, 19–21
theory of mind, 9, 28, 238, 292
third-party behavior, 249
third-party emotions, 411, 416
third-party perspective, 334, 356
third-party well-being, 250, 252, 256*n*6, 307, 311, 389
See also altruism; suffering
third-person, 181–183, 193, 220
Thomson, J. J., 39, 42, 68, 88
time. *See* reaction time
Timmons, M., 104*n*14, 114–117
Tolhurst, W., 206*n*3
Tomb, I., 225*n*5
torture
Abu Ghraib, 369
by adolescent girls, 323, 340, 343, 346, 351, 366, 370
and obedience, 370

Tranel, D., 187, 196, 339, 383
Trevethan, S. D., 176, 203
trolley problem
  consequentialist view, 39, 42, 65
  deontology view, 74
  and do and allow, 160
  and double effect, 160
  and emotions, 68, 111
  versus footbridge dilemma, 107
  and intuition, 70, 84–87, 86f, 99, 106, 110
  neuroimaging study, 106
  and (im)personality, 41–44
  and psychopathology, 110
  variations, 82, 108, 112
true community antisocials (TCAs), 155–157, 156t
trust, 54
truths
  conceptual, 382, 396, 398
  and justificatory rationalism, 422
  mathematical, 394n8
  See also moral truths
Turiel, E., 231, 267

uncertainty
  and behavior, 304, 322
  brain area, 309, 319
  and consonance, 298
  and temperament, 309
the unexpected, 309
universal order. *See* cosmic concern
Urbach-Wiethe disease, 126
utilitarian(ism), 65, 91, 107–108, 110–111, 114, 116–117, 412
  See also consequentialism

Valdesolo, P., 111
value(s)
  ascription of, 263
  and fear, 32
  nonnormative, 261
  normative, 261

as projection, 410
and suffering, 401, 425
Van Horn, J., 159
Vartanian, L. R., 333, 334
Veague, H. B., 364
vegetarianism, 287
Veit, R., 136
Velleman, D., 261
Venables, P. H., 138
ventral striatum, 16, 21, 144
ventromedial frontal cortex
  age factors, 186, 198
  and behavior, 184–188, 192, 221
  and externalism, 204, 218
  and moral judgment, 178, 182–189, 196–201, 218, 225n5
  and moral reasoning, 183, 192, 221
  and remorse, 186
  and skin conductance, 178, 187, 200, 225n5
  and social judgment, 222
  and sociopathy, 188, 383
ventromedial prefrontal cortex
  damage, 195
  and psychopathy, 151, 364
  and temperament, 310, 318, 321
vicarious distress
  and Asperger's syndrome, 278
  and autism, 253, 256n7, 266, 293–295
  in children, 301, 322
  versus empathy, 255n2, 256n7
  versus obedience, 269
  and psychopaths, 231
  and psychopathy *versus* autism, 259
victims
  identifiable *versus* statistical, 43, 48–50, 53, 76
  pianos as, 263
viewing pictures, 187, 199, 200, 274
violations
  and autism, 276, 293
  and behavior control, 362
  child view, 299, 301, 322

components, 276
cultural factors, 12
faux pas, 276, 294, 296*n*2
harmless, 57, 78*n*8
media effect, 305
of moral *versus* conventional rules,
    276 (*see also* conventions)
(im)personal nature, 44, 106, 109
and psychopathology, 362
and rationality, 380, 400
and reaction time, 109
of social norms, 12, 13, 14, 15, 21, 27
by TCAs, 156
of trust, 54
violence
  by adolescent girls, 323, 340, 343,
    346, 351, 366, 370
  (im)personal, 43
  and psychopathy, 155
  statistical improbability, 367, 370
  and ventromedial frontal cortex, 186
violence inhibition mechanism (VIM),
    276
virtue
  and ideal *versus* action, 298
  and peer group, 338
  and social category, 303–307, 312,
    314, 321
virtue ethics, 75
viscera, 330, 339, 346, 362
voice, 177, 203

Waddington, C. H., 339
Walker, L. J., 176, 203, 337
Wallace, J., 175
wealth, 45–47, 76, 116, 306
westernization, 56–58, 78*n*9
Whalen, P. J., 321
Wheatley, T., 58
Wheelwright, S., 279
will, weakness of, 381
Williams, B., 412
Williamson, S., 134

Williamson, S. E., 170
Wilson, T. D., 61
wrongness
  versus bad, 276
  emotivist view, 376
  "gut" feelings, 324
  and intuition, 36, 63, 83
  and juvenile justice system, 357

Yamaguchi, S., 141
Young, L., 111, 196

Zahn, R., 151
Zimbardo, P., 269, 368